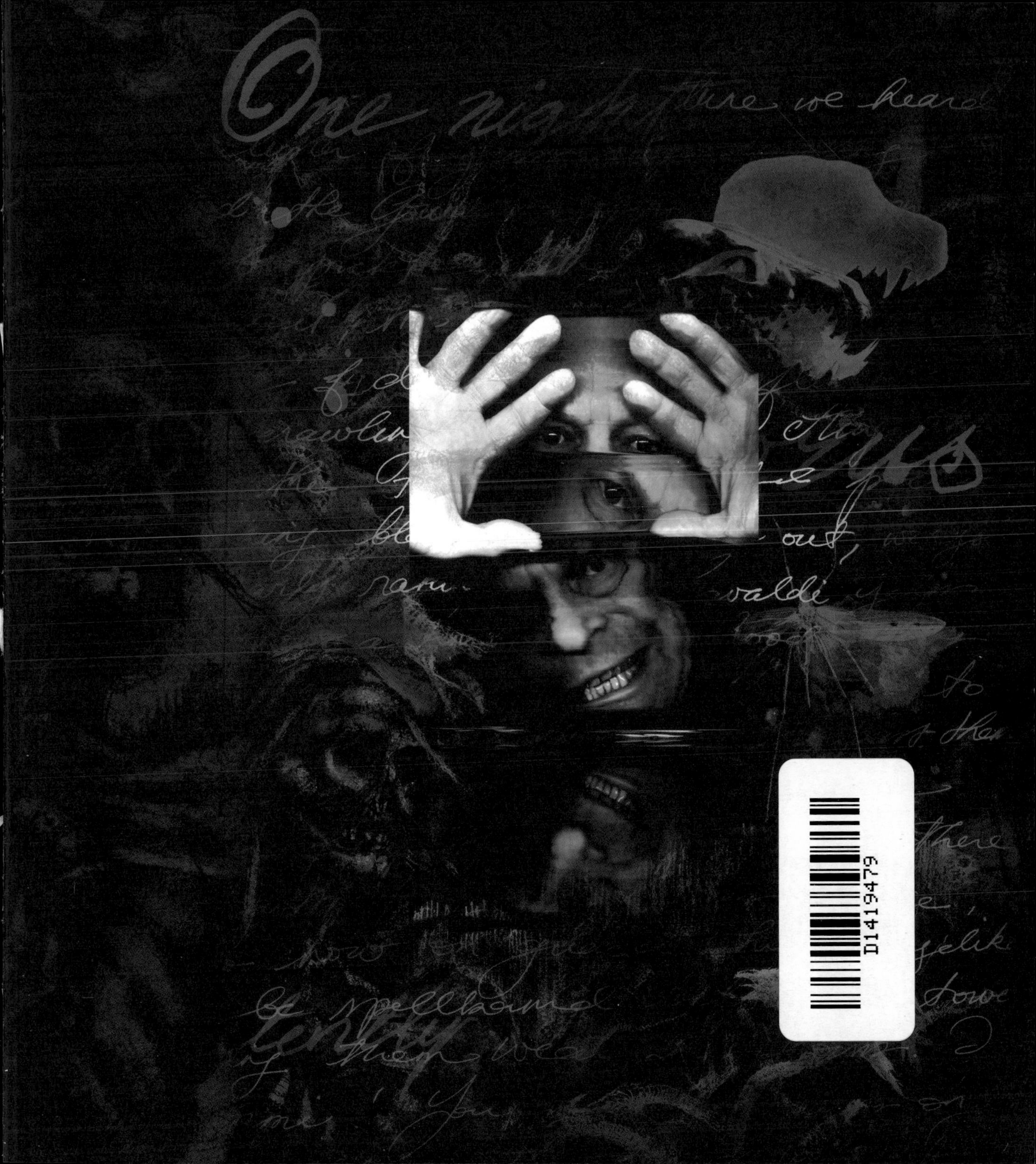

Dreams and Nightmares

By the same author

Clint Eastwood: Quote Unquote

John Travolta: Quote Unquote

George Clooney

The Exorcist: Out of the Shadows

Dark Knights and Holy Fools: the Art and Films of Terry Gilliam

Sean Connery: A Biography

Brazil: The Evolution of the 54th Best British Film Ever Made

The Authorised Biography of Ronnie Barker

The Pythons Autobiography by the Pythons

The Rough Guide to Comedy Movies

The Life of Graham: The Authorised Biography of Graham Chapman

Dreams and Nightmares

Terry Gilliam, The Brothers Grimm,
and Other Cautionary Tales of Hollywood

Bob McCabe

HarperCollins*Entertainment*
An Imprint of HarperCollinsPublishers

HarperCollins*Entertainment*
An Imprint of HarperCollins*Publishers*
77–85 Fulham Palace Road,
Hammersmith, London W6 8JB
www.harpercollins.co.uk

Published by HarperCollins*Entertainment* 2005
1 3 5 7 9 8 6 4 2

A catalogue record for this book
is available from the British Library

ISBN-13   978-0-00-717556-7
ISBN-10   0-00-717556-6

Printed and bound in Italy by Lego Spa

As always, my heart lies elsewhere –
with Lucy, Jessie and Jack.

Introduction

AT THE END OF 2002, filmmaker Terry Gilliam began pre-production work on a film titled *The Brothers Grimm*, set to be shot in Prague the following summer. The movie was financed in part by Metro Goldwyn Mayer, and by Miramax, a hugely successful independent production house, formed and run by two brothers, Harvey and Bob Weinstein.

The finished film was not released until the dog days of summer 2005. In the time in-between, Gilliam had very publicly fallen out with his producers, and the Weinsteins had opted to part from Miramax's parent company, Disney.

The book that follows is not your standard "making of" book; what it is instead is a collection of snapshots – some crystal clear, some blurred – from the middle of a hurricane, occasionally finding release in the eye of the storm. This is how *The Brothers Grimm* appeared to some of those on the inside as the days went by, before, during and after.

Hindsight is never a factor.

Bob McCabe, 2005 – after the event.

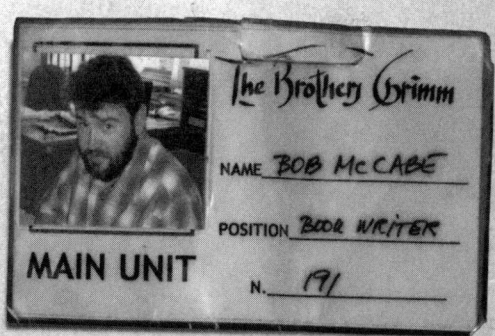

Once upon a time...

The Road to Marbaden

O**N 22ND MAY 1998** Terry Gilliam's *Fear and Loathing in Las Vegas* opened in American cinemas. It opened that Memorial Day weekend partly as counter-programming to what was perceived to be that summer's lizard-led behemoth, *Godzilla*. Over their shared opening weekend, *Godzilla*'s overall box office haul was $55.7million; *Fear and Loathing* came in at $4.3million.

Fear and Loathing proved not to be overly popular with audiences, but also managed to divide critics – some of whom thought Gilliam perfectly captured the surreal insanity and generational divide of Hunter S. Thompson's ground-breaking book; others who felt he simply abused it; still others who weren't really sure what to think about a movie that had already incurred the wrath of the European press after a very vocal screening at the Cannes Film Festival.

It would be another seven years before Gilliam would have a movie hit the big screens of the world.

Despite his reputation as a unique visionary filmmaker, his successful box office track record, his ability to attract big name actors and draw often their best work from them, the simple reality was that Terry Gilliam couldn't get a movie made.

Not for want of trying. Over those intervening years numerous projects came and went, some briefly, some consuming years of time and development, one even going as far as filming for a handful of days before disastrously falling apart.

As *Fear and Loathing* was finishing its run, Gilliam was attempting to move on to a number of other projects.

The first of these involved a step back – "Time Bandits 2". Revisiting his hugely successful 1981 children's fantasy, Gilliam was re-working the premise with original co-writer Charles McKeown. The central character this time was to be a young girl into computers and the internet, who teams up with the dwarves who repair the holes in time, whilst also taking some time to plunder history along the way. Originally, the plan was to make it as a theatrical movie, with Gilliam only producing ("It's an odd one to go back to… there's this slight feeling of repetition in how you deal with time.") with the story exploiting the (then) pending millennium. However, the backing for the movie never materialised.

It was revived in 2001–2 as a two-part series for Hallmark television, budgeted at $60million, but once again interest waned, plus Gilliam felt "the events of 9/11 panicked Hallmark into pulling investment out of their TV/entertainment expansion".

But by then Gilliam had moved on. For years, he had worked on developing "Don Quixote", a task that had foiled many a filmmaker over the years, Orson Welles included. None of them had ever succeeded in finding the right take on it. Now working with his new regular collaborator Tony Grisoni, Gilliam had worked out what he felt was the way in to Cervantes' classic tale.

"The Man Who Killed Don Quixote" became a time-travelling tale of life in the media world of the early 21st century that hurtled itself back to the days of the man who tilted at windmills. Johnny Depp signed on very early to play the part of Toby Grosini, a soulless modern-day advertising executive, currently shooting a TV campaign based on the character of Don Quixote (whilst also working on a jingle called "Let's Fuck up the World"). When wandering around the remote Spanish location he is shooting in, he is somehow transported back into the days of the real Quixote, inadvertently – and unwillingly – assuming the role of Sancho Panza.

It was a bawdy, funny, hugely inventive twist on the original legend and started to attract finance. Right from the beginning Gilliam was determined, however, to make it a European film, not wanting to turn to Hollywood for any form of financial help. This was a difficult proposition – but not an impossible one. Hachette Premiere – who had worked on such big-budget European successes as *Cyrano de Bergerac* – came on board and helped assemble a financing cartel from various other countries (three French companies, three Spanish, one German, one British), something that proved difficult to maintain.

The film was obviously a sizeably budgeted and very complicated one, but the budget was weaned down to $32million; Jean Rochefort was Gilliam's first choice to play Quixote, despite the fact that, now in his seventies, he would have to learn English. The money was raised, the locations were chosen, and a great cast was assembled, including Miranda Richardson, Christopher Eccleston, Sally Phillips, Bill Paterson and more.

After a long haul, Gilliam was set to make his first film in what by then had been three years. Filming began on location in Spain in September of 2000. ("I spent so long preparing to make this film, I think I was already exhausted by the time I got there.") It lasted five days.

email from Terry Gilliam to Bob McCabe – Friday, 6th October 2000:

"Jean Rochefort is ill in bed in Paris – no definite date for return. Flash flood wiped out set and equipment. 1st and 2nd assistant directors have resigned. Shooting has been stopped for two weeks. Completion bond has arrived. I have gone catatonic and am hiding in my flat. Incommunicado. We have a couple of minutes of film – but only one complete scene… does that qualify as a movie? FUN???!!! You must be fucking joking."

The problems were manifold, but two, more than anything, predicated the collapse of the movie – Jean Rochefort's health, (he was later diagnosed with a double hernia making it impossible for him to ride a horse, something he was required to do for most of the movie); and the weather. On the second day they were hit by a storm that rapidly turned into a flood, which ruined the costumes and washed the sets and equipment away.

"This storm, it was really wonderfully apocalyptic," recalls Gilliam. "It was Old Testament stuff, it was everything you'd ever hoped, because it's coming and you can see it coming over the hills, it's moving this way and it went sort of yellow and the wind came first, so we're running round saying 'Toto! Where's Toto? Toto, To-to!' and the wind is coming in and this thing just came, it was like a tornado. Everyone was in this little box canyon area, huddled under a tent, trying to drag the equipment in and then it hit, *wham!*

And I said: 'Fuck, I'm not going to stay under this thing, it's all cramped,' and by then I'd gone crazy because I knew, here it was, the rain I'd been terrified of and thinking about for months has now arrived and I just walked out into the middle of it and found myself on a great overhanging rock, and just sat there. It was better than anything you see in the movie: the lightning, the sound effects, just brilliant, and it went from rain to hail stones and the place was just flooding and I'm looking away, I didn't see what was going on behind me: waterfalls were appearing over the edges of these things. It was just outrageous. And I'm out there like King Lear howling at the storm, laughing and howling in equal measure, and then it finally passed; it only lasted 45 minutes, and I turned back and the tent's gone, everything's gone, it's just been washed away."

The crew held out for a few days in the vain hope of re-starting; there was talk of beginning to shoot again in either November of that year, or January of 2001, but the insurers moved in and put an end to it all, selling off costumes and props – despite constant claims the project would go forward again – in an attempt to recoup some of the $16million they eventually paid out in insurance. It was one of the greatest disasters in modern movie making (and is extremely well documented in Keith Fulton and Louis Pepe's superb documentary, *Lost In La Mancha*).

It was, however, a huge blow for Gilliam, who returned home somewhat beaten and unsure of what his next move should be, admitting at the time that the collapse of the film had left him severely depressed.

"The weird thing is it's actually really hard for me to imagine how to make a film again. This has killed me. It's not worse than *Munchausen* but in some ways it is, because on *Munchausen* at the end there was a film, for better or worse there was a film. There's nothing here after all that time and it's a strange one."

The rights to the movie were tied up in vast amounts of Euro-litigation and Gilliam has still to win back the rights to his own (and Grisoni's) script so he can one day attempt to make his dream movie a reality.

Nonetheless, after some down time, another potential movie option did appear. Terry Pratchett and Neil Gaiman's immensely popular comic fantasy novel, *Good Omens*, tells the tale of a devil named Crowley, an angel named Aziraphale and the impending end of the world, due to happen next Saturday, just after tea (according to Agnes Nutter). Both have been stranded on earth for 6,000 years awaiting the part they are due to play in the Apocalypse, but in that time both have grown accustomed to the ways of the world and neither of them want to see it all end, so they must join forces to prevent the end of the world.

Gilliam warmed to the project (which had been gestating alongside "Quixote") immediately and once again enlisted the aid of Tony Grisoni to adapt this sprawling comic epic into an epically sprawling screenplay.

"It's a rather wonderful book," says Grisoni. "It's a very popular book as well. It's interesting because Terry Pratchett, of course, has got this vast readership; but for all those who aren't completely sold on his world, Neil Gaiman makes the equation beautifully. It's a great mix between those two. The only thing that made me slightly nervous was that the book is full of stuff that *so* points to Terry as director. Here and there it felt a little too cosy.

"The thing is its tone, which is kind of extraordinary: a fast adventure movie tone which is very funny but with wonderfully dark moments as well."

Despite the unusual nature of the material, things progressed swiftly.

Charles "Chuck" Roven came on board as producer and the initial budget was set at $83million, something that proved to be unfeasible, despite needing to display the Four Horsemen of the Apocalypse, the Garden of Eden and the near-end of the world on screen. It was whittled down to a more manageable $60million but remained dependent on the casting of the two central roles. George Clooney was interested at one point, but passed. By early 2002, however, Gilliam had secured Johnny Depp for Crowley and Robin Williams as Aziraphale; both, Gilliam claimed, were doing it for less than their usual fee, out of friendship. Their pulling power at the time, however, was not strong enough.

"Robin's films haven't done too well recently and Johnny's haven't done too well," said Gilliam at the time. "And when you go out there it's the most depressing thing because the approach is always: 'What's Robin done recently that's done well? Can't think what Robin's done recently. And Johnny's been around but the films haven't been doing that well.' That's how they think, I mean I feel like saying 'Johnny and Robin. Fuck! That's great!' And it's like: 'Well, you know, Russell Crowe's a lot better these days.' That's what the Hollywood mentality is.

"Plus I've got very pissed off with Chuck, because he's just dragging his feet and I've waited too long on too many projects with him that haven't come together; this will be the fourth and either he can make it happen or he can't make it happen."

As it turned out he didn't make it happen, with Gilliam even positing that nobody wanted to make a movie about the end of the world in the wake of 9/11.

Nonetheless, it is a project that both he and Grisoni would like to revisit at some point.

"I'm not sure if we will ever continue with it," adds Grisoni; "I'd love to, but I don't know if that's possible. It's got this very weird structure, which… well, it's not that weird, but people involved in making mainstream movies have decided to call almost anything 'weird'. So, you start off the tale with a demon and an angel who have been here since Eden and have come to a kind of arrangement to make life easier. They actually both enjoy the world quite a lot and the angel is deeply into secondhand bookshops and things, and the demon does what demons do; and they have a bit of a battle, but it's in the background so they can just get on with life. And you're with them right up until they lose the anti-Christ. So you get to know these two and you're involved in their tale. Then we switch to the humans' story. New characters, new settings, new tale. Panic! It's, 'Oh, wait a minute, we lose them! For how many pages do we lose them?' [rapid flicking of script pages] 'Thirteen pages they're not in the story! We can't do that!' We worked on it for about a year, a year and a half."

By now, desperate to work, Gilliam did something he is normally reluctant to do – he agreed to direct a commercial. Not just any commercial – this was the Nike World Cup spot – the one in which the world's top soccer stars play a grudge match in the belly of a massive oil tanker.

For the job, Gilliam brought along his favourite one-eyed Italian director of photography, Nicola Pecorini, but as was typical of Gilliam's frame of mind at the time, he didn't really enjoy the job, making an advert when he should have been shooting a movie.

"It was awful. I went to Rome and did this thing, but the only good thing is I got to meet all the hot players and they signed this football for my son, Harry. You get out there and it is an agency that is so nervous, worried about losing the account, I think, and they can't make up their mind what they're doing and the players turn up and I have no idea what the commercial is anymore. We shot 250,000 feet of film, just for a 60-second commercial. That's a movie. It's just ridiculous and everything I was doing, the agency would be saying, 'I'm really worried about that,' and so I said, 'You just tell me what you want, you go and rehearse it and I'll shoot it,' and that's how it was done."

When he had to go back to shoot the re-match version of the spot, Gilliam threatened to just go along, let the creative head direct it and he would be his assistant. "I don't want to sit there and say, 'I'm doing this,' and them saying, 'No, Terry, I don't think we ought to do that.' I said, 'You don't need me, then. I'll go and be paid to direct it and just be his assistant.'"

During this period there was brief talk of trying to resurrect *Anything For Billy*, an adaptation of a western novel by Larry McMurtry that Gilliam had first read back whilst shooting *Twelve Monkeys* and toyed with the idea of making shortly after. This project was a particular favourite of Gilliam collaborator, (actors' coach) Stephen Bridgewater, and was at this point being mooted as a possible movie or mini-series for television, but discussions never went very far.

A screen adaptation of Mitch Cullin's book, *Tideland*, had already arisen as something Gilliam really wanted to make and Jeremy Thomas had gone so far as to announce it at the Cannes Film Festival in 2001 with the director attached. But, given the difficult nature of the material, it was not proving easy to finance.

In the meantime, two further projects had emerged via Tony Grisoni and Gilliam's previous agent, Jack Rapke. The first of these was based on a true story from the mid 1970s and was originally titled "The Man Who Robbed

The Pierre" (as in the Pierre Hotel in New York). It was soon retitled "Blue Ribbon Operation".

"I thought that 'Blue Ribbon' was absolutely amazing," says Grisoni. "The dialogue was so fantastic, so smart. I really enjoyed it, though it wasn't the sort of thing to which I'd have had anything to offer. I don't think it needed me. I think it would just go back to the guy who wrote it, because he just knew what he was doing so well. It was such a clear vision. In fact, I thought that that's what he ought to work on. It doesn't immediately strike you as a Terry movie, but what I loved about it was that the characters in it were just wonderfully drawn. They were droll and they were ironic. The whole thing was this character piece. I think if he'd flipped it around it could have been very much his movie."

Gilliam did proceed and got as far as talking to John Cusack and Dustin Hoffman about it, both of whom expressed interest.

However, plans to progress on this project were superseded by the other screenplay Grisoni had been looking at. This one had the financing in place, appeared to be a done deal, would offer Gilliam the largest budget he had ever worked with, show Hollywood he could make a big-budget costume piece (with a view to resurrecting "Quixote") and, more than anything, get him back to work. So it was that *The Brothers Grimm* broke Gilliam's dry stretch. And almost Gilliam himself.

"Why am I making this film? Because I've had four go under before it."

Terry Gilliam, *somewhere in Prague, 2003…*

'If You Go Down To The Woods Today . . .'

The Brothers Grimm On-Set Diary

So THE REALITY WAS THAT – barring the five days of actual physical shooting on "The Man Who Killed Don Quixote", before its tragic demise – Terry Gilliam hadn't made a film in seven years. "Quixote", "The Defective Detective" (a dormant project he had co-authored with *Fisher King* scribe Richard LaGravenese), "Good Omens", "The Man Who Robbed The Pierre", which, less it need restating, bore the promise of the potential dream casting of John Cusack and Dustin Hoffman ("And this is the old Hoffman," Gilliam stated. "This is 'Ratso' Hoffman.") – these had all gone the way of dust. Gilliam, an Oscar nominee and a man with a fierce and loyal following both in the world of fandom and within the movie industry itself, just simply couldn't get a film made.

He was author J.K. Rowling's first choice to bring Harry Potter to the big screen; the film company behind it, Warner Brothers, feared Gilliam would make it "too dark". While the Potter movie launched a relatively anodyne billion-dollar industry, Gilliam paced his attic workspace in North London, reading scripts, taking meetings and struggling to get back the rights to "Quixote", still his dream project.

But he needed to work. And that opportunity presented itself in a script by Ehren Kruger that "re-imagined" (a popular Hollywood phrase at the time) the brothers Grimm as a pair of 18th-century con men, spinning tales of enchanted forests and haunted barns in order to scam local townspeople out of their money. Until, that is, they discover a real enchanted forest and have to drag all their mythological folklore into the real world, to save themselves and everyone else.

It was a high-concept idea from a writer who was currently flavour of the month in Hollywood, having stepped into the breach and saved the *Scream* horror franchise. (Kruger took over scripting duties on *Scream 3* when its creator Kevin Williamson had jumped ship; he had subsequently delivered another $100million-grossing success in the form of the American remake of the cult Japanese horror movie *The Ring*.)

In short, this was a hot script, but one that still came with its fair share of development nightmares, something Gilliam was no stranger to.

After reading the script, Gilliam was at first dubious. He wanted to rewrite it with the man who was by now his regular collaborator, Tony Grisoni. MGM agreed and Gilliam and Grisoni proceeded, albeit somewhat cautiously; after all, they'd been here several times before in the last few years. Yet all the signs looked good.

But as budgets started to be drawn up, MGM began to make noises about backing out. This was not a small movie, and if anything the Gilliam/Grisoni rewrites were making it a more complicated picture, and by default a more expensive one. As it teetered on the edge of collapse, Gilliam was unsure for once what to do. "I guess the whole 'Quixote' thing left me more depressed than I realised."

The cavalry arrived in the form of Harvey and Bob Weinstein and the Miramax offshoot Dimension Films. But it was a bed that, right from the off, Gilliam was unsure he wanted to get into. He had to relinquish final cut, something he was loath to do, and had the good sense to realise that the combination of himself and Harvey and Bob might well be an incendiary one. Given the fact he had stopped talking to them by the first week of production, he was probably right.

The Brothers Grimm shot on location in Prague – after many months of pre-production – from the 30th of June 2003 until the 28th of November of the same year, six days after the 63rd birthday of its co-writer and director, Terry Gilliam. By the very scale of the production it was a long and difficult shoot, one that finished three weeks behind schedule and around $5million over its originally conceived $75million budget. This is not unusual for a production of this scale and complexity, particularly given that those actually actively making the film on a day-to-day basis in Prague felt it was under-financed to begin with. "They gave us $75million when the lowest budget we ever presented – and this is after we cut stuff – was $78million," says Gilliam. "But they wouldn't budge."

The following is a series of extracts from a number of diaries kept during the production. It is by no means meant as a definitive version of everything that went on during the making of *The Brothers Grimm*; rather it is intended more as a subjective look at the process – how one talented and lauded filmmaker struggles to get the film he wants to get made, actually made.

It is, therefore, a document of the difficult birth of a hopefully beautiful baby.

Those contributing include:

NICOLA PECORINI (NP) – the Director of Photography, there from the beginning and fired three weeks into production by Miramax/Dimension;

NIKKI CLAPP (NC) – Script Supervisor, keeper of daily production log/diary;

BOB McCABE (BM) – author/journalist, there to document the making of the movie at Gilliam's request, and escorted away from the set three weeks before the end of production by Miramax (and two large Czech security guards);

TERRY GILLIAM (TG) – leader of the banned.

From the Diary of Nicola Pecorini (NP):

Los Angeles: Monday, 18th November 2002

NP: Well, more or less everything started to come together in the last ten days. But let's start at the beginning.

Three weeks ago while I was still in Italy, Terry called me from London saying that Chuck Roven was committed to going ahead and that in all honesty he found *The Brothers Grimm* – however flawed and in need of heavy rewriting – very much more suited to his studio than it could ever have been with "Blue Ribbon Operation". In fact, for some time Terry continued to ask me (and, I suppose, to ask himself) whatever could he do with a script like this?

My reply was that there was nothing wrong in taking the money that they kindly offered, and sitting down to enjoy watching the fine actors put on a play, so long as I and, above all, he knew very well the enormous limitations of the story.

The problem is that Terry needs to work; it is not just a crime against the art of cinematography, and a reflex against human understanding and acceptance at the highest level, that Terry Gilliam doesn't succeed in realising his projects how and when he feels like it. He, as a person, needs to create: it's a question of his sanity. For which "Blue Ribbon" would do fine, not because it would be who-knows-what story, but because it seemed possible.

So now *Brothers Grimm* seemed possible… And not just that, *Brothers Grimm* offered more space and possibility to fly. And to fly high!

I had read the script a little while before and in all truth I fell about laughing. The problem was that it was shallow. It was a well-conceived series of gags but it completely missed the point, and Terry's works are fantastic simply because of the incredible depth (or height) that he manages to reach. But it was an appealing starting-point (and I can't wait to see Terry's rewrite).

Even more, Terry is also exasperated by the continued indecision and lack of commitment to any project since "Quixote". "Good Omens" was another bitter blow, we got so close and then frustratingly everything went back to square one. So, let's go for *Brothers Grimm*!

Talking of the script and characters (which according to Terry were the real weak spot in the story) we went on to talk of the cast.

Clearly Terry wanted to work with Johnny [Depp] again but equally clearly he understood that to antagonise the studio at the beginning would really be starting off on the wrong foot. Therefore, he asked for a shortlist of the studio's preferred actors so that he could choose from a favoured few. The market demanded that on this list there would be Heath [Ledger]'s name… As expected, Heath is enthusiastically embracing the idea of working with Terry and Johnny; it's exactly the kind of challenge he's looking for. When I gave the script to Heath, I felt like very much the producer – I understand the challenge and satisfaction of putting together a project, getting a team, finding the right chemistry. Perhaps when I grow up I can try it…

The following week Heath and Terry met in London where, to my great disappointment, Terry wasn't keen on Heath (there goes my producing career…). After this meeting Terry went to Los Angeles, where he started working on the script with the writer to get the project going in the right direction.

It would be shot in Prague at the beginning of spring.

The budget would be $68million.

Why shouldn't we be able to make a movie for that money?! We were given the go-ahead for eight weeks' preliminary pre-production…

Wednesday, 20th November

NP: The incredible thing that we didn't take into account was that I would do it, and even Chuck Roven seemed to have no problems about it! I thought that there would have been doubts, not only with the studio (which I took as read) but in some way with Terry himself.

The facts: yesterday evening I had dinner at Chateaux Marmont with Terry, Heath and Chuck. Heath, even tipsy, was the Heath I'd learned to know and appreciate: nervous, witty, provocative, sparkling with ideas. And Terry immediately responded to him. So much so that the morning after, when I took him the tape of *The Sin Eater*, he spoke positively and above all agreed with my impression (as usual instinctive and not elaborate) that Heath and Johnny have at least one common denominator, something in their DNA is the same but at the same time the opposite. Nothing better for screen brothers.

Chuck was the same person I'd begun to know (but not yet appreciate!). He was uncomfortable (which made you uncomfortable) and if you talk of anything remotely not connected to Hollywood, he's completely lost and looks as if he's just arrived on the planet. (His face, when Heath mentioned the Australian viewpoint that the CIA had placed the Bali bomb to get Australia's support for the war in Iraq... priceless!)

Wednesday, 4th December

NP: Talking with Wolfgang [Glattes – line producer], I gave him names and numbers of [sound mixer] Ivan Sharrock and [cameraman] Pete Cavaciuti. A bit early but better safe than sorry. He confirmed that they'd like to make a "British" film but also confirmed that he thought this very improbable. However, they've made an offer to an English set designer [Guy Hendrix-Dyas, who designed *X-Men 2*] and if everything goes to plan we will be in Prague next weekend. Barrandov is booked and everything's at our disposal. Seems as though it really will be spring in Prague...

Interview with Terry Gilliam

TERRY GILLIAM (TG): Chuck Roven sent it to me and started hassling... Originally, [producer] Daniel Bobker got that script to me earlier. MGM basically told Chuck that there was no way Terry Gilliam would direct that film. In fact, Chuck first put forward Raja Gosnell as director, but Raja went off to do *Scooby Doo 2* and so I guess I was Chuck's second choice. But apparently Daniel Bobker said it got to him even before Chuck was involved. Daniel doesn't have much experience and Chuck had been patching up projects for MGM, like *Rollerball* and *Bulletproof Monk*.

So anyway, he was Mr Fix-it there, and he got drawn into it because he had the experience with something of this scale and then I read the script and I didn't like it because here were a couple of contemporary Hollywood guys going into the 19th century in Germany and being smart-asses and it all seemed to be a compendium of all your favourite moments from all your favourite successful fantasy movies and I didn't like it.

BM: Did you turn it down straight away?

TG: Yeah. And then there was this project I was working on called "Blue Ribbon Operation" with John Cusack, and then I got Dustin Hoffman involved and the studio got all sniffy about lots of things and it collapsed. Chuck had been on top of me, obviously pushing me to do "Grimms" and so I said, "Okay, I've got to do something," and reading it I saw I could make an interesting world and maybe if I could rewrite the thing I could make a better film. But then Chuck said MGM was rejecting it, there was no way, so that was the end of that for a while.

BM: They then rejected you?

TG: Me. Wrong guy, too dark, too dismal, too disturbing, three Ds, and then Chuck orchestrated a meeting between me and Michael Nathanson and Chris McGurk, who are the top honchos at MGM, when they were over in London checking out the latest Bond film and by the end of lunch they said, "The only guy who can make this film is Terry Gilliam."

BM: To which you responded...?

TG: Well, it was the right thing to say because I *am* the right guy for the material. At least, if I could turn the material into what I wanted it to be.

BM: So it was always the case that you wanted to rewrite what was there. That was it, from day one.

TG: Yeah. Because I thought it was two-dimensional characters chasing a narrative, trying to keep up with a narrative and the stuff just seemed not to be coming from the heart of the piece, which was fairytales and a lot of the things that happen in it were nothing to do with Grimm's fairytales. There were a lot of things that are no longer in the script for a variety of reasons.

Monday, 9th December

NP: Terry's left for Prague!

You can hardly believe it – not even "Good Omens" was this far ahead.

couldthisbecouldthisbeit?

Thursday, 12th December

NP: I talked with Heath. They've gone through the new version of the script – as far as he knows, agents and lawyers are still talking and everything's going according to plan.

For my part, I've tried to get my hands on a copy of the new draft, but to no avail. The Christmas spirit has already infused Los Angeles and the offices aren't working with the necessary clear-headedness.

This town is so cut off from the world that it goes into a frenzy when asked to join in something that has a "planetary" significance. Except you then discover they're incapable of taking part (look at what they were able *not* to do for the new millennium).

London: Sunday, 15th December

NP: I called Terry. He came back yesterday evening from Prague. Hopes are still high. Heath is champing at the bit, Johnny hasn't officially yet said yes.

Monday, 16th December

NP: Met Guy.

Sat down with him and Terry.

Went through whole script.

Where, what, somehow, how?

Stage or real?

All that...

Fantastic locations.

References: back to Dore. Breughel the Elder. A kind of *Alice in Wonderland*.

Went to London bookshop Foyles; couldn't find much about the Grimm brothers as humans. Found amazing book about extraordinary trees and the oddest thing is that not one of the photographs showed the tops of the trees; the intriguing part is the root, but the danger then is to go down the anthropomorphic path and risk falling into a certain iconography like Roger Corman. Given to Terry.

Dinner with Ray [Cooper], he is sceptical about the movie being good for Terry.

My point is that, with the right people and right locations, it could be fantastic – maybe not as deep and universal as all of Terry's other movies, but certainly a "TG-movie".

TREE SLOWLY CRACKS

Tuesday, 17th December

NP: Back to the office. Guy is very nervous to "do a good job" – who would not be? Back in '97 I was even more nervous, and I still am.

Daniel Bobker arrived and met Terry, and they've begun to work on the storyboards. We've talked at length of the moving forest and how to realise it, dividing it into models and fast-cuts.

Wednesday, 18th December

NP: I left out that I arrived in Tuscany in time for [assistant costume designer] Carlo Poggioli to call me and ask for clarification and advice. On the one hand I'm pleased that they consider me one of Terry's Fifth Column, perhaps that means that I'm visible. But on the other hand it's worrying, not just because it gives me a lot of responsibility but because at this long distance it could be a double-edged sword. However, for the moment it's fine.

Carlo and Gabriella [Pescucci – costume designer] are absolutely fixed on taking part, and I don't think anyone's more suitable than they are. Not only this, they're already in Prague for another job so everything should be smooth and straightforward.

I passed this on to Terry.

Wolfgang has talked to Carlo and Gabriella, the seed's planted, now we need to water it. Carlo assured me that they're even agreeable to being English if necessary...

Friday, 20th December

NP: Terry called me in a panic because Johnny still hasn't arrived. I immediately sent e-mails and placed a few phone calls, just in case. I spoke with Mathias who told me that Johnny sounds very fed up with the buccaneer picture [*Pirates of the Caribbean* – the movie that would land Depp a Best Actor Oscar nomination] and therefore he hates the whole movie business at the moment. A classic!

Interview with Terry Gilliam

BM: Why Prague? Just financial or the space?

TG: Because the then production line producer, Wolfgang Glattes, had done *Hart's War* here and knew the set-up and said, "We could save a lot of money, blah, blah, blah." And you know, so off we went to Prague.

BM: So was the film budgeted at this point?

TG: Well, there was a kind of sense that the budget was around $75million, $70million, whatever.

BM: Was that realistic?

TG: No, no, no, everybody said it was... those who weren't trying to impress the studio always said it was going to be more, but then there's always the reality of what will they jump in for, at least to start the process, so it was around that number.

BM: How committed are you to it at this point?

TG: I'm not.

BM: You could just walk away at any time?

TG: Many times a week we would say we could just go away from the whole thing.

Saturday, 21st December

NP: The barrage had some effect. Johnny wrote to Terry, not to say "yes" or "no" but at least he's alive and his computer works.

I talked briefly with Terry about who else could play Johnny's role. I suggested Guy Pearce, he told me that Matt Damon is interested but he doesn't like him much.

John Turturro would love to play Cavaldi, I always knew that Turturro is clever, Cavaldi at the moment is definitely the best role.

Terry also said that back in Hollywood everybody would love to be part of the project (same as in *Fear and Loathing*); the only one who's not jumping at the chance is Johnny. (Bastard!)

Terry is also convinced that Johnny is somehow threatened by Heath, just because he's younger...

Christmas Day

NP: Spoken with Mishka [Cheyko – associate producer]. I told him to find the French edition of Mastroianni's bio *I Remember, Yes I Remember* so that we can give it to Johnny and he can read how Marcello, when he realised that he was ageing, started playing older roles so that anybody recognising him in the street would think, "He's actually younger than he looks on screen!"

I'll never understand why someone as beautiful and charismatic as Johnny could have similar insecurities.

Monday, 13th January 2003

NP: Terry called me. Johnny has said "no". He's played too many parts of that period, and to listen to him you'd think they hadn't done him a bit of good. Also, while talking to Terry, it came out that Vanessa doesn't like Prague... And here's how sometimes the "story" can change: just because Johnny was a bit of a hooligan in Prague a couple of years ago, now he can't take part in *The Brothers Grimm*!

Terry took it philosophically; after all, it will be enough that Johnny comes back if and when he can pick up "Quixote".

So now Matt Damon is leading the field, especially as Ivan and Oliver have told me that he's a pleasure to work with. So much the better.

Tuesday, 14th January

NP: I spoke on the phone with Guy Dyas. Unfortunately, I'll miss him completely in London: he's going to Prague tomorrow. But he's in good spirits and has been able to put together a very good crew. He's going crazy with the budgeting aspect of it but it seems that Wolfgang is happy with the numbers. His main concern is the timing: he needs at least twelve weeks of heavy duty construction to be ready in time, therefore they need to commit ASAP.

London: Wednesday, 15th January

NP: Received Guy's drawings and plans (the really good designers make me mad); it's begun to take visual shape, and of course it gets more and more complicated.

Dinner with Terry – he's still very optimistic and upbeat and doesn't seem to suffer Johnny's defection too much.

He also believes at this point they cannot really back down.

Thursday, 16th January

NP: Spent the day with Terry: went through a lot of "visual references", mostly romantic, strong lights where you need to see, black on black for the rest. I'm intrigued with the idea of making "day for night" in the studio, that's the route I've been taking for some time:

darkness not as a lack of light but as the presence of shadow. It's early days, but if we don't go over the top we should do a good job.

Friday, 17th January

NP: Today's the deadline of the 8th September pre-pre-production. Damon should give us an answer on Tuesday, then we'll see.

Los Angeles: 19th January

NP: Talked with Wolfgang, who confirmed that everything hangs on Matt Damon's reply. If it's positive it will be like passing Go without collecting the money: the film will become bigger, which means we'll have to revise everything including the dates and (listen, listen) the budget!

Tuesday, 21st January

NP: Fateful day, we haven't heard anything, and to compensate Terry's vanished...
    Bad sign? Good sign?

Wednesday, 22nd January

NP: Fear is kicking in... Terry has gone, Damon did not answer, fuck me it's another folded project...
    Fuck Hollywood, fuck them all. Not only are all my numerous agents not in town but they're off skiing and having a great time at the Sundance film festival. Fuck them too.

Later still: 22nd

Email from Terry, he is coming tomorrow. Maybe Hollywood is not that rotten after all!

Thursday, 23rd January

NP: Terry has arrived; Damon is "interested" but he mainly wants to know why Terry would be interested in *him*. Good question, probably because with him he could make this bloody movie...

Terry is still upbeat about it, does not think that with Damon things would change much. He seems to have the right attitude to make things happen, I guess that the work done on the script with Tony has produced good results – so good that Terry now feels stronger for the project. Good.

Monday, 27th January

NP: And we're waiting again...

Today Terry is meeting everyone and tomorrow he has to go to Minneapolis to meet Josh Hartnett, even though part of him knows he isn't the right choice. He's just going to please the studio; what a waste of energy, time and money.

Wednesday, 29th January

NP: Terry went and came back from Minneapolis, "for lunch", as he said. He did meet Josh Hartnett and confirmed his opinion of him: boring!

It makes sense given that they are making him become the new Tom Cruise. Tom Cruise: boring. Perfect icon for the average boring American.

The good news is that they said "yes" to Robin Williams playing Cavaldi; maybe Turturro would have been better but on the other hand it shows commitment to making the movie. Thiscouldbeitthiscouldbeit!

Discussed again with Terry the possibility of filming in 3perf. His point is that so far nobody asked us to save money on film-stock and he believes that the advantages (25% less cost in film stock, prints and lab) are inferior to the disadvantages (not being free to have a work-copy screening anywhere, have to plan in advance so carefully because it would be difficult to get additional 3perf cameras on short notice, etc) therefore he suggests we keep it in our back pocket in case we clash on a cost issue.

Terry can't wait to leave, his autonomy in LaLaLand is more or less reduced to less than a week: it's a physiological not intellectual fact. I understand completely...

Thursday, 6th February

NP: Lunch with Wolfgang. Finally something that begins to resemble an official commitment. Terry will be back next week to talk again with Matt Damon who now wants to play Wilhelm... too bad that Heath has been promised that part... what's wrong with their egos sometimes?!

If all goes well, then Terry should meet with the BIG BOSS of MGM somewhere in Nevada (sounds very alien!) because "he has this habit of meeting a director before green-lighting a project". And what if he does not like the director in question? Piranhas! Poor Terry, the shit he goes through.

But the news from London is good, despite the weather: the script is shaping up, we flash back to their youth and a wonderful episode with magic beans and tragedy. Can't wait to read it.

They are also considering a partnership with another studio to make it happen.

Left lunch somehow lighter, maybe we are going to make it! Then the tough job will start...

This is turning into a story of mealtimes: dinner with Terry; the appointment with the extraterrestrials in Nevada has become a "vision meeting" here in LA and all because Terry refused to stay in LA longer than necessary and therefore they would have had to buy another first class ticket... However, tomorrow will certainly be a crucial day in our destiny, let's hope for the best!

Monday, 10th February

NP: I called Wolfgang: our destiny is still uncertain, but to make up for it he's sending me a new version of the script... still, it's moving on!

Wednesday, 12th February

NP: The facts: around 9.00am I cannot take it any longer and I call Terry (who's staying at Chuck's house). Chuck answers: "No, Terry is back in London, he left last night with the movie he wanted in his pocket!"

I can't believe it. I immediately called Ivan, Carlo and Gabriella. Mishka and poor Guy are lonely, without news, in Prague. Not even two hours later, Guy calls back: "Spoken with Wolfgang, absolutely no green light yet! Cannot commit, I'm losing my head people, nobody believes me any more, will not make the date, I'll have to write a memo."

Good thing he reminded me, I'm not sure how I feel about memos: yes, it can be a way to cover your ass but also as a way to produce "evidence" that will be used *against* you! I guess it all depends on the kind of relationship you have with your co-workers...

Talked to Wolfgang, no green light but very, very close, like we've never been so far. (I hope so, this thing has been going on for three months now.)

Thursday, 13th February

NP: I talked with Terry, who told me the ball is in MGM's court. Matt Damon's on board, Heath as well, and so is Robin Williams. It's up to them to say "yes" or "no".

Of course, Matt wanted to play Will, the role that Terry gave to Heath, so Terry met with Heath to explain the situation. But before he could talk, Heath told him that after reading the new script (which, by the way, is much stronger than the last one: good old Tony Grisoni...) he actually would rather play Jacob. Great! Terry agrees and they both go to meet Matt Damon, who at this point (24 hours later) reconsidered and actually wants to play Jacob as well! *They're great*!!

Saturday, 15th February

NP: World Peace Day: even in Hollywood there were lots of people. How insignificant can a movie be?

TG: So then they won't do Robin's deal and so Robin's out of the picture, which is great, it's wonderful, my buddy Robin, we get him and they push him out. That's a good start.

Tuesday, 18th February

NP: We're off! Not that we've been given the green light yet, the green light implies too many commitments and expenses, but we go to Prague on Sunday to pre-pre-scout and make it happen! I almost don't believe it.

Sunday, 23rd February

NP: On the plane to Prague via Frankfurt.

The plane is packed and overbooked: I really cannot see this "Great Airline Crisis", since 9/11 planes are more and more full and more expensive, there is something definitely rotten in a system that takes advantages of tragedies.

I'm very curious to see Prague after all these years. Last time I was here was June 2000 while prepping for "Quixote"(!)

Yesterday before leaving I went to do some homework and watched *The Lord of The Rings: The Two Towers*. Definitely an impressive piece of work but at the same time a "fantasy" piece that allows you to do anything; the forest — you never know whether it is night or day, the nights always have a full moon, and our heroes never get hurt or spill a drop of blood.

From what Terry told me so far we are contrary to this; we have to be real and make sure that the viewer doesn't know where the boundaries between reality and fantasy are so that they can share the brothers' experience.

So, finally, there's something really important to report about the film, the making of it… but now's not the time to lose one's head!

Later: Prague

A classic… I'll try to put it in sequence:

There are eleven of us here: Terry, Guy, Wolfgang, Mishka, Keith (who I know from *Cutthroat Island*!), Kent, Steve, Andy, Roger, Danieli and me. Then there are Alex, Veronika, Martina, George, Pepino and all the locals who for some years round here haven't stopped working. Chuck decided not to come. Guy & co. have made models of the village and the forest. Of course, the first thing Terry wanted to do was "play" with the models. And to justify that he was right, it immediately came out that there were endless flaws: the height, the space, the use of these, the height and distance of the village in relation to the forest…

But above all, one thing has become *very* clear: it will be a very difficult and complicated film, and bound to be littered with problems where there is no easy way round.

The good news is that everyone seems to know what they're doing and have a very positive and proactive attitude (with the exception of Andy, SFX, who gives the impression of being an expert but is also a pain in the butt). Tomorrow we're going on location: Kutna Hora, Ledec, forests…

Thursday, 27th February

NP: It's not possible! It's happened again: MGM woke up Wolfgang this morning ordering him to pull the plug, everybody home ASAP! They have no intention of keeping it going. It doesn't matter that they have a cast, a crew, locations, stages, a script – it does not matter

that Chuck came up with 60% of the budget. They probably simply do not get the movie, they are too stupid!

TG: They were still putting up the money, flew people in from LA, Paris and on Tuesday we had a recce; then on Thursday morning, we're about to head out and I get a call from Chuck saying, "MGM have pulled the plug". That Thursday, they put everybody back on planes to where they came from. The show was basically over and I had dinner that evening with Gabriella, who stayed on, and Nicola and Wolfgang, and when I got back to my room there was a phone call from Chuck saying, "Dimension want on board".

BM: And what did you think of that, initially?

TG: Well it was better than nobody, I guess. I thought, well let's check it out. I always said I'd never work with those guys but I was kind of into it and it was their thing. So anyway, I flew out to LA.

BM: Given that MGM had pulled the plug, was Dimension saying they'd take the whole thing on?

TG: Well, MGM were looking for a partner to do 50/50. Chuck had actually got Intermedia on board, or it looked like they were going to be, and they were willing to put up 60%, but for whatever reason the deal was that MGM preferred to go with Dimension. So then it was a matter of going out to meet Bob and Harvey Weinstein.

NP: I cannot believe this is happening again. Terry does not deserve this; the art of cinema does not deserve to be served by stupid hotel managers who do not have any clue about beauty, spirit and life.

The only hope is that Chuck can come up with something. I don't know what, but something. He has forty-eight hours. On Monday we are going to lose the stages and then it will definitely be over... So we went to the "last supper" at Kampa Park, taking Matthew Modine with us. The only goal is to hit MGM with a last expensive tab, great wine, good caviar... In the middle of dinner, Chuck phoned to say that as he's found other people interested in putting money into the project; now, all of a sudden, MGM is thinking it over and maybe they want to do it after all...

I cannot believe their stupidity.

Going back to LA tomorrow, in any case. Hopefully, Terry will come too; I believe he is the only one who can put the whole thing back together, even if he rightly says that he wants to direct, not produce.

Los Angeles: Friday, 28th February

NP: Back in LA.

Absolutely raging against the whole situation: it's not only for *Brothers Grimm*, it is the symptom of a deeper "malaise" within the movie industry. If they cannot jump to the occasion of such a project when will they ever make something worth making?!

Of course, here everybody already knows everything about the collapse. But by the end of the day the rumour is that Miramax is picking it up...

Saturday, 1st March

NP: It's all true!

When MGM passed, regardless of Intermedia's 60%, Miramax stepped forward and offered to take over with Intermedia. At this point MGM said, "Wait a minute, if Miramax wants it then we want it!" Result: Intermedia is out of the picture, MGM will distribute it internationally and Dimension (Bob Weinstein), domestically. It seems that Harvey threw his weight into the proceedings, calling Matt Damon personally etc.

Terry sounded upbeat and confident (even though he has not spoken with Chuck since Thursday evening, or maybe because of it).

My main concern is: given Miramax's and the Weinstein reputation would it not be better to forget about the whole thing and concentrate on something else ("Quixote" to say one!). What those fat bastards did to Kapur on *Four Feathers*, Scorsese on *Gangs* and Minghella on *Cold Mountain* should have advised Terry to stay well clear of them.

The rollercoaster of conflicting news and unexpected events is exhausting.

Prague: Sunday, 16th March

NP: Back to square one: Prague!

We are all regrouping in the Hilton hotel lobby tomorrow morning at 8.00am to go scouting....

Just wasted two and a half weeks!

But still no green light, of course not!

First they want to know if we can "cut" the budget... they want to trim $3million below the line and $6million above the line.

Personally I could not care less about the above the line. (Even though the rumours are that Robin Williams got offended at the new offer and does not want to be part of it anymore. Not encouraging but on the other hand it would reopen the door for John Turturro.)

It's difficult to concentrate on the future of a film when at stake is probably the future of the world, with that asshole Bush going to war...

Monday, 17th March

NP: We scouted Ledec, Kutna Hora and the real forest. Ledec will be Karlstadt, Kutna Hora as Frankfurt.

The forest is the problem, not just practically but also psychologically. One of the reasons Terry was convinced to go ahead with the *Grimms* adventure was this incredible location, which seems made for the film: now we find out that it's a protected zone, full of tourists and therefore "they'll never give us authorisation"!

Terry is furious (bearing in mind the limitations of his furies…) and after they took us to look at an "alternative", which was nothing at all like the first, he persuaded them to go back to the original place so that they could at least take into account exactly what was needed.

The place is amazing; I understand Terry's disappointment.

But the biggest problem is caused by Miramax's stupidity: while we were going back to Prague, Robin Williams had a long phone call with Terry, who began stroking his hair (a real sign of impatience). The problem: Miramax, in its efforts to cut the budget and with the priority of keeping Matt Damon, has offered $10million to Damon and $1million each to Robin and Heath! Not that $1million isn't a lot of money by Hollywood standards, but it's an insult to an actor like Williams. Why are they so stupid?

Consequently, I can't yet commit to the project; I still see it too much in the air, too many ifs and buts.

However it goes, it's still a pleasure being on the road again with Terry, the energy he's able to unleash is so positive that it's a great experience at every step, even this far from shooting.

Friday, 21st March

NP: The first day of spring, a lovely Prague day, it's even warm…

Tuesday we went to Krivoklat to look for a reasonable "forest edge" (no luck) and the interior of the mayor's office, then we all met up to try to put our ideas together and consider, given the time and resources available, whether it was still realistic to make the film.

The project is becoming more complicated and difficult. Out of 175 scenes, we've counted six where the filmmaking is straightforward; all the others have at least some VSFX! On top of this, with the size of the sets and all the complications of real size, miniatures, blue-screen, CGI...

The good news is that the human elements are motivated, committed and experienced enough to somehow guarantee that we can actually make this movie, and make it well.

The problems are the suits back in LA who still cannot commit, and they still do not understand that to make this film you need to move quickly, and above all that to make it well means having the budget and that's the money to spend. It's no good beginning a job like this if you then find yourself halfway through with your pants down. Not only useless, but dangerous. Terry is still paying for the consequences of the wicked management of *Munchausen.*

I still can't bring myself to leave. I can't commit completely until I know we are really making it and the same can be said of Terry, who for the umpteenth time has to fly back to Los Angeles to meet (yet again) the Weinsteins who should then give the green light (and we hope that they win something at the Oscars on Sunday, so at least on Monday they'll be in a good mood and perhaps hung over from the parties...)

Monday, 24th March

NP: Dawn of Monday morning, it will be jet-lag, it will be tension, but this morning I really can't sleep and keep picturing Terry looking at me shaking his head...

The last two days in Prague were frenzied. Lots of nervous energy, not necessarily positive and certainly not optimistic. Chuck's main concern is to lower that budget to $75million, nothing more, nothing less, regardless of the needs, regardless of the reality. And this translates into a great waste of that energy. Meanwhile we are also trying to keep going forward and get as much ready as possible, given the circumstances. We had the longest SFX meeting ever, almost two days of going through every detail.

I've been meeting people for crew; I must admit that is always terrifying to have to make choices based upon a brief meeting. Choices that we might eventually deeply regret and can cause high distress to the proceedings. Now I understand why certain colleagues never ever change crew. On the other hand it's exciting somehow to be able to make the right choices and to work with great people. The only problem is that I haven't seen many of those in Prague...

The War is going on and in a little while will become "normal"; the Oscars took place and we LOVE Michael Moore!

With Terry we were wondering if it would have been preferable to have a winning or a losing Weinsteins Bros on this Monday morning, the outcome provides a decent balance: they won but they did not sweep it, therefore maybe they'll be more inclined to listen to others.

Whatever, as long as a decision is taken today. It has been dragging on for too long and we are on the verge of losing the momentum.

Afternoon

Terry came by on his way to the meeting: he was not exactly looking forward to the moment. After last night's party, he desperately needed a strong coffee...

Night

Spoken with Terry; they said that they will give an answer within 48 hrs! MORE FUCKING WAITING!!!

But the deal with Matt Damon seems done so it looks very much as if they want to make the movie, but they want to shrink the budget… they really are nuts!

Wednesday, 26th March

NP: 2 hours to the 48 hours...

che stressssssssssssssssssssssssssssssssssssssssssssssssssssssssssssssssssssssss.

Thursday, 27th March

NP: I cannot believe it: the boys in Prague managed (I do not know, nor do I want to know how) to scale down to $75million and now those assholes want it even lower!

Terry is furious, everybody is depressed and I really do not know what to think/hope/wish.

Yes, I want to make this movie but I am not so sure we can work at our best with such assholes...

For Terry's sanity it would probably be better to drop it all together; he will not go crazy and grow frustrated and they would not have their stoopid savings...

Friday, 28th March

NP: Yet another day of uncertainty and indecisions...

Terry is kind of hiding, the boys in Prague are growing more and more frustrated, I'm trying not to think about it or to think as little as possible.

I parked the script/work folder on the side and I promised myself that I will not open it again till it's green lighted...

Sunday, 30th March

NP: Terry called and said that he had decided to make the movie whether they want it or not!

As I was starting sulking in desperation here comes the maestro who gives up all his deal (final cut, retainer etc.) and saves the movie!

AND THEN HE REFUSES TO BE CREDITED AS PRODUCER: HE IS THE REAL PRODUCER.

It also seems that Miramax is trying to get rid of Chuck, and that's a reason for the delay in the switching to green.

In any case he's flying back to Prague tomorrow.

We'll see.

TG: Chuck by now has been terminated. They wouldn't do his deal. His deal was not going to be done. I don't know it directly, it's just hearsay; it was a rich deal which was based on him bringing a lot of money to the table. Anyway so they didn't like the deal, he wasn't going to give up on it and they ended up at loggerheads and they terminated it. Somewhere before this occurred though, Wolfgang Glattes had quit and John Schofield had come on. He's been great, he's been really keeping it going. And Roberto [Malerba – production manager]. And then they keep telling me to lower the budget, keep the schedule down while all this is going on and so I'm pulling some big eye-candy out very early on, that they really liked, such as a creature made of bones held together by bugs. So originally in the final confrontation, it's not the forest on fire it's a thousand of these skeletal warriors, taking on the army.

Wednesday, 2nd April

NP: This morning at a production meeting in Prague Jake (Bloom)/Dimension said that we do not have the green light yet but that we can go ahead spending!

Too bad there is no accountant or account!

But it's good news; we now have to make this darn movie!

Evening

It's official – WE HAVE THE GREEN LIGHT!

Monday, 14th April

NP: In Prague, the enthusiasm has come back.

John Turturro has got the script and we should have a reply soon. Tomorrow Terry goes back to London to begin casting.

Thursday, 17th April

NP: I've been back in Prague four days. A load of things has happened. A brief recap:

John Turturro passed; family problems stop him from being too far for too long.

Terry does not really know who to cast, he's thinking of giving Cavaldi to Jonathan Pryce and Delatombe to someone like Vincent Cassell.

Miramax is pushing for someone else, like Ben Kingsley.

I suggested Roberto Benigni, or Colin Firth.

There is some kind of offer out for Nicole Kidman to play the queen...

Things are moving on in Barrandov.

Trees are starting to go in, the village is starting to go up.

The weak points start to show...

Terry is growing impatient with various elements of the team, and as usual it's the "poor" architect who bears the brunt. The problem is that Terry chose him at the time when nothing about the movie was very clear, and he said yes just to move things along more than anything else. And now he regrets it!

We will probably go to London next week for a screen test for Samantha Morton, but she has been sick and she needs to look her best. We'll see.

Tuesday, 22nd April

NP: Facts: Easter is finally gone and we should not suffer any more disruptions.

There was too much work last week: the most important thing we accomplished is that we met Mike and Kent on Thursday and Friday in front of a model of the forest stage. The result is that we took the decision of doing the whole of the forest on stage! Terry feels that it's the best solution, to control as much as possible and to work in comfort…

The backlot is growing fast, at least that is a tangible sign of things moving along…The ravens have hatched and they look so sweet and clumsy, and that's another place where we are in good shape: the animals!

Tony Grisoni has been here all of last week and we should soon receive a new version of the script.

Terry still has no idea who will play Cavaldi; he's more and more leaning towards giving the role to Jonathan Pryce. I'm still not convinced by it.

Today some big Miramax boss is coming from NYC with Jake. What to do, we do not know, but he's coming anyway.

Tuesday, 29th April

NP: Back to Los Angeles for two weeks, and then I'll be back in Prague for good.

Found an apartment close, too close, to the American Embassy. Security is great(!) the problem will occur if they do put a bomb there. But it is really beautiful and I'm looking forward to it.

Work is going ahead full steam and I suppose this week even more steaming because a lot of the crew were supposed to start on Monday: SFX workshop, plasterers; stages 6 and 7 should have been started.

The backlot is proceeding fast, and it makes sense.

It's somehow hard to be away from there because my brain is so involved in it that the physical distance just makes it difficult. I'm in the stage of rapid evolution of ideas and being there is important, but "they cannot afford to pay me more than ten weeks' prep". Therefore they flew me back. On the one hand I would say, "Fuck it" and just stay with no pay, but in the great scheme of things I do not believe this is correct. Miramax is making the movie to make money. I cannot give them too much of my free time, I did already and I will for one week, but enough is enough.

The guy from Miramax turned out to be John Gordon EVP (I guess that means Executive Vice President, but I'm not sure at all...); better executive than expected, not that I had much to deal with him but according to Terry, Roberto and the others, he likes the script and rows in the right direction. They are *so* corporate! This is really one of the things about America that I have a really hard time understanding: the corporate thinking (that is so much more than just "loyalty" to your employer, it's a mix of fears...)

Friday, 2nd May

NP: Bob Weinstein doesn't like Samantha Morton, he wants Liv Tyler(!!) Terry, of course, does not want to give up.

Personally I believe that Liv is not right: too big for our two boys *and* too clumsy. On *Stealing Beauty* she was clumsy but we all figured that she was still quite young and therefore not used to her "big" body yet. But she is still clumsy in *The Two Towers*, even when she tries really hard to have a "pose".

I haven't spoken with Terry for days now, I don't want to bother him but I soon will.

Last Friday at the camera test it was fantastic to see Terry's eyes and mind when he saw the "camera" (even though it was a stupid HD video camera), I always forget that for him being on a set (even a disgraced one) is an event. He has not been on a set since Nike – that's eighteen months ago!

NP: I went to the screening of Jim Sheridan's new film *In America*, pleasantly disturbing. With Samantha Morton! (Nothing new, but very good – considering nothing surprises or shocks me any more. Am I turning into a snob?)

What in the meantime has become the real fly in the ointment is that Bob can't even look at it any more, and Terry can't give up! It became somehow the watershed, it will define who has the power and it will dictate the relationship of that power in the next few months.

Terry is very cleverly using the "Matt Damon leverage factor". Matt is on board for one reason over all the others: Mr Gilliam! Therefore, if he is the "golden boy", he'll be Terry's best ally.

I'm really curious to see how far he'll be able to push it. Somehow I'm happy not to be in Prague for this part of the business, it can really get ugly. They already told me about furious phone calls and insults, worse than small boys...

BM: Samantha Morton was a big issue with Terry. This is one of the things that has delayed him getting into this film, because he spent so much time dealing with that. But you were standing in the same corner.

MATT DAMON: The way I think about it is when you sign on with a director you're signing on to their vision and that's why. Look, it's fucking Terry Gilliam, I love his movies and I really admire him and have so much respect for him. When he says something, when something lights a fire in him, that can only be good for the movie. So that's something that you fight for… so that was my feeling about Sam. Plus I had my own opinion about her when I worked opposite her (in screen tests), I think she's just fucking great. So I would have taken the same position, but the fact that Terry was so passionate about her made it kind of a no-brainer and something to really dig in over.

Prague: Wednesday, 14th May

NP: Here I am, back in Prague to stay this time!

As I arrived at Barrandov I was kidnapped by Terry and we went to see both the forest stages and the backlot. The boys have been working really hard and doing a wonderful job. The village is particularly breathtaking and we can already see that it will offer wonderful opportunities.

The stage is a bit more difficult, but it's shaping up. I'm still very worried about the backdrop. Given that there is not enough space, it becomes crucial that the backdrop will be believable and I still haven't seen even a sketch; it really worries me...

Thursday, 15th May

NP: The Samantha Morton situation is worse than I imagined, so bad that Terry went for his medical and did not pass it for high blood pressure! That fucking Bob is managing to stress him beyond belief, but he will not let go. He said that his goal is to make justice of this stupid attitude the Weinstein Bros. have of "punishing" someone simply because they do not like her and/or because she said "NO" once (by the way, she said no to the *Four Feathers* simply because she just had her baby and did not feel in shape enough to take the job).

Matt Damon is still not fighting strongly enough along with Terry because his contract has not been signed yet and he feels that it would not be productive to put his weight down in such circumstances.

Heath cut his hair short (yet again) and Terry is furious.

TG: I knew that it was going to be rough, but I just felt if I didn't do it, I'd probably go crazy, because to let it drop again having spent many, many months on it and then starting to get on something else, I felt this is stupid. I didn't like the feeling of the thing, but I have to work. So now Chuck's gone and various people from Dimension/Miramax are on the case trying to fill the gap and all that really is supposed to be happening is that Bob W. and I are supposed to be talking all the time because Bob's a filmmaker, like Harvey, and they want to be participants in the "creative process".

And with all these phone calls, I found I'm dealing with somebody I don't even know how to talk to because all he can talk about is clichés, other films, like, "Oh, remember that scene where they ride the bicycle; oh, we've got to do that thing from *Titanic* – "King of the world," and I'm saying "I don't think that's actually this film," so we're having this dance and every time he calls, my blood pressure goes up.

So I went through a whole period with very high blood pressure, which I'd never had before. And I don't have it now in the middle of all this stuff, I don't have high blood pressure, it's dealing with *them*. It's these people who I basically despise, is the simple word, who've treated so many filmmakers like shit. They are what they are and I sort of find myself in bed with them and thinking can I control all this stuff? So my blood pressure's going sky high, Chuck's been fired, Robin's out of the picture and we're trying to put this fucking thing together again and it's just marching on. And the girl, I said, has to be Samantha Morton.

Friday, 16th May

NP: I went for my medical and I passed, did not have the time to get over-stressed yet!

The Samantha situation is getting worse and worse if only for the fact that the days go by and no decision is taken. The most stoopid aspect of them all is that Bob keeps saying NoNoNoNO but he is not coming up with viable solutions and ideas. It's just that he does not like her, plain and simple.

Meanwhile, speaking with Mishka we came up with the idea of Roman Polanski playing Cavaldi – script is off to him, he's intrigued, we'll see.

On the Queen side, at one point it seemed that Nicole Kidman passed and Terry spoke with Uma Thurman, but now Kidman has dropped out of another project and might be available again.

Meantime the weeks go by…

Sunday, 18th May

NP: The casting/power stall is still the main problem, days go by and no decisions get taken The most staggering thing is that from the side of the Weinsteins there is no real evident effort to find a sensible solution, they keep sending tapes of total disasters, not even pretty faces, just bad actresses.

TG: We're in production and Harvey's first comment is, "Samantha Morton? You must be kidding! You think Matt or Heath want to fuck that?" I'm saying, "She's perfect! She's fantastic, I'll find a screen test of her," and John Gordon, who's one of the Miramax minions, comes over, knowing that Harvey's against her and it ain't gonna work and by the end of the screen test day he's completely convinced she's the girl. So I think well, we've won it and then it was just a matter of "We've sent the tapes off, so how are they going to respond to it?" Are they going to admit they were wrong gracefully? Are they going to demand a quid pro quo? What's the price of this thing? But, no question, she's the girl, she's fantastic.

And then we get the message back: "Nope, don't get it, she's cold…" I said, "What are you talking about?" This is something that's being described that has no bearing to what's on tape. And then you're getting a phone call with Bob, basically him shouting at me, and I say, "I'm really not sure I can make this movie without Samantha."

He'd lost control. These guys, they're like Tourettes' Syndrome, they just started howling, screaming, because nobody threatens them, nobody tells them what to do and I said, "Bob, there's a real problem here, our tastes may be just different to the point that this isn't going to be good to anybody. I'm not saying right, wrong, good or bad, I'm just saying different. It's a terrible way to start but this is it, the girl's perfect; I'm not sure I can make –" This is the irony, when I said I don't know if I want to make the movie without her, that was like this huge threat, "Oh he's going to walk off." That blew it and the screaming started.

Tuesday, 20th May

NP: The stages and the backlot village proceed at an amazing pace, it's always quite astounding to witness the creation of fiction… it will always fascinate me.

The stall situation is still at a stall: Chuck Roven (who has been rehired so that "someone" could "talk" to Terry…) is coming back today. Nobody really knows what to do, supposedly he is obsessed with reducing the budget and shrinking the schedule, like if they were too big and too long! That's not the problem; the problem is to allow Terry to make his movie; a Gilliam movie should be guided by Gilliam's vision, not Bob's.

Morning: Thursday, 22nd May

NP: Chuck arrived yesterday. We were all anxious to see what he was coming with (ideas? threats? blackmail? solutions?) but he came practically empty-handed (and headed…) No solutions, no ideas, just a generic will of even further "shrink the budget and the schedule". When, meeting him in the toilet with (literally) his dick in his hand, I explained my worries, it seemed at that moment as if he'd fallen out of his tree. I don't think he understood the situation, I hope he does now he's spent the whole day with Terry.

Samantha was offered another job (four weeks in August, and they are paying her more than she was offered here for twenty weeks...). It's getting more urgent than ever to find someone else. I suggested to Terry to look outside the English-speaking countries and find a beautiful German, Swedish, Danish face...

Yesterday evening, after an afternoon of sinking into a semi-depressive state ("I'm on the verge of telling them: you cast! you decide! I just shoot and get the fuck out of here!") Terry had a long conference call with Chuck, the lawyers and the agents. After this he called to tell me he had to go to London because, to be fair, we should test some of the other girls with the same care and attention that we spent on Samantha... personally I much prefer for them to come here.

9.30am

NP: Terry arrived from his doctor: his blood pressure reads 110 over 170!

Not good news. He's red with rage and what annoys me most is that I'd really like to punch Bob in the face.

11.30am

NP: As everyone's taking it for granted that Ben Kingsley is on board, I called him: he is more than sceptical about them reaching an agreement: too little money, above all the back-end. "I have to think of my family," he said(!).

Afternoon

NP: Chuck, who seven weeks ago was moving heaven and earth to cut budget and schedule in unrealistic figures, now wants reality: "Add ten days' shoot and the necessary funds." What a world of pricks!

Friday, 23rd May

NP: A long talk to Chuck this morning. He expressed his worries, the fact that as usual Terry is causing chaos, the fact he becomes aggressive and won't listen to reason. He begged me to keep an eye on him (that's one eye gone...) but he did seem to me to want to work closer on the film. We'll see!

Monday, 26th May

NP: Terry has returned, the blood pressure hasn't gone down.

I met Matt (he arrived on Friday): he's charming, a bit babyish, but appealing. But Terry is absolutely right: his neck is too big and stiff! He absolutely has to stop working out, I don't know if tango lessons would be enough.

Five weeks to go and we are still missing three main characters out of five, it could make us all suicidal...

Wednesday, 28th May

NP: Terry's mind is finally coming around to how to shoot the movie, instead of producing. Good. Even if the casting fuck-up is in full swing.

Now we have two girls, both called Sienna(!) both English and both looking like models(!). Tomorrow we will "test" them.

TG: It reached a point that she [Samantha Morton] may be the best but they aren't going to let her be in the thing and we've got to do something because we're running out of time, I mean all the departments were screaming like mad, costume in particular, and we'd arranged riding lessons and archery lessons, they had a lot of stuff to do to get ready for the thing and by now Matt just thinks she's fantastic, there's no question about it, and Chuck basically pushed me into a situation where I didn't give a fuck anymore. So we tested two girls, the two

Siennas, they'd been chosen as their girls that would need a screen test. I said, "You guys pick who you want and let me know because you're refusing my choice, so tell me who you want? Choose the two best out of the whole thing with the screen testing with Matt and Heath." Matt and Heath are now here in Prague. And we do it and they're both really nice girls, end of conversation. Neither of them are up to the role.

And I said, "This is fucking stupid because I want Sam to do it," and I'm on the phone to her agent and the fight is non-stop, this is just going on and on. I'm on to her agent saying that's who I want and her agent is refusing to let them get near to Hugh Jackman, who they want for something else, because she's the same agent for both of them; all this shit's going on, everything's going on to apply pressure. I'd even finally reached the stage where I said, "Quid pro quo: Ben Kingsley for Sam. To have Sam we'll take Ben, even though I don't think Ben is right for the part; he's a wonderful actor and somehow we'll make it work. All I really want is Sam." And Bob said, "No."

I said, "What the fuck, what is the game that is going on here now? Here's somebody that *you* want that I've got doubts about and here's somebody *I* want that you've got doubts about: let's just swap." And so that's the point when I said, "I don't know what the rules are now. This is fucking ridiculous, not even a quid pro quo like that," and all we know is that Harvey is giving Bob advice… Bob, I don't think, knew. I think Bob could have gone any number of ways.

Thursday, 29th May

8.00am

NP: Testing day. We have to be "as fair" as we were with Samantha. The difference is that this time Matt will be here! Good Luck.

1.00pm

Details on the testing: it was Miramax who insisted personally that Matt should be part of the test, which he did not want at first. Last night was crazy, telephone calls back and forth.

Anyway, we have shot the tests, same exact light and set-up as Samantha's test in London. The two poor girls do not stand a chance (don't even talk about No 2, who has a fantastic line in moustaches...). The only problem now is if Bob likes moustaches...

Saturday, 31st May

NP: The pinheads in New York didn't even deign to look at the "test Siennas", after so much bother, cost, wasted time. To compensate, they've again gone on the attack with the budget: we have to tighten our belts, we need to spend less.

I get the impression they do it just to exercise pressure, to demonstrate power.

CO-WRITER TONY GRISONI (TGr): I think the trouble started with Terry wanting Samantha Morton to be in it, who could fire a bow and

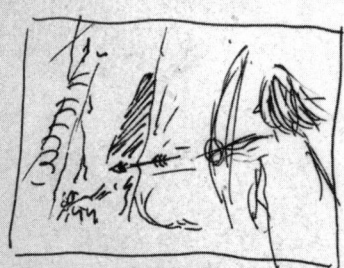

arrow, she was strong and she could stand up to the men and you just didn't believe it. It looked like she'd been created by a guilty conscience. She was this strong woman without a single fracture in her at all, so

one of the ways of developing her character was we gave her the whole business about her father being the centre of her weakness. She was haunted by him, and in love with him. She loses her father to this evil queen. It's not a million miles from the reality of when someone's dad falls in love with some other woman.

And so we worked up all of that so she wasn't just a huntin', fishin', shootin' all-round girl and so the idea of casting Samantha Morton pushed it even further. It was also an interesting choice because Samantha Morton is not your regular big epic movie heroine: she's multi-faceted, there's a fractured quality to her nature. That's what's interesting and exciting and dangerous about her. Samantha Morton in that role – playing a love scene with Matt Damon – is very different from someone else.

So it was a bold move, I thought, and Samantha was very up for it and although it's not unheard of for producers and directors to have disagreements over casting, I think we were all a bit surprised because the word was "No, she would not be cast." So the pissing competition starts there. I got the impression that what you need in a situation like that is a broker. Because if it really is just a pissing competition, that's the most destructive thing you could possibly have. Basically the fight is not about what someone has decided is best for a movie, the fight is about "I have to win." So who could have been the broker? Or was that not possible? I think for all the terrible things people say about Miramax and the Weinsteins, I don't think they can ever be accused of pretending to be other than what they are. I think they've always been very, very clear.

NP: But they're taking huge risks. For example, yesterday morning at the production meeting there were moments of panic (especially from Guy, he is definitely on the brink of breaking up. Maybe that is the way he works, but he is definitely on the edge...) because we have been told that Uma Thurman would only be available in August, which would mean a complete re-shuffle of the schedule, constructions, revamps, etc etc. Just huge and costly, even if it were possible. Later in the day Terry had the brilliant idea of calling Uma personally: she is available, but definitely *not in August*! Problem solved. No, wait a minute, there has never been a problem; those jerks at Miramax were trying really hard to create one.

Terry was furious and in the evening he started shouting during a conference call. I wasn't in the office at the time (dammit!) but I heard it was some show. Knowing Terry, he probably made it grow once he began: never losing it, on the contrary, using all the leverage of an explosion of legitimate outrage.

Chuck then called to tell Terry that according to reaction at the other end, the outburst achieved its goal: they were definitely shocked. He also said that the time has come, no more bullshit, he is coming back next week and why not test Samantha again with Matt and Heath in Rome?

That's one of the most stupid contradictions in terms I've ever come across, "The time is up, let's lose some more"! Brilliant.

We then went to listen to a fantastic Gypsy Music Festival and danced/sweated away the tension… Heath has arrived, he's in great shape and enthusiastic and we painted the town red the whole weekend. We also got the good news that they finally closed the deal with Jonathan Pryce, bless their souls! It took about eight weeks!

Monday, 2nd June

NP: It seems strange: a good decision has to be counterbalanced by a shit one. Bob and Harvey have definitely said *no* to Samantha; no explanations, just a final *NO*. Chuck told Terry, who is on his way to Rome and is going to stir Heath and Matt to attack the Weinsteins with a well-coordinated barrage. We also have to switch the schedule to accommodate not having Angelika for the first two weeks.

Personally, I'm very depressed at the moment: I can't believe that after eight months we are still on the verge of collapsing…

Tuesday, 3rd June

NP: Terry is in Rome, he sounded very determined and serene. No news from the jerks in NY, no other names but the stupid idea of Liv Tyler.

Official: Ben Kingsley is *not* Cavaldi. (Why should we ever believe these assholes?)

The stage work is proceeding, the branches canopy is going in, the lights are getting attached and connected, we are getting closer... HELP!

Evening

It seems that Bob gave in: he can live with Samantha, but now it's up to Harvey.

TG: Harvey finally got it on his radar – before this it was Bob's movie and not Harvey's – Harvey wants to win Oscars and Bob makes their most successful movies.

So ultimately Harvey was saying Sam was fine – but it was Bob's call.

Wednesday, 4th June

NP: The real drama occurred: Terry, Matt, Heath and Chuck came back from Rome.

Conference call with Harvey, John Gordon, Terry, Matt, Chuck, "No No NO!" to Samantha, do not want to hear that name again, etc etc". Screams. Shouts. "You are nobody, your movies never make any money. I'm the MOST successful producer of all times." Blahblahblahblah. Really painful and utterly stupid.

But he does not seem to budge, and no reason for it whatsoever...

Terry is seriously considering other girls, but by now we are so far behind we are going to lose time anyway. [Casting agent] Irene [Lamb] did not have anybody up her sleeve and I think that's very naughty.

[Actors coach] Steve Bridgewater is here and that's good for Terry.

Thursday, 5th June

NP: Walked through sets with everybody. As we feared (but even worse than we feared) things are looking difficult for the SFX department, especially on the fire in the forest situation. As Billy Friedkin would shout, "You fucked up, now unfuck it!" Only time will reveal if they are capable of unfucking it. The branches canopy on set is going ahead, slowly, but it's getting there. The problem is that we need three levels, we'll be lucky if we get one.

Tuesday, 10th June

NP: Heath and Matt have entered into the spirit of the game and began to interact: enthusiasm is really good, and at the moment the only problem is that Heath overtakes Matt by quite a few lengths. But Steve Bridgewater and Gerry [Grenell – Dialogue Coach] are working side by side, so we'll soon see results (I hope).

The good news is that Terry is really loving what Heath is doing. He is really pushing it and is already focused on what he wants to do with his character.

The saga of the actress is reaching an abysmal level of stupidity: undoubtedly, objectively, Samantha outclasses all the other "contenders" as an actress and by her presence.

Now it seems that she's arriving tonight and tomorrow we'll have another test, this time, to be fair, she will have to work with Matt and Heath. And then the idea is that Matt and Terry will fly to NYC to convince the Fat One that Sam is *The Girl*! One positive note is that it's become Matt's battle, Terry is just going along... It's a great strategy, we hope it pays off.

Wednesday, 11th June

NP: And the shit hit the fan...

Those stupid jerks of two fat brothers! After reassuring (personally reassuring!) Matt that they would call him before any decision was made, they actually sent out an offer to

Lena Headey (the second girl tested on Monday) without telling anybody. Matt, Heath and Terry are furious.

We had dinner at Café Colonial last night and Samantha joined us around 11.30. The poor girl knows the situation and I must admit I was impressed to see how cool and under control she was.

TG: Liv Tyler even did a screen test and she's just not right; there's a fine line, and Matt and Heath were there to watch it and they agreed and the next thing I hear is Harvey on the phone saying "Matt really liked Liv". It's just they'll say anything basically.

So Chuck finally said, "We've got to have somebody, just a couple of good actresses, I don't care. Someone who can act, we'll start with that." And there were more phone calls and blah, blah, blah with casting and Irene said, "Well, Lena Headey's a good actress." She didn't screen test because Irene knew I wanted Sam. And then we tested Laura Fraser, who is a good actress, and so they were flown out here to screen test with the boys and they did and neither of them were really right and I said, "I really don't think either of them can do it," but I had said to Chuck, "Just get me two and I'll pick one of them, just to end this whole fucking thing, one of them will do." It was one of those stupid moments when I say something like that, just to fuck off, just get me two and one of them will do it.

So then there's Bob on the phone, and I'm – suddenly – a man who's lied to him. I lied to him because I'm now saying neither of them is right. "You said you'd pick one of them." "Yeah, I know I said it but neither are right, Bob." And it was just going on and on and I'm going crazier. When the two Siennas came out, Bob at that point had said, "All right, test a couple of girls and you can test Samantha as well with the guys."

At the time I didn't do it, so because I didn't do it then I couldn't do it now. I guess there's a time limit on this thing and if I'd done it then I guess I would have been all right; but now we've done Lena and they liked Lena and then the phone calls start. I mean Matt was on for a couple of hours to Harvey and Bob just pleading for Samantha, because he'd seen the tape and said, "This girl is perfect, she is great." And Harvey had actually said to Matt that he'd give him a call before they did anything. I actually was on the phone begging Bob. I said, "I know, I fucked up, but just let Sam have one more chance with the guys. She just acted with somebody else, let her have a chance, let me show you; what's to be lost, just let me show you what she could do and give the guys a chance?" And he said, "I'll get back to you," and the next thing I know I hear from Chuck that they've taken up the offer on Lena Headey, because when Lena and Laura came down they'd done pre-test deals, which means if they liked the test, the deal was done and then he said, "It's done." By that point, I had actually said to Sam, "Come out, we'll do a screen test. I'm willing to pay and I'll pay your airfare, I want to do it." And then I hear on the way home that Lena's been cast.

So Samantha gets off the plane to discover that Lena's been cast and we all came here to Café Colonial, we were sitting in this very room here – Matt, Heath, myself, Sam – just getting pissed, and Heath sat on the phone to his agent screaming and shouting. And Matt's going crazy. We're out in this restaurant and then the world's biggest ever lightning crash happens, a thunder strike, boom, and the rain was pouring down. Matt's on the phone to Bob, pleading saying, "Samantha's the one," and it was like the elements had said no, the decision's been made by greater authorities… I like to think they're on my side occasionally, but they haven't been lately.

So this is going on and we're just sitting outside in the rain, saying, "Fuck it all". Sam gets drunk, we all get drunk and have a wonderful time and I get on the phone to Bob, and Bob's so excited because I never call him. I said, "Bob, you just made the biggest fucking mistake in your life!" and slammed the phone down. Nobody does that to him.

BM: Did he call back?

TG: No, he didn't know what to say. I mean, "Fuck you," – I'm never speaking to these bastards again in my life! So we did the screen test the next day, which was fucking wonderful. And then on the way in the next morning before the screen test I get a phone call from John Gordon, who is looking after things saying, "Bob says all right, he has agreed in good faith he'll let you do the screen test and give you an honest and unbiased opinion and look at the tests with an open mind." He'd previously said that the arbiter of the whole thing would be Harvey; he'd already abdicated.

At this point those fat bastards have to pay, not because they chose the "wrong" actor, but because the way they handled the whole issue is not only inhuman, but offensive and unforgivable.

NP: Today we will shoot film of the boys and Samantha, at least to leave a testimony of what the movie could have been. (The most extraordinary thing is that after all this shit, Miramax already sent another script to Samantha! They *really* are assholes!) The good side to all this is that Terry and the boys now have a very strong connection: they have been in the trenches together!

Of course, everybody is freaking out, they think that this is the end of Terry's career, that you can't step on the Weinsteins' toes, that this is suicide, etc etc. Personally, I'm very proud of Terry and pleasantly surprised that Matt is going along.

Interview with Matt Damon

BM: You mentioned at Nicola's birthday party that you didn't want to get back in the fold at Miramax.

MATT DAMON (MD): I think a lot of people have that love-hate relationship with Miramax. There's a certain part of me that has always felt an intense loyalty to them, but you talk to other people within the business and *Good Will Hunting* made them more money at the time than in their entire careers.

And the way I've always thought of Harvey, I said this to someone else who was writing a book about Harvey and I don't know if he put it in or not, but have you ever heard the little tale of the frog and the scorpion? Where the scorpion comes up and he's on one side of this lake and he says, "I have to get to the other side," and the frog says, "No, you're a scorpion. You're going to sting me." And the scorpion says, "No, I won't, I'll be indebted to you." And blah, blah, blah and he convinces the frog to give him a lift to the other side of the lake at which point he immediately stings him and as the frog is dying he says,

"Why did you do that?" And the scorpion says, "I'm a scorpion, it's in my nature." And that's the way I think of Harvey. There's a part of him that's like that. He's one of the most immensely charming people you'll ever meet, if he focuses on you; if you come on to his radar he can wow you with his charm.

He's incredibly entertaining also; he's incredibly fun to spend time with when you're around him. He's a fun, entertaining guy, but at the heart of it he wants to know what he can get out of you and he's a really fantastic businessman, a shrewd businessman and that's what he is. And so at a certain point every time something like this happens I get furious and I go, "God!" but also I get mad at myself for coming back and working for him.

BM: Technically there's nothing wrong with a businessman being a businessman.

MD: No, but Harvey masquerades as something else and that is, I think, the thing that people take offence to.

BM: And what would you say that was? He masquerades as...?

MD: As family, it's this kind of wannabe mob boss slash, you know...

BM: God, we're going to get sued on this!

MD: Well, Hyperion [a Miramax-owned publishing company] will probably get the book and then it'll never be in there. But I think that's the thing that I bump into, whether it's directors or other actors, I've heard so many people swear they'll never work with him again and then you see them again and they're working for him and you say, "What are you doing? You're working for him again?" You know, good-natured ribbing goes on, and people say, "Well, he had the material this time, he had the script that I wanted to do," or "So and so was directing it."

People say, "I'm not really working for Harvey, I'm working for this director who I really want to work with." Because often times to the people making the movies, they don't really care what the studio is, they care who the director is and what the project is and the people they're going to be spending their days and nights with for the next six months, or what have you. Yet Harvey finds a way to kind of insinuate himself into the production, which kind of causes a lot of headaches for the people who would rather just get on with it and work with each other. So, yeah, although I said that, I was furious when I said that, and I said as much to him.

BM: Have you had the same conversation with him?

MD: Well, we haven't spoken for a long time.

BM: But you'd happily say it to his face?

MD: Yes, yes. It's nothing that would shock him. The last conversation I had with him we yelled at each other, I hung up on him, we didn't talk for a while or I wouldn't take his call; and then he got me, because he'll call you all hours until he gets you. Oh no, no, his first one, he turned to somebody and said — this I love — he said, "I gotta send Matt the letter."

BM: What is the letter?

MD: It's like a fucking "Dear John" letter and it shows up and it's like "Dear [blank], I am terribly sorry for my behaviour during the [blank] conversation that we had, it was absolutely inexcusable. I'm ashamed of my conduct." — It was just this bizarre form letter.

BM: But it felt like a form letter?

MD: It was an absolute form letter. It was literally "the letter" that he sends and at the end of it, there's this paragraph where he's apparently reaching out and apologising and it's like two sentences of "I still think my decision about Samantha Morton was correct. I stand behind that, I will not waiver from my position" and you know, "regards".

NP: We did the test: she was magnificent! And Heath even more... The problem is going to be Matt; he has to push to keep up with Heath! Anyway, the test was really good. The simple fact is that Terry's instinct was right, she belongs in Marbaden!

All of a sudden what was Terry's desperate move (paying for her ticket, taking the risk, etc) became endorsed by Miramax too. Therefore we shot the test on video (with a slightly worse camera than before) and then we scrambled to edit it on the most obsolete on-line suite I've ever experienced(!) to funnel it down to NYC. At 2am they realised they lost the sound in the process... We haven't heard any reactions yet. We'll see...

Afternoon

Still no news. Harvey is supposedly flying to Italy on holiday.

Terry wants to go back to London and not return till he gets a positive answer.

The SFX department is more and more a cause for concern. This morning they managed to start a fire in the backlot while testing a smoke gun for "chimney smoke" effect!

The stage is getting there – the amount of lights rigged up is quite staggering but it starts to look like a real forest, strong contrasts, patches of light, sense of depth. Now it will be up to Roger [Holden – Greens Department] to make it "feel" like a forest.

Tested the torture chair: it works! The funny thing is that we all seemed quite surprised that it did work. We weren't expecting much from the SFX, but perhaps it's time we started to have a show of faith.

At dinner with Terry, Heath, Matt, Steve, Gerry, and then joined by John and Rochelle. Long phone call between Matt and Bob, Matt is really trying hard (at least listening to his reports) but the two fat bastards still do not get it! Every single person who has seen all the "tests" agrees that Samantha is by far the best. Not those two arrogant bastards.

Maybe this is an omen: while Matt was on the phone the sky opened up and there was a real downpour (Armageddon). Of course we did not move, and we got so drenched so fast, really liberating.

Friday, 13th June

NP: The camera arrived! We're getting closer.

Stages 6 and 7 are now getting there light-wise… the scent is fantastic; it really helps to create the right atmosphere.

Evening

Definitely *no* and that's it!

They called Matt back and told him (at least this time they did it).

Terry's called from London to say we'll know in two days!

What a shit situation!

Saturday, 14th June

NP: So many things run through your mind: this kind of arrogance is disgusting, and to know that you have to work with the Weinsteins isn't pleasant. I hope that Terry finds the strength to channel his anger positively: after all, the film is about two brothers – Angelika is important, but isn't one of them.

Sunday, 15th June

NP: I spoke briefly with Terry; he's disgusted and doesn't want to do the film any more. "If I don't believe in something, I'm not able to do it."

TG: All the shit that's gone on, it's just been constantly dealing with that, wanting to get off this thing and stop the nightmare, but I don't know.

NP: The crew wanted me to send him an SMS giving their support to whatever decision he takes but at the same time their determination is to make "a great piece of cinema" and, in the process, pay back the Weinsteins. The ideas are actually flocking in: the most popular is to have the mud-mimic (that looks like a turd...) have the Weinsteins' features. I believe this can be a very subtle and sweet revenge, also because I'm convinced that in their vanity they would just leave it in.

Terry told me that he may come back Wednesday. Certainly he will not come back before Chuck: he feels totally betrayed by him and he is not ready to listen to him any more. He's convinced that if he hadn't listened to him at all, by now we would have Samantha and not someone who worries about being pretty at every moment. A totally wrong attitude for Angelika who, on the contrary, should be scruffy, dirty, and appear through that rough bark with the strength of youth and beauty.

Tomorrow we'll start rolling film. Without a director, but that's a detail...

Monday, 16th June

NP: We rolled the first footage: Stages 6 and 7, Forest. Trying to finalise the looks; tried different solutions of mist, dry ice, atmos. With the naked eye I would say the starker the better, but you never know what comes out on film.

Terry is still in London (where I am sure his wife Maggie is mellowing him down).

No news, he does not talk to nobody.

Tony is here.

Chuck is coming tomorrow, Lena is arriving Thursday.

From the diary of Bob McCabe (BM):

Tuesday, 17th June

Arrive at Barrandov Studios. Picked up by George, who is TG's driver and used to be a physiotherapist – but is now working here as his practice was washed away in the big floods of 2002.

Meet up with Amy Gilliam, who is having a great time working for her dad – who is absent. Still.

After weeks of trying to convince Dimension to cast Samantha Morton – even going as far as paying for a final screen test out of his own pocket – last Friday (the 13th no less) – they said "No" once and for all. And Gilliam has gone AWOL.

The sets are amazing – staggering interior forest, exterior village accompanied by exterior real-life forest – ripe for burning apparently – all real trees, re-planted on the backlot. They were guaranteed not to turn brown before the end of the shoot when they're burned down. They're already turning brown.

Meet crew – a mix of generally British department heads and locals filling up the ranks.

Meet Nicola, the DP, and Stephen Bridgewater – larger than life US acting coach who's worked with Gilliam since *The Fisher King*.

Matt Damon arrives with tinted eyelashes, plucked eyebrows, a wig and a new nose – a *real* transformation. Friendly and courteous.

After lunch, sit in on rehearsals with Matt and Heath.

Matt is very active, dynamic, works himself hard, knows how to push himself – and seems to enjoy doing so.

Heath is a bundle of fidgets/nerves – more insular- staying in character.

Both speak in Brit accents the whole time.

Dialogue coach Gerry Grenell, a tall soft spoken Irishman, helps with the accents. Matt is apparently having trouble with his Ls.

A serious amount of training has gone into this for Matt – yoga for posture, diet to lose weight, and attempting to re-train his facial muscles to accommodate the new accent. It's working, apart from possibly the Ls.

Tony Grisoni (in car on way back to hotel): "I think Heath is just one of those to whom everything just comes easier. He would've been the one who still passed his exams even if he stayed up all night the night before. Matt's like the rest of us. He has to work at it."

In TG's absence, Stephen Bridgewater is all but directing the performances, along with Tony G. There's good work being done and Tony is incorporating numerous ideas from their script-based improvisations. Matt is extremely fond of calling his on-screen brother a "fuckin' cunt" in improv – falling into a deep East End accent when he does so, unintentionally different from the plumier tones he employs for the rest of his performance, which is more Hampstead than Walthamstow.

Still everyone is happy that things are now progressing with work on the text. They feel they're getting there.

Gilliam himself is also getting here – he's due back this evening.

NP: Screened the tests: let's put it this way, we are definitely on the right subway line, we just need to decide at which stop to get off. My main problem is to deliver an interesting look (3 to be precise) but at the same time do it in such a way to be fast, not fuck up the stage and switch over from day to night (or vice versa) fast.

The forest definitely needs more branches, more green, more moss.

Shot more tests especially to determine the red of the red moon.

Terry is still in London but will arrive tonight. Maggie succeeded; he will behave responsibly and accept the idea of being a hired gun in a rotten system. I still believe that we can make a good movie, but I am sure that something broke within him, he had to give up his "integrity" somehow, at least I'm sure that is what he feels.

He told Tony that he was not coming back 'cause after being away 3 days he realised that we can make the movie without him, so why bother!'

Typical, like on Nike…

Wednesday, 18th June

BM: Terry has arrived; as has Chuck Roven with his list of "suggestions".

Relief. TG seems in good spirits but is comically negative. Cannot decide how sincere this attitude is… I don't think he can either.

Watch test shots of Matt and Heath's stand-ins in the forest set. The chocolate filter seems to work best but Terry and Nicola are still not convinced they have the right look.

TG on phone to Lena Headey: "We've basically starting by running as fast as we can and then when we get tired we sit down and work out where we are." TG checks out the props department – nearly always adding on to what's been delivered, developing details that will barely register on screen. Wants Cavaldi's men to be all in silver and black – "They're the SS."

First day of shooting tests for Matt and Heath in costume – their first time before a camera on this movie. Test for hair, make up and costume – and in Heath's case, underwear. He looks remarkably incongruous in filthy long johns and red Converse hi-tops (by no means a bad fashion moment). Matt: "Should I hold up a sign asking for '$3million more for our movie please?'"

Boys relaxed and funny on camera. Matt keeps repeating his favourite line – "It's like being inside Jacob's head."

Matt suggests that the climactic rescue of Angelika be given to Heath's character as it fits the romance better. It's agreed.

TG: "I haven't got a single shot in my head yet. To be honest, I'm getting a bit worried."

BM: Tests followed by meeting with Chuck and his suggestions:

Studio wants to keep the budget at $75million and shave off ten days.

Chuck goes to bring in Jake Myers, Miramax/Dimension's man, to the room. Chuck seems distinctly uncomfortable with having a journalist in the room taking notes and TG seems to be taking a distinctly perverse pleasure in watching him squirm. As Chuck leaves to track down Jake, Terry whispers to Tony Grisoni – "He [Jake]'s not here today. Am I getting mean?"

The 1st assistant director/associate producer Mishka Cheyko and executive producer John D. Schofield are brought in to the meeting.

Lena is arriving this evening. It's now rumoured that she's a vegetarian – which will make the scene where she has to gut a rabbit more difficult.

TG suggests putting Grisoni's name first on the latest draft due later today. This is vetoed by Roven in favour of original writer Ehren Kruger.

TG: "This film is like a fucking albatross."

Roven: "I call it a virus."

Bob Weinstein has sent a memo via Jake Myers – he wants to save time on scenes 21–25 by using the second unit.

Wants to lose flying Greta's shawl. TG is adamant – "The shawl is the magic thing."

Roven: They want us to cut the page length.

TG: But that doesn't do anything.

One scene is to be cut to save half a day's filming. But TG is not happy.

Roven: "This is a pretty harmless cut. And we have a $3million problem here."

TG leaves the room momentarily and Roven lays his cards on the table – "We have to give them something."

The current schedule is 93 days and a further 7 for blue-screen work.

They suggest "re-considering" one of the major set pieces – when the forest comes to life.

TG: "This is turning into *The Four Feathers* again… exactly the same – they brought in a different girl and then a week before they started filming they brought in a new script."

Matt must leave 31st October – to be insured for his next project. (He needs to have two weeks off – contractually – before starting *The Bourne Supremacy*, in Berlin.) This leaves the blue-screen work at the end very tight. TG suggests changing his contract – this is a no go.

Uma Thurman still has not replied to the offer to cameo as the Tower Queen.

The second unit has to shoot for 62 days out of the overall shoot. It is suggested that Stephen Bridgewater direct Matt on the blue-screen work to get Damon away on time.

Everyone is on edge – any overages eat into Terry's pay for the movie; Chuck Roven was previously fired and off the project for 8 weeks, and gives the impression that he doesn't seem to feel he's in too strong a position now he's back.

From day one, John Schofield has told them – Miramax/Dimension – it was never a realistic budget.

Schofield: "We're only eight days away from shooting? How are we gonna do this, fellas?"

They've spent all their time resolving the casting issue and not the financial issue.

Schofield: "This is the tightest schedule I've dealt with in a long time, and this fucking weather could kill us."

At that moment Peter Stormare (now cast as Cavaldi) arrives and lightens things up.

Back to the meeting:

TG: "What we should be doing now is concentrating on the movie. I've spent the last month having one battle and now we're about to have another one. They're going to have a director on their hands who is in no way ready to direct this movie. The reality is I've got no shots in my brain… *The Four Feathered Brothers Grimm*???"

Need to persuade Matt to give up 5 of his Saturdays.

Attempting to trim the Mud Mimic scene down from 4 to 3 days.

TG: "They've beaten the shit out of me… Right now I want to get on with pretending I'm making a movie."

Roven: "They don't think you're out of control."

TG: "They don't want to exaggerate an inflammatory situation? They did last week!"

Everyone is concerned that there is no contingency time for any problems that arise during filming.

Roven: "The odds are stacked against us. Because of the money. But that's the deal with the devil we made."

TG: "They fucked me and I also feel they also fucked the film, and that's what makes me mad."

Matt arrives, complete with English accent. Roven mentions the idea of him giving up his Saturdays. He agrees – a team player.

The script meeting resumes – the atmosphere is more relaxed now they're back to simply talking about the script and not schedules and budget problems.

Some debate over whether Angelika should kiss Will or not.

Chuck Roven remains uncertain over the whole inclusion of the Mud Mimic sequence.

Storyboard artist Danielli Auber shows me a virtual rendering of the key effects scenes in the movie. It has been storyboarded in extreme detail; the movie exists here, if not on celluloid. "It's great fun working with Terry because he's so full of ideas for his characters and great at bringing them to life for you."

Later:

Gilliam watches rushes and visits department heads. It looks like he can finally get down to making his movie, even if he's not ready to do so. Still, he insists I watch the Samantha Morton screen test – he's like a dog with a bone on this one. She's good; in fact, she's the best of the tests I watch.

His final comment of the day – "Are you getting plenty of good dirt?"

Lena Headey arrives tonight. TG is meeting her for dinner.

NP: Terry is back, and in a better mood than I expected. Shot hair and make-up tests with the boys; Matt is looking great with his nose a la Brando, and the sideburns and wig really work.

Screened the tests, everybody is getting excited, even if it's a bit too early, but that's the power of film rolling.

Trying to give more of a "sunset" feel to the forest, going with warmer rays. Terry too is not convinced about the atmos on the stage, not to mention the fact that Kent [Houston – VFX supervisor] does not want any smoke!

Peter Stormare arrived: great addition, it seems, a great guy to work with, full of energy, wit and ideas. I believe he will bring new challenges, especially for Heath, who already starts being bored and cannot wait to start shooting.

Dinner with Terry and the boys (plus Tony and Johnathan); waiting for Lena, making a big effort to heal the wound ASAP. We are there at Café Colonial and a phone call comes to say she missed the plane and will not make it tonight. Terry immediately said: "That's it, she is off the movie!" He is really trying but it's going to be a long and painful battle.

Thursday, 19th June

NP: Today we do the test of the forest fire and the various lighting of the village. Angelika's stunt double arrived: her name is Samantha Martin! If you were writing a script you couldn't come up with a sadder coincidence.

Terry seems in good form, for the moment he's accepted the situation and is behaving responsibly. I'm not so sure it will last long, though.

The tests are done. I wonder if this SFX crew will ever do something right and surprise us. I make better fires for New Year's Eve. Make-up and hair tests were really encouraging. The Brando-esque nose is definitely a big improvement.

BM: Morning rehearsal scheduled for: Matt; Heath; Peter Stormare; Lena Headey; Johnathan Pryce; Stephen Bridgewater; Gerry; Tony G; TG.

Stephen and Gerry both feel that Matt and Heath are now more or less there – need less work. Now have to devote what's left of their time to the newly arrived.

Peter Stormare – described by TG to Matt: "The hurricane has arrived" – needs his Italian accent addressing. Some early work involving voice tapes from Gerry failed to arrive, so he's behind.

Morning – read through of script.

TG to Heath: "I love your terrible French… play it straight at this point."

Matt plays with the line "Every second counts" – then adds for Terry's benefit – "That's what you're gonna get Bob Weinstein telling you in about six months!

Johnathan Pryce is keen to join in – opts to read one of the other absent characters. The tone of the read through is very light, with much laughter and messing around. Heath's sunglasses are ever present.

TG plays the witch and the boys really go for it. It is a loud, boisterous reading with TG screeching away as the old hag of a witch.

Matt: "We want to be overacting in that bit."

Johnathan: "Well, you've got that down."

Matt: "Moving on…"

Johnathan Pryce insists on playing all the small parts, each with a more outrageous accent than the last one. He's especially good at the very butch mother of the young Grimms, while Matt is happily camping it up as his younger self.

Peter is late for the read-through – citing jet lag. An AD arrives to say he'll be here in 5 minutes.

It turns out Angelika's stunt double is called Samantha Martin – not a million miles away from the uncast Samantha Morton.

TG: "It's not going to go away."

TG has flu pending ("I should be ready to start, but I'm ill.") – but still extremely energised, singing and miming the role of the tavern band. He and Matt are up and dancing round the table; everyone else remains seated.

TG explains how the tavern scene should be "like Casablanca when the Nazis show up" – an odd comment from a man who recently criticised Bob Weinstein for constantly relying on references from other movies.

Matt quizzes Gerry about how his accent is coming along. He also quizzes me – I tell him it sometimes moves from North London to the East End – which isn't a bad thing for a con man. He tells me that mine is rather good – I explain I've been working on it most of my life.

Peter arrives – it is the first time he has met Johnathan and Heath. His accent is in place, very broad and very funny. Everyone relaxes, laughs.

Peter is really playing around with his lines – despite his casual impression, he has obviously spent some time working on Cavaldi and has clearly thought it all through.

Pryce meanwhile is heading into Clousseau territory (but loving it).

The first reading of Delatombe and Cavaldi's scene plays very funny.

Matt: "I don't want to be in any scene with you guys."

(Peter also plays his own horse, providing suitable sound effects.)

They reach Angelika's introduction – break for 15 minutes to wait for Lena Headey. Lena – who it has been determined is definitely a veggie – arrives.

Heath: "Now we've got a female…" – he responds by putting on some deodorant.

Matt (to Lena): "You should see the ham that's going on in this room."

TG: "We're a ship of fools about to set sail."

Lena is more restrained than the others. While appropriate for the character, it's also quite flat – nerves?

Johnathan turns the Minister character into a raving Scotsman and lets fly.

Matt reads the Mud Mimic as a dead-on impression of Harvey Weinstein.

Lena fills in and reads the Mirror Queen.

Matt has a tendency to repeat words he's uncertain of accent-wise – testing himself.

Overall it's a big success. Up and running.

Still some script concerns – TG feels there should be more for Delatombe in the torture sequence. There are more script amendments to be made, ad-libbed lines to be incorporated etc. Tony G and Heath run new lines.

Stephen Bridgewater: "There's a lot of work still to be done."

Matt is leaving – he's working all night filming a cameo for "The Ugly Americans", (later renamed "Euro Trip") also shooting in Prague, a favour for a friend.

After the read through, we drive out to see the village set with TG, Lena, Johnathan and Peter – none of whom have seen it yet.

They are suitably in awe of the work Guy Dyas and his team have done.

Lena: "God, I feel rather intimidated now."

TG: "This is the way to waste the Weinsteins' money."

Post-mortem – Matt needs to relax into it more and not work so hard – but TG is convinced he'll have it in time. "Heath is amazing. This is gonna surprise a lot of people."

Johnathan was competing with Peter – but it can be brought down, no worries at present. (Dimension were apparently willing to pay more for Ben Kingsley to play Cavaldi, ironic given that they seem unwilling to up the budget to meet the demands of the production.)

Thursday night – Nicola shoots tests on the village – for lighting, cannon fire etc (there will be 13 different types of explosion, apparently, according to the FX guys). Plus, need to check the potential reflective problems of the Grimm's mirror armour.

Tuesday, 24th June

BM: This evening, Terry is due to be lifted up by an Indian guru – famed for lifting people up.

Richard Ridings – who plays Bunst – arrives, full of life and willing to have all his hair shaved off.

TG: "Cavaldi's kind of claimed the bald bit. He's not done a limp or a lisp yet – he's left those alone."

TG discusses the costume work: "With Gabriella, she just does beautiful, beautiful stuff and then we destroy it."

All departments gearing up.

Meeting with Stephen and Gerry – they both want a movement coach for Matt, who may have to pay for it himself.

TG seems more concerned about Matt than the others do.

TG discusses the work they've done with Lena. There is much debate about Angelika's character/motivation.

Stephen: "Why does it have to be this complicated? What if she thinks she's the wolf?"

TG: "If I had written this script from scratch, we wouldn't have written *this* script."

A props guy shows up with a new crossbow (for Heath's character in the Mill Witch sequence, early in the film). They're still building key props – aiming for the first day of next week. TG wants to add a "safety" to Heath's crossbow. (This will be one of the props Gilliam takes for himself at the end of production.)

The Great Oak Leaf debate – are the greens people using real oak leaves or SFX oak leaves? This must be known.

An actress who was booked in for the "pre-shoot" has been rushed into hospital – needs to be re-cast.

Matt and Heath are both still wasted from Friday night. Matt went go-karting yesterday – Sunday – and has forgotten to bring his script today.

Another major read through – though this time with the newly arrived Mackenzie Crook and Richard Ridings. Mackenzie wears a woolly hat and appears nervous. Stormare has now had his head shaved.

TG spent the previous night at a Gypsy music fair – and now wants to score the movie to this music.

They work on the mill scene to help the newcomers get the feel of it.

Matt: "We're overacting just to inspire you."

Mackenzie needs to rehearse his wire-work – both he and Richard do the read-through with their character teeth in to practice saying the lines round them.

Stephen [On Pryce]: "John arrived with a chip on his shoulder." – Turns out he was more eager to play the role of Cavaldi, i.e. the funnier role.

The script has certain details omitted – like a guillotine that is needed – so as not to panic the financiers.

TG directs the new arrivals – playing up Mackenzie's nervousness and Richard's size and bluster.

Stormare storms – TG: "Peter, what's left for everyone else to do?"
Stormare responds by suggesting adding lines.

The first scene involves the snails in the torture room and is set for next Monday.

Guy, Mike and others discuss rigging Mackenzie – general design/stunt meeting.

The snail head casing – there is some concern over whether it will steam up once the actors are in it. And whether or not the actor will be able to breathe.

TG has added a musical saw for Cavaldi to play.

Tuesday evening, 7.30pm, Terry is lifted (literally, on a specially designed piece of machinery) by Sri Chinmoy, an Indian guru who has also lifted Mandela, Gorbachev, Mother Teresa and others (as it says on his promotional literature). He does this "for the betterment of mankind" – lifting up those who have uplifted us. That's the gist.

He sits there, eyes closed the whole time, drinking Evian, occasionally pausing to lift up various heads of neuroscience institutes, etc. He is accompanied by a chorus of sari-wearing women. He lifts two female professors and then gives them a gold medal on a rainbow sash.

They are followed by a professor of physics.

A flag behind him bears the legend – "Lifting up the world with a oneness-heart." Signs on the side display the

weights of those being lifted; announcements are made in both Czech and English. He only lifts them an inch or two. He's wearing perforated plastic shoes and white socks.

Terry appears very moved by the whole experience (weight 191lbs/apparatus 17lbs/total w. 208lbs.); he appears to be in tears twice. Amy is also lifted alongside him.

Afterwards we are summoned for a private meeting with the guru, who despite all his spirituality seems to know a good photo op when he sees one. Turns out he's a big Python fan (they're everywhere) and extols its "childlike" values, rather than its "childish" values as Terry had said.

Dinner afterwards with TG and Nicola. Terry is still not up for making this film, firmly viewing himself as "a director for hire on this one".

I ask Terry about the two recent movies that seem to loom over this in style and tone:

Sleepy Hollow? "Not an issue. We don't look anything like that."

Shrek? "Ah. *Shrek* was a much better film than this."

Thursday, 26th June

BM: This morning – big production meeting with all department heads. The big day is looming.

Nicola argues that all the second unit gear has arrived but no one has looked at it yet.

NP: "This is suicidal. We need to be looking at it Thursday. We start shooting Monday."

It is not resolved. They go through a scene-by-scene breakdown in terms of the schedule – what's going to be shot day to day for the first week.

Need to test the actor in the guillotine.

Last night in the car, FX man Kent Houston confessed that there are a lot of surprises being thrown at him – if something proves problematic there's a tendency to hand it over to the CG people in post-production – but at least these things are being thrown at him now, not later. KH: "At least I hope that's the case."

The horses have arrived.

Cavaldi needs to practice driving the carriage, although the stunt guy inside is really driving it.

TG on Guy Dyas: "He's working himself crazy on this. He's got his wife working for nothing… he really wants this to be the one…"

BM: Since the collapse of "Don Quixote", Tony Grisoni has been writing the adaptation of Mitch Cullin's *Tideland* for Gilliam; before this was "The Man Who Robbed The Pierre" (renamed "Blue Ribbon Operation") amongst others – "Great dialogue. This one was shit. But it moved forward." He and Terry are doing this because Gilliam needs a gig, basically.

TGr: "Terry doesn't believe in directing actors. He leaves that to Steve and Gerry."

TG: "I don't direct actors. I can't teach them to act. Steve and Gerry can do that… I make them feel comfortable, but I can't teach them…"
Full of praise for Steve and Gerry – "They should be on every film."

BM: Corner Guy Dyas in the fly-infested food tent. (Admittedly, the flies do seem to add to the state of the local cuisine.) Guy is warm, personable, a very decent bloke and, seeing his designs for this movie, a real talent. Having developed his craft in design, he found himself designing *X Men 2* for director Bryan Singer, and suitably impressed Gilliam enough to land his sophomore gig on *Brothers Grimm*. Given the forests, tower and town he's built – with the detail always paramount – he more than knows what he's doing. He also knows the prestige of this job, working round the clock to keep everyone as happy as can be, soliciting his wife to help him on what surely must be twenty-hour days. However, he never appears to hit a bad mood and manages to keep his team in equally decent spirits. We talk late at night as the shoot drags on.

Interview With Guy Hendrix Dyas

GD: Before I started in movies I did a Masters degree
in Industrial Design at the Royal College of Art and I
subsequently got hired and went to Tokyo for three years
and worked designing walkmans and discmans — the more
technical end, measured drawings, making moulds and
tooling machines and doing the whole end of things
that way.

Quite honestly, after about three years it got a bit
boring, so I started doing my own exhibitions and at the
same time furniture, crossover furniture, electronics,
paintings, everything, just anything to keep me busy
really. It was a concoction of stuff, and at the same time
George Lucas was doing a retrospective exhibition. I think
it was called "The Art of ILM" [Lucas's effects company,
Industrial Light & Magic] and it was a travelling
exhibition that started in Tokyo and actually ended up
in the Museum of Modern Art in San Francisco.

Anyway, the curator and art director of that
exhibition happened to see my tiny little exhibition that
was off in some gallery in Tokyo and left an ILM business

card. I thought someone had printed it up as a joke, but I called the number late at night and he answered. His name was Mark Moore. He was an ILM art director who himself had studied industrial design and said that they were gearing up for the new *Star Wars* films, the three new *Star Wars* films, and no, they weren't hiring me for those but they wanted me to replace some of the people in the art department at ILM who *were* going up to do them.

So that's how I got into the movie industry, quite by default. I wasn't going to say no, I'd had enough of walkmans and discmans and it seemed like a fresh new opportunity. So then I spent three years at ILM and that was more like going back to film school, really, because I learnt everything from storyboarding... I even directed a couple of music videos there, which I won't even mention anything about those — it's not my forte! Then I started production designing commercials, and did that for three years, and decided to move to LA and basically go for bigger fish, try to do a feature film. Once there, I started illustrating and conceptualising for producers and people who had scripts so that I could get more involved in that side of things and eventually got my break with Bryan Singer on a TV pilot that didn't go, but then I did his sequel, *X-Men 2*, so that's it in a nutshell.

BM: So that pilot would be *Galactica*?

GD: Yeah, it was *Battlestar Galactica*, and I believe they did end up doing the pilot and using some of my designs. So that's the long version of it!

BM: So how did this one come about? Did you pitch for it or were you approached on the back of *X2*?

GD: A bit of both, I think. I mean, *X-Men 2* wasn't exciting enough to someone like Terry Gilliam for him to come looking for me. He's definitely, from the get-go, one of those few directors who you want to work with. He's a legend. He himself has come up through the artistic side of filmmaking so there's a very strong appeal and every single one of his films is close to perfection, as far as I'm concerned: he's never had a miss. Some of the best directors in the world have had the odd miss, but he just never has, and I wanted to be a part of that process and see how he did it, see what was unusual. You know, when you've met people who have worked for him you want to hear what the complaints were, what the praise was, what is he made of, so I actually really pursued the project.

BM: How did you hear about it?

GD: I saw it in the trades. I saw that there was this film that was being developed called *Brothers Grimm*. It seemed like a very interesting topic from the get-go, especially for my personal sensibilities and things that I draw and design. Plus the name Gilliam was attached so that was it, I just had to go for it. So I tried to approach Terry and I think subsequently either one of my phone calls got through or I got an opportunity to meet him; it might have even been that the Royal College of Art connection made him curious about me because Terry used to lecture there. I was this British guy living in the States who was production designing, and he thought, "Oh, let's see him," and we hit it off immediately at the meeting. I brought every single conceptual drawing I'd ever done for people like Oliver Stone, Tim Burton, I pulled out all the big guns and he really responded to the designs and ideas.

BM: But you had nothing there for *Grimm*? You hadn't done anything in advance?

GD: I hadn't done anything in advance but I was absolutely prepared to say, "Look, if I get an opportunity, give me a trial run," which is sort of what they did, to tell you the truth. Chuck Roven and Terry were slightly cautious, perhaps because of other experiences he'd had, so I was pretty much on trial, I think, till about last month when my contract finally came through.

In the meantime, I just drew the hell out of the show and some unfortunate things that happened to the show in terms of its schedule worked out beautifully for me. I was stranded here in Prague, for about a month where absolutely nothing happened on the show, and I was stuck in my hotel room and I didn't know anybody at all. So I started to just forget about the politics of the situation and all the troubles that Terry was having in terms of putting his show together, and he was really trying, and I just concentrated on the artwork and the design and kept feeding him with drawings and designs and getting feedback that way and we worked a lot through e-mail. Terry was great, he'd look at a lot of my sketches and send his doodles over the top, always making everything more complicated and deeper and in-depth and we just worked that way.

So by the time the film was officially green-lit essentially most of the designing was in place, and I've spent the entire duration of the real pre-production tweaking designs, changing things as per Terry's needs as the scripts changed, and proceeding this way and being very hands-on. I've been painting, plastering...

BM: I've noticed, yes.

GD: I've had to because, although I have an amazing group of key people, the talent pool here is somewhat limited and we've had other productions here, firstly things like *Hellboy*, that came before us, and *Van Helsing* that swallowed up a lot of the basic talent here, so you have to muck in to get something done. But you know it's going to be worthwhile so you don't care, you just go for it.

BM: It strikes me that with a film like this you can't impose something on a naturalistic environment, so you're designing every single thing to fit in as part of the created whole. How does that cross over between departments? I mean, you're designing props for the props department to make presumably as opposed to leaving them to their own devices — does that extend to costumes as well?

GD: Yes. Gabriella and I immediately knew that we wouldn't want to have too much communication in terms of, for example, the villagers' costumes or the costumes that would appear in the tavern, because it was taken as read that everything would gel. I mean, I saw Gabriella's sketches, she saw mine, we saw each other's colour schemes and that was fine. The one that we were really excited about and are still developing even now is the Queen's costume and how that's going to relate to the various mattresses and the colours in the tower; it's really got to work. She's got to pop in that set, but at the same time Terry wants something really special for the climax of the film. So as much as I'm doing, I think, a very elaborate and very detailed set, I'm having to pull the reins back a little bit to make sure that our actress really pops in that background. It's a really fine balance and very exciting, just because I've never done anything like that before.

BM: But very early on you were looking for a forest as opposed to building a forest?

GD: We were definitely looking for a forest clearing in which to build a lower portion of the tower. It became clear very early on that because of the weather patterns here — it's not like California — you can't guarantee it's all going to be a certain type of weather. I was therefore very keen to get the sets into controllable environments so Terry can shoot day or night, whatever he wants to do.

    It's available and it's cramped, but it's worked; I think the forest looks spectacular, the stuff they've done so far. I'm very excited about the ruins, fingers crossed for that, and again even things like the top of the tower, we're doing that in a very, very confined space on a small stage where we've got lots of sets crammed together, but I think we'll somehow be able to pull it off. We've planned it so that by shooting across the stage you can avoid the other sets and still get far enough back for Terry's lenses to get all of the set in.

BM: Where do you find trees in Prague, just out of interest?

GD: Well, the nice thing is that from the get-go we knew we would not use any natural forests. All the trees we've used in the entire production have been Forestry Commission trees, trees that basically are being grown to be used as wood. So we would go to a plot of land that was ready to be cut to make, for example, IKEA furniture, and we'd say, "Okay, we'll buy two hectares," and it sort of went like that. I think we got up to something just short of 2,000 trees, pine trees, on our three mounds at the backlot for our village and I think if Terry had had his way we'd have had a further mound for the perspective, but it worked out quite well. A lot of trees, but I have a feeling we'll still be putting in trees.

BM: You also have other things like the torture chamber, for example, which is an incredibly elaborate set, but also again completely out of someone's imagination. There's not really a reference point for that apart from certain individual items in it, but as a whole it's a unique space, isn't it?

GD: The torture chamber was a lot of fun. That was a location space; it was a shell, if you like. In both Terry's and my fantasy world we would have used something absolutely monstrously huge like a Pironese drawing, something that had multi layers, but it was the only space that we could find that was reasonable. I mean, cost does come into it: we couldn't spend all our money on the dungeon because we had so many other things to build, and it wasn't a large portion of the film. Anyway, it gave us the tiering effect, with different levels of cooking and torture going on all at the same time with the potential, funding provided, for Kent to do CG extensions if we ever got around to it. I don't think we did, unfortunately; that's something he'll have to save for another film, but certainly the impression is there that this torture dungeon goes on for many, many levels above and below. A very elaborate set.

Oddly enough, the thing that Terry definitely has to take full credit for designing are the torture devices — they were complete Gilliam designs. For example, with the Angelika rig with all the spinning cogs and things, basically he showed me images of things and said, "This is what I want the torture device to look like," and it was up to me to tap into my more technical side to get all the cogs working, get all the wheels working and make some sort of logical sense of the machine.

Then again with the Hidlick and Bunst rig, where they're hanging upside down with the snails inside their glass boxes, Terry already had that mapped out on the day we met and there was a fantastic sketch he'd done of that. And that was as clear as day to me, it was just a case of, "Okay, that's what he wants, let's build it."

BM: Is he a difficult man to satisfy?

GD: Absolutely. He will never be satisfied. I will never satisfy him but I'll absolutely love it and die trying. And if he's half-satisfied I'll be a happy man.

BM: It has been a difficult shoot in every sense — there have been politics, there have been weather issues, how has that impacted on you?

GD: I think the biggest disappointment for me was while we were building the village during the early months of the year, we had some of the most fantastic skies I've ever seen. I mean skies that would do painters like Constable proud, just the most unbelievable colours, all through the build, and I was just rubbing my hands together thinking, I do not believe this, we are building a set with a natural matte painting that is going to be changing on a daily basis.

By the time the summer rolled round we moved into apparently what is one of the hottest summers the Czech Republic has ever seen. It might as well have been southern California; it was an absolute fight to keep any greenery alive in the village, and of course we are dealing with a damp, decaying, muddy village — that's what Terry wanted. This illusion was largely created with greens that were painted together with a lot of painted sawdust splattered on the walls like lichen and greenery that was

growing up the walls, but it was absolutely blistering hot
and that was probably the only huge disappointment for me.
I wish we'd had the same weather patterns that we'd had
earlier in the year, with a finished set. I think he'd have
been over the moon. We all would have been.

BM: The town you've had to build here, you told me it cost
something like $400,000, which is astounding when you see
what it is because that's value for money.

GD: Yeah, it really is, I think that's largely down to the
workforce and the cheapness of the materials here. Also, I
think that the Czech Republic is very, very geared up to
using those kinds of period type towns, villages, that type
of architecture, they're extremely good at it; and with
good guidance, from department heads that I brought over
from the UK, it has all worked beautifully. I'd always
intended the rooftops to be crooked and the buildings to
subside and quite honestly a lot of that's happened quite
naturally due to the building techniques and we haven't
corrected it, we've just let it all go. You'd have thought
Prague and the Czech Republic would be fantastic for
locations, but interestingly enough Terry and I did close
to a month of scouting right at the beginning. We went
through all these beautiful forests: one of the favourites

was Ruba Skala, which had an incredible rock formation that Terry just instantly fell in love with, but we couldn't shoot there because it is a national treasure, and the trees were not thick enough for Terry's liking and they certainly weren't, I think, "Gothic". They didn't reflect the Arthur Rackham illustrations that we'd all been drooling over when we came to be doing this film.

So it was very obvious that to control the environment and get all the lighting, the forest had to be built on stage, which would be a huge build on stage. The stages at Barrandov are very limited, but thanks to Mishka, our first AP, there was some careful coordination, and we've been able to pull it off. But without the careful coordination we probably should have really had more stages and we're only doing it by the skin of our teeth, we really are.

BM: Was it always designed to be as functional as it is, because everything works on your sets; that's what's so nice about it. When you walk into the house — it's got an interior.

GD: Yeah, I think you can go off the deep end with the fantasy: that happens a lot. This is a fantasy film but it is buried in reality as well; you've got to make an audience believe it's real as we know otherwise you lose them, it just becomes a big, flamboyant joke, really. We have tried to strike the balance between fantasy and reality and we've pushed it in certain areas where we felt it would make a strong visual impact and would suit the story.

I think there's going to be a really magical flavour to the queen's tower based on traditional Gothic architecture, but the furniture is completely of my own design, completely unfounded, there is nothing really traditional architecturally about the bed or the chair that she sits in. These are things that were designed from scratch and have elements of Celtic and Gothic influence but they are completely new designs, they're modern designs in Gothic spaces and hopefully it will work — we won't know until the furniture's in there, really.

It doesn't end: there's always something to do. Always another layer of paint, another layer of plaster. My construction coordinator has had lots of arguments with me. He always says most people put on three or four layers of paint; I tend to put on ten or fifteen, but again I'm working for a director who has an eye that will spot the short-fallings of a set. He'll know if it's not looking realistic and he'll point them out to me, you know: "Dyas, you didn't do that." He'll know, so you have to get it right.

Mishka runs the meeting, round the table:

* TG wants a couple of street dogs in the courtyard for when they shoot scene 87 next week.
* For the dungeon scene in week one, air conditioning needs to be provided to get rid of the heat and smell of the meat.
* Wednesday July 9th – will they need to bring in mud or will there be enough mud there?
* Kent: "Are we removing someone's legs?"
* Scene 8: haven't booked a background carriage, and there's less than a week to go.
* Have decided to go with lots of CG rain, as opposed to practical.
* Discussion as to how to set fire to a horse's tail.
* A few ravens will always be needed for the forest set. Four or five birds need to be available every day when on this set.
* No Kraft service on set as it will be invaded by the ravens.
* TG adds 25 geese to the background of scenes 36–7 – scheduled for July 16th – to the exasperation of executive producer John S.
* Little Red Riding Hood is scheduled to shoot her scenes on July 17th and will need to come back for two days in October.
  Exec prod John mumbles, "That's a bad idea," under his breath (implying that she may well have grown by then). Also need two doubles for her to avoid time constraints on kids performing.
* SFX guy Mike still saying horse rig won't be ready for a couple of weeks. TG is showing distinct worries about his choice of FX people.

Mike says the moving trees are arriving at the weekend, and the animatronic wolf will be arriving a week before it is being used. TG pushes Mike to make it earlier – "A week before makes me nervous."

* 50 snails are required for the first day of shooting.

* Hans and Greta are scheduled for the 18th of July.

* Matt, Heath and Steve are scheduled to shoot blue-screen scenes on Wednesday 23rd.

* July 29th will be the first day on the backlot.

* Wednesday August 7th – shoot animatronic *trees* on stage 7.

* The tree that grabs Angelika: they only have two days for this scene, so it's decided to shoot for two days and one night.

* Steve thinks TG should be working more with Lena. She's feeling left out and TG acts like he's not really bothered about her.

* Discuss how the first day will not be easy on the boys – it really is a case of throwing them in at the deep end – with snails, torture rigs, being trussed up in gunny sacks etc.

    Plus also shooting the flashback childhood/snow scene.

* By day 3 we will see the first appearance of Hidlick and Bunst, as well as the horses, the carriage, a huge crane shot, 30 odd soldiers and Angelika. Not a light schedule.

* Day 4 will see an animatronic kitten getting minced.

2ND UNIT

REACTION TO MACHINE START

SILVER TASTE STILL ON SOMEWHERE

C/U ANGELIKA CHAIN TUGGED

DOG'S ENTRY

ANGELIKA DOUBLE

VICIOUS DOGS – PIECE OF KITTEN

JAKES FEET BEING HIT BY PEGGED COGS

QUARTET

WITH A SLIP FROM VIOLINIST ON KITTEN DEATH

KITTEN PURRING RUBBING VIOLINIST LEG

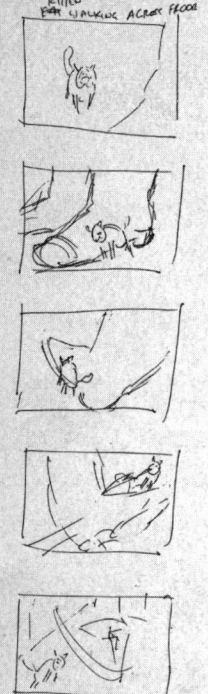

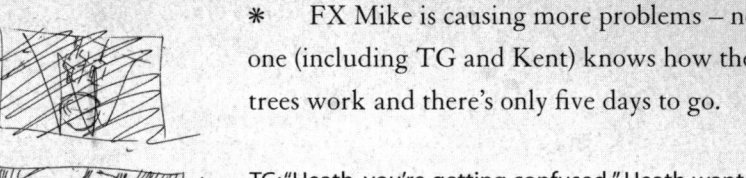

* FX Mike is causing more problems – no one (including TG and Kent) knows how the trees work and there's only five days to go.

TG: "Heath, you're getting confused." Heath wants to make his own compendium/Grimm notebook – he's been shown some dummies but wants to make his own.

TG is not happy with the executioner costume. He's unsure if it's correct to the period. Of Gabriella he says, "She's gone silly."

TG: "I'm very relaxed knowing that we can't possibly make this film. I can feel my angina."

Nicola is still shooting tests to establish the look of the forest.

TG checks out Lena's hair and scars and is pleased with the result.

Tony G. is very pleased with the way her performance is coming along under Steve.

TG confers with Johnathan P. He wants to change some of his lines so Tony G. is ushered out of rehearsals with the other actors to make minor alterations. Refers to TG as "His Maestro".

Later in the week – the decision is made for Lena to play it with an Irish accent. Bridgewater: "It makes her more of an outside, wilder."

NP: Hit the ground running on Monday; on top of it there is a visit and meeting from lawyers for the "Quixote" fuck up.

Should never forget that "Quixote" is the real (and only?) reason that we are here; make this one to then be able to finish "Quixote".

I am sure this is the main reason (together with respect for the crew and the work done so far) for Terry to come back and "give in".

The Grimmsteins (as we now refer to them) are more and more of a nuisance. They still want to cut budget and schedule.

Chuck is back and the other night at dinner (all the actors there, finally some sort of bonding/relaxed circumstance) he managed to annoy Terry so much that he exploded (literally, spreading wine and glass everywhere).

Great show of support from the cast, they all got up leaving Chuck there with the bill and (hopefully) his questions.

Personally I'm quite fed up with the whole story, I cannot wait until we start shooting. (Actually, yesterday we shot the Dinner Banquet blue-screen scene, fantastic costumes and hair-dos; if just for the energy and creativity of Gabriella & Co. and all the others we have to keep going.)

So far my crew seems well assorted, but I do not feel tensions between the various nationalities and habits… Trying to stay focused on the actual shooting. Hopefully tomorrow I'll be able to sit down with Terry, Pete and Ivan and talk about what we want to achieve.

Numerous additional fuck-ups from our fantastic SFX dept!

As Roberto put it yesterday: "We are now looking into the next necessary step: replace them!"

A bit too late, now none of the good ones is available

Friday, 27th June

NP: More tests: Wilhelm nose was wrong this time, too broken.

Cavaldi & Delatombe are fantastic.

Jacob is definitely there.

For Matt & Lena it is another story but we knew it.

SFX are constantly surpassing themselves, this time with the little "germanveteranhandpropelledtrycicletrolley", they were able to have the chain come off every time it steers(!) Solution? Weld the steering (can't he go straight?) They are really hopeless, every day I hope that something would go right and smooth for them.

Three days to go; I feel pretty ready (as ready as we can).

Terry is already working on the "editing" plan; given that the Grimmsteins want to lower the budget, Tony is now working on cuts that take away completely the big forest battle at the end, leaving the final duel between the Grimms and Delatombe as a "character" duel not as big-time action *kaboom*.

Very clever from Terry, I would be surprised if the fat ones buy into it.

More tests today (including a new one on Matt's nose: I'll bet you this will be the next titanic clash) and then last scouts in Kutna Hora/Kacina and Krivoklat.

Saturday, 28th June

NP: The nose IS an issue: they're paying him $10million – why on earth would they want him with a different face, even if a better one?

By the way, no sideburns either.

Maybe they are afraid that he looks period(!)

It's serious: Terry's had it and he does not want to have to worry about all these continuous interferences. The Samantha issue was, yes, a fight about vision [and he lost it thanks to the suggestions of his "friend" Chuck], but was perhaps more some sort of "preventive strike" of the Grimmsteins against "Saddam Terry".

Now it's all about vision; Terry does not give a shit about the "power", he just needs/wants to make a movie he can believe in, and with Matt's untouched face he cannot.

As simple as that!

Now it is panic, they are flying over. (Not the Grimmsteins themselves yet, John Gordon and Andrew Rona.)

If Terry does not budge and the assholes neither, not only do we risk not rolling on Monday but not to roll at all.

I cannot believe it; after all these months and efforts, 24hrs before the start we are at this point.

Tonight's kick-off party might become the wrap-party…

Sunday, 29th June

BM: "THE DAY OF THE $3MILLION NOSE".

The Weinsteins are reportedly not happy with Matt's new nose. For the part of Will he is sporting a tousled wig, sideburns and a prosthetic nose. Everyone else – Matt included – thinks it's a great look. "Like a young Brando," Bridgewater says.

Days ago, he took some digital shots of the make-up and sent them over to Miramax/Dimension in the US, presuming they'd really love the look. It appears no one took any real notice until Sunday – the day before shooting – and Harvey W. wants it gone.

Still looking for the additional $3million for the budget, Gilliam says they tell him he can have anything he wants – if he loses the nose. That's a big price to pay for a piece of putty.

Gilliam argues that, "he's been working in it for five weeks. You can't do this to him the night before." But he remains calm

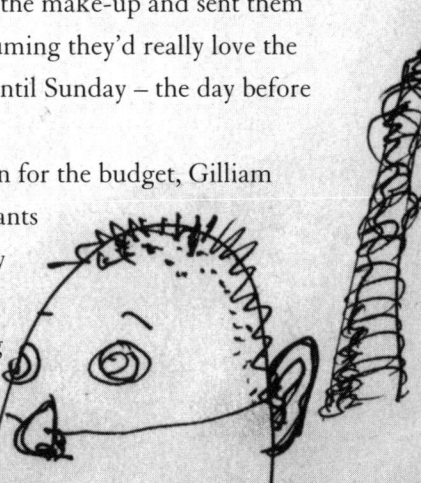

and goes to bed telling them that if there's still a movie in the morning, he'll shoot it, if they want to fire him, fire him.

"I think they were expecting me to be angry and explode. This way I really unnerved them… Harvey doesn't exist for me on this movie anymore. Anything he wants can go through Chuck.

"We got the call, in fact, to go to Chuck's flat. They'd sent in their minions to deal with this thing and they were basically saying, 'if you put the nose on, we close this film down'. But at the same time they were offering me the $3million we needed if I would give up the nose. And I said, 'Fuck it, there's no way. I'm not doing a deal on this; it's not about that.' Then we get to Chuck's flat and we have this conference call, with Bob on the other end – and it's the first time throughout this whole thing that I actually felt some sympathy for Bob, because it became clear that he was totally at a loss, and he didn't know how to deal with the whole thing. And it's clear that Harvey is behind the scenes there. You could just feel that Bob was caught between me and Harvey. And he was saying, 'I just don't know what to do'. And I was saying that *I* didn't know what to do.

"Then we went to dinner and I was sitting there with the minions and I said, 'I don't give a fuck any more. I've had it with this project. I'm tired, I can't stand dealing with you people, I've lost all my enthusiasm for it… and I might just go home. I've had enough of this shit.'

"Later, I was in bed and the phone rings: it's Chuck and he says, 'Basically, I've been through this experience before with another director and here's what happens – you *will* put the bump on his nose, they *will* close down the production, they *will* then take you to court for the costs up to now of the production, because you are not following orders. It *will* go into court, it'll take a year and you, Terry, *will* win. Is that what you want to do with a year?' So we went to work and I was working at half-mast. And it's one of those things that hangs you in that 'I'm thinking what would have happened if I put the bump on his nose? Was it a bluff?' Even when I went to work in the morning I was going to put the bump on his nose – I was going to scare the shit out of them. But Matt said, 'Come on, I really want to do the film.'

Days later, Gilliam elaborates on what he worries the piece of putty may have done to him. "The nose was when I think I lost self respect. That's when the self-loathing set in. That was when I thought, 'Fuck, what have I done?' Contractually we're supposed to have an even vote in all the main decisions – the Weinsteins and me – but if there's a stalemate, they have the final vote. So what's the point of even putting this in a contract?"

NP: The party was strangely subdued.

Heath came back from Amsterdam, and in his reading Matt feels defeated, not a good thing.

Learned that also on *The Hours*, Harvey did not want Nicole Kidman to put the nose on, and only Scott Rudin's tenacity kept them going.

Let's see if we have a Scott Rudin!

Monday, 30th June

BM: The first day of shooting, on location at Krivoklat.

Gilliam is still employed, which is less than can be said for Matt's nose.

From the Production Diary of
Nikki Clapp – Script Supervisor:

NC: Slightly late starting rehearsals… By the hour… Started at 08.00 until 08.45 then sent the actors for wardrobe whilst we set up on stunt doubles coming out of sack, 1 shot on each of them.

Then we had a good day, but only managed to complete the first part of the scene.

We finished with Will/Jacob around 19.35 and sent them home, then we lined up for boys' POV OF HILDICK/BUNST in chairs in dungeon pit… setting up 2 cams for this, but we wrapped before shooting it as it would have taken too long tonight. We will start this in the morning.

Also we still owe CLOSE SHOT DELATOMBE & MAIDEN as cover for the first part of the scene, which we will do 2nd up in the morning before getting the boys…

Tuesday, 1st July

BM: An early morning drive through some spectacular local forest scenery prompts the question of why the production felt the need to build their own (two) forests.

Gilliam's reply: "Because it's raining today. And with a production this tight we have to stay in control."

The day is largely devoted to filming the torture scene, with the boxes of snails. Gilliam confers almost solely with DP Nicola, the producers who mill about seem largely extraneous. Terry is in his Cannes jury "Can Be Bribed" T-shirt.

Gilliam: "It's a fucking terrible day." The machine that suspends the actors isn't working correctly and both Mackenzie Crook and Richard Ridings need down-time – literally – as they can only remain suspended upside down for so long.

The day over runs and they are unable to complete the days' filming. Tomorrow morning – which was scheduled for exteriors – is now put aside to finish off the interiors from today.

NC: …the first take was a nightmare. Keeping the actors upside down for over 3 minutes whilst everyone futzed around… Poor Richard (Bunst) getting very claustrophobic in his snail box for this long a time. He had to have a rest when we finally turned him upright again, and so the day went on… We did not finish our shots on this scene today.

Wednesday, 2nd July

BM: Driver George gets stopped by the police for speeding, trying to get Gilliam to the location on time.
Last night Guy Hendrix Dyas and the props team arrived with Cavaldi's elaborate black carriage, on a flatbed truck.

Dyas: "On the way down the trees were so low that we lost a couple of birds off the top. Some super glue and some plaster should sort it out."

Finish up yesterday's scenes, this time with the camera on

Delatombe (Pryce). From the courtyard outside, Heath can be clearly heard bellowing his lines from the grand room upstairs.

Exteriors being lit – Terry is thrilled with the carriage and arranges it for the horses.

Damon arrives for his 9.30 call at 10.25, but is forgiven.

The horses arrive – around twenty of them, including four to go with Cavaldi's night-black carriage/prison, described by Guy as "very fairytale like, but the stuff of dark fairytales".

Gilliam seems to be getting a lot of coverage – nerves perhaps? He is constantly shooting with two cameras: "Because we have two cameras. Which is not the best reason in the world. I hate two cameras! – but we have to cover ourselves in case anything goes wrong."

Despite the need to move on, Gilliam lets his actors improvise through numerous takes – Pryce and Stormare especially, working on making Cavaldi scarier in particular.

Lena's first day – she's been here all morning in costume – with nothing to do now until after lunch. Bridgewater still has his doubts – "I don't think she's got a thing to offer."

Running late – with sets in front and behind the castle being rigged simultaneously. In less than two hours the castle's courtyard has been transformed into a period street complete with blacksmiths, soldiers and, naturally enough, horse shit. An irate assistant director asks the horse's trainer (in costume) to do something about this. The local just shrugs his shoulders as if to say "It's a horse – that's what they do."

Busy afternoon – Gilliam plots the courtyard scene as a series of stedicam moves. Again the two leads like to improvise from take to take – with both moves and dialogue, thus the first shot runs to twelve takes.

The shoot runs late, but the big crane shot – involving dozens of extras, the carriage leaving and an execution by guillotine is nailed in three takes, as the clock ticks past 9 pm and the light is all but gone. Only a 90 minute drive back to the hotel now.

Thursday, 3rd July

BM: Late call today – 12.00pm due to late run last night. Drive to new location, the Prague National Museum, a large palatial mansion 1½ hours from the city, to shoot the interiors of the dungeon, a dense, elaborate three storey set.

Gilliam, in car on the way there – "What I'm doing on this movie is not really caring as much about the things I usually care about."

Gilliam and Grisoni have heard that already there are rumours in Hollywood of "Chuck Roven vs. the Weinsteins." They laugh, somewhat incredulous.

Both are extremely impressed with Heath; Matt still occasionally apologises for losing his accent.

(Gerry adds later – "He has to stop being a car salesman.")

Gilliam: "Johnathan just makes his character more and more disgusting. They're going to hate that bit when he eats the food. Fuck it – we'll make a movie even more disgusting than the Farrelly brothers."

And then the flood arrives! What is it about Gilliam's films and floods?? "Quixote" was washed away – last year so was Prague. Good thing this didn't happen yesterday when it was all exteriors. The catering tent's roof has just collapsed flooding the place where many of the extras were taking shelter.

Gilliam receives a FedEx parcel containing a present from his agents – a pair of red boxing gloves and a sparring helmet. The card reads – "Dear Terry. No matter what happens, your friends at Endeavour will always be in your corner."

The set itself was constructed in just one week – it is immensely detailed on three levels, a full circle effect with nooks and crannies and torture devices all around, waiting to be filled with heavily made up extras. One of them – in a boiling vat of oil – takes his place in the liquid, wearing an incongruous pair of red Speedo swimming trunks.

Chuck has asked to see Lena's audition tapes again today – he appears worried from yesterday that the studio will not go for her Irish accent. She may have to be English again – even though she has only uttered one line to date – "Nice one Jake."

Gilliam has insisted that real meat be used in the torture chamber. Due to an initial lack of stage blood, two of the props guys are rubbing down a vat with what appears to be a large cow's liver. Surely this must contravene some health and safety act? I guess that's why we're in Prague.

Lena, being a vegetarian, does not realise that she has to get into this vat, dressed with real meat, and now being drenched in some recently located stage blood.

The meat is being stored in fridges over night. By Monday – under the lights – who knows how it might smell.

The first shot rolls at 3.30pm, although the crew has been prepping since close to dawn. Before he goes on, Gilliam and Gerry are worried that Peter Stormare may not be fully heeding their advice, wanting to do things his way. He is – he and Johnathan Pryce improvise numerous lines over the next five takes, each of them eager to out do the other.

Apparently last night the Miramax people in Prague saw the first two days' worth of dailies and really liked them.

Stephen Bridgewater comes clean: "Terry wasn't even taking Chuck's calls till Sunday. At one point it got so bad, he was asking me to talk to him."

But today everything in on schedule and Gilliam seems to be finally enjoying himself, especially when he gets Lena in the meat-tastic vat. "I've got to train her. I've got to stop being so nice to her."

Bridgewater is still concerned: "The big battle is still to come. Editing. He hasn't got final cut....I rode in with the boys this morning (Matt and Heath) and they were asking how they could connect more with him...Up until this week he wasn't even talking to them."

Friday, 4th July

NC: The least said about today, the better!! Lots of that old chemical testosterone flying around the set and not possible to duck every bit of it!!

All rather time consuming as Will and Jacob hanging in harnesses and it is very tiring for them. They are doing their gallant best.

Some glitches with the old machine...which took up some rehearsal time and practice with getting the blades spinning at the correct speed...but then TG not really happy with the speed they went...but by then, we had shot with the blades and not CG blades.

Anyhow, we have finished week 1... sort of on schedule, which is really quite a miracle!!

Saturday, 5th July

NP: No, we did not have a Scott Rudin. We started without the nose and $500,000 more in the budget.

As I expected Matt did not have the balls.

But we started.

After 5 shoot-days we are still on schedule. Footage looks great: a Terry Gilliam movie! Finally!

The actors started studying each other, it's always extremely intriguing to observe the dynamics in such occasions, they are all smelling and circling to define their territories, in this case than even more 'cause both Jonathan and Julian did "compete" for Cavaldi's role and were very keen to play it. But Peter Stormare is bigger than life and brilliant, therefore they have to compete from their positions…

I'm trying to step back and let Terry and Pete become accustomed to each other, my crew seems to be working great, grips and electrics work well together and I'm very pleased with the choices…

The set is often a mess, especially in Krivoklat where it was logistically badly organised and we paid a heavy toll in time just to keep it quiet and clean (I'm growing more and more inpatient with the assholes who litter the set!)

Heath is great (focused, inventive, surprising at every turn), Matt is trying real hard and is getting somewhere, but I have the impression that he really should learn not to "think" so much, he should let go and trust his instincts.

Monday, 7th July

BM: Lena films her scene in the torture chamber with blades descending on her in the vat. There is some concern over how realistic it was – i.e. if the FX guy doesn't hit the stop button on time, it could be far too effective. At one point she is almost corkscrewed.

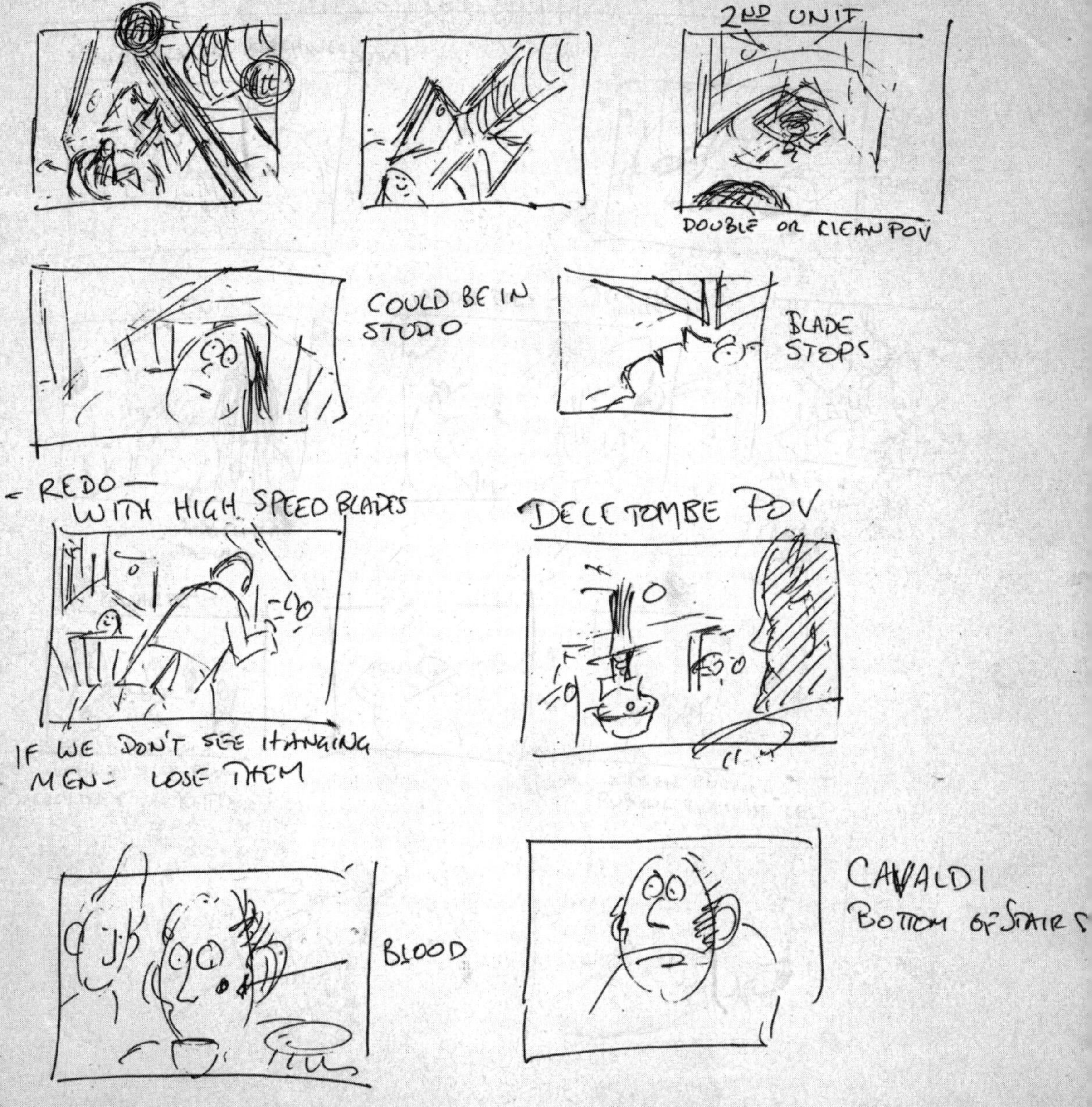

2ND UNIT

DOUBLE OR CLEAN POV

COULD BE IN STUDIO

BLADE STOPS

←REDO—
WITH HIGH SPEED BLADES

DELLE TOMBE POV

IF WE DON'T SEE IT HANGING MEN— LOSE THEM

BLOOD

CAVALDI
BOTTOM OF STAIRS

Gilliam not too happy with the previous week's shoot – "There were lots of mistakes in the rushes… stupid things. But the first week is always full of mistakes."

Bridgewater: "Today's the first day he's been up to it. Today he came prepared. By his standards I'd give last week a one out of ten… but to be fair to him, he stood up in front of everyone and took the blame."

Peter Stormare stands around, concerned that they won't get everything they need today.

Have lunch with Stephen Bridgewater. He hasn't really worked with Lena. She already knew Gerry so it was decided it would be best to leave her to him, keep her comfortable. After all the commotion over Samantha Morton not being cast, she clearly feels uncomfortable enough already.

Terry took great delight in recounting the moment when Lena's stunt double was required, calling "Lena out – Samantha in." Oh the irony.

A quiet, straightforward day, mostly doing pick-ups shots from Friday. The promise of an early break as the unit has to move location tomorrow.

Matt avidly watches/studies Johnathan Pryce in close up on the monitor.

Early end is lost as things fall behind yet again. They were due to finish at 6.30 so the crew can disassemble and move on, but filming carries on until 9.50pm.

Gilliam is doing many takes and some frustration from the crew at this is barely hidden.

The day ends for most – although the 2nd unit has arrived to continue shooting coverage (with Lena). They finish post 11.00pm – at least one of them is sleeping in their car tonight, to avoid the long journey back to the centre of Prague.

Stephen Bridgewater phoned Guy Dyas after having watched rushes on Sunday night to tell him that basically he'll never satisfy Terry no matter how hard he tries – no one can. "They all try to put that extra effort in because it's 'a Terry Gilliam movie'. But they never really satisfy him. I mean how can you give him what he's seeing in his head at that moment? He's a hard bastard sometimes… I say the same to his face."

BM: A lot of people I've spoken to say they're only doing this film because of Terry Gilliam.

TG: Which really pisses me off!

BM: Why?

TG: Because I don't think it is a Terry Gilliam film, it's already been compromised a lot. It was compromised early on and that's been the reason for my attitude most of the time. It's one thing for me to make the mistakes as I go forward, at least I start with something that at least in my mind is pure and good and as good as it can be and then I fuck it up along the way, but to have something fucked up in many ways before we even begin – by other people, I think is unforgivable.

NC: Peter S [Cavaldi] banged his head very hard… doing a sort of stunt fall into some sacks. He saw stars… Eva [set nurse] applied ice and we all cooed at him and he soldiered on. These actors are the SWEETEST and so funny still and polite after seventeen hours wrapped in hot sergey, tweedy costumes in a stinking, meat rotting infested gaseous cupola with a sweaty smelly crew!!!

Tuesday, 8th July

BM: New location today, where a church crypt is doubling as Delatombe's dining room. It is surrounded by seven ornate mirrors, but as people start to arrive on set the props are still being painted and the set is still being dressed.

Gilliam is very active but he appears to only conceive of the final design once he's in the middle of it, constantly developing his initial ideas, shifting pre-set props as he goes.

Peter Stormare is all good nature, keeping everyone's spirits up; Johnathan Pryce less so, constantly on the phone and leaving the set when not needed.

Gilliam spent little time with the other departments during prep, seemingly another victim of the Samantha Morton battle, so things could be smoother.

Lunch is served outside St Barbara Cathedral, everyone eats on the run as the production has opted largely for ten-hour continuous days, as opposed to breaking for food… which is a good thing as the first shot only rolls at 2.30pm.

Nicola popped his knee on last night's shoot and arrives today hobbling; by lunchtime he is on crutches – the first physical injury of the production. (There already seem to have been several psychological ones.)

Gilliam's children, Holly and Harry, arrived yesterday. 15-year-old Harry is making his acting debut in the movie as the Stable Boy and nervously runs his lines by his dad.

When the first shot is more than an hour later than expected, Gilliam is noticeably angry – "Just fucking shoot! We've now just got six and a half hours to do everything we need to get done today."

There is a tense atmosphere for the first few takes – Cavaldi's entrance into the dinner is constantly mis-timed. It takes over twelve takes to get, and many of them are not completed due to these mistakes.

Gilliam constantly re-blocks the moves. Is this a regular habit or is he simply not prepared enough for this film?

By late afternoon things have relaxed and silly season has arrived. Delatombe has Cavaldi up against the wall and both actors can't help cracking up at the sight of Cavaldi's wig in his mouth.

By 8.00pm there is one hour left and three more shots to get. Another late night.

NC: …it was also a very FILTHY black nostril day again. Think it's these parafinny candles they have…

Wednesday, 9th July

BM: Still in the mountain town of Kutna Hora, where Guy and his crew have constructed another remarkable set. Based over a bridge and an old fortress town tower, this is to be Karlstadt town square.

Harry Gilliam makes his screen debut and to mark it the ADs have re-christened Gilliam's trailer – the notice on the door that formerly read "Director" now reads "Stable Boy". He is nervous, excited and needs to eat. His sisters protectively fuss round him.

Gilliam Sr. professes to not being nervous – "He's just another fucking extra. Just get the lines right and let me move on," he laughs.

In the town the director is actively trying to master the "cripple car" and rides it round the square as the shots are set up.

Predictably (given Prague's unpredictable weather) it is a glorious sunny day, just when Gilliam wanted heavy rain. They test the rain machines and hardened dry earth is quickly turned into heavy mud, which runs downhill into the stable, which floods.

The horses arrive as do the actors, Stormare still buzzing over the bit of business with the wig the previous night – "I've never seen that done before."

On the way in this morning, Stephen Bridgewater was talking about the phrase "Going postal" – an Americanism that kind of implies there is worse to come. He refused to be drawn on why he had brought it up.

Gilliam still seems to be working out all his shots on arrival. So far things are running 2 hours behind. It's 11.00am and nothing has been shot. Gilliam has just asked for a crane to be brought in and a track to be built.

11.30 and the square is really coming to life – costumed extras, including numerous marching soldiers, horses, two goats, a dozen chickens, etc. Plus the taverns and shops are dressed with dead pheasants and fish.

The first take is at 12.50 – Matt and Heath are present in costume, but stunt riders do the scene. This is the only shot done before lunch-break and it takes an hour and a half to get. Some locals wander onto the supposed "high security" set to see what's happening.

Gilliam definitely seems to be making it up once he's on set – constantly adding to each take, reworking things, refining. The shots get better, the choices get better, but it does mean delays.

NC: Here we are gathered on this enchanting set and blow me down, it is SUNNY... which is a word no one wants to hear really... as this is a rain sequence and we don't have actors for weather cover.... Whoopsie daisy!

At 9.45 we looked at a rain test on the set... looks good and thankfully... it CLOUDED OVER. Gawd is on our side, honeychild! So... lining up the crane for shot of Will and Jacob entering town... with loads of lovely Background action, brilliantly trained geese and goats and horses, and also townsfolk who didn't moan about being soggy and wet for hours.

Started shooting at 13.00... after 3 takes we decided to move the legless beggar in his cart more into the foreground. Did the next take which was great but Jake's horse knocked into the cart by mistake, which kinda broke it and legless beggar fell out into the mud, causing approx 15mins delay to fix it. Mind you, the mud is not helping it move and it seemed to be falling apart anyway. Was from an original design found in some book... Obviously not L. da Vinci's...

Sunday, 13th July

NP: Sunday – We certainly did better this week than the first one.

Still a bit of a mess on the set, still losing too much time at the start of the day but the scenes are more "organic".

The real problem is that Terry still does not feel the movie is HIS OWN.

He feels raped and unamoured.

Had a long lunch with him and Chuck (he's back!): quite frank, hope it will be useful

Going on stage tomorrow. Now it seems that Terry Glass will take over, a bit suicidal on his part...

Cavaldi and Delatombe are getting more and more outrageous and funny. Of course Miramax does not get it...

Monday, 14th July

BM: Gilliam:"Just remember – birds fly forward."

Bridgewater: "That's the old Terry I know... He must have got some sleep or something."

The production has moved back to Barrandov studios. "Day one of how many years on this set?" jokes Gilliam.

Standing round the back of the forest set, two Miramax execs are overheard quietly talking enviously of the opening weekend haul of £46million just brought in by *Pirates of the Caribbean*. You can see the wheels turning – maybe this could be the next big swashbuckler?

TG:"If they wanted another *Pirates* it's too fucking late for that now."

NC: And we all thought: Fantastic... Easy peasey studio... UNTRUE. Hellhole of dust and blackness!

BM: *cont'd*:
Off camera – the Queen has still to be cast. Lists are being emailed – Cameron Diaz or Gwyneth Paltrow? Gilliam wants Angelina Jolie; Bridgewater favours Winona Ryder (after all, Prague is a good town to shoplift in).

It is a long slow day on the backlot, essentially filming the group's ride into the forest from every conceivable point of view. Even so, it remains unfinished. The day wraps at 7.30pm. Bridgewater is currently giving Gilliam a five out of ten. Gilliam:"I just don't know what I'm doing yet... hopefully it will come."

Bridgewater is not concerned by the amount that's being shot – "I would say this is the least amount of coverage I've ever seen him shoot."

NC: All I have to say for today is thank you to the wonderfully amiable horses and mules, even though Matt doesn't agree I'm sure, for plodding up and down and up and down with crashing and bangings all around them. Not even a nicker or whinny.

Tuesday, 15th July

BM: Start the day with a crane shot of the ride into the forest. Gilliam explains he wants a "raven's eye view" of the thing. As the cameraman reaches the roof, first AD Mishka adds "And get a haircut," to that direction.

Stormare is exercising in his trailer doorway – "My early morning Marine routine," he jokes on the same day that a US Marine is reported to have run off to Paris with a 12-year-old girl.

Gilliam confers with his head of FX, longtime collaborator Kent Houston. "You can be bolder with the smoke."

"As long as you observe the rules of continuity," Houston replies. They both laugh with what feels like almost a siege mentality.

Gilliam: "I'm just too tired… what I'm doing is concentrating on the battles. They're just so contained so you can avoid the rest… Films are what happen to you when you're busy making other plans." (John Lennon, reportedly, rolls over in his grave.)

Bob Weinstein is due to arrive for dinner tonight, so that means the day will wrap on time. Gilliam's blood pressure is up and he is checked on a daily basis for it (soon an oxygen tank will appear in his trailer). "I'm enjoying this movie now. I've abdicated any sense of responsibility."

With the lack of walkie talkies, Nicola must shout up to his cameraman. "It's a fantastic DVD extra," he jokes. "'Hear The Fucker.'"

Nonetheless it's gallows humour from the DP – "I watch the dailies at 6.30. In case I fucked up – there's an 8 o'clock plane."

FX man Karl Derrick passed up a job on *Troy* because he wanted to work with Gilliam. "Two things on the page made me want to take this job – the names Terry Gilliam and Brothers Grimm." Karl and his department are currently concentrating on an animatronic wolf, the make-up for Mackenzie as the Mill Witch and designing the make up for the Queen, something which is proving to be a long job, especially as the role has still to be cast.

Bob Weinstein arrives just as Gilliam is leaving the set – "I'm trapped."

Bob takes Matt – whom he apparently describes as "his rascal" – to dinner that night; Gilliam is invited for the following night. The phrase "divide and conquer" comes to mind.

Meet Paul Feldsher from Miramax, later described by Gilliam as "the hit man who wants to be loved". He already knew who I was – "I had you checked out yesterday." When he hears the book is already set up at a publisher, he replies, "That's okay. We'll buy them!"

View first assembly of scenes between Delatombe and Cavaldi. Mention to Gilliam that they seem quite cold and austere. Minutes later he says, "It is cold, you're right. That's my fault… I just haven't got it yet."

Later, tell Bridgewater how Terry feels he still hasn't got it or connected with the material. Stephen seems genuinely concerned – "I wish he wouldn't keep saying that in public."

NP: Bob arrives! Just minutes before the wrap, just in time for the dailies. My first impulse is to bail out, let Terry meet and mingle. Then, moved by compassion, I headed to the screening room to help him out, only to find that he'd bailed on me! So I find myself in the room with Bob (I swear I tried to say, "Nice to meet you," when they introduced me, but I just couldn't do it, it was too much, he's disgusting at first sight, even with all my background knowledge. So all I said was, "Welcome to Prague.")

Nothing was said during screening, except "Is this supposed to night or day?" At that point I understood that the man (and with him, all his brown-nosers) were hating it. I walked out before the end just because, not having Terry there, I didn't want to show my anger. They saw me outside when they left but no one called me over or even came near me.

Wednesday, 16th July

NP: I could feel the tension on set. The movie was too "dark", not enough close-ups of the boys, not enough coverage. Bob was on set, Terry was friendly enough but cold.

BM: The spectre of Bob W. looms large – although the man himself isn't present. He arrives at (high) noon to see the assembled footage.

The first roughly edited footage is viewed – it has been prepared for Bob's arrival. It is the material shot in Delatombe's room and the torture sequence, plus Will and Jake in the town square. Gilliam declares that Mr. Weinstein is happy with what he has seen.

Gilliam, John Schofield, Chuck, Nicola and Roberto are in for a breakfast meeting. Michelle Pfeiffer is now a distinct possibility for the Queen. Gilliam wants her.

First shot is done before 10.00am – a first in itself.

Heath and Matt hang out between shots, riffing on lines from *Life of Brian*. Heath is particularly fond of "I'm Brian. And so is my wife."

Matt is getting bored and jokes, "Rehearsal is for pussies – let's shoot." They do – but only after another half-hour delay.

Everyone is lining up tickets to see the Rolling Stones play Prague next week. Gilliam has been invited to Mick Jagger's 60th birthday party; he also went to Jagger's 40th, and arrived an hour late to find Mick, Jerry Hall and Mick's mum and dad sitting on the coach. Alone, with no one there yet. (He is planning on being fashionably late this time.)

Bridgewater suggests mic-ing Terry up for his dinner with Bob W. He is only half joking. "He's my new best friend," deadpans Gilliam.

The first raven arrives on the set and is the only performer in the scene who seems to get it right.

Went to see the town set of Marbaden this morning – the trees are becoming browner and browner, like they're dying incrementally…

Stormare and Bridgewater spend the interminable wait after lunch joking over past failed relationships. Peter in particular is very high energy… Then it's time for Heath's performing horse (it dances) – it hits its mark every time, even though it has taken 90 minutes to set up the shot. (Within a week it will be dead, the production's first fatality.)

NC: Brilliant. Jake's horse doing a dance though we do seem to go over the top in testing it out and its little veins are standing out… This is a very fine horse… half-Spanish half-English…. with the sweetest disposition… and it loves

peppermints! Ssssh! Then we line up for yet more of this lovely horse dancing and Jake trying to get on it… by now the creature is quite tired and we do take after take till we decide that it is not quite happening and perhaps it is better to let the 2nd unit get another go at this another day. Hmmmm. I've no more to say on paper, but ye can all guess!!

BM: *cont'd*:

Before the shooting starts, Steve frankly tells Matt, "You've got fat," and suggests he take up smoking again. (Within days, he has.) Three weeks in Matt has hired a personal hypnotist to help him break the habit. Despite their praise for this wonderful human being, soon everyone that's seen the hypnotist is back on twenty a day and rising. Given the combustible nature of the forest set – and the fact that everyone patently ignores the "no smoking on set" notices, it's amazing that only one very minor fire is reported.

Still, it's a frustrating day – the second AD Ricky Graysmark says, "I'm only coming to work for the last fifteen minutes of the day – then I can go again, because the rest is a waste."

NP: Terry had dinner with him [Bob Weinstein] and he finally went back home in his private jet much more happy and satisfied with the movie. He is a simple man, after all: all he needs is to be in constant control (or at least feel that way) and to be loved…

Thursday, 17th July

NC: …We then tried to get some shots of the LITTLE GIRL (Little Red Riding Hood), but discovered that (she) is and will be a nightmare. Several crew members wanting to rattle her… a real drama queen… then we shot with her

DOUBLE… very good double actually. In fact, so good that we did several blooming shots that were really close on the DOUBLE! YIKES!! However, she turned into ugly pills and has obviously gone to the same acting school as the first one…

Friday, 18th July

NC: Started off first thing with the little s**t (mistress of the blank expressions!), Red Riding Hood picking bloody berries and pricking her finger. I won't write any comments that were flying around "video village" (where we view the playback), but leave it to your fertile imaginations!! Those two shots took until 11.10… that is FOUR HOURS SINCE CALL!!! Should we RECAST? Lots of discussions going on… We then reversed onto her from the cave looking out on the back of her head, which was the best place to be shooting from and everyone calmed down… phew, relief, no angina pains… the sequence will work and then we have 5 weeks for her to get some ACTING LESSONS before we start running her around the meadow set…

Sunday, 20th July

NP: Hansel and Gretel are real good, but I over lit it! Yes, I can bring it down and de-saturate it but I still over lit it… We've done a great shot for the Little Red Riding Hood scenes, flying just above ground to leap after her and keep flying looking down, but again I fucked up (a tree is far too bright!) but it has lot of CGI blue-screen work so we can take it down.

On Saturday morning, big panic attack for some veiling on the above-mentioned shot… luckily false alarm but the Saturday was gone.

We have to pay more attention to details, all of us.

Thursday, 24th July

BM: Lena is still very unsure. Gilliam takes her to dinner to reassure her before re-shoots next day.

The dancing horse has died; from colic, apparently.

Saturday, 26th July

NC: Just SO SO SAD to learn of that beautiful horse suffering such an untimely passing to the other side. May he rest in peace. For the little time I knew him, he cheered me up enormously. I really feel for those poor people who were so close to him…

TG got hold of a pan glass from somewhere and now has his beady eye on the contrast… Nicola look out!!

On a painful note… during scene 93A, our focus puller the lovely JJ on the A-cam was slammed into a set tree. He was riding the Quad bike for the shot and it zipped around another tree a bit too fast and tipped over slightly, slamming him (in the back as he was looking the other way) into a tree… OUCH!! He didn't even whimper… but Eva, our nurse, made him go to the hospital for an X-ray… his back was scraped and bruised and his left arm punctured. He walked off the set and I saw him at wrap still upright! We did slow the Quad bike down after this.

Sunday, 27th July

BM: Majority of crew and cast off to see the Stones tonight – Vaclav Havel introduces the show.

NP: Rolling Stones concert tonite!

Survived another week of passion: switched to the night look on Monday, in the midst of the ongoing argument about the darkness of dailies…

Notwithstanding my insistence, they keep making-up Matt with too much black around the eyes: he's already got a sideboard of a forehead, if you then give him black eyes the light sucks in everything. You want to put light on him to show up his blue eyes, but if you put too much then he starts to squint...

I worked a lot with Lena and the first day has been a bit of a disaster: she could not concentrate and the results on screen were dreadful! Not only that, it cost a lot of time to produce such poor results and on Friday, after a long dinner with Terry and Lena, we had to re-shoot it all (this time with better luck).

During the disastrous day the Miramax boys were very nervous: for the loss of time, for the quality of the acting, for the work and energy required. Assholes! They forced her on Terry and now they can't cope with the fact that it's counterproductive. Double assholes!

Lena, poor wretch, is in a shitty position: it's also her own fault because she should by now have some idea in her little head, even a wrong one but some idea. She has nothing. We're trying every way to make her feel confident and loved (in fact, she threw a pretty successful party on Saturday night) and I find myself even lying. Terry Glass has arrived and I have to say that even if he's his usual indolent, lazy self, everything immediately got better. For example, the smoke and atmosphere on stage are finally working.

The set is chaotic, and Terry is so good at stirring up the chaos! The other day I nearly shouted at him to stop it; he came up with something he wanted at the very last moment, and then was angry because it didn't work! The level of attention to detail is getting better, but we need to do more.

Tomorrow we get into the backlot, let's hope it will be very cloudy for the whole week, it will be a sin to have full sun in Marbaden.

Monday, 28th July

BM: On the Marbaden backlot – Gilliam is still worried about Matt, gives him direction constantly, while giving hardly any to Heath. For example, when Will is asking Angelika's name, it takes in the region of 18 takes and Matt only nails the intonation on the last one. Still, he did nail it…

Gilliam is now referring to Bridgewater as "Bilgewater"…

Everyone is knackered after the Stones, Gilliam got less than three hours sleep last night. "I really can't see myself up for this one…" he says in the car on the way in. "I think I'm making this one to prepare myself for making a real film. I've never had this kind of money before and I never will again… At the moment it's just work. I'm filming it in the most pedestrian way… it's not exciting."

Stephen Bridgewater is looking increasingly worried.

Gilliam: "There's just no organisation round here… I don't think I'm getting that much coverage… certainly not enough… There just isn't enough time to do all this."

The main shot of the day – the carriage ride into Marbaden – doesn't come off and is postponed till the next morning. They rehearse an interior scene in the church but it is too late to film it.

Gilliam: "We're two days behind, but they're saying one. That's a lot to be behind this early in the shoot."

Tuesday, 29th July

BM: Gilliam – in the car on the way to the set – "I wish a producer would actually produce this film… Chuck's probably leaving soon now that Paul Feldsher's here. He'll take his million and go. Nice way to make money."

Gilliam is confident of starting by 8.00am. The crane is already in place… but it's gone 9.00 by the time they start – and as the day starts to brighten up, the shot is once again lost to the weather. Because of the unexpected decent weather, the set has to be watered down to keep the mud – the studio's fire truck and hoses are brought in to do so.

Peter Stormare always seems to be the first actor on set and goes out of his way to keep people's spirits up.

I walk out with Nicola at the end of the day. He is not a happy man – "This was a shitty day for me… those assholes from Miramax… they are so relentless. I'll be happy when they put me on the plane and send me home, which I know they are thinking of doing."

This has not been a good day – the introductory scene of the brothers arriving in town has been abandoned both yesterday and this morning. Gilliam decides to carry on despite the change in the weather. Everyone sits and waits for some kind of cloud cover time and time again for the rest of the day. Then torrential rain arrives and ruins the final shot of the day – a scene on the way into the town that is set up, but abandoned.

Throughout the day there are flocks of geese, a pair of cows, horses, goats and more milling around – it's a good deal of detail but Gilliam is still unsure: "I don't think I'm capturing it. And it's all so dark." His thoughts turn to Miramax – "I don't think I'm giving them what they want."

It's just been announced that there's a conference call tonight between Gilliam, Roven and Miramax. Gilliam's blood pressure sky-rockets at the news. Bridgewater: "He turned red."

Matt picks up on the prevailing attitude – "Everyone seems very on edge today."

Terry is yelling and Mishka finally loses it, yelling "I'm not going to fucking kill myself if people are not doing their fucking jobs…" He turns to the Miramax execs – "And I want Miramax to back me up on this." They look like they're about to laugh, like naughty schoolboys. Unfortunately, Mishka's explosion takes place in front of a young child actor Laura Greenwood, (who's playing the young girl, Sasha).

Wednesday, 30th July

BM: Ride in with Gilliam, who says the conference call was a big success. Bob Weinstein is apparently very pleased and has offered to give Terry whatever he needs – "I was hoping they would fire me."

Shooting on the backlot today, which once again requires wetting down – i.e. turning into a sea of mud.

Saturday, 2nd August

NP: One fine morning that filthy rattlesnake, Paul, came up to me and said, "I want to talk to you." We went back to town by car. (What an idiot I was to let other people drive my car; they managed to ruin the clutch! Ten days later I'm still waiting for the part. Fuck off.)

And he started, "They actually expect me to tell these things to Terry himself, but given that I'm seeing him get his enthusiasm for the movie back, I don't want to bug him and I'd rather talk to you. The fact is that Harvey hates, hates what he sees – it's too dark, too stark and you can never see Matt's eyes. He has convinced Bob that it has to change, that we are doing a comedy. Not any other kind of movie, it has to be a comedy. And he keeps saying that, given this movie will never be a contender for an acting Oscar(!), then it should be for the technical categories, like cinematography. And we know that not only are you a good friend of Terry's and a world-class cinematographer, but this photography is not

Academy Award-savvy and things have to change. What do you want to do about it?" In simple words: we hate what we see; either you help us to stab Terry in the back, again, or else it doesn't matter how good your friendship is, you're history! A great offer, in real *Mafiosi* style. At the time I didn't pay enough attention, but looking back it was an ultimatum from The Godfather, Act 2000.

My reply was polite but not terribly diplomatic (how odd, that I can't be diplomatic to shits!). "I understand you're worried and I'll take it into account. But my only artistic reference is Terry and I do what he wants in accordance with my own sensibility and technical ability, even on the rare occasions when we disagree. It has to be like that, it's the only way I can interpret my craft: for the movie, for Terry's movie. Incidentally, it just so happens that I don't give a damn about the Academy Awards. The only thing I agree with you about is that Terry has no enthusiasm; the problem is that he believes he's been 'raped', twice already, and now they are expecting him to show enthusiasm towards the outcome of that. Isn't that a bit like expecting a raped woman to love the child of violence as much as a love-bed child? Since the beginning of time, that's been impossible." I must admit, I was really proud of the metaphor.

I left, saying I'd think about what he told me and come up with some ideas of "what to do". I also insisted that if the look was the issue and my job was at stake, I expected them to have the decency to look at the dailies in a projection room, and not on a shitty VHS transmitted via satellite.

He warned me not to tell Terry of our conversation. I, of course, immediately phoned Terry to tell him.

Mishka almost cracked under the pressure and the next day he exploded in an unbelievably vile and uncalled-for outburst on set, when he lost his grip of the set and then started on me. Maybe that's what friends are for, but given the circumstances and the attacks we're suffering from those assholes, our best bet is to stay together and talk frankly about our problems, no good pointing the finger at this or that. Evidently Mishka does not think so, he was very quick to point the finger at me! I tried to talk to him, but he won't see it. Strictly professionally speaking, he's been a real disappointment. His department is leaking like a sieve and he's never ready to think of a solution to the usual unexpected problems which crop up.

I suppose this is all part of life's rich pattern, the friendships you make and which last, as long as you don't change so much as to be on a different wavelength. Good Lord, what deep thoughts, and all because we've found ourselves buried in so much shit it's ruining the film.

I've taken all this calmly and philosophically enough. Being sacked in the past certainly helped me to absorb the inevitable anguish that the prospect of being thrown out of a job, to which I've given so much time and energy, provoked. On the other hand, this type of pressure helps you to focus better when you're working on the set.

Objectively, I believe that until now the photography has served the film well. In fact, given Terry's state, the only thing that brought the film on track in keeping with Gilliam's abilities is the cinematography, the use of wide-angle lenses, the compositions, the different levels of storytelling.

Sunday, 3rd August

BM: Nicola is officially fired by Paul Feldsher. He's glad to be going but is nonetheless pissed off.

NP: And go!

Yesterday evening, about midnight, coming back from dinner with Terry, Tony, Steve Bridgewater and Matt.

I'd just about sat down, when shitface Paul arrived. "I cannot just sit there with you here. I need a minute of your time." So we sat on a nearby table, and off he went: "That's it, the decision has been taken, you are off the movie. The decision was made by Bob and Harvey two weeks ago, they hate the look of it. And you have to admit that the footage doesn't look great. Don't you?"

Why I should agree with the fact that my work is shit is a mystery to me... And from then on I almost laughed at the thought of the poor wretch who they chose in my place: he would not be in for a fun ride. With hindsight I think that the time and way Paul chose to tell me show he was looking for a fight, a real one. In that way he could pass some of the blame on to me. But I didn't bite, I stayed calm and bright and I asked him if he realised the consequences of such a stupid decision, that in the best-case scenario it would mean shutting down for days, and Matt's end date is still standing. Terry is dreading the thought of having months and months of this kind of torture. He regrets the compromises he's made so far, and this would be a fantastic way out. A bit like Samson and the Philistines.

One thing is certain, they haven't anyone else in mind, not here or in Prague, so to my question, "What would you like me to do on Monday? Stay home?", he replied, "Absolutely not, we would like you to come and shoot." That's totally out of the question. I will not go there to create an incredibly uncomfortable environment; it wouldn't be fair to the crew, or to me. I've spoken with Terry and John and they agree. They are going to have a meeting with Paulshitface at noon...

Evening

The lawyers are at work. Terry wants out, he cannot bear the thought of having to live in this shit for the next year.

Tomorrow I'll go to work not to be in breach myself. It will be a fun day at the office.

Monday, 4th August

NP: 7.00am at base camp, the news broke. The average reaction was between incredulous and enraged, but more toward the incredulous, after all I was still there, therefore the act was not over yet.

On the set Paul Feldsher arrives and comes to me with his hand out: "I want to congratulate you and thank you for your professionalism in being here today!" I stared at his hand and after quite an embarrassing long moment (45, 50 seconds?!) I shook it, saying "Snake!" so that everybody could hear, and walked away. Was a great little moment, the timing turned out just right, and he was really taken aback by the episode. My impression though is that the whole thing has been so badly handled from the beginning that I do not see which way they can go in order to save the movie.

The immediate result of my "snake" was that Paul and Jake disappeared from the set and we finally experienced some freedom, even some fun. There was so much rage and frustration in the air that when we approached scene 91 it turned into an unexpected, surprisingly violent scene (so much so that the next day both Tony and Matt, after seeing rushes, felt that it had to be re-shot completely). But it was fun to work with the boys and Terry. There was an amazing level of energy, also helped by the fact that we were in Angelika's house therefore only a few people could fit. I realised that this is the way movies should be done.

At the end of the day we had a powwow where we agreed that I should keep shooting the next day while Terry would have his lawyers/litigators dealing with Miramax. The plan was that somehow we would disregard the firing and behave as though nothing ever happened. Meanwhile, Terry would discourage anybody coming to replace me… My instinct was to hurt them as hard as possible. But Roberto and Steve talked me out of it, fearing that not having had anything written on Miramax/Dimension letterhead I could have been in breach myself.

NC: Ooooerrr matey… NOT a good day. Dare I say anything more… or will I be 4 the chop suey soon, eh? Oh dear, I can't resist. Best advice – don't go into a restaurant… Nicola our famoso DeePee was told he was history… yet, bless him, in true professional style, he turned up today to help TG out of a jam as the alternative would have been a blasted day and that spells a lorra dosh.

Tuesday, 5th August

NP: Back to work again. My entrance on set was unforgettable: as I'd had my hair cut I arrived ten minutes late. When I turned the corner, everyone turned to look and were dumbfounded, particularly when I said, "Hi, I'm the new cinematographer!"
Another little moment of crew fun, which we should have more often.

Wednesday, 6th August

BM: Receive text message from Steve Bridgewater: "We are closed down. Nicola not working anymore."

Evening – Gilliam meets with Tom Siegel, the newly appointed DP.

Gilliam faxes Bob Weinstein:

"…Once again you have made an arbitrary decision which has harmed the film I am trying to make. From the beginning of this project I have said that our tastes are very different – with each of your acts, from the forcing of Lena Headey on me to the willingness to close the film down because of a make-up on Matt Damon that made him look right for the character of Will Grimm, to the criticism of Peter Stormare's performance to the present firing of Nicola Pecorini, I am convinced the film in your head is a different one from mine.

In the case of N.P.. I think you fired the wrong man – his work was beautiful, dark and magical – exactly what I wanted. Exactly right for the story…"

NP: I arrived at Barrandov. Terry is poisoned: Miramax have threatened to sue if he tries to walk or obstructs their decisions. In other words, he cannot refuse to meet DoPs. Not only that, they have the tiebreak control, therefore they can impose anyone at any moment.

We should have started to work inside the barn today, the witch sequence, the long, complicated and difficult scene 15! Let alone the gloomy atmosphere, nothing was ready. The stunts did not work, the set was not completely dressed, the SFX were keeping their standards consistent… And my head was empty. I could not come up with any feasible solution. For the first time in my working life I found myself empty of ideas. Scary! After a quick call to Sue at ICM in London, I gathered Terry, John, Roberto, Mishka, James and Paul in Terry's trailer and said, "On stage, a few moments ago, for the first time in my professional life I found myself empty, my mind was blank. The reason is that I can't begin such a difficult sequence, establish such a complicated look, knowing that I will not be allowed to finish it. I need an answer to a question, a basic question before I can even start considering whether to keep working. If you fired me because I am not good enough to shoot a Miramax movie why do you want me to keep shooting a Miramax movie?"

They could not answer, they could not admit that it was merely for financial reasons. I tried to get it out of them, I tried to give them a way out. Let's talk about vulgar, dirty money and maybe I could consider finding in myself at least the same "motivation" I have when I shoot a commercial. But no, they are so utterly stupid that they blew even this possibility.

Terry "enjoyed" my show, I could tell. He found it extremely well handled. Even in these crises we have the same reactions. From their sick point of view they've seen it right: I was Terry's best friend and ally. If their sick plan is to cripple Terry, they started with the right foot.

Thursday, 7th August

BM: Tony Grisoni flies out to offer moral support.

Today and tomorrow are now rehearsal days for the actors. Nicola volunteers to come in and work for free to keep things moving, but four days of filming have been lost and the movie is now a week behind schedule.

Sunday, 10th August

BM: Arrive back in Prague just in time for Nicola's birthday party, which is also his (thankfully, non-permanent) wake. Everyone is there and everyone is sad to see him go; all think it's the wrong, tokenistic decision. Even Matt is speaking out against Miramax, saying he doesn't want to work with them anymore: he's not happy with the way they treat people/do business. (Matt has his mother and sister in town – possibly for support. It's the week Ben Affleck's *Gigli* has just opened, so Matt takes some comfort in the fact that he's not the only one having a rough week.)

Gilliam has been in retreat back in London for the last two days, but flies in for Nicola's party. "It's totally unfair that Nicola is going... I said to them you're firing the wrong man. It's me you should be firing... They do this to everyone they work with, you have to sell your soul to them."

The party empties out mid-evening, with only a few stragglers left – Nicola, Steve B, Gilliam and myself. We finish off the wine and drag ourselves back through the streets to our – admittedly picturesque – temporary homes. Gilliam is thinking of buying his; his wife Maggie is pleased when the whole idea doesn't work out.

"Marvellous" Monday, 11th August

NC: Last week was a RUMMY OLD WEEK… We shot for a couple of days and then me old darlings, it reely went reel… Nicola really was fired and I think they did stick the tail on the donkey and found poor unsuspecting Tom (yep, we'll be gracious for a bit!!) lurking around in the pisspot of Europe and we SNAFUed him into our lair as a spy in a flider's wed – oh no, sorry – fly in a spider's web, I meant. I was going to comment on the fact that he showed up wearing the same clothes both days I've seen him, but then I learnt that his suitcase went walkies so I'll resist.

With everyone DREADING Monday morning, it's arrived!! And it's like we're starting again… Not much to say about today though – doing 2 biggish shots which took ALL BLOOMIN' day and a lot of muttering about SETTLING IN TIME… that's a new movie phrase that will enter our vocab like 'TURN OFF YOUR CELLS/MOBILES'.

BM: Tom Siegel's first day – he works well but it is a long day involving Mackenzie swinging in the barn. This is the only scene scheduled and again it is a 10-hour continuous day.

Tom is asked by a crewmember how to spell his name. Tom replies, "I don't know if I want my name on this."

Chuck is not here as, according to Terry, Miramax wouldn't pay for his transport. Are they deliberately trying to get rid of Terry's support group? First Nicola, now no Chuck.

Terry speaks to Tony G on the phone and unloads on him – he's currently got his lawyer looking into it, trying to find grounds under which he can quit. Is sacking his chosen DP some form of restraint of trade/creative freedom?

Matt is pissed off with Miramax, Heath is a friend of Nicola's — last week you had two very angry actors and a director who was, according to publicist Patric Scott, "incandescent with rage". Patric vows never to work with Miramax again.

Gilliam wonders if it'll be Mishka or John Schofield who goes next. "Schofield's doing a good job but he has no real power."

Another Miramax exec flies in just for the day. TG:"I said 'Hello' to him – that was about it."

Is paranoia setting in? – TG:"I think they thought I was going to go 'politically slow' today."

Terry takes Nicola out for a farewell dinner.

Tuesday, 12th August

BM: Gilliam:"Tom takes longer to light than Nicola – I don't know what this is doing to the budget. They've got this guy staying at the Four Seasons – none of us have stayed there! It's got to be $80million – it could go to a hundred.

"I've proved to myself I can still shoot a film. I don't need to finish it… anyone could finish it at this point."

Over breakfast John Schofield castigates him: "Stop saying that. You're still making a Terry Gilliam film." Gilliam doesn't look so sure. This reminds me of something Bridgewater said at Nicola's party: "I came here because I thought I was making a *Terry* film – now I'm not sure."

Tuesday morning: TG is rehearsing actors by 7.15am – a swift start for once. It is the scene where Mackenzie's Mill Witch reveals himself. Terry sets up the master shot; Tom spends the next three hours lighting it, saying – loudly in front of a large amount of the crew – that they

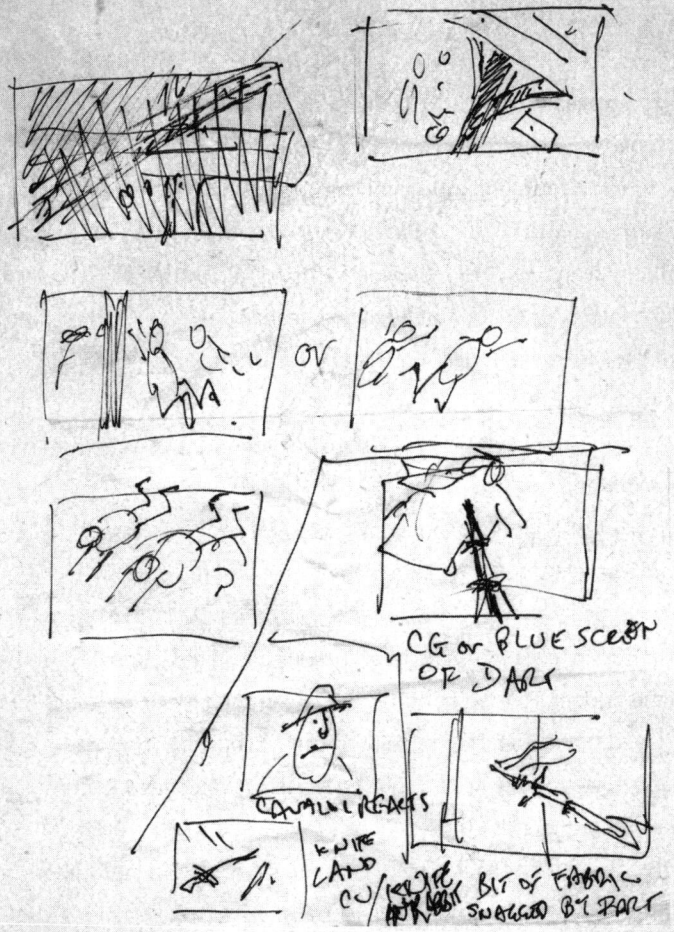

probably won't end up using most of the master. Is he undermining Gilliam?

TG tells me that the crew are now referring to Paul Feldsher as "the loneliest man in Prague".

Gilliam has requested no press on set; publicist Patric Scott has to liaise with Dimension in New York, who claim to be unaware of any problems on set.

TG: "I want to teach them a lesson. It's time somebody did, because they hire talented people and then they screw them over."

Much of Lena's early stuff is having to be re-shot. TG: "They shouldn't have fired the DP – it's the lead actress they should have fired. And they realise that now. They know she's miscast." [Nikki Clapp agrees.]

It used to take about two hours to prep and light a scene – currently four hours in…

Nikki got lost in Prague last Saturday and went into a cinema. It was showing *Brazil*. She went in and watched it; said it reconfirmed her faith.

There is increasing dissent and disharmony amongst the ranks:

NC: "I work for Terry. I don't work for them."

Chrissie, from Make-up: "Yesterday Tom said my make-up was too heavy. Matt likes it that way – it's his job to light him!"

It's now noon and nothing has been shot – TG, loudly: "Let's get something on film today."

Mishka calls for "Quiet!" but the chicken clearly isn't listening.

Mishka: "It's impossible to work here. You have to have discipline, guys."

TG: "Wake up, guys. This is the first shot of the day – and it's noon."

The shot is about to be abandoned due to trouble with marks being hit when at the last moment TG places a dead rat by Matt's foot. Heath suggests drawing a chalk line round it.

From this Friday, the original camera team of Sky, Pete and JJ are being moved down to the B team. Tom has his own team on hand. Gilliam: "Hooray. The Marines are here to save us."

Peter Stormare: "This happens a lot on Hollywood movies. When they watch rushes they have their girlfriends or mistresses there. So there are a lot of opinions."

TG: "The hardest thing on this film has been to keep a rhythm going. We keep starting and crashing… There's no energy here on set. Matt's crashing, Heath's crashing… but now Miramax have admitted they've fucked up. So now Tom's on board they're going to leave us alone to get on with it. Finally, we get to get on with it."

Tonight is the Prague premiere of *The League of Extraordinary Gentlemen*, a film that many of the crew here worked on last year, before it was forced to relocate due to the floods. Tomorrow night is Flood Night, a celebration of the flood. Sean Connery is in town for both and many of the crew want to finish on time tonight to get to the party.

Gilliam seems unable to relax, as does everyone else – "Mishka's just not pushing everyone hard enough. He thinks he's going to be the next to be fired."

They're changing over from an Arriflex camera to Panavision, which is Tom's preference. For once the budgetary additions don't seem to be an issue…

Gilliam on Tom: "It's very difficult when you replace someone who was as loved as Nicola. So I'm giving him some space to settle in… he doesn't like Steadicam. He likes tracks, so it takes longer. I tell him what I want, I go away, I come back two hours later and they haven't done what I asked for… I've been shooting a lot on Steadicam because it's quicker – it's rougher at times but they haven't allowed us enough time to shoot this. When Tom came in he said this was such a complex script. There's a lot going on in every scene. Chuck said the same thing. None of the other producers seems to realise that. There isn't enough time in the schedule they've given us. And Matt has to be away to do 'Bourne Again'."

Some worries are expressed about whether Tom's style will match Nicola's footage.

Stormare is emerging as the heart and soul of the thing – he shows up when not working, determined to keep spirits and energy up.

Tuesday afternoon – the stunt where Bunst falls down the ladder – takes ages to set up and rehearse. The Czech stuntman keeps mis-timing his cue. Gilliam is *really* frustrated – "Mackenzie is ready. Why aren't we?"

They eventually go for a take – the stuntman's cue [a light] goes off, so he stops and the scene is lost. Gilliam [under breath]: "Jesus, what is that asshole doing?"

On the second take he breaks only one rung and slides down the sides, Navy style. TG: "That's exactly what I didn't want. *I* could do this fucking stunt." He is stressed and incensed.

NC: Took forever and a day to get the first shot this morning… shot turned into a complete nightmare as we were now on a dolly for a move round Hidlick to reveal stunt-double Bunst falling down the ladder with breakaway rungs… THEN a poor electrician had been asked to flag off a lamp on the upper level and went charging onto the set and tried to climb up the ladder…

Guess what? The rungs broke!!! JJ just managed to stop him breaking the whole bleeding lot, but by then a torrent of nasty words had left the guvnor's mouth, and a load of stifled giggles from the rest of us. Poor guy went as red as a beetroot and beat a hasty retreat.

BM: One of the horse trainers was sent back to Paris to tend the horses. She was due to go on the bus, which was a thirteen-hour journey; when Matt heard, he paid for her to fly club class.

Paul Feldsher is ill. He jokes that his ass is bleeding. No one shows any concern even if this is only a joke.

Possibly in response to the Panavision invasion, there seem to be a large number of crew sporting Arriflex T-shirts on set today.

Paul F. is now referring to me as "the face I most fear on the set".

Late afternoon – two cows and a pig are brought onto the already ripe set. The pig has remarkably good timing, the actors are not far behind.

Gilliam, despite the high blood pressure which is measured regularly, has gone back on the coffee. "Miramax now finally acknowledge they've made mistakes and from now on we can do it the way we want to. So why are all these 'producers' still here?"

NC: We're off to meet with Nicola, who've we've arranged to have dinner with despite the fact he's just had his mobile disconnected and his underpants taken away! Here's looking at tomorrow.

BM: Last night, the second unit set up the "witch on the water" to shoot plates for Kent Houston to blue-screen.

Today is just pick-ups of the barn scene – Richard/Bunst's close-up takes about a dozen takes – but filming does start by 8.20am.

Main cast not required – I spent the first part of the morning playing dice with Johnny Chicco (aka Johnny Cheeks), Heath and Annabel Schofield. (Cheeks has been brought along by Matt, and is a real character – he's the one who persuaded the props department to make him a portable, green-baize lined dice table.)

Johnny Cheeks is technically known as Matt Damon's stand-in. But he serves many other functions on this movie. Not only is he the proverbial life and soul of the party, who never seems to have any down time when it comes to his ebullient personality, but he also styles himself as essential party man and friend to the stars. When people need to blow off steam at the weekend, Cheeks is your man – he knows the best places and he makes sure the club managers know they are due a visit from a certain amount of Hollywood elite that night.

He got to know Matt via their mutual work on the Farrelly brothers' conjoined twins comedy *Stuck On You* and appears to have been a fixture in Damon's life ever since, travelling with him and sharing his New York apartment, a venue that neither have seen much of lately. He is great company, persuaded the prop department to make his just-off-set dice table – out of the film's budget – and has aspirations one day to land a gig performing on *Saturday Night Live*. He is in his own unique way a crucial part of the infrastructure behind this movie and on current evidence he might well get there one day.

Interview with Johnny Cheeks

JC: Giovanni Vincenzo Cicco is my given name. But people just call me 'Cheeks' and it's kind of stuck.

BM: How come you're here, and what are you doing here?

JC: I feel like the luckiest guy. I mean, I *am* the luckiest guy in the world, and I've had arguments with people, also on the crew, who say, 'Hey, *I'm* the luckiest guy in the world.' But literally, I'm Matt's stand-in but I think I'm a terrible, terrible stand-in.

BM: You said to me the other day that you were the one who knew exactly how somebody should move because you'd done it before and you knew exactly what was right.

JC: I know how to be a stand-in, but a lot of times it's, "Where's Johnny Cicco? Can you get Johnny Cicco in here?" And someone will say, "He's coming, he was just playing dice at the table down by the trailers!"
    You see these other stand-ins, the local stand-ins that are right there sitting on set with a walkie talkie, and when they say "check the gate" they fly right onto set and they're waiting, standing by. And, you know, I take

the easy way out, I wait to see if Matt's going onto set or if Matt's there, because I know the deal. They go in to rehearse, then you watch rehearsal, then the stand-ins stay there. In fact, you can fuck off and do whatever you want to do, because you've seen the rehearsal and then you've seen takes, and throughout they're running tapes back and forth so you can just check 'em out, see the gist. But I definitely do know the art of standing-in, in theory. It's just I've got too many social... I'm a social butterfly. That's really what I think my role is on this.

BM: So how does that bring you and Matt together? How do you know him?

JC: I'm actually an actor and I was cast in one of the Farrelly Brothers movies, just this last one, *Stuck on You*. I only met Matt in February. I play a porno director in the movie. Lines like, "More, deeper, more, all right, take it out!" But we met, and he's from Cambridge, Massachusetts. I'm from Cranston, Rhode Island. So we have the New England connection, and I literally went up to him and was like, "Matt Damon, Johnny Cicco, Cranston, Rhode Island." And he was like, "Hey, Cambridge!" and I was like, "I know!" So then we just got talking... and we've got a pretty tight bond, being from New England. It just sounds good.

But I was cast as a porno director and it was only three days in Miami. Now, I'm friends with Bob Farrelly so I would say, "Bobby, please, there's gotta be something I can do. I want to go, I want to film in LA for three weeks then I want to go back to Rockport, Massachusetts and film for a week and I really, really want to go to Miami for two and a half months to shoot there. What can I do?" He was like, "Can you do any lighting stuff?" I was like, "Nah, you get shocks off electricity and it's bad." He's like, "You know how to grip?" "Grip? Is that the things with the black flags in the way? Nah, I can't do that." And he was like, "Well, we need stand-ins," and you would just think that Matt would have his own stand-in, because some actors do. So I was originally supposed to be Greg Kinnear's stand-in but on the first day of shooting a guy comes up and he's like, "*I'm Greg Kinnear's stand-in.*" I was like, "Oh shit!", and I was like, "Oh, *all right*, I'll stand-in for Matt." And then we just met and he's one of the nicest, real people that I've ever met. I mean that goes a long way, especially in this business, to be able to hang, to be with somebody, talk to somebody that's genuine and who actually follows through. You know actions speak louder than words, and it's like he's never ever been anything but a true champ. I'm a big, big fan of Matt Damon.

BM: So you came straight here from *Stuck on You*?

JC: I had a month off. Matt had a week off and then he had to come to Prague and get into character, learn the dialect, you know, and I went home to Rhode Island. I was living in LA and I went home to Rhode Island to hang out with my parents because I knew I wouldn't see them for three or four months.

I couldn't wait to get here and on my first day I came down and he was up in the make-up chair and he had the big wig on, which was funny because it changes him completely and that's great. And Matt was like, "Hey Terry, this is Johnny Cheeks, my stand-in." And he's like, "Oh my God, he's got the nose!" Because I literally had the hair and everything and I would wear the wardrobe. For a few weeks I was wearing Matt's wardrobe, so Terry a couple of times would come up to me and say, "You know, Matt..." I'm like, "No. Johnny Cheeks!" And then, of course, he'd run away and go find Matt.

I talk to everybody on set, from the gardener and PAs all the way up to the directors and the executive producer. I mean I literally talk to everybody. So I'm like a social butterfly around set. I bring people together and people start hanging out. I'm all about camaraderie on the set, not like... everything is cliquey, you know those

little cliquey places, but I like to oversee stuff like that
and bring all those groups of people together.

And I love Peter Stormare. He is wicked funny. "Wicked"
is a Rhode Island thing. "Wicked funny." I'm going to keep
in touch with him; we'll keep in touch, Peter and I. He has
the kind of style that I like. That's how I act, the way he
acts. But some people don't like that. Some directors can't
handle it because you know you burn film trying to get that
really funny... but it always happens on the day.

BM: A lot of improvisational stuff.

JC: A lot of improv. Like I can prepare the shit out of a
role, prepare, prepare, know the lines down cold but the
magic won't happen until the camera's rolling on the day. I
can rehearse. It'll be good. I can prepare, but things just
click. Especially if you're working with an actor who's
giving you something or not giving you anything and then
you've got to adjust. I haven't really experienced the
whole pounding the pavement, trying to go to 100 auditions
a week just to try and get that one little break. I work
best on set, so if I can get onto a set stuff will start
happening for me from then on, you know what I mean?
Throughout my life, working in film, it's been, "Oh my God,
I've been cast as an extra and... oops, I found myself on
set and started talking to people and then..." I've
literally fallen into it.

BM: Taking over when you get there.

JC: Trying to, but I do it in a way that makes it look like I'm not pushy, Mr Bully pushy, and "Hey look at me!" At least I try and do it in that way.

BM: This has been at times a troubled set though, hasn't it?

JC: Yeah, but only on the days that I have off. The days I have off, I don't know what happens, the whole place falls down!

BM: The days that I show up there are problems!

JC: It's crazy. The drama and all the political stuff, like from studio to production house to the actual crew and everything that goes in with it, I stay as far away from that as I can. I am here to do what I want to do and what I'm here to do and I do it and then at the end of the day if it doesn't have anything to do with me, you know I'm fine with that. That's why I'm convinced... not convinced, but I really want to produce some day and I'm so confident that I'm going to be an outstanding producer because —

BM: Nobody likes producers though.

JC: They'll like me. They'll like me because... I've met a couple of producers that I really, really dig but I mean I want to produce some day and I don't know... Actually I do know. I'm going to be an outstanding producer.

BM: There's something you want to do in between though.

JC: The *Saturday Night Live*? Yeah, that's my baby. I'm hoping, but that is going to take some help because it's a very political show. My game plan is to go to LA. This is the structure that I'm going to try and follow: go to LA and go to Groundlings Theatre; it's this theatre company in LA that is actually an improv school, you have sessions, you give them a bunch of money, you go in and work with other actors doing improv stuff, coming up with skits, just bouncing off of different actors and the Groundlings Theatre is one of those places, one of those stocked ponds.

Saturday Night Live will pick actors out of there. They'll pick actors from Second City Theatre in Chicago. You go in and you do these sessions. One session is three months, and if you're good enough they'll ask you to come join the cast. And from there you do shows and they say, 'Wow, this is their cast for this year and they only have two spots open for like a hundred people in there,' so it's very, very competitive. But I know a couple of people who work on *Saturday Night Live* and some actors said —

BM: Mentioning no names.

JC: Right. They said that they would totally help me. So I'm going to take all the help that these people want to give me and if they can put me in the door, I'll do what I do once I'm in the door and I should be fine. I just can't help but fall into doors...

Matt's been so great. I mean I'm here. You don't take a stand-in to Europe. You don't. You don't do that unless you're a great guy and it's not so much about wanting to help me because I don't want to be a professional stand-in but I did want to come over and meet Terry Gilliam. And meet all his boys, you know what I mean, and be able to talk to them. And who knows, he might hate me, but I don't know. He smiles.

TG: "Mishka just wasn't keeping it all moving fast enough… I have to keep it all going, keep the spirits up. But I can't find it."

Karl Derrick, FX, on Mackenzie: "He's the best actor in a prosthetic I've ever worked with… He's a very good actor and he just becomes part of the team."

Gilliam is still downbeat, although finding some humour in the often apparent futility of trying to keep things moving along at a decent pace: "This is like Napoleon's retreat from Moscow – we're trapped in the snow and we can't get home. We can't get home to Kansas. That's it! – It's Dorothy's retreat from Moscow. I just don't know if I'm Dorothy or Toto."

Meanwhile, back in the main office, someone has graffiti'd the following slogan on Terry's office door: "Are you sure you're sexy enough to stay in the Czech Republic?" No one has any idea what this means or where it came from.

Due to the schedule running over, it has been decided that Mackenzie has to come back for six days in September to finish his scenes. (He's going back now to do *The Office* Christmas specials.)

Karl Derrick is also feeling the tension: "You can cut the atmosphere with a knife. I've never been on a shoot like it."

Cameraman Pete Cavaciuti: "I've never known anyone to be treated as badly on a film as Nicola."

TG: "If only people were doing their jobs."

Afternoon – reverse shots with the pig once again stealing the show as it moves out and starts eating the dead rat prop. Matt, not wanting to be outdone, improvises a kick up the pig's arse.

Kent spent last night supervising the second unit shoot: "We're screening the 2nd unit rushes in five minutes, Terry, if you're interested."

"Good luck," replies Gilliam. He doesn't go.

Today is the hottest day so far – both inside and out.

Finally, on take 6, the pig lets everybody down by wandering off mid-camera/scene.

Amongst the boredom, the dice game is slowly taking over…

Matt jokes about stealing Heath's close-ups. On his last film – the Farrelly's conjoined twins epic, *Stuck On You* – him and Greg Kinnear referred to themselves, jokingly, as "opponents".

Gilliam refers to Matt's look for the movie – "He's the new Doug McClure."

It's the final shot of the day and the chicken cannot be found. Mishka bellows out: "One minute for the smoke and the chicken is coming…!" – not something you often get to say.

Matt, whilst waiting for the chicken: "I'm sweating like a rapist." Four shots completed, it's a wrap for the day, then off for a meeting with the FX department, where Karl is still working on his animatronic wolf.

Then another meeting – this time with John Schofield – there is some concern over stunt master Mario Luraschi. TG is worried about some of the second unit stuff he's been shooting. Mario takes offence and says that if Terry doesn't like his work, maybe he should quit. TG: "I thought I was the only one allowed to do that."

Then off to editing – the roughly cut footage already looks good, although Cavaldi and Delatombe's big scene from the first few days need trimming (less Peter, basically, too indulgent).

Editor Lesley Walker reveals that Miramax has asked for the last two days of film – as in the physical film – to be shipped to the States. Gilliam is surprised: "Jesus, are they going to start beating up on Tom now? I bet they are."

Gilliam is more than willing to admit he fucked up/made mistakes in the first two weeks: "And those bastards charged right in and overreacted," – i.e. Nicola.

All the Italian members of the crew held a farewell party for Nicola last night.

Paul is still known by just about everyone as "the loneliest man in Prague". TG didn't even know he was on set today, although he does leave the set, joking/sparring with Miramax's Jake:

TG: So how's Bob's movie going today?

JAKE: It's going really well.

TG: Is it going anything like my movie?"

Thursday, 14th August

BM: Ready to shoot by 7.30am? NO!

DP Tom spent last night watching *Time Bandits* and is quoting Cleese as Hood – "Have you met the poor?"

Over breakfast they are still debating who's going to play the Tower Queen. TG is against Diane Lane; he wants Michelle Pfeiffer. It is still not cast.

Terry is finally enthused – after last night's viewing of the footage. He tells Matt and Heath about the ride into town – "We've made a western."

The first reaction shot is played at half-speed – "Half-speed acting," as Terry calls it. "Story of my week," replies Matt, who seems concerned. "You can't tell a chicken to go half speed."

In downtime Matt references Python's *Holy Grail* – it seems everyone here is here for Terry and that legacy.

Shooting by 8.10am.

The pig man is threatening to take his pig home if Matt kicks it again. A pork strop? Interesting. The pig, to be fair, doesn't seem to care either way.

As a rule, Heath always checks his performance afterwards on the monitor; Matt, less so, but soon is following Heath's lead.

Tellingly, no one from Miramax is on set today.

It's a fast moving day, but dull in that it largely consists of pick-ups/coverage etc.

Terry's wife, Maggie Gilliam, is coming out for the weekend – calm heads will prevail.

Bridgewater: "This is the worst set I've ever been on… I know Terry would love to re-film those first two weeks." Steve is frustrated that he can't get Lena to work – "I'm used to winning these things. The day when she was skinning the rabbit, she was very off, apparently she said it was her period."

Gilliam cracks a joke on set: "What's my motivation? The paycheque."

To which Tom replies, "Don't fucking go there. That's what it's come to – from the height of *Monty Python* to a fucking paycheque?"

But a quarter of Gilliam's paycheque is being held against

overages – he's presuming that the extra expenses that have come about as a result of hiring Tom and co are authorised and he's not paying for them.

Friday, 15th August

BM: A flyer has started to circulate round the studio and stages. It features a photo of Nicola, looking the worse for wear and washing his feet in the sink, accompanied by a quote from Christopher Isherwood's *Prater Violet*: "You see, the film studio of today is really the palace of the sixteenth century. There one sees what Shakespeare saw: the absolute power of the tyrant, the courtiers, the flatterers, the jesters, the cunningly ambitious intriguers. There fantastically beautiful women, there are incompetent favourites. There are great men who are suddenly disgraced. There is the most insane extravagance, and unexpected parsimony over a few pence. There is enormous splendour, which is a sham: and also horrible squalor hidden behind the scenery. There are vast schemes, abandoned because of some caprice. There are secrets that everybody knows and no one speaks of. There are even two or three honest advisers. There are the court fools, who speak the deepest wisdom in puns, lest they should be taken seriously. They grimace, and tear their hair privately, and weep."

Monday, 18th August

NP: Disgusted and scorned, I abandoned the attempts of keeping this diary updated; now that I'm in Tuscany let's try to recapitulate the "bitter ending".

We were left inside Terry's trailer and the jerks not being able to handle in a sensible way the casino they triggered. When they did not answer my very basic question, nor would they consider making me an offer in order to keep shooting, I told them that, given the circumstances, I did not feel capable of giving Terry the quality he deserves and expects from me. I acknowledged the fact that they fired me and wished them luck for the rest of the shoot, even though it is not luck that they need, but brains!

My substitute, Tom Siegel (with whom I share my agent), arrived the same evening. And they put him in a suite at the Four Seasons (a detail that really pissed Terry off, he himself has never been treated in such a grand scale). The shoot is shut down for the rest of the week; at $235,000 a day it makes nearly a million dollars.

Terry went back to London to get out of this deep shit. He consulted with his lawyers regarding the breach of contract but they are so cautious that they are not pursuing that road. What they are aiming for is to demonstrate that Terry has been denied the tools to implement his vision and therefore he wants out!

Miramax threatened to sue him if he walks, and with the precedent of *Munchausen* that's the last thing Terry wants to cope with.

So he came back, just in time to come to my birthday/farewell party on Sunday afternoon. Great Party! Everybody (almost everybody) showed up and there was great sorrow in the air. More than any "wrap-party" I've ever been part of. It is interesting what happens when you get unjustly fired: it's a bit like attending your own funeral; you get to know what people really think of you.

Heath has been extremely sweet: when told of my definitive "dismissal" he told them that when he is on set he performs for few people, and I was one of those people, therefore by taking me away they were taking away a big part of his performance.

I've never received such an amount of presents in 46 birthdays, not even when I was a kid!

I probably should do it again! (Just kidding.)

On Monday they went back to work at an unbelievably slow pace; by Wednesday afternoon they achieved 7 set-ups! Not only that, but they are switching over to Panavision at a cost of about $750,000, plus they are flying in a key grip, a gaffer, 3 camera people... I thought that there was no money left! These are the miracles of the studio world... The reality is that they are digging themselves deeper and deeper into a money-hole. Terry called over the weekend. He sounded really depressed… I really believe that he should get out of there, not only to preserve his sanity but because at this point he will definitely not be able to make the movie he has in his mind/heart. 'Cause now they are already talking about cutting the script and chopping a few more heads off (Roberto and John have been threatened to be fired if "in 2 weeks you do not straighten things out!")

For my part I promised Terry that I will get him out of there, no matter what it will take. The basic idea is to hit the backlot with a Sikorsky double-blade helicopter, throw down a rope ladder and get him out of there while the whole set is flying away...

Tuesday, 19th August

BM: Terry keeps referring to Tom's burly camera crew as the Marines having arrived. The Brits are not too happy. Tom's been acting as his own camera operator, but after a few days Pete now has his job back. There seems to be some give and take between the camera crews after all.

All this week is devoted to the Tavern scene. It goes well.

TG:"I still haven't found the floor under me yet, but it's getting there."

Wednesday 20th August

NC: 5 HOURS BEFORE WE SHOT. TG doing his nut… but this is time consuming stuff as a lot of extras need instruction and then that has to be misunderstood – whoops, sorry – translated…

Thursday, 21st August

BM: There is clearly dissent amongst the crew. Inspired by the turn of recent events, one "senior crew member" decided to put pen to paper and confront the powers that be. In the end the letter was never sent for fear of job loss. But its sentiments ring true and reflect the atmosphere on set at the time. Spleen is vented.

"To whom it may concern

21st August 2003

A personal view

"Brothers Grimm" has come to the end of week 7. The creative processes for this fantastic movie are becoming bogged down due to personality differences and basic chains of command on the floor. The Director, Terry Gilliam, in my opinion is being over-ruled on choice of set-up by an operator who does not seem to understand what a Terry Gilliam film is. TG has lost his basic collaborator, Nicola Pecorini, and has had to, it seems, accept another camera person not of his choosing. Whilst lighting may have been an issue, the operating and choice of shots is what makes a TG movie exciting, interesting and talked about years after the movie was made. Some people call this art. The fundamental and significant person who translates TG's ideas has been replaced for 'Artistic Differences'. We have ended up with an operator who sets-up shots, usually on a dolly or crane, which are then changed by TG to something that he had asked for in the first place. This has accounted for an incredible amount of time-wasting and energy.

Creativity is being destroyed!
 So the questions you have to address are:
 Do you want to make a Terry Gilliam film?
 Are you committed to this project as Terry sees it?
 Or are you trying to make a committee film with no one's
 vision but the accountants'?

So the answers are:

If it is a TG film then those in charge should recognise this fact and give
him the tools to make it his way.
 One above applies if you are. If not, fire him!
 That is what we seem to be making at the moment...

Positive Thoughts.

So the first suggestion is to get rid of anyone who comes on the set
with negative ideas of why we cannot do this and this and this...! Let
the Director Direct! The crew (AND WHO CARES WHAT THEY
THINK - AFTER ALL THEY ARE EXPENDABLE) are demoralised
and, along with our leading actors, wish to return to the spirit of
this film that we had at the start in July, i.e. WE WERE MAKING
and COLLABORATING IN "A TERRY GILLIAM MOVIE" - AND
NOTHING LESS!

To rekindle the spark of collaboration I am suggesting the following:

Newton Thomas Siegel is now the DoP. Whilst this appears to be a "fait accompli" the new camera crew have asserted themselves as THE filmmakers of the "Brothers Grimm" i.e.:

to quote the new Grip/trician (whatever that is - TV?) "We are here to sort out this mess";

and whilst make-up is being applied to Matt Damon a quote from the DoP: "Matt, would you like a hot dog?"

Matt: "What?"

DoP: "Would you like a hot dog with mustard 'cause it would match your make-up!"

This was in front of Matt, the chief make-up artist and others... what a complete asssssssssssssss. And it was not said as a joke - if it was, then that sense of humour should be confined to kindergarten.

To this end it is perfectly obvious that the present DoP, Newton Thomas Siegel, is getting above his station. He sets up shots which are classic, locked off and uninteresting - a movie going nowhere with no vision.

In the nicest possible way, tell Newton Thomas Siegel that he is ELEVATED to the position of Maestro - THE "DoP" on a par with the Oscar-winning DoPs such as Vittorio Starraro, Freddie Young,

Freddie Francis, David Watkins and John Alcott, all of whom had excellent operators and were able to concentrate on the lighting.

Immediately re-instate Peter Cavacinti as first camera operator. This would give back to the Director at the very least some of his authority, and a person with whom he has a rapport, and save considerable time on the set. . As Terry's "opus operandi" is to change the set-up during rehearsals this would surely save time as Peter would be able to adapt whilst Newton gets on with the lighting.

Keep all non-essential people off the set. It's wasted air and vibes because the only reason most of these people are there is to ascertain the reasons for not going any faster without the bollocks to be able to do anything about it. This makes for frustration and negative vibes. Best left to the production office. On a Harold Pinter set you could hear a pin drop whilst lighting... On a Kubrick set there was nobody... On a Scorsese set there was no Scorsese...

Confine video playback to the end of the last take of any slate. Nobody - but nobody and most of all the actors (as they then change performances/action to suit themselves) - should have access to video playback. This is old school, basic command time - video is for damage control, not for egos. And besides, video playback costs more time on a film than any other factor. Think about it. No Video, No Playback - let's do one for Lloyds and on to the next set-up, 'cause the operator just said the last take was good for me, Guv! But seriously, think about its use: great tool, but...!

So in conclusion, we have in our hands a project with great potential. I would respectfully suggest that to get this project back on course that:

If we have to live with Newton as lighting cameraman, then his crew should go home as they are expensive and not needed given that the first camera will be operated by Peter C. and JJ, and the very experienced, inexpensive Czech crew could be reinstated to operate the second camera.

I'm sure we've all noticed the improvement in the budget visually due to the Panavision cameras... Yeah, right!

Come on guys, let's make a TERRY GILLIAM that we all signed up for with all its dark sides, quarks and quirks and not make, "Shakespeare in bloody Barf Love".

Yours, the filmmaker and no friend of anybody 'cause I'm too old, been there and done that!'

Saturday, 23rd August

NC: A lovely scene, with Will in bed with the blondey twins wearing a cute little bonnet... and poor old Jake on the other side of the room sucking his thumb & hugging a pillow with cotton wool stuffed in his ears... then Jacob's bed collapsed... So, one minute there we were quietly shooting and the next minute about 4 burly guys were charging into the set, mattresses were being flung off, props discarded this way and that... drills were screwing in screws... saws were going... chaos! Then it was quiet till – you guessed – THE OTHER BED COLLAPSED. On ran our burly team with tools once more and burrowed about under the double bed in record time again...

Bridgewater celebrates his birthday with Stormare and Damon, in his own special way.

Monday, 25th August

BM: Finish off guessed the scene with Cavaldi discovering the two twins in bed with the Grimms upstairs and then it's back to the body of the Tavern scene – i.e. the boys being dragged out of it.

Initially, it's moving pretty quickly and then things fall apart after what appears to be an impromptu POV shot of the ropes tied to Matt and Heath is suggested by Terry and duly added. (Turns out this was storyboarded but had fallen through the cracks) Tom S. and Nikki C. are both quietly complaining that they don't have time for, or need, all the shots Terry is outlining, often on the spot.

TOM (to NIKKI): "Are you gonna be the one to tell him?"

At one point there are eight men hunkered down around the dolly, trying to fix the ropes which are deemed to be too high.

Matt and Heath arrive and are strapped into skids to be dragged across the tavern floor. They are, several times, followed by numerous pick-up shots. Matt jokes: "So, how's your day been, Heath?"

Matt is always asking Terry for advice? Insecure, or just trying to establish a rapport?

Mishka decides that tomorrow should be a twelve-hour day with a lunch break.

Tuesday, 26th August

TG in car on way in: "I realised last week that I'm now committed to this. I'm stuck with it for the rest of my life."

Back to the backlot – Marbaden Square – it's the big ride out of town towards the forest. Shooting, of course, doesn't begin on time and when it does, it is slow and problematic. Terry moans about the horses – "I should never work with fucking horses."

Back at Nicola's birthday/leaving party – when I accused him of being too old to have a ponytail, he explained that it was only there to cover a head injury that was a result of a horse-riding accident that occurred during the filming of *Twelve Monkeys*, so I guess you can see why he's gone off horses.

One and a quarter hours later everyone is more or less satisfied and moves on.

NC: First up was a complete mishmash. Blocking the scene was chaos. In fact, TG was like a mother hen and we were all his chicks following him around back and forth and up and down in a sort of mad group – just like the geese, but less beautiful. Finally, we got a set-up – by this time half the crew were peeing in their pants, as there was no loo on set and they were waiting to hear where the first shot was before they placed the toilets. Then we got out every camera we had and set up a crane and a Steadicam and another cam only to find we didn't have an operator for that camera. So TG braved the handles and got some beautiful shots…

BM: Matt has pulled a hamstring and is having trouble getting on his horse – echoes of Jean Rochefort?
Terry says that Miramax are still refusing to pay Chuck Roven's travel fares so he is still absent. He should never have left.

The Miramax reps are – at least currently – no longer making their presence felt on set.

Lena has returned for the first time in weeks. She does not look happy to be back and no one has made a big deal of welcoming her back.

In a corner of the set, Stephen Bridgewater quietly opines: "Only 144 shots left to do."

The biggest time worry is still losing Matt when he has to move on to *The Bourne Supremacy* and *Ocean's 12*, back to back.

Filming exteriors still – the ride out of town with the various animals etc. Gilliam is most impressed with the geese – "The thing is I just don't care about the shot. That's what worries me. The geese are good. The Prague people are good. It's just what we're doing with them is a complete disaster."

Meanwhile, on the other side of the town square, the loneliest man in Prague sits alone at his monitor, reading today's script pages in an attempt to look busy. All day he sits on the other side of the village, with Terry and co over on the shooting side. There is no attempt at communication between them.

Tom is constantly being sarcastic. Both Nikki and Amy (amongst others) have voiced complaints over it. Example – after a long time spent setting up a crane shot of the boys' first departure (with Cavaldi and the geese) the film jams in the camera on the crane. TG jokingly shouts, "This never happened with Arriflex."

Tom's reply is, "Yes, but you were working with an inferior Spanish mind." (A comment that is wrong on several levels.)

Tom seems very wilful, to the point where he goes ahead and goes against the director. Gilliam vetoes the second half of one crane shot but Tom ploughs on: "Well we'll try it anyway and see how it looks."

The 12-hour day is being expanded to 13 – everyone is told late in the day that they're working till eight. There's talk of rebellion in the ranks, but they move on.

The last shots of the day are of the arrival at Angelika's house – it takes ages.

Gilliam is very unhappy with Lena's half-hearted performance. Even the always-amiable Heath is complaining, saying that he can't hear her lines and thinks she needs to be stronger. Terry says he's not even going to bother to talk to her – he sends Gerry and Steve in to do the job.

The last half hour gets blackly comic: Terry's old head wound is leaking – "Because I'm poking it with a sharp pencil," he says. (To elaborate: when shooting *Twelve Monkeys*, Gilliam suffered a horse-riding accident that cracked the back of his skull. When he was being sewn back together some of his hair was sewn inside; subsequently, he has an unsightly gash that occasionally emits pus under stress. It also accounts for his fondness for his generally in evidence ponytail.) Heath and Steve lighten the place with some long distance sign language; then Stormare takes over with Cavaldi rocking back and forwards on his horse with his mouth wide open for people to throw tennis balls into. Sadly, there are no tennis balls around.

Then Gilliam takes over – sparring with Bridgewater, bemoaning his existence in general and his life on this film in particular.

TG: Bridgewater's blessed. I'm cursed.

SB: I think it's darker than that.

During the Lena crisis, despite the humour, TG is getting really pissed off with her.

SB: "He can do himself real damage, you know."

Terry only half-jokes with producer Jake about the fact that they're shooting right now with only a fraction of the crew and it's going much smoother. "That's my problem, there's too many people on this set and they have nothing to do so they sit around and talk. And nothing gets done." Jake as ever – as is his job – is effectively evasive.

Despite the good humour that eventually develops, Terry tries to get four shots in forty minutes, so the crew aren't kept any later. He fails – his perfectionism and Lena proving too much. It wraps at around 8.30pm with a 7.00am call for the next day. But it's generally agreed that Lena now gets it – Bridgewater explains that it was when Terry actually went and spoke to her personally that she started to get there.

Back at his trailer after the shoot, Gilliam is in a more serious, reflective mood: "The trouble is I don't know what any of these shots mean. Some of them may look nice but I keep trying to find out what they mean."

BM: Does every single shot have to mean something?

TG: "Yeah. Or at least I used to think so."

BM: Terry Gilliam's film has given me bronchitis! Given the dust and detritus layering the backlot and the sets, it seems everyone is hacking up a lung here and there. The on-set medic is a very busy lady.

Little Laura Greenwood is back again – she's very sweet, talks to everyone and really doesn't want to leave, which she has to do after her work this morning is complete.

Terry continues vibing on his theme of this movie (off-screen) being one big community – there are so many people here, they've actually become a real village. "They get up early in the morning, without complaint, to come here, meet up, stand around and talk and share – some will probably even get married. It's just such a shame that making a movie has to get in the way of all this." It's sarcastic but tinged with a good deal of how he really feels about the thing (even if he does seem to be channelling Woodstock.)

Interview with Lesley Walker

The Brothers Grimm marks the third time that British film editor Lesley Walker has worked with Gilliam — following on from 1991's *The Fisher King* and 1998's *Fear and Loathing in Las Vegas*. (They would shortly collaborate again on *Tideland*.) In a prestigious career, Walker has worked as Editor on such movies as *Letter to Brezhnev* (1985), *Mona Lisa* (1986), *Waterland* (1992) and Richard Attenborough's *Shadowlands* (1993) and *Grey Owl* (1999.)

During the production of *The Brothers Grimm*, she is both editing on location and making a regular base in an editing suite at Barrandov Studios.

BM: It's August 27th, how far in are you in terms of what you need to do?

LESLEY [LW]: I'm fairly up to date. I'm actually really only a day behind them at the moment on a rough cut because it is roughly put together, and if I do have time then I do a little bit of finesse. But part of the reason for just chopping it together any old how, is to see if there's anything missing, really, while the sets are still standing. For example, tomorrow they're taking the barn down and I'm not sure that they've got enough plates at the moment for the witch sequence, so I've actually just cut that sequence together and I'll let him have a look at it and see if that works.

BM: Technically how does this work? Because whatever they shoot today, for example, this gets processed overnight?

LW: Absolutely. It's done on site, below us, in fact.

BM: And that gets to you on 35mm?

LW: It comes in to us on 35mm and on separate sound. Then it's put onto Beta, actually overnight, in the early hours of the morning. Here, we only have a slot at 4 o'clock in the morning because there are two other American pictures who are in ahead of us, so I get it back into the Avid the next day. My assistant does that and then transfers the whole thing. He syncs it up in the Avid separately because it's a first generation as against taking it off the magnetic. So he does that in the morning while the others actually do the film. I'm not the greatest fan of Avid, I have to say; I did resist for a number of years and I still think that cutting on 35mm is much more interesting.

BM: But presumably you do that afterwards?

LW: No, no, no. In some cases — though not on this film —
we did a picture a couple of months ago which was all shot
on 35mm and printed on 35mm and we conformed it to 35mm
for showings for previews, etc. On this film there's no
point because there are so many visual effects, half the
film's visual effects, so I wouldn't have it on film because
it costs too much money. So we're going to be previewing
off tape.

Then we scan the negative; I have never done this
before: we're digitally grading, so we're not neg-cutting
per se. Normally, when we have 35mm we have a 35mm cutting
copy which is exactly what everybody's agreed to and we've
dubbed to and everything else, and that 35mm goes to the
laboratory and they match the negative to it. In this case
we're not doing that, we're scanning the negative in
digitally, and then they're going to grade it rather like
going through an Avid, so we're never going to physically
touch the negative. So it's a new one for me, but it's the
only way we can do this and get all the visual effects in,
because I don't think we're going to get the last one,
according to the schedule, until after we've actually
dubbed. So I don't know what's going to happen. We're
supposed to finish at the end of June 2004 and the last
effects come in in June 2004 and I think they're supposed
to dub or mix in early June. So we shall see, it's rather
like a piece of string.

BM: How's Terry been on this film compared to the other times you've worked with him?

LW: Well, he's actually been up here on the Avid watching things a bit more than he's done in the past. I tell a story of when I first worked with him on *Fisher King*: he never saw any cut material at all, none at all, and we cut it on 35mm — I think he saw maybe two sequences on that. It was the first time I actually worked with him; and we came to the first screening of the film with him at the end of the shoot, in the viewing theatre back in London, and he said, "Well, what's the matter?" as I was pacing up and down, and I said, "I'm rather nervous," and he said, "Why?" I said, "Well, you haven't seen anything, I might have it totally wrong," and he just said to me, "If there are any mistakes, I made them." And that was it and so we had the screening and it was great. I mean, great and overlong like a lot of my first cuts are because you might as well have it in otherwise you do throw the baby out with the bath water. On *Fear and Loathing* he didn't really come into the cutting room very much, but he's come up here several times, two or three times a week, actually. I think it kind of helped because it's such a complicated piece, in as far as the witches are doing this and you have your imagination, so you have to cut blank pieces of film and what's the wolf supposed to be doing in this part? And Red

Riding Hood? So I think if you see something physically you can think, "ah, yeah well, I can see how that's going to work". So I think that may be why he's up here a little bit more.

BM: I think it's also partly because he doesn't go to rushes very often.

LW: No, no. He sees his rushes on the Steinbeck here, but he's always said to me about dailies that he normally starts off seeing them quite a lot and then he says, "Well, I know what I've shot so I don't really have to see them."

BM: There's obviously been some controversy on this film, in that Terry's not taken well to Miramax. Does that impact on you in any way?

LW: It hasn't done really because I'm kind of divorced from them, at the moment. I think it's going to get tough for me in post-production, actually for both of us to be very honest, because that's where they come from. That's where they pounce on you, and unless we've got previews that are made in heaven with 100% audience saying it's great then they'll just march in. They always do and they always have done. And maybe it's tatty-bye me then and somebody else comes in, it's quite possible. I don't think they really care as long as they do what they want to do and I think that'll happen for me a little later down the line. They've seen a bit of the cut material. They saw some very early on.

BM: What have they seen so far?

LW: They saw the dungeon and the opening, them riding into Karlstadt and the mayor's office.

BM: So that was in the first couple of weeks really, wasn't it?

LW: Yes, they saw that and Bob Weinstein who saw it here, said — I don't know if he was being funny — but he said "Don't touch a frame and carry on cutting." But you take a lot of that with a large pinch of salt, so I don't think they interfere in the editing part and please God, touch wood that they don't, but I think it's more shooting and time and getting enough close-ups really.

BM: One of the things they seem to be doing, whether intentionally or not, is removing some of Terry's support group here.

LW: Yes, absolutely. In fact, actually, I think it's one of the silliest things they did. I think there were other ways round it. I think they were determined to get rid of Nicola and it was a prop of Terry's, it was a mate, as well as Terry chose him, he chose Nicola to light it. And it's the third thing they did to him: the actress; the nose make-up; and then Nicola. And to be quite frank, they've got their own way with the new lighting cameraman and until such time they'll carry on not taking Terry's props away if everything's going to plan but if they want to they'll haul another one out. Actually Kent and I laughed which one it was going to be, either he or I?

BM: They're getting rid of people one by one. The other one is Chuck Roven, of course, who they're not letting back, in essence.

LW: No. So he's been sort of made the sacrificial lamb as well, and I just think they're stupid actually, I really do. There are other ways of handling all this and it's because they didn't like the way Nicola was not over-lighting, and yes, in some cases, he didn't light the actor's eyes, but it was exciting. It was far more interesting in my opinion than what's happening at the moment. Nicola had an element of danger in his lighting and that's not the case here.

Also, they ditched re-grading. We can do far more than with a 35mm grade, you can alter things dramatically. But I don't think it's as interesting and, like I say, it's a different style, it's a totally different style that I'm not that keen on.

BM: How would you define the difference?

LW: Well, he [Newton Thomas Siegel] has very, very set rules. He doesn't like shadows, the new man, he doesn't like cross-shadows, he doesn't like anything that's out of focus. And I know people say, "Well, nor does anybody," but there are times on films that a little bit of soft focus, especially in, say, a running shot or something, is fine. It works and I'm a person who thinks that most rules are there to be bent anyway, so there shouldn't really be any hard and fast rules. Terry's got control and he's using the lenses he wants to use and is using Pete (Cavaciuti) on the Steadicam as he wants to use him, because if you suddenly started having huge close-ups of everybody continually, then it wouldn't be a Terry Gilliam film. It just wouldn't. It's ridiculous even to think about it and I was a bit worried to start off with. They kept on popping in close-ups of Matt in certain scenes, which I know we don't have to use, but it was just like, come on, you know why you're doing them.

BM: They still have to take an hour to film them.

LW: Exactly, or longer. In fact it's been a lot slower since Nicola left. We've had less footage, actually about half. But they've won on that one; I don't think it seems to matter. So I'm getting worried by the "let's cut the script" thing that's come in again.

BM: Does it have the feel of Terry's work? This is a very early stage, obviously.

LW: Some of it does, but not totally. That's a tricky question, actually. It's such a different subject, I mean for me, because I've worked on two, *Fisher King* and *Fear and Loathing*, and it's actually so different for both of us, to be honest, I've never done anything with visual effects before. There are elements in there and once it's pulled together, once we get the right thing flowing as we've worked together, I think it will become very, very obvious that it's a Terry Gilliam film. If he's allowed to do so. I'm afraid, though, that if he starts using another favourite lens, or something, and they want loads of close-ups then there's no way it's going to look like a Terry Gilliam film.

BM: I know he's worried that he hasn't connected with it. That's his main concern and it's quite a significant one, because I think even when he's worked with other people's material, he's made it his own.

LW: Yeah. He said that from the word go, actually. He was saying it still last week.

BM: He said it last night.

LW: Did he? I was hoping, because yesterday he looked slightly jollier at lunchtime.

BM: No, yesterday was a really bad day.

LW: It got worse again. You see I saw him at lunchtime and he was sort of okay.

BM: Well, he doesn't like the scene and he doesn't know what to do with it or what it's about really, and everyone was there till 8 o'clock as well because of overruns and he was thinking, "Well, why are we doing this because I don't even know what I'm doing?" But then he says that a lot.

LW: He does, yes.

BM: Has he done that in the past?

LW: No, this is different; this is totally different in that way. He normally knows exactly what he wants and no, it has been a different Terry in that way. That is unusual. On *Fear and Loathing*, he knew very positively what he wanted. I do think a lot of it's to do with the fact that he was excited at one point about this film and I think he started off with every good intention, but they did knock his legs away from him. I do think that was the Samantha Morton thing. Well actually, when MGM couldn't fund it and Miramax stepped in, I think that was the start of it because they don't listen and they are extremely rude and Terry, really, he's always had respect and I don't think they respect anybody. He may fight with producers, in fact he and I ran out of Hollywood on *Fisher King* because Terry wanted to keep a scene and they wanted it out. So we just wouldn't answer the phone and we got back on the old jumbo and came back to London, but they would talk to him and they did respect his point of view, whereas I don't think they respect any point of view whatsoever. So that was number one and then the Samantha Morton thing was number two and anything he wanted to do with make-up, the look of it, has been taken away from him, and I think that's just knocked the stuffing out of him. I try and jolly him along and say, "It'll be fine," and all the rest of it, but some days you can win on that one but not a lot, and I think it kind of shows on the floor, actually. It's so slow.

BM: Yes, and he's not hiding the fact that he doesn't want to be there. It sounds like a joke, but there's only so many times you can make that joke in front of 200 people. However, on Monday he said, "I finally realised I'm committed to this and I'm finding my feet," and then I think yesterday threw him completely.

LW: It is weird, actually, because Cavaldi was back and the scene had gone well on Monday, and he was much jollier. He came back up here to the office on Monday night and then yesterday lunchtime he was still bubbling a bit, but then I think he must have lost it. I don't know what

else he can do really, to be honest? I don't know, I don't
think there are any actors coming in. I mean certain
actors help him get bolstered up, like Peter playing
Cavaldi... and Heath he's very fond of and then he's got
Johnathan Pryce coming back in about a week's time. But
he's got to go back into the forest and I think he got so
fed up with the first forest set, and I think the new one's
up for the next ten weeks and it's a hard one. It would
have been nice if they could have simplified the last third
actually slightly. I remember saying to Patric, the
publicity man, "They should really have got a script
doctor in." Someone who just reads that last third and
says, "Well, they go in and out of the forest, and out and
in and up to the town and down to the town, let's simplify
that curve." I think it would make their life easier. But
at the moment it is highly complicated.

I find it extraordinary that it's taken him so long to
get another film made. I really find it extraordinary; and
he is not a waster. He works bloody hard.

After pick-ups for the return to Marbaden, it's off to do interiors in Angelika's house. Gilliam keeps it a fairly closed set for rehearsal.

Today is Peter Stormare's birthday – he won't be drawn on how old but the ADs have worked out it's his 50th. His wife, mum and dog have flown in for the occasion.

He arrives on the backlot for the scene in Angelica's house and everybody sings him "Happy Birthday" in a gloriously sunny valley, surrounded by a fairytale 18th century town. He is delighted and embarrassed – he has been called here specifically for this – now he can go for the rest of the day. He's off to play his guitar, after jokingly trying to persuade Terry, Heath and Matt to star in the video for his band.

Amazingly, there are three producers on set today – is everyone finally trying to get along?

Afternoon spent on set, shooting interiors with Lena. At the end, TG embraces her and says, "Thanks for showing up for my movie. What took you so long?" She clearly appreciates it.

End of the day – they rehearse and block scene 91, although the dialogue issues that crop up are not addressed.

Then off to stage 7 to check out the pond. Gilliam wades straight in in his wellies and walks it through, re-designing it as he goes – not good news for the FX guys.

Then more FX/props meetings, deciding how the caskets should open, etc.

Then dinner.

Thursday, 28th August

BM: Finally heard from Sky who works on the camera crew. He's told me on several occasions now that there's something he wants to say, get off his chest. He does so. "The thing is this was really a family film – that's why we all really wanted to do it. Not only are there a lot of people here who are children of some of the others – I mean, I've known Amy since I was 9, and most of the Italian set. So we've all known each other for years. And that was one of the reasons we all wanted to work on this. That and the fact that it was a Terry Gilliam film. But by doing what they've done, [bringing in the US camera crew] they've ruined that. They've turned it into a 9 to 5 job – and none of us wanted that." As he told me this, Sky didn't realise that new DP Tom was standing right behind him.

Morning – re-shoot scene 91 (the argument between Will and Jake) – one long take. Matt wanted it re-done. It was previously shot in the wake of Nicola's firing and Matt and Tony in particular think he may have played it just too aggressive.

TG: "Matt's concerned about words. He thought he was too aggressive – he needs to rationalise everything."

Experience what can only be described as a "playful" verbal joust with Paul trying to lose that "loneliest man in Prague" moniker – people are talking to him now, although admittedly mostly Miramax people and others on their payroll. I'm also talking to him as he was the one who kindly diagnosed the fact that the level of smoke, dust and – basically – shit on the set has given me bronchitis. And he sent me to the crew nurse.

Interview with Terry Gilliam

I meet Gilliam for dinner at the Café Colonial, which has become the restaurant of choice for the A-list talent on this movie whilst in Prague. (Tellingly, many of the crew are dining at another place further down the street.)

BM: As of today, which is 27th August, how do you feel about the movie overall at this point?

TG: I don't know. I don't know what I feel about the whole thing because I *can't see* the whole thing. I can only see bits and pieces. Some of the bits and pieces are good. Some are less good. But I think I've reached the point that I guess I have to make the movie.

BM: You're no longer in denial?

TG: I think that's probably it, I'm in de-Mississippi!

BM: I knew I shouldn't have said that. How do you see the way forward then?

TG: We're just one step at a time now, just march forward day by day. I think the main thing is I suppose a kind of acceptance has crept over the whole operation. There's no way out that I can see, no way out, and the dangerous thing is some of the things I see and like, they make me get enthusiastic about it which makes me even more fearful because I'm waiting for the next depredation and that's my only concern. Because, I mean, at this point it's been seven weeks to deal with all the shit being thrown at us, which is a long time in a movie. So I'm waiting for the next thing they come up with, the next thing that will happen. Let me tell you, I don't know what it is.

BM: But you think there will be more?

TG: Clearly... I think it was just this last week it's kind of okay, time to just admit to it. Here we are, we're stuck, we're going to be in here for the next year and my aim is to try to get on with it. It's a strange feeling.

BM: Do you ever see yourself enjoying it?

TG: I enjoy moments all the time. That's what it is, but it's individual things, not the overall thing. It's just grabbed moments. We've got a really nice crowd of people here, and there's some people working very hard and doing very good work, so since I'm stuck with the responsibility and cause of much of it, I felt it's time to grow up and accept the job.

BM: Did you think you were letting them down in any way by your attitude?

TG: I'm told I've let them down by my attitude, by certain people. I'm not sure if I have or haven't. The main thing is I've kept going, and we keep doing the work and I think the work is good, most of it, and that's it. That's the whole reason I stuck with it because there were too many good people who'd worked too fucking hard who were so determined to do it, so one went on with it.

BM: Let's go right back to the beginning then: when was it offered to you and what was your response to it?

TG: Oh fuck. I don't know. It must have been the middle of last year [2002]. Then when they got hot on it, then I was actually put on the payroll for eight weeks, so I got Tony involved, came out here, did some recces, started putting the piece together, choosing a crew, Guy Dyas, first choice, Nicola.

BM: How did Guy come about? Where did you know him from?

TG: I didn't. He was just thrown at me; he had just done *X-Men 2* and he came in with incredible enthusiasm and he's an incredible artist, he's brilliant, very smart, very energetic, not as experienced as a lot of other people but, boy, you know he has a determination. He's worked seven days a week for months, for half a year or more.

BM: So when were you doing these recces?

TG: I think we first came out here at the end of October, beginning of November... But then you start working on a thing, as one does, so it's getting involved, finding some good locations; Bob's interesting, Guy's doing brilliant work, we're putting together the whole thing. We've got a team, Gabriella and Nicola and Mishka. Then Wolfgang put us together with Reformer Films.

BM: Who are Reformer Films?

TG: We've asked that question many times... There used to be two main companies out here in Prague, one called Ethik and the other they called Stilkin, and both had been highly recommended. And Reformer is an offshoot of Ethik. So we've been working on the thing and at one point we have a meeting with all the heads of department from LA with the big go, this is going to be in January, and we're getting everything together, and we go on a recce and at the last meeting with MGM, this guy named Alex Yemenidjian, who is the *capo* there, — it didn't go well. Chuck and I are doing a song and dance with Guy's brilliant drawings, budgets are talked about and then

Yemenidjian says, "Why do ya wanna make this morbid film about animals eating children?" So, I think that started the deterioration.

BM: Then Miramax came on board. Had you met the Weinstein brothers before?

TG: I'd met Harvey several times, and by this time we had on board Matt, Heath, Robin Williams, Samantha Morton, Jonathan Pryce.

BM: Who'd got those on board?

TG: Chuck and I. This is for MGM; that was why the movie was marching forward. To be honest, I didn't actually have Samantha then but I knew she wanted to work with me.

BM: And Matt and Heath were your first choices?

TG: The first time we talked about this thing, our first choice was Johnny Depp and Heath Ledger, but Johnny didn't want to come back to Prague. That was our original cast.

BM: How did you get to Matt?

TG: It's who you're interested in is where you start from. Matt I'd met in London when he was doing a play and he was keen to work, and so that was good. Heath was there because of Nicola, as Heath had done *Sin Eater*, the Brian

Helgeland film with him. "This guy's really good," Nicola
said. "Like Johnny. He's really got the stuff."

So Heath was the first one on board. I was still
talking to Johnny about it. But with Heath, I met him,
talked to him on the phone and he was in without even
reading the script. So gradually Matt comes round to
Chuck's place to talk about the film and the first thing he
says is, "I want to play Will." I'd actually been thinking
of Heath playing Will, because that would be the straight
casting and Matt argued all the reasons and I argued all
the reasons why he shouldn't play him and why he should
play Jake.

BM: How was that resolved?

TG: At the end of the evening, he said, " Well, whatever
one you want me to play, I'm on." So the next morning
Heath comes by to talk about the script and parts and I
said, "Which part do you want to play?" and he says, "I
want to play Jacob." So I said, "Well, you're on." And then
I took Heath over to meet Matt, who was shooting this
Farrelly brothers film where he plays a Siamese twin
[*Stuck On You*] and I go and I say, "Matt, meet Jacob."
And he said, "What? You talked me into playing Jacob last
night," and I said, "No, you talked yourself into playing
Will."

And then Robin was desperate to play Cavaldi and Jonathan was there for Delatombe and that was it.

Then it's time to come out to LA, so I get out there the night of the Academy Awards, and I go to the Vanity Fair party, something I've never done and I'm quite excited, and Bob's there with Marty Scorsese, the loser [he had been nominated for the Miramax-funded *Gangs of New York*] and I said, "Marty, listen, it hurt Harvey a lot more than it hurt you," because Harvey set out to get him that Academy Award and failed. So anyway I talked to Marty about whether I should do this thing, having publicly stated I'd never work with them, and after a long time he said, "Just give it a go; it won't be easy, but just give it a go." So the next day we were meeting with Harvey and Bob and their minions.

BM: Of whom there are many, it appears.

TG: Exactly. And Harvey comes in with all the bluster and bullshit you can imagine and he just talks crap, and we talked about the cast and you see the real reason he got involved is because Matt's the prodigal son.

BM: And they want him back.

TG: Yes. And the first thing he said was, "Why do you want Heath Ledger?" I said, "Because he's perfect, and really good." Heath had had a run-in with them on *Four Feathers*, coming to Wes Bentley's defence and Shekhar Kapur's defence and they didn't like that. So we went through the other stuff and I said, "Samantha Morton," and Harvey said, "No fucking way," and that was the beginning of it. Oh, a good start...

But the deal was eventually done. It was 50/50, but Miramax run the show, or Dimension as it is. It's a weird contractual thing: MGM, if they don't like it, cannot take it, so Dimension get the whole thing 100%, and they want it 100%. They want the budget cut down, they said, "Do it for $75million," and off we go, and so around that time Wolfgang Glattes, first line producer, quits: he couldn't stand Chuck. Chuck was always trying to get the budget down and Wolfgang said, "Not possible," and he always felt compromised. It had been going on so long by that point, my feeling was I just had to go to work despite it. I had actually, originally, when the whole project started, set out to make a commercial film, because it was all in aid of getting "Quixote" off the ground. Contractually, it's a very retrograde step I've taken on this film.

BM: Do you want to elaborate on that?

TG: Not really. No. But it was retrograde — very.

BM: But you haven't got final cut, which the Weinsteins never give, it appears, and you're in financially for some of the overage. Is it fair to say that?

TG: It's fair to say that. I'm not in as good a position as I have been on previous films. I guess that's how keen I was just to go back and work, just do something. But I didn't want to do this kind of shit. That was the thing I was loath to get involved in. We have lots of special effects. I just didn't want to do it, to be quite honest. From the beginning I just wanted to get away from that kind of stuff. From the beginning, I have been telling everybody, this is much more complex than you can imagine. This is a really complicated, difficult film and nobody seemed to accept this. Except the people who are actually in the business of making it, they'll understand it, but Chuck didn't ever seem to accept it. It's more complicated than *Scooby Doo*. It's a nightmare, this one, there are no simple scenes. There's horses, there's special effects, monsters and bugs. I don't know, it's shit.

And all through this process it's been very weird because I've only been halfway there. That's why Nicola was so incredible, his energy was like Guy's. I always thought Nicola was like one of the producers; he was pushing things together to make it happen. He has an incredible energy.

BM: Did you feel equally distant from it when you were in the process of rewriting it?

TG: There were parts of it that were always there and that I never touched, so it was basically a case of trying to do two things: make the characters three dimensional, push the brothers' relationship to its limits, stretch them further and further; and try to make the magic in the fairytale, have the events come out of that as opposed to a bunch of clichéd special effects.

BM: Do you feel you got there?

TG: No, no. We got somewhere. From the beginning it's just floating along into it; it's been very strange, just to keep going. I think the process is much longer and in more detail than I imagined. You start losing confidence in your ability to ever make films again. Anyway, I did a lot of work on the script and did a lot of improvements, I feel. And it's just been this huge juggernaut marching on all the time, keeping up with all the things that need to be made, designed, developed, discussed. It was just marching on the long march. So all that's going on. There was all this pressure to get the budget down — after $75m was agreed, then they wanted it lower.

BM: So they want the big action adventure movie without paying for it?

TG: Without paying for it. Things like *Van Helsing* are sitting in Prague at like $150million and we're expected to do similar work for half that... And Chuck, you know, the producer, gets pushed out. And then we're going, we're just rocketing now. And I'm just resolutely marching on in some dumb, fatalistic mindset, but I had to make the movie because if I didn't work I would go crazy.

BM: But at the same time you told Miramax you might walk — did you intend it as a threat?

TG: No, I'm just stating a fact! They're not threats, I'm just saying that's what I think. And so this is the thing: I'm the one who's realised I just have to keep talking calmly in my conversation with them, with Bob, and I put the phone way out there while the screaming just went on and on and on... threatening me! "We'll close the fucking thing down! Fucking nobody tells me anything! And we'll put John Madden on this..." They were going to replace me with John Madden... So I kept the call going, I didn't hang up, and I suddenly realise, whoa, I don't like this way of working. Then we got Harvey on the phone the next day, he was there to protect his little brother.

BM: Did he have the same approach?

TG: Yeah.

BM: So he was yelling as well?

TG: They can't stop themselves.

BM: I thought you might have had good cop/bad cop in reverse happening there, but obviously not.

TG: But that time Harvey said I was going to be replaced by Anthony Minghella. I'm moving up, in the world, aren't I? "I don't want to hear that name said again. Samantha Morton. There's no way she's doing the film. Okay, Terry, okay, I don't want..." and Chuck was listening to that phone call and was just astonished. Astonished!

BM: What do you think the reasoning behind that was?

TG: I have no idea. I've spent weeks, months, trying to understand what it was that they were determined was wrong about her. They even called her London agent... They don't know who she is. I don't think Bob knows who she is. And at the same time Harvey's on to her agent, saying "There's no fucking way she's going to do this movie but she is going to work for me one day and she is going to win an Academy Award, the girl's a genius!" This is the kind of "on the one hand he can do one thing and on the other..."
   So (at this point) I just want out of here, I just want out of this fucking mess. And then for Cavaldi, they

wanted Ben Kingsley. Sir Ben Kingsley. And I met Ben and I like Ben, he's a wonderful actor but I just didn't think he was right for the thing. I said, "The character's a buffoon. He's dangerous and he's a buffoon." He's all sorts of things and Ben thought about it for a long time and they were putting huge pressure on and were offering him more money than was in the part, blah, blah, blah. It's when they want something, they will pay anything for something they want. But if it's something the film *needs* or should have, nothing. It's all about whim. It's the whim of the despot is what we're dealing with and all their minions are terrified of them. They wake up trying to find out what kind of mood they're in before they approach them on various matters. Two guys who've worked their way up and now control their little world and will do it their way...

All this shit's going on. Bob just isn't used to doing big films like this. This is twice the budget of most of his stuff. But then he's always been smart, he's stayed doing the money-making films as opposed to the ones that Harvey makes, they cost money and often lose money. And then my old roommate, Joel Siegel, from New York, the film critic on *Good Morning America*, bumped into Harvey, and he e-mailed me and said "Oh, Harvey said his brother Bob is such a sweetheart, he's letting him work with Terry Gilliam on this film."

BM: That says it all.

TG: But he drives Bob crazy. They wind each other up something terrible. But Harvey wants the kudos, he wants the class.

You know, as he screamed at me, that he's the greatest movie producer in the history of motion pictures, he said, "Fuck you, don't talk to me about art. I mean, I make art films, I'll tell you about art films. I make Portuguese films, you know, Portuguese films, I mean Brazilian films in Portuguese." That's what he said. "I make Iranian language films, so don't fucking talk to me." So it goes on.

We have the Bob thing, on the phone, and everyone's trying really hard to be nice to each other so they don't explode, and they're just like, "Fuck this." Then there was this period of about six weeks or longer of screen tests for anybody but Sam Morton. All these girls coming forward, everyone they could think of, you know. The two Siennas... I don't even know the names of most of them because they don't mean anything. And these tapes kept coming forward and so all this was going on, these girls were coming forward from Irene Lamb [casting director], and I'm thinking this is just crazy, because everybody knew Samantha was right for the part; the casting director for Miramax said she was perfect.

And so this is going on and on and on, and while this is happening we're trying to get the budget down and the budget's going this way, and all the normal things of just dealing with them. The problem with Miramax is that nobody there is really empowered and it's a film without a producer, because Chuck isn't there and John Schofield isn't given the authority to produce and to run the show. And the Miramax people all live in fear, is what they do.

I was reading *The Feast of the Goat*, the Mario Vargas Llosa book, about Trujillo, the dictator of the Dominican Republic and his assassination; I'm reading it and it's describing perfectly the way the Weinsteins work. One minute they're gracious and they're handing out gifts and rewards and then the next... [makes cutting sound]. That's what Harvey was saying: play ball, be nice to Bob and they will reward me. He wrote me a note and I'm just, "Fuck you!" I'm not doing it that way. I'm not playing that game. And I guess I confused them quite a bit because they don't get me.

BM: Well, people don't speak back to them.

TG: Yeah and people don't say, "Fine, well get me out of here, fuck you and I'm happy to go home." So anyway, the Samantha thing went on and on and on and then Chuck came back on. Now Chuck was planning to sue them, but Chuck has now decided not to sue; they come back to Chuck, and Chuck has been brought back on because they've no producer and somebody's got to deal with me. It's like I think they decided at a certain point they couldn't deal with me anymore because I wouldn't play ball. So let's get Chuck on because Chuck is going to sue them, they're going to have to pay him a pile of money, no matter what, so if they're going to pay him the money they might as well get something for it and so they brought Chuck back on. Schofield has always said that he had a brief of two things: get the budget down and get rid of Sam, whether that's true or not I don't know, but Chuck very quickly, at least, had to agree that Sam was the best of all these twenty, thirty people who were being hauled up.

BM: So they didn't respond by saying, "Okay you don't have to have Ben Kingsley if you lose her"?

TG: No, no, they still wanted Ben Kingsley

BM: But Lena's already cast?

TG: But it could have been backed off, because Miramax do it their own way, they could have pulled that. So we do the next screen test with Sam and everybody's just leaping up and down with joy that we've got the girl. Bob just sort of said, "It still doesn't make any sense." He can't see it.

BM: It was never going to happen at that point; that was tokenistic really, wasn't it?

TG: But he thinks that somehow by doing that he's done his due diligence, and all that stuff is bullshit. Afterwards, there was still nonsense going on because Lena was thinking she wouldn't do it, but her agents told her Miramax would sue her if she didn't because she had a contract.

Paul berates me – tongue somewhere near his cheek – for the book he thinks I am writing: basically Terry is all good/Miramax are all evil. I give him gum, in part to shut him up. "How much longer are you here? So we can stop behaving well and work out who's going next." There are several contenders, or at least people who think they may be.

Set-up time is spent throwing down dice with Heath and the ubiquitous Johnny Cheeks, on the dice table Cheeks had the prop department build for him. (So that's how budgets escalate.)

More "fun" banter – with the Miramax twins:

MIRAMAX: "Wait till we buy out Simon and Schuster – then you'll be sorry."

I tell them this book is not being published by Simon and Schuster, but Harper Collins – "At least buy out the right publisher. I wouldn't want Miramax to waste their money."

MIRAMAX: "We'll buy your book and that'll be your last printed word. You'll end up working in a video store."

"Really? I thought I'd end up being offered a job as an executive at Miramax."

OTHER MIRAMAX: "That's not a bad idea…"

People are discussing what the commemorative crew shirt should look like: One suggests the film's title with a picture of Bob and Harvey Weinstein underneath; another goes for the same picture with the title changed to "The Brothers Grimmer".

New title suggested for movie – "King Kong vs. Godzilla, Part 2 – The Miramax Story".

Gilliam catches me having lunch with Steve Bridgewater. "So it's all about him now is it?" Book is briefly re-titled "Bridgewater – Lust For Glory."

More and more people seem to be smoking in and around what is still a highly combustible set. Paul F. is on 20 a day after having given up for eight months. Bridgewater made use of Matt's hypnotherapist – next day he said he'd given up and has felt no desire for a cig and was never going back. Two weeks later he's smoking like a chimney.

Monday, 1st September

NC: Saw *Pirates* [*of the Caribbean*] at the weekend, which was a mightily boring load of crap apart from our WONDERGOD JOHNNY… Christ, who invented sword fighting…? Yawn! YAWN! YAWN! Let alone ships with holes, then no holes… hellooo? Story…??? But apparently Captain Jack Sparrow's performance was so beguiling that even our leads started mincing around OUR 18th-century set. Oh mi good gawd! I mean, one day watching JD and we get mincing… 1 day with someone from SOURF LONDON and the accents have gone AWOL. Where has STABILITY gone??? Gerry – get your skates on…

Tuesday 2nd September

BM: It's been reported in the press that Cameron Diaz – an option for the Queen – has broken her nose whilst surfing, and that Ben Affleck and J. Lo are getting married on the 14th – Matt is expected.

Bridgewater: "Oh well, our luck couldn't last forever."

Monday, 8th September

BM: Production is only one day behind at this point.

Tuesday, 9th September

BM: The week of hellish night shoots begins. Long anti-social hours – call is for 6 pm, working through to 5 am – also known round these parts as "dawn".

Wednesday, 10th September

BM: The call is for 7.00pm.

DP Tom Siegel is being his usual tactful self – he constantly photographs everything and says, "When I see light I've just got to shoot it – then to an Italian crew member – like when you see pasta, you've just got to eat it, I guess."

Johnathan Pryce has been away for the last ten days. He gets back about 11.00pm and pops by the set to say hello.

The night begins with Little Red Riding Hood (surely it's way past her bedtime?) being chased out of the forest back to town – part of the movie's opening. It's a crane/POV shot of the wolf jumping on her – but it's not working. TG re-directs the action – from the leap to the girl's fall to the speed of the camera to how close it gets to the girl's face. By the end of all this it's not necessarily a new shot, but certainly a different one to what the night had begun with. And it works. Now it's just a case of getting the right take.

It is a long night – the shot of the girl running away requires 20 takes.

Gilliam's mum Bea is there. She sits all night, huddling to keep warm, checking her son's work out on the monitor. I sit with her and we take bets on how many takes he's going to go to on each shot. It starts with

Bea betting 3 and me 5; then she goes to 7, I go to 11. Technically I get closest when I bet 21.

Then it's down to the town bridge to shoot the Gate Keeper. He's old and can't walk on his wooden leg and can't see a thing without his Coke-bottle glasses. On two out of five takes he falls over backwards out of shot as "ACTION" is called. This is not intended (but at least keeps everyone awake via the stifled laughing at his expense).

TG: "Wouldn't it be nice if we could see his lack of leg in the shot… perhaps we can replace his lack of leg with a huge shaft of light emanating from where the leg should be."

It's late.

2.00am – Paul F. shows up in good spirits. "It's going real well. After the initial problems we finally have agreed on a path and a direction for this movie – Terry's."

At 3.00am Matt, Heath, Lena and Peter are finally called for their shots. Everyone is tired… except Johnny Cheeks, who is a ball of energy and is having the fucking time of his life!

He met Matt courtesy of the Farrellys and he has been on board ever since, as a curious mixture of good friend and court jester.

He's the kind of guy who within minutes of landing in Prague knew all the right places to go and all the right people to know, to get whatever it was you were looking for.

Things start to get playful around 3.00am, with Cheeks doing his act at Stormare's request. It keeps everyone going. He's a good man; Lorne Michaels take note.

TG is pushing ahead and the shot is finished just before lights up.

There is a mad scramble for the mini-vans back to various hotels.

As the first assistant director, Mishka is, in essence, the guy who runs the floor. During the course of the night, "A Brief Guide to Mishka-speak" is devised:

"People, we're one minute away from shooting" – at least half an hour;

"Let's go again, right away" – twenty minutes;

"5 minutes away" – forty-five minutes to an hour;

"Time to go" – there is a rumour going round that every time Mishka says this, he's actually tending his resignation, but no one's accepting it as they don't realise that's what he's doing. It's a language barrier thing.

Thursday, 11th September

BM: A big scene tonight – Delatombe bids the Grimms adieu. Peter is on horseback with loads of soldiers around him.

Peter is convinced he's met me before in England – "Were you in a Welsh band called The Man around 1979–84?"

No!

TG: "It's going okay but I'm really not that inspired that often. Last night was the perfect example. It all looks so mediocre… Even when I look at the edited stuff, some of it is mediocre."

Paul F. has apparently put an offer in today to Monica Bellucci's "people" in regard to her playing the Queen.

Another difficult shot is readied – Delatombe firing the cannon from the town. 2nd unit supervisor Ricky arrives to report on his night's work – Lena and the lake. Turns out Lena is not too comfortable around water

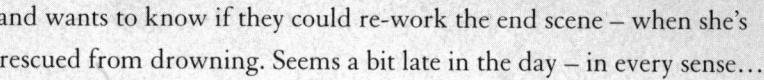

and wants to know if they could re-work the end scene – when she's rescued from drowning. Seems a bit late in the day – in every sense…

Paul F. notices me writing in my notebook. He calls over "You're killing me Bob, you're killing me!"

The big scene should be ready: Johnathan Pryce is on his horse – but they haven't sorted the cannon out yet. He sits there, trying not to fall asleep in the saddle for another half hour.

Surely this should have been done earlier? Everything on this movie seems to work one thing after another, instead of various departments working concurrently. While they were lighting the set, surely the cannon people should have been doing their bit, not waiting until the lighting people had finished, and then taking their "turn".

Nonetheless, when it is readied, the scene works spectacularly well with the cannon deafening all those around. The only worry was how Delatombe's skittish horse would react – it doesn't even like the noise of people talking near it, God knows how it will react to a large blank cannon charge.

In the end it handles it remarkably well, all six times. It's only the humans whose eardrums are bleeding.

Having spent hours setting up and shooting the last two shots, the final shot of the night is done and dusted in just under half an hour.

At the end of the night/morning/whatever – TG: "Well, we're halfway through now, I guess we'd better keep going."

Friday, 12th September

BM: The Day Of The Royal Visit.

Prince Andrew is stopping by today to check out the amazing sets. (Rumours that he's here to nail Lena are a gross exaggeration…)

NC: We were delayed as we had a RIGHT ROYAL interruption. Apparently the visiting ex-Mr. Fergie was heard to say to someone and I quote: "There's a lot of faffing about that goes on, isn't there?" Oh dear… is it soooo apparent? Bet it's like that in the FIRM too. Oh well… they didn't stay long… that shiny old suit was causing us so many reflection problems that we got out a huge wind machine that blew them away and into a Eurotrash party. Poor Annabel said it was sooo boooring that she came back to the set in her glad rags and wellies just to tell us all.

BM: TG – earlier: "The actors are asking to look at the edited footage now. They shouldn't be allowed to. They shouldn't even look at playback. This is what holds everything up. They should just go on and act. Only the director and editor should look at the footage."

Gilliam is keen to debunk the myth of the auteur – after all, Steve and Gerry work with the actors, Mishka calls action on set and runs the crew, others contribute to shots from DP Tom to cameraman Pete, and so on.

Evening – I manage to bump into Prince Andrew – literally – as we fight for space all round the monitor. We both apologise and his bodyguards stop talking into their sleeves and stand down. After a couple of remarkably quick takes of Little Red Riding Hood running out of the forest, HRH departs and the production hits its real groove: damn slow, re-take after re-take of the same – apparently – simple scene.

Paul F. has been detailing how he spends his evenings in Prague – "I go home, cry into my pillow: 'Nobody likes me' – then I phone my accountant, find out what I've earned, try to find a reason to get through the day."

I have managed to get him hooked on sherbet lemons – his shrink will not approve.

A few minutes later Paul lets out what can only be described as a primal whine – "Bob, are you gonna say lots of terrible things about Miramax and bring your book out before the film?"

He has mistakenly been informed that the book is being published early – it's impossible, the story won't be finished.

The good news of the evening is that earlier today he landed Monica Bellucci for the role of the Queen. Overweight crewmen start to drool openly…

Later – Gilliam falls asleep on the set of the Engineer's workshop – while they are setting up. Tom decides to shoot the rehearsal, Peter S. hams it up, as Gilliam sleeps through the whole thing. (Expect to see it on the DVD extras.)

TG [By way of explanation]: "It's about time – everyone else has been asleep on this set…"

It's another long night (they're all long nights) – one long scene in the Engineer's room – only two decent takes.

It's the weekend, so return home. Meet Gilliam on the plane by chance. He talks about how active Chuck still is – daily phone calls, etc.

Monday, 15th September

BM: Monica Bellucci arrives for make-up and costume tests; spends several hours having her face moulded.

Tuesday, 16th September

NC: It seemed sooo feasible... sooo easy – a snip we all thought. How wrong could one get!!

Basically, it seemed the lights go up and we then fit the actors into the lights, and then if they get into shot (the lamps you ninnies... not the actors) we change the shot. Then it becomes a boring shot, then TG doesn't like it, then we change things, then those things are unplanned, so everyone is not at all ready and excuse themselves with the fact that they didn't know about it beforehand, so we then compromise and by the time EVERYONE is confused as to what is REALLY WANTED and everyone becomes headless chickens, or else socialites without a party to go to, then everyone turns to their neighbour and whinges and by this time HOURS go by and tempers start to fly and the actors start to moan about ungainly positions that HURT!

Thursday, 18th September

NC: Today was a bit alarming really... We suddenly decided to reshoot half the shots on the meadow that we had done before, as the PERSPECTIVE element hadn't quite worked... So with a brave heart, considering he had a whole forest to burn and a posse of VIPs breathing down his neck, TG set up lots of little miniature haystacks and teeny altars and we moved closer to the forest and then dragged in THE HOODED

QUEEN, who ran around and puffed and panted, and then we moved back and forth and haystacks went up and down and became pointy then rounded, and huts moved clockwise then counter clockwise, and clods of earth flew up and down and phew! We finally finished at 12.45am... Lots of VIPs now visibly sweating!!! But to give them their due they only hovered like beautiful butterflies instead of descending as locusts.

BM: Gilliam reinvigorated by his previous weekend away. Tonight is the night they set fire to the forest – a big, one-take-only deal.

Miramax have a release form they want me to sign. Bridgewater: "This may be the last time they have you on!"

When the document duly arrives it is prefaced by a letter from Miramax's legal film, O'Melveny & Myers LLP, which states that Miramax "has a policy of not permitting journalists, documentary crews and all press to be present at productions or production related events unless it is a circumstance that has been mutually agreed upon in writing prior to such production. This is a Miramax precedent." I am subsequently informed that due to "special circumstance out of respect for Mr. Gilliam, his previous collaboration with you, as well as your reputation as a film historian" that I am allowed to be on the set that I have been on for the last several weeks.

There is, however, a catch. I am asked to sign an attached three-page document and return it at my "earliest convenience". The reality is that my earliest convenience would be sometime around November, after the film is finished shooting, so that I can avoid acquiescing in any way to the highly restrictive contents of said document, which includes such points as:

"Point 1 (a): The timing of location of McCabe's visits must be approved by a Miramax representative (other than Terry Gilliam) prior to each such visit…" – so far, fairly reasonable. "Point 2: McCabe hereby grants to Miramax the sole right of approval, to be exercised in writing and in a reasonable manner, over the content of the Book with respect to (i) all matters concerning Miramax…"

Okay, getting a bit more difficult here…

"Point 4: In further consideration of Miramax's permission to access the shooting set, McCabe hereby further agrees that: (a) …the Book shall not include any confidential material or confidential information (collectively 'Confidential Information') concerning (i) the business of Miramax; (ii) any motion picture or television property or production or Miramax; (iii) any officer, director, employer, employee or agent, unless previously authorised in writing by Miramax."

Getting a touch restrictive now, in a 'say nice things or go away' kind of way…

"4 (b): The Book shall not be derogatory to or critical of the entertainment industry…" (What? The *whole* entertainment industry???)

"Point 5: McCabe shall not, nor shall McCabe permit others to, use the name 'Miramax' or the name(s) of any Miramax

officers, employees, agents or affiliates, parent or subsidiary
companies for any purposes in connection with the advertising
and publicizing of the book…"

It was very clearly turning into a long night… until finally some of it
made sense:

"Point 10: This agreement shall be deemed null and void
unless this agreement is fully executed by both parties." It
wasn't. I never signed it.

Gilliam is aware of the papers they want me to sign. He says it's likely
they're fine with me monitoring as long as I don't mention Miramax by
name. Discuss turning this diary into an obscure fairytale piece in which
everyone assumes a character name. Not quite sure which one's the
wicked fairy though. (Oh no, hang on…)

As Gilliam says, "They can't sue you for libel if you call someone a
'fucking piece of shit'. That's an opinion – it's not presented as a fact."

TG on Paul F. – "He's read your books and he really likes you, but he has to
do this because he's a bad guy. He's the hit man who wants to be loved."

Back on set – Terry the FX man calls loudly to an Italian crew member to
put out his cigarette – he has a point, after all he is standing next to three
large fuel tanks here to set the forest aflame.

The fire scene – currently taking three hours to set up and
counting… Six cameras set to cover it… it involves setting fire to the
kindling beneath the tied-down Grimms. The lack of organisation
becomes apparent – the scene is being readied to go (itself a protracted

process) when Gilliam notices there is not enough kindling. The cameras are ready, the scene is being rehearsed but there's nothing to burn.

Everyone with a spare hand decamps to the forest in the dark to scrabble for twigs. The greensmen are hacking pieces of wood apart with axes for a scene that should have been ready ages ago. The wind is kicking in but still temperatures are rising – this is a one-shot-take: it can't go wrong.

TG: This was supposed to be a simple shot.

Bridgewater: It's only simple if you know what the shot is…

Bea Gilliam is ready to go home but TG insists she stay to watch this first – her son wants his mum to watch him burn shit down. How strangely touching.

Finally, the wood is in place. "Action," is called, the soldiers set their torches. The burning goes well – with one exception – one of the soldiers/extras is being careless with his torch and has set fire to his hat. He stands to attention, oblivious to the fact that his head is on fire.

Gilliam keeps the cameras rolling as long as he can to cover his shot, then someone yells "Cut". (TG: "It wasn't me. Some pansy yelled 'Cut'.")

And 3rd AD Nathan Holmes darts across the field like a hare on heat (which is how he's appeared to be for most of the shoot, especially around Lena) to knock the burning titfer from the still-unaware soldier's bonce. Said soldier becomes the subject of much piss-taking among his compatriots.

Amy Gilliam is looking after her father – "I gave him moral support – I smiled at him."

It's a tense atmosphere but Miramax exec Jake Myers is still distracted, playing games on his mobile phone.

Five hours and counting. They wait until the last minutes before sunrise (predicted incorrectly on the call sheet) – then it's one take on the big one…

It's hot dozens of yards back; there are big explosions – everything works – followed by a spontaneous round of applause after the event. TG: "Now that's a forest on fire." It was worth it in the end.

NC: We then waited… and waited… and waited… the dawn chorus had started… all the early planes were leaving Prague… the sky was about to turn into that beautiful blue… the VIPs were lined up, their brows furrowed. TG was PACING! Then… the magic word… READY! My God – FANFUCKINGTASTIC! – just everything worked brilliantly… the soldiers marched up and lit the kindling… then marched back again… then the pines caught fire and ROARED. And then Johnathan instructed the explosion… but no one heard him!! We waited and waited as the flames licked hundreds of feet into the sky and then BOOM!!! The first tree fell in a shimmering mass of sparks and fire. The line of cavalry skedaddled… and then a DOUBLE BOOM and a HUGE FIREBALL leapt up into the sky. Boy, am I glad I wasn't in a plane leaving Prague right then. Black clouds of smoke billowed out into the ether and then went on burning for over 12 minutes. Brilliant. Well done our lovely SFX boys for a safe nite. How can we go to sleep now??

Stephen Bridgewater – Snatches from a late night conversation:

It's late. Bridgewater has retreated to his spartanly furnished office. It's some time between 2.00 and 3.00am. We're all waiting for the fire.

Steve has worked with Terry since *The Fisher King*. He is technically billed as an Actors Coach, but with Gilliam he is more than that – he is friend, sounding board, emotional buffer and often an uncredited form of associate director, working as he does primarily with the actors.

An arms-bearing Christian, Bridgewater has an eventful past. He was a radio DJ until both his father and son died (his father from natural causes, his five-year-old son accidentally drowned). He then decided to reinvent himself – "just give it a shot".

He relocated to LA, came across the script for *The Fisher King* and made a short film of the first 10 pages of the script using friends and associates – he knew the world of the DJ, as in Jeff Bridges' character in the movie. He then borrowed a Federal Express uniform from a friend, having heard Gilliam was up for the directing gig, and phoned around the best hotels in LA. "There are about ten hotels in LA he's going to be staying at. He was pretty easy to find." [Stalkers take note.]

He went to reception dressed in the FedEx outfit and said he had to deliver this tape personally – into Gilliam's hand – and did so without saying a word. TG got in touch saying, "Obviously you're good with actors" – and he landed the job coaching Bridges and Brad Pitt.

"I prefer to be off-camera. I don't go looking for much on screen; if something comes to me, I take it."

Bridgewater was on board *Grimm* early on – Matt was very worried about putting his English accent out there, as there were a lot of English people on set. Eventually Steve and Gerry said if you're worried about it you have to do it all the time. So he did – result!

"Matt has worked so hard on this film and that's gonna get noticed when it's released… There's nothing he can't do… but he has to work at it. He works when he's alone, really intensely, so he's always ready… Lena's the only one I can't get a handle on on this… she refuses to work with me or Gerry. And I don't mind if she's off doing her horse riding or whatever, I know she can act. She's the hardest job I've ever had and I don't think I've got it."

In the middle of the interview – around 2.30am local time – the actor Robert Patrick (*Terminator 2*, *X-Files*, etc.) calls up. He's one of Bridgewater's clients and is asking for advice. Bridgewater hands the phone to me so I quiz Patrick long-distance – he's the first and only acting coach Patrick has ever used. "He's just so good at offering up ideas."

"That's what it's about," Bridgewater concurs; "it's about offering actors choices. I know I'm good at seeing things from a different point of view and that helps them."

Patrick agrees that all the best work he does with SB is in rehearsal/preparation. By the time he gets on camera, he's got it.

Post-Patrick, Bridgewater continues on Grimmer things: "Terry hasn't helped this film. I think he's really depressed, and when someone you love is depressed, it's difficult to help them. But he's been so vocal in all of it, he's not done himself or anyone else any favours.

"He spent all of his pre-production time concentrating on two things – Sam Morton and Matt's nose. Now if Bob Weinstein had come to him early and said, 'We're gonna have a problem with casting the female lead,' – if they'd said that early on, I don't know if he would have had a problem with it. But they didn't, so it became a problem. And it took up most of Terry's pre-production time. So he is not prepared. He hasn't been on any of this... On a scale of 1 to 10, the best I've seen him is an 8, and that's only once or twice. I would say he's averaging a 5–5½."

Bridgewater was supposed to be on for the whole shoot, but there is now talk of him leaving early.

"I'd be happy to stay on if this was a 'Terry Gilliam Film'. But I'm not sure it is. He still doesn't seem to have committed to it and I'm not sure why.

"He's not got that many films left in him... He's smarter than Kubrick, I think that's why many of the executives he has to deal with worry about him, because when he gets in the room with them, he's the smartest one in there.

"The moment when this production changed – for the worse – was when they fired Nicola. A lot of people were affected by that.

"What I want to know is why is Terry letting Tom direct parts of this film for him? Ask him why he didn't stand up for Nicola?"

Some hours later Gilliam explains his take on the firing of Nicola...
TG: "As far as fighting for Nicola, there was no fight. They have the final vote and that's the reality. Early on, Feldsher had given me this gift of a little doll's head. It was almost his joke – as in 'heads will roll'. And then he came in with another little doll's head and I said, 'I'm not taking it', because I knew whose head it was.

This little game went on for almost two days, and he was trying to find some time to talk to me, and I was deliberately avoiding him.

"According to the Director's Guild of America's rules – which we're sort of working under although this isn't a DGA film – the idea is that they have to consult with me, they couldn't fire Nicola without consulting with me first. So I was stalling. Then Nicola called me and said, 'You won't believe what Feldsher's just done – he fired me.' And my first reaction was, 'We've got the bastards!' We both thought – they are dead. All I could think of was punishing them and now I can get out. I thought I'm going home now – and both me and Nicola thought this was great… Then they brought in Tom Siegel and we had lunch at the Four Seasons. The hotel that none of us could afford to stay in…"

Friday, 19th September

BM: Filming Woodcutter flashback on Stage 6. Another 12 hour day – as in night ("lunchtime" is around midnight.) Then decamp outdoors again for more scenes with Cavaldi.

Meanwhile, back on set – they're still shooting the Woodsman and Paul F. is still hooked on sherbet lemons. He says to me – "Have you been served your papers yet? You will be."

After the shoot there is a meeting about the catapult at the Queen's tower. At one point Gilliam stands in a mock graveyard, his minions before him, looking incredulous as he explains his desire for a stuntman to fly up, hit the wall and slide down. As he leans alone on a gravestone, it's a strangely poignant sight.

TG & Guy use red laser pens to "spot," the points they want to hit on the tower; Tom uses a green light – "Who has all the best toys?" he laughs. "Who's being paid too much??"

Saturday, 27th September

NC: Today was our last day EXTERIOR in Marbaden Village... and goodbye for a bit to some of our charming extras who seem to have taken root and become Marbadians... but according to Guy (the set) is worse than Venice and is sinking at the rate of knots... Perhaps we could make "Death in Marbadia" with Cavaldi?

We finished up a lot of left over bits today: First up was Hidlick and Bunst trying to ride into the town and react to the Mud Mimic... neither of them can ride... but boy are they game lads and they bounce around in any direction the horses care to go. Mind you, all they had for an eyeline was a dead rat on the end of a pole and TG running around like a loony bin escapee cackling in the background with a megaphone! He really does put his 150% into it... I was laughing so much, I couldn't check eyelines. Think he may have been working off the excitement of 'gypsy brass' nite – well, that's what I was told and believed it when he turned up in the same t-shirt as yesterday. Or could it have been for stills continuity for the end scene, so we looked as if we filmed it really quickly! All in one day!

Glory be but today was the end of WEEK THIRTEEN!...

Wednesday, 1st October

BM: The shoot has now finished with the backlot – last week saw the "happy ending" dance shot, and Gilliam managed to get the Bulgarian folk music for the scene that he has been angling for.

Today I hang out with Matt, who has been licking a toad – "It was okay until the lady doctor told me to take these three infection pills after," he says. "But I still got her number."

We discuss what has now become known as "Benifer" – the very public relationship between his best friend Ben Affleck and current fiancé, Jennifer Lopez. Apparently some tabloid magazine has been stalking Matt to see if he'd left Prague, meaning the potentially secret wedding was on. He claims to have no idea what's going on – "He should just have it at his mother's house."

I ask if he's seen Ben's recently aired advert for L'Oreal shampoo, because, after all, Ben's "worth it too". He has and says, "How cynical is that?" Good point.

Later – Matt and Johnny Cheeks are having a quick fag break – thankfully off set so the fire risk is being slightly adhered to. "It's a tinderbox in there," says Matt, who continues to use his British accent when off screen.

Bridgewater has still not left the country – he's struck down with bronchitis. (I swear this film is creating long-term health hazards – it's like asbestos back in the 60s.)

Matt – on set – "You check your nose after ten minutes in here and everything that comes out of it is black."

The camera operator Pete is getting fed up with the slow rate of shooting: "That's because there's two directors here – one up there and one down here!" He indicates Tom as the former and Terry as the latter.

Later I ask him where he thinks the root of the problem lies. "In

England the camera operator works with the director. In America the DP is God. It's a different approach, but it does cause problems…"

Matt: "Terry's getting really excited now. Early on he would sometimes say: 'It's a bad day.' Now he says, 'That was really good.'"

However, today does turn out to be a bad day – very slow with little achieved.

The child actress Laura Greenwood is back – this time floating in the on-set pool, looking for all the world like a pre-Raphaelite carbon copy. Thomas Hanak as the Woodsman has to be sewn into his costume every time he's on set – things go slowly and despite going an hour late, not all the work is done and the last shots are postponed until tomorrow.

That morning – one industry veteran working on the film tells me he has never worked on a movie before without an active producer. Chuck is still on the phone all the time, but not here in person.

Meanwhile, producer Daniel Bobker – one of the good guys – takes me to see the Miramax double act that is Jake and Paul. Paul is not happy that I haven't called their lawyer before arriving. I explain that the publishers' lawyers are still going over the document Miramax want me to sign. (In reality, they're laughing at it.) "I think you're a bit more savvy than you let on in showing up here." This is intended as something of a compliment, and he's right! I have no intention of signing that hugely restrictive piece of work. As Gilliam says, "If you do, you don't have a book." It's labelled an "agreement" – but I don't agree.

After a polite and cordial slap on the wrist – and Paul asking if I've brought him any sherbet lemons (I sensed he was jonesing for them) – it's more than apparent that they're not too bothered, they just don't want to end up in the shit with Harvey and Bob.

The threat of my imminent departure is left hanging in the air.

I call my publisher in London to get him to talk to their lawyer in LA – then go and play dice with Matt and Johnny Cheeks – his dice table is still being redefined and re-built into the finest in the land. If only Miramax knew where their money was going.

Gilliam to Damon – after a day when things haven't gone with too much speed – "So what have you been doing all day?"

Damon: "Fuck all. How about you?"

The day ends.

Ride back to my hotel with Johnny Cheeks. He has plans on moving into Matt's New York place – with his dice table – whenever Matt gets a chance to get back there. (In the meantime he's travelling with him on the upcoming *Bourne Supremacy* and *Ocean's Twelve*.) They seem like good friends.

Thursday, 2nd October

BM: Early morning – no producers in sight – things are looking good!

Slow start – as ever – but I do discover that Johnny Cheeks not only got laid last night, but he also got the lady in question to cook him dinner and watch a video – Johnny Depp in *Blow*. The man embraces Prague more than anyone else on set.

Have been invited to Matt and Lena's birthday party on Saturday night.

Still stuck on stage 6 – Laura is back in the water.

Johnny Cheeks normally rides home with Heath to smoke. They seem like good friends as well.

Speak to Terry Glass (SFX floor supervisor) – he says this is a hard shoot, with things changing every day. He's been based in Prague for a number of years now – the work keeps him here. He lost his workshop in the floods last year, whilst working on *The League of Extraordinary Gentlemen*.

Bump into Mackenzie Crook coming out of the toilet in half of his Mill Witch make up – a very odd moment.

Karl Derrick meanwhile has modelled Monica Bellucci and her double – the make-up for the aged Queen currently takes eight hours to apply.

Mackenzie spends his day suspended against blue-screen – flying as the Witch.

Karl: "I think the second unit is vastly underrated in every sense." He's right – all the blue-screen work they're doing defines the first act of the movie. Plus, they're on schedule and getting on without hassle.

I visit the backlot – the town of Marbaden – which is now finished with. It's like looking round a fairytale ghost land.

Interview with Matt Damon

Following numerous on-set conversations, Matt Damon sat down to talk in-depth in early October. He was keenly aware of the situation between his director and his producers, and seemed eager to back the former. He had previously tried to help out in the situation regarding Gilliam's argument with Miramax/Dimension over the (non) casting choice of Samantha Morton, and the subsequent battle that ensued. The interview took place between set-ups in Damon's trailer at Barrandov Studios.

BM: The first day I arrived on set, Terry said, "It's the $3million nose." What was your point of view on that, because it was a very strange thing?

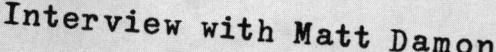

MD: I thought clearly they felt strongly about it. They were kind of sheepish because the Samantha thing had just happened and they had sworn up and down, "Oh you won't be hearing from us again." This was really it, and then right on the heels of that came this other realisation on their part that I was going to wear this little tiny prosthetic piece on my nose. I thought it was a good look. I'm going to use it in another movie. It was really interesting to see. It was kind of eye opening to see how much can be altered with make-up by making little alterations. I got really excited about that.

BM: Did it help you get the character?

MD: No, the character wasn't the nose. It wasn't that. I wasn't going to sit there and have a tic where I touched my nose or constantly pose for the camera. It was something that went on my face and I forgot about it. I did see it very vaguely in my peripheral vision, however, and so I think that did change something and might have brought something interesting, I don't know.

But the fact that they were taking that away was just another detail, and Terry's a master of detail, he's successful in creating these other worlds because he's thought of every single nook and cranny. He shoots everything between a IO and a 2Imm lens. If you're going to do that you have to understand every little nook and cranny of the world you're creating and you have to have a hand in it and micro-manage all of that stuff and that's what he does and that's what he loves.

So it became another little lightning rod and so
I spoke to them and I'd already kind of given them my
position on the Samantha thing. What I had done early was
when I heard all this stuff was going on before I got to
Prague, I had them make me pay or play on the movie
because I figured they're paying me a shitload of money,
so I figured if I was pay or play, they know that come what
may, they'd have to pay me. If the movie shuts down, they
have to pay me.

BM: So you did that to protect the movie rather than
yourself?

MD: Yeah, yeah, yeah. That was my ace up the sleeve,
I figured, and I kind of proudly announced it.

BM: Can I ask how much?

MD: $IOmillion. Believe me, I'm as fucking shocked as you
are! Do I feel I deserve it is a whole 'nother discussion.

BM: I've always been curious as to actually how much of
that do you take home after agents, managers, taxes, etc.
What does $IOmillion really mean?

MD: It's less than half that. It depends, I think, on how
many people you have. I have an agent and a lawyer and
those people are on a percentage. Some people have

managers, which is another 10 per cent, and some people have business managers and managers and agents. You start doing that and you can turn a paycheque of $20million into $5million, which is still very good pay for a few months' work. Talking about banking that money, that's pretty incredible. But you can turn half of that into the same thing if you don't put everyone on the payroll.

BM: You said you were a fan of Terry's and you admired his work; what was the difference between the admiration you brought to this movie and the reality of working with him? Was it what you expected?

MD: It's exactly so far what I expected. I think what's been a surprise has been the production hassles. They would argue with Terry and Terry would argue with them. You know, I figured when I showed up it would be wide-angle lenses and a lot of waiting around; because you look at his movies, the detail that's in every shot, I mean they're really gorgeous and they're really interesting and they're really unique. And so it's not a case of putting on a 200mm lens and having these kind of shots with all this diffusion, these kind of glory shots, it's a really different look for a film in that regard. Then in just talking to him and listening to how he works and how he thinks has been really

what I'd hoped would happen; and also as someone who wants
to eventually direct it's been invaluable.

BM: So it's a real learning curve?

MD: Definitely, definitely. And I'm asking a lot of
questions too.

But what I didn't anticipate was all this. I really
thought when it was Dimension, I really thought, well
okay, they'll bust his chops a little bit in pre-production
and they'll come after him in post- but they'll leave us
alone while we make the movie and they'll leave us alone.
They'll defer because, in my experience, the one thing
that they respond to is passion, and if somebody is truly
passionate about something they are capable of kind of
grudgingly supporting them and saying, "Okay, well I
think you're wrong but I'll give you this one," because
they'd try and do some quid pro quo. I mean, they do it on
stuff they agree with; they disagree just to get something
from you later. They're sharp businessmen.

BM: Nothing wrong with that.

MD: But I do think the movie became something different. I
do think something did happen in that suddenly Bob had the
'class' project and I think it irked Harvey. And this is me
absolutely hypothesising, I have nothing to back this up;
but, based on their actions, Bob was a lot more reasonable

and a lot easier to talk to, from my perspective, in the
instances when I was involved.

Then he'd go away and he'd come back, and to me it
felt like Harvey was in his ear telling him, "Oh, well
you're fucking up and they're taking advantage of you,"
and there was such a lack of trust from the beginning from
them that I just sensed something kind of going on between
those two guys. They don't want to get played by anybody.
They'd rather fail than get played by somebody. That's
kind of the hustler mentality of these kids. I mean I call
'em kids because it's like a childlike impulse and it's
something they've carried with them from their childhood
and they became very successful because they pay
attention to stuff like that, and they look at the world
that way.

Bob said to me at one point that he was willing to pull
the plug on the movie. The night before shooting we had an
in-depth conversation, this was over the nose. So when we
came to work that day, that to me was what I thought was
funny — they approved some overages that were being
argued over, which admittedly they probably would have
had to approve anyway and I think they might have known
that, but the nose became the issue. So suddenly they
said, "Okay, we'll give you $3million for the nose." So I
was sitting in this make-up chair at 5.30 in the morning
and Terry said, "All right, what do you think?" and I

looked down at this tiny fucking piece of gelatine and it was the size of the tip of my pinkie and I just started laughing, and I said, "Are you kidding me? What do I think? Look at that thing! That's $3million right there! Let's go. Let's make the movie!"

BM: It's just the most ridiculous kind of bargaining you can think of in one way.

MD: It's so bizarre!

BM: There's a couple of things I've heard on this film that I just want to run by you. Firstly, one of the reasons for Dimension/Miramax making this film is because they want to bring you back into the fold. Do you feel that way or not?

MD: No, I don't know what that's about. I don't think I was necessarily out of the fold at that point. I had a bad experience with them on *All the Pretty Horses* and I went away and had some good experiences with other studios, particularly on *The Bourne Identity*. That had production problems that were twenty times what these are and we had a studio that absolutely backed us up, 100 per cent, and I would go out of my way to work for those people just because I've seen them in the worst production disaster I've ever been witness to and seen how they handled themselves.

BM: Because it was delayed for ages, wasn't it?

MD: Oh, delayed and re-shot and it was testing well and we went back and begged them for more money even after it was testing well and they said yes, even though they had no reason to believe that they should dig any deeper; I mean it was just great.

Their faith ended up getting rewarded, which was really nice to see because things don't always work like that. But no, I don't think I was really out of the fold. I'm more out of the fold now than I was, after this experience, because it goes into the "life's too short" category. The other thing is Harvey's business has kind of changed over the years, because before he would have the material and he would cry poor but once Disney got him, suddenly his business plan, his business model changed. He couldn't go up and say, "Well I don't have any money," because everyone would go, "Fuck you, you just made $150million on that movie you just did."

So he's constantly trying to redefine his niche and not be a big studio when in fact he kind of is. He's trying to use the things that he used to have to his advantage that he doesn't really have any more. He also doesn't have the material any more, because they make more movies now, they put out a lot of movies which aren't as good. They aren't the quality that they used to be.

His business used to be different because he used to acquire and so he'd get movies that were already made, and one thing he always did have was a really good eye, and so he could take a movie like *Cinema Paradiso* or *The Crying Game* and then market the shit out of it because he's really savvy about that. But now he's built up so much bad will with the way he handles himself during the award season itself, which I think has lost so much credibility. It's just a giant kind of silly machine at this point.

BM: Said the Oscar-winning screenwriter.

MD: Yeah, but I think at least it gives me a chance to say it. Look, it was great. I was really happy about it. It was obviously a huge thrill but it certainly wasn't *the* defining moment in my life by any stretch.

BM: Why Will Grimm as opposed to Jake? I believe both you and Heath were talked about for each role. Why did you want Will?

MD: Because I was doing *Stuck On You*, this movie that's going to come out from the Farrelly Brothers. And Greg Kinnear was playing the "Will" role and I was playing the "Jake" role, basically. Terry said that in real life Heath's more like Will and I'm more like Jake. Getting to know Heath more, I don't know that that's true, in the sense that Heath isn't that cynical and there are a lot of qualities that Heath has that Will doesn't have. But what I think he meant, and what it felt like to me that he meant at the time, is that Heath is this dashing leading man and I'm more of an internal person, and Jake is kind of in his world of books, and so it would have been a much easier fit, I think, to do it that way. It would have been less distance to travel for either of us, which was kind of boring.

And Terry said, "When we were doing *Twelve Monkeys* I wanted to cast Bruce in Brad's part and Brad in Bruce's part and they both wanted to play the other parts." It's more exciting when you're swapping like that, and it gives the actors more of a challenge. It ended up meaning that I needed an hour of make-up in the morning and Heath doesn't even go at all.

BM: You've done a lot of preparation work with Stephen Bridgewater and Gerry Grenell.

MD: I've never worked with an acting coach before. Francis [Coppola] had one on the set of *The Rainmaker*, which was really great because it was somebody who was at the behest of the actors.

Terry called me. I think he thought I might be offended by it and he said before the movie shot, "Do you mind if I have this guy here? He's been on a stash of my movies." He

was talking about Bridgewater and I said, "No, that's
great." With Steve it was more about finding the characters
in the pre-production stages in the months beforehand and
just talking about different choices, and different ways to
do things, different ways to play scenes. Basically, we
were just doing a lot of the busy work so that when we got
here and we were shooting, as many questions as possible
had been asked, and all these avenues had been explored,
and we'd come up with five or ten ways to play a scene that
we thought were good — maybe a few versions that we
thought were best, and I really liked that. That's the fun
time, to kind of fuck around before.

BM: What are your hopes for this film, because on one level
it strikes me as a fantastically commercial movie, on
another level it strikes me as a complicated, difficult
movie — what do you think?

MD: I hope that it's both! I think that a movie can work on
different levels for people. People go to the movies for
different reasons. A lot of people bust their ass at work
all week and some will go to a museum if they want an
artistic experience; but most people, at least most people
that I know, go to the movies because they want to just be
entertained and zoned out and have a good time.
     I think it's great when a movie can work on both

levels, where it can entertain people and provide an
artistic experience, and I think a movie like this is going
to be so rich with detail that you can watch it again and
keep finding new things. Like the scene in the workshop,
with Terry and I and there's five actors in the scene and
five different things are going on, and Terry doesn't use
close-ups so you're watching all of them from these
different angles at once and you can really choose any of
the people and follow them through the scene and it'll be a
slightly different experience.

You don't see that a lot. People shy away from wide-
angle lenses just because they're not as flattering. With a
long millimetre lens your focal point is so short that you
have to look at what the director's telling you to look at,
whereas with a wide-angle lens you can wander around and
have your own experience and it's a really fun way to
watch a movie.

BM: The chemistry between you and Heath seems to be there.

MD: Definitely. That was another part of coming out here
early, just going out with the guy who's going to play your
brother and spending time getting into trouble and
building up a kind of reservoir of comic experience — that
always helps. It's bizarre, I think: if you're doing a play
with somebody you're going to spend four weeks in

rehearsal with them, so how is it that on a movie that's costing two hundred times that you're meant to show up the day you start work and be somebody's brother? Yeah, an actor can do that because you can say, "well I have a brother in real life, I know what this relationship's like," but I think it's always better for me when there's something else behind the eyes of people, people who have a real experience together.

Jake is there with Josh, a young Miramax intern who looks about twelve years old. TG is later introduced to him on set – "Hopefully you're not here to cause trouble," he says. "There's already been enough lives lost."

Spend part of the afternoon talking with Matt in his trailer.
As I leave I tell Matt that it's looking likely I may be booted off the set because I won't sign Miramax's so-called "agreement" – the one we have now re-christened a "restraining order". He tells me not to sign it and, "If they throw you off, come back anyway; we'll go out one evening and have dinner and catch up that way."

Rode home with Mishka – he's happy with the way things are going, even if it is so slow.

Friday, 3rd October

BM: Ride in with Terry – talk of latest machinations to do with book – turns out Harvey W. has been asking to buy the US rights to it. Publisher Trevor Dolby is now looking forward to wheeling and dealing at the upcoming Frankfurt Book Fair. The need to retain editorial control is (thankfully) paramount to all those concerned – Trevor seems to think that it will be okay (although he has the lawyers on speed dial).

One of the make-up ladies, Viv, is desperately ill in hospital with some advanced form of glandular fever – no point in sending her flowers as she's being kept unconscious and being pumped chock full of drugs. Terry always says that the making of his movies reflects the story of them – now he has his sleeping Queen, admittedly minus the Tower.

TG still not happy with Mishka – "He just seems to wait until everyone tells him they're ready rather than hurrying them along… he blames others or he blames me and my eccentric ways, which is fine, but he's hired to keep my eccentric and demanding ways in check. Sometimes I think he's hoping to get fired... Tom's getting fed up with him too..."

Has paranoia finally set in??

Morning shooting – a continuation of yesterday. Laura is (in a pleasant way) described as being "12 going on 50". She certainly knows what she's doing and points this out without any guile – "That's what they're paying me for," she says in a manner that would be precocious if it wasn't so charming.

She spends the morning lying dead in a crypt and being rescued by Will. On one take, Matt is worried that he bumped her back. "Child abuse! YES!" Gilliam cries triumphantly.

TG to Laura: "You're a natural at being dead. I think you've found your calling in life... just remember this is as good as it gets. It's all downhill from here."

We watch tape of Heath and his "mirror double" – TG is worried about the thinness of his neck. Matt suggests, "Maybe we could take all the prosthetic noses we have left and thicken it up." Heath arrives to check himself out, full of energy as always.

Matt spends the rest of the morning falling over and ducking from an axe to be CG'd in later.

Matt's throwing a birthday party tomorrow night; one of his entourage offers to add me to the list of the select few he is making hash cakes for. A long night is anticipated.

Mackenzie Crook has over the last few years made a name for himself, largely as the nerd-like worker and Territorial Army wannabe, Gareth, in the BBC's worldwide sitcom success, *The Office*. Having begun in character-based stand-up, he is now rapidly forging a well-earned reputation in Hollywood movies, co-starring alongside Johnny Depp in both *Pirates of the Caribbean* and *Finding Neverland*.

In *The Brothers Grimm* he co-stars as the brothers' assistant Hidlick, spending much of his time in full body make-up as the bogus Mill Witch. Still a disconcerting sight in full make-up, Mackenzie has a contractual hour off to rest his eyes from the contacts he has to wear for the Mill Witch sequence. His elongated nails mean he can't really do much, so I light his cigarette for him and we talk.

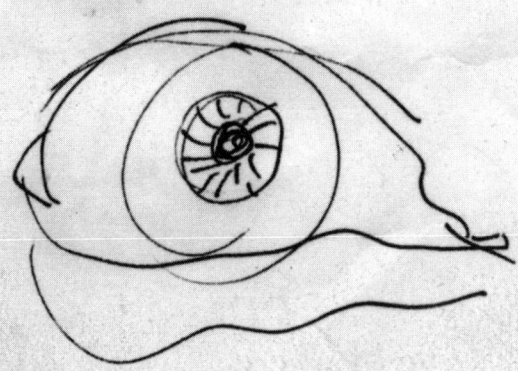

Interview with Mackenzie Crook

BM: This looks like a very uncomfortable situation to be in; as you say, a walking nightmare.

MC: Yeah, I'd have to think very seriously again about doing something involving prosthetics.

BM: What does it actually entail physically?

MC: We've got it down to 2 hours now for the basic make-up, which is pretty much a piece of rubber glued entirely onto my face. Well, they tape down an eye first, and then put it on. I have my real hair glued down and then this wig stitched to it.

BM: When you say "glued down", what do they actually do to you?

MC: It's this super-strength gel, and they just glue it to my head and then stitch the wig into my hair, which is actually the most painful bit because my hair is just pulling the whole time. I shouldn't sit here complaining about it, but it's incredibly uncomfortable and then the one eye that I have free I have a huge black contact lens, and false teeth, finger extensions, so I can't visit the lavatory or do any of my normal functions.

BM: That must get very awkward at certain points.

MC: Luckily, I've done nine days of this and I've never had to have a wee halfway through, thank God, otherwise it would be someone like yourself, perhaps, helping me.

BM: Oh well, I think I might draw the line at that point. A cigarette's okay!

MC: And then just in case I had any senses left they dropped some black stuff into my mouth, which is really bitter, so all my sense of taste is taken away. But, you know, I'm complaining now because I'm in it, but I'm pleased that I'm doing it.

BM: How much of an incentive for doing it was Terry's involvement? A lot of people say they're here because it's a Terry Gilliam film, that's the impression I get.

MC: Yeah, quite a bit, I've got to admit. I play Hidlick, who is one of the Brothers Grimm's henchmen, and this part, the Mill Witch part, was originally going to be done by a stunt double. But I wanted to do it, as I thought there should be a performance in there, which I wanted to do, so I sort of put my name forward, saying, "As much as I possibly can do, I would like to."

When my agent phoned me up and said, "Terry Gilliam wants to see you," it was one of the most exciting days of my life, I've got to admit, without being too sycophantic; he's a bit of a hero of mine and to find myself working with him is a dream come true.

BM: It's different from BBC TV, isn't it? It must be a change of pace, much slower here, especially with all the blue-screen and the make-up and effects.

MC: Yes it is, it's a completely different experience, except both with *Pirates* and *The Office* and with this as well I've had a feeling right from the beginning that it's something particularly special that I'm involved in. I had a big feeling about *The Office* as soon as I read the first pilot script; I knew that it was going to be a massive hit and the same with *Pirates*. And also with this, though it's different from anything I've ever worked on, probably more difficult than anything I've done before.

BM: Is that just physically?

MC: No, I actually mean politically. The whole production seems fraught. Not so much anymore, but at the beginning they got rid of Nicola, the DOP, and things like that. I've just never experienced stuff like that, the tension and the politics.

BM: You're aware of it, but you're not involved.

MC: Yeah. I think they keep it away from the actors, unless you want to get involved. But it makes it exciting as well. It does make it exciting and I think it's going to be a great movie. I really do think it's going to be something that people haven't seen before.

BM: Tell me a little bit about Hidlick: what do you do when you approach that character on the page; what works about it for you?

MC: He's an actor when it comes down to it. I tend to play henchmen or sidekick characters, which I'm completely happy to do, but whereas in *Pirates of the Caribbean* I was the brainless one and my partner was the brains of the operation, in this one I feel I'm more the brains of the operation with Bunst being my sidekick. So I almost decided to camp it up a bit. He's an actor; I'd imagine that he'd answered an ad somewhere that was advertising some travelling theatre company and instead he's found himself dressing up as a witch and scaring peasants. So it's just an opportunity to make him a little bit ridiculous, a little bit camp almost. He's a luvvie and he's always complaining.

BM: What do you think of the scale of the production?

MC: As I say, I think people won't have seen anything like this. I've seen things on this movie that I never thought I would see. It's so obviously Terry's vision, it's like a look into his mind when you go into these sets and you go to the village or you see this costume that I'm wearing now. Of course, there's been fantasy movies before but there's so many different elements to this one. Every scene is going to be spectacular.

BM: Does that make it harder for you as an actor because every scene is being worked through to be the best it can be, meaning lots of takes, lots of time? Because Terry is very methodical and on take 17 he suddenly gets a new inspiration — is that good or bad for an actor?

MC: It's good. It's got to be good. If he suddenly comes up with a different idea and wants it in a slightly different way then that can only be good, to make it fresh and keep on, and I don't think anybody gets bored making a Terry Gilliam movie, you can't really get fed up with it. And that's the great thing — if you can come up with a suggestion that Terry's into it's a great feeling. So it makes you want to think more about your part, think more about your role and come up with ideas of your own and suggest them. I feel completely comfortable trying that.

BM: And this is your last day, I gather?

MC: Tomorrow, I do one more scene, the hanging upside down with snails on my head scene.

BM: Not a pleasant one to finish up on. It's not been an easy job for you, has it?

MC: You're telling me. Pretty much every single scene has had something at least uncomfortable if not dangerous involved. And this is the second movie where I've had to have a huge contact lens in one of my eyes. It's not actually as bad as the one in *Pirates*. That one was a hard lens; this one is only a soft one, so I can keep it in for longer. For *Pirates of the Caribbean* that was the first time I'd worn a lens, but luckily it turns out I'm alright. I have the right-shaped eyes.

Post lunch – spend some time talking to Daniel Bobker, the man who has fostered this project from the get-go.

"Ehren Kruger I had known for over ten years, since he interned for me when I was a publisher… Then he wrote the film *Arlington Road* and that drew him to the attention of Bob Weinstein. And he was kind of an in-house writer for Miramax and Dimension for about three years after that.

"Then I was talking to him about working together, around the time he became free from Miramax, and he told me he had this original screenplay he'd written on spec. And I loved it. So first I took it to MGM, who really liked it and wanted to make it… Then I sent it to Terry's London agent and she sent me back a message saying that Terry Gilliam would be perfect for this. So way back at the beginning she had this idea that I thought was perfect… but it was still difficult to buy into the idea of this individual auteur and this film.

"Then what happened was MGM were going to back out because they heard Miramax had made a much higher bid – and the thing was, they hadn't. They saw Ehren's early treatment and turned it down. Then he showed them his first draft and they passed on that.

"So eventually MGM took it on board in February 2001, and about a year and a half later we got Chuck Roven on board as co-producer. Chuck was going to bring in over half the money we needed, in exchange for European rights. But things are cyclical and by then they were changing and there was a lot of trouble with film financing out of Germany, so then it wasn't going to happen.

"So the day I got that call – at 9.30am – I was scrabbling around to save this picture. MGM had heard that another company had made this huge offer for this film – and they hadn't. So I had one morning to try and convince them that none of this was true – and that's how Miramax became involved. We went to them to co-finance it once MGM came back on board."

Saturday, 4th October

BM: It's Matt's birthday on Wednesday and Lena's yesterday, so they take over a Prague club to throw a joint birthday party at ZD Lounge, Kremençova 10. Most of the cast and crew are there early – the bar is on the stars – and margaritas are the order of the night. The place is a hot house but still a place to blow off steam, what seems like a much-needed communal night out for all those involved in the movie. Clad in combat trousers, Heath mans the decks and DJs for the first couple of hours. Matt stands by the wall, his regular cohorts on show, eyeing the room like a man who's recently become single. Everyone else is, frankly, pissed.

Tuesday, 7th October

NC: ...then did a hysterical shot of the Woodsman running to a stop near the crypts... well, every take he kept crashing into the crypt!! I mean, what is going on? We found out that his hat slipped so low the poor bloke is going by guesswork... we have sooo much material for OUTTAKES it's not true! Don't print them, as don't know if we can really spend some dosh for a joke or not??

Wednesday, 8th October

[Problems with the Tower Queen's hair, which needs to fall – Rapunzel-like – from the tower, to enable Jake to make his escape.]

ROPE BREAK!

Bull turn to the pos

corner

Terry
Gilless
to checka

Au Trees selle

NC: There we were in a buoyant mood, with TG munching on egg and fruit and enthusing about some of the cut stuff dear Lesley had shown him to cheer him up… when up trolls Rickay with his cute little bobble-less hat rolling his huge blue eyes from side to side. He was finally noticed and opened his mouth and said, "Hair Guv, I think you'd better take a look…"

There, strung up 4 storeys high, was a rather dubious looking CURLY white hair rope descending way below us… This was the day we'd been waiting for, when our WHITE hair arrived rather than the misunderstood BLACK lot that we seemed to have obtained before… Suddenly TG is spied down the hall. All eyes swivel to him and wait anxiously and then go out on stalks. John Schofield's heart is sinking, in fact he is now thinking he will go and dye his own hair red as he NEVER wants anything to do with white hair ever again… Then *poof* – TG dispels the solemn mood and says with a bit(!) of work here and here, he thinks it'll be okay… PHEW, PHEW, PHEW – so the 35-metre length is carried ceremoniously onto the set and set up high in the scaffolding.

We then tie poor Heath on a rope when he is feeling like shit with a raging temperature and the sweats – huge flu – he wraps himself in white hair and BANG! we drop him from a rather great height down onto the Woodsman. Marvellous… but something was not at all right and we had to go for take 2.

It then took practically all the available crew, including JAKE, in a long line all standing together picking blooming LEAVES AND TWIGS out of the ruddy hair!! Would you credit that? 45 minutes of time it took and even JAKE grabbed hold of the worst bit and joined in our cotton-picking song... a lot of team effort and it worked... just why can't we MAKE IT GO QUICKER??!!!

Thursday, 9th October

NC: ...TG had gone off set and when he came back he wasn't happy with the framing as things seem to have been shifted AROUND rather, so this new shot wouldn't really match our wide shot... so we then spend another 1/2 hour or so re-jigging the winch into position to ameliorate things. This involved a lot of digging and shifting... then the camera had to move and then because they are on the top of tall legs, the boxes for the people standing near the camera had to be moved...

Complete frightmare. You can easily see how one little stitch unravels a jumper sooo quickly. The clock is ticking! We started to shoot... TG kept leaping up to fix the rope position in the frame, but by the time he got back things had changed again...

We then line up for Will's walk around the base of the tower. Well, for some reason, (Matt) is not a happy bunny with this scene... found that he couldn't say the words required and yet still be concerned with his brother up top, and boy did this show in the takes... we just couldn't seem to get the sense right... and we shot take after take after take and analysed it more and more, but it just didn't seem to have the flow. By the end he was begging TG to omit the scene from the film. In reality, the brothers' relationship has changed a bit since this scene was written and that is possibly the hitch up...

Monday, 13th October

BM: Heard from my publisher in regard to last week's Frankfurt Book Fair (basically where the deals are done for the coming year's titles) – Johnathan Birnam has made them an offer on behalf of Harvey W. for the book.

Meanwhile Paul F. doesn't want me on the set. Calls are being made – I've been asked by Paul not to come back to Prague at the moment; he's even offering to refund the airfare I've already laid out. I go anyway, at the request of Amy Gilliam, who thinks I should be there as things get weird.

So I'm back in Prague – that night Paul asks me not to come to Barrandov, even though he has no say over that.

I temporarily agree, allowing various people time to make various calls.

NC: We completed a couple of shots fairly well but then it turned into a rather miserable day with TG puking up for most of it, poor chap. We don't know if that was a reaction to some crewmember or the catering! But we had to get notes by remote control as he curled up with a bucket back at base.

The day then continued as best as we could without our really main man around… the other main man (DAMON) was chatting about his finish date quite a bit. Hey… can't he fly back on Sundays to finish off with us? I mean he's only in Berlin! With the same entourage!! They could fill a jet or 2…

Tuesday, 14th October

BM: The day the shit hits the fan.

I sleep late – publisher Trevor calls lawyer Brian Birken in the US to assuage any and all fears. Still, Paul F. has pleaded with me once again not to come to Barrandov.

I go anyway but have to avoid the set. So I spend the day in Gilliam's trailer, watching DVDs, beginning with Woody Allen's *Sweet and Lowdown*. I'm halfway through *Field of Dreams* – and for some reason on the phone to a German friend/producer – when Paul F. comes to the trailer. He has a noticeable cut on his forehead and already the rumours are rife about what he got up to at the weekend. Either way, he's not in a good mood.

He's throwing me off the set – given the fact that I'm not actually on the set at the moment, this would seem to be a difficult thing to do. But he takes that in his stride. "You can either do this the easy way – and walk out to the bus stop, or we can do it the hard way." The hard way involves the two Czech security guards he has with him. I peer outside to see them and they are desperately trying not to laugh at the ridiculousness of the situation.

Out of politeness, I agree to leave, once I've packed my things together and phoned Amy Gilliam to let her know what's going on. Paul is adamant that I will not pack my things away – they can be sent on to me. Naturally I refuse, pointing out to him that I do not want to add to Miramax's already max-ed out budget and that I am nowhere near the set and while he may have charge over that, neither he – nor Miramax – actually own Barrandov Studios, and I am here in this trailer at the invitation of both Terry and Amy Gilliam.

He replies with a "Yes, actually I do own this studio," which for some reason reminds me of all my favourite moments from *This Is Spinal Tap*, so top-heavy is it with its sense of deluded self-importance. I try not to laugh but absurdity is the nature of the day. I pack my stuff away and call Amy to let her know I'm off – Paul paces and fumes outside the trailer. Did I spend longer than needed packing up? Of course I fucking well did! The result being that Paul has laid on a car to drive me back to my hotel. (Good thing too, because I didn't have a clue which bus to get.)

As I'm leaving, Johnny Cheeks wanders by and tries to get me to throw down some dice. Sadly, I tell him my shooting hand is all but hung up – "They're kicking me off." He is relatively stunned. Everyone else who hears the news thinks so too – I have several emails in the following days along the lines of "What the hell?" But I'm gone. Paul paces as he watches me leave. But then that's middle management for you – actually taking a real decision must have scared the hell out of him. Bless.

NC: Very glad to see TG back in good form despite enlarging zit on nose. He won't even have the pleasure of squishing it and the contents landing on the mirror as it is INTERNAL. Now I'm being REALLY GROSS as I'm catching it from a lot of the "shermans" on the shoot, who seem to delight in sending their mucous back along their nasal passages as fast as they can snort it there and right into my lughole… Whoopsie, shouldn't say that word, should I! "Snort"… not "lughole"!

Thursday, 16th October

NC: We were all winding everyone up about a 3RD UNIT, and the corridor polisher who wants to be up for the lighting job… he's found that if you switch a few back-lighters on and a few off, it all comes out in the wash for quite a lot of dosh – and who knows, he may get the job.

Wednesday, 22nd October

NC: TG was as happy as Larry as unit after unit approached him for their brief and he doshed out notes and squiggles and then sat back and reminisced about the old days when he (was allowed to) direct all the film!

November

BM: Matt's finish date was supposedly 31st October – this has long been a thing of the past. He is still here and still in the thick of things, even though he is supposed to be taking some downtime and prepping for *The Bourne Supremacy*, shooting in Berlin imminently.

The movie itself was scheduled to wrap on November 5th – this has also become the stuff of long ago and far away.

The Brothers Grimm is over budget and behind schedule – though not drastically. Nonetheless, the series of battles that have defined the production have slowly taken their toll on most concerned, and as the show rolls on the atmosphere is changing to one of exhaustion and a desire to be gone, something that is not even buoyed by the arrival of fresh blood, in the shape of Monica Bellucci, the Tower Queen.

Tuesday, 4th November

NC: ...it started about dawn when some mysterious plane flew in with a new hairy thing that came from the Bible days. This all turned out to be MB. Well, I suppose we have had it really lucky with our down to earth, no nonsense thesps so far. Our good luck seems to have run out! We came to do a line-up and – oh dearie me – no sign of her "Back at the hotel" we are told... Luckily TG threw a conniption fit and Miss oh-someek-and-mild turned up full of sweet cherubic smiles. So we'll refrain from further comments until we get the dress and the wig and the hair extensions and the crown all ON! And then, the buggers that we are, only then will we judge!

Now, a teeny something has caught my attention... old Isaac has taken to bringing a little black book on the set – those little books like policemen carry in England... complete with elastic band and licky index-finger-type syndrome!! Now just what is being scribbled all during the day??!!

Wednesday, 5th November

NC: To quote – "Today started out as dreadful and then got worse." – And that's from the horse's mouth...

The ANCIENT QUEEN decided to take after her younger version, MB, and turn on the dramatic tap!! First of all, she slumped in a chair and wailed because the contact lenses were scratching her eyeballs and she refused to have them in any more... we then had to stick this huge great corona affair on her head complete with antlers.

Apparently, this crown was very heavy... well... heavy for a 24-year-old girl with a previously broken neck apparently... and then the damn antlers caught in the throne she was sitting in and yanked her neck so badly that after every take, even before we had cut the camera, she got her assistant to whisk her off, which dragged bits of hair all over the place, and then about 50,000 people went in and fiddled and so each take TOOK BLOOMIN FOREVER. Miss Drama Queen, and this is DAY ONE with her, and we've only seen her from the rear-side view.

I have NEVER in my life seen so many people on the set! The cocktail party is getting larger… not a spare inch to move in and not a crumb of silence all day…

Wednesday, 12th November

NC: What can we say… we are in everyone's bad books as we didn't finish and we are very naughty, naughty people and now we will probably have to shoot at least one more week after the official finish date… and then some.

Thursday, 13th November

BM: Day 100 of a proposed 98-day shooting schedule. Peter Stormare finishes his role and departs the shoot.

NC: 13.30 and we finally moved back to Stage 5 where we lined up for a shot on the Mirror Queen turning into the Old Queen in the Woodsman's arms. Poor old Thomas Woodsman, I don't believe he knew he'd be carrying all sorts of female shapes and sizes around our sets. Thank god he has a VGSOH and a VSB (very strong back) as those tits can't be light!

Actually, he told me that Miss Belchi apologised to him for being so heavy and he said, "Don't worry, you are like a cloud." One of those really dark rain clouds that appear just before a storm, perhaps, but by this time she wasn't listening as she was checking her cleavage in the mirror… But she is a real pawn in the game as the real old bat was much, much lighter and despite all the latex, so much younger (but SO old and heavy in spirit that it was almost impossible to look at her). The vibes of hate that emanated from her eyes just zapped around us like crackling electricity. Uneffingbelievable!! But we managed to get ONE shot… starting 17.20.

(What is wrong with us??) Why does it take four hours to get one shot on a set we have already shot on?

We are really going to crack that schedule, eh!! 7 more days to shoot!! Oh yeah…

Friday, 14th November

NC: It was going really well until rather a lot of envelopes with pink paper were distributed on the set… Yup, it's really true… this truly wonderful saga is about to collapse in front of our eyes.

Saturday, 15th November

BM: The night of the official wrap party – even though the movie is still in full swing. It is a grand affair complete with fireworks over the Charles Bridge, a screening of an hour of cut footage from the movie (designed to bolster waning spirits), a display of shots from the movie arranged by the editing department, and music provided by an authentic gypsy band, complete with ten-year-old drumming protégé.

Monday, 17th November

BM: Matt Damon completes his last shot and leaves the shoot, more than two weeks late for *The Bourne Supremacy*, which has adjusted its schedule to accommodate the Grimm delays.

(*The Bourne Supremacy* will open on time the following summer in July 2004 to an opening weekend US gross of over $52million, confirming Damon's status as an actor more than capable of opening a film. His follow up to *Bourne*, *Ocean's Twelve* – the sequel to *Ocean's Eleven* – films shortly after *Bourne*, once again in various European locations, Damon's erstwhile home for well over a year by then. *Ocean's Twelve* opens on schedule in February 2005. During the release period of both of Damon's subsequent movies, *The Brothers Grimm* remains in post-production.)

Shortly after Matt's departure, Paul Feldsher leaves town. It is noted by all that he says goodbye to no one before leaving.

Thursday, 20th November

NC: ...a few departures – Matt of course... he was quickly followed by the pilchard who was too enamoured with us all to even say goodbye, so he snuck off on a prayer and a wing... that is what we are into folks – COST CUTTING instead of much more film to cut. Yep, I'm told all the DEAD WOOD are being ferreted out and truncated and next week will see a little heap of people left to struggle on gallantly!! I DON'T think...

...have there been a lot of squabbles on the set or what? Most of us have resorted to being our age – that is, of a spotty 13 year old. Ask a department something and they tell you to talk to another department. Ask that department and they deny they were ever involved with the matter. Ask the other matter and they say they don't speak the language. Ask the language and they say they never learnt to speak one and that wasn't part of their job description! Ask for their job description, and they say they tried not to be hired as they knew they weren't up for the job but the other person INSISTED!! We seem to have crumbled from a great height...

Friday, 21st November

BM: But it wasn't all grim news on the Grimm set, despite the recent issuing of pink slips: Vocal coach Gerry Grennell and his wife Rose announced towards the end of production that their time away on location had resulted in the beginnings of a baby. Debate instantly ensued that if it's a boy it should be called Wilhelm or Jacob… hopefully its birth will prove to be a lot smoother than that of the *Brothers Grimm*.

Saturday, 22nd November

BM: Terry Gilliam celebrates his 64th birthday – one year away from his bus pass – behind schedule and over budget in Prague. Gilliam is more than surprised when his wife Maggie walks onto set with his cake – he is surprised not so much to find she has snuck into Prague but by the fact that she is walking, having spent the last few months with her leg in plaster following a horse-riding accident earlier in the year.

Monday, 24th November

BM: That's it – it's official, it's all over – *The Brothers Grimm* has officially wrapped… only thing is, they're still here, working…

NC: …Sssssshhh – we are ALL still here! Calling ourselves a reduced unit though the only crewmember that seems to have left is "the lighting dude" as he had Thanksgiving. So what did the rest of the Americans have, eh? Forgivings, perhaps? But at least now we are snot free.

Today got off to our usual slow pace with a little light starter on the Queen on blue-screen. This turned into a HUGE NIGHTMARE as we are having to set up 5 cameras for each size that we shot on the set. Getting all the cameras aligned and positioned didn't actually take that long… but we had forgotten the BELCHING factor – about 3 people have to trail her, carrying the vast amounts of hair, then another 3 stagger on behind carrying her dress, and getting them all in sync is a feat. We had crowns on and off and mirrors summoned and getting the lighting checked – oh yes, she is a shrewdie, this one, and then she screamed and screamed and screamed till we had it in 5 sizes… but by this time we were well into the afternoon.

Monica Bellucci has left the building!

Wednesday, 26th November

NC: And here we are and we are cracking. Heath has found some energy as he is determined that we will finish with him today. His bags are packed and his dogs are in the suitcase too.

…we do a quick (Ha!) little insert of the Woodsman double throwing a ring. Nothing is EVER quick… we are only seeing his HAND! Anyone could have done it and should have as it proved rather tricky to get the throw quite right… Stressed out as we are, we print out a whole lot and just HOPE that we have got one… All shot in extreme slo-mo, so we don't even have time (or the patience) to see it back on the video to check. Half of us were back on stage getting ready for the finale… BUT… we weren't ready so WHAT WAS THE RUSH!!?? Great communication, eh?

We finally shake the room about and drop dust and rubble everywhere and Jake climbs in between the huge mattress and the whole bloody contraption falls… We do 3 takes and that's it. GOODBYE TO MR. LEDGER – God bless him, what a lovely, clued up, generous, polite, on the ball bloke he is… we all had a cheer that lasted for ages.

NC: All units STILL seem to be shooting. We are down on the blue-screen stage where they are squashed in the HOVEL set… though could have fooled all of us that it was a set first – so TG spent the next few hours getting the place ready with a feel and a few spiders and then it was fine. And we started on a very apt last-day shoot with our YOUNG JAKE AND WILL… who were brilliantly cast.

We then lined up for little Greta and her buggy shawl on a flat bit of wall that has become our CAVE SET. Talk about compromising… but we sort of hotched a shot together; of course it didn't work, of course Kent will fix it and as little Greta screamed as a black shadow fell over her, the whole crew SCREAMED WITH HER!!! What a great finish!

BM: And so it came to an end – 118 days after it began. Those left behind wended their weary ways home or to holiday destinations, matched by their desire to lie down, sleep off the last few months and forget… until it was time to recommence the battle. The words of the long-departed Steve Bridgewater hung in the air as Gilliam approached the next stage of birthing his movie – "The big battle is still to come. Editing. He hasn't got final cut…"

Poem heard on set of *The Brothers Grimm*, Friday 14th November 2003, the day cast and crew were handed their pink slips announcing the end of the movie –

"Miramax, Miramax on the wall
What is the most incomplete film of them all?

The Brothers Grimm."

Post-Production, Tideland and the Long Road Home

WITH A WEEK OFF TO RECOVER from the last strained months, Gilliam was back in the editing suite before Christmas 2003. Lesley Walker, who had been working continuously throughout, was once again back in London, which at least meant that more often than not they were being left to their own devices, with the numerous producers awaiting initial results.

Even so, things were afoot, props and costumes were impounded in New York and Miramax had taken possession of the actual film stock.

The film was clearly unfinished, certainly on the CGI FX front – the wolf, for example, was barely realised, but everyone was adamant that, given the film was already over budget, their was no more money to throw at it, despite the fact that such key elements had to be finalised.

It was also a time for those involved to reflect on the events of the previous few months. Tony Grisoni had spent the latter part of the shoot working on the screenplay for what would be Terry's next movie, an adaptation of Mitch Cullin's Southern Gothic *Tideland*, which was committed to shoot in 2004.

Grisoni recalls: "To be honest, I sometimes think that some of Terry's so-called friends, such as me and Nicola, should really have dissuaded him or tried to dissuade him from taking on that film in the first place. When I first read the screenplay, which was end of 2002, it was a kind of rollicking adventure yarn, but it didn't seem to offer up anything new for him; in fact, a lot of it seemed very familiar. It looked like it was derived from stuff that Terry had done before. But I know that he wanted and needed to make a picture, make a big picture. His sights were always fixed on doing "The Man Who Killed Don Quixote" and this was similar in budget and scale, and if it turned out well then it might be more possible to get "Quixote" financed. That was one of the main reasons for going ahead. But the first thing I was brought in to do was to write up some characters. That made me feel like a character mechanic or something. But when you come in to fix characters it means you're touching everything else around them.

"I remember one of the first phone calls was a conference call with MGM before they backed out," Grisoni continues; "one of the things they were saying was, 'The brothers haven't got any history and the brothers haven't got any weight to them.' So I suggested having a sequence where the brothers were kids, because if you've got a story which is really about the fairytales they collect and tell, it would have shown that their childhood is where all that stuff begins.

"They were horrified at the idea; you'd have thought the entire movie was about to be a flashback, but we went on anyway and used that sequence. And then for me it was very like working with Terry on any other film we've worked on together; it's constantly going over the screenplay. And by the end, there wasn't a scene or page we left unchanged.

"But looking back, I feel that we should maybe have started from scratch and dug over the soil much more. That's easy to say in retrospect. At the time, it was happening! Matt Damon's there, Heath Ledger's there, we're making a film; the notion of saying, 'Well, wait a minute, maybe we should scrap the whole thing and start afresh and rethink' – it's not practically going to happen, is it? But there were narrative problems which, the deeper we got into filming, the clearer they became. We found ourselves trying to fix things a little too late in the day sometimes."

By late February/early March, Gilliam had completed a rough cut of his movie, and started to show it to a few friends and colleagues.

Miramax people talked of re-shoots, but this at first seemed extremely unlikely at any time in the near future, as both Damon and Ledger were committed to projects throughout most of the year and the very elaborate sets in Prague had been destroyed.

Plus there was the not inconsiderable fact that the movie was contractually bound to be delivered by April or the production would incur a further $12million in leaseback costs. The movie's planned release date of summer 2003 was postponed to the autumn at the earliest, as Gilliam ploughed on editing the film into something approaching his final cut.

The film runs easily past its April deadline. At the beginning of June Bob Weinstein comes to London to view a couple of reels of the film and is apparently not pleased. "Bob looked at a couple of reels," Gilliam recalls, "and said, 'That's it, that's the last time you'll see your masterpiece.' And we had this little meeting and I said, 'I don't know how to make it any better. I mean, we think it's a good film and we don't know what to do to make it into what you think it is, Bob, because we think we're talking about different films.' So he leaves and we get the champagne out. It's the happiest day on the film so far when I'm out of it. Well, they never came back. They went to various Oscar award-winning directors, asking them to come on board."

Another trimmed cut – still incomplete and unfinished – receives its first public test screening in a cinema in New York. The reaction is gauged to be lukewarm. Miramax start to make suggestions about bringing other people in. In a similar situation, the editor Pietro Scalia has been refining another project (*The Great Siege*) for them for some fifteen months or more. They suggest that Terry and him should meet to discuss his re-editing the movie, but both men seem reluctant to do so.

Another Miramax "family" member, Oscar-winning director Anthony Minghella, has also been asked to take a look, to offer suggestions.

Meanwhile, two more screenings are put on in London – firstly at the Odeon, Leicester Square and at a local cinema in Wandsworth. In both cases the movie is played before a family audience with a lot of younger kids and in both cases – particularly the latter – it gets its strongest response to date.

"The great thing is that once it started, the minute it started with Red Riding Hood, you could hear the kids calling, 'Red Riding Hood'; they were right into it," states Gilliam. "Any reference to the fairytales and they were just totally into it. At one point I had to go and take a pee and a group of about four boys came running in because they wanted to do a pee quickly and get back in there, saying it was, 'Really spooky!' And so suddenly it played the way it's meant to play and this is what I've been telling Miramax, it's an innocent movie. It's not a cool movie. And then we had a dinner afterwards and we went through all this stuff and they said, "Will you release it now?" And I said, "Of course I'll release it now, I'd back it totally."

The Weinsteins had wanted Minghella to attend the Wandsworth screening, unbeknownst to Gilliam, until a memo stating this arrived on his desk by mistake.

"They'd told him that I was too busy doing my next film to really finish this one properly, so could he take a peek at it? And as a result of this Bob called to apologize about me seeing the memo. We still haven't had a fight since early on, it's like he went to his anger management classes and I put on my Gandhi loincloth and homespun and we went to work. That's why this Gandhi-esque approach I'm doing is the only way."

Despite all the good signs coming from these screenings, they were still pushing to have the movie re-edited.

"They said, 'Okay, you won't call Pietro, but if he called you would you take his call?' I said, 'Yeah, why not?' and he said, 'What would you say to him? What would you say?' and I said, 'Well, I'd say good luck.' 'Does that mean you won't sit down with him?' 'No. I'm not going to.' I said, 'Take the film away, cut it the way you want, add scenes, do whatever and come back and talk,' and nothing has happened.

"They hadn't contacted anybody, except they tried to get Anthony Minghella involved, and they tried to get Pietro to look at it. They only seemed to be interested in hiring Academy Award winners. That's what they want because they don't believe in people just being talented, you've got to win awards, it seems to me. And they've discovered that the kind of people they want aren't going to come forward without me asking them in. And that's why I'm not going to ask anybody else. I like this film. I mean we could always trim it. We could do bits and pieces, but there it is. Because I still deeply suspect they are talking about a different film. As long as I feel that, I'm not going to play games. You guys work out what you think the film is. And so it ended up in a stalemate as usual and I said, 'What do you want me to do?', and I hinted that I might take my name off if I didn't like it.

"Again they don't think things through in advance and then they say, 'Oh, they've got a problem.' 'I could have told them the problem months ago.' Also, they're arrogant enough to think if they snap their fingers people will rush in to get on board. It may work when you've got a first-time director, but not with me; so I've put them in a very strange situation and then I keep hearing rumours lately that maybe that Bob is fast coming to terms with the fact that it's not the film he thought it was going to be."

After an early screening of *The Brothers Grimm*, Gilliam is already thinking ahead to his next project, *Tideland*, and confesses, "This one's different. I have every shot of it in my head already." After the countless days of being unsure what to do on the set of *Grimm*, that's a relief to hear. "I'm really moving fast on this thing. Making decisions really quickly: I see a few photographs, decision. Never done this before, so this is going to be fun.

"We've been to Canada, checked out all the locations. The guy who owns this great bit of land that could be South Africa or Texas or anywhere, turns out to be Dallas Jensen and he's a Python fan and a Born Again. Interesting character. It's all coming together incredibly smoothly. You always get very nervous because this is like filmmaking should be. Good people and good fun. I'm just dreading Regina. Regina, Saskatchewan is going to be home for many a month. Mike Palin reminded me that we played there when we did the Python Canned Canadian tour; we played Regina, so by going back the circle is complete."

As easily as *Tideland* appears to be coming together, however, the *Brothers* are still experiencing a wealth of problems. The original writer of the movie, Ehren Kruger, was also apparently approached to offer any suggestions on how to "improve" the film as it stood. Again, he seemed reluctant to get involved without Gilliam asking him, and Gilliam had no intention of asking, as the writing credits on the movie were also becoming an issue.

The hoped-for credit was to be Kruger, Grisoni and Gilliam, but the Writer's Guild of America somewhat unfairly suggest that if you are brought in as a second writer on a project you must prove to have written more than 50% of it to receive co-authorship. However, if you are also the project's director that figure rises to 60–70%. In order to ensure Tony gets a credit, Gilliam had decided to remove his name from it; as a mark of respect for his co-writer, Grisoni informed the Guild that he wanted no credit.

"It's like a recurring nightmare," elaborates Grisoni. "We're getting back into this credits nonsense [a similar incident occurred with the WGA on their screenplay for *Fear and Loathing in Las Vegas*]. What happened was that Hardware Corporation/Miramax put in the temp credits, and they submitted the script with Ehren's original title page, which didn't mention us, for the screenplay and we said, 'Wait, haven't you made a mistake?' 'Oh yes,' they said. 'We've made a mistake.' Then there was silence and then they came back after a lot of fluffing around and said, 'Oh no, we've made a mistake, it will be story by Ehren Kruger and screenplay by the three of you." Then more silence. And sure enough they'd decided to give Ehren sole credit.

"But then you have to go through this whole boring thing with the WGA where you put up screenplays and say, 'This is the screenplay I started working on and this is the one where I took over from Ehren Kruger, and here's how vastly I've improved the screenplay," and all this very negative stuff. It doesn't feel very good because it's always at the expense of the other guy, to be honest, and it's not like Ehren didn't write an original screenplay; he did and people were prepared to turn it into a movie. That's no small feat.

"But the whole thing turned into a stupid battle; would Ehren Kruger get sole screenplay credit or would he share it with me. It reached a point where I didn't want to go through that kind of stuff any more. Any joy that I might have had from working on the film, and there was some, was rapidly disappearing and it just seemed stupid and a waste of time.

"So I then went back to the WGA and said I thought Ehren's name ought to be included along with anyone else who contributed anything to the screenplay. I said I wanted Terry's name on the screenplay credits and they said, 'What are you doing to us, Tony?'" Because apparently writers don't do that, you don't go back and say, 'Oh, it's not just me, there are others too.' They were befuddled by it.

"And I said, 'Look, I think it's a true and honest reflection of what went on. That's what this is meant to be about. Terry wrote stuff for the screenplay, right. If he didn't write stuff for the screenplay I would not be putting his name up for it. I wrote stuff for the screenplay. Ehren Kruger wrote stuff for the screenplay.' And that was that. They arbitrated and decided we shouldn't have a screenplay credit. I have to say I feel a lot better for it, for not getting a credit."

By the summer of 2004, the movie is as complete as it can be. The production office is long gone, the editing suite is closed down, no score is being recorded, and the FX people – who are working on in some capacity – are not being paid.

There are still talks of doing re-shoots on the film even as late as mid 2005, but no one has yet spoken to Matt or Heath about such a possibility. To all intents and purposes Gilliam is finished with the movie and gearing up to work on *Tideland*. But Miramax do not think so.

"I don't know what is going on but it's over two months since I told Bob, 'Why don't you just take it away and play?' I haven't spoken to him and I'm not planning to again. Nobody speaks to Bob, they speak to the minions. Nobody seems to be able to say or do anything because it's the Ministry of Wind and there's all this talk."

The priority is *Tideland*, and this needs to be negotiated. There has been some discussion that Gilliam might go away and shoot it and then work in post-production on both of them simultaneously. But with such an offer there is of course a catch. They are claiming they have "first priority" on Gilliam, and by exercising it they can effectively kill *Tideland* dead in the water.

"All they can do is that they can send a letter to *Tideland* saying we have first priority on Terry. Now, as I've explained to my lawyer, Tom Hunter, which he has explained to their lawyer, what are they fucking talking about? There's no cutting rooms, there's no music recording, there's nothing. What does first priority mean if there's nothing to work with? But it wouldn't stop them doing it just because they can do things like that. It's their first knee-jerk reaction to anything, which is to lever it as much as they can and just generally disrupt. So the threat of closing down *Tideland* is just terrifying. Our producer Jeremy Thomas was really worried about it. They were ready to send the letter. So I needed to negotiate. The minute we started negotiating, then they tried to get everything they can."

It is custom and practice for Hollywood directors to be bound by restrictive contracts. It may well have been that Gilliam was obliged to sign just such a thing.

For legal reasons, it would have been so restrictive that no one else was allowed to see it – although Grimms Brothers legend doth suggest it may have included the words "settlement" and "release", and incorporated such ideas as if the original filmmaker (often known in such contracts as the 'Artist') would go on to another movie (say *Tideland*, for example) the man known as 'Artist' would in no way discourage anyone else – be they editors or Academy Award-winning filmmakers – from helping complete his film in his absence. This might seem fair.

Also, it may have been the case that, when it came to publicity, the original filmmaker (who may by this time be off making/or have made another film) would in no way ever say anything disparaging about this original film, its cast or producers whilst promoting this film; would always say he was happy about both the funny bits and the serious bits of that film, and state that he was happy about any or all of the changes made in his absence whilst he was off doing something else anyway (if that were the case). Smiling, whilst doing this, was apparently optional.

Now of course, this may not have been true in any way (because no one ever saw the contract in question) and because, once you enter the enchanted forest, all reality is lost, as we know from the film.

"A lot of it I'm not worried about because I can be very positive and very damning at the same time by being so positive, and I just love the idea of being on the *Letterman Show* and being asked, 'How do you feel about your film?' 'Well, I just can't remember exactly.' And then just pull out the piece of paper and say, 'Oh shit, I don't have my glasses, can we see this bigger please?' and get the whole audience to come along and see it because I'm a man who abides by my contracts and I'll play it right, contractually, right down the line."

With this reluctantly agreed to, more demands were made, with Gilliam being required to agree, in the film's advertising, to the use of the phrase, "A Film By Terry Gilliam". This one he didn't see the humour in.

"They went back to them and said, 'Terry won't agree to it,' and Bob said, 'I insist on it. I'm not going to budge on this one.' And suddenly we were in a position of here goes the letter that would destroy *Tideland*. Just as I'm getting into pre-production.

"Tom was trying to really argue because Bob was unrelenting. Apparently his lawyer said, 'Well, Bob's in his office. If Terry wants to call and plead with him, he'll be there.' Plead with Bob. Oh good. He just wants a relationship, that's all. And Tom was really arguing; if it wasn't for *Tideland* I'd say get fucked, but they can destroy *Tideland*. So I said, 'Okay, fuck it. I don't care any more. It's war. I'll just burn everything. Just tell them to get fucked… I don't care anymore. I'm just going to burn the whole fucking thing.' What are they going to do? They're going to have to get an injunction to stop me doing *Tideland* because I'm just going to go to work on it and ignore them.

"If Jeremy and I could convince the bond company and everyone that they don't have first priority on me in this situation, and that's a very big 'if', and Tom said, 'Well, they'd probably have to take an injunction out to stop you and that would probably be difficult,' so I said, 'Let's just burn all our bridges and tell them to get fucked.' And Tom said to them, 'All right. Get fucked.'

"Thirty minutes later they called back and said, 'Bob's relented.' So what is it with these guys? Is it all bluff? Is it all just push, push, push because that's all they know how to do? Because the situation's being negotiated they've got to extract every pound of flesh? I don't know. Anyway, we're marching on, but we're also at the same time getting them to write more of the script of what I'm supposed to say on talk shows. I want as much as possible."

Pietro Scalia did eventually look at the film and told them it was all there. It could maybe be trimmed a bit, but otherwise it was there. Bob, apparently unhappy with this response, replied, "I don't need to talk to you then," so while Grimms remained on hold, Gilliam moved on to *Tideland*.

Mitch Cullin's darkly beautiful tale mixes shades of *Alice in Wonderland* with a world completely unique to itself. It focuses on a ten-year-old girl named Jeliza-Rose, who after the death of her junkie mother moves with her equally addicted father to an isolated, dilapidated farmhouse in rural Texas.

As her father takes root in his armchair, seemingly lost in a drug-induced stupor, Jeliza-Rose explores her new world, whilst also increasingly moving into her own fantasy one, accompanied by her only real friends, a collection of disembodied Barbie doll heads, each replete with their own distinct personality. Soon she meets fireflies, discovers the nighttime presence of the monster-like bog men, finds a real friend in the form of a retarded boy named Dickens, and deals with his mother, an eccentric local taxidermist.

It is a very delicate tale mixed with some brutal elements and implications, a balance that attracted Gilliam on his first read when Cullin sent the novel to him directly. He swiftly passed it on to Tony Grisoni, who had the same reaction, as did Oscar-winning (*The Last Emperor*) producer Jeremy Thomas, who began to raise the money to make it, announcing it first at the Cannes Film Festival. Although considerably less expensive than *The Brothers Grimm*, it still proved to be a tough sell, given the unusual nature of the subject matter. But now everything was in place, and filming was to take place in Saskatchewan in Canada (standing in for Texas) in the autumn of 2004.

"*Tideland* is a dream of a book to adapt," Grisoni enthuses. "We used practically all of Mitch's dialogue. He's just got the ear for it. It's also a dark little parable, a dark, Gothic little tale, but it's told with such simplicity because it's all told through this girl, Jeliza-Rose, and she is the best modern Alice I've ever come across. It's too good. There's too much there. I think he's going to have a ball with it and I think he's really going to enjoy himself and I think we're going to see a very, very interesting, strange little film.

"I think *Tideland* is the angel of the piece, almost the result of *Grimm*. I'm sure Terry will feel pressure. A lot is riding on *Tideland* because Terry's going to have a lot of control, total."

Gilliam was eager to re-team with his old *Fisher King* star, Jeff Bridges, for the role of the father, but in defference to producer Jeremy Thomas it was a part also offered to Billy Bob Thornton (who eventually passed in favour of a movie with a much larger paycheque) and Sean Penn, who also turned it down. Bridges then took the role (as intended); Jennifer Tilly as the mother, and ten-year-old Jodelle Ferland as Jeliza-Rose. The production set up shop on the cold wheat planes of Canada and began to shoot.

Back in the USA, however, things were also happening with Miramax, as rumours became rife that their long-term financing/distribution deal with Disney might be coming to an unpleasant end. (Back in June the Brothers graced the cover of industry bible, *Variety*, ironically under the headline "The Brothers Grim" – in the article Harvey was quoted as saying he had placed an ad in the *LA Times'* classifieds saying, "Two execs looking for company to run. Resumes available upon request.")

There were said to be many contributing factors. One was the indication that Disney wanted to scale back their annual $700million production budget. Another was Michael Moore's 9/11-themed documentary *Fahrenheit 9/11*, which Disney had originally been due to distribute. When Disney took the unusual decision of passing (it was widely held that they did not want to be seen to be involved with such an incendiary movie in a Presidential election year, and that the Republican Mouse House could not be seen to be supporting a movie that openly criticised George W. Bush) Miramax took the unprecedented action of buying the film back and distributing it themselves, unexpectedly producing a $100million hit in the process.

Others blamed the strain of the relationship with Miramax on the increasing growth of the budgets of their movies, with what had once been seen as a boutique operation now regularly looking to finance such big-budget epics as *Cold Mountain* and *Gangs Of New York*, in their ongoing desire to win Academy Awards and be accepted as serious filmmakers rather than as businessmen.

Indeed *Gangs* was another big-budget costume drama that had seen similar problems to *Grimm*. Here, they had taken a noted auteur (in *Gangs'* case, Martin Scorsese) and seemingly made his life very difficult, by increasingly trying to control his vision. In this case Harvey had been in charge; now here was Bob – the man who ran Dimension, the sister company that made relatively low-budget films for big profits (i.e. the *Scream* trilogy) – now seeming to be going down the same path, with *Grimm*'s budget reported to be passing the $80million mark, with more work still to be done.

As *Tideland* continued its peaceful shoot, there was talk of Miramax laying off staff — as high as a third of personnel. In the end it was 13%. One of the reasons that was cited was how some movies' budgets were getting out of control, nothing of course to do with any unwanted interference in their making.

"It's an interesting period for them though," Gilliam noted, "because they do seem to be in freefall for the first time."

Tideland finished on budget and schedule. During its shoot, Gilliam worked most of the week on *Tideland*, spending the weekends editing *Grimm*, taking some dramatic moves in the process of re-structuring the film: moving the flashback of the Grimms as young boys to the top of the film (thus losing the much dreaded "flashback"); shifting Little Red Riding Hood to where that moment had been; and dropping one of the movie's most expensive FX shots, involving the attack of the big tree in the forest, a move he had long considered and finally had the courage to go ahead with. Some of these suggestions came via Steven Soderbergh, who offered advice on the film via Matt Damon.

All in all these proved to be strong improvements, good work from a man who in order to be freed up to make *Tideland* had had to hand back a quarter of his fee on *Grimm* (and, given the fact he'd also had to give up a third when MGM dropped out, this was becoming more and more of a thankless task). But the movie was getting better, and that's what mattered more.

"You could argue I lost a million-four on this deal. A director of my calibre is supposed to be getting five million a film. But I didn't get it and I gave up a lot of money because the MGM deal was the best-paid job I had had. It was higher than I had been paid before. Now I was being paid two, back to my old price of twelve or thirteen years earlier. But, I still walk away with money.

"This was about them blackmailing because we wanted to make *Tideland* and they had the upper hand and they squeezed every bit. They said, 'These are the rules and if you want to do it it's going to cost you. You're going to have to sign this thing with your script.' I'm actually handing over the film to another director, if they want to bring another director in to do it. I signed everything over, plus a quarter of my salary."

Back in London, the editing of *Tideland* was going smoothly, while Grimm was still proving grim. Peerless Camera, the FX company, still had much work to do, but there was still no money coming forward. Jake Myers at Miramax drew up a list of the remaining FX shots, pointing out how many of them could easily be dropped. The date to deliver the final cut is now the end of May 2005, but while all the haggling is still going on, many of the animators essential to finishing the film have been forced to move on to other jobs. When the decision is finally taken to put up some of the money, this budget is swelled by the need to buy some of the key personnel out of their new contracts.

However, they are still arguing for some of the effects not to be included. Gilliam plays his trump card – contractually now, *Tideland* has first priority on him until its completion on April 5th. He tells Miramax he won't come back till then, leaving it impossible for them to get their finished movie by the end of May. "They bring out the worst in me and I really do despise them so much."

The money is found, part of it ironically from the salary payback they took from Gilliam, so he's now financing his own film, finally working for himself.

The movie is scheduled for a July 29th release in the US (although Chuck Roven is wisely trying to persuade them to put it back to August to avoid that summer's collection of *Batman Begins*, *War of the Worlds*, *Fantastic Four* and *Charlie and the Chocolate Factory*. In the end, August 26th will be decided upon, during an intense period in which Miramax release twenty of their long-delayed projects in a matter of weeks, so they can clear their slate before losing the Miramax/Dimension brand names.

Harvey Weinstein is in London and trying to get hold of Terry, who is studiously screening calls on his mobile and switching it off when he realises it's Harvey calling. He does not want to take the call and says to his lawyer, "I'll take his phone call if he pays me the $400,000 he's taken away from me. So we can have a $3million nose/$400,000 phone call. You know there's a lot of ways of doing this. Which is pretty cheap compared to a $3million nose. And I said, 'I'll take a phone call for that money, but that's the only way I'll take the phone call.'"

Harvey wants to come to the editing room to hook up but Gilliam puts him off, claiming they are too busy. Harvey's assistant shows up at the office, but is deterred.

Eventually a meeting is agreed to – this movie does need to be sold and burnt bridges must be mended, at least in part, to do so.

"It was just Harvey doing what he's good at. He loves the film. They love the film now and they're going to go out and sell the shit out of it and make it a hit, and so you sit there and let him go on and on. And he was immediately apologetic about Samantha Morton. This is what I love about him. He's really sorry that all that went down and 'I know that created a very bad atmosphere,' blah, blah, blah, but she's in Miramax's *The Libertine* and she's wonderful. Isn't that a great line, if you can do that? So that's all right then, Harvey; isn't that great? Telling the guy who really wanted her in the film that she's great in another film, and that's wonderful, isn't it? We should all be happy. This is like madness."

In the lift on the way out from the meeting, Harvey suggests that wouldn't it great if the film could be cut into a PG as opposed to a PG-13, because you can't advertise a PG-13 on children's television. He even has a list prepared of suggested cuts – take out the horse eating the girl scene, and so on. Gilliam asks to keep the list, but it is on Miramax-headed paper and Harvey is instantly suspicious. "He didn't want me to have it because he said, 'This will go in the book.'" They offered to send Gilliam a copy without the logo, but it never arrived and the idea was never mooted again.

A few weeks before *Grimm* was due to be delivered, Gilliam was in Air Studios in Hampstead, London watching as the final touches were being recorded for the movie's score, with composer Dario Marianelli and full orchestra. Now with everything but the promotion of the film behind him, he took time out to assess how he felt about the experience of the film he has devoted the best part of the last three years of his life to.

"I regret a lot of it," he says quietly, "but there's a lot that I really like. I think we've done some really good things. But I don't think it got me out of my depressive loss of confidence state, it made it worse. That's why with *Tideland* I was not even thinking, so it's instinctive what I'm doing. But *Grimm* was absolutely debilitating. It was like this endless sickening fall – that's what it felt like.

"I don't care about the success of it, frankly. I just want it to be out there. It would be great if it's successful, but I don't really care at this point. I'd just like the film to be out there and see if there's enough people out there who like it. And I think there are. I think I like it. I think I'm just so numb now, it's better than hating it. The first few times I saw it I said, 'I don't know what this movie's about any more because this is so affected by the making of it,' and so I was only seeing the bad stuff. It really has been hard and I just know that as you go on you get more attached to it. There's a parenting issue here. And no matter how difficult the birth, my name goes on it and the last thing you want is to be depressed and to get some really bad reviews and do no business. That would hurt. That would probably really finish me but at least it's given me high blood pressure.

"I keep thinking now that if they'd cut it and I had to go out and promote it, I would promote it really heavily. Because the joy of all this is to be able to go, 'I've always said I've supported new filmmakers and here's my chance, helping a new filmmaker, Bob Weinstein. You know, we assembled his team, we go and shoot for 111 days, we bring this whole thing together, we edit it, we sort of shape it and then we let him exercise his genius and take credit for it. The only sad thing that I feel is I can't share the credit with him, I have to take the credit for directing the film, which is clearly me as an egomaniac as opposed to sharing the credit, which I'd like to do, with Bob, the man who made this film what it is today. Welcome: new filmmaker.'

"I can live with it. One day I might even like it. All I can say is I like parts of it a lot. I think parts are brilliant, fantastic. And maybe one day when I've forgotten everything about the making of the film, maybe I can look at it and say… well, I hope I live long enough for that."

In mid-May, the day before he leaves to briefly attend the Cannes Film Festival, Gilliam screens the finished print of *Tideland*. It is a wonderful, disturbing, often dream-like piece, filled with startling images, moving constantly between light and dark in this amazing landscape. It also looks set to spark controversy, with its early scenes of a young girl cooking up heroin to inject into her junkie parents, an uneasy implied sexuality between Jeliza-Rose and Dickens, and the later sight of Jeff Bridges' bloated body being cut open and stuffed. Not a light ride but a thoroughly haunting one. And one that is already proving too strong for some. The intention was to have the film ready for competition in Cannes; Jeremy Thomas was convinced they had a Palme d'Or winner on their hands. The Cannes committee felt otherwise, rejecting the film.

"They just didn't know what to make of it," Gilliam admits, surprised at the reaction. "They were embarrassed by it, confused by it. And then we did more work on it, not cutting it, but getting it further along. And they saw it again and they actually had kept the space open for us, a secret surprise, up to the last moment. Saw it again and rejected it again. And the argument was, that they were protecting Jeremy and me from the mob because they didn't want to have happen what happened with *Fear and Loathing* in Cannes, where we were torn apart by the mob, and they were protecting us. I don't need protection. Jeremy doesn't need protection. I'm not saying it's an easy film. But that's what festivals are about, aren't they? Doing dangerous things, pushing the envelope, taking chances, but I don't think that's what Cannes is about these days. They get *Star Wars* down there."

So Gilliam ended up in Cannes not with *Tideland*, but promoting *The Brothers Grimm*. The night before he left he explained he was travelling out with Harvey – "My new best friend."

Harvey is in Cannes to sell the movie with his usual charm and finesse, joking that the reason *Grimm* is so late is that they made a $150million movie for $75million. It's a good line but for some, it's a bitter joke. Around twenty minutes of the movie are screened. The new trailer features the on-screen credit: "From acclaimed director Terry Gilliam." Terry leans in to Harvey and says, "Harvey, it should say 'reclaimed director'. That would be better."

Harvey now wants to be Terry's best friend again. He has lost a lot of weight in the last year or so, is leaving Miramax behind and claims he is a changed man.

"Harvey may be a changed man, but I'm not!"

There is an image of Terry Gilliam as a filmmaker who looks for the fight. He battled to bring his vision of *Brazil* to the screen; he was a man under siege during the production of *The Adventures of Baron Munchausen*, fought the Writers Guild of America and was booed off the screen at Cannes with *Fear and Loathing in Las Vegas*, tilted at windmills as he saw his beloved "The Man Who Killed Don Quixote" fall apart, and publicly brawled with two of Hollywood's most successful self-styled moguls throughout the long, delayed gestation of *The Brothers Grimm*.

Maybe it invigorates him as he works, maybe he needs it to achieve the best in him, maybe he just is the kind of person who seems to attract that kind of response through a combination of unique talent, tenacity, a strong desire to maintain the integrity of his work ("I'm right, and the people around me are right and a couple of fat bastards were wrong!") and sheer bloody-mindedness.

Gilliam himself sees it another way. He doesn't always fight – he cites *Fisher King* and *Twelve Monkeys* as perfect examples of such – but if he has to, he'll step up.

"If I'm forced to fight, I'll fight and I'll make the most of it; that's what it's about, it's as simple as that. But I really don't want to do it because I'm tired. On this, I think maybe I learned to walk away from the film a bit and I had to play a mind trick on myself to do that, to fool myself into not loving it.

"But by letting go of it I think I won. I won the battle, by running away, by giving up. I won by not doing what I normally do. Sometimes when you're dealing with bullies that's the only thing to do. Give it to them and gamble on that.

"Maybe I've gotten wise… But it's also unfortunate when you find yourself with people you really don't like who have got a history of fucking around other people, then you kind of feel that's the moment when you've got to slap on the armour. It's a dirty job but somebody's got to take these fuckers on. There is that."

Despite all the difficulties, the lost battles, the interference, the loss of hope and will, the catering in Prague, and the protracted post-production, *The Brothers Grimm* has emerged unscathed on screen, a striking movie that fits well within Gilliam's body of work, invoking the fairytale worlds its heroes tell of in glorious detail, surrounded with strong performances and Gilliam's unerring visual style.

It may well have been a difficult birth, but a beautiful baby definitely emerged.

Acknowledgements

THE MAKING OF THE BROTHERS GRIMM was in many ways a delight, and there are a number of people to whom I am eternally grateful.

First and foremost of course is Terry Gilliam – for his wanting me to be there, his enduring friendship and support, for always being a font of indiscreet information at 6 a.m. and for the numerous lifts in at said time.

I am more deeply indebted than I ever knew I would be to the best cinematographer I know: Nicola Pecorini, who also turned out to be a wonderfully passionate writer, and whose diaries he graciously agreed to share with this book and which shape it in so many ways.

For the same reasons, I thank Nikki Clapp, not only for her incredible tenacity and goodwill during the shoot, but also for her wonderful, undiminished sense of humour along the way.

Guy Hendrix Dyas was a total star – as can be evidenced from his work on screen – and in the additional exclusive artwork and cover he delivered to us for this book. It is exemplary – but then again so is he.

For long dark nights of the soul (and the lunchtimes) Stephen Bridgewater is fantastic company. Also in the same vein, I would like to thank for their time and consideration Lesley Walker and Amy Gilliam – without whom nothing would have happened on this film. Matt Damon was a towering fort of honesty, and Heath Ledger throws both a mean football and a cool dice – a delight in both cases to be around.

At Harper Collins, this book would simply not exist without the tireless work (and purse strings) of the fine editors who are Chris Smith and Trevor Dolby.

Overall I am genuinely indebted to the entire cast and crew of this film, some of whom I will not name (as they want to work again) but all of whom worked harder and longer than required in difficult conditions, always remaining gracious, generous and friendly – even to a pesky journalist with an ever-present notebook.

It was, more than anything – and at times in the strangest of ways – a lot of fun.

Prague, I believe, is still reeling.

Bob McCabe

Osseointegration in Craniofacial Reconstruction

Osseointegration in Craniofacial Reconstruction

Edited by

Per-Ingvar Brånemark, MD, PhD
Professor
Institute for Applied Biotechnology
Göteborg University
Göteborg, Sweden

Dan E. Tolman, DDS, MSD
Professor Emeritus of Dentistry
Mayo Medical School
Emeritus Member, Section of
Oral Diagnosis and Oral and
Maxillofacial Surgery
Mayo Clinic and Mayo Foundation
Rochester, Minnesota

Quintessence Publishing Co, Inc
Chicago, Berlin, London, Tokyo, Paris, Barcelona, São Paulo,
Moscow, Prague, and Warsaw

Library of Congress Cataloging-in-Publication Data

Osseointegration in craniofacial reconstruction / edited by Per-Ingvar
    Brånemark, Dan E. Tolman
       p. cm.
    Includes bibliographical references and index.
    ISBN 0-86715-337-7
    1. Head—surgery. 2. Osseointegration. 3. Maxillofacial
prosthesis. 4. Ear prostheses. I. Brånemark, Per-Ingvar.
II. Tolman, Dan E.
    [DNLM: 1. Osseointegration. 2. Craniofacial Abnormalities—
surgery. 3. Maxillofacial Prosthesis. 4. Maxillofacial Prosthesis
Implantation—methods. WE 705 084 1998]
RK521.083 1998
617.5´1059—dc21
DNLM/DLC
for Library of Congress   98-21397
                                        CIP

quintessence
books

© 1998 by Quintessence Publishing Co, Inc

Quintessence Publishing Co, Inc
551 Kimberly Drive
Carol Stream, Illinois 60188

Members of the Section of Publications, Mayo Clinic
and Mayo Foundation, provided editorial assistance.

Printed in Singapore

Contents

Contributors

Tomas Albrektsson, MD, PhD
Professor
Department of Biomaterials/Handicap Research
Institute for Surgical Sciences
Göteborg University
Göteborg, Sweden

Kerstin Bergström, CDT
Department of Otolaryngology
Sahlgren's Hospital
Göteborg University
Göteborg, Sweden

Per-Ingvar Brånemark, MD, PhD
Professor
Institute for Applied Biotechnology
Göteborg University
Göteborg, Sweden

John B. Brunski, PhD
Professor
Department of Biomedical Engineering
Rensselaer Polytechnic Institute
Troy, New York

Peder U. Carlsson, PhD
Postdoctoral Associate
Department of Applied Electronics
Chalmers University of Technology
Göteborg, Sweden

Keith D. Carter, MD
Associate Professor
Department of Ophthalmology
University of Iowa College of Medicine
Iowa City, Iowa

Ronald P. Desjardins, DMD, MSD
Professor of Dentistry
Mayo Medical School
Consultant, Section of Prosthodontics
Mayo Clinic and Mayo Foundation
Rochester, Minnesota

Steven E. Eckert, DDS, MS
Assistant Professor of Dentistry
Mayo Medical School
Consultant, Section of Prosthodontics
Mayo Clinic and Mayo Foundation
Rochester, Minnesota

Elof Eriksson, MD, PhD
Professor
Harvard Medical School
Division of Plastic Surgery
Brigham and Women's and Children's Hospital
Boston, Massachusetts

Ann Fyler, BS
Director
Anaplastology Clinic
Department of Otolaryngology, Head and
  Neck Surgery
University of Iowa Hospitals and Clinics
Iowa City, Iowa

Gösta Granström, MD, DDS, PhD
Associate Professor
Department of Otolaryngology, Head and
  Neck Surgery
Sahlgren's Hospital
Göteborg University
Göteborg, Sweden

Susan W. Habakuk, BS, MEd
Clinical Assistant Professor
The Craniofacial Center Department of
  Surgery
College of Medicine
University of Illinois at Chicago
Chicago, Illinois

Bo E. V. Håkansson, PhD
Associate Professor
Department of Applied Electronics
Chalmers University of Technology
Göteborg, Sweden

David Harris, FDS, FFD
Senior Lecturer
School of Dental Science
Trinity College Dublin
Dublin, Ireland

Patrick J. Henry, BDSc, MSD
Director
The Brånemark Osseointegration Center
West Perth, Australia

Kenji W. Higuchi, DDS, MS
Director
Spokane Center for Tissue-Integrated
  Reconstruction
Spokane, Washington

Kajsa-Mia Holgers, MD, PhD
Specialist in ENT and Audiology
Departments of Audiology and Anatomy and
  Cell Biology
Göteborg University
Göteborg, Sweden

Ian T. Jackson, MD
Director
Institute for Craniofacial and Reconstructive
  Surgery
Southfield, Michigan

Eugene E. Keller, DDS, MSD
Professor of Dentistry
Mayo Medical School
Consultant, Section of Oral Diagnosis and
  Oral and Maxillofacial Surgery
Mayo Clinic and Mayo Foundation
Rochester, Minnesota

William E. LaVelle, DDS, MS
Professor Emeritus
College of Medicine
University of Iowa
Iowa City, Iowa

Neil Meredith, BDS, MSc, FDS, PhD
Associate Professor
Department of Oral and Dental Science,
  Bristol Dental Hospital
Bristol, United Kingdom
Department of Biomaterials/Handicap
  Research
Institute for Surgical Sciences
Göteborg University
Göteborg, Sweden

Eric K. Milliner, MD
Assistant Professor of Psychiatry
Mayo Medical School
Consultant, Division of Child and Adolescent
  Psychiatry
Mayo Clinic and Mayo Foundation
Rochester, Minnesota

Jeffrey A. Nerad, MD
Professor of Ophthalmology
University of Iowa School of Medicine
Iowa City, Iowa

Marcelo Ferraz de Oliveira, DDS
Private Practice
São Paulo, Brazil

Stephen M. Parel, DDS
Private Practice
Visiting Professor, Baylor University
San Antonio, Texas

Julian J. Pribaz, MD
Associate Professor of Surgery
Harvard Medical School
Division of Plastic Surgery
Brigham and Women's and Children's Hospital
Boston, Massachusetts

David W. Proops, BDS
Consultant Otolaryngologist
University Hospital Birmingham
Birmingham, United Kingdom

David J. Reisberg, DDS
Director
Maxillofacial Prosthetics
Department of Surgery
College of Medicine
University of Illinois
Chicago, Illinois

Robert W. Sargeant, BA, JD
Attorney at Law
Seattle, Washington

Richard Skalak, BS, PhD*
Professor of Bioengineering
Department of Bioengineering
University of California, San Diego
La Jolla, California

Anders Tjellström, MD, PhD
Associate Professor
Department of Otolaryngology
Sahlgren's Hospital
Göteborg University
Göteborg, Sweden

Denton D. Weiss, MD
Harvard Medical School
Division of Plastic Surgery
Brigham and Women's and Children's Hospital
Boston, Massachusetts

Ann Wennerberg, DDS, PhD
Assistant Professor
Department of Biomaterials/Handicap
  Research
Institute for Surgical Sciences
Göteborg University
Göteborg, Sweden

Gordon H. Wilkes, BScMed, MD
Clinical Professor of Surgery
Co-Director, COMPRU
Department of Plastic Surgery
University of Alberta
Edmonton, Alberta, Canada

John Wolfaardt, BDS, MDent, PhD
Professor
Co-Director, COMPRU
Faculty of Medicine and Oral Health Sciences
University of Alberta
Edmonton, Alberta, Canada

*Deceased August 1997

Osseointegration of the Craniofacial Implant

1.

Tomas Albrektsson, MD, PhD
Neil Meredith, BDS, MSc, FDS, PhD
Ann Wennerberg, DDS, PhD

- Biomaterial
- Design
- Surface
- Clinical Measurement of Implant Stability and Osseointegration

The first study in which a direct bone anchorage was suggested as a clinical possibility was published in 1969,[1] and the term "osseointegration" was first used in 1977.[2]

Of the numerous publications on osseointegrated craniofacial implants, the majority represent various types of clinical reports; there are only a few investigations that deal with experimental analyses. The first craniofacial osseointegrated implants were placed in 1976, based on the experience of previously placed oral implants[3] combined with data gathered from experimental investigations of skin-penetrating implants.[4] If interfacial conditions are stable, evidence had indicated the possibility of maintaining a problem-free skin penetration. The stable interface was established through bone anchorage of the implants and reduction of the soft tissues in the implant region.

Holgers[5] dealt with soft-tissue reactions to craniofacial implants. Holgers described an accumulation of inflammatory and immunocompetent cells in soft tissue close to skin-penetrating implants without these findings being correlated with adverse skin reactions. Holgers speculated that there was some sort of cellular defense barrier protecting the breach in the skin barrier. Jacobsson et al[6] and Granström et al[7] analyzed implants placed in irradiated bone with soft- and hard-tissue histologic examination of cut and ground bone tissue samples. The authors observed intact, keratinized epidermal layers around the abutment and normal soft-tissue and hard-tissue conditions adjacent to implants retrieved 2 and 7 years after irradiation. In one case, irradiation was performed 6 years after placement of the implant. In the postmortem analysis of this implant, good integration was described. The stability of osseointegrated, temporal bone implants was investigated by Tjellström et al[8] and Yamanaka et al.[9] The authors used a torque gauge instrument (Johnichi 15 BTG-N) to remove clinically osseointegrated temporal bone implants. At 3 to 4 months after their placement, there was an average removal torque of 42.7 N·cm needed to loosen the implants. After longer times of implantation (4 months to 3 years), the removal torque was, on average, 67.9 N·cm. At 3 to 6 years after placement, an average removal torque of 96.4 N·cm was found.

The limited number of experimental investigations of craniofacial implants is because there is no proper animal experimental model that mimics the situation of skin-penetrating implants in humans. Much of our basic knowledge about craniofacial implants, therefore, originates from studies of oral implants in which conditions are relatively similar and there are substantially more results available. The focus of the major part of this chapter is on knowledge gained from studies of oral implants.

During the 1970s we had frequent discussions about the concept of osseointegration in Brånemark's laboratory, and we envisaged this mode of implant anchorage as depending on hardware and software. These discussions led to our presentation[10] in 1981 of six factors that were regarded as important to control for a reliable bone anchorage to ensue. These factors related to hardware, implant biocompatibility, design and surface conditions, and various clinical conditions for the establishment of osseointegration. How do we look on factors such as implant biocompatibility and design and surface conditions, and is it possible to learn from experimental and clinical studies how to optimize these factors in our attempts to manufacture the ideal implant? Unfortunately, oral implantology has not exactly been a field characterized by sound scientific methodology followed by carefully monitored clinical investigations. Instead, based at best on some short-term animal studies, we have seen a rapid development of new clinical products that have been marketed without any attempts to first investigate the clinical efficacy of these new designs. It is an important task for the future not only to change this uncritical marketing approach but also to learn as much as possible about the true outcome of some implant designs to avoid unnecessary human suffering. The lack of osseointegration of an oral implant may be diagnosed as clinical failure, but this does not imply that osseointegration is identical to implant success. Only if osseointegration is maintained with time is there clinical success. We have learned that some commonly used implant materials, designs, and surfaces will not result in an optimal tissue interface.

Our own research group has concentrated its scientific investigations on the above-mentioned factors. We present an up-to-date overview focused on the implant hardware and its importance for the long-term clinical outcome. In addition, we present a novel mode of diagnosing osseointegration that we believe may have possibilities lacking in other techniques.

Biomaterial

Reports of research on different types of biomaterials have long dominated many scientific and clinical meetings. Some tested materials, such as various types of glass ceramics, have been used predominantly experimentally, whereas others, such as different calcium phosphates, have been introduced clinically. We will summarize the knowledge on clinically used metals such as commercially pure (cp) titanium, titanium-6-aluminum-4-vanadium alloys, niobium, and tantalum and on clinically used ceramics such as various types of calcium phosphates.

Metals

The original research on osseointegration was based entirely on studies of cp titanium.[1,2,11] At that time, osseointegration was not regarded as a possible mode of anchorage for any metallic biomaterial. It is, therefore, understandable that osseointegration initially was limited to the material for which it was proved, namely cp titanium. Today, it is known that osseointegration, if defined as direct bone-to-implant contact, occurs to a wide range of metallic materials, which has led some researchers to look on osseointegration as a primitive wound healing response.[12] However, there are clear quantitative differences when the bone response to various metallic biomaterials is compared experimentally. Furthermore, there is only limited clinical evidence of osseointegration for a few metals. It is a different situation to find a piece of unloaded amalgam to be bordered by bone tissue, as reported by Donath et al,[12] than to see this same material functioning as a load-bearing device. Cp titanium remains the only metal with a proven oral implant long-term record.

Clinical function is the ultimate mode of testing. However, because the reason for implant success or failure is multimodal, it is largely unknown whether clinical failure depends on the use of unsuitable materials or on other factors. There are, for instance, high percentages of hip and knee survival reported over long follow-up times for arthroplasties anchored by acrylic cement, despite those materials being poorly tolerated in bone.[13] One possible explanation for this contradiction is that acrylic cements function through tissue interdigitation, and the interfacial strength of this type of cemented prosthesis does not depend on tissue vitality. This is in sharp contrast to the osseointegrated implant, where long-term function results from a gradual implant adaptation to loading.[14] Therefore, it seems likely that the magnitude of the bone response is associated with clinical success in the osseointegrated implant. This does not mean that we are able to couple percentage of bone to implant contact with clinical function, even if some knowledge has been gathered from retrieved implants.

We have examined several hundred retrieved Brånemark-type implants that were removed from patients despite being clinically stable. Reasons for implant removal include ongoing bone resorption, implant fracture, pain on chewing, psychologic disorders, and postmortem cases.[15] Almost every implant analyzed demonstrated 60% or more direct bone-to-implant contact. The degree of bone anchorage reflected the analyzed jaw in that mandibular implants showed, on average, approximately 80% bony contact compared with approximately 60% for maxillary ones, provided the devices had been loaded for more than 3 years (Fig 1-1). When loaded up to 1 year, the implants in both jaws had an average bone contact of about 40% (Tsuboi Y, Tsuboi N, Bolind P, Sennerby L, Johansson C, Roos J, Albrektsson T, unpublished

data). We believe the higher degree of bony contact of mandibular implants reflects the different bone morphologies of mandibular and maxillary bone.[16] The increase in bone contact percentage with time of loading probably reflects the different stages of bone remodeling during healing and adaptation. With respect to the individual implant, there was likewise a shift in bone response in that bone defects were seen mostly at the bottom of threads in unloaded implants, whereas in loaded implants bone defects were seen predominantly at the tip of threads. Presumably this finding reflects a stress concentration in the tip region. We have analyzed many other types of metallic and ceramic implants, but there are a sufficient number of only Brånemark implants from which to draw any quantitative conclusions[17] (Fig 1-2).

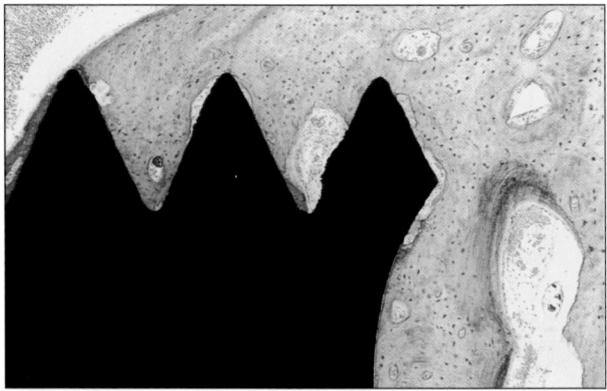

Fig 1-1. Brånemark-type implant retrieved 16 years after its placement in the maxilla because of psychologic reasons. The overall bone-to-implant contact percentage is, on average, 20% lower in the maxilla compared with the mandible.

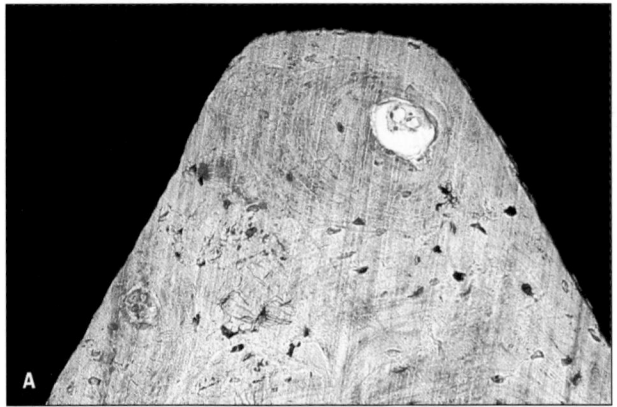 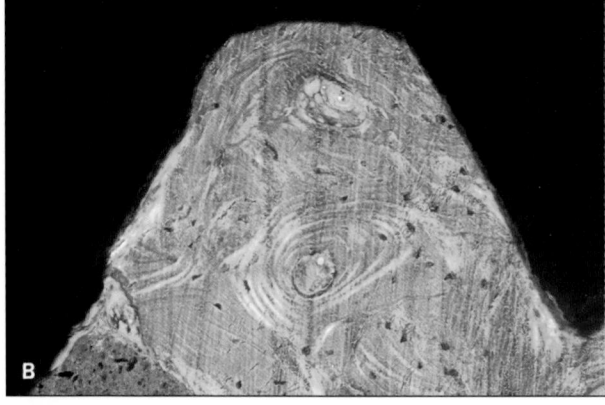

Fig 1-2. *A,* Brånemark-type implant removed because of progressive bone resorption from the mandible of a patient 4.5 years after placement. There was an average of 90% bone-to-implant contact in this case, based on an evaluation of the six threads available for analysis. *B,* Fluorescent light image demonstrates haversian systems of another implant from the same patient.

Looking at types of metallic biomaterials other than cp titanium, there is clinical documentation of one conical, porous-coated titanium-6-aluminum-4-vanadium implant—the EndoPore implant—and one screw-type implant of the same material—the Screw Vent. The results of EndoPore implants at 3 to 4 years of follow-up indicated a cumulative success of 94.8% and a cumulative bone loss of about 0.7 mm for implants placed in the anterior mandible.[18] This indicates quite positive results, but the contribution of the material, implant design, and surface as well as software parameters for this positive outcome is difficult to evaluate because there were no control implants used.

De Bruyn and co-workers[19] compared 85 Screw Vent titanium alloy implants with 107 Brånemark implants and found the latter gave a better clinical result in the maxilla at 6 months of follow-up. Interestingly, with an increasing follow-up time, the Screw Vent mandibular implants have indicated a higher degree of bone resorption than the Brånemark devices (De Bruyn H, Collaert B, Lindén U, Flygare L, unpublished data). However, it is difficult to be certain that this poorer outcome with the Screw Vent implant is to be attributed to the implant material. There are other potential differences between these seemingly look-alike implants, such as slightly different surfaces and designs,[20] and it is difficult to state with certainty if the biomaterials used are the incriminating factor to explain the inferior results of Screw Vent implants. The same is true with respect to the Core Vent implant made of titanium alloy, which showed unacceptable bone resorption.[21] This titanium alloy design and the possibility of maintaining osseointegration around it will be discussed under Design.

Nevertheless, experimentally there is strong evidence for titanium alloy having an inferior bone attachment compared with cp titanium. The first evidence was published by Johansson,[22] who demonstrated a significantly stronger bone reaction to cp titanium compared with the alloy at 3 months of follow-up. There were no differences noted between these two materials with respect to soft-tissue reactions.[23] Johansson et al (Johansson C, Han CH, Wennerberg A, Albrektsson T, unpublished data) and Han et al (Han C-H, Johansson CB, Wennerberg A, Albrektsson T, unpublished data) confirmed the presence of significantly higher removal torques for cp titanium compared with titanium alloy implants at 3, 6, and 12 months of follow-up in a rabbit model. The inferior bone response to titanium alloy was explained by leakage of aluminum, as indicated by Secondary Ion Mass Spectroscopy observations. Aluminum has been hypothesized to compete with calcium during early bone formation.[22] Ektessabi et al[24,25] found evidence of a vanadium leakage too. In fact, Thompson and Puleo[26] demonstrated that Ti-6Al-4V solutions suppressed expression of the osteoblastic phenotype in an in vitro model by strong inhibition of osteocalcin synthesis. This resulted in reduction of calcium levels, and the authors suggested that this may contribute to implant failure by impairing normal bone deposition, thereby supporting Johansson's 1991 theory.[22]

Tantalum and niobium have been suggested as suitable implant metals. They have demonstrated quite good biocompatibility in different studies.[27-30] However, the only clinically used oral implants made from these materials that we are aware of are blade-vent designs that have no proven longevity. Whether tantalum or niobium can be used successfully for oral implants remains to be seen.

Ceramics

Various types of calcium phosphate coatings (such as hydroxyapatite [HA]) were launched clinically during the latter part of the 1980s on the basis of short-term animal experiments.[31,32] The attractive characteristic of HA was its rapid incorporation in bone tissue. Unfortunately, few if any long-term quantitative experiments and no controlled clinical trials were done before clinical launching of this new biomaterial. Potential risks associated with coat fractures, coat loss, and coat resorption were described during the 1980s.[33] Plasma spraying has remained the dominant mode of coat application. Plasma-sprayed HA coats have a minimal thickness of 30 to 50 µm.[34]

Gottlander and co-workers[35-38] performed a series of investigations of different types of HA-coated implants. They confirmed the rapidity of the bone response to HA-coated implants compared with noncoated controls, and in most cases they found that with longer times of follow-up (6 months-1 year) the difference in bone anchorage disappeared between coated implants and noncoated controls. Furthermore, when examining the amount of bone adjacent to the two implant types, Gottlander[34] reported 50% to 75% more bone in the uncoated titanium compared with the HA-coated implant interface. The suggested explanation for this impairment in bone volume around HA-coated implants relates to loosened HA coats and a subsequent cell-mediated phagocytosis with less bone volume as an end result.

The described bone resorption in experimental long-term studies has an interesting clinical link. Johnson[39] reported that, after longer follow-up, initially successful HA-coated implants demonstrated considerable bone loss, resulting in rapid failure that had been observed with an alarming frequency. Wheeler[40] confirmed a much poorer survival rate of HA-coated cylinders compared with noncoated titanium implants.

Even if the experience with the first generation of HA-coated implants has not been positive, calcium phosphates remain interesting materials because of their documented capability of inducing rapid osseointegration. Our experiments with HA-coated implants, therefore, continue. Very thin coats, applied with techniques other than plasma-spraying, may share the same advantages without having the disadvantages of thicker coats. As thin a coat as 0.3 µm has promoted the early bone response in our ongoing experiments.

Design

We believe that implant design influences the maintenance of osseointegration. Original Core Vent hollow cylinders gave rise to bone saucerization in high numbers, despite evidence of preliminary osseointegration.[15,21] Loss of osseointegration in many cases occurred within 5 years of placement. There is overwhelming evidence that a similar secondary loss of osseointegration occurs with different types of cylindrical IMZ implants without threads.[41-47] Bone loss seems to occur slowly but continuously without any tendency toward steady state, even for implants placed between the mental foramina. This leads to acceptable *survival* rates at 5 years but unacceptable *success* figures at 5 to 10 years when the bone resorption results in clinical problems in many cases. Dietrich and Wagner[46] described an accelerating bone loss around cylindric implants between 5 and 10 years of follow-up, coupled with a parallel decrease in implant survival rate from 93% to 70% for implants inserted mainly between the mental foramina. These data are in contrast to those for threaded screws, which have demonstrated steady state bone in many studies.[48-53] In a compara-

tive study in a matched patient group of 175 threaded Brånemark implants and a similar number of unthreaded IMZ cylinders, there was a statistically significant difference in bone loss, with a clear tendency to steady state bone with Brånemark implants in contrast to the cylinders.[41] Another interesting comparison can be made between ITI implants of the first generation, without threads, and those of the later generation, with threads. Only the latter demonstrated steady state bone levels.[54]

To our knowledge, there are no clinical studies documenting steady state bone with nonthreaded cylindric implants.

Surface

Williams[55] stated that ultrastructural, microstructural, and macrolevels of the surface topography are known to influence the behavior of the adjacent tissue. The author indicated that surface measurements on different scales are important for understanding the influence of surface topography on implant incorporation. For complete ingrowth of bone, there is a need for at least 100-µm spaces. However, this does not exclude the importance of surface roughness on the micron and nanometer scale (Fig 1-3).

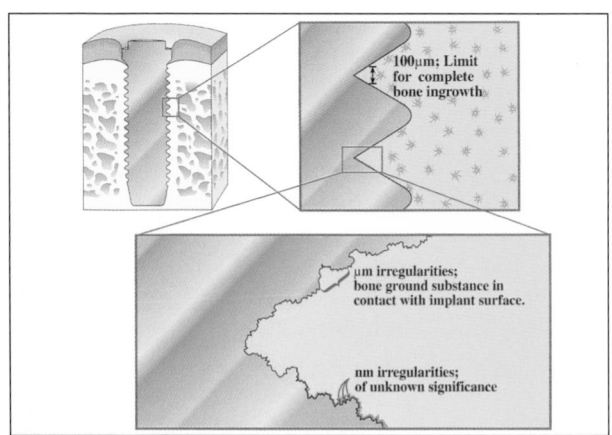

Fig 1-3. Schematic of the importance of surface roughness. Ingrowth of complete bone with vascular supply would need a pore of 100-µm minimal thickness. Parts of bone tissue may invade pores in the 1-µm range and thereby contribute to the development of a biomechanical bond of the implant. Surface irregularities in the nanometer range have been suggested as important for the process of osseointegration, but there is no precise documentation for this hypothesis.

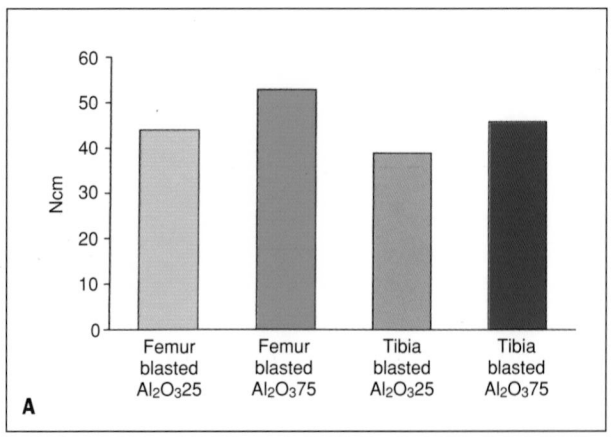 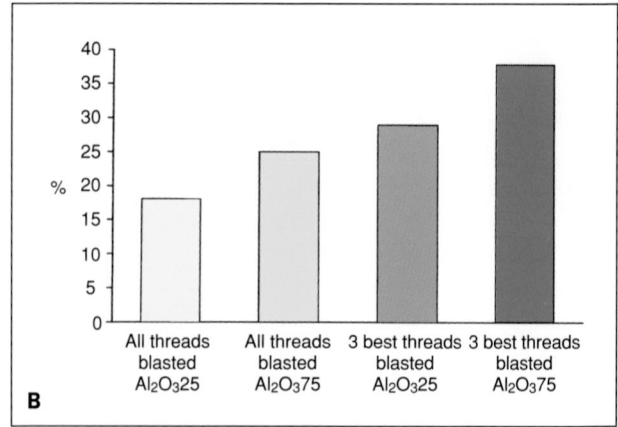

Fig 1-4. *A,* Diagram shows the removal torque of screws blasted with 25- and 75-μm particles after 12 weeks in rabbit bone. *B,* Diagram demonstrates the bone-to-implant contact for screws blasted with 25- and 75-μm particles after 12 weeks in rabbit bone.

Meyle et al[56] found the contact between tissue and implant was influenced by the micromorphology in an in vitro study. They found fibroblast processes extended into the grooves of microtextured surfaces (1 μm × 1 μm), resulting in an extensive contact between tissue and implant. Boyan et al[57] stated that environmental factors such as microtopography may influence whether mesenchymal cells differentiate into fibroblasts, chondrocytes, or osteoblasts. The authors hypothesized that if the surface topography allows vascular ingrowth osteogenesis is favored, and if only limited vascular ingrowth is possible it is more likely that chondrogenesis will occur. Small deposits of bone were found in 1- to 2-μm pores after push-out tests and observed with scanning electron microscopy.[58] These findings indicate that close contact of mineralized tissue to the implant surface, although without cells, is important for bone fixation.

To investigate the importance of surface roughness on the micrometer scale, a series of experimental studies was undertaken.[59-61] By blasting cp titanium implants with different-size blasting particles and leaving some implants with the original turned surface, four clearly differentiated surface structures were achieved. This was shown qualitatively as well as quantitatively with help of an optical profilometer especially adapted to measure threaded implants (TopScan 3D, Heidelberg Instruments GmbH). The TopScan system has some advantages over other optical measuring equipment such as better resolution owing to suppression of the out-of-focus information. There is a long working distance, which is important when the samples need to be tilted, and a higher numeric aperture by using standard objectives (i.e., more light can be collected), which is important when measuring porous or tilted surfaces.

After surface modification and characterization, 318 screw-shaped implants were inserted in rabbits. Four weeks, 12 weeks, and 1 year after the implants were inserted in the tibia and femur, they were evaluated with respect to removal torque and the amount of bone in contact with the implant surface. The results from the animal experiments demonstrated higher removal torques and higher percentages of bone-to-implant contact for implants blasted with 25- and 75-μm particles than with 250-μm particles or turned implants (Fig 1-4). The corresponding average height deviation for these four surfaces was 1, 1.5, 2.1, and 0.6 μm. When comparing implants blasted with 25- and 75-μm particles, screws in the latter condition showed stronger bone fixation (Fig 1-5). The implants blasted with 75-μm particles had a surface structure without a dominating pattern, an average surface height deviation of about 1.5 μm, an average wavelength of about 11.1 μm, and a developed area ratio of 1.5 (Fig 1-6).

Whether or not the results from animal studies are valid for humans remains to be determined. After all, the greater the surface irregularities, the greater the corrosion. Potentially negative effects due to corrosion or ion release may be detectable

Fig 1-5. Photograph of screw blasted with 75-μm particles of Al₂O₃, with a surface roughness (average height deviation) of about 1.5 μm.

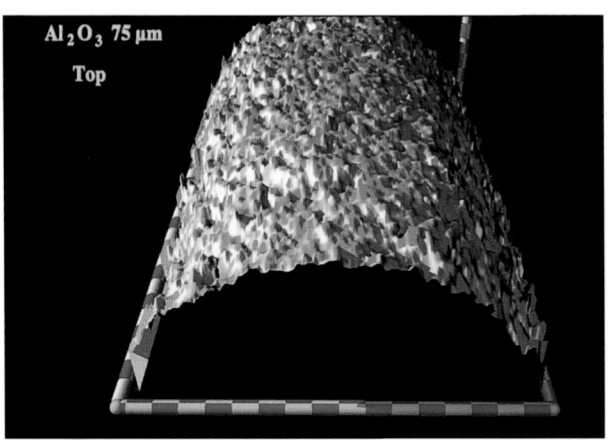

Fig 1-6. Computer-generated three-dimensional image of the surface topography of a screw top blasted with 75-μm particles of Al₂O₃. Each section of the x, y, and z bars represents 10 μm.

only after several years. However, the results from the above-described series of rabbit studies serve as encouragement for controlled clinical studies in humans. We strongly believe that increasing knowledge about implant surfaces will lead to the manufacture of better functioning implants in the future.

Clinical Measurement of Implant Stability and Osseointegration

The success rate for threaded, bone-anchored titanium implants can be high. Friberg et al[62] reported 69 failures of 4,641 consecutively placed implants. There is an increase in the number of failures seen in irradiated and grafted tissues. Bone quality also plays an important role, and healing and bone formation at the implant-tissue interface may be prolonged in tissues where there is a more open trabecular network.[30]

The currently available clinical methods for measuring implant stability and osseointegration are simple and rather subjective. Radiographs can be useful in assessing the quality of the implant-tissue interface and the degree of fit between implant fixtures and abutments, but it is often difficult to obtain reproducible and standardized radiographs clinically. Sundén et al[63] suggested that the probability of predicting implant stability from a radiographic examination may be low in populations in which the failure rate is low. The practice of tapping an implant with a mirror handle to elicit a ringing sound is not dissimilar to that of a railway engineer tapping a wheel to elicit a crack. However, this test is highly subjective and probably tells more about the implant than the interface. There is considerable interest in the development of a quantitative noninvasive method to measure bone quality, implant stability, and osseointegration. Friberg et al[64] described the application of thread cutting forces measured during tapping an implant site before implant placement to determine bone quality. The results clearly showed a relationship between cutting resistance and bone density, and it has been proposed that this method may be used to measure bone quality at the time of implant placement and thereby predict the optimum healing period. One of the difficulties associated with the technique is the sensitivity of the results to the sharpness of the cutting tool. The components

Fig 1-7. Resonance frequency transducer attached to implant abutment for in vivo measurement.

need to be manufactured to a close tolerance, whether it is a tap or self-tapping implant.

In the search for a noninvasive method to monitor implant stability, many clinicians[65-70] have used the Periotest (Siemens AG, Bensheim, Germany) in attempts to measure implant stiffness. The Periotest is an electronic instrument developed to provide a quantitative measurement of tooth mobility.[71] The Periotest comprises a handpiece containing a metal slug that is accelerated toward a tooth by an electromagnet. The contact duration of the slug on the tooth is measured by an accelerometer. The software in the instrument has been designed to relate contact time as a function of tooth mobility. The result is displayed digitally and audibly on a scale of –8 (low mobility) to 50 (high mobility). In a review of the literature, Olivé and Aparicio[65] described Periotest values that had been obtained when making measurements on several implant systems. Typical values were –5 to 5 for the ITI implant system. This forms a narrow range over the scale of the instrument. One of the limitations of the use of the Periotest to measure implant stability is that the range of stiffness observed between osseointegrated and failing implants is quite different from that of a tooth supported by a periodontal ligament. In addition, the

scale of the Periotest is nonlinear and was designed to follow Miller's classification for tooth mobility, thus making interpretation of implant stiffness difficult.

In an assessment of the use of the Periotest for mobility measurements of craniofacial implants, Derhami et al[72] reported good interexaminer reliability but highlighted variables that may influence Periotest values. These were problems associated with the use of a handheld probe and included the vertical measuring point on the implant abutment, the handpiece angulation, and the horizontal distance of the handpiece from the implant.

Elias et al[73] investigated the use of another impact-type method; a small hammer, mounted as a pendulum suspended in a frame, provided a controlled lateral impact to an implant in vitro. Unlike the Periotest, which measures contact duration, Elias et al[74] recorded the force with which the hammer struck an implant as a function of time. It was reported that it was possible to record slight differences among interfaces surrounding dental implants in vitro and that the technique may be modified for use in vivo.

A noninvasive test method to measure implant stability was described by Meredith et al.[75] The technique eliminates problems associated with a handheld probe by attaching a small transducer directly to an implant or abutment (Fig 1-7). The transducer is excited with a small electrical signal and the response is measured. Typical results for an osseointegrated and a failing implant are shown in Figure 1-8. The technique is able to monitor several parameters, including bone quality at the time of implant placement and changes in stiffness at the implant-tissue interface attributable to bone formation during healing. The method is noninvasive and measures the resonance frequency and damping of the transducer. It has been shown in vivo that the resonance frequency of the transducer-implant system increases after implant placement during healing as bone forms at the implant-tissue interface.[76,77] It is also evident that there is a decrease in resonance frequency and an increase in damping if an implant fails to integrate because of fibrous tissue formation at the interface. Potential applications for resonance frequency analysis are not only as a research tool but also as a clinical aid in diagnosis. However, it is only a combination of techniques that can lead to a complete understanding of the host response to implant placement.

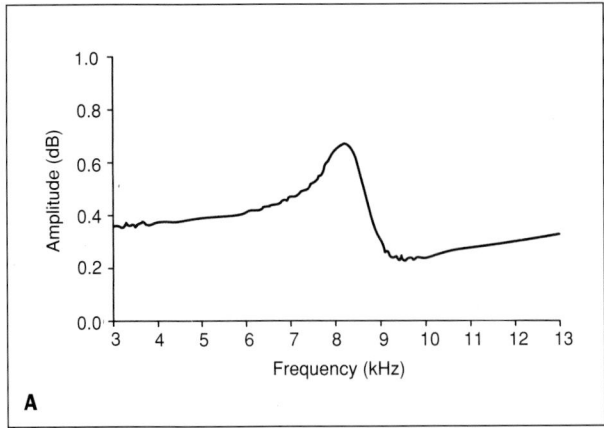 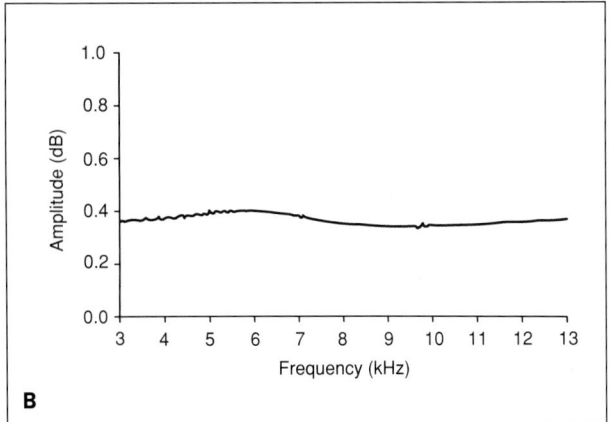

Fig 1-8. *A,* Frequency response curve of osseointegrated stable implant (resonance frequency is taken at the point of maximum amplitude). *B,* Frequency response curve of failing implant. Note flat response with low resonance frequency and high damping.

Conclusion

The clinical introduction of a new implant cannot be based on findings in various experimental studies. The step from animal to human is not a short one, and there is a considerable risk that unobserved or ignored biomaterial problems in animal experiments may prove to induce failures when the same material is being tried in humans. We can learn new, potentially interesting ideas from basic scientists, but this cannot replace careful clinical monitoring. Uncritical manufacturers have overlooked this problem in their desire to succeed in marketing different designs and, unfortunately, uncritical clinicians have accepted too easily that animal results reflect the clinical reality. Many of these acceptable designs clearly are harmful, as evidenced by controlled, prospective or retrospective clinical studies. Even if primary osseointegration has been achieved with different oral implant designs made of different materials and with different surface conditions, this does not mean necessarily that the same designs will demonstrate maintained secondary osseointegration and clinical success. We foresee that several of the implant designs that today are being frequently used will result in such severe problems with time that their future use will be questioned.

From a positive standpoint, we believe that altering the implant surface conditions may lead to improved clinical results, particularly in so-called compromised bone beds. Again, it is imperative to avoid a too rapid clinical application of preliminary findings in experimental animals. For instance, there are potential benefits as well as risks associated with increasing surface roughness of an implant. Continued research and development coupled with controlled, prospective clinical studies should guide the clinician in the future. Brånemark's original osseointegrated implant was not available for routine clinical use until it had been studied and documented sufficiently, a fact that should inspire our clinical colleagues to avoid using untested oral or craniofacial implants.

References

1. Brånemark P-I, Adell R, Breine U, Lindström J, Hansson B-O, Ohlsson A. Intra-osseous anchorage of dental prostheses. I. Experimental studies. Scand J Plast Reconstr Surg 1969;3:81.

2. Brånemark P-I, Hansson B-O, Adell R, et al. Osseointegrated implants in the treatment of the edentulous jaw. Experience from a 10-year period. Scand J Plast Reconstr Surg 1977;Suppl 16:1.

3. Tjellström A, Lindström J, Hallén O, Albrektsson T, Brånemark PI. Osseointegrated titanium implants in the temporal bone. A clinical study on bone-anchored hearing aids. Am J Otol 1981;2:304.

4. Brånemark PI, Albrektsson T. Titanium implants permanently penetrating human skin. Scand J Plast Reconstr Surg 1982;16:17.

5. Holgers KM. Soft Tissue Reactions Around Long-Term Clinical Skin-Penetrating Titanium Implants. Monograph, University of Göteborg, Göteborg, Sweden, 1994.

6. Jacobsson M, Tjellström A, Thomsen P, Albrektsson T, Turesson I. Integration of titanium implants in irradiated bone. Histologic and clinical study. Ann Otol Rhinol Laryngol 1988;97:337.

7. Granström G, Tjellström A, Albrektsson T. Postimplantation irradiation for head and neck cancer treatment. Int J Oral Maxillofac Implants 1993;8:495.

8. Tjellström A, Jacobsson M, Albrektsson T. Removal torque of osseointegrated craniofacial implants: a clinical study. Int J Oral Maxillofac Implants 1988;3:287.

9. Yamanaka E, Tjellström A, Jacobsson M, Albrektsson T. Long-term observations on removal torque of directly bone-anchored implants in man. In Yanigihara N, Suzuki JI (eds): Transplants and Implants in Otology. Amsterdam: Kugler Publications; 1992:245.

10. Albrektsson T, Brånemark P-I, Hansson H-A, Lindström J. Osseointegrated titanium implants. Requirements for ensuring a long-lasting, direct bone-to-implant anchorage in man. Acta Orthop Scand 1981;52:155.

11. Albrektsson T. Healing of bone grafts. Thesis, University of Göteborg, Göteborg, Sweden, 1979.

12. Donath K, Laass M, Günzl HJ. The histopathology of different foreign-body reactions in oral soft tissue and bone tissue. Virchows Arch A Pathol Anat Histopathol 1992;420:131.

13. Morberg P. On bone tissue reactions to acrylic cement. Thesis, University of Göteborg, Göteborg, Sweden, 1991.

14. Strid K-G. Radiographic results. In Brånemark P-I, Zarb GA, Albrektsson T (eds): Tissue-Integrated Prostheses: Osseointegration in Clinical Dentistry. Chicago: Quintessence Publishing Company; 1985:187.

15. Albrektsson T, Eriksson AR, Friberg B, et al. Histologic investigations on 33 retrieved Nobelpharma implants. Clin Mater 1993;12:1.

16. Friberg B. Bone quality evaluation during implant placement. Thesis, Göteborg University, Göteborg, Sweden, 1995.

17. Albrektsson T, Åstrand P, Becker W, et al. Histologic investigations of failed dental implants. A retrieval analysis of four different implant designs. Clin Mater 1992;10:225.

18. Deporter DA, Watson PA, Pilliar RM, et al. A prospective clinical study in humans of an endosseous dental implant partially covered with a powder-sintered porous coating: 3- to 4-year results. Int J Oral Maxillofac Implants 1996;11:87.

19. De Bruyn H, Collaert B, Lindén U, Flygare L. A comparative study of the clinical efficacy of Screw Vent implants versus Brånemark fixtures, installed in a periodontal clinic. Clin Oral Implants Res 1992;3:32.

20. Wennerberg A, Albrektsson T, Andersson B. Design and surface characteristics of 13 commercially available oral implant systems. Int J Oral Maxillofac Implants 1993;8:622.

21. Malmqvist JP, Sennerby L. Clinical report on the success of 47 consecutively placed Core-Vent implants followed from 3 months to 4 years. Int J Oral Maxillofac Implants 1990;5:53.

22. Johansson C. On tissue reactions to metal implants. Thesis, Göteborg University, Göteborg, Sweden, 1991.

23. Johansson CB, Albrektsson T, Ericson LE, Thomsen P. A quantitative comparison of the cell response to commercially pure titanium and Ti-6A1-4V implants in the abdominal wall of rats. J Mater Sci Mater Med 1992;3:126.

24. Ektessabi AM, Otsuka T, Tsuboi Y, et al. Application of micro beam pixe for detection of titanium ion release from dental and orthopaedic implants. Int J PIXE 1994;4:81.

25. Ektessabi AM, Otsuka T, Tsuboi Y, et al. Preliminary experimental results on mapping of the elemental distribution of the organic tissues surrounding titanium-alloy implants. Nucl Instrum Methods Phys Res B 1996;109/110:278.

26. Thompson GJ, Puleo DA. Ti-6A1-4V ion solution inhibition of osteogenic cell phenotype as a function of differentiation time-course in vitro. Biomaterials 1996;17:1949.

27. Pflüger G, Plenk H Jr, Böhler N, Grundschober F, Schider S. Bone reaction to porous and grooved stainless steel, tantalum and niobium implants. In Winter GD, Gibbons DF, Plank H Jr (eds): Biomaterials. New York: John Wiley & Sons; 1980:45.

28. Plenk H Jr, Pflüger G, Böhler N, Gottsauner-Wolff F, Grundschober F, Schider S. Long-term anchorage of cementless tantalum and niobium femoral stems in canine hip-joint replacement. In Ducheyne P, van der Perre G, Aubert AE (eds): Biomaterials and Biomechanics. Amsterdam: Elsevier Science; 1984:61.

29. Johansson CB, Hansson HA, Albrektsson T. Qualitative interfacial study between bone and tantalum, niobium or commercially pure titanium. Biomaterials 1990;11:277.

30. Johansson C, Albrektsson T. A removal torque and histomorphometric study of commercially pure niobium and titanium implants in rabbit bone. Clin Oral Implant Res 1991;2:24.

31. Cook SD, Thomas KA, Kay JF, Jarcho M. Hydroxyapatite-coated titanium for orthopedic implant applications. Clin Orthop 1988;232:225.

32. Hayashi K, Uenoyama K, Matsuguchi N, Sugioka Y. Quantitative analysis of in vivo tissue responses to titanium-oxide- and hydroxyapatite-coated titanium alloy. J Biomed Mater Res 1991;25:515.

33. Lemons JE. Hydroxyapatite coatings. Clin Orthop 1988;235:220.

34. Gottlander M. On hard-tissue reactions to hydroxyapatite-coated titanium implants. Thesis, University of Göteborg, Göteborg, Sweden, 1994.

35. Gottlander M, Albrektsson T. Histomorphometric studies of hydroxylapatite-coated and uncoated CP titanium threaded implants in bone. Int J Oral Maxillofac Implants 1991;6:399.

36. Gottlander M, Albrektsson T, Carlsson LV. A histomorphometric study of unthreaded hydroxyapatite-coated and titanium-coated implants in rabbit bone. Int J Oral Maxillofac Implants 1992;7:485.

37. Gottlander M, Albrektsson T. Histomorphometric analyses of hydroxyapatite-coated and uncoated titanium implants. The importance of the implant design. Clin Oral Implant Res 1992;3:71.

38. Gottlander M, Johansson CB, Albrektsson T. Short- and long-term animal studies with a plasma-sprayed calcium phosphate-coated bone implant. Clin Oral Implant Res (in press).

39. Johnson BW. HA-coated dental implants: long-term consequences. Calif Dental Assoc J 1992;20:33.

40. Wheeler SL. Eight-year clinical retrospective study of titanium plasma-sprayed and hydroxyapatite-coated cylinder implants. Int J Oral Maxillofac Implants 1996;11:340.

41. Quirynen M, Naert I, van Steenberghe D, Duchateau L, Darius P. Periodontal aspects of Brånemark and IMZ implants supporting overdentures: a comparative study. In Laney WR, Tolman DE (eds): Tissue Integration in Oral, Orthopedic, and Maxillofacial Reconstruction. Chicago: Quintessence Publishing Company; 1990:80.

42. Dietrich U, Wellman O, Wagner W. Nachuntersuchungen von IMZ implantaten Typ I und Typ II. Z Zahanärztl Implantol 1991;7:221.

43. Richter EJ, Jovanovic SA, Spiekermann H. Rein Implantatgetragene Brücken: eine Alternative zur Verbundbrücke? Z Zahnärztl Implantol 1990;6:137.

44. Schramm-Scherer B, Behneke N, Reiber Th, Tetsch P. Röntgenologische Untersuchungen zur Belastung von IMZ implantaten im Zahnlosen Unterkiefer. Z Zahnärztl Implantol 1989;5:185.

45. Flemmig TF, Höltje WG. Periimplantäre Mukosa und Knochen bei Titanimplanten. Die Rolle von Plaque, Zahnstein, Befestigter Gingiva und Suprakonstruktion. Z Zahnärztl Implantol 1989;5:185.

46. Dietrich U, Wagner W. Zur frage des Knochenabbaus bein IMZ-implantaten. Z Zahnärztl Implantol 1992;8:240.

47. Dietrich U, Lippold R, Dirmeier Th, Behneke N, Wagner W. Statistische Ergebnisse zur Implantatprognose am Beispiel von 2017 IMZ-implantaten unterschiedlicher Indikation der letzten 13 Jahre. Z Zahnärztl Implantol 1993;9:9.

48. Adell R, Lekholm U, Rockler B, Brånemark P-I. A 15-year study of osseointegrated implants in the treatment of the edentulous jaw. Int J Oral Surg 1981;10:387.

49. Adell R, Lekholm U, Rockler B, et al. Marginal tissue reactions at osseointegrated titanium fixtures. I. A 3-year longitudinal prospective study. Int J Oral Maxillofac Surg 1986;15:39.

50. Lekholm U, Adell R, Lindhe J, et al. Marginal tissue reactions at osseointegrated titanium fixtures. II: A cross-sectional retrospective study. Int J Oral Maxillofac Surg 1986;15:53.

51. Cox JF, Zarb GA. The longitudinal clinical efficacy of osseointegrated dental implants: a 3-year report. Int J Oral Maxillofac Implants 1987;2:91.

52. Albrektsson T, Dahl E, Enbom L, et al. Osseointegrated oral implants. A Swedish multicenter study of 8139 consecutively inserted Nobelpharma implants. J Periodontol 1988;59:287.

53. Chaytor DV, Zarb GA, Schmitt A, Lewis DW. The longitudinal effectiveness of osseointegrated dental implants. The Toronto Study: bone level changes. Int J Periodontics Restorative Dent 1991;11:112.

54. Behneke A, Behneke N, Wagner W. Klinische Ergebnisse mit transgingival inserierten enossealen Implantaten (Bonefit-System). Z Zahnärztl Implantol 1992;8:97.

55. Williams DF. Biocompatibility: performance in the surgical reconstruction of man. Interdisc Sci Rev 1990;15:20.

56. Meyle J, Gültig K, Wolburg H, von Recum AF. Fibroblast anchorage to microtextured surfaces. J Biomed Mater Res 1993;27:1553.

57. Boyan BD, Hummert TW, Dean DD, Schwartz Z. Role of material surfaces in regulating bone and cartilage cell response. Biomaterials 1996;17:137.

58. Wong M, Eulenberger J, Schenk R, Hunziker E. Effect of surface topology on the osseointegration of implant materials in trabecular bone. J Biomed Mater Res 1995;29:1567.

59. Wennerberg A, Albrektsson T, Andersson B. An animal study of c.p. titanium screws with different surface topographies. J Mater Sci Mater Med 1995;6:302.

60. Wennerberg A, Albrektsson T, Andersson B. Bone tissue response to commercially pure titanium implants blasted with fine and coarse particles of aluminum oxide. Int J Oral Maxillofac Implants 1996;11:38.

61. Wennerberg A, Albrektsson T, Lausmaa J. Torque and histomorphometric evaluation of c.p. titanium screws blasted with 25- and 75-microns-sized particles of A1203. J Biomed Mater Res 1996;30:251.

62. Friberg B, Jemt T, Lekholm U. Early failures in 4,641 consecutively placed Brånemark dental implants: a study from stage 1 surgery to the connection of completed prostheses. Int J Oral Maxillofac Implants 1991;6:142.

63. Sundén S, Gröndahl K, Gröndahl H-G. Accuracy and precision in the radiographic diagnosis of clinical instability in Brånemark dental implants. Clin Oral Implants Res 1995;6:220.

64. Friberg B, Sennerby L, Roos J, Lekholm U. Identification of bone quality in conjunction with insertion of titanium implants. A pilot study in jaw autopsy specimens. Clin Oral Implants Res 1995;6:213.

65. Olivé J, Aparicio C. Periotest method as a measure of osseointegrated oral implant stability. Int J Oral Maxillofac Implants 1990;5:390.

66. Teerlinck J, Quirynan M, Darius P, van Steenberghe D. Periotest: an objective clinical diagnosis of bone apposition toward implants. Int J Oral Maxillofac Implants 1991;6:55.

67. Manz MC, Morris HF, Ochi S. An evaluation of the Periotest system. I: Examiner reliability and repeatability of readings. Dental Implant Clinical Group (Planning Committee). Implant Dent 1992;1:142.

68. van Steenberghe D, Quirynen M. Reproducibility and detection threshold of peri-implant diagnostics. Adv Dent Res 1993;7:191.

69. van Steenberghe D, Tricio J, Naert I, Nys M. Damping characteristics of bone to implant interfaces. A clinical study with the Periotest device. Clin Oral Implant Res 1995;6:31.

70. Carr AB, Papazoglou E, Larsen PE. The relationship of Periotest values, biomaterial, and torque to failure in adult baboons. Int J Prosthodont 1995;8:15.

71. Schulte W, Lucas D, Mühlbradt L, et al. Periotest: ein neues Verfahren und gerät zur Messung der Function des parodontiums. Zahnärtzl Mitt 1983;73:1129.

72. Derhami K, Wolfaardt JF, Faulkner G, Grace M. Assessment of the Periotest device in baseline mobility measurements of craniofacial implants. Int J Oral Maxillofac Implants 1995;10:221.

73. Elias JJ, Carollo JS, Brunski JB, Scarton HA. Noninvasive method for measuring the integrity of implant-tissue interfaces. Bioengineering Division, American Society of Mechanical Engineering 1993;24:327.

74. Elias JJ, Carollo JP, Scarton HA, Brunski JB. Comparison of shock absorption of Brånemark and IMZ implants in vitro (abstract). J Dent Res 1992;71:115.

75. Meredith N, Alleyne D, Cawley P. Quantitative determination of the stability of the implant-tissue interface using resonance frequency analysis. Clin Oral Implants Res 1996;7:261.

76. Meredith N, Shagaldi F, Alleyne D, Sennerby L, Cawley P. The application of resonance frequency measurements to study the stability of titanium implants during healing in the rabbit tibia. Clin Oral Implant Res (in press).

77. Meredith N, Book K, Friberg B, Jemt T, Sennerby L. Resonance frequency measurements of implant stability in-vivo: a cross-sectional and longitudinal study of resonance frequency measurements on implants in the edentulous and partially dentate maxilla. Clin Oral Implant Res (in press).

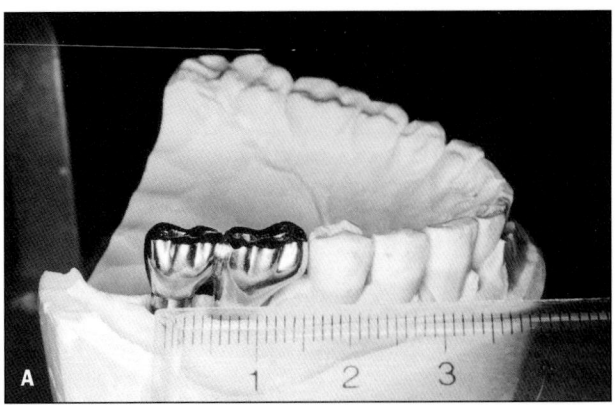

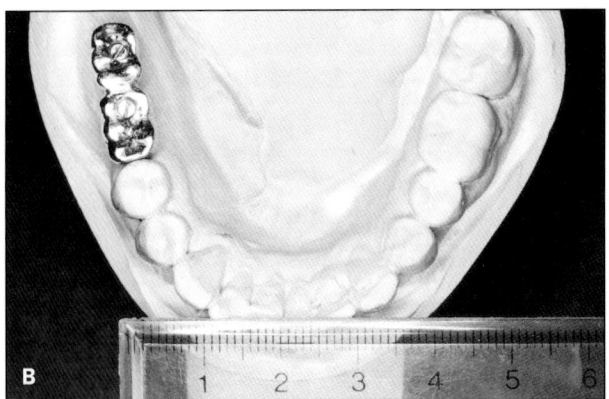

Fig 2-2. *A,* Partial prosthesis in the molar mandibular region. *B,* Occlusal view of same case pictured in *(A). C,* Problem formulation: find loadings on implants 1 and 2 when force P acts at point Q. *D,* Problem simplification: three-dimensional to two-dimensional. *E,* Problem simplification: ball-and-socket joints at bridge-implant connections. *F,* Solution of a representative two-dimensional rigid-body static-equilibrium problem.

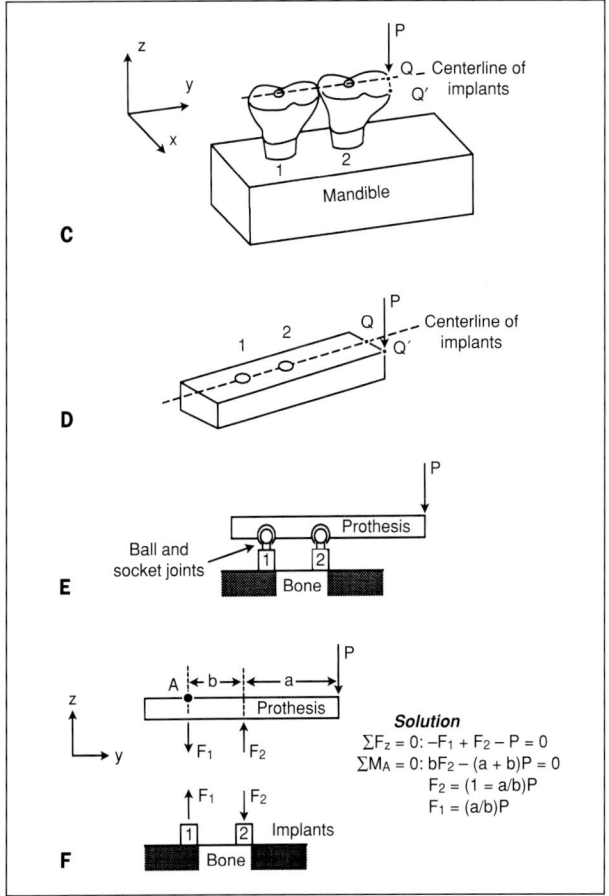

Another way to analyze the above case would be to apply the 1983 model of Skalak.[4] However, this model was developed originally to solve the more general problem of predicting vertical and horizontal force components on more than two abutments supporting a rigid prosthesis (Fig 2-3). Like the seesaw model, the Skalak model assumes that the bridge-implant connections are ball-and-socket joints, which can transmit forces but not moments. The Skalak model assumes that each abutment acts like a spring with a known axial spring constant. The Skalak model has been used to analyze fully edentulous cases. It is useful in developing guidelines for how many implants to use and where to place the implants.[5]

However, it is important to appreciate how two seemingly minor changes to the original partially edentulous case create difficulties in using the seesaw and 1983 Skalak models. First, suppose that the

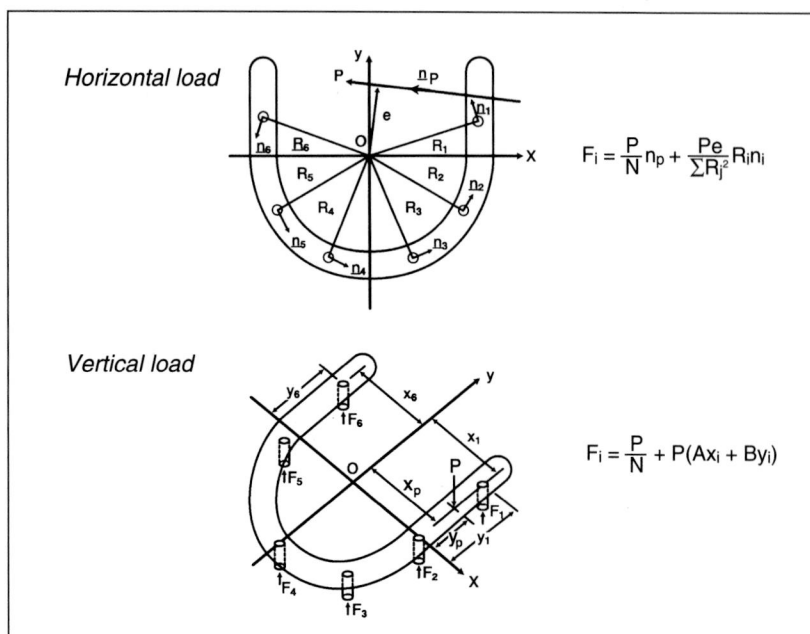

Fig 2-3. The Skalak model can predict the horizontal and vertical force components on each abutment when the prosthesis is loaded by horizontal and vertical forces, P_h and P_v, respectively. (From Brunski JB, Skalak R. Biomechanical considerations. In Worthington P, Brånemark P-I [eds]: Advanced Osseointegration Surgery: Applications in the Maxillofacial Region. Chicago: Quintessence Publishing Company; 1992;15. By permission of publisher.)

Horizontal load

$$F_i = \frac{P}{N}n_p + \frac{Pe}{\sum R_j^2}R_i n_i$$

Vertical load

$$F_i = \frac{P}{N} + P(Ax_i + By_i)$$

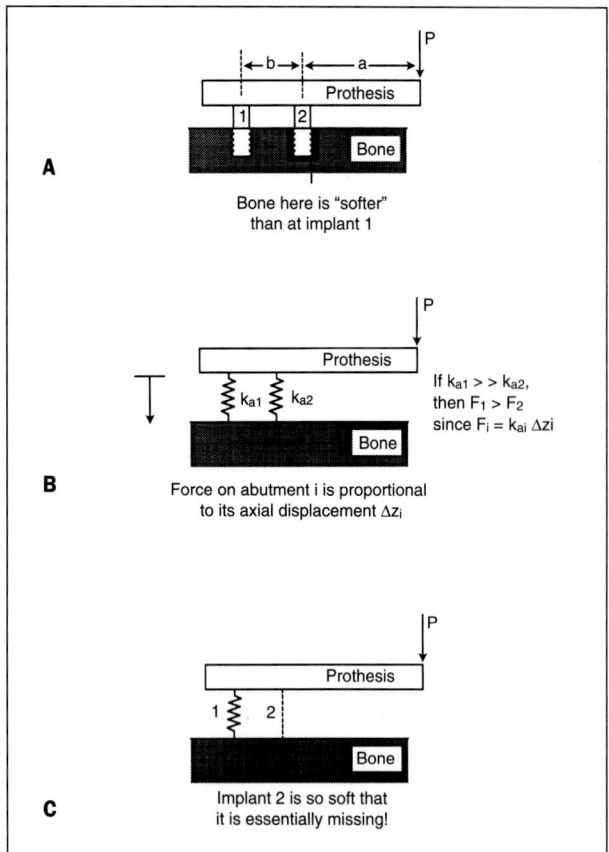

Fig 2-4. *A,* Implant 1 is in normal-stiffness bone, but implant 2 has a soft interface. *B,* Implants 1 and 2 are idealized as springs; axial force in a spring is proportional to its deflection Δz through the spring constant k_a. *C,* Implant 2's interface is so soft that it carries essentially no load.

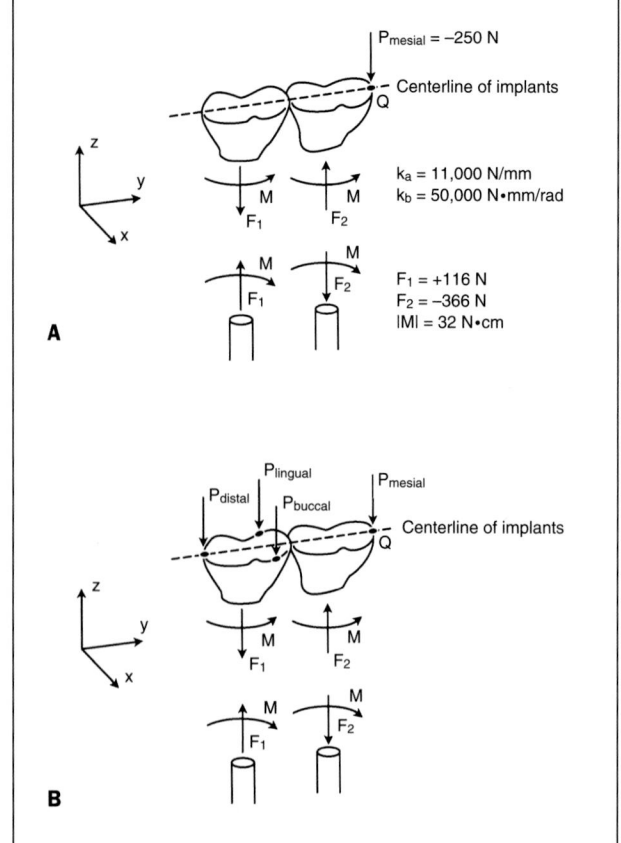

Fig 2-5. *A,* Predictions from the Brunski and Hurley (BH) model for P = −250 N at point Q; k_a = 11,000 N/mm, k_b = 50,000 N·mm/rad. *B,* Axial forces may act at various points on the prosthesis (see Fig 2-6 for results).

Fig 2-6. Axial forces and moments on implants 1 and 2 predicted by the Brunski and Hurley model when the prosthesis is loaded at mesial, distal, buccal, and lingual locations as shown in Figure 2-5*B*. (Modified from Brunski and Hurley. Implant-supported partial prostheses: biomechanical analysis of failed cases. In Hochmuth RM, Langrana NA, Hefzy MS (eds): Proceedings of the 1995 Bio-engineering Conference. Vol. 29. New York: American Society of Mechanical Engineers;1995:447. By permission of publisher.)

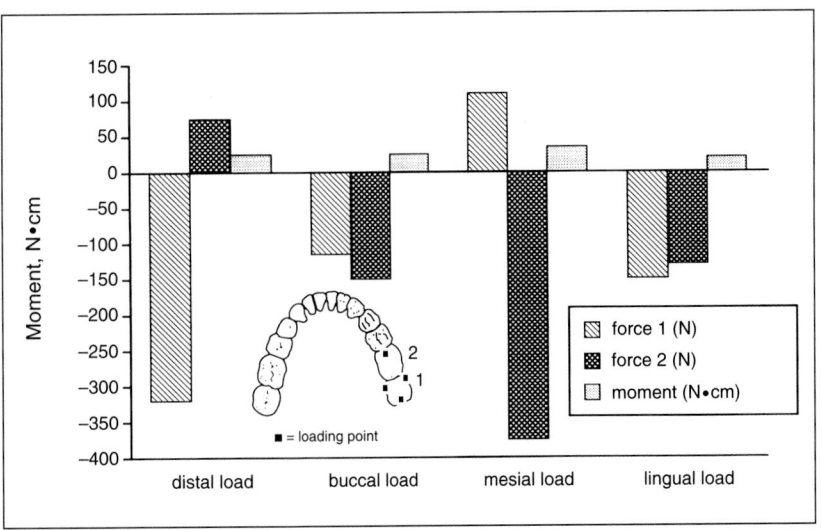

downward force P acts at a point Q′ rather than Q, where Q′ is not exactly on the centerline joining the two implants (Fig 2-2*C*). As a second complication, suppose that implant 2 is surrounded by soft (lower stiffness) bone compared with the bone around implant 1 (Fig 2-4*A*).

For loading at Q′ rather than Q, a little thought will convince the reader that the bridge will be unstable if connected to the implants by ball-and-socket joints. This is because ball-and-socket joints can support forces but not moments; such joints would not prevent the bridge from tipping about the centerline joining the two implants.

If abutment 2 was much softer than abutment 1, we could solve this problem approximately by using common sense and intuition. For example, Figure 2-4*B* idealizes the abutments as two springs having different spring constants. If k_{a1} is much larger than k_{a2}, one can imagine that abutment 1 would essentially do all the work when the bridge is loaded by the force P, as shown (Fig 2-4*C*). (This assumes that abutment 1 can support a moment.)

The point is that neither the seesaw model nor the 1983 Skalak model accounts for the two complications noted above. However, other engineering models can account for different sorts of bridge-implant connections and different abutment stiffnesses. For example, the 1993 model by Skalak, Brunski, and Mendelson (SBM)[6] allows for different axial stiffnesses among the abutments while still assuming ball-and-socket joints at the bridge-abutment connections. The 1995 Morgan and James (MJ)[7] model assumes built-in bridge-implant connections that can withstand a moment as well as

force under horizontal or vertical loading of the prosthesis. The 1995 Brunski and Hurley (BH)[8] model combines certain aspects of the SBM and MJ models to analyze forces and moments on variable-stiffness implants supporting a bridge that is loaded vertically.

To illustrate how these newer models differ from the seesaw and Skalak models, note that the BH model predicts forces and a moment on abutments 1 and 2 in the partially edentulous case that is under discussion (Fig 2-5*A*). For a vertically downward force P = –250 N at point Q, the BH model predicts F_2 = –366 N (compression), F_1 = +116 N (tension), and a moment of magnitude 32 N·cm on abutments 1 and 2. For comparison, the seesaw model predicts F_2 = –468 N and F_1 = +218 N.

The newer BH model can also be used to explore how the forces and moments on abutments 1 and 2 depend on the point of action of the downward force P (see various loading points in Fig 2-5*B*). For example, a distal versus mesial loading of the prosthesis by –250 N completely reverses the signs of the forces on abutments 1 and 2, while the magnitude of the moment stays about the same (Fig 2-6). This means that the two implants can experience quite different axial loads—sometimes tensile, sometimes compressive—depending on where the force P acts on the prosthesis. In turn, the interfacial bone also is loaded differently, depending on where P acts.

With regard to different axial stiffness of abutments, the SBM and BH models allow each abutment to have a different axial stiffness, k_a. As suggested previously, the meaning of axial stiffness (k_a)

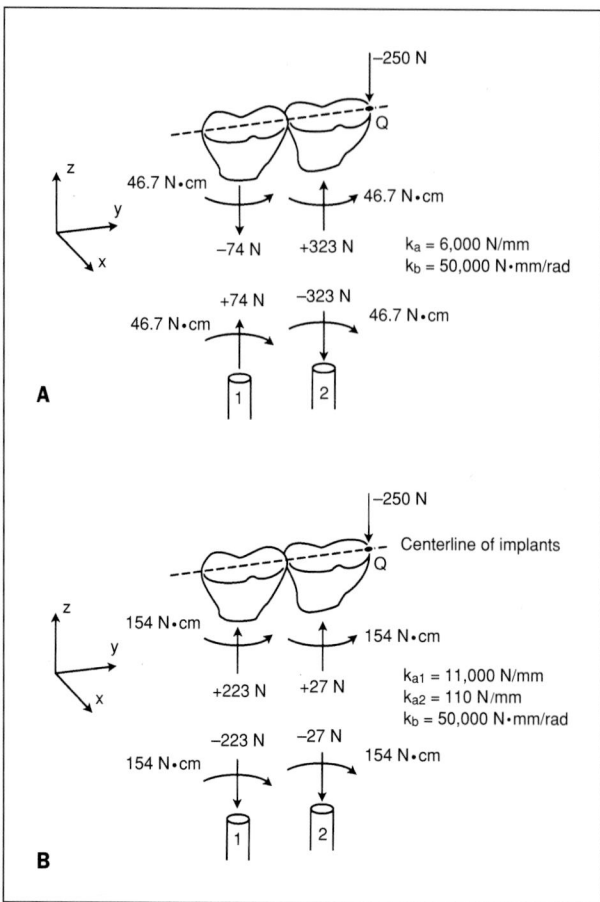

Fig 2-7. *A,* Predictions from the Brunski and Hurley (BH) model for the prosthesis loaded at point Q: k_a = 6,000 N/mm, k_b = 50,000 N·mm/rad. *B,* Predictions from the BH model for the prosthesis loaded at point Q: k_{a1} = 11,000 N/mm, k_{a2} = 110 N/mm, k_b = 50,000 N·mm/rad.

comes from modeling an abutment as a spring whose axial displacement Δz is linearly proportional to the axial force F in the equation $F_i = k_{ai} \Delta z_i$ (Fig 2-4*B*). Some engineering models also permit an abutment to have a bending stiffness, k_b, which is a constant relating bending moment to angular deflection (for more details, see Morgan and James.[7] The BH model combines parts of the MJ and SBM models to account for axial (k_a) and bending (k_b) stiffnesses of abutments supporting a rigid bridge loaded by a vertical force.

Abutment stiffness values can make a large difference in the predicted forces and moments on the bridge abutments. For instance, in our partially edentulous case, if the axial stiffnesses of abutments 1 and 2 remain equal but are decreased from 11,000 N/mm to 6,000 N/mm, while the bending stiffness remains at 50,000 N·mm/radian,

then the abutment loadings decrease to F_2 = –323 N and F_1 = +74 N, while the moment on each abutment increases to 46.7 N·cm (Fig 2-7*A*). These results compare with F_2 = –366 N, F_1 = +116 N, and M = 32 N·cm from the first BH simulation (Fig. 2-5*A*).

As another example, if abutments 1 and 2 do not have the same axial stiffness—e.g., abutment 2 is softer than abutment 1, k_{a1}/k_{a2} = 100, then the predicted loadings are F_2 = –27 N, F_1 = –223 N, and M = 154 N·cm (Fig 2-7*B*). These results differ substantially from those in previous simulations. Moreover, if the stiffness ratio is increased still further to k_{a1}/k_{a2} = 1,000, then abutment 1 shoulders about 90% of the total bite force and a correspondingly large bending moment while abutment 2 hardly supports any load. This confirms our commonsense, intuitive solution of this situation; in the limit of an infinitely small stiffness of abutment 2 (k_{a2} = 0), abutment 1 does all the work (Fig 2-4*C*).

All of the engineering models discussed so far (i.e., seesaw, Skalak, SBM, MJ, BH) assume that the prosthesis is infinitely rigid or undeformable. While at first glance this may appear to be a reasonable assumption for many prostheses, especially those made from metals and ceramics, it is conceivable that some actual prostheses are not infinitely rigid. For example, some clinicians have used all-acrylic or metal-backed acrylic bridges in fully edentulous cases.[9] However, tests of such bridges indicate that neither type of bridge behaves as an infinitely rigid structure (Fig 2-8).[10] In general, the rigidity of a bridge in bending or torsion depends on the elastic modulus of the bridge material and the bridge's size and shape.

To account for bridge deformability in intraoral or craniofacial cases of implants, one approach is to use computer simulation methods such as finite element analysis (FEA). An FE model can simulate the size, shape, and material properties of the prosthesis, implants, and bone. As an example of what can be accomplished with FEA, the three-dimensional FE model in Figure 2-9[11] simulates the two-implant partially edentulous case that we have been discussing. As with all models, the FE model has many assumptions that have to be evaluated against reality and the goals of the analysis. For example, this FE model considers only a 30-mm-long segment of the patient's mandible. It assumes that the segment is rigidly supported at each end and has an elliptical cross section with 2-mm-thick cortices. It also assumes that the mandibular bone is homogeneous, linear elastic, and

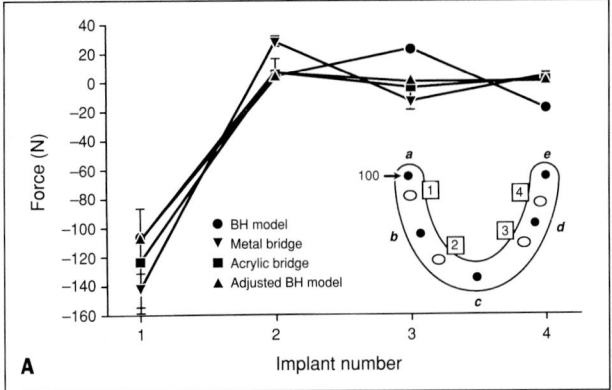
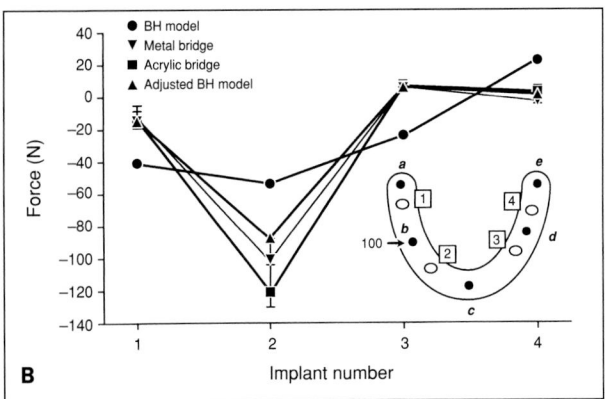

Fig 2-8. Comparison between measured and predicted forces on implants supporting an all-acrylic or a metal-backed acrylic bridge(10). The disagreement between theory and experiment arises in part from the fact that the bridges are deformable and not infinitely rigid. *A,* 100 N applied to the prosthesis at point **a**. *B,* 100 N applied to the prosthesis at point **b**. *BH,* Brunski and Hurley.

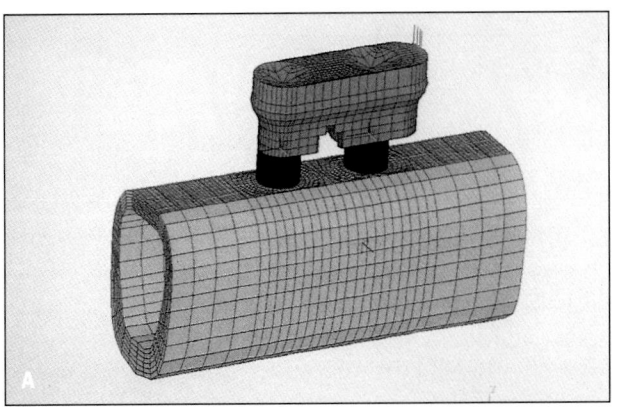
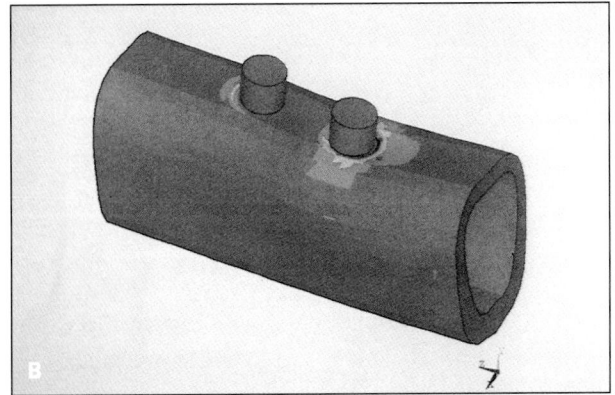

Fig 2-9. Finite element (FE) model of the two-implant partially edentulous case of Figure 2-2 (implant 2 is on the right). *A,* FE mesh of the problem. *B,* Selected FE results, here showing contours of high strain near the crestal region of implant 2 (on the right). (From Prabhu and Brunski.[11] By permission of the American Society of Mechanical Engineers.)

anisotropic (different elastic properties in different directions). Moreover, the model assumes that the implants are bonded to interfacial bone (i.e., no slippage at the bone-implant interface). Finally, the prosthesis is assumed to have the elastic properties and actual geometry of a precious metal alloy prosthesis.

Results from the FE model (Fig 2-9) indicate that for a downward –250 N load at the end of the mesial cantilever of the prosthesis, F_2 = –325 N (compression), F_1 = +75 N (tension), M2 = 30 to 50 N·cm, and M1 = 11 to 12 N·cm (the range in moment values is the result of approximations that have to be made when computing moments from the raw strain data in the FE model). Although the force values approximately agree with the results from one of our earlier BH simulations (e.g., Fig 2-5*B*), the FE

model predicts different moments on the two abutments. This is because the prosthesis is modeled as deformable in the FE model but infinitely rigid in the BH model. As the bridge's rigidity is increased in the FE model, there is closer agreement between the FE and BH models.

Summary of Models of the Partially Edentulous Case

Table 2-1 summarizes key results from the models that have been discussed. Generally, the seesaw model overestimates axial loading and neglects bending moments, but it has the advantage of being extremely simple. The Skalak, SBM, MJ, and BH

Table 2-1 *Summary of Predictions for the Two-Implant Case in Figure 2-2A and 2B*

Model*	F1, N	F2, N	M1, N·cm	M2, N·cm	Axial stiffness, k_a (N/mm)	Bending stiffness, k_b (N·mm/radian)
Seesaw	+218	−468	Not predicted	Not predicted	Not prescribed	Not prescribed
MJ, BH	+116	−366	32	32	11,000	50,000
MJ, BH	+74	−323	46.7	46.7	6,000	50,000
MJ, BH	−223	−27	154	154	k_{a1}/k_{a2} = 100, k_{a2} = 110	50,000
MJ, BH	−247	−2.87	163	163	k_{a1}/k_{a2} = 1,000, k_{a2} = 11	50,000
FE	+75	−325	11-12	30-50	†	†

*The cases listed under MJ, BH refer to the four examples discussed in the text, in which axial stiffness values differed among the cases.

†Stiffness values are not prescribed specifically as part of the finite element model.

BH, Brunski and Hurley; FE, finite element; MJ, Morgan and James.

models are all more complex than the seesaw model, but they are more powerful and can account for multiple implant support, horizontal and vertical loading, bending, and variable abutment stiffness. Although calculations for the seesaw, Skalak, SBM, MJ, and BH models can be accomplished with pencil and paper or personal computer, FE models generally require much more user expertise and computational power.

Interestingly, for our example partially edentulous case, the simpler models can give a reasonably accurate picture of implant loading; for some purposes, these simple models may be sufficient. However, if one wants to examine detailed stress and strain distributions in bone around the implants, then FEA is required. During the initial stages of case planning, any of the foregoing simple engineering models would be a good starting point for a biomechanical analysis. However, one problem is that at the case planning stage, when implants have not even been placed, the clinician generally does not know precisely what stiffness values or other properties should be used in any of the models. In time, a database will be established to supply the needed input data.

Interpreting Results From Biomechanical Models

After predicting forces and moments on bridge abutments, it remains to be determined whether the predicted loadings are safe or dangerous. (This is

the purpose of the evaluation step depicted in Figure 2-1, "Compare results with data. . . . ") The definition of safe versus dangerous loadings in a given case involves two topics: loading of prosthetic hardware and loading of the bone–implant interface.

Load Limits for Prosthetic Hardware

Prosthetic hardware includes the bridge, screw joints, abutment screws, and implants. For analyses of the loading limits of hardware in intraoral cases, several references provide useful data about the properties of casting alloys used in the frameworks[12]; fatigue and tensile properties of gold screws, abutment screws,[13,14] and implants;[15] bending limits for screw joints;[16,17] and misfit of prosthesis and abutments.[1,18,19] However, because differences exist between craniofacial and intraoral hardware, strength data for intraoral prosthetics will not apply necessarily to craniofacial devices. In any case, the in vivo loads on craniofacial hardware most likely will be significantly less than those on intraoral hardware; this statement is supported by load estimates developed later in this chapter.

There are only a few reports about the load limits of actual craniofacial prosthetics. For example, a study by Del Valle et al[20] reported tensile retention values in the range of 3 to 36 N for various types of ball-and-socket systems, magnet systems, and facial prosthetic adhesives. The authors noted that the mechanical retention systems (e.g., ball and socket, bars and clips) were superior to magnet or adhesive systems in situations where tensile and shear forces exist.

Load Limits of the Bone-Implant Interface

Defining safe versus dangerous load limits for bone in intraoral and craniofacial cases is the most difficult problem in biomechanical case planning. The following summary of research data will assist decision making in intraoral and craniofacial applications.

Design of Craniofacial and Intraoral Implants. A review of the literature shows that intraoral implants have been designed in a vast array of different sizes, shapes, and biomaterials. The particular design of the threaded pure titanium Brånemark implant that has been so successful in intraoral sites is not accidental; this design is predicated on several key principles, including the biomechanical principles discussed in upcoming sections.

With craniofacial implants, one difference is that craniofacial bone sites will differ from intraoral bone sites. The craniofacial bone will generally be thinner than in intraoral sites. The effective implant length in craniofacial sites is often only 3 or 4 mm. A notable difference between intraoral and craniofacial implants is that the craniofacial implant has a flange above the threaded portion. This feature affords initial stability of the implant during the healing period and especially helps prevent tilting of the implant under the action of lateral forces and moments. Also, the flange helps prevent accidental perforation of the implant through thin bone sites that may be encountered in the craniofacial anatomy.

Micromotion at the Bone-Implant Interface. For osseointegration to occur, a biomechanical prerequisite is that the implant must be nearly immobile in the healing tissue immediately after implant placement. Excessive relative motion, or micromotion, of an implant in healing bone will prevent proper bone regeneration (osseointegration) and instead stimulate repair, which in the case of oral implants is often characterized by formation of a substantial amount (e.g., 50 to several hundred microns) of noncalcified, collagenous, poorly vascularized, mechanically nonsupportive scar tissue at the interface.[21-23] The term "relative motion" means a shearing or normal (perpendicular) displacement of the implant surface relative to bone in which the implant is placed. In this context it is appropriate to use the term "osseointegration" to mean a bone-implant interface that has formed by the process of bone regeneration as opposed to repair.

It has been hypothesized that the mechanism underlying scar tissue development around implants experiencing micromotion involves mechanical damage to cells and vasculature that populate the healing site during early stages of bone healing. However, a key unresolved question about micromotion concerns the minimum amount of micromotion that stimulates formation of scar tissue. Studies in the 1970s[24,25] plus work by Søballe[26] and by Pilliar et al[27] indicate that a shearing type of micromotion on the order of 50 to 150 microns is sufficient to disrupt the early stages of normal bone regeneration. Notably, this limit is largely independent of the implant biomaterial; Søballe's work showed that both porous Ti and hydroxyapatite-coated porous Ti were surrounded by a noncalcified fibrous membrane after about 4 weeks of micromotion in dog tibia.

Scar tissue at a site of micromotion appears undesirable for biologic reasons, and it also seems unfavorable biomechanically. For instance, in a collection of stiff and soft abutments supporting a loaded bridge, load sharing among the abutments depends on the stiffness of each abutment, as discussed earlier. In a collection of soft and stiff abutments, the stiffer implants will tend to take most of the load. Because a fibrous tissue interface is considerably less stiff than an osseointegrated interface,[28] implants with fibrous tissue interfaces would tend not to take their fair share of the load when supporting a prosthesis, shunting most of the load to the stiffer abutments.[2]

In view of the negative effects of micromotion on interface development, the conclusion is to avoid biomechanical conditions that predispose an implant to micromotion. It is especially critical to avoid micromotion in the early period after implantation (e.g., days, weeks). The original loading protocol for Brånemark implants, which specified an undisturbed healing period,[29] minimizes the chance of implant-bone micromotion during the healing period.

Immediate Loading of Implants. If there is early loading of an intraoral or craniofacial implant in bone, must there be micromotion and subsequent formation of interfacial scar or fibrous tissue? The answer is not necessarily; several other factors, especially implant geometry and tightness of fit of the implant in the bony site, also influence what will happen.

For example, a polished, smooth-surfaced cylindric implant in an overdrilled hole in bone is much more likely to undergo significant micromotion when loaded than a screw-shaped implant placed in a carefully threaded bone site. This is because the screw-shaped implant interlocks firmly in the threaded site, whereas the smooth-surfaced cylinder is not well stabilized in the overdrilled (oversized) hole.

In principle, it should be possible to obtain osseointegration even in the presence of immediate loading, provided the implant remains immobile in bone during the early healing stages. Notably, experiments with immediately loaded implants support this idea. Corso et al[30] reported that immediately loaded screw-shaped oral implants with various surface coatings were osseointegrated after loading for 180 days in the premolar regions of canine mandibles. In clinical studies, Schnitman et al,[31] Bijlani and Lozada,[32] and Salama et al[33] reported that immediately loaded screw-shaped implants in human subjects showed mobility values and radiographic characteristics consistent with osseointegration. Similarly, in orthopedics[34] immediate loading of noncemented hip and knee prostheses can be followed by a direct bone-to-implant interface. Although the data are promising, it is too soon to conclude that immediate loading of intraoral and craniofacial implants is an acceptable protocol for the long term.

Stress Analysis and Load Limits of Bone-Implant Interfaces. If an oral or craniofacial implant has achieved osseointegration during immediate loading or after a period of no loading, does an osseointegrated interface have a load limit? How much can implants be loaded before they fail? To answer these questions, it is useful to summarize stress analysis and its role in single-cycle failure as well as failure after cyclic loading or fatigue.

In single-cycle and fatigue failure of any material, the type and magnitude of stress and strain in the material determines much of what happens. Therefore, it is important to be able to predict the stress and strain states in the material under the expected loading. In conventional stress analysis of materials, one computes the stresses and strains in the material and then interprets the values in terms of well-defined strength limits for the material, which are often listed in tables of material properties. In the case of single-cycle failure, relevant material properties include 0.2% yield strength, yield strain, ultimate strength, shear strength, compressive strength, and strain to fracture. For fatigue loading, relevant material properties include the fatigue limit.

Tabulated strength properties come from relatively simple, well-controlled mechanical tests in the laboratory, such as uniaxial tension or compression tests in single-cycle loading or rotating-beam

bending tests in the case of fatigue. One of the difficulties is that data from simple uniaxial or bending tests do not usually apply directly to complex real-world loading conditions. In fact, deriving multiaxial failure criteria for materials in complex loadings is a central problem in stress analysis, which goes beyond the scope of this chapter. Suffice it to say that for the special case of bone around a loaded implant, the stress analysis problem is multiaxial and quite complex, so theoretical predictions of failure modes in single-cycle or fatigue loading of bone are not at all straightforward. In view of these difficulties in the theoretical approach, it is more convenient to try to develop a database on failure by doing experiments with actual bone-implant systems, as suggested below.

Single-Cycle Overload of Bone-Implant Interfaces: Pull Out. From data on the mechanical behavior of bone per se,[35] it is known that many variables can affect the strength of bone. It follows that the same factors should influence the mechanical properties of the bone-implant interface. The single-cycle strength of the bone-implant interface depends on factors such as type of loading (tension, compression, bending, torsion); type of bone (cortical or cancellous); healing time; shape of the implant (threaded or not); diameter of the implant; surface coating and roughness of the implant; and surface area of the implant in contact with bone. Strength values also depend on whether the tests have been done on dead bone in the laboratory or on implants in living or freshly killed and retrieved bone.

P-I Brånemark et al[36] reported pull-out strengths of 1,000 N and 350 N for osseointegrated screw-shaped implants in dog mandibles and maxillae, respectively. These data were for an unspecified subgroup from among 67 screw implants that had healed in dogs for 6 to 8 weeks followed by a prosthetic loading period of up to 60 months. R. Brånemark et al[37] reported pull-out forces of about 1,550 N and lateral failure loads of about 210 N for osseointegrated Ti screw implants (3.7 × 6 mm) that had healed for 14 to 18 weeks in the proximal metaphyses of dog tibiae. They also reported a failure torque of 31 N·cm about the centerline of the implant.

Using hydroxyapatite-coated cylindric implants that had osseointegrated in dog mandibles for 15 weeks, Block and Kent[38] measured pull-out strengths as follows: for implant diameters in the range of 3 to 4 mm and lengths of 4 to 15 mm, pull-out values were 15 to 38 pounds (67 to 169 N), with the smaller values for 4-mm-long implants. For a given implant length, the pull-out strength increased modestly with increasing implant diameter.

Using freshly placed 7-mm-diameter Brånemark implants in the mid-diaphyseal cortices of dog tibiae, Hoshaw et al[39] measured pull-out forces of 1,450 ± 190 N for fresh-frozen tibiae having a mean cortical thickness of 2.6 ± 0.3 mm. In similar experiments with dead, wet bovine cancellous bone, Balon[40] found that the pull-out strength of Brånemark implants depended strongly on the apparent density of the bone sample (mass divided by sample volume as determined from external dimensions); pull outs could occur in low-density bone at forces as low as 100 to 300 N (Fig 2-10).

Single-Cycle Overload of Bone-Implant Interfaces: Torque Test.

Another common test of single-cycle interface strength has been the so-called torque-out test, as performed by Johansson and Albrektsson[41] in Sweden. In this test, a torque is applied in a reverse direction from that used to screw the implant into bone; a handheld torque gauge or similar instrument is used to apply and measure the torque. The maximum torque that the bone-interface can withstand is recorded when the implant breaks loose from the bone. For example, using 3.75-mm-diameter and 10-mm-long Ti screws in rabbit tibiae, Johansson and Albrektsson reported that torque values increased from 16.8 to 77 N·cm as the healing time increased from 1 to 6 months. Similar values have been reported for implants in baboons[42] and other species; R. Brånemark[37] presented an extensive summary of this type of measurement. Gotfredsen et al[43] reported larger torque-out values for TiO2-blasted (i.e., rough-surfaced) Ti screws in dog mandibles, namely 120 to 150 N·cm; presumably the larger values are partially related to the rough texture of the oxide-blasted screw surfaces.

Sullivan et al[44] used similar reverse torque methods to test Brånemark intraoral implants in human subjects as part of a program to develop an ad hoc clinical test of whether an implant was sufficiently integrated at the time of the second-stage surgery. They measured torque-to-failure values between 45 and 58 N·cm for three implants in one human volunteer.

Tjellström et al[45] appear to be the only group to have measured torque-to-failure values for craniofacial implants. Their failure torques were 26 to 60 N·cm (mean, 42.7 N·cm) for 3.75-mm-diameter and 4-mm-long Ti implants in human mastoid bone for 3 to 4 months.

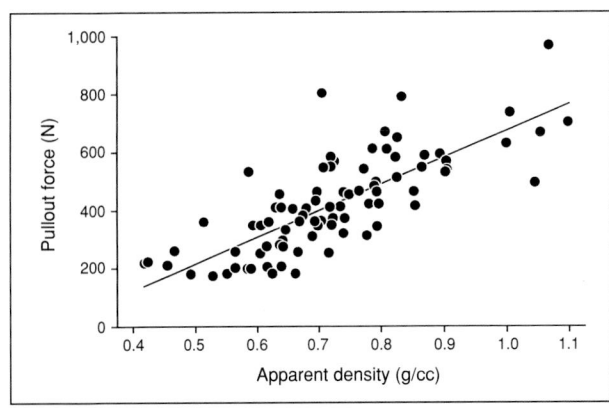

Fig 2-10. Correlation between pull-out strength (3.75 x 10-mm Brånemark implants) and apparent density of bovine trabecular bone in vitro.

Clinical Significance of Pull-Out and Torque Tests.

The clinical significance of these data is that they provide order-of-magnitude estimates for how much axial and lateral force an implant can withstand in vivo and likewise for torque about an implant's axis. Such data can be used along with the load predictions from engineering models discussed earlier to estimate safe versus dangerous axial loading limits of implants.

For example, axial pull-out force values of ≈ 1,000 N are up toward the high end, and perhaps even beyond the expected regimen of normal biting forces, depending of course on the patient's chewing habits and prosthetic situation. But pull-out values of 100 to 300 N, as measured for implants in low-density cancellous bone in vitro and in vivo and for cylindrically shaped hydroxyapatite-coated implants in dog mandibles, are definitely low compared with normal biting forces and related implant loading. To appreciate this fact, recall that the axial forces on implants in the two-implant case analyzed earlier were larger than 100 to 300 N.

With regard to the meaning of torque-to-failure data, torque about the long axis of an implant is not a common loading mode for most intraoral implants, except for the case of implants used for orthodontic anchorage. On the other hand, in craniofacial applications, torque about the long axis of the implant is more likely. This follows from the fact that many craniofacial prostheses are loaded by transverse rather than axial loads, as discussed in the examples at the end of the chapter.

Multicycle Failure (Fatigue) of the Interface.

Stress analysis of bone around implants is complicated theoretically and often impractical. As an alterna-

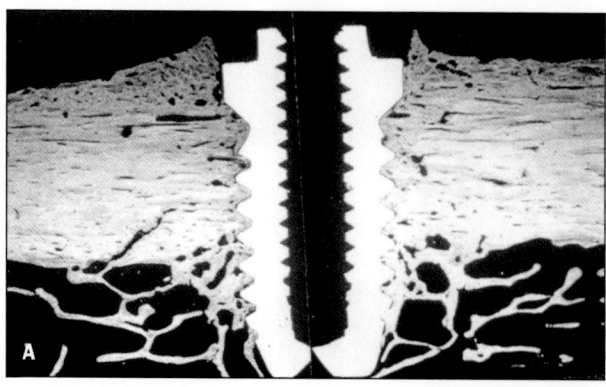 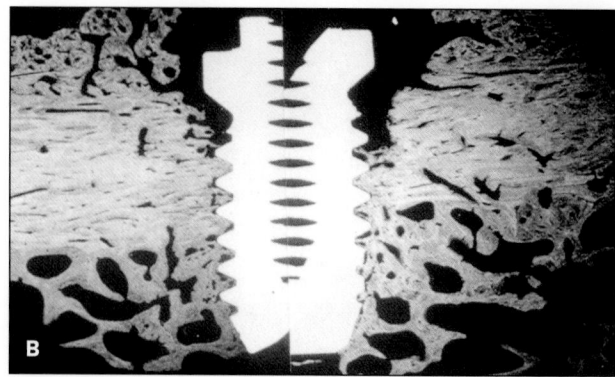

Fig. 2-11. Bone reaction around control *(A)* and loaded *(B)* Brånemark implants in a dog tibia model. The implants had healed for 1 year before any direct loading occurred. The loaded implant was subjected to cyclic axial tensile loading with a peak of 300 N; loading occurred 500 times/day for 5 consecutive days. These backscattered scanning electron micrographs were obtained from bone samples taken at 3 months after the end of the loading period. (From Hoshaw et al.[48] By permission of Quintessence Publishing Company.)

tive, fatigue tests on whole bone-implant specimens can provide direct evidence about the load-bearing capacity of the bone.

For example, using 3.75 × 7-mm implants in disks (2 mm thick × 18.3 mm diameter) of dead bovine plexiform bone, Hoshaw et al[39] reported a semilogarithmic relationship between the axial force amplitude on the implant and the number of cycles to failure (e.g., at 600 N, the number of cycles to failure was 100, whereas at 400 N force, the number of cycles to failure was about 10,000). The authors noted that the mechanism of interface failure involved accumulation of microscopic damage at stress concentrations in the bony interface (e.g., cracks and delaminations at notches of threads cut into the bone), followed eventually by macroscopic crack propagation throughout the specimen and complete fracture.

For implants in living bone, fatigue tests are much more complicated to conduct but ultimately more relevant because they can simulate the functioning of implants in typical patients and allow investigation of possible bone reaction to cyclic loading of the bone-implant interface. Unfortunately, there have been only a few controlled experimental studies to explore this important subject.

Brunski et al[46] subjected 3.75 × 7-mm Brånemark Ti implants to controlled axial loading in mandibles and long bones (radii) of mature beagle dogs. Five implants in healed mandibular premolar extraction sites received cyclic (square wave), axial compressive loading characterized by a peak force of 110 N; frequency, 0.5 cycles/second; and 500 cycles/day for 5

to 7 consecutive days. A group of control mandibular implants was not loaded. A loaded group of implants in radii received axial tensile loading with the same cyclic characteristics as the mandibular cases, except for a peak load of 50 N for two dogs and 100 N for four dogs. Histologic examination was done at 6 days (radii) and 20 days (mandibles). No statistically significant differences were found between histologic results from loaded and control groups in radial and mandibular cases, with one exception: there was slightly more modeling activity on the periosteal surface of mandibles with loaded implants. Generally, the levels of loading (50–110 N) were not sufficient to provoke any differences in bony response around loaded compared with control implants. However, a weak point of this study was a rather short time between implant loading and tissue analysis; it is now known that the remodeling cycle (sigma[47]) in dog bones is about 3 months, which represents the minimum time for bone to manifest a remodeling response, if one is to occur in reaction to loading.

Hoshaw et al[48] performed essentially the same type of in vivo fatigue experiment as Brunski et al,[46] but they used larger loads on the implants (300 N axial tension), a more uniform bony site (dog tibia), and waited longer (3 months, or about 1 sigma) before analyzing the bone for possible differences between loaded and control groups. They reported differences between loaded and control groups, including more bone loss at the crestal region of the loaded screws (Fig 2-11). In view of results from FE stress analyses and histometric measurements of the bony response, Hoshaw et al[48] concluded that their experiment supported the hypothesis that bone-implant interfaces can be overloaded during cyclic loading. Moreover, they suggested that the likely overload mechanism involved excessive strain in the bone (e.g., greater than bone's yield strain of about 0.7%), which, in turn, damaged cells, bone matrix, and vascular elements and stimulated local bone remodeling and modeling in an effort to repair the damage.

As indirect support for the theory by Hoshaw et al, there is a strong similarity between their findings and the pattern of crestal bone loss often reported in clinical cases of suspected overload.[49] Also, Isidor[50] reported results from an experiment on the loss of osseointegration caused by occlusal load of implants. He implanted five screw-type implants per mandible in four monkeys and allowed a 6-month undisturbed healing period. There were two implants in each lateral segment and one implant in the frontal area. In each animal a fixed partial prosthesis was mounted on the two implants in one of the lateral segments. The prosthesis was designed to be in supraocclusal contact with a maxillary splint that had been placed earlier. The prosthesis was deliberately designed to cause a lateral rather than axial excessive occlusal load on the implants. The implants supporting the prosthesis were cleaned once a week, whereas the other implants were never cleaned and had cotton ligatures placed crestally to promote plaque accumulation. Isidor found that 4.5 to 15.5 months after occlusal loading, five of eight implants with occlusal loading lost osseointegration, as judged by mobility and peri-implant radiolucency (Fig 2-12), but none of the implants with plaque accumulation lost osseointegration.

Clinical Reports of Overload. A typical problem attributed to biomechanical overload is so-called late failure, characterized by excessive bone loss after several years of implant function. In late failures, the bone–implant interface rather than the implant components is the weakest link. For example, in a retrospective study[51] of 69 patients, excessive marginal bone resorption (> 1 mm) after the first year of loading was correlated with implant overload. In another study,[52] most of the failures occurred soon after implant placement, especially when implants were placed in low-density, fat-infiltrated type IV bone in the maxilla. Rangert et al[53] studied a group of 39 patients in whom implants fractured often after bone loss due to resorption at the marginal (crestal)

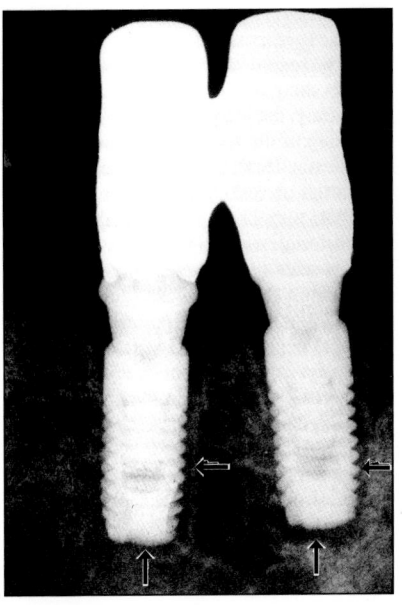

Fig 2-12. Radiographic evidence of loss of osseointegration around overloaded screw-shaped implants *(arrows),* as reported in a study in primates by Isidor.[50] (From Isidor.[50] By permission of Munksgaard International Publishers.)

region. Thirty-five of the fractures (90%) occurred in the posterior region of the jaw. Furthermore, 30 of the prostheses (77%) were supported by one or two implants and exposed to a combination of cantilever and other load-magnification factors plus bruxism and heavy chewing forces. The study concluded that partial prostheses supported by one or two implants of standard 3.75 mm diameter replacing missing posterior teeth were subjected to an increased risk of overload due to bending. Rangert et al[53] also noted that in the 5-year study by Lekholm et al,[54] the number of implants that failed after the start of loading was nearly equal to the number that failed during the early healing period. This differs from the results with full-arch prostheses, for which there are usually fewer failures after loading than before loading. Rangert et al[53] stated that in many instances partially edentulous cases are more susceptible to overload and that "overload-induced bone resorption seemed to precede implant fracture in a significant number of the patients."

As further support for the statements above, it is instructive to review the two-implant case shown in Figure 2-2. In this case, bone loss was seen around the crestal region of the mesial implant at 1 to 2 months after function started (Fig 2-13), and this was

29

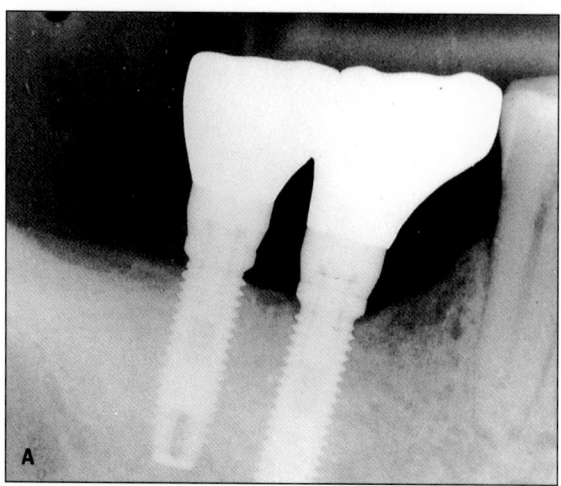
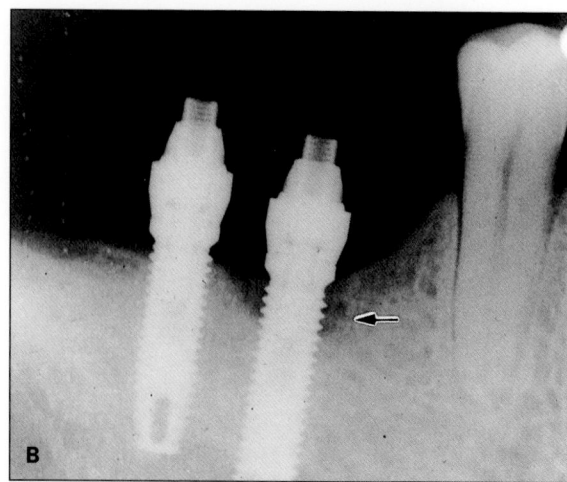

Fig 2-13. Clinical example of suspected overload of an implant. A, Radiographic appearance of the two Brånemark implants supporting the partial prosthesis already described in Figure 2-2. *B,* Radiolucency at the mesial implant. This implant also eventually fractured after about 2 months of function. Note the crestal bone loss *(arrow).* (From Prabhu and Brunski.[11] By permission of the American Society of Mechanical Engineers.)

followed by fracture of the mesial implant. Notably, during typical loading of the prosthesis, the FEA of this case (Fig 2-9) showed high strains (> 1%) at the crestal bone. Therefore, it is plausible that the crestal bone loss occurred in reaction to local damage to the bone, per the hypothesis of Hoshaw et al.[48]

Biomechanical Analysis of Typical Craniofacial Cases

To illustrate biomechanical models and treatment planning concepts in craniofacial cases, this section analyzes typical auricular, orbital, and midfacial prostheses described in the literature. In each of the cases, the selected loadings of the prosthesis are merely examples; many other situations could be explored, but the ones chosen illustrate the basic ideas.

Auricular Case, Two Implants[55]

In this case (Fig 2-14*A*), two titanium implants were used to support a metal framework that allowed a prosthetic ear to be clipped onto it by means of Hader clips. A biomechanical model of

the case seeks to predict the loadings on the two implants when a test load of magnitude 10 N is applied in the negative y-direction at a particular point on the framework (Fig 2-14*B*). We will consider a horizontal load in the plane of the prosthetic bar, perpendicular to the long axes of the two implants in the bone. Note that 10 N is used only as a nominal test load; no data are available on actual forces on this type of prosthesis in vivo. If actual forces become known, the results could be scaled accordingly.

The Skalak or BH model of this case predicts the implant loadings shown in Figure 2-14*B*. With reference to the coordinate system shown, both implants are loaded by x- and y-components of force. The y-component of force on implant 2 is slightly more than that on implant 1, whereas the x-components are equal. Another way to describe these results is to say that the x-components of force set up a counterclockwise couple-moment that is equal but opposite to the clockwise moment produced by the 10-N force acting at a distance from the line connecting the implants. The forces on the implants are quite small compared with any of the danger limits that have been mentioned in this chapter.

If, for the sake of discussion, implant 1 or 2 acted alone in this case, it would have to resist the entire

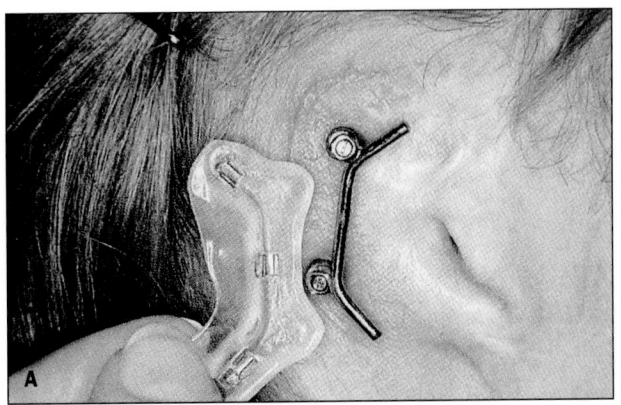
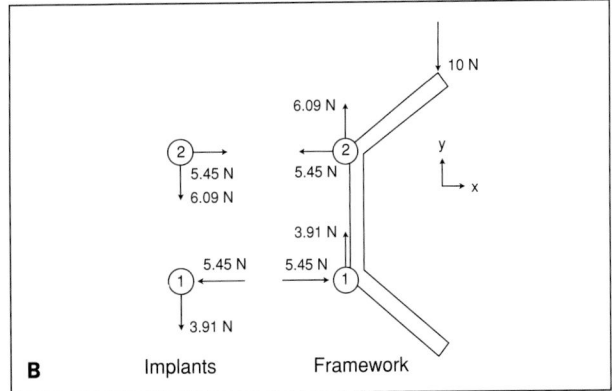

Fig 2-14. Auricular case. *A,* Two implants support a metal framework that can attach to an auricular prosthesis. *B,* Skalak model predictions of framework and abutment loading when a 10-N load acts in the negative y-direction at the point shown. (*A* from Tjellström et al.[55] By permission of Quintessence Publishing Company.)

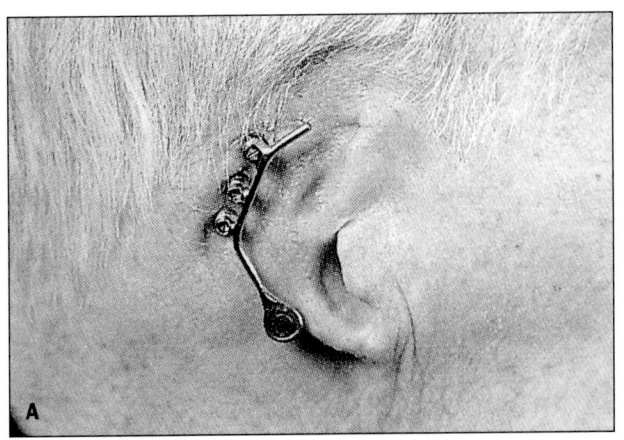
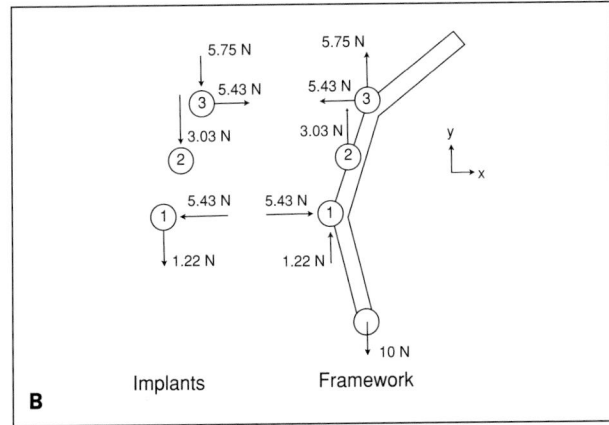

Fig 2-15. Auricular case. *A,* Three implants support a framework that attaches to an auricular prosthesis. *B,* Skalak model predictions of framework and abutment loading when a 10-N load acts in the negative y-direction at the point shown. (*A* from Thomas.[56] By permission of Quintessence Publishing Company.)

moment produced by the 10-N force. A ball-and-socket connection between bar and implant would not be able to resist such a loading, but the MJ model allows for a connection that could resist a moment about the long axis of the implant during horizontal loading of the bar. Depending on the exact geometry of this case, the moment on the implant could be as large as 10 N × 1 cm = 10 N·cm, which is about 25% of mean torque-out failure for implants in mastoid bone, as reported by Tjellström.[45] However, for the 10-N direction shown, the sense of the moment would actually tend to tighten the implant in the bone.

Auricular Case, Three Implants[56]

This auricular case (Fig 2-15*A*) resembles the first case except that three implants are used. For a 10-N test load applied in the horizontal plane (Fig 2-15*B*), the implant loads predicted by the Skalak or BH model are again rather small; none is larger than about 6 N, as in the first case. Again, there are no moments predicted about the axis of any implant; there are just x- and y-forces. Note that implant 2, the middle implant in this arrangement, does not see any x-component of force; this is because implants at positions 1 and 3 together supply the counterbalanc-

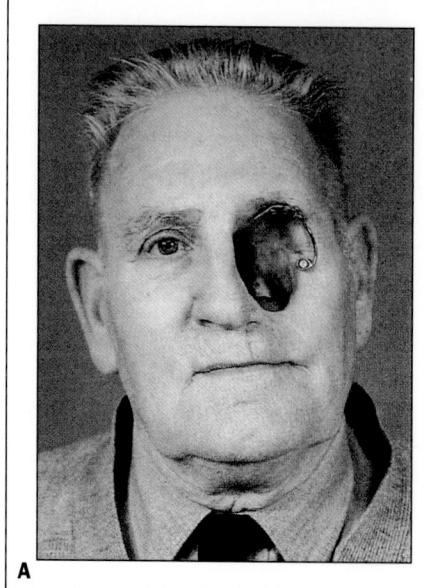
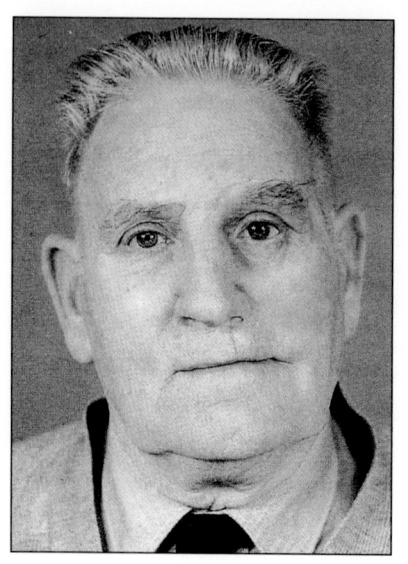

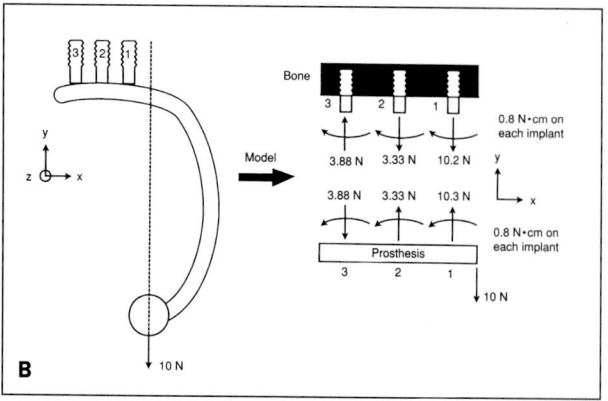

Fig 2-16. Orbital case. *A,* Three implants support a semicircular framework. *B,* Skalak model predictions of framework and abutment loading when a 10-N load acts in the negative y-direction at the point shown. (*A* from Thomas.[56] By permission of Quintessence Publishing Company.)

ing couple-moment on the framework to resist the moment from the applied 10-N force.

Orbital Case[56]

In this case (Fig 2-16*A*), three implants support a framework on which an orbital prosthesis is attached. To enable a simple analysis, we assume that the three implants are in a straight line and aligned parallel to one another in an x-y plane parallel to the page. The interimplant spacing is about 4 mm. The framework is assumed to be attached to the implants by joints that can support vertical forces and moments about an axis perpendicular to the plane of the page.

For a 10-N vertical load parallel to the axes of the implants, the BH model predicts different axial forces on each implant but the same moment of magnitude 0.8 N·cm (Fig 2-16*B*). The forces are tensile on the implants nearest the applied load, whereas implant 3 sees an axial compression. The force magnitude is 10.3 N on implant 1 nearest to the loading point of the prosthesis. As discussed earlier, none of these loadings on the implants appears large enough to cause concern, although no data on bone properties at this orbital site are readily available.

Midfacial Case[56]

To simplify analysis of this complicated case (Fig 2-17*A*), we assume that the three implants are parallel to one another and perpendicular to the x-y plane of the (infinitely rigid) framework. The

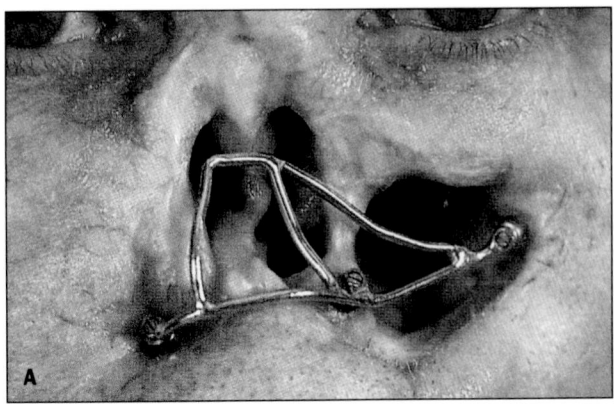

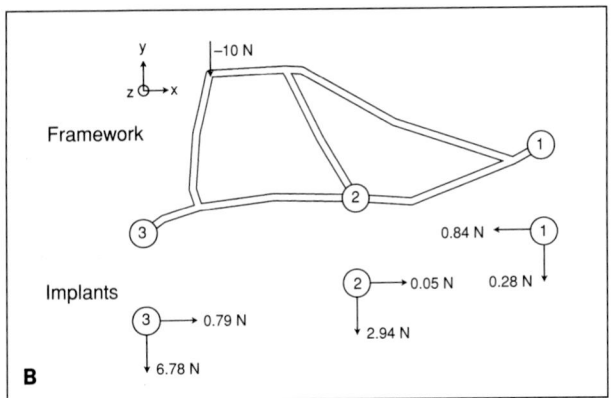

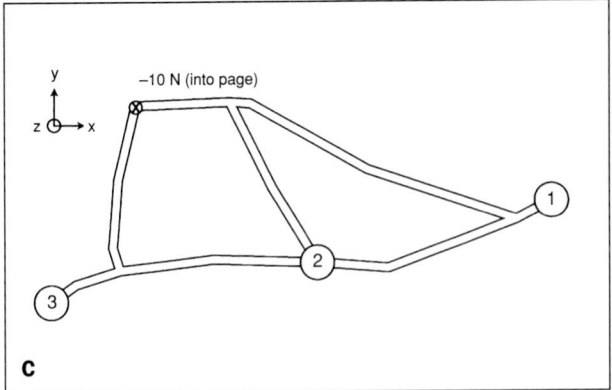

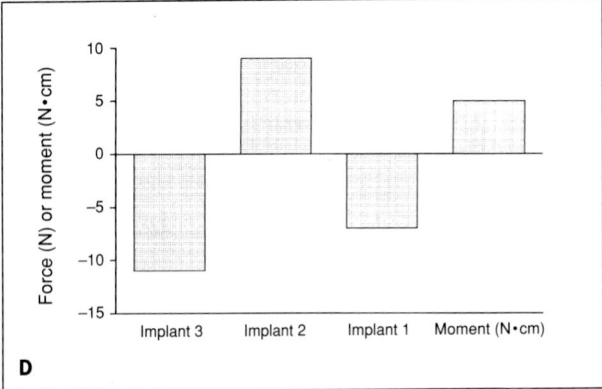

Fig 2-17. Midfacial case. *A,* Three implants support a framework for a midfacial prosthesis. *B,* x- and y-components of loading on the implants when a 10-N force acts on the framework in the negative y-direction at the point shown. *C,* Diagram showing a 10-N force acting on the framework in the negative z-direction (into the page) at the location shown. *D,* Forces and moments on implants 1, 2, and 3 for z-component loading of framework. (*A* from Thomas.[56] By permission of Quintessence Publishing Company.)

framework is loaded by a test load with two components: a horizontal force of 10 N in the x-y plane of the framework and a vertical force of 10 N in the negative z-direction, perpendicular to the framework.

As seen in Figure 2-17B, the BH model predicts that for horizontal loading only, implant 3 nearest to the loading point is loaded by the largest x- and y-components of force, whereas implants 1 and 2 see relatively inconsequential forces. For vertical loading of 10 N at *x* (Fig 2-17C), implant 2 is subjected to tensile loading whereas implants 1 and 3 see compressive forces (Fig 2-17D). This force distribution is consistent with the slightly staggered arrangement (noncollinear) of the implants, which tends to make the framework rotate about a line between the three

implants when the loading acts at *x*. According to the model, each implant is also subjected to a moment of magnitude 5.4 N·cm.

As with the other craniofacial cases that have been discussed, load levels in this midfacial case are small compared with typical loads with intraoral implants. Because the implant sizes are about the same as for intraoral implants, it is expected that these craniofacial cases will succeed biomechanically. However, until more is known about load-bearing capacities of craniofacial bone, it will remain difficult to evaluate the significance of the above-noted loading levels. A recent analysis[57] of an implant-supported bar for treating a midfacial case gives a good example of what can be accomplished with more extensive finite element computer techniques.

Conclusion

Based on research in biomechanics, it has been possible to synthesize the basic building blocks of a biomechanical approach to case planning. The engineering models and research database on safe versus dangerous loading of implants allow a clinician to anticipate and avoid potential problems with loading of implants. For those clinicians working with intraoral and craniofacial implants, it is likely that increasing use of this approach and additional research into some of the topics that still remain troublesome—such as the biologic significance of certain stress and strain states in the bone—will improve the health care of patients.

Acknowledgments

The authors thank Mr. J. A. Porter, MS, Department of Biomedical Engineering, Rensselaer Polytechnic Institute, for preparing the drawings in this chapter.

References

1. Brunski JB, Skalak R. Biomechanics of osseointegration and dental prostheses. In Naert I, van Steenberghe D, Worthington P (eds): Osseointegration in Oral Rehabilitation. London: Quintessence Publishing Company; 1993:133.

2. Brunski JB. Biomechanics of dental implants. In Block MS, Kent JN (eds): Endosseous Implants for Maxillofacial Reconstruction. Philadelphia: WB Saunders Company; 1995:22.

3. Rangert B, Jemt T, Jörneus L. Forces and moments on Brånemark implants. Int J Oral Maxillofac Implants 1989;4:241.

4. Skalak R. Biomechanical considerations in osseointegrated prostheses. J Prosthet Dent 1983;49:843.

5. Brunski JB. Biomechanical factors affecting the bone-dental implant interface. Clin Mater 1992;10:153.

6. Skalak R, Brunski JB, Mendelson M. A method for calculating the distribution of vertical forces among variable stiffness abutments supporting a dental prosthesis. In Langrana NA, Friedman MH, Grood ES (eds): Proceedings of the 1993 Bioengineering Conference. Vol. 24. New York: American Society of Mechanical Engineers; 1993:347.

7. Morgan MJ, James DF. Force and moment distributions among osseointegrated dental implants. J Biomech 1995;28:1103.

8. Hurley EP. Force and moment distribution among abutments supporting partial and full dental bridges: preload, positioning, and stiffness effects. M.S. Thesis, Rensselaer Polytechnic Institute, Troy, New York, 1995.

9. Balshi TJ, Wolfinger GJ. Conversion prosthesis: a transitional fixed implant-supported prosthesis for an edentulous arch—a technical note. Int J Oral Maxillofac Implants 1996;11:106.

10. Smerek J, Brunski JB, Wolfinger G, Winkelman R, Balshi T. Implant loading with all-acrylic vs. metal-supported-acrylic prostheses (abstract). J Dent Res (Special Issue) 1997;76:263.

11. Prabhu A, Brunski JB. Finite element analysis of a clinical case involving overload of an oral implant interface. In Chandran KB, Vanderby R Jr, Hefzy MS (eds): Proceedings of the 1997 Bioengineering Conference. Vol. 35. New York: American Society of Mechanical Engineers; 1997:575.

12. White GE Jr. Osseointegrated Dental Technology. London: Quintessence Publishing Company; 1993.

13. Patterson EA, Johns RB. Theoretical analysis of the fatigue life of fixture screws in osseointegrated dental implants. Int J Oral Maxillofac Implants 1992;7:26.

14. Jaarda MJ, Razzoog ME, Gratton DG. Ultimate tensile strength of five interchangeable prosthetic retaining screws. Implant Dent 1996;5:16.

15. Morgan MJ, James DF, Pilliar RM. Fractures of the fixture component of an osseointegrated implant. Int J Oral Maxillofac Implants 1993;8:409.

16. Rangert B, Gunne J, Sullivan DY. Mechanical aspects of a Brånemark implant connected to a natural tooth: an in vitro study. Int J Oral Maxillofac Implants 1991;6:177.

17. McGlumphy EA, Robinson DM, Mendel DA. Implant superstructures: a comparison of ultimate failure force. Int J Oral Maxillofac Implants 1992;7:35.

18. Smedberg JI, Nilner K, Rangert B, Svensson SA, Glantz SA. On the influence of superstructure connection on implant preload: a methodological and clinical study. Clin Oral Implants Res 1996;7:55.

19. Carr AB, Brunski JB, Hurley E. Effects of fabrication, finishing, and polishing procedures on preload in prostheses using conventional "gold" and plastic cylinders. Int J Oral Maxillofac Implants 1996;11:589.

20. Del Valle V, Faulkner G, Wolfaardt J, Rangert B, Tan HK. Mechanical evaluation of craniofacial osseointegration retention systems. Int J Oral Maxillofac Implants 1995;10:491.

21. Brunski JB, Moccia AF Jr, Pollack SR, Korostoff E, Trachtenberg DI. The influence of functional use of endosseous dental implants on the tissue-implant interface. I. Histological aspects. J Dent Res 1979;58:1953.

22. Brunski JB, Sumner R, Hench LL, Lemons JE, Pilliar RM. Influence of biomechanical factors at the bone-biomaterial interface. In Davies JE (ed): The Bone-Biomaterial Interface. Toronto: University of Toronto Press; 1991:391.

23. Pilliar RM, Niznick G, Bonfield W, Parr J, Sauk JJ. Quantitative evaluation of the effect of movement at a porous coated implant-bone interface. In Davies JE (ed): The Bone-Biomaterial Interface. Toronto: University of Toronto Press; 1991:380.

24. Brunski JB. The influence of force, motion, and related quantities on the response of bone to implants. In Fitzgerald RF Jr (ed): Non-Cemented Total Hip Arthroplasty. New York: Raven Press; 1988:7.

25. Szmukler-Moncler S, Reingewirtz Y, Weber HP. Bone response to early loading: the effect of surface state. In Davidovitch Z, Norton LA (eds): Biological Mechanisms of Tooth Movement and Craniofacial Adaptation. Boston: Harvard Society for the Advancement of Orthodontics; 1996:611.

26. Søballe K. Hydroxyapatite ceramic coating for bone implant fixation: mechanical and histological studies in dogs. Acta Orthop Scand Suppl 1993;255:1.

27. Pilliar RM, Deporter D, Watson P. Tissue-implant interface: micromovement effects. In Vincenzini P (ed): Materials in Clinical Applications, Advances in Science and Technology. Faenza: Techna Srl; 1995:569.

28. Brunski J, Hipp JA, El-Wakad M. Dental implant design: biomechanics and interfacial tissue. J Oral Implantol 1986;12:365.

29. Brånemark P-I, Hansson BO, Adell R, et al. Osseointegrated implants in the treatment of the edentulous jaw: experience from a 10-year period. Scand J Plast Reconstr Surg Suppl 1977;16:1.

30. Corso M, Fiorellini J, Sirota C, et al. Clinical and histometric analysis of osseointegration of immediately loaded implants in dogs (abstract). J Dent Res 1997;76:24.

31. Schnitman PA, Wohrle PS, Rubenstein JE. Immediate fixed interim prostheses supported by two-stage threaded implants: methodology and results. J Oral Implantol 1990;16:96.

32. Bijlani M, Lozada J. Immediately loaded dental implants—influence of early functional contacts on implant stability, bone level integrity, and soft tissue quality: a retrospective 3- and 6-year clinical analysis (abstract). Int J Oral Maxillofac Implants 1996;11:126.

33. Salama H, Rose LF, Minsk L, Klinger E. Immediate loading of TPS root-form implants in the human mandible (abstract). Int J Oral Maxillofac Implants 1996;11:125.

34. Fitzgerald RH Jr (ed). Non-Cemented Total Hip Arthroplasty. New York: Raven Press; 1988.

35. Cowin SC, Van Buskirk WC, Ashman RB. Properties of bone. In Skalak R, Chien S (eds): Handbook of Bioengineering. New York: McGraw-Hill; 1987:2.1.

36. Brånemark P-I, Adell R, Breine U, Hansson BO, Lindstrom J, Ohlsson A. Intra-osseous anchorage of dental prostheses. I. Experimental studies. Scand J Plast Reconstr Surg 1969;3:81.

37. Brånemark R. A Biomechanical Study of Osseointegration. Thesis, Göteborg University, Göteborg, Sweden, 1996.

38. Block MS, Kent JN. The integral implant system and the science of hydroxylapatite-coated implants. In Block MS, Kent JN (eds): Endosseous Implants for Maxillofacial Reconstruction. Philadelphia: WB Saunders Company; 1995:223.

39. Hoshaw SJ, Brunski JB, Cochran GVB. Pull-out and fatigue failure of bone-dental implant interfaces. In Torzilli PA, Friedman MH (eds): 1989 Biomechanics Symposium. New York: American Society of Mechanical Engineers; 1989:205.

40. Balon BE. Pull-Out Strength of Screw Shaped Dental Implants in Bovine Cancellous Bone. Thesis, Rensselaer Polytechnic Institute, Troy, New York, 1993.

41. Johansson C, Albrektsson T. Integration of screw implants in the rabbit: a 1-year follow-up of removal torque of titanium implants. Int J Oral Maxillofac Implants 1987;2:69.

42. Carr AB, Papazoglou E, Larsen PE. The relationship of Periotest values, biomaterial, and torque to failure in adult baboons. Int J Prosthodont 1995;8:541.

43. Gotfredsen K, Nimb L, Hjörting-Hansen R, Jensen JS, Holmén A. Histomorphometric and removal torque analysis for TiO$_2$-blasted titanium implants: an experimental study on dogs. Clin Oral Implants Res 1992;3:77.

44. Sullivan DY, Sherwood RL, Collins TA, Krogh PH. The reverse-torque test: a clinical report. Int J Oral Maxillofac Implants 1996;11:179.

45. Tjellström A, Jacobsson M, Albrektsson T. Removal torque of osseointegrated craniofacial implants: a clinical study. Int J Oral Maxillofac Implants 1988;3:287.

46. Brunski JB, Hipp JA, Cochran GVB. The influence of biomechanical factors at the tissue-biomaterial interface. In Hanker JS, Giammara BL (eds): Biomedical Materials and Devices. Materials Research Society Symposium Proceedings. Vol. 110. Pittsburgh: Materials Research Society; 1989:505.

47. Roberts WE. Bone tissue interface. J Dent Educ 1988;52:804.

48. Hoshaw SJ, Brunski JB, Cochran GVB. Mechanical loading of Brånemark implants affects interfacial bone modeling and remodeling. Int J Oral Maxillofac Implants 1994;9:345.

49. van Steenberghe D, Tricio J, Van den Eynde E, Naert I, Quirynen M. Soft and hard tissue reactions towards implant design and surface characteristics and the influence of plaque and/or occlusal loads. In Davidovitch Z, Norton LA (eds): Biological Mechanisms of Tooth Movement and Craniofacial Adaptation. Boston: Harvard Society for the Advancement of Orthodontics; 1996:687.

50. Isidor F. Loss of osseointegration caused by occlusal load of oral implants. A clinical and radiographic study in monkeys. Clin Oral Implants Res 1996;7:143.

51. Quirynen M, Naert I, van Steenberghe D. Fixture design and overload influence marginal bone loss and fixture success in the Brånemark system. Clin Oral Implants Res 1992;3:104.

52. Jaffin RA, Berman CL. The excessive loss of Brånemark fixtures in type IV bone: a 5-year analysis. J Periodontal 1991;62:2.

53. Rangert B, Krogh PH, Langer B, Van Roekel N. Bending overload and implant fracture: a retrospective clinical analysis. Int J Oral Maxillofac Implants 1995;10:326.

54. Lekholm U, van Steenberghe D, Herrmann I, et al. Osseointegrated implants in the treatment of partially edentulous jaws. A prospective 5-year multicenter study. Int J Oral Maxillofac Implants 1994;9:627.

55. Tjellström A, Jansson K, Brånemark P-I. Craniofacial defects. In Worthington P, Brånemark P-I (eds): Advanced Osseointegration Surgery: Applications in the Maxillofacial Region. Chicago: Quintessence Publishing Company; 1992:293.

56. Thomas KF. Prosthetic Rehabilitation. London: Quintessence Publishing Company; 1994.

57. Anderson JD, Kasra M. Engineered bar design for a midface defect: a case report. Int J Oral Maxillofac Implants 1996;11:400.

Psychologic Aspects of Craniofacial Defects

Eric K. Milliner, MD

> - Basic Concepts
> - Premorbid Personality
> - Accommodating to Facial Disfigurement

The concept of the tissue-integrated prosthesis supported by the osseointegrated implant was introduced by P.I. Brånemark in 1965. An important aspect of this new reconstructive technique was its positive effect on the quality of patients' lives.

Candidates for craniofacial reconstruction are patients whose psychology can be as diverse as the physical conditions that bring them to the surgeon's attention. Little systematic attention has been given to the emotional, behavioral, and psychosocial aspects of these patients' experience or to the predictors of psychologic outcome postreconstruction. Despite lack of data for this unique population, a spectrum of psychiatric principles may be useful for clinicians working in the field of oral and maxillofacial reconstruction.

Blomberg and Lindquist[1] and Blomberg[2,3] assessed the psychologic acceptance of complete removable dentures in a controlled study before and after treatment utilizing the tissue-integrated prosthesis. The majority of the patients reported a significant improvement in their quality of life. Tolman and Taylor,[4] in their report of a 24-center prospective study involving 145 patients treated with a bone-anchored craniofacial prosthesis, discussed the patients' perceptions and acceptance of this osseointegration attachment system. Their entry and follow-up questionnaires and post-treatment telephone survey did not provide quantitative data. However, there was an indication that quality of life had significantly improved when patients compared their experience of the osseointegration implant system with prostheses that had been previously available. The importance of psychologic assessment has been discussed by Chinellato[5] and Blomberg.[6]

Basic Concepts

The premorbid personality of each individual patient and the level of adaptive functioning before illness or trauma are the most reliable predictors of coping capacity. In addition, the patient's perception of the circumstances in which the problems began and the patient's subjective impression of how the case has been managed may influence the outcome as much as the facts of the pathology and the expectations of medical professionals for the patient's prognosis. Therefore, it behooves clinicians to become sufficiently acquainted with their patients' internal world to appreciate how the illness and its treatment are most likely to be integrated in the patients' views of themselves and their life experiences.

Premorbid Personality

Each individual develops a mental self-representation through the accumulated impact of life experiences since birth. In addition to constitutional determinants of intelligence, temperament, and the capacity for state regulation, each infant is born with a propensity for psychologic attachment to primary careproviders: the biologic mother or surrogate is the most frequent object. Through experiences in that original dyad, the baby organizes a sense of self at a psychobiologic level of emotional nurturing and physical need gratification, long before language development and memory allow for cognitive self-observation. However, at a fundamental level of basic trust, the child develops a preverbal awareness that basic needs will be met, important interpersonal ties will be maintained, and the surrounding environment can gradually be explored and mastered with reasonable safety and competence. Most importantly, if basic neurophysiologic endowment is adequate and the nurturing environment is good enough, the child develops a cohesive sense of identity as a discrete, separate, and valued individual with capacities to cope with internal impulses and the dictates of the social environment.

The developing child also has an ever-expanding awareness of bodily functions and competencies, so that by age 3 to 5 years the child shows clear awareness of being distinct in identity from careproviders. The child's pride in psychologic separateness is matched by a delight in mastering physical potentials. At the same time, the earlier infantile omnipotent and grandiose qualities in viewing the world are gradually replaced by a more realistic awareness of causality and practical limitations.

Fundamental to a child's self-esteem and sense of optimism in later life are the qualities of affirmation, acceptance, and love experienced with the original careprovider. The careprovider's ability to sustain such an attitude depends partially on the practical

and emotional significance of the child in the caretaker's life and partially on whether the child sufficiently matches preexisting fantasies of the caretaker so as to not be a severe disappointment.

However, even during emotionally traumatic circumstances, many parents have the capacity to accommodate to their disappointments and to provide sufficient positive affirmation for their child to develop in a reasonably normal fashion.

Accommodating to Facial Disfigurement

A difference in psychologic challenge and outcome would be expected if comparisons were made among patients whose equivalent disfigurements were the result of 1) severe congenital anomalies, 2) accidental trauma, or 3) surgical intervention for destructive tumors or malignancies. Even though all three categories of patients might suffer severe social inhibition, their internal view of themselves and their disfigurements and especially their response to cosmetic reconstructions are likely to differ appreciably.

Disfigurement Associated With Congenital Malformations

Patients with congenital lesions are likely to be the most diverse group psychologically. Their sense of personal identity has included an awareness of being disfigured since their earliest memory. In this regard, they experience their appearance as "the way I am, and the way I have always been," and to that degree they are spared the trauma associated with an abrupt change in body image.

Their self-esteem and sense of self-worth, however, are likely to be highly variable, based in part on the degree to which their primary careproviders were able to tolerate their appearance and to convey a sense of genuine love and acceptance of the child by age 3 to 5 years. Other parents, because of guilt, self-blame, or personal narcissistic vulnerability, accommodate less well to having a disfigured child; marriages, childrearing approaches, and the child's self-esteem may suffer as a consequence. Children in this group, like the others, face varying degrees of social ostracism, which can be particularly devastating to the emerging psychologic identity of young children. Consequently, from the psychosocial perspective, optimal outcome likely will be achieved if gross defects are corrected at the earliest reasonable age (preferably before preschool). Conversely, additional surgery is likely to be most psychologically difficult during early to midadolescence when pubertal changes add developmental complexity to a young person's sense of body image and self-esteem. Also, logic dictates that cosmetic outcome may be best if final reconstructions (if necessary) are postponed until physical growth is complete in the latter part of the 2nd or early 3rd decade.

A comparatively rare, but uniquely problematic situation occurs in those patients who are profoundly distressed by their change in appearance, despite an excellent cosmetic repair. Most often, these patients have worked arduously and successfully to integrate their original appearance as part of their positive mental representation of body image and self-esteem. Consequently, they may experience change (even change that other people would readily assert was for the better) as a profound loss of their internal view of themselves on the one hand and of their lifelong project of adapting successfully. Paradoxically, for some severely disfigured individuals, the daily struggle to overcome their disability may have provided an important focus of sustained effort and sense of accomplishment.

Thus, it behooves the surgeon to be thoughtful and perceptive, to inquire about and accept the patient's own personal views, to evaluate whether the patient has a realistic concept of anticipated outcome, and to assiduously avoid pressuring for surgical intervention if the patient indicates a preference for leaving things as they are.

Case Example. A 60-year-old man had a congenitally absent pinna in association with total deafness in his right ear. Intermittent drainage of malodorous pus had been problematic since early childhood, and he recalls being held back for 2 years in elementary school as a result of recurrent otitis media.

As the fourth of 10 children, the patient denies ever being teased by siblings or peers, but he recounts feeling exceedingly self-conscious from a young age. For example, a family portrait when he was age 6 years shows him hiding the right side of his face behind the arm of his older sister. His family circumstances were unique in that another sister had a similar congenital deformity, and cousins with normal pinna had branchial cleft cysts. He grew up with

the belief that his anomaly is inherited but tends to skip a generation or two before coming back.

The patient's first prosthesis was designed at the Mayo Clinic in 1946. It was sculpted from latex and was held in place with liquid adhesive. He recalls that the material would curl and become disfigured after 2 or 3 weeks and that the cost of replacements ($5.00 each) seemed exorbitant at the time. Serous weeping of the skin covered by the prosthesis became problematic and led to increasingly frequent failures of the adhesive.

His first osseointegration implantation was performed in 1984. Although less than perfect, the new technology has proved vastly superior to the previous latex and adhesive design. An elevated bar is attached to three implants, onto which the pinna prosthesis adheres with several small magnets. After surgical recontouring of the periauricular base, the margins of the molded prosthesis feather almost imperceptibly against the surrounding skin. Precision sculpting and coloration make the prosthesis virtually indistinguishable from the contralateral normal ear, which itself was revised with a cartilage implant years ago.

The result for the patient has been exceedingly gratifying, as reflected by his confidence that most observers now judge his appearance to be totally normal. Moments of embarrassment occasionally still occur; for example, at the funeral of his first wife, a well-wisher inadvertently dislodged his prosthesis when giving him a hug of sympathy.

The patient's disfigurement has not deterred him from remarrying; from having two children (who proved to be normal) after accepting the risk they might be congenitally affected; and from actualizing the advice of an older brother who admonished, "Don't feel sorry for yourself" as the family struggled through the aftermath of the 1929 Great Depression. He embodies the emotional stability and resilience often attained by patients with congenital anomalies whose developmental experience has been otherwise normal.

Disfigurement Secondary to Traumatic Injuries

This group includes individuals whose facial disfigurement is the result of accidental trauma. They tend to be the most angry and litigious group, and they have the highest risk for reactive depression and suicide. On the other hand, they come to their experience of traumatic disfigurement with a well-integrated mental self-representation of being previously normal. Their psychologic vulnerability to trauma is often proportional to the degree to which their sense of personal adequacy rested on their physical attractiveness. Their original, actual beauty or handsomeness is not nearly so important. Rather, the critical factor is whether or not the patients' feelings of self-worth rested primarily on their attractiveness alone. If confident in their other assets, many patients cope with profound traumatic disfigurement while remaining psychologically intact. Unfortunately, for others whose identity is tied strongly to appearance, an apparently minor blemish can prove psychologically overwhelming.

Another important predictive factor is the patients' perception of blame or responsibility and their internal comfort level with anger. Those who tolerate their own anger poorly may be more susceptible to reactive depression, resulting when normal rageful emotion is countered by internal prohibitions of conscience, and the anger is then redirected against themselves.

A key factor influencing anger is whether or not the patients believe the trauma was preventable. In addition, whether they judge themselves or others to have been negligent in causing the trauma is exceedingly important. Equivalent disfigurements will be coped with much differently by persons convinced that it was truly no one's fault compared with persons who angrily hold themselves or someone else to blame.

A corollary of fault is the issue of reparation and whether or not the patient feels the outcome was fair in compensable cases. Litigations (whether won or lost) are unavoidably stressful and constitute one of the most frequent secondary burdens for trauma victims.

Psychologically, the optimal outcome is likely to be determined by how close the surgical reconstruction approximates the patient's original appearance. In this regard, the surgeon's narcissism and the patient's magical desires may collude to the detriment of both parties. Namely, if physicians or dentists reinforce the patient's understandable wish that everything be restored to the way it was before the accident, the surgeons have only themselves to blame if the patient is later dissatisfied. Reality-based disappointments are virtually inevitable, because restorations never reconstitute the patient's normal anatomy and function or even appearance. Thus, surgeons will do themselves and patients a service by not being drawn into false promises or unattainable perfectionistic goals. Instead, there should be a frank discussion of surgical limitations and the probable blemishes and defects in outcome when the goals of treatment are first introduced to the patient and family.

Physicians and dentists should be aware of the frequency with which patients unconsciously displace old attitudes and unresolved conflicts from previous interactions into the physician-patient relationship. Predictors of problematic transference include patients with a past history of difficult relationships with previous careproviders and authorities (especially parents). It is also easy for patients to unconsciously shift the blame or anger for unresolved trauma away from those originally responsible and onto the provider (especially in circumstances in which the actual outcome fails to match the unchallenged, magical expectations that the patients believe were promised by their physicians or dentists preoperatively).

Reactive dysphoria, including strong feelings of anger and grief at the loss of previous appearance, is normal after traumatic injuries, especially those involving disfigurement and loss of function. Thus, a pathologic significance should not be inferred each time such patients are angry or upset. However, some despondent patients in need of support may progress to self-injury or suicide if their needs are unrecognized. It is the surgeon's responsibility to be aware of patients' emotional struggles, to avoid glib reassurances (which may give patients the impression that their distress is disallowed or discounted), and to ensure that any case in question is brought to the attention of a mental health professional for evaluation.

Case Example. An 18-year-old male had just completed his first year of junior college when a motor vehicle accident resulted in the traumatic amputation of his left ear. He sustained back injuries and required auditory canal reconstruction (which preserved 80% of his hearing); an abdominal graft was used to cover the defect in facial skin.

Even now, the patient has complete amnesia from the night before the accident until the end of his initial 6-week hospitalization. It was then he first learned (or can remember being told) the extent of his injury. He recalls being scared and initially questioning, "Why did this happen to me?" He elaborates that "at age 18, it's supposed to be the best time in your life," in contrast with the 26 operations and innumerable emotional challenges that he had to face in the next several years. However, he feels no one was to blame, faults neither God nor himself, and seems confident in the formulation that such things occasionally happen to people, just by chance or coincidence.

Initially, he was offered a conventional prosthesis affixed with adhesive, but after learning that adhesive can sometimes fail without warning, he declined to consider it for fear of social embarrassment. Consequently, he returned as a college sophomore without an ear and without a prosthesis and struggled for a year to hide his disfigurement. It was 18 months after his initial trauma that he came to the Mayo Clinic, and he admits in retrospect that he needed a lot of encouragement and support to consider osseointegration implantation.

Three titanium implants were positioned in the auricular bed, and a C-clamp framework attached to the abutments allows the prosthesis to be held in place with five magnets. The patient's satisfaction with the result in appearance is reflected by his confidence that he now looks normal and that people can hardly tell he wears a prosthesis unless they scrutinize him carefully.

Yet the approach has not been without complications. Initially, skin breakdown occurred between two implants that were positioned close together, and regrafting was required. Also, because of position, the patient finds it difficult to perform his own skin care and hygiene; he relies on his older brother to clean his implants and to manage occasional infections. Wearing the prosthesis has not been free from social embarrassment; the device occasionally becomes dislodged with vigorous athletic activity and while he functions in his job as a high school teacher and basketball coach.

In retrospect, the patient feels that strong family ties and the support of his small rural community have helped a lot to get through it without feeling in need of any mental health services. In actuality, he complied with 6 weeks of counseling recommended by and provided through his insurance company, with little if any appreciable benefit.

In his own judgment, coping with trauma at the age of 18 years caused him to grow up a lot and prompted him to rethink his priorities. It furthered his determination to pursue personal goals (i.e., to become a teacher, rather than farming as his parents anticipated); it drew his parents closer together in their marriage and enhanced his own relationship with them (especially his mother, who was at his side through most of his hospitalizations); and despite initially being treated with kid gloves by his siblings, it eventually brought the five children closer together.

Interestingly, the truck involved in the accident belonged to his employer, a company owned by his brother-in-law. Despite litigation regarding compensation, the patient perceives the suit to have been filed against the insurance company, and he denies any anger or perception of his brother-in-law or his company being to blame. The patient asserts that his relationship with his older sister and brother-in-law remains cordial and essentially unchanged. Only the patient's younger brother (2 years his junior) evidenced jealousy over the time and attention that the parents paid to the patient after the accident, an attitude that proved short-lived and spontaneously resolved.

Currently, at age 30 years, the patient still lives at home. He completed his college degree and has been teaching for 2 years. Most people in his small community know of his trauma, including his current girlfriend who has accepted it very well. He perceives himself to be more self-confident and socially outgoing now than if the accident had never occurred; the notoriety actually forced him to overcome his originally shy and retiring demeanor. He has tried to "go on and not let it bother me" when embarrassed. Occasionally, he resorts to humor when his prosthesis is dislodged in public, easing the shock or dismay he has noted in startled observers (especially the boys on his basketball team). However, he acknowledges that it is still a sufficiently sensitive issue that he would never joke about his prosthesis spontaneously. His comfort at home is sufficient, however, that he does not wear his prosthesis when only family members are present.

Again, the patient credits the strength and emotional support of his family for facilitating his recovery and current excellent adjustment. He believes that other patients, with different backgrounds and family experiences, might cope differently with equivalent physical trauma and disfigurement.

Surgical Disfigurement and Neoplastic Lesions

The final category includes patients whose disfigurement is the result of destructive tumors or malignancies and those whose appearance (at least temporarily) may be worsened by surgical interventions. As with the group of trauma victims, patients in this category come to their disfigurement with a sense of loss and change in previous appearance and body image. Many of the same principles elaborated in the previous section apply.

However, some important differences distinguish the tumor or cancer patient from those disfigured by accidental trauma. The issue of blame and responsibility is much less prominent, and anger (especially toward external, willful, or negligent perpetrators) is less common. Instead, these patients tend to be more inwardly focused, blaming personal misdeeds (for example, cigarette smoking, cocaine addiction), bad luck, cruel fate, or God for their misfortunes.

On the other hand, because aspects of their disfigurement may be the direct consequence of surgical intervention, their ambivalence (both conscious and unconscious) toward their dentists or physicians may be far more conflicted and problematic than for the congenital and accidental trauma groups.

Perhaps most importantly, this group of patients is struggling with primary disease that is often life threatening. Some may experience tremendous gratitude that the surgeon's efforts may save or prolong their lives. Others, with identical aesthetic outcome, may focus on blemishes in actual or perceived appearance as a psychologic displacement away from, and defense against, their fears of potentially lethal disease.

Consequently, the risk for serious distortions in the physician-patient relationship is high among tumor and cancer patients. Being aware of this liability should help the physician or dentist avoid overpersonalizing the blame or counterattacking or abandoning the patient.

Case Example. Through videotaped and published testimonials, a woman offers insights that complement and contrast with the above generalizations. As a teenager in the early 1940s, the woman received radiation therapy for facial acne before the danger of such treatments was appreciated. In her 3rd decade, she was diagnosed with skin cancer and underwent a series of palliative operations. Nevertheless, she married, had three children, and lived a full and productive life devoted to her family and church.

In 1983, 6 months after her husband's death, she underwent a right orbital exenteration, plus the removal of her nose, hard palate, upper lip, most of her teeth and gums, and much of her right facial musculature. Through a series of 10 operations at the Mayo Clinic in a 3-month period, a skin graft from her chest was used to fashion an upper lip; her bottom lip was recontoured using sections of tongue; and a remaining tooth was used to anchor an artificial, removable palate. Six exposed titanium implants around her orbit became points for magnetic attachment of her facial prosthesis. Except for a brief period after her initial reconstruction, she was provided with a series of oral and facial prostheses throughout her treatment that restored her physiologic and cosmetic deficiencies.

The patient promised herself in the hospital, "If I ever got to go home, I would never complain about things." Instead, it was her conviction that "God gave life back to me, and now it's up to me to show Him and the rest of the world what can be done with a face that has been deformed by cancer and surgery." She credited God and the support of her family for her ability to recover without needing professional counseling. In fact, she provided counsel for other patients after their facial surgeries, wrote a patient information brochure for individuals who had lost an eye, and considered writing a book about her experiences.

In early 1989, the malignancy recurred and she faced the possibility that her left eye might need to be excised. Her initial intent was to decline the operation rather than risk having her remaining eye removed and being blind. She counseled with her minister who assured her that it would not be suicide nor would God be angry if she abided by that decision. However, she reversed her stance after her family made clear "they would love me with or without my eyes . . . I was their Mom . . . and their response made me realize my worth to my children." In fact, palliative resection did not require removal of her eye, in which she continued to have functional vision until her death at age 71 years in June 1996.

It was her testimony that "material things don't mean much when a person is lying in a hospital fighting for life" and her conviction that "our family has been brought closer together by this crisis." The patient's psychologic resilience was sustained by her unswerving faith, "I somehow sensed God's purpose to give us life that is more than just living," and by her internalized awareness of the love and unquestioned support of her children and extended family.

Conclusion

Patients' allegations are always to be taken seriously but are not always to be accepted at face value. If patients know that their complaints have been fully heard and that their dentist or physician has empathy for (although not necessarily agreement with) their perceptions, they are likely to be far more receptive if it becomes evident that referral to a mental health professional is necessary.

However, most individuals without preexisting psychiatric conditions cope adequately with trauma if given sufficient emotional support. And a few are challenged by tragedy to new levels of spiritual growth and developmental maturity.

References

1. Blomberg S, Lindquist LW. Psychological reactions to edentulousness and treatment with jawbone-anchored bridges. Acta Psychiatr Scand 1983;68:251.

2. Blomberg S. Psychological response. In Brånemark P-I, Zarb GA, Albrektsson T (eds): Tissue-Integrated Prostheses: Osseointegration in Clinical Dentistry. Chicago: Quintessence Publishing Company;1985:165.

3. Blomberg S. Psychological aspects of treatment results and patient selection. In Worthington P, Brånemark P-I (eds): Advanced Osseointegrated Surgery: Applications in the Maxillofacial Region. Chicago: Quintessence Publishing Company;1992:347.

4. Tolman DE, Taylor PF. Bone-anchored craniofacial prosthesis study. Int J Oral Maxillofac Implants 1996;11:159.

5. Chinellato MCMP. Psychological aspects in the treatment with bone-anchored prosthesis. In Brånemark P-I, Higuchi KW, Oliveira MF (eds): A Team Approach to Rehabilitation of Complex Cranio Maxillofacial Defects: The Challenge of Bauru. Chicago: Quintessence Publishing Company; (forthcoming).

6. Blomberg S. Psychological considerations in the treatment of patients with cancer. In Brånemark P-I, Oliveira MF (eds): Craniofacial Prostheses: Anaplastology and Osseointegration. Chicago: Quintessence Publishing Company;1997:118.

Cost-Effectiveness in Craniofacial Implant Rehabilitation

Kenji W. Higuchi, DDS, MS

- Cost-Benefit and Cost-Effective Analysis
- International Survey
- Future Considerations

When the shape of the body is deformed, it changes the disposition of the soul

Aristotle

Internationally over the past several decades, there has been concern about increasing health care costs. In an era when medical technology is skyrocketing, health care resources are increasingly more limited. Craniofacial implant rehabilitation is an example of new technology that provides an improved quality of life not previously available to children and the elderly with facial disfigurement. Highly favorable outcome studies demonstrating the safety and effectiveness of this approach are well known.[1-5] These reports document the predictability of skin-penetrating osseointegrated implants as supporting elements for facial prostheses as well as their salubrious aesthetic and functional benefits. These types of studies examine effectiveness of treatment; investigations providing data on the costs to achieve these outcomes also are necessary. This chapter addresses economic, time, and effectiveness implications of this therapeutic alternative.

Cost-Benefit and Cost-Effective Analysis

Cost-benefit analysis (CBA) and cost-effectiveness analysis (CEA) are methods used to evaluate financial costs and clinical consequences associated with an intervention. These approaches have been used to develop models to analyze the relationship between costs and therapeutic outcome results of diagnostic and surgical care.[6-9] These terms sometimes are interchanged incorrectly; important differences exist. In CBA, all costs and consequences are expressed in monetary terms, with the net benefits being the difference between the total monetary costs of an intervention and the consequences of that treatment, which also are expressed in economic terms.[10] CBA requires the difficult task of assigning a monetary valuation to life. An improved quality of life from craniofacial rehabilitation may be truly a benefit, but expressing it in dollars is difficult and controversial.[11]

This complex task of designating monetary value to life and limb has encouraged the use of

Table 4-1 *Alloplastic Compared With Autogenous Ear Reconstruction: Economic Costs*

Procedure	Cost, Can$
Osseointegrated implant auricular prosthesis (3 implants)	8,877
Four-stage autogenous reconstruction	9,050
One-stage temporoparietal flap	6,500

Data from Wilkes and Wolfaardt.[21]

CEA, as witnessed by the explosive growth in the number of CBA and CEA publications in the scientific literature in the last decade.[10] In CEA, the results are expressed as a net cost necessary to produce a certain unit of outcome measured in terms of health. This outcome in health improvement may be difficult to measure quantitatively, especially when quality of life issues are involved. In a large multicenter study in the United States, a gain in self-esteem, improved psychosocial status, and confidence were reported after craniofacial implant-retained prosthetic treatment.[12] No attempt was made to compare these observations with parallel therapy using non-implant-retained prostheses. Application of CEA involves quantifying outcome effectiveness using both methods and then comparing the financial costs necessary to produce those results. The effectiveness of an implant-retained prosthesis has been attributed to the more stable and secure anchorage of the facial epithesis based on osseointegrated implants, which permit the construction of a prosthesis with finer margins and better aesthetics. Doublet and associates[13] pointed out that cost-effective is not necessarily synonymous with cost-saving. An intervention may be considered cost-effective if compared with other interventions it is relatively efficient or requires relatively lower costs for the same unit of outcome. Measurement of outcome effectiveness is central to CEA and allows for these outcome results to be evaluated on their own merits instead of having to be converted into monetary benefits.

A large number of authors[12,14-20] reported on the functional and psychosocial benefits of osseointegrated implants in dental and maxillofacial rehabilitation. There have been few publications examining the relationship between financial costs and outcome effectiveness in the management of the craniofacial implant patient. Wilkes and Wolfaardt[21] examined criteria for treatment using osseointegrated alloplastic ear reconstruction compared with autogenous ear reconstruction. They reported similar financial costs comparing autogenous and craniofacial implant reconstruction of an external ear (Table 4-1).

At present, no universally agreed on criterion exists that measures outcome results specific for craniofacial implant-anchored prostheses compared with the alternatives of an adhesive-retained prosthesis and autogenous reconstruction. Clearly, there are a large number of patients who are either medically or financially unable to proceed with the rigors of autogenous reconstruction and who would have suboptimal results with a non-implant-retained prosthesis. In these compromised situations, an osseointegrated implant-retained prosthesis may be the only reasonable option. The primary objective of an implant-retained prosthesis is to provide secure anchorage for a lifelike prosthesis that replaces a lost portion of facial anatomy. Quantifying relative improvement in aesthetics and an enhanced sense of security is difficult, and although these quality of life issues are elusive, it is important to acknowledge that they are indeed real and meaningful for the patient treated.

The therapeutic and financial impact of any medical intervention must be assessed not only on outcome results and monetary costs but also in the context of time. There will be significant economic differences in ongoing maintenance costs between young and elderly patients based only on longevity. Information compiled at the Craniofacial Osseointegration and Maxillofacial Prosthetic Rehabilitation Unit (COMPRU) at Edmonton, Alberta, Canada, projects that in 20 years there is a potential savings of 31% for the craniofacial osseointegrated implant-retained prosthesis compared with an adhesive-retained prosthesis (Table 4-2). This analysis is based on anticipated costs of treatment and does not reflect comparative effectiveness or outcome results (Table 4-2).

Table 4-2 *Extended Financial Costs of Treatment for an Auricular Replacement (Alberta, Canada)*

Time interval, yr	Cost, U.S.$		
	Adhesive retained	Craniofacial osseointegrated implant retained	Autogenous reconstruction
1	3,056	6,419	9,220
5	8,418	7,946	
10	15,278	12,748	
20	28,518	19,077	
Maintenance costs†	2,910	2,565	
Total costs	31,428	21,642	
Potential savings‡ = 31%			

*Costs are calculated on present value and are not inflation adjusted. Adhesive-retained prostheses costs are based on annual replacement, with a new mold being constructed every third year. Craniofacial osseointegration implant-retained prostheses costs include all hospitalization costs (at the rate for residents of the United States). The costs are based on a mold being constructed at every third remake. Autogenous reconstruction includes all hospitalization (at the rate for Albertan residents) and surgical costs.

†Maintenance costs over 20 years.

‡Potential savings of a craniofacial osseointegration compared with an adhesive-retained auricular prosthesis over 20 years.

Courtesy of Dr. John Wolfaardt.

International Survey

In October 1996, questionnaires seeking information related to time and economic issues were submitted to 14 international centers experienced in craniofacial implant rehabilitation. Six centers, three from the United States and one each from Canada, Australia, and Sweden, responded to this survey concerning auricular replacement. Table 4-3 summarizes the range and median values for economic costs and the time required to provide the surgical and prosthetic services for an auricular prosthesis after the placement of two craniofacial implants.

Although the number of respondents limits the application of descriptive statistics, several consistent response patterns were observed. For all six centers, the financial costs for providing the prosthetic and anaplastology services were greater than the surgical charges, excluding operating room and anesthesia fees. These costs were influenced by the extent of governmental coverage and the country of origin. While the combined median surgical (2,790 U.S.$) and prosthetic (4,015 U.S.$) fee totaling 6,805 U.S.$ is not insignificant, this amount represents 50% to 60% of typical charges in the United States for the

Table 4-3 *International Survey, October 1996: Total Initial Costs for Auricular Prosthesis*

Treatment	Initial cost, U.S.$	
	Range	Median
Examination and consultation	113–555	250
Surgical fee and components (two implants), excluding operating room and anesthesia costs	1,800–4,124	2,790
Prosthetics, anaplastology, and laboratory services	2,500–4,850	4,015

commonly prescribed five-implant hybrid mandibular bridge (Wolfaardt J, personal communication, September 1997). A significant disparity was reported in the treatment time required for prosthetic and anaplastology treatment (22.5 hours) compared with the median surgical time of 3 hours (Table 4-4).

Including the 1.5 hours of yearly follow-up, a median combined treatment time of 29.3 hours was anticipated from the multispecialty surgical-prosthetic team to provide the initial implant-retained auricular prosthesis. A meaningful investment of

Table 4-4 *International Survey, October 1996: Total Initial Treatment Time for Auricular Prosthesis*

Treatment	Initial treatment, h	
	Range	Median
Surgical time for implant (two) and abutment procedures, no skin graft	1.4–4	2.3
Surgical time for implant and abutment procedures, with skin graft	1.75–4	3
Prosthetics and anaplastology treatment	8–32	22.5
Yearly follow-up treatment	0.5–3	1.5

time and economic costs is therefore necessary during the first year of treatment, and additional ongoing costs in the years ahead must be considered. The cost of remaking the prosthesis varied significantly depending on geographic location, but the most frequent response was equivalent to 50% or less of the original expense. The methods of payment also differed from country to country and within regions of the United States. The Swedish and Canadian teams reported that governmental support provided comprehensive coverage for their citizens, whereas the three American and one Australian team depended heavily on private insurance and patient self-pay, with limited governmental support. There was consistent agreement among teams that the prosthesis should be remade on average every 2 years.

Future Considerations

There have been few publications concerning the relationship between economics and craniofacial implant rehabilitation. CEA has not yet been reported for this treatment modality. Objective documentation of the effectiveness of a treatment method is challenging because both short-term and long-term CEA must be considered in the assessment. Because craniofacial implant prosthetic rehabilitation is a relatively new alternative outside of Sweden, few international centers have long-term data, especially in the treatment of children. In 1989, the Swedish Council on Technology Assessment in Health Care published a report[22] examining economic benefits of extraoral implant treatment of facial defects. This study projected economic long-term savings for auricular, nasal, and orbital implant-retained prostheses compared with conventional methods. Associated with the economic savings were benefits such as an improved cosmetic result, safe anchorage, and less anxiety about prosthesis loosening.

When compared with existing conventional methods of autogenous reconstructive surgery and non-implant-retained prostheses, craniofacial implant rehabilitation appears to be more expensive in the short term but is likely to be less expensive in the longer perspective. Importantly, in most cases, an osseointegrated implant-retained prosthesis affords a significantly improved outcome in terms of limiting surgical morbidity, achieving superior aesthetic results, and providing well-established psychosocial improvement. In the years ahead, clinicians providing this form of therapy are encouraged to document outcome effectiveness using variables to which CEA can be applied. Global scientific validation of superior patient benefits will be necessary as we work toward the goal of securing improved governmental and third-party insurance coverage for this area of reconstructive surgery.

References

1. Tjellström A, Rosenhall U, Lindström J, Hallén O, Albrektsson T, Brånemark PI. Five-year experience with skin-penetrating bone-anchored implants in the temporal bone. Acta Otolaryngol (Stockh) 1983;95:568.

2. Albrektsson T, Brånemark P-I, Jacobsson M, Tjellström A. Present clinical applications of osseointegrated percutaneous implants. Plast Reconstr Surg 1987;79:721.

3. Parel SM, Tjellström A. The United States and Swedish experience with osseointegration and facial prostheses. Int J Oral Maxillofac Implants 1991;6:75.

4. Wolfaardt JF, Wilkes GH, Parel SM, Tjellström A. Craniofacial osseointegration: the Canadian experience. Int J Oral Maxillofac Implants 1993;8:197.

5. Tolman DE, Taylor PF. Bone-anchored craniofacial prosthesis study. Int J Oral Maxillofac Implants 1996;11:159.

6. Miller MJ, Swartz WM, Miller RH, Harvey JM. Cost analysis of microsurgical reconstruction in the head and neck. J Surg Oncol 1991;46:230.

7. Levine MN, Drummond MF, Labelle RJ. Cost-effectiveness in the diagnosis and treatment of carcinoma of unknown primary origin. Can Med Assoc J 1985;133:977.

8. Bass EB, Pitt HA, Lillemoe KD. Cost-effectiveness of laparoscopic cholecystectomy versus open cholecystectomy. Am J Surg 1993;165:466.

9. Koenig WJ, Lewis VL Jr. The physician cost of treating maxillofacial trauma. Plast Reconstr Surg 1993;91:778.

10. Elixhauser A, Luce BR, Taylor WR, Reblando J. Health Care CBA/CEA: an update on the growth and composition of the literature. Health Care 1993;31 Suppl:JS1.

11. Hurley J. What does economics have to offer risk-benefit analysis? Can J Publ Health 1991;82:S21.

12. Kent G, Johns R. Effects of osseointegrated implants on psychological and social well-being: a comparison with replacement removable prostheses. Int J Oral Maxillofac Implants 1994;9:103.

13. Doubilet P, Weinstein MC, McNeil BJ. Use and misuse of the term "cost effective" in medicine. N Engl J Med 1986;314:253.

14. Kent G. Effects of osseointegrated implants on psychological and social well-being: a literature review. J Prosthet Dent 1992;68:515.

15. Anderson JD. Diverse applications of the osseointegration technique: the maxillofacial patient. Int J Prosthodont 1993;6:163.

16. Tzakis MG, Linden B, Jemt T. Oral function in patients treated with prostheses on Brånemark osseointegrated implants in partially edentulous jaws: a pilot study. Int J Oral Maxillofac Implants 1990;5:107.

17. Lorant JA, Roumanas E, Nishimura R, Beumer J III, Wagman LD. Restoration of oral function after maxillectomy with osseous integrated implant retained maxillary obturators. Am J Surg 1994;168:412.

18. Blomberg S, Lindquist LW. Psychological reactions to edentulousness and treatment with jawbone-anchored bridges. Acta Psychiatr Scand 1983;68:251.

19. Kiyak HA, Beach BH, Worthington P, Taylor T, Bolender C, Evans J. Psychological impact of osseointegrated dental implants. Int J Oral Maxillofac Implants 1990;5:61.

20. Weischer T, Schettler D, Mohr C. Concept of surgical and implant-supported prostheses in the rehabilitation of patients with oral cancer. Int J Oral Maxillofac Implants 1996;11:775.

21. Wilkes GH, Wolfaardt JF. Osseointegrated alloplastic versus autogenous ear reconstruction: criteria for treatment selection. Plast Reconstr Surg 1994;93:967.

22. Hallén O, Magnusson S, Jacobsson M, Marké L-Å. Bone-Anchored Implants in the Head and Neck Region: Report From a Conference. Stockholm: The Swedish Council on Technology Assessment in Health Care; 1989.

Medicolegal Risk Analysis

5.

Robert W. Sargeant, BA, JD

> - Malpractice Litigation
> - Product Liability Litigation
> - National Data Bank Reporting
> - Testimony Under Oath
> - Insurance Policy Coverage

The practice of health care has evolved significantly in recent years. State-of-the-art clinical techniques are no longer the sine qua non for a successful career. Health care has become a business as much as a learned profession. To practice effectively, today's clinician must develop and use risk-management philosophies and procedures. In specialized areas of medicine and dentistry such as oral and maxillofacial surgery, otolaryngology, and plastic surgery using osseointegration in craniofacial reconstruction, the tools of medicolegal risk analysis are invaluable.

This chapter provides the modern clinician with an analysis of the problems and risks presented by the judicial and related systems, and it offers methods to handle these problems and risks. It is only through a command of the controlling medicolegal issues and procedures that professional liability risks can be managed and counterproductive results prevented. The discussion on medicolegal risk analysis explores in detail malpractice and product liability litigation, with a cautionary note on the National Practitioner Data Bank. Included are guidelines for testimony under oath and other aspects necessary for compliance with requirements of the legal system. The analysis addresses an increasingly important concern: successful risk management requires health care providers to understand insurance policy coverage issues and to be aggressive consumers of insurance products and services. In the practice of health care, one is compelled to understand, use, and continuously improve medicolegal risk analysis to protect the provider and the patient.

Malpractice Litigation

The mention of a malpractice lawsuit creates many unpleasant and disturbing thoughts. It is seldom offered as part of the medical or dental school curriculum. A new graduate licensed to practice has little if any training in the rigors of the justice system. Even though all health care fields are exposed to lawyers and litigation much more than most professions, health care educational institutions do not equip their students and faculty with the tools necessary to minimize the drain on precious resources that litigation can create. The foundation for a risk management program is an understanding of the bases for professional liability; only with a firm command of the concepts of malpractice can health care professionals survive within the system.

Theories of Professional Liability

A patient can sue at any time and for any reason. There is no absolute prophylactic for a lawsuit. The concern, correctly articulated and understood, is to prevent a successful lawsuit, i.e., one that results in the payment of a settlement or judgment against the provider. With the understanding that all health care providers are vulnerable to claims and lawsuits, regardless of whether the lawsuits are meritorious, and knowledge of the legal theories under which a provider may be held legally responsible to a patient, lawsuits can be defended, even discouraged, and often prevented.

Theories of professional liability, often referred to colloquially as "malpractice," have evolved considerably. The same legal theories governing liability apply consistently to physicians, dentists, and all other health care professionals. The grounds for liability originated in the appellate courts; judges decided why and when health care professionals could be held liable to patients for money damages claimed to be the result of challenged diagnosis, treatment plan, or other aspect of health care. Each case was decided on its facts, which created problems in that the standards applied were often unpredictable and inconsistent. The rule applied in one court's decision may be different or rejected entirely in another. Professional liability is a function of state law, and the law of one state often differs substantially from that in another state.

To combat the inherent unfairness of overlapping and changing legal precedents, state legislatures have adopted statutes designed to clarify and standardize legal theories governing malpractice lawsuits against health care providers. Although professional liability remains primarily within the purview of state laws, most states have enacted statutes that are largely uniform. There remains an element of judicial precedent in determining which legal theory applies and to what extent, given a particular set of facts, but much of the uncertainty and inconsistency has been removed. The statutes providing for legal liability for health care providers, including but certainly not limited to osseointegration in craniofacial reconstruction, generally focus on the issues explained below.

Substandard Diagnosis and Treatment. The primary, and most frequently recurring, theory of liability in a malpractice lawsuit alleges that the injury resulted from the failure of a provider to follow the accepted standard of care. The patient suing must prove by a preponderance of the evidence (i.e., it is more probable than not) that the provider failed to exercise that degree of care, skill, and learning expected of a reasonably prudent provider at the time of diagnosis and treatment, in the profession or class to which that provider belongs, in the state where the care was provided, acting in the same or similar circumstances. The patient must prove further that it is more probable than not that the failure to follow the accepted standard of care was a proximate cause of the injury or harm about which the patient complains in the lawsuit.

Articulating and defining the standard of care applicable to a particular provider's care and treatment of a patient's condition are the most difficult and often the most strenuously disputed issues in a malpractice lawsuit. The standard to be applied is a state standard, not a national, community, or university standard. The standard of care for a health care provider in Los Angeles, California, may not be the same standard governing another practicing in Albany, New York. The standard of care can, and often does, change over time. A surgical procedure performed in 1990 by an ophthalmologist, oral and maxillofacial surgeon, otolaryngologist, or plastic surgeon may require a substantially greater standard of care in 1998; the accumulation of knowledge and experience over time does not necessarily apply retroactively. The standard is a minimum level of expertise below which a provider may not practice, not state-of-the-art treatment modalities using the most recently published research data.

Proving the standard of care to which an individual is held requires expert testimony. An expert is a witness capable of rendering an opinion that is admissible under the rules of evidence for the court in which the trial is to be conducted. Generally, a layperson may not express an opinion admissible into evidence in a malpractice trial. The reason is that the layperson without sufficient education, training, and experience does not have personal knowledge of the applicable standard, even though that particular witness may well have an opinion. In most malpractice litigation, the patient must proffer sworn testimony that the provider being sued failed to meet the standard of care, and that it is that failure that was, more likely than not, a cause of the injury claimed. An expert in a malpractice lawsuit does not necessarily meet the same test for expertise as most providers would expect. An expert witness in a dental malpractice lawsuit may be a general dentist who asserts to have personal knowledge of the applicable standard of care, even though the procedure about which the patient complains involves specialized oral surgery techniques.

A maloccurrence is not tantamount to malpractice. Under most state laws, the fact that a poor result was obtained in any particular situation does not necessarily support the conclusion that the provider failed to meet the standard of care. The provider making a diagnosis and treating the condition diagnosed does not serve as a guarantor that an optimal result will be obtained. The provider is required only to exercise that degree of care, skill, and learning expected of a reasonably prudent provider. It is not uncommon for a patient to sue for malpractice based on a misunderstanding or a miscommunication concerning the result to be anticipated. In many malpractice lawsuits, several qualified experts may be called to testify as witnesses. It is not uncommon for lawyers representing the patient and the provider to call several experts as witnesses on the issues of standard of care and causation. The experts may be called to address different areas of practice or levels of specialization within an area of practice. The fact that the experts disagree as to the applicable standard of care is not in and of itself evidence of malpractice.

One of the more disturbing realizations for any health care provider sued for malpractice is that, where experts express differing opinions, admissible in evidence at trial, as to whether the diagnosis and treatment that are the basis for the lawsuit met or failed to meet the standard of care, a judge or a jury must decide which is to be believed. It is most discomforting to learn that a jury of one's peers seldom, if ever, contains any of the provider's peers. Few judges are health care providers or have specialized education, training, or experience in specific procedures. Jurors are most often pooled from state and county voter registration and driver licensing data banks. If a dentist was seated on a panel from which a jury was to be selected in dental malpractice litigation, that person would probably be challenged or dismissed peremptorily by the attorney representing the patient. The person or group charged with the legal responsibility to decide whether a dentist met the standard of care in a civil action for dental malpractice is most often not qualified or knowledgeable in dentistry.

The basis (i.e., the evidence on which a judge or a jury decides a malpractice lawsuit) is in large part the expert opinions admitted into evidence by the witness called by the lawyers and qualified through their oral testimony. When experts express expert opinions that differ significantly, it is the fact finder's responsibility to decide which is more credible and which is to be believed. Trial lore is replete with cases decided on the personalities rather than the qualifications of the expert or the rationale for the opinions rendered. It is possible for a patient to prosecute a civil action for malpractice based on the testimony of expert witnesses proffered by lawyers, in which the experts professed anything but expertise. Nonetheless, if the witnesses are able to testify under oath that they have personal knowledge of the standard of care and the judge or jury is persuaded that the testimony is credible, a judgment against the provider may be the result in the litigation, even though the world's best and brightest testified to the contrary on behalf of the provider being sued.

Proximate causation is a difficult concept to master in a malpractice lawsuit. There may be numerous causes for a condition. The claim of malpractice requires proof that an injury or harm was suffered by the patient. Most lawsuits find their origin with some claim of injury or harm to varying degrees and in differing conditions. It is not necessary for the harm to be significant or the injury to be devastating to initiate litigation. Regardless of the nature or scope of the harm or injury claimed by the patient suing, the judge or jury must be persuaded that the condition about which the patient complains was more likely than not caused by the provider's failure to meet the standard of care. As with the applicable standard of care, this requisite element for any prima facie cause of action for malpractice must be proved by expert testimony. Although many laypersons may conclude that an unanticipated or unfavorable result occurred, the provider may not be held legally liable unless there is sufficient evidence from those qualified to express professional opinions that the harm or injury would not have occurred but for the provider's failure to meet the standard of care.

Failure to Obtain Informed Consent. A second theory of liability often alleged in malpractice lawsuits asserts that the provider failed to obtain the patient's informed consent for the procedure performed before beginning treatment. The informed consent claim is rooted in a long-standing public policy that people should have control over their bodies and the ethical principle that no health care provider should perform any act without first obtaining the patient's knowing and willing acquiescence. The informed consent theory of liability, like the standard of care theory, is grounded in state law; a uniform standard for informed consent does not exist.

To establish a prima facie case for failure to obtain informed consent, the patient must prove by a preponderance of the evidence that the provider failed to inform the patient of a material fact or facts relating to the treatment, that the patient consented to the treatment without being aware of or fully informed of such material fact or facts, that a reasonably prudent patient under similar circumstances would not have consented to the treatment if informed of such material fact or facts, and that the treatment in question proximately caused injury to the patient. Most state laws provide that a fact is defined as or considered to be a material fact if a reasonably prudent person in the position of the patient would attach significance to it in deciding whether to submit to the proposed treatment. This factor requires an evaluation of the statistical probability that the harm may occur in conjunction with or as a result of the procedure involved with the treatment plan or the qualitative significance of the harm that may be anticipated or expected even though improbable, or both.

As with the standard of care, material facts must be established by expert testimony. Experts, and the admissibility of opinions proffered by witnesses called as witnesses at trial, are determined by their personal knowledge and not by their academic, clinical, or professional qualifications. Material facts concern the nature and character of the treatment proposed and administered; the anticipated results of the treatment proposed and administered; the recognized possible forms of treatment; or the recognized serious possible risks, complications, and anticipated benefits involved in the treatment administered and in the recognized possible alternative forms of treatment, including nontreatment. Although detailed and thorough records are useful and often persuasive to a judge or a jury in the defense of a malpractice lawsuit based on failure to obtain informed consent, they are not dispositive. The fact finder must critically evaluate and weigh all of the evidence and decide what and who to believe. Failure to use a form for documentation of informed consent is not admissible as evidence of failure to obtain informed consent.

The two most difficult issues for health care providers confronted with malpractice suits based on failure to obtain informed consent are the probability or risk of harm and the patient's option to elect nontreatment. Certain forms of harm often are not documented in the literature to have causes clinically proved to be related to a certain procedure or treatment modality. Nonetheless, even though the statistical probability for a particular harm or untoward result may be insignificant, if the nature of the harm is substantial, informed consent is required. For a patient who is in a category less than likely to suffer harm and who can be protected from the harm by a relatively simple or noninvasive procedure, it must be performed. This is true even though the provider may determine that the applicable standard of care does not require the test, diagnostic procedure, or other action. Much more frequent is the situation presented by the provider who fails to advise the patient that nontreatment is an option. In many cases, nontreatment may not be the favored option, or it may seem perfunctory to the provider asked to evaluate treatment options. It is most embarrassing to be cross-examined in a malpractice lawsuit and forced to concede that the consultation did not include a discussion of the option to forgo treatment.

Breach of Contract and Misrepresentation. State laws make actionable a provider's breach of promise to the patient that the injury suffered would not occur. The lawsuit for malpractice for breach of an oral contract need not be supported by formal contract negotiations. When the provider promises a certain result or that an injury or form of harm will not occur, and the result is less, liability can be a consequence. It is unusual for this theory to be alleged, and incidence of this result is low. It is instructive to recall this area of law. In the course of the consultation and during the treatment, a reasonably prudent provider is always cautious not to create overly optimistic patient expectations. A corollary to the breach of promise or contract theory of liability is misrepresentation under state law. Most states have adopted a rule of law establishing legal liability for an intentional or an unintentional misstatement of a material fact, when the patient justifiably relies on the provider's statement and harm or injury results from the reliance. The salient point is that zealous efforts to inspire patient confidence, or to ease anxiety, can be counterproductive.

Misrepresentation is a viable consideration in using specialized products, instruments, or techniques in conjunction with the informed consent theory of liability discussed above. There are numerous product manufacturers of implants and other similar products in use around the world. Some of the manufacturers' products are designed and built with the support of empirical clinical data. These data justify representations to patients in obtaining informed consent with regard to the risks related to a procedure or inherent in the use of the product; some, unfortunately, do not. Approval or certification by a governmental agency or a professional organization does not automatically mean that the clinical data supporting a statement or representation about a particular risk or predicted result should be applicable to all similar products, instruments, or procedures. Extreme caution should be exercised by the clinician using one product but relying on the research data and literature documenting the performance of another, albeit similar, product. Liability for misrepresentation of the product used and the risks and benefits to be anticipated may be the consequence.

Res Ipsa Loquitur. Latin for "the thing speaks for itself," the doctrine of res ipsa loquitur may be applied to a malpractice action when an occurrence producing an injury is one that does not ordinarily occur in the absence of negligence, when the act is so palpably negligent that it may be inferred as a matter of law, when the general experience and observations of humankind teach that the result would not be expected without negligence, or when proof by experts in an esoteric field creates an inference of negligence. The rarity of an occurrence or the fact of a bad result is insufficient by itself to establish that an injury was the result of negligence. This common law principle not uniformly codified by state statutes may be applied only when the facts and circumstances involved reasonably imply that the event causing the injury or damage would not ordinarily occur in the absence of negligence, that the provider controlled the instrumentality that caused the injury or damage, and that the injured patient in no way contributed to the causative event.

Res ipsa is often alleged as a catchall theory of liability in malpractice lawsuits. It more commonly is used in product liability or general negligence lawsuits. Thus, in the specialized field of osseointegration in craniofacial reconstruction, res ipsa serves as an important caution. Implant placements, osteotomies, or other procedures using state-of-the-art products and instruments can have unsuccessful or even harmful results through no fault of the provider. This is a defense to a malpractice action for substandard care, but testimony to support this assertion is not sufficient to defeat a res ipsa claim. A successful defense may at times require proving a negative—an admittedly difficult task. When an instrument malfunctions or a product fails, it may be necessary for the clinician to prove the absence of negligence. This is often required in conjunction with the application of the learned intermediary doctrine discussed below.

The problems associated with misrepresentation discussed above should also be considered in conjunction with the res ipsa theory of liability. The harm or injury alleged to have resulted "but for some negligence," although difficult to specify or to articulate by expert witnesses, should be anticipated with the use of one product based on the research data and clinical literature of another product.

Unfair Business Practices. Consumer protection legislation exists in most states. These statutes prohibit "unfair or deceptive business acts or practices" that result in harm to the consumer. Appellate court decisions tend to distinguish business practices actionable under consumer protection laws from professional expertise or judgments exercised in providing health care. Nonetheless, allegations of violation of consumer protection laws are increasingly made in malpractice lawsuits. When the claim arises solely as a result of a provider's clinical judgment or ability in making a diagnosis, obtaining informed consent, performing treatment, or addressing complications that may arise, a consumer protection law violation is unlikely. However, when the claim goes beyond the care and treatment performed and joins conduct related to the business or financial aspects of the practice, there is an additional risk of liability.

Several examples are available. One is the claim that a clinician has a "diagnosis just looking for a disease or condition" for patients with temporomandibular joint syndrome. There are providers not trained in specialized treatment methods who operate mills for motor vehicle accident victims. Many similar complaints are treated with standardized plans, without regard for the particular nature or extent of the symptoms presented. When the evidence tends to show that the provider makes diagnoses or prescribes treatment plans based more on the income that will be generated for the provider's practice than on the condition presented by the patient, a risk of liability exists. The same can be said for use of osseointe-grated implants. Is the treatment plan based on an accurate diagnosis and a reasonable assessment of the options available to the patient or on the size of the surgical and other fees to be paid to the clinician? Although these questions are rarely answered by providers from the outset, they should be a touchstone for any medicolegal risk assessment policy.

When the patient can prove that a claim for damages exists separate from an allegation of negligence, based on the entrepreneurial aspects of the practice, and that the damages (not necessarily personal injury) were the result of unfair or deceptive acts or practices of the provider or clinic, which is within the sphere of trade or commerce, statutory penalties, attorney's fees, and court costs may be awarded to the patient. This statutory violation award of damages and penalties is in addition to any recovery for professional negligence. Care must be taken in any new and rapidly evolving area of practice, especially in the area of osseointegration and reconstructive surgery, to avoid and prevent claims resulting from the business aspects of the practice.

Professional Licensing Standards Violation. Prevention and defense of a lawsuit are not the sole concerns of medicolegal risk analysis. All states have licensing requirements for health care providers. Many states and local jurisdictions have peer evaluation and dispute resolution systems in place. The same sorts of concerns about professional malpractice lawsuits should be evaluated in light of potential licensing complaints. Many times patients with a grievance file a complaint for administrative rules and regulations governing licensing; often the tests applied in disposition of such complaints are the same as the applicable state laws controlling malpractice lawsuits. The licensing or regulatory violation about which patients complain may be exclusive of a malpractice lawsuit or it may be in addition to a civil action. Careful consideration of the state and local administrative rules and regulations is also an important aspect of any medicolegal risk analysis program.

Proving Negligence in Court

The theoretical bases for malpractice lawsuits must be evaluated together with requirements under state law for proving and recovering on a claim of negligence. In essence, a professional malpractice lawsuit is grounded in negligence, the same as lawsuits based on alleged liability for personal injuries resulting from a motor vehicle accident, a slip and fall, or any other tort claim. Although a malpractice lawsuit concerns a professional practice and usually requires rather than permits expert testimony to establish legal responsibility of the defendant sued, the manner in which a plaintiff must plead and prove the case to recover money damages in the form of a judgment is the same. The patient suing a provider for malpractice must allege and prove that the provider owed a specific and identifiable duty to the patient; that the diagnosis, consultation, treatment, or follow-up breached or violated that duty; and that the breach of duty was *a* (not necessarily *the*) proximate cause of the harm or injury claimed. An assertion of violation of duty is not actionable without evidence of harm or injury.

In the case of a malpractice lawsuit against a health care professional, duty is premised on the existence of the doctor-patient relationship. Breach or violation of the duty owed by a provider to a patient is defined as an act, error, or omission to exercise the requisite degree of care, skill, and knowledge of a reasonably prudent clinician under the circumstances or to obtain informed consent, as discussed above. Breach of duty and proximate causation are both proved by expert testimony. The term "proximate cause" is not well defined in the law, although there are volumes written on it. It encompasses the factual considerations that generally concern the causes for a condition or problem about which a patient complains; it also includes legal policy issues as defined by appellate court judges who must decide whether the liability of a defendant in a particular case is just or fair. The testimony in depositions and at trial that a patient has suffered injury or harm is often lengthy and emotional. It is an understatement to observe that in many if not most malpractice lawsuits the patients suing often relate all of the ills falling on them to the substandard care or the treatment to which the patients deny consenting.

When a malpractice lawsuit actually goes to court, proving liability and damages is far more difficult than is usually envisioned. After preliminary motions and rulings by the judge, usually on matters relating to the nature and scope of the evidence that may be presented to the jury in court, lawyers for each side make a speech to the jury about what they think the evidence will show. This is called an opening statement—first the attorney representing the patient speaks and then the attorney representing the provider. The patient calls all of his or her witnesses, sometimes including the provider being sued, and introduces into evidence all of the evidence supporting the malpractice claim (and other claims such as violation of consumer protection laws). The reason the patient's entire case is presented first is because the patient has the legal burden to prove the theories of liability and damages alleged by a preponderance of the evidence. If the evidence meets the minimum requirements, the provider's lawyer presents the provider's case; if the evidence is insufficient, the case is dismissed. The patient has a chance to put on witnesses in rebuttal. Occasionally, witnesses testify by deposition or on videotape, but most often live appearances are required. Scheduling treating providers and expert witnesses in a malpractice lawsuit is an enormous project. After all the evidence is presented to the jury, the lawyers for each side have an opportunity to present legal arguments. Arguments reflect the way in which the lawyers think the jurors should apply the facts of the case to the law as articulated by the judge. The judge instructs the jury on the law, and deliberations follow immediately. The entire process is time consuming. One of the most significant reasons for the modern health care professional to develop and implement aggressive medicolegal risk analysis policies and practices is because the defense of a malpractice lawsuit, even if successful, requires such an enormous and inordinate amount of time that the result, even if a verdict for the provider, is seldom rewarding. Avoiding the process of malpractice litigation is essential for any successful practice.

It is a complicated and treacherous task to prove in court that a provider should be held legally liable to a patient. Most malpractice lawsuits that have merit (i.e., the patient's attorney clearly demonstrates an ability to prove the requisite elements for a prima facie cause of action) are settled by the provider, counsel, and insurance company well in advance of the trial date. Defense lawyers and the malpractice insurance carriers are not in the business of wasting precious resources by taking cases to trial when there is little or no chance the provider will win. The cases that go to trial do so for either of two reasons: the patient's proof of liability is weak or the patient's claim for money damages is excessive. When a malpractice case is tried, it is because the provider's attorney has made a strong recommendation to the insurance claims representative and the defendant provider on the defendant's ability to win or because the dollar amount of the patient's claim,

even if the patient is successful in establishing liability and after incurring the significant expense necessary to defend a malpractice lawsuit, will be less than any reasonable offer of settlement made on behalf of the provider before trial.

Product Liability Litigation

It is not sufficient to conclude an analysis of medicolegal risks inherent in osseointegration in craniofacial reconstruction with a review of malpractice law. Where products are used in surgical procedures, the ophthalmologist, oral and maxillofacial surgeon, otolaryngologist, plastic surgeon, and other health care professionals assisting in the delivery of products and related services are at risk for product liability litigation. Product liability litigation follows much the same procedures as malpractice lawsuits. The differences primarily are found in the legal theories of liability. The focus of product liability litigation is the product manufacturers and distributors; however, health care professionals are routinely joined as parties to these lawsuits. An understanding of the basic principles of product liability law is an essential first step to avoid the process and the risk of exposure to liability in product litigation.

Defective Design and Manufacture

There are two grounds for product liability. Although there are applicable federal statutes and regulations concerning product liability, they affect the product engineer, manufacturer, and distributor. Those laws of concern to clinicians, insofar as dental and medical products and instruments are concerned, are found in state statutes. The first theory of product liability relates to the design and manufacture of a particular implement or instrument. A product manufacturer and distributor may be held liable for money damages, for injury or harm arising from a product failure, and for the design and manufacture of a product that is not reasonably safe. Technology, cost, and specification are all considerations in determining what is and what is not reasonably safe. The tests used by the courts in resolving product liability claims revolve around the reasonableness of the design, materials, assembly, and packaging of a product challenged on a case-by-case basis.

Adequacy of Warnings and the Learned Intermediary Doctrine

Some products, no matter how well designed and manufactured or distributed, are inherently dangerous. Where the need for a lawful product exists but the technology does not exist to produce that product in a manner that is free of risk, the product is viewed as dangerous. A dangerous product may be designed, manufactured, and distributed, even though it may not be reasonably safe. Readily apparent examples of such products are firearms, explosives, ladders and scaffoldings, motor vehicles, and construction equipment. If the use of a product as intended by its manufacturer and distributor cannot be reasonably safe (i.e., it is inherently dangerous or its use necessitates exposure to a danger of some sort), warnings must be given. The tests here are concerned with the adequacy and reasonableness of the warnings, not the product. The warnings must be in writing and specific about the aspect of the product that is dangerous as well as about the nature and scope of the risk inherent in the use of the product. The kind of injury that may occur and the severity of the harm to be expected must be adequately disclosed. Even the design, wording, color, and size of the warning labels are relevant issues in product liability litigation.

The adequacy and reasonableness of warnings in product liability litigation are the most frequent concerns for health care professionals using osseointegration in craniofacial reconstruction. It may be that the technology does not exist to design, manufacture, and distribute risk-free surgical implants and instruments. The same is true for many prescription drugs and for certain diagnostic tests. When this situation is present, it is incumbent on the manufacturer and distributor to provide adequate warnings to consumers. Rarely, if ever, does the surgical patient have the opportunity to view or evaluate product warnings. The patient usually never actually sees the product but is affected by it nonetheless. The warnings are provided to the surgeon and those working to assist in the surgical procedure.

This is the point at which the surgeon becomes vulnerable to risk. Whether the surgeon is given adequate warnings becomes a crucial issue in the litigation. The reasonableness of the warnings and their presentation are important. At a minimum, patient litigation for product liability creates the risk that the provider will be deposed. The worst-case scenario is that the manufacturer defends the lawsuit by arguing that the warnings were given and were adequate, but the surgeon failed to note the warning or failed to appreciate and use effectively the information contained in the warning. Thus, the surgeon becomes the target of the litigation, either for liability or for considerable testimony in deposition or in court.

The defense alleged in this situation is called the learned intermediary doctrine. It provides that a product manufacturer or distributor may defend a product liability lawsuit by contending that the product cannot be designed in a manner that is without risk or danger to some degree and that adequate warnings were given. If the intended use and application of the implement or product envisions a professional, such as an ophthalmalogist, oral and maxillofacial surgeon, otolaryngologist, or plastic surgeon, making the ultimate delivery or performing adjustments or maintenance, the manufacturer is required to provide adequate warnings to that professional. It is axiomatic under this defense that the consumer relies completely on the care, skill, and knowledge of the professional who delivers or places the implement or uses the instrument. It is the legal duty of the professional in exercising the standard of care and in obtaining informed consent to understand and follow the warnings fully. Failure of the professional, the learned intermediary, to understand and follow the warnings may absolve the product manufacturer and distributor from legal liability to the ultimate consumer (i.e., the patient). A successful learned intermediary defense may also result in malpractice liability for the surgeon.

The surgeon relies on the manufacturers and the distributors of implements and instruments used in placement of implants in craniofacial reconstruction to provide adequate product warnings, research data, literature, instruction, updates, and support. Moreover, the surgeon using products in this category of medicolegal risk must provide patients, the consumers protected by product liability laws, with adequate information and warnings. If this requirement is not met by the manufacturer and distributor, the surgeon using the products accepts an unnecessary risk of liability and participation in the product liability litigation.

National Data Bank Reporting

Recent federal laws and regulations implemented by the United States Department of Health and Human Services mandate reporting of malpractice claims against dentists and physicians. The law requires that this information is confidential and not available for regular public inspection. Absolute privacy is not always possible. Whenever a provider or a lawyer, claim representative, or other agent working with or on behalf of a provider makes a payment to a (usually former) patient in consideration for a release of liability, it must be reported to the proper authority. This applies equally to the payment of a judgment incurred as a result of a finding of liability in a civil malpractice or product liability lawsuit and to a confidential settlement agreement entered into and performed before trial.

The statutes creating and regulations implementing the National Practitioner Data Bank are important to the provider in any medicolegal risk analysis. Reporting of claims in compliance with the law should be a part of any practice. Making sure that the information is reported accurately, timely, and fully, both by the provider subject to the claim and others involved in the claims process, cannot be omitted.

Testimony Under Oath

It may seem unfair, and at times overly burdensome, but it is inescapable that the provider may be required to give testimony under oath in conjunction with litigation. The justice system in the United States and in several other countries requires citizens to provide information necessary to the resolution of disputes before its courts. Providers can be compelled by subpoena and by summons to provide records, give testimony, and provide other information relevant and necessary to the operation of the courts. Providers frequently are requested by their patients and attorneys representing them in litigation to provide records, information, and opinions and to participate in the process. Because health care professionals are in the business of treating patients who suffer from some condition that may require diagnosis, treatment, or other forms of assistance, the probability that a provider will be affected by or involved in some aspect of the litigation process is significantly greater than for a layperson. Knowing the rules for giving testimony under oath and complying with the requirements of a particular part of the process are essential.

Expert and Fact Witness Responsibilities

Health Care Provider Exposure to the Judicial System. Providers are exposed to two markedly different kinds of responsibilities to the justice system. Understanding the difference between these responsibilities and meeting each without incurring unnecessary or avoidable loss of resources can result in substantial benefit. In the course of the doctor-patient relationship, the provider can be either a fact witness or an expert witness. A fact witness is any person with knowledge of facts or information relevant to an issue or claim subject to the jurisdiction of the court. A provider who makes a diagnosis or performs treatment on a patient who is a party to a lawsuit is no different legally from a person who witnesses a motor vehicle collision, a liquor store robbery, or a fall in a restaurant. Any person who has personal knowledge of relevant facts may be compelled to appear in court or at a deposition and to give testimony under oath concerning the facts witnessed or the information held.

The problem is that providers are often requested to provide copies of records, summarize cases, prepare reports, give deposition testimony, and testify in court without an expectation that they will be reimbursed for their costs or paid for their time and effort. Under state laws, providers are subject to subpoena, with only nominal compensation for a witness fee and mileage reimbursement. It is not fair to require a high level of cooperation and input without some form of compensation.

Most providers expect of themselves more than the system expects from them. All that a provider is required to do is provide the records requested or answer the immediate questions asked in a deposition or in-court examination under oath. The facts concerning the history given by the patient, the condition observed by the clinician, the diagnosis made, the diagnostic tests used, the treatment plan, the patient's cooperation and performance, and the prognosis are all that is required. The answers are usually in the records concerning the patient; for the provider to be expected to go beyond this information in the usual course of business is not reasonable.

Formulating and Rendering Opinions. Where most providers get into trouble in preparing reports or in giving testimony under oath is in rendering professional opinions. As a fact witness, a treating provider, either in a personal injury action generally or in a malpractice or product liability lawsuit, is not required to render professional opinions beyond those connected with the course of treatment. Many feel compelled to do so, and that is where they get into trouble. A person's opinions, whether lay or professional, belong to no one else. A provider cannot be compelled to testify to professional opinions unless the provider is serving in the capacity of an expert witness. Caution should be exercised not to express opinions unless they have been formulated well in advance of the testimony and with knowledge of all the necessary information.

This is not to say that providers should avoid completely the role of an expert witness. It is necessary for providers to serve as experts in reviewing records, in formulating opinions, and in giving testimony. Opinions should be expressed in a cautious and responsible manner. A provider can agree to serve as an expert in only a consulting role, without obligation to give testimony under oath. After a complete review of the records and preparation of an analysis of the issues raised in the litigation, a professional opinion is invaluable to a fair resolution of any personal injury litigation. When a provider agrees to serve as an expert, to render and testify opinions admissible in court, the expert should expect to be paid a reasonable fee. What is reasonable depends on the qualifications of a particular expert, the level of expertise required by the issues joined in the litigation, the amount of time required to participate in the process, comparable fees commanded by other experts in the field, and the provider's experience in serving as an expert. Fees vary from case to case and from time to time. A standardized fee schedule for expert witnesses does not exist.

Standards and Guidelines. Litigation support services is a developing industry. Some qualified health care providers solicit business completely unrelated to providing care; they are in demand. This sort of activity results in a disservice to the patient and to the justice system. Although qualified professionals who are able to assist lawyers and the courts in conducting litigation should be able and willing to serve in selected cases, as needed, when the time spent in consulting and testifying on medicolegal issues exceeds the time spent caring for patients, there is a problem. Many of the health care disciplines and the boards representing the specialist in

the fields have formulated guidelines for those who are able and who choose to serve as experts. Generally, these guidelines require responsible, accurate, candid, and unbiased conduct. When the provider clearly is not qualified or the information provided is patently incomplete, it is wise to withhold an expression of any opinions; on the other hand, when all of the criteria for responsible testimony are met, experts should be comfortable rendering opinions without concern for the party who is aided by the opinion expressed.

Ex Parte Communications With Attorneys

State laws make the information obtained by a treating health care provider in the course of making a diagnosis, preparing a treatment plan, delivering care and treatment, or obtaining informed consent from a patient absolutely privileged. A provider may not be called as a witness by a party or person other than the patient or the attorney representing the patient. Extreme caution must be exercised in releasing any information about a patient or the care provided. Records must not be released without a release satisfactory under state law; information of any degree or in any amount concerning a patient must not be disseminated except pursuant to a valid subpoena. Violation of these guidelines exposes the clinician to unnecessary risks of liability. Any communication with a party other than the patient or with a lawyer other than the patient's is considered ex parte. Most state laws and court rules governing ex parte communications prohibit any violation of the doctor-patient privilege.

Every communication with a person other than the patient in any capacity other than in the course of providing treatment is suspect to violation of the laws and rules prohibiting ex parte communications. The simple rules of practice are: release records only on written request with a written release signed by the patient or the patient's attorney or in compliance with a court order or enforceable subpoena, discuss a patient's case with persons other than the patient only with the patient present and written permission, give testimony concerning a patient's condition and treatment only pursuant to subpoena or court order, and express opinions concerning any case only with a current recollection of the pertinent facts and on thorough review of a complete set of records and relevant testimony.

Liability for an Incorrect Opinion

It is common for a provider to be asked by report, on deposition, or in court to give an opinion about future events or requirements. Given a course of treatment and a known prognosis, a provider may be asked to express an opinion about the cost of future treatment to be reasonably expected. Unwitting clinicians often comply, in an effort to assist the patient, by expressing opinions about the future expenses in a given case. This is a trap that must be avoided zealously. Once on record by report, on deposition, or in court, that opinion is usually the basis for settlement before trial or an award of money damages at the conclusion of a trial. If the patient recovers a sum certain based on the opinion of a qualified treating or expert witness, the witness may be liable for expenses incurred in future treatment in excess of the opinion rendered, even though the clinician who gave the testimony was attempting little more than to help a patient to make a good faith recovery.

Payment for Services and Testimony

A fact witness can be compelled to give testimony under oath concerning information relevant to a legal proceeding about which that person has knowledge. State laws provide for little or no remuneration to the fact witness, except for mileage and a nominal appearance fee. How then should a provider asked to release records or subpoenaed for deposition or for a court appearance avoid the unfair loss of income and expense? In most states interprofessional committees made up of health care professionals and lawyers have attempted to resolve this problem by agreement. Most state laws do not provide for hourly fees or expert compensation.

The quid pro quo is that attorneys must make a good faith effort not to impose excessively on health care professionals and must reach agreement to pay reasonable fees for services provided in conjunction with giving testimony or related information. At the same time, health care professionals are expected not to take advantage of the situation and their unique position, expecting only reasonable compensation for their time and consequential expenses. This is a delicate balance, leaving what is reasonable to be decided on a case-by-case basis. When a provider is called to give testimony as a fact witness, the fee to be expected should reflect the provider's

ability to use the time and resources to generate income from his or her practice. When a provider is called as an expert witness, the fees may be substantially greater, reflecting the ability to testify in the capacity of an expert witness.

Legal Requirements for Maintaining Records

Most state statutes and administrative regulations specify the minimum time that a record must be maintained and available for inspection by a patient, a licensing board, or officers of the court. The periods usually range from 5 to 10 years after the date that the patient was last treated or was last seen in the provider's office. Absolute compliance with these laws and regulations is strongly recommended; failure to keep sufficient records for the requisite period may subject a clinician to sanctions. It is not a defense to a licensing inquiry or investigation that someone else was responsible for this task or to respond with a lack of knowledge about the status of the records requested.

To be sure, it is advisable to maintain records for substantially longer than required by these rules. Many states have common law adopting what is generically referred to as the discovery rule. The rule holds that for tort claims under state law the applicable statute of limitations does not begin to run until the claimant discovers each of the elements of the claim—duty, breach, causation, and harm. The discovery period may extend well beyond the state licensing requirement for retaining and maintaining records. In many states, the statute of limitations, that is, the period within which a claimant may file a civil lawsuit or the claim is time-barred, governing tort claims, which includes malpractice and product liability, is between 1 and 3 years. The statute of limitations in most states does not even begin to run against a minor until that person reaches the age of majority under state law. Some states have special rules applicable to enforcing a statute of limitations on claims against health care providers, but they are often enforced far too flexibly. Under the discovery rule and related exceptions to the statute of limitations, claims may be brought and prosecuted successfully long after the patient's treatment has ended or the patient has been seen in the practice or clinic. This is a better, stronger reason to comply with these licensing statutes and regulations.

The possibility or even the mention of being in the unenviable position of defending a malpractice lawsuit without adequate records should be sufficient to encourage a provider to maintain records for as long as practicable, even for much longer periods than may be required by state law. Adequate, extended maintenance and retention of records for a minimum of 10 to 15 years, depending on the applicable licensing laws and regulations and the governing statute of limitations and relevant exceptions, is an important part of medicolegal risk analysis.

Insurance Policy Coverage

Medicolegal risk analysis is incomplete without a discussion of the issues concerning insurance coverage. Clinicians in private practice, in clinics, in universities, or affiliated with public health hospitals need to consider at least four separate questions about the policy or alternative form of protection available to them. First, is the financial condition of the underwriter, institution, or other source for indemnification and defense sufficient to cover fully these expenses in the event of a claim, demand, or loss? Second, how is the period for coverage or protection determined? Third, what is an adequate amount at which to set the limits of the policy, or how much coverage is enough? Fourth, what is the scope of the coverage afforded under the precise language of the policy? Not addressing and resolving these questions, at a minimum on an annual basis, is irresponsible; engaging in any form of practice without satisfactory answers to these questions can be devastating for the clinician and the patient.

Financial Strength of Underwriter

Little concern is usually given to the company, institution, or other entity issuing the coverage; most health care providers ask only about the price—the amount of the annual or other premium charged by the underwriter. Most states' laws create a fund to protect insurance consumers in the event that the company issuing the policy is insolvent. To participate in a state insurance guaranty fund, the policy must be submitted to the state insurance commissioner or similar regulatory authority for review and approval, and the company, institution, or risk retention group must satisfy rigorous minimal financial requirements. The purpose is to restrict from doing business in the state companies that are not likely to be able to stand behind the policies they issue to their insured, in the event of a major loss or a series of catastrophic losses during the same period. If an insurance company goes bankrupt or refuses to honor its policies, the state guaranty fund steps in, defends the lawsuits, and handles the claim; the insured and the claimant are protected.

Regardless of whether a fund exists in any particular state, the concern that the insurance company issuing a policy will be ready, willing, and able to defend and indemnify the provider who is covered needs to be addressed regularly. An insurance policy, contrary to many marketing efforts by underwriters, is not a security blanket or an absolute protection against liability claims. It is a contract for indemnification in the event of a loss. The policy provides the insured with a defense of the claim or litigation arising from a claim. This can be the most important aspect of the protection afforded by an insurance policy. When the malpractice liability is disputed by the provider and a reasonable determination is made to litigate to a conclusion by jury verdict or appeal, the attorney's fees, court costs, and expenses incurred in the litigation usually run into tens of thousands and often hundreds of thousands of dollars. Retaining lawyers and experts, preparing and presenting a successful defense, and surviving a civil malpractice lawsuit are difficult and expensive.

The policy also provides the insured with a promise to pay a loss covered by the policy, defined as either a settlement of the claim in consideration for a full release agreement and a dismissal of the pending lawsuit or a payment of a judgment entered against the insured at the conclusion of the litigation. Whether for defense costs or payment of loss, the insurance policy is only a contract of indemnification, and the contract has value only if the insurance company has the ability to perform under it.

The same rule applies to alternative forms of liability protection offered to employees of institutions, members of larger professional organizations, or participants in risk-retention groups or similar actuarial pools. The most important question that should be asked of any organization is, Does it have the financial resources and the business strength to stand behind any and all claims that may be presented to it during the applicable period? It may be difficult to ask these questions, and it may be even more difficult to get answers. It is absolutely essential for any clinician who treats patients to obtain a satisfactory response to this concern. What are the financial resources of the risk-retention group? How much money has the underwriter approved by the association paid in claims for malpractice in the last 10 years? What are its reserves for future claims? What coverage is available if the practice changes or is discontinued? What other relevant information about the insurer's claims history for malpractice claims is used in offering coverage? Who owns the company or participates in the group, pool, or institution, and what is its interest in providing long-term protection against malpractice liability? Do you know the answers to these questions as they relate to your practice?

Claims Made Versus Occurrence Policy Forms

Insurance policies or similar products are written on either a claims made or an occurrence basis. These terms relate to the period during which a claim will be covered. This is the case for property, casualty, personal, and professional liability insurance. It is important to know which form of coverage is being offered and to make an affirmative decision whether this is appropriate for the practice to be protected against loss.

A claims made policy covers only loss arising from a claim that is made against the insured and presented to the insurer during the policy period. Most policy periods for malpractice policies are for 1 year. An angry threat made orally to the provider or to an associate, staff member, or another clinician is usually not sufficient to give rise to a claim covered under the policy. To present a claim to an insurer and request protection under the terms and conditions of the policy, there usually must be some kind of demand for action by the provider— waive a fee, pay for supplemental treatment, pay money for consequential expenses, and pay compensation for pain and suffering are all common examples of demands made by patients that are covered under a policy. Some insurance contracts require that the claim must be made to the provider in writing and tendered to the claims rep-

resentative for the insurer in writing. A summons and complaint for a formal settlement demand package from an attorney representing the claimant is most often not a prerequisite for accepting tender of a claim under an insurance policy or similar coverage. The key point is that the claim must be made to the provider and tendered to the provider's malpractice insurer within the claims made period; otherwise, there will be no coverage.

Applying medicolegal risk analysis tools to insurance-related claims mandates careful scrutiny of claims and potential claims and timely notice to the insurer of any information that may result in a demand for payment of a loss or a lawsuit. In deciding whether a claims made form policy is appropriate for a particular provider's practice, it is important to evaluate the retroactive date included in the declaration sheet specifying coverage terms and conditions. It is insufficient to develop and enforce an aggressive claim management program if the policy affording coverage has a prohibitive retroactive date. The retroactive date term in a malpractice policy is related to an arbitrarily designated date—sometimes the date that the policy first went into effect, sometimes the date that the provider first purchased malpractice liability coverage, and sometimes a date without determinable importance to anyone other than the underwriter or agent writing the policy. The term means that for claims presented during the claims made period, and arguably covered under the policy, if the diagnosis, records, consultation, treatment, or related events or facts occurred before the stated retroactive date, even though the claim was actually made during the policy period, there is no coverage.

The retroactive date for a claims made malpractice policy can precipitate an unusually harsh result. Imagine a claim made during the coverage period for one insurance company's policy that is based on events or facts that occurred long before the current policy went into effect and during the period of coverage for a policy issued by a company no longer in business or that no longer provides coverage under the terms of the policy in effect at the time. This is not an unusual situation. Insurance underwriters use the retroactive date term in their policies as an effective method of limiting or reducing claims against the company; an unnecessarily recent retroactive date provision in a policy can have unfavorable consequences for the provider unaware of its effect.

Analytically, an occurrence policy form is the opposite of a claims made policy. An occurrence policy form looks to the date of the occurrence of the diagnosis, consultation, records, treatment, or follow-up that is the basis for the claim. Under an occurrence policy form, the date the claim is made and tendered to the insurer is largely irrelevant. A claim under an occurrence policy may be tendered years after the policy period expires and many years after the patient last presented to the provider or the clinic (or, as is more often the case, failed to present). Thus, it is the date of the occurrence of the events and facts from which the claim may arise that is the dispositive criterion under an occurrence policy.

Most insurance companies have discontinued issuing malpractice liability insurance policies on an occurrence basis; with few exceptions, policies are currently issued on a claims made basis. Check to see which form is proposed before purchasing any malpractice liability insurance policy. It is important that consideration be given not only to the instant policy coverage proposed to be issued but to the policies previously issued. Are previous policies claims made or occurrence based? Will the coverage from prior policies work in concert with the current coverage proposed, or will gaps exist for which there may not be any coverage? How will the retroactive date for a new claims made policy function in conjunction with prior occurrence policy provisions? Insurance company marketing representatives are capable of answering these questions; make sure they do before buying any coverage.

Setting Policy Limits

The dollar amount of malpractice liability coverage that is necessary is a variable constantly changing and dependent on several factors relating to the provider requiring coverage. Insurance policies customarily set two limits for the amount of the indemnification for which the insurer may be liable to the insured under the terms and conditions of the policy, often expressed as a ratio. The first figure, usually given as the numerator, is the maximum the insurer will pay on behalf of an insured provider to an individual claimant in the event of a loss covered under the policy. The second, usually given as the denominator, is the maximum an insurer will pay in total to all claimants for claims made against the insurer during the policy period that are covered under the policy. Most insurance policies issued in the United States have a minimum policy limit of $1,000,000.00. A policy with lesser limits should be scrutinized carefully.

Policy limits with greater amounts usually are available, and may be advisable depending on the nature of the practice and the coverage requirements of the provider. The additional premium charged to increase the loss limits for a policy usually is nominal compared with the initial premium.

It is also important to know how the limits are calculated and applied to a particular claim or group of claims. First dollar defense is a valuable additive. With some policies, the policy limits term applies to the total cost to the insurer to indemnify an insured in the event of a loss. This means that the total amount of money spent by the insurer to pay attorney's fees, court costs, and expenses incurred in defense of a lawsuit or claim is applied to the limits. For example, if the policy limit is $100,000.00 and the defense of the litigation requires $50,000.00, the effective limit is reduced by half. With first dollar defense, the limits do not apply to the defense fees, costs, and expenses; a lawsuit may be defended, from the provider's perspective, without regard for the total amount paid to conclude the litigation. Although this does not translate into a complete disregard for cost effectiveness in defending lawsuits, it is a tremendous advantage to the provider who is already losing a tremendous amount of time and professional resources in defending a lawsuit.

Scope of Coverage Under Policy Language

All of the considerations and observations discussed in this section on insurance policy coverage are useless if the terms of the coverage are overly restrictive. What is a covered act, error, or omission under the policy may change from company to company and from year to year. What events or claims are excluded from coverage must be stated clearly in the language of the policy. The manner in which the insurer drafts what is commonly referred to as an adhesion contract may be defined broadly or narrowly. Read the policy. It should make sense and should be understood by the provider; a juris doctor degree should not be a prerequisite for this exercise. There is little or no opportunity to negotiate the general terms of coverage. There are several competitors in this field. The most conservative recommendation is the best: the provider who is an informed and aggressive consumer, not only in price comparisons but on all terms and conditions of coverage available, will be rewarded.

Conclusion

Medicolegal risk analysis is a dialogue. It is only by raising these issues and obtaining sufficient information that the risks of liability and loss can be avoided and defended. The intent of this chapter is not to provide all the answers. That would be impossible. Any lawyer or insurance salesperson who suggests otherwise should be held suspect. An absolute bulletproof checklist does not and cannot exist. The law is always evolving—so too must the process of medicolegal risk analysis. This process is an effective tool, but only when it is exercised vigorously and regularly. By the time a claim is made or a summons is served, it may be too late. Preventive medicine is the most effective manner in which to visualize the concepts used in medicolegal risk analysis.

Medicolegal risk analysis begins with the theoretical foundation for malpractice liability. Substandard care, failure to obtain informed consent to treatment, breach of contract and misrepresentation, unexplained but unexpected untoward results, unfair business practices, and professional licensing standards can be grounds for legal liability. The theories of potential liability should be viewed in the context of the requirements for proving negligence in court. Relevant and at times troublesome consideration must also be given to product liability law. Although a product manufacturer may be held liable for money damages for personal injuries sustained by a patient, the ultimate consumer, the reasonableness of the design, engineering, and construction of the implement or instrument may be only the beginning of the analysis. For products that cannot be manufactured completely free of risk of harm to the patient, adequate warnings are mandated. The reasonably prudent provider must obtain and understand all relevant information concerning necessary warnings and incorporate this information into the consultation at which informed consent is obtained. Misuse or misrepresentation of product information, including research data and clinical literature, may be grounds for liability to the consumer. The learned intermediary doctrine is a defense to product manufacturers and distributors and should be a caution sign for the unsuspecting provider.

Federal laws and statutes require reporting to appropriate authorities. Medicolegal risk analysis requires management of claims information and compliant dissemination and maintenance of this information. The same is true with insurance-related information. Claims should be reported in an accurate, complete, and timely manner. Failure to do so may result in uncovered liability claims.

In purchasing and using insurance products effectively, many questions need to be asked. The operation and form of the policy are relevant. The limits of coverage, the amount of limits, and the terms and conditions of coverage are all necessary information in making risk-management decisions with regard to purchasing coverage for malpractice liability claims.

Testimony given under oath is an important aspect of medicolegal risk analysis. The context of the testimony requested should be understood clearly before any action is taken by the provider. Whether the provider is called as a fact witness or as an expert witness must be determined. If the situation is not clear, the necessary questions must be asked. A fact witness may be compelled to give testimony pursuant to subpoena, without payment of a fee other than statutory reimbursements for mileage and nominal appearances. A provider is not required to express personal professional opinions beyond the scope of the history obtained, the diagnosis made, the treatment provided, the result obtained, or the prognosis given. When expressing opinions admissible under the rules of evidence, caution must be exercised to obtain and review thoroughly all pertinent records and testimony before giving testimony. Whereas a fact witness may not be able to insist on payment of a professional fee for services in giving testimony, an expert may. What is a reasonable fee and what is an unreasonable fee depend on the qualifications of the expert asked to render an opinion, the difficulty or complexity of the case, and the amount of time and resources that must be expended to perform the work requested. Most jurisdictions have interprofessional committees or task forces that have reviewed the ongoing work between health care professionals and trial lawyers. These organizations require fair and responsible conduct from both perspectives. Candor, integrity, professionalism, and fairness are the watchwords for expert witness performance under numerous professional guidelines.

Finally, ex parte communications in violation of the doctor-patient privilege are to be avoided. Requirement of a signed, written release for records and for medicolegal consultations with attorneys should be made. Testimony, either in court or in deposition, should be given only pursuant to a valid subpoena or court order. Caution is necessary in giving testimony, with consideration for the privilege, the accuracy of the testimony, the expression of professional opinions admissible into evidence, and the context of the testimony. A provider is not an advocate, and the testimony should be considered for the benefit of the court, not one party or the other.

Medicolegal risk analysis is designed to raise questions constantly. Viewed as intended, this chapter will assist the clinician, researcher, instructor, and related professionals to raise and to revise these questions and the answers constantly. It is only through this process that the techniques of medicolegal risk analysis will continue to be beneficial.

International Perspective on Treatment Outcomes

6.

John Wolfaardt, BDS, MDent, PhD
Anders Tjellström, MD, PhD
Stephen M. Parel, DDS
Gordon H. Wilkes, BScMed, MD

- History of Craniofacial Osseointegration
- Individual Implant Success
- The Skin Response
- Innovation in Relation to Craniofacial Osseointegration

Per-Ingvar Brånemark was not the first to introduce the concept of skin-penetrating implants. This prompts the question of why Brånemark's work on skin-penetrating implants in facial reconstruction has aroused such international interest across a broad spectrum of clinical and research disciplines. In considering the international perspective on percutaneous osseointegrated implants in craniofacial reconstruction, the remarkable and unique contribution of Brånemark is evident. The purpose of this chapter is to consider the international perspective on craniofacial osseointegration through an appreciation of treatment outcomes.

A percutaneous implant has been described as an "object foreign to the body placed through the skin such that a permanent defect is created."[1] The prospect of establishing a permanent percutaneous connection has numerous applications and has challenged medical science for many years. As recently as 1981, von Recum and Park[2] concluded that there were no studies that consistently demonstrated percutaneous devices being maintained in humans or animals for longer than 3 months without failure due to infection. Historically, a clinical need for permanent percutaneous connections is found in nephrology, cardiology, neurology, urology, otolaryngology, orthopedic surgery, plastic and reconstructive surgery, and many other clinical disciplines. Clearly, this demonstrated a pervasive need for developing means to establish a permanent percutaneous connection.

Head and neck reconstruction is one area of clinical endeavor in which investigators have long expressed a desire for permanent percutaneous connection. Autogenous head and neck reconstruction is not always possible, may not be desirable, or may be delayed. Prosthetic reconstruction becomes the treatment modality of choice in such circumstances. In these situations, a permanent percutaneous connection anchored in underlying bone supports facial prostheses.

For a facial prosthesis to be successful, it must meet criteria of aesthetic acceptability, functional performance, biocompatibility, and longevity. Inherent mechanical retention within the defect or the use of adhesive systems frequently has proved problematic or unacceptable.[3-13] The use of adhesives remains controversial, and this arises from long-expressed concerns of unpredictable performance, placing adhesives on compromised tissue surfaces, difficulty of manipulation, decreased durability of the prosthesis, and added cost to the patient.[3,4,7-9] As a result of the problems encountered with adhesive systems, advocacy of the use of mechanical retention has been made. In the past, mechanical retention has involved the engagement of divergent undercuts within the defect or the use of external retention to headbands, elasticized retention, spectacle frames, or other methods of varying ingenuity. Frequently, inherent retention within the defect is absent or external forms of retention are unacceptable to the patient. With the prevalence of these historically crude approaches to facial prosthesis retention, it is not surprising that methods of retention continued as a source of debate with little resolution and remained the primary limiting factor to success with prosthetic reconstruction. With the introduction of osseointegrated implant biotechnology to facial prosthetics, there was opportunity to provide secure retention of prostheses without jeopardizing the integrity of the skin and underlying tissues or the prosthesis.

The use of osseointegration biotechnology in facial prosthetic restoration was hailed in 1986 as the most significant advance in the field of facial prosthetic restoration in the past 25 years.[7] A statement as strong as this merits consideration of the impact that craniofacial osseointegration has had on the international perspective.

History of Craniofacial Osseointegration

The principles of osseointegration are well documented and the outcomes of this modality of treatment in the management of edentulousness were already scientifically established by the early 1980s in longitudinal[14] and replication studies.[15] In 1975, Brånemark postulated that a skin-penetrating implant should be possible based on the principles of dental implants.[16] Following the pioneering work by Brånemark and his co-workers, the first clinical trial on skin-penetrating osseointegrated implants was conducted in 1977 at Sahlgren's Hospital in Göteborg, Sweden, where specifically designed implants were placed in the mastoid region to support a bone conduction hearing aid (Fig 6-1).[16,17] In 1979, the first implants were placed in the mastoid region to retain an auricular prosthesis (Fig 6-2).[18] In May 1984, the biotechnology was released internationally with the introduction of training courses in Göteborg, Sweden.[19] In February 1988, the Bone-Anchored Hearing Aid (BAHA) was approved for use within the Swedish health system by the Swedish National Social Welfare Board.[20] A state of the art conference was held in Göteborg, Sweden, on September 1, 1988, to consider bone-anchored implants in the head and neck region. A report on this landmark conference was compiled by the Swedish Council on Technology Assessment in Health Care.[21] This report was the founding document on the introduction of craniofacial osseointegration in head and neck reconstruction and was the first document to provide data on cost of care delivery. Since 1986, international conferences on craniofacial osseointegration have been convened and reports emanating from that time have confirmed the efficacy and predictability of craniofacial osseointegration.[22-29]

Individual Implant Success

Since the introduction of craniofacial osseointegration in 1977, there have been essentially two variables used to evaluate treatment outcome in the literature: individual implant success and skin response. More recently, other variables have been reported and, importantly, among these is patient response to treatment.

The Swedish Experience

In 1980 Tjellström et al[30] published a report on BAHAs. Subsequently, in 1981 Tjellström and co-workers[17,31] published two papers on the use of titanium implants in the temporal bone; one specifically dealt with an implant-retained ear prosthesis. These early descriptive reports first introduced the concept of skin-penetrating osseointegrated implants supporting facial prostheses and BAHAs.

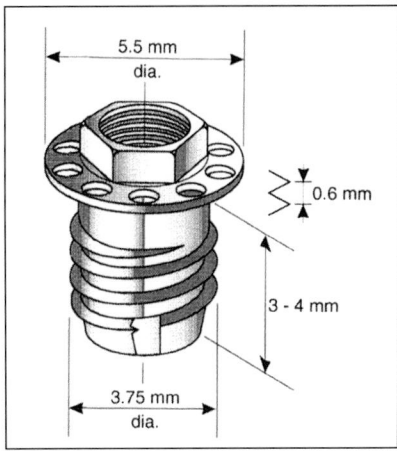

Fig 6-1 Dimensions of the 4.0-mm cranio-facial implant introduced in 1984. *dia*, diameter.

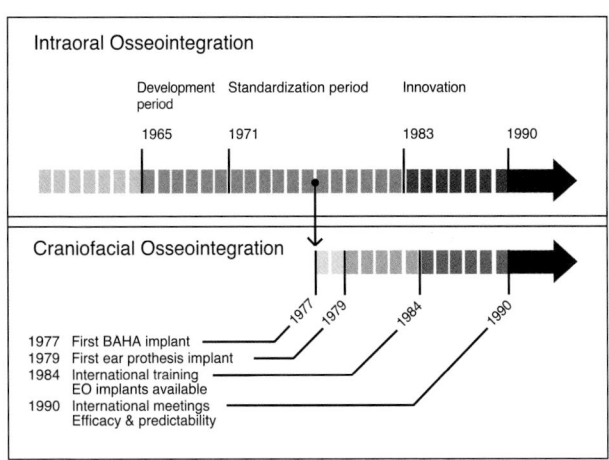

Fig 6-2 Historical development of craniofacial osseointegration in relation to the development of intraoral osseointegrated implants. *BAHA*, Bone-Anchored Hearing Aid; *EO*, extraoral.

In 1983, Tjellström et al.[32] reported a 1- to 5-year follow-up on the Göteborg experience with craniofacial osseointegrated implants in the temporal bone for retaining facial prostheses and for BAHAs. This early report assessed 14 implants placed for BAHA and 44 implants placed for retaining facial prostheses. This study concluded that threaded titanium implants could be osseointegrated in the temporal bone for periods of 5 years or more and that it was possible to achieve a permanent skin penetration in the temporal region without adverse tissue reactions. In a 1985 report on 5 years' experience with bone-anchored auricular prostheses, Tjellström et al[33] discussed 159 craniofacial osseointegrated implants that had been placed in 38 patients for retaining auricular prostheses. The study reported the loss of integration of one implant and the removal of two abutments because of skin inflammation. By this time, the surgical technique was well described in the literature and the sense of need to consider treatment outcomes with greater sophistication in terms of individual implant success and skin response emerged.

A later development was to extend the clinical applications of craniofacial osseointegration to or-bital and nasal reconstruction. In 1987, a publication by the Göteborg group[16] presented an evaluation of treatment outcomes on 389 skin-penetrating implants in 174 patients. Within this group of patients, 103 were treated with BAHA, 49 with an auricular prosthesis, 18 with orbital prostheses, 2 with nasal prostheses, and 2 with reconstruction of other facial deformities. Of the 389 implants placed, 6 were not integrated at second-stage surgery, and the study reported an overall success rate of 98%. Importantly, five of the six failures were in irradiated bone. Therefore, it was concluded that the success rate was 99.7% in nonirradiated bone and 85.3% in therapeutically irradiated bone. This study also found that skin reactions were mild or nonexistent, with 92.1% of 951 clinical observations showing no adverse skin reaction. The study concluded that potentially serious skin reactions occurred in only 2.8% of observations. This paper was significant in that it drew attention to several issues that would be important for the future: the extended applications of craniofacial osseointegration beyond the temporal region, the importance of therapeutic radiation on individual implant success rates, and the significance of monitoring skin response to percutaneous abutments.

Eleven years after initiating treatment for ear replacement with craniofacial osseointegrated implants, Tjellström[18] published 10-year follow-up results on 94 patients treated for auricular replacement with implants. Of these patients, 30 had been followed for more than 5 years and 52 for more than 3 years. A total of 303 implants were for ear replacement and 244 abutments had been connected, with no patients lost to follow-up. The discrepancy between implants placed and abutments connected was attributed to the early approach of additional implants being placed in case of implant failure. In the early experience, three or four implants were placed. However, this report confirmed that only two implants were necessary to support an auricular prosthesis. Remarkably, only 2 of the 94 patients were reported to not wear their prostheses. This report added substantially to our knowledge of outcomes of craniofacial osseointegration treatment. First, it confirmed the individual implant and skin response success rates during a 10-year period. Second, the study indicated that two implants in the mastoid region were sufficient to retain an auricular prosthesis. The report also defined several factors leading to implant failure and abutment removal. In this way the contributing factors of soft-tissue infection, percutaneous abutment hygiene, and behavioral factors became better understood in treatment selection.

Clinical research on craniofacial osseointegration was providing an understanding that craniofacial osseointegrated implants yielded treatment outcomes that were distinct from those of the dental implants as understood at that time. A 1992 study[34] evaluated osseointegrated skin-penetrating titanium implants used to retain facial prostheses for a 5-year period. In this evaluation, the prosthesis had to have been worn for at least 6 months. The evaluation included 70 auricular and 17 orbital prosthesis patients. The study found that achieving integration in the orbit was not as successful as in the mastoid region. In the mastoid region, the success rate continued to be predictable: 95% success rate for implants placed, exposed, loaded, and connected. In the orbit, for implants exposed, the success rate was 72%. A further difference was that the failures in the mastoid occurred within 6 months after insertion, whereas orbit failures tended to occur later, with losses reported as late as 6 years after insertion. Of the 19 implants in the orbit that were found not to have integrated, 16 were in therapeutically irradiated bone.

The success rate in irradiated orbits was calculated as 62.7% and in nonirradiated orbits, as 92.1%. Clearly, placement of implants in irradiated bone had been identified as a challenge. This publication was particularly important because it attempted to describe criteria for evaluating individual implant success in craniofacial osseointegration. Although in 1986 criteria for success for dental osseointegrated implants were proposed by Albrektsson et al,[35] it was in 1988 that the report of a conference defined similar criteria for skin-penetrating implants for extraoral and BAHA applications.[21] Subsequently, in 1992 Jacobsson et al[34] proposed revised criteria for success for craniofacial implants (Table 6-1). These success criteria address individual implant success. Currently, no internationally accepted criteria exist for assessing success in terms of patient-perceived outcomes of treatment for either BAHA or implant-retained facial prostheses.

A two-stage surgical technique was fundamental to Brånemark's approach. More recently, one-stage procedures have been undertaken in the mastoid region. Tjellström and Granström[36] reported their results of patients treated with one-stage or two-stage procedures for BAHAs and auricular prostheses. The one-stage surgery group showed a 16% graft failure, which was attributed to altered vascularity because of the nature of the one-stage procedure. The two-stage group showed no graft failure. Apart from this finding, the two groups were not different in terms of the success rate for stable implants. These workers suggested the use of a 4.0-mm-length implant for one-stage procedures. They recommended that the one-stage procedure be used only for the mastoid and not in children or irradiated bone.

By the early 1990s craniofacial osseointegration had taken several new clinical research directions, and the training programs were having an impact on rapidly emerging international involvement. The international involvement in craniofacial osseointegration has been heavily influenced by the role of medical device regulatory bodies and the introduction of other implant systems. Treatment of the irradiated patient and the use of hyperbaric oxygen therapy, increased interest in skin response to percutaneous abutments, one-stage procedures, biomechanics, treatment selection, and imaging are some of the many areas evoking clinical and scientific interest. Some of these issues will be considered further in this chapter.

Table 6-1 *Criteria for Success of Craniofacial Osseointegrated Implants*

The Swedish Council on Technology Assessment in Health Care	Jacobsson et al.
1) The implants are immobile, as verified by clinical examination	1) Individual unattached implants should be immobile when tested clinically
2) No prolonged symptoms, such as pain, infection, tactile disorders, or nerve damage, should be present in connection with the implants	2) Soft-tissue reactions around skin-penetrating abutments should be of types 0 (reaction free) or 1 (slight redness, not demanding treatment) in more than 95% of all observations
3) Penetrated soft tissue should be free from irritation in at least 85% of the regular outpatient postoperative checkups	3) Individual implant performance should be characterized by the absence of persistent or irreversible signs and symptoms such as pain, infections, neuropathies, or paresthesia
4) At least 95% of the temporal bone implants and at least 75% of other extraoral implants should be functional after 5 years	4) In the context of the above, a success rate of 95% in the mastoid process and 90% in the orbital region, in nonirradiated bone tissue, at the end of a 5-year observation period should be a minimum criterion for success
Modified from Hållen et al.[21]	From Jacobsson et al.[34] By permission of Quintessence Publishing.

The International Experience

In 1986, Parel et al[7,37] published several reports on the experience with craniofacial osseointegration at the University of Texas at San Antonio. The first implants in this study were reported to have been placed in 1982. These publications indicated the number of implants placed but did not report on treatment outcomes.

A study by Parel and Tjellström[38] of the experience with craniofacial osseointegrated implants involved the work of 1 Swedish and 13 United States centers. These authors investigated the number of implants placed into patients who had or had not received radiotherapy. Although no experience with BAHAs was reported from the United States, the Swedish experience was included. Several important facts emerged from Parel and Tjellström's report. The study indicated that implant placement in the mastoid region had a high success rate based on individual implant evaluation, with a combined center success rate of 98.3% in nonirradiated patients. Orbital implants in nonirradiated patients provided an equally impressive combined success rate of 93.9%. Success rates in the midface and in irradiated patients proved more variable. The combined center individual implant success rate for irradiated patients was 61.1%. In some anatomic locations the number of patients treated was too small to draw firm con-

clusions. In this early evaluation, it appeared that the nonirradiated patient could be effectively treated with osseointegrated implants to retain a facial prosthesis in various areas of the facial skeleton. These investigators concluded that the therapeutically irradiated patient should be approached with care and in an environment that fully appreciated the risks associated with external-beam therapy.

In 1993, the Canadian experience with craniofacial osseointegrated implants was reported.[19] This study looked at the early Canadian results and combined them with the Swedish and United States results. The combined result reported the treatment of 603 nonirradiated patients (Table 6-2). In this patient group, 1,221 extraoral implants were placed and 1,190 were regarded as stable at the time of reporting, thereby providing an individual implant success rate of 97.5%. The experience in all three countries provided similar rates of individual implant success. A much smaller group of therapeutically irradiated patients had been treated, with 34 patients being reported on. In this study, 100 of 144 implants successfully integrated, for an overall success rate of 69.4%. In the therapeutically irradiated group of patients, the success rate was highest in Canada, followed by the United States and then Sweden. Importantly, these differences were attributed to time of follow-up, number of cases treated, and distribution of

Table 6-2   Success Rates of Swedish, United States of America (USA), and Canadian Experience* With Craniofacial Implants

	Patients treated, no.	Implants inserted, no.	Implants integrated, no.	Success rate, %
Nonirradiated				
Sweden	435	767	755	98.4
USA	84	268	253	94.4
Canada	84	186	182	97.8
Total	603	1,221	1,190	97.5
Irradiated				
Sweden	16	57	33	57.9
USA	11	51	33	64.7
Canada	7	36	34	94.4
Total	34	144	100	69.4
Total	637	1,365	1,290	94.5

*Number of centers: Sweden = 1, United States = 13, and Canada = 6.
From Wolfaardt et al.[19] By permission of Quintessence Publishing.

case type treated. As each of these factors increases, it appears that the success rate can be expected to decline toward an as yet unestablished baseline for irradiated patients. It must be remembered that at that time hyperbaric oxygen therapy was not routinely considered in the management of the therapeutically irradiated patient treated with osseointegrated implants.

Roumanas et al[39] reported a 6-year follow-up on the University of California at Los Angeles experience with craniofacial implants. This study reported on 30 patients treated between 1987 and 1993 with craniofacial osseointegrated implants for retention of facial prostheses. Of the 92 implants inserted, 86 were connected, but of these 8 subsequently were buried because of soft-tissue problems. Failure to achieve osseointegration occurred in 15 implants. The reported success rates (with number of patients in parentheses) in the nonirradiated patients were: auricular 91.9% (9), nasal 75% (9), and orbital 75% (3). The reported success rates (with number of patients in parentheses) in the irradiated patients were: auricular 100% (1), nasal 50% (2), and orbital 58.3% (5). These authors concluded that placement of implants in therapeutically irradiated sites is not a predictable procedure. Hyperbaric oxygen therapy was not administered to patients treated in this study. These authors speculated on the relative merits of hyperbaric oxygen therapy given that they thought that not every patient would be able to af-

ford hyperbaric oxygen therapy. Their approach was to place additional implants to overcome expected implant loss in the irradiated patient.

On January 13, 1995, the Food and Drug Administration provided clearance to Nobel Biocare USA, Inc. to market the Brånemark craniofacial implant system. Tolman and Taylor[40] reported on the results of the trial initiated in 1988 in the United States for the Food and Drug Administration. This prospective study involved 24 centers and 145 patients who were treated with craniofacial osseointegrated implants to retain facial prostheses. Of the 145 patients, 115 were evaluated throughout the study and were followed up for at least 30 months. A total of 452 implants were placed in the following regions: auricular (318), orbital (98), and nasal (36); 77 implants were not evaluated because they were left as "sleepers" or were not uncovered. The individual implant success rates (with number of patients in parentheses) reported for the nonirradiated group followed throughout the study were similar to those reported in previously cited studies: auricular 99% (85), nasal 94% (6), and orbital 100% (14). In the irradiated group, the results were somewhat different from previously cited studies in that fewer losses in the orbit were noted. The individual implant success rates (with number of patients in parentheses) reported for the irradiated group followed throughout the study were: auricular 100% (2), nasal 100% (1), and orbital 90% (7).

Table 6-3 *Results of Quality of Life Assessment*		
Assessment	Before enrollment in study, %	18 months after prosthesis connection, %
Stability of prosthesis	50	93
Acceptable appearance of prosthesis	31	72
Self-conscious about prosthesis	36	77
Placement of prosthesis	39	91
Removal of prosthesis	58	91
Able to practice good hygiene	55	65
Activities not limited by prosthesis	38	83
Remove prosthesis no more than once a day	68	89
Data from Tolman and Taylor.[40]		

Table 6-4 *Classification of Soft-Tissue Response to Percutaneous Titanium Abutments*	
Class	Description
0	No irritation: epithelial debris removed if present
1	Slight redness: temporary local treatment
2	Red and slightly moist tissue; no granuloma formation: local treatment; extra controls
3	Reddish and moist; sometimes granulation tissue: revision surgery is indicated
4	Removal of skin-penetrating implant necessary as a result of infection
R	Removal of implant for reasons not related to skin problems
From Holgers et al.[41] By permission of Quintessence Publishing.	

Tolman and Taylor[40] attempted to assess quality of life issues associated with craniofacial osseointegration treatment. The assessment was conducted by questionnaire and telephone survey. The questionnaire was administered at enrollment into the study and at 6 and 18 months after prosthesis connection. A particularly important finding was that 93% of patients rated the implant prosthesis stable at 18 months, whereas only 50% of those patients with a non-implant-retained prosthesis before the study rated the prosthesis as stable at the time of entering the study. A summary of the results of the questionnaire reported in the study is provided in Table 6-3. Of the 30 patients who participated in a telephone poll, 19 wore the prosthesis more than 12 hours per day. Remarkably, 24 patients reported that they saw the prosthesis as an extension of themselves. Tolman and Taylor[40] concluded that craniofacial osseointegration provided an important alternative to conventional reconstructive surgery and demonstrated a significant improvement in quality of life compared with previous retention systems for facial prostheses.

The Skin Response

Individual implant success rates have been used most frequently to evaluate treatment outcomes.

Additionally, skin response has also been considered as an indicator of success by rating the skin response on a five-point scale. This five-point scale emanated from the work of Holgers et al[41] in 1987 and has been adopted widely, with variation, in the literature (Table 6-4). The technique that has been used with this grading scale is to report on all clinical observations of skin response during an interval. Holgers et al[41] evaluated 136 implants for auricular prostheses during a 3- to 66-month period. They made 708 observations of skin response and found 647 observations (91.4%) of no response and 27 observations (3.8%) of slight redness. They concluded that the failure rate was similar to that observed in cardiac pacemakers. In a similar study on percutaneous abutments for BAHAs, Holgers et al[42] evaluated 313 observations on 67 BAHA abutments. Of the observations, 292 (93.3%) showed no reaction and 13 (4.2%) showed slight redness. It was concluded that grading of slight redness could be clinically questioned and that the success rate could be considered 97.5%. Holgers et al[43,44] have since published on various aspects of the skin response, including morphologic and microbiologic aspects of the skin response to percutaneous titanium abutments.

Albrektsson et al[16] conducted 951 clinical observations of skin response around 389 abutments for BAHAs (243 observations) and auricular prostheses (708 observations). Of the observations, 92.1% showed no skin response and 3.9% showed slight redness. Potentially serious skin responses occurred in only 2.8% of observations. Tjellström[18] reported on 244 skin-penetrating abutments used to retain auricular prostheses. He compared the skin response in this group at three periods separated by 2-year intervals. For the three sequential periods, grading of no reaction was 92.9%, 88.8%, and 89.3% over the 4 years. Interestingly, this study reported that 15% of patients accounted for 70% of skin reactions. A small group of patients may have had repeated adverse skin reactions.

Tjellström et al[45] considered the skin response in children. Eight patients ranging in age from 6 to 11 years were included in the study. Evaluation of 113 observations of skin response on 26 abutments revealed 95 observations (84.1%) of no skin response. It was reported that problems were encountered with two of the subjects when they entered adolescence, as a result of behavioral problems and lack of compliance with hygiene measures.

It had been unclear whether the skin response would be different in skin that had been in the path of a therapeutically irradiated field. Jacobsson et al[34] examined the skin response in the mastoid and orbital region in patients treated with craniofacial osseointegrated implants. In the mastoid region, 88% of observations showed no skin response and 7.8% showed slight redness. In the orbit, 92.6% of observations showed no response and 5.4% showed slight redness. It was concluded that the frequency and distribution of the adverse skin reactions were the same for mastoid and orbital areas in spite of the fact that many patients with orbital implants had received radiotherapy. Granström et al[46] did an extensive analysis of titanium implants lost in irradiated tissue. These researchers found no statistically significant difference between the skin response of the control group and that of the irradiated group at 3 months and 1 year after implant surgery. This study included patients treated with implants in the orbit, midface, and temporal bone. Interestingly, irradiated patients treated with hyperbaric oxygen showed improved skin responses during the first year but not at later periods.

In 1994, Holgers[47] published a monograph based on doctoral work that examined skin response to skin-penetrating titanium implants. This comprehensive work considered grading of skin response as well as morphologic, microbiologic, and immunologic aspects of skin with permanent, percutaneous titanium abutments.

Gitto and co-workers[48] assessed the skin response in seven patients treated with BUD implants (BUD Industries, East Aurora, New York). Five patients were treated for auricular prostheses, one for an orbital prosthesis, and one for a hair replacement prosthesis. Various factors were assessed, including sebaceous crusting, presence of a peri-implant exudate, skin cultures, implant mobility, and tissue response characterized by type, thickness, contour and attachment, mobility, and reaction. The factors described will prove useful to those considering research on skin response to titanium percutaneous implants. Interestingly, these researchers proposed a four-point grading of skin response based more on a typical inflammatory response. Only two patients had a skin response: one had a mild response and the other had a moderate to severe response. All cultures grew normal skin flora except for those from the two patients with adverse skin reactions which grew *Staphylococcus aureus*. This finding was in agreement with that of Holgers.[47]

Toljanic et al[49] examined the microflora of five subjects treated with orbital percutaneous implants. They found 17 distinct microbial strains, which could be categorized as those that are constituents of the skin and upper aerodigestive tract and those that commonly are found in the intestinal tract. It was suggested that the presence of the intestinal tract organisms was due to the iatrogenic environment created within the crevicular space around the abutment. Additionally, the frequency of occurrence of each organism did not appear to be related to the level of hygiene practiced by the patient. Staphylococci were the most prevalent organism among those isolated. Because all implant sites studied were clinically free of disease, it was concluded that host defense factors must be operating.

Tolman and Taylor[40] reported on 1,872 observations of skin response based on the Holgers et al[41] five-point grading system. During the 30-month period of assessment of patients with orbital, nasal, and auricular prostheses, 4.0% of observations recorded an adverse tissue response.

Innovation in Relation to Craniofacial Osseointegration

With the rapid escalation of interest in craniofacial osseointegration, there is much innovation surrounding this biotechnology. This innovation spans many aspects of care delivery to the facial prosthetic and BAHA patient.

Hyperbaric Oxygen Therapy

The problem of higher rates of implant loss in therapeutically irradiated bones has been well established in the literature. The use of hyperbaric oxygen therapy has been shown to substantially decrease the loss of craniofacial osseointegrated implants in irradiated bone. In 1988, Jacobsson et al[50] reported the loss of 5 of 35 skin-penetrating implants. This 14% loss was higher than expected in nonirradiated bone. The rationale for these situations was to place additional implants that could be used later if losses occurred, to delay implant placement for 12 months after radiotherapy, and to allow the implants to heal for 9 to 12 months before connecting them through the skin. These delays placed additional burden on irradiated patients requiring craniofacial osseointegrated implants. Granström et al[51,52] reported the use of hyperbaric oxygen therapy to decrease the risk of implant loss in the irradiated patient. In 1994, Granström et al[46] reported that with the use of hyperbaric oxygen therapy no implant losses had occurred during a 5-year follow-up period of 48 implants placed in irradiated orbital, nasal, and temporal regions. Granström et al[53] have also considered the possibility of having implants installed and then having to irradiate the patient or subject the patient to chemotherapy. They found that skin dehiscence occurred in a significant number of patients who were irradiated, and 2 of 32 implants were lost with induction of chemotherapy. They suggested that successfully integrated implants should be disconnected and buried if they are to be irradiated. Hyperbaric oxygen therapy has been an important development in decreasing implant loss in therapeutically irradiated patients. It significantly decreases treatment time of irradiated patients because the 12-month waiting period after radiotherapy before placing implants[50] is no longer necessary. In addition, with hyperbaric oxygen therapy, the second-stage surgery can be done 6 months after implant installation.

Biomechanics

Biomechanics has assumed an ever-increasing importance in establishing, enhancing, and preserving the integrity of the bone-titanium interface. Del Valle et al[13] did a mechanical evaluation of craniofacial osseointegration retention systems and found them to be more predictable than the adhesive retention systems. Additionally, these authors suggested that preformed bars were superior in retention performance to cast bars in bar and clip retention systems. The new magnet systems developed for retention of facial prostheses by way of osseointegrated implants were found to be of improved and acceptable performance. This study also found that the loads delivered by the retention systems were not to be considered trivial. Rangert[54] made recommendations based on principles of biomechanics as to how craniofacial osseointegrated implants should be spatially arranged and how superstructures should be designed. This author also considered the relative merits of stand-alone and connected implants in prosthesis design. Anderson and Kasra[55] have applied engineering principles to the design of a superstructure for an extensive midfacial defect. This approach was adopted in an attempt to control forces and moments on the implants supporting and retaining the facial prosthesis.

Imaging

Siting craniofacial implants has proved difficult in certain situations such as in children with congenital anomalies. The result is that implants are positioned in less than favorable sites for prosthesis construction or BAHA positioning. Surgery may have to be abandoned if adequate bone volume cannot be found. Watson et al[56] developed means of digitally overlaying three-dimensional laser scanning and computed tomographic scanning so that the image of the desired implant location on the skin surface can be correlated with the underlying bone image. The result is that once implant sites are selected from the imaging study, a surgical template is milled numerically to identify the implant positions for the surgeon.

Autogenous and Craniofacial Implant Ear Reconstruction

Autogenous auricular reconstruction remains a challenge for the reconstructive surgeon. The introduction of craniofacial osseointegration provides a technique of ear reconstruction that had not previously existed. The relative use of autogenous reconstruction and craniofacial implant-retained prosthesis reconstruction has been considered.[57,58]

Wilkes and Wolfaardt[59] developed criteria for treatment selection based on the belief that autogenous reconstruction and craniofacial osseointegration are not competing technologies but rather are complementary. These authors consider that the important issue is to select the right treatment modality for the patient.

Innovation now extends beyond what is possible to discuss in the available space. The literature on craniofacial osseointegration is expanding rapidly. The development of techniques for prosthesis construction, for enhancing the aesthetics of prostheses, treatment planning techniques, and BAHA technology are all areas receiving much attention in the literature on craniofacial osseointegration.

Conclusion

The clinical history of dental osseointegrated implants is in excess of 30 years, with the technology having been available to the international community for the past 14 years. The number of dental osseointegrated implants placed each year is now in the hundreds of thousands. Craniofacial osseointegration has a history of almost 20 years, with use in the international community for approximately 12 years. Owing to the nature of conditions treated and the more difficult regulatory environment associated with introducing new biotechnology, the number of patients treated with craniofacial osseointegrated implants is relatively small compared with the number of patients treated with dental osseointegrated implants. It is estimated that several thousand patients have been treated with BAHA and facial prostheses. These factors make craniofacial osseointegration distinct from dental osseointegration. Other issues that make it distinct are that it functions in a percutaneous environment that is less forgiving than the oral environment, it is exposed to the external environment, frequently it is used in situations where the tissues are compromised by combined modality cancer therapy, and it is often indicated for use in children. For these and other reasons, the decision to use craniofacial osseointegration biotechnology should be made with concern for the patients' needs and with care not to misuse a valuable biotechnology for patients with special rehabilitative needs.

References

1. Mooney V, Schwartz SA, Roth AM, Gorniowsky MJ. Percutaneous implant devices. Ann Biomed Eng 1977;5:34.

2. von Recum AF, Park JB. Permanent percutaneous devices. CRC Crit Rev Bioeng 1981;5:37.

3. Chalian A, Bogan RL, Sandlewick JW. Retention of prostheses. In Chalian VA, Drane JB, Standish SM (eds): Maxillofacial Prosthetics: Multidisciplinary Practice. Baltimore: Williams & Wilkins; 1972:121.

4. Russouw C. The Bond Strength of Facial Prosthetic Adhesive Systems. Thesis, University of Witwatersrand, Johannesburg, South Africa, 1987.

5. Page K. Assessment of the mechanical properties of some facial prosthetic adhesives: a preliminary report. In: Proceedings of the International Congress on Maxillofacial Prosthetics and Technology, ed. 1. Southampton, England, UK: Millbrook Press; 1983:410.

6. Bonner E. The Need for and Value of a Maxillofacial Prostheodontic Service in the Witwatersrand-Vaal Area. Thesis, University of Witwatersrand, Johannesburg, South Africa, 1984.

7. Parel SM, Brånemark P-I, Tjellström A, Gion G. Osseointegration in maxillofacial prosthetics. Part II: Extraoral applications. J Prosthet Dent 1986;55:600.

8. Rahn AO, Boucher LJ. Maxillofacial Prosthetics: Principles and Concepts, ed 1. Philadelphia: WB Saunders; 1970:113.

9. Roberts AC. Facial reconstruction by prosthetic means. Br J Oral Surg 1967;4:157.

10. Parel SM. Diminishing dependence on adhesives for retention of facial prostheses. J Prosthet Dent 1980;43:552.

11. Hulland CV, Hulland SM, Turner TD. Adhesion to skin: principles and applications. In: Proceedings of the International Congress on Maxillofacial Prosthetics and Technology, ed. 1. Southampton, England, UK: Millbrook Press; 1983:402.

12. Wolfaardt JF, Tam V, Faulkner MG, Prasad N. Mechanial behavior of three maxillofacial prosthetic adhesive systems: a pilot project. J Prosthet Dent 1992;68:943.

13. Del Valle V, Faulkner G, Wolfaardt J, Rangert B, Tan HK. Mechanical evaluation of craniofacial osseointegration retention systems. Int J Oral Maxillofac Implants 1995;10:491.

14. Adell R, Lekholm U, Rockler B, Brånemark P-I. A 15-year study of osseointegrated implants in the treatment of the edentulous jaw. Int J Oral Surg 1981;10:387.

15. Zarb GA, Symington JM. Osseointegrated dental implants: preliminary report on a replication study. J Prosthet Dent 1983;50:271.

16. Albrektsson T, Brånemark P-I, Jacobsson M, Tjellström A. Present clinical applications of osseointegrated percutaneous implants. Plast Reconstr Surg 1987;79:721.

17. Tjellström A, Lindström J, Hallén O, Albrektsson T, Brånemark P-I. Osseointegrated titanium implants in the temporal bone. A clinical study on bone-anchored hearing aids. Am J Otol 1981;2:304.

18. Tjellström A. Osseointegrated implants for replacement of absent or defective ears. Clin Plast Surg 1990 April;17:355.

19. Wolfaardt JF, Wilkes GH, Parel SM, Tjellström A. Craniofacial osseointegration: the Canadian experience. Int J Oral Maxillofac Implants 1993;8:197.

20. Williams E. A Matter of Balance, ed 1. Göteborg, Sweden: Akademiförlaget; 1992:145.

21. Hallén O, Magnusson S, Jacobsson M, Marké L-Å. Bone-anchored implants in the head and neck region. Report from a conference. The Swedish Council on Technology Assessment in Health Care, 1988.

22. van Steenberghe D. Tissue Integration in Oral and Maxillofacial Reconstruction. Amsterdam: Excerpta Medica, 1986.

23. Laney WR. Eyes, ears, and noses too (editorial). Int J Oral Maxillofac Implants 1990;5:319.

24. Rydevik B, Brånemark P-I, Skalak R. International Workshop on Osseointegration in Skeletal Reconstruction and Joint Replacement. Göteborg, Sweden: Institute of Applied Biotechnology; 1991.

25. Ars B (editor). Congenital External and Middle Ear Malformations: Management. Amsterdam: Kugler Publications; 1992.

26. Laney WR, Tolman DE. Tissue Integration in Oral, Orthopedic, and Maxillofacial Reconstruction. Chicago: Quintessence Publishing Company; 1992.

27. Albrektsson T, Jacobsson M, Tjellström A. Implants in craniofacial rehabilitation and audiology. Third International Winter Seminar of the Biomaterials Group, Lech, Austria, March 3-8, 1991.

28. Wolfaardt JF, Wilkes GH. Craniofacial osseointegration Canada '93. The First Conference on Craniofacial Osseointegration in Canada, Lake Louise, Alberta, March 11-12, 1993.

29. Albrektsson T. Biomaterials Club. Fifth International Winter Meeting of the Biomaterials Group, Ischgl, Austria, February 12-17, 1995.

30. Tjellström A, Hakansson B, Lindström J, et al. Analysis of the mechanical impedance of bone-anchored hearing aids. Acta Otolaryngol (Stockh) 1980;89:85.

31. Tjellström A, Lindström J, Nylen O, et al. The bone-anchored auricular episthesis. Laryngoscope 1981;91:811.

32. Tjellström A, Rosenhall U, Lindström J, Hallén O, Albrektsson T, Brånemark P-I. Five-year experience with skin-penetrating bone-anchored implants in the temporal bone. Acta Otolaryngol (Stockh) 1983;95:568.

33. Tjellström A, Yontchev E, Lindström J, Brånemark P-I. Five years' experience with bone-anchored auricular prostheses. Otolaryngol Head Neck Surg 1985;93:366.

34. Jacobsson M, Tjellström A, Fine L, Andersson H. A retrospective study of osseointegrated skin-penetrating titanium fixtures used for retaining facial prostheses. Int J Oral Maxillofac Implants 1992;7:523.

35. Albrektsson T, Zarb G, Worthington P, Eriksson AR. The long-term efficacy of currently used dental implants: a review and proposed criteria of success. Int J Oral Maxillofac Implants 1986;1:11.

36. Tjellström A, Granström G. One-stage procedure to establish osseointegration: a zero to five years follow-up report. J Laryngol Otol 1995;109:593.

37. Parel SM, Holt GR, Brånemark P-I, Tjellström A. Osseointegration and facial prosthetics. Int J Oral Maxillofac Implants 1986;1:27.

38. Parel SM, Tjellström A. The United States and Swedish experience with osseointegration and facial prostheses. Int J Oral Maxillofac Implants 1991;6:75.

39. Roumanas E, Nishimura R, Beumer J III, Moy P, Weinlander M, Lorant J. Craniofacial defects and osseointegrated implants: six-year follow-up report on the success rates of craniofacial implants at UCLA. Int J Oral Maxillofac Implants 1994;9:579.

40. Tolman DE, Taylor PF. Bone-anchored craniofacial prosthesis study. Int J Oral Maxillofac Implants 1996;11:159.

41. Holgers KM, Tjellström A, Bjursten LM, Erlandsson BE. Soft tissue reactions around percutaneous implants: a clinical study on skin-penetrating titanium implants used for bone-anchored auricular prostheses. Int J Oral Maxillofac Implants 1987;2:35.

42. Holgers KM, Tjellström A, Bjursten LM, Erlandsson BE. Soft tissue reactions around percutaneous implants: a clinical study of soft tissue conditions around skin-penetrating titanium implants for bone-anchored hearing aids. Am J Otol 1988;9:56.

43. Holgers K-M, Paulsson M, Tjellström A, Bjursten L-M, Ljungh Å. Selected microbial findings in association with percutaneous titanium implants. Int J Oral Maxillofac Implants 1994;9:565.

44. Holgers K-M, Tjellström A, Thomsen P, Tjellström A, Ericson LE, Bjursten L-M. Morphologic evaluation of clinical long-term percutaneous titanium implants. Int J Oral Maxillofac Implants 1994;9:689.

45. Tjellström A, Jacobsson M, Albrektsson T, Jansson K. Use of tissue integrated implants in congenital aural malformations. Adv Otorhinolaryngol 1988;40:24.

46. Granström G, Bergström K, Tjellström A, Brånemark P-I. A detailed analysis of titanium implants lost in irradiated tissues. Int J Oral Maxillofac Implants 1994;9:653.

47. Holgers K-M. Soft Tissue Reactions Around Long-Term Clinical Skin-Penetrating Titanium Implants. Monograph, University of Göteborg, Göteborg, Sweden, 1994:58.

48. Gitto CA, Plata WG, Schaaf NG. Evaluation of the peri-implant epithelial tissue of percutaneous implant abutments supporting maxillofacial prostheses. Int J Oral Maxillofac Implants 1994;9:197.

49. Toljanic JA, Morello JA, Moran WJ, Panje WR, May EF. Microflora associated with percutaneous craniofacial implants used for the retention of facial prostheses: a pilot study. Int J Oral Maxillofac Implants 1995;10:578.

50. Jacobsson M, Tjellström A, Thomsen P, Albrektsson T, Turesson I. Integration of titanium implants in irradiated bone. Histologic and clinical study. Ann Otol Rhinol Laryngol 1988;97:337.

51. Granström G, Jacobsson M, Tjellström A. Titanium implants in irradiated tissue: benefits from hyperbaric oxygen. Int J Oral Maxillofac Implants 1992;7:15.

52. Granström G, Tjellström A, Brånemark P-I, Fornander J. Bone-anchored reconstruction of the irradiated head and neck cancer patient. Otolaryngol Head Neck Surg 1993;108:334.

53. Granström G, Tjellström A, Albrektsson T. Postimplantation irradiation for head and neck cancer treatment. Int J Oral Maxillofac Implants 1993;8:495.

54. Rangert B. Biomechanical considerations for implant-supported orbital prostheses. J Facial Somato Prosthet 1995;1:43.

55. Anderson JD, Kasra M. Engineered bar design for a midface defect: a case report. Int J Oral Maxillofac Implants 1996;11:400.

56. Watson RM, Coward TJ, Forman GH, Moss JP. Considerations in treatment planning for implant-supported auricular prostheses. Int J Oral Maxillofac Implants 1993;8:688.

57. Federspil P, Delb W. Treatment of congenital malformations of the external and middle ear. In Ars B (ed): Congenital External and Middle Ear Malformations: Management. Amsterdam: Kugler Publications; 1992:47.

58. Portmann D, Boudard P. Agenesia of the ear: therapeutic attitude. In Ars B (ed): Congenital External and Middle Ear Malformations: Management. Amsterdam: Kugler Publications; 1992:71.

59. Wilkes GH, Wolfaardt JF. Osseointegrated alloplastic versus autogenous ear reconstruction: criteria for treatment selection. Plast Reconstr Surg 1994;93:967.

Part II

Soft and Hard Tissue Defects: Pretreatment Evaluation

Surgical Considerations

7.

David Harris, FDS, FFD

- Patient Assessment and Selection
- Minimizing Patient Risk During Surgery and Anesthesia
- Patient Information and Preparation

Successful outcomes in reconstructive surgery depend on meticulous attention to detail in all aspects of patient care. The preoperative assessment and preparation of the patient should be considered as the first step in a continuum of care that extends through the planning and performance of the surgical procedure to the postoperative care and long-term follow-up.

Craniofacial reconstruction based on the principles of osseointegration is always an elective procedure. Because of this, it must be done only under optimum conditions on carefully selected patients for whom the potential benefits have been weighed carefully against the known possible complications and risks. Additionally, patients should be well prepared physically and psychologically, be kept fully informed about all aspects of the nature of the treatment, and be given a realistic view of the likely outcome.

Several considerations are involved: 1) patient assessment and selection, 2) minimizing patient risk during surgery and anesthesia, and 3) patient information and preparation.

Patient Assessment and Selection

In selecting a patient for a particular reconstructive procedure, attention should be focused exclusively on whether this represents the optimum form of treatment in light of an individual's physical, psychologic, and personal circumstances and perceived quality of life. Many factors and variables need to be considered carefully, including age, the presence of any concurrent disease process, and the significance of any previous therapy. A decision to proceed should be based on an evaluation of an overall risk-benefit analysis, taking into account alternative available treatments and the patient's own wishes. At all times the welfare of the patient must remain paramount.

When evaluating the potential improvement that might be obtained, it is necessary to analyze the extent to which the existing condition affects the patient physically and psychologically. Some tissue defects favor a clear objective measurement of the degree of the functional deficit. However, the psychologic consequences to the patient may not be evaluated so easily. For example, it can be expected that a facial deformity may have a significant impact on a patient's self-image and ability to function and interact socially. The extent of the patient's perceived disability, however, cannot necessarily be assessed objectively and reliably. The emotional impact and consequent interference with quality of life may be far greater than that which might be suggested by either the quantity or nature of the tissue deficit. In general, most patients readily volunteer an insight into their physical disabilities but are often reticent to disclose or discuss their deepest underlying emotional concerns. Given the lengthy and complex nature of many reconstructive procedures, every opportunity should be taken at an early stage to listen to and understand the patient's reasons for seeking help and expectations of the eventual outcome.

In a small number of people, the existence of an undisclosed hidden agenda could result in inappropriate selection of a patient who may appear eager to proceed. Such an event might well produce a patient who can never be happy with the results of treatment and who will focus on, and can be most intolerant of, any minor complications that might occur. When any doubt exists, the patient should be referred for a more complete psychologic or psychiatric assessment, preferably before surgical treatment!

Special care should be exercised in evaluating children. In many situations all information regarding the effects of the condition will be gained from the parents, with little or no input from the child. Even with young adults, a parent may have become overprotective as a result of a child's facial defect and insist on answering all questions. Although the parents' concerns are of course most important and indeed their wholehearted support for all phases of the rehabilitation is essential, it is vital in all cases to understand the problem from the patient's viewpoint. When the dynamics of the child-parent interaction preclude the establishment of a satisfactory physician-patient relationship, a psychiatric consultation should be sought.

Techniques used in rehabilitation, based on the placement of osseointegrated bone anchorage elements, may be in one of three categories. First, there are techniques that now have substantial published experimental and clinical documentation to support their routine application. A second category consists of procedures that have produced promising results in the short to medium term but still await the publication of sufficient clinical data to corroborate their long-term benefits. Last, there are some techniques that are still in the early stages of development and must be considered experimental. Applications within this last category should take place only at specialized centers as part of a carefully documented and ethically supervised clinical trial.

The placement of implants and associated reconstructive surgical procedures are planned to allow for the retention of a prosthetic device. The surgical objectives will be to provide a stable long-term anchorage for the prosthesis while preserving the integrity and biologic functioning of the bone and overlying soft tissues. They should also facilitate the design and provision of a prosthesis that can restore the tissue defect, provide for the maximum improvement in long-term function and comfort, and allow for the optimum restoration of aesthetics when required. A further objective will be to ensure that the health of the soft tissues adjacent to the implants can be maintained effectively by the patient.

If all these objectives are to be achieved, it is essential that an idealized normal model for the individual patient is visualized as part of the preoperative planning and is reconciled with the clinical possibilities. In most circumstances involving craniofacial reconstruction, developing a treatment strategy necessitates a multidisciplinary approach with significant input from other professionals who will be participating directly in the rehabilitative process. This may involve colleagues expert in the fields of anaplastology, maxillofacial prosthodontics, oncology, audiology, psychology, and social work. Optimum planning necessitates that the different clinical perspectives are collated at an early stage and consolidated into a surgical plan that can provide the best treatment outcome. This objective includes planning surgical conservation and reconstruction measures that can minimize functional deficits and support easier maintenance in the completed case. Clearly, it is imperative that one team member accepts overall responsibility for coordinating the various diagnostic and evaluation protocols.

A successful prosthetic construction may impose definite requirements for reconstructive surgery and on the type, number, and position of implants placed. The surgeon must fully appreciate the key demands of the prosthetic prescription and identify in advance those surgical requirements that cannot be met or need to be modified. When possible, the fabrication of a locating template showing optimum positioning of implants from a prosthetic standpoint is an invaluable guide during the planning and the operative stages.

Clinical examination should include a total assessment of all the available tissues, including the quality and quantity of the bone stock, skin, mucosa, and muscle. Where implants are to penetrate skin or mucosa, the type, thickness, mobility, and physical characteristics of these tissues are established. The need for secondary alterations to tissues at second-stage surgery can be considered. Any pathologic features adjacent to, or at, the proposed surgical sites should be identified. Infective processes are common in the jaw and the sinuses, and, if required, such problems are best dealt with before elective surgery.

Supplementary information may be obtained from plain radiographs and, when indicated, other imaging techniques, including tomography, computed tomography, magnetic resonance imaging, and ultrasonography. The type and number of radiographic studies undertaken should be designed to ensure that the patient receives the lowest radiation dose and restricted to those investigations that are likely to provide useful clinical information.

When insufficient or unsuitable tissues are present, consideration can be given to the use of augmentation techniques. It should be decided if these need to be done as a separate preliminary procedure or in conjunction with implant placement. Available techniques include free or microvascular grafting of autogenously derived bone and skin or soft-tissue grafts. Potential donor sites need to be evaluated to ensure they are suitable and can provide the type, quality, and quantity of tissues that are needed.

Attention should be given to the potential involvement of, or damage to, any important adjacent anatomic structures, nerves, or vessels and to the possible inadvertent removal of tissues that might subsequently compromise function. In the case of treated preexisting malignant disease, the proposed intervention must not interfere with future site inspection for signs of tumor recurrence.

In young patients in whom the proposed surgery necessitates alteration to or removal of existing tissues, special consideration must always be given to whether the resultant change in tissue topography could possibly jeopardize the application of future and more beneficial developments.

The patient's past or current medical history or condition may directly affect the prognosis. Previous radiotherapy to the area or to adjacent structures may have adversely affected the healing capacity of the tissues or have produced conditions for osteoradionecrosis to occur postoperatively. Full details of the nature, frequency, date, duration, and total dose received are required. This information provides a basis for judging the advisability of treatment, the timing of the procedure, and the necessity for prophylactic measures such as preoperative and postoperative hyperbaric oxygen dives.

Some medical conditions can predispose the patient to delayed healing or to an increased propensity for infections to develop. These include uncontrolled diabetes, any cause of general disability or immune depression, or when large doses of steroids are prescribed. Active, generalized bone conditions such as Paget's disease, osteomalacia, osteoporosis, or hyperparathyroidism can pose serious dilemmas for bone healing. Long-term retrospective studies on implants placed for intraoral reconstruction have shown a statistically significant increased failure rate in smokers.

Soft-tissue considerations, such as the occurrence of severe psoriasis, might create problems where skin penetration of implants is involved.

A patient's ability to collaborate fully, during the procedures and in the long-term perspective of continuing maintenance, may be influenced by several variables, including the patient's social condition or mental state or the presence of any physical or mental incapacities. Patients undergoing active psychiatric care need a careful evaluation in conjunction with their attending physician. A history of alcohol or substance abuse should be assessed critically.

Minimizing Patient Risk During Surgery and Anesthesia

Elective surgical procedures impose a particular onus of responsibility in identifying and anticipating any factors that might contribute to an increase in morbidity or mortality. This is especially true given the current trend for an increasing number of procedures to be done on an outpatient basis. It is common practice that the anesthesia evaluation may take place after the patient has been admitted. This could, on occasion, result in a procedure being postponed pending further investigations, with consequent waste of time and resources. This situation is also particularly frustrating for a patient who is prepared psychologically to proceed and has detailed personal and social plans in place for the anticipated perioperative period.

Table 7-1 Sample Protocol for Preoperative Tests*	
Tests	**Indications**
Urinalysis	All patients
Hematologic	
Hemoglobin	All women, men > 60 yr, risk of bleeding, major surgery
Prothrombin time and partial prothrombin test	Anticoagulants, liver disease, bleeding history, malignancy
Biochemical tests	
Serum electrolytes	> 60 yr, kidney disease, diabetes, diuretic or steroid therapy or bowel preparations
Serum creatinine	> 60 yr, kidney disease, diabetes, high blood pressure, nephrotoxic medication
Electrocardiogram	> 50 yr, cardiovascular or pulmonary disease, diabetes
Chest radiograph	> 60 yr, cardiovascular or pulmonary disease, malignancy, risk of tuberculosis
Pulmonary function	Symptoms or risk of lung disease, smoking > 20 pack-years†
Echocardiogram	Consider in heart failure and valvular heart disease

*Based on Medical Knowledge Self-Assessment Program.
†One pack-year = 20 cigarettes daily for 1 year.

A comprehensive preoperative evaluation is based on a detailed medical and social history and physical examination. Individual situations dictate the necessity for special screening tests, communication with the patient's attending physicians (present and past), or referral for a specialist's opinion. The presence of risk factors alone should not necessarily exclude a patient for elective surgery because, with appropriate management, many hazards may be minimized or eliminated. Once risk factors have been identified and evaluated, they can be reviewed in relation to the potential benefits of any proposed treatment. Medical conditions and therapy should be stabilized for at least 6 weeks before operation.

A detailed medical history includes particulars of all symptoms and treatment of present, past, and intercurrent disease as well as details of any previous operations, special investigations, or hospital admissions. Systematic inquiry is essential, with special emphasis given to current drug therapy; any bleeding or hematopoietic disorders; cardiorespiratory, endocrine, renal, neurologic, or liver disease; infections; allergies; or previous adverse drug reactions. In female patients of childbearing age, the presence or likelihood of pregnancy should be established, as should the use of hormonal contraceptive control.

The ever-growing list of investigations and special tests that can be done appears to be almost unlimited. Overinvestigation is wasteful of resources and not in the best interests of the patient. Apart from the medical history, several considerations can influence the scope of the screening protocol (Table 7-1). The likelihood of undiagnosed symptomless disease increases in individuals older than age 60 years. Some of these patients may not have had occasion to undergo any kind of health screening in the past. More extensive investigations may be appropriate for the elderly subject or for heavy smokers. The extent of the surgery, type of anesthesia to be used, length of hospital stay, and any postoperative restrictions need to be considered. The strategies adopted for special investigations should be dictated by common sense and the possible presence of known risk factors. They should focus on the probability of providing information that can anticipate or help in the management of problems in the individual patient.

In most cases a patient's current drug therapy should be continued with as little modification as possible. Medications given orally may need to be changed to parenteral administration before anesthesia or during the perioperative period, with consequent adjustment of dosage and frequency. Additionally, optimum dosage of different types of replacement therapy may need to be modified in response to the altered metabolic conditions resulting from the surgery and anesthesia. These include medications such as adrenal steroids and those used in the control of diabetes and thyroid insufficiency. To avoid increased risk of bleeding from reduced platelet function, nonsteroidal anti-inflammatory agents should be discontinued 5 to 7 days preoperatively and acetylsalicylic acid (aspirin), from 7 to 14 days.

When indicated, consideration should be given to referring the patient to a specialist for a full systems review and for specific advice and help in medical management preoperatively and postoperatively.

Thromboembolism

The risk of developing a deep vein thrombosis in the perioperative period increases in the presence of several factors: procedures during general anesthesia in excess of 30 minutes and those involving abdominal and thoracic interventions, patients older than age 40 years, obesity, prolonged immobilization postoperatively, or a history of previous deep vein thrombosis or pulmonary embolism. When indicated, appropriate prophylactic physical and pharmacologic measures can be prescribed. These include the use of external pneumatic compression, graduated compression stockings, low-dose heparin or enoxaparin given subcutaneously, or intravenously administered dextran solution.

Preoperative management of the patient should include measures designed to ensure good systemic health and to minimize the possibility of a wound infection. These include providing optimum control of diabetes, treatment of anemia, prevention of smoking, ensuring a good nutritional state, and eliminating any adjacent or remote sites of infection.

Antibiotic Prophylaxis and Infection

The use of antibiotics may be indicated prophylactically during operation to help avoid the development of wound infection or to minimize the possibility of a transient bacteremia developing into a chronic infection around existing prosthetic devices or damaged heart valves. The latter indications are well documented for all surgical procedures and should be considered mandatory.

There are increasing concerns about the development of antibiotic resistance and the possible inappropriate or incorrect use of antibiotics in clinical practice. Additionally, the risks of causing any of the adverse effects associated with using antimicrobial agents must be weighed against their potential benefits. Peterson[1] lists four guiding principles in considering antibiotic prophylaxis.

1) There should be a significant risk of infection associated with the type of surgery undertaken.
2) The correct antibiotic must be selected (i.e., it should be active against the type of organisms likely to be involved).
3) The dosage must be high enough to produce an effective concentration within the tissues that may become contaminated.
4) The timing and the duration of administration must be optimum.

When it is considered that there is a risk of a bacterial infection during an operative procedure, the organisms likely to be involved and their susceptibility to the antibiotic used should be known. The antibiotic should be present within the tissues, in sufficient concentration, at the time of contamination, and for no less than 4 hours afterward.

Commensals in the oropharyngeal region are predominantly aerobic and anaerobic streptococci, *Staphylococcus aureus*, peptococcus, peptostreptococcus, and many anaerobic gram-negative bacteria including *Bacteroides* species. Additionally, the nasal flora can harbor staphylococci, *Streptococcus pyogenes*, *Streptococcus pneumoniae*, and *Haemophilus* species. Skin flora include staphylococci and diphtheroids. In the oropharynx, anaerobic bacteria are more common than aerobic by a factor of 10.

The cephalosporin cefazolin in sufficient dosage is effective against most organisms encountered in clean contaminated surgery of the head and neck, including anaerobic bacteria. A suggested adult regimen is 2 g cefazolin administered intravenously 30 minutes before operation or at induction of anesthesia, followed by two repeat doses at 8-hour intervals. Alternatively, clindamycin 600 mg plus gentamicin 1.7 mg/kg is administered in three doses at 8-hour intervals as for cefazolin. Continuation of antibiotic prophylaxis beyond 24 hours postoperatively has not been shown to confer any advantage.

Surgical interventions have been classified into four categories that form a basis for predicting the risk of infection developing.[2] Reconstructive procedures with osseointegrated implants are considered to be in either category 1 or 2.

1) Clean: Uninfected operative wound in which the respiratory, alimentary, and genitourinary tracts and the oropharyngeal cavities are not entered. Clean surgery has an infection rate of approximately 2%, decreasing to 1% with good surgical technique.
2) Clean-contaminated: Operative wounds in which the respiratory, alimentary, or genitourinary tract is entered without unusual contamination and under controlled conditions. The predicted infection rate is 10% to 15%, decreasing to 1% with excellent surgical technique and prophylactic antibiotics.
3 and 4) Apply to procedures involving gross contamination and dirty or infected wounds.

It is acknowledged that the insertion of a foreign body in the tissues further increases the risk of infection, especially when combined with bone grafting and lengthy operative procedures. Host resistance may also be compromised in older patients as well as by underlying medical conditions or previous therapy. Some late failures in hip prostheses have resulted from a low-grade bacterial infection traced to contamination at the time of surgery.

Although in many situations the risk of wound infection is low, the consequences for the patient of implant failure and associated revision surgery can be considered a reason for antibiotic prophylaxis in the absence of any specific contraindications.

The need for any special requirements in the postoperative period must be considered in advance for each individual case to ensure that adequate facilities are available. Such measures include the need for a period of intensive nursing, intravenous fluid regimens and parenteral feeding, special diets, and physiotherapy. Written postoperative instructions should be available regarding nursing care and monitoring. The surgeon's instructions for wound management, mobilization, and medications must be clear.

Patient Information and Preparation

Patients need and appreciate comprehensive and clear information on the expected course, duration, and nature of the postoperative healing period. It is vital that they know in advance exactly what to expect and what is expected of them so that they can make the appropriate arrangements for the perioperative period. In particular, they need to be aware if any restrictions are to be placed on their normal activities. It should be ascertained in advance whether their social circumstances will facilitate any special care that is required after dismissal from the hospital, especially when outpatient surgery is envisaged.

It would be wise to inform patients if it is anticipated that the immediate recovery phase will involve special measures such as admission to intensive care, a period of immobility, placement of a urinary catheter, administration of fluids intravenously, or the necessity for nasogastric feeding. It can be helpful if they speak to other patients who have undergone similar procedures.

Both oral and written preoperative instructions should be provided. These include details on fasting and any alteration in medications before anesthesia. Outpatients must be made aware, and confirm in advance, that suitable transport and escort arrangements are in place after their dismissal from the hospital. In addition, they should have received and discussed postoperative written instructions before surgery.

Upper respiratory tract infections pose particular hazards for patients who are to undergo anesthesia. In such circumstances, the increased associated risks in the perioperative period normally dictate that elective surgical procedures should be postponed. Patients should be asked to report immediately if they feel they have a sore throat, cough or cold, or flu-like illness at any time before admission.

Patients must give consent for the proposed treatment. If this is to be informed, then they must understand and have been made fully aware of all aspects of their proposed treatment.

References

1. Peterson LJ. Antibiotic prophylaxis against wound infections in oral and maxillofacial surgery. J Oral Maxillofac Surg 1990;48:617.
2. Topazion RG. The basis of antibiotic prophylaxis. In Worthington P, Brånemark PI (eds): Advanced Osseointegration Surgery: Applications in the Maxillofacial Region. Chicago: Quintessence Publishing Company; 1992:60.

Prosthetic Considerations

8.

Steven E. Eckert, DDS, MS
Ronald P. Desjardins, DMD, MSD

- Diagnostic Media
- Defect Etiology
- Anatomic Areas

Prostheses have been used for centuries to replace missing facial structures. Early prostheses generally were made from metals, fabrics, leathers, or waxes.[1] These prostheses were designed to protect the underlying structures and to restore external contours, but they did not provide satisfactory cosmetic replacements of the missing facial structures.[2-4] In the last half of the 20th century, numerous synthetic materials have been developed that provide texture, contour, color, and pliability that mimic the facial structures.[5-8]

When considering prostheses for patients with missing facial structures, one must evaluate subjective as well as objective factors.[9] Patient experience with previous prosthetic interventions must be elicited. A history of successful prosthesis use may be a good indicator of future success if the patient has not recently experienced significant changes in the supporting structures. Conversely, patients who have never experienced satisfaction with facial prostheses are unlikely to find significant improvement with a new prosthesis unless their chief complaint has been one of poor prosthesis retention. If retention is identified as the cause of prosthesis failure, the benefits obtained through the use of endosseous implants for prosthesis support and retention may be profound[10] (Fig 8-1). Complaints regarding color, contour, texture, or the removable nature of the prosthesis will not, however, be altered by techniques that are designed to improve prosthesis retention.

Objective considerations are related to the size, shape, and location of the defect. Residual structures must be assessed for their capacity to support and retain a prosthesis. Osseous structures are evaluated to determine the potential for endosseous implant placement if this method of retention is considered. If adhesive retention is anticipated, the soft tissue surrounding a defect is studied to ensure that the potential for prosthesis extension is sufficient to provide a zone for adhesive application.[11] Likewise, undercuts within a defect may provide mechanical retention when other forms of retention are insufficient.[12]

Numerous factors must be assessed when facial prostheses are planned. This chapter discusses many of these considerations. However, it is important to realize that each patient is an individual with specific concerns and needs. This material may provide general direction, but the reader is cautioned to apply sound clinical judgment to satisfy patient demands.

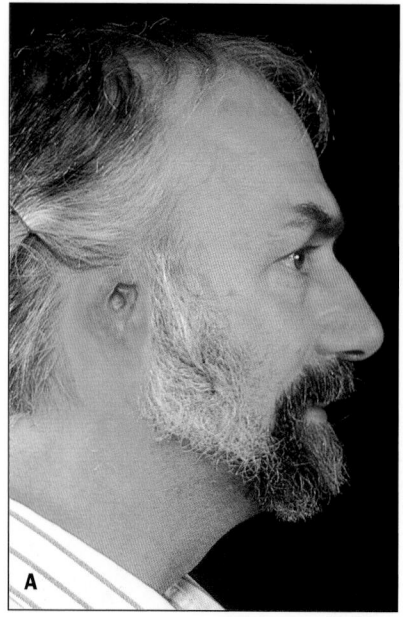 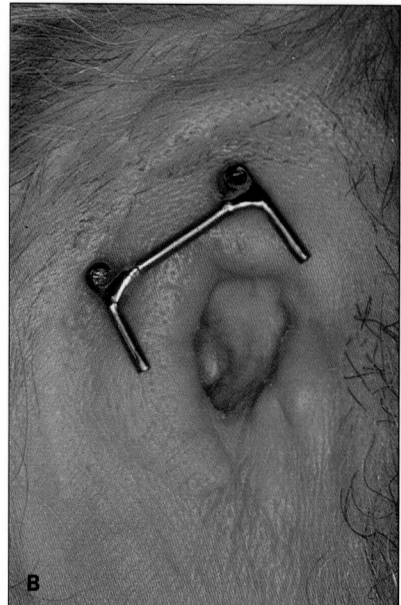 

Fig 8-1 *A,* Congenital absence of right ear with history of poor retention with adhesive-retained prostheses. *B,* Endosseous implants joined by connecting bar. *C,* Implant-supported and -retained prosthesis supports eyeglasses and is not dislodged during physical activity.

Diagnostic Media

Diagnosis and treatment planning depend on the accumulation of sufficient data to allow the restorative team to develop a comprehensive analysis of the needs and findings. Extensive problem-oriented examinations are performed. Examination must include a thorough review of the bone and associated soft tissues in the area of concern as well as an analysis of all pertinent radiographs. Facial moulage impressions are made for diagnostic purposes.[13] After the fabrication of diagnostic casts, wax trial prostheses are made, with particular attention to the orientation of these prostheses to the frontal, sagittal, and coronal planes.[14]

Diagnostic casts and oriented wax trial prostheses are reviewed to assess potential areas for prosthesis retention. These aids provide visual information regarding alternative means of mechanical retention for the facial prosthesis. The wax trial prosthesis is made after evaluation of presurgical photographs, presurgical casts, contralateral anatomy, and estimation of normal anatomic forms.[14] When no other data are available, blood relatives may be assessed for facial similarities. Once all material is gathered and the potential for adhesive and mechanical retention is determined, a decision is made regarding the need for auxiliary retention in the form of endosseous implants.[15]

Defect Etiology

Congenital and acquired defects are responsible for most facial defects requiring maxillofacial prosthetic intervention. Treatment decisions usually are based on knowledge of the current status of the disease state and an understanding of the patient's future needs. The etiology of a defect may provide the clinician with information regarding the prognosis and the potential for further surgical procedures in the near future. When the defect has stabilized postoperatively, reconstructive efforts, including placement of endosseous implants, may be considered to provide definitive solutions to anticipated prosthesis retention concerns. Conversely, if further surgical intervention is anticipated, endosseous implant placement may not be practical at that time.

Congenital Defects

Congenital abnormalities are unlikely to result in complete absence of the eyes or nose. In contrast, microtia or agenesis of the ear is associated with several congenital syndromes.[16] Treacher Collins, Crouzon's, and Pierre Robin syndromes are examples of the syndromes that are associated with facial deformities, palatal clefts, hearing loss, and significant malformation of the external ear.[17] These conditions often require multiple surgical procedures throughout the early years of life to provide the patient with near-normal physiologic functions of mastication, deglutition, and respiration. These patients may experience numerous surgical attempts to reconstruct the external ear but often find cosmetic results lacking.

Once adolescence is reached, continued surgical revisions are unlikely because a point of diminishing returns often is met. Because a stable defect is anticipated, definitive reconstruction using a synthetic prosthesis is common. One may anticipate a tissue bed that has been significantly altered by prior reconstructive efforts. Cicatricial changes, loss of anatomic landmarks, and alteration of normal architecture are common. Adhesive retention for auricular prostheses is usually successful if tissue irregularities such as tissue tags or residual anatomic structures are present. In the absence of anatomic landmarks that can be used for prosthesis orientation, adhesive retention may be a compromise because it is difficult for the patient to repeatedly position the prosthesis for maximum adhesive contact with the underlying skin. In this event, endosseous implants may provide retention and support that would not otherwise be available for facial prostheses.

Acquired Defects

Acquired defects may cause the loss of any facial part. The traumatic or neoplastic etiology is important for determining the type of treatment. In contrast to the patient with a congenital defect, patients with acquired defects caused by the surgical resection of a neoplasm have a high propensity for tumor recurrence and the associated need for subsequent surgery.

Neoplasm. Benign and malignant neoplasms may cause the loss of facial structures. Basal cell carcinoma is the most common form of skin cancer in the head and neck region. Basal cell tumors normally are excised with narrow tumor-free margins. This surgical approach is recommended because basal cell tumors are unlikely to exhibit local or regional metastasis.[18] Unfortunately, sun-induced skin changes may cause multiple primary tumors, resulting in a need for multiple surgical procedures in a small area. Significant facial defects from benign lesions are usually the result of multiple contiguous operations.

Malignant lesions more frequently result in loss of facial structures. Skin cancers such as squamous cell carcinoma and melanoma are more aggressive, both locally and distantly, than basal cell carcinoma.[18] Tumors located deep to the skin may require more extensive surgical resection that can result in the loss of facial structures. The potential for recurrence of any of these tumors may influence consideration of implant placement.

Trauma. Traumatic events such as motor vehicle accidents, explosive injuries, and gunshot wounds can result in the loss of facial structures.[19] Tissue damage due to trauma lacks the level of predictability seen with surgical excisions of tumors or in the surgical reconstruction of congenital defects. These defects can be associated with large areas of tissue damage, resulting in a lack of tissue foundation for restorative endeavors. Traumatically induced tissue loss, however, is unlikely to recur.

Anatomic Areas

Auricular

Prosthetic replacement of the external ear normally has a favorable cosmetic result. Adhesive retention of these prostheses is often less than satisfactory as a result of 1) the lack of facial contours that may assist in the accurate positioning of the prosthesis (Fig 8-2) and 2) movement of associated facial structures with mandibular movement.[20] Residual structures such as the tragus, helix, or lobe may provide excellent points of orientation but they may be malpositioned or movable as a result of prior surgeries, thus jeopardizing the cosmetic or retentive results.[16]

Endosseous implant support and retention for prosthetic replacement of the ear has been well documented in the literature.[21] Implant survival has

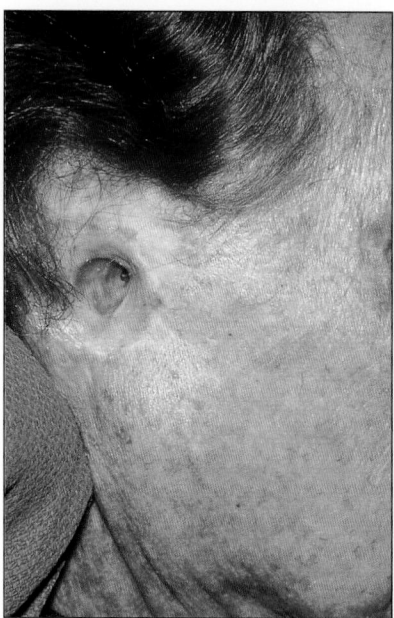

Fig 8-2 Flat anatomy associated with a congenitally missing ear makes orientation of an adhesive-retained prosthesis difficult. Implant retention could be a valuable asset in prosthesis retention.

proved to be so predictable that the historic recommendation of three implants now may be decreased to two implants.[22] From a prosthetic standpoint, fewer implants make implant and bar splint interference in prosthetic design less likely.

The restorative team must provide the surgical team with information regarding the ideal placement of the endosseous implants. Anatomic landmarks assist in the location of implants, but diagnostic wax patterns of the ear may prove more valuable in determining implant location.[23] Orientation of the implants relative to the external auditory canal, as suggested in previous papers, may place the implants in unfavorable positions relative to the final prosthesis if the position of the canal has been altered from its normal anatomic location. A diagnostic impression followed by development of a wax trial prosthesis oriented to the facial structures is most likely to result in better implant location. Once the wax trial prosthesis is complete, implant location should be planned within the bulkiest portion of the prosthesis.

Nasal

Nasal prostheses must gain adhesive retention from a wide extension of the prosthesis beyond the defect, which may negatively influence the cosmetic result (Fig 8-3). Mechanical retention by extension into the defect or through contact with eyeglasses may augment adhesive retention.[24]

Movement of the muscles of facial expression may either dislodge a nasal prosthesis or encourage space to become evident between the prosthesis and the skin (Fig 8-4). This movement, when encountered in the inferior half of the nasal area, may be counteracted through the use of endosseous, implant-retained bar-clip assemblies. Two implants are placed in the floor of the nose to support a custom-made retention bar. Implant survival in this area should approximate the rate found in the anterior maxilla.[22] Implants placed in the glabellar region are not expected to achieve high survival rates, making the use of adhesive or mechanical retention (or both) in the superior portion of the nasal prosthesis essential.

Implants for nasal prostheses are placed vertically into the floor of the nose. The implants should be placed such that the implant body is within the confines of the nasal prosthesis. Normally, this arrangement requires two implants, with one implant placed to the left and one to the right of the maxillary midline. Presurgical planning requires communication with the surgical team. Description of the ideal implant location may be sufficient; however, if doubt exists regarding the location, diagnostic impressions and a diagnostic wax pattern may further clarify the intended implant location.

Orbital

Replacement of the orbit and its contents through the use of an adhesive-retained prosthesis is a predictable procedure (Fig 8-5). Defects should be lined by a skin graft to ensure adequate tissue for prosthetic support.[25] It is only when the orbital contents as well as contiguous facial structures are lost that implant retention becomes more critical (Fig 8-6). Implants may be placed in the lateral and superior aspects of the orbital rim with a reasonable expectation of success.[26]

Implant placement should be well planned to ensure that implant angulation or implant body or subsequent bar splint placement does not interfere with normal contours of the facial prosthesis. Implant

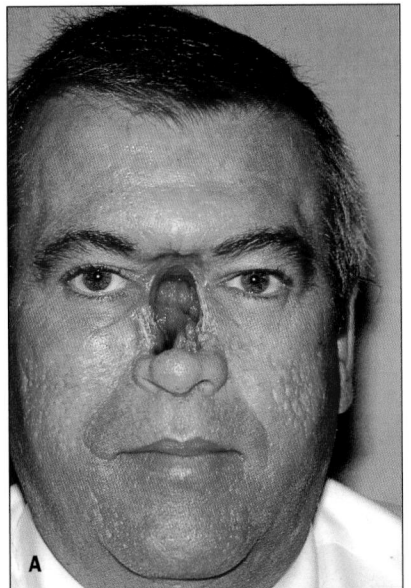
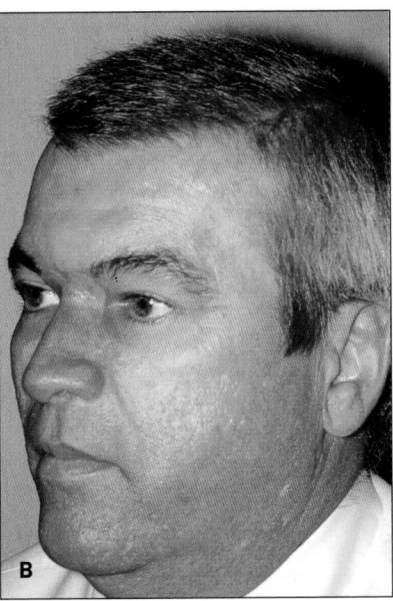
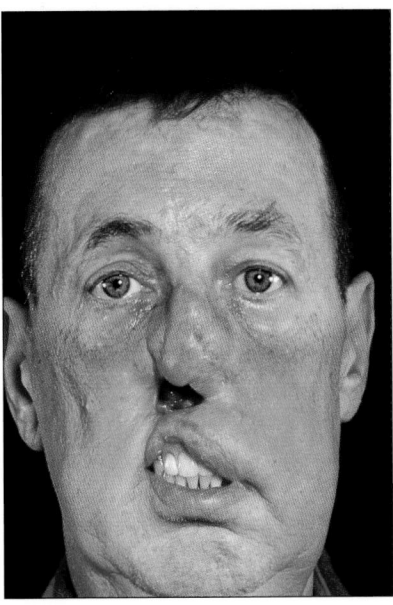

Fig 8-3 Small prostheses for replacement of a portion of the nose are often difficult to extend for adhesive retention, but the defect may not be amenable to placement of endosseous implants. *A*, Defect. *B*, Prosthesis in place.

Fig 8-4 Narrow defect margins as a result of proximity to movable tissue and facial hair decrease the potential for adhesive retention. Endosseous implants placed into the nasal surface of the maxilla may be used to provide prosthesis support and retention if mechanical retention within the defect is not possible.

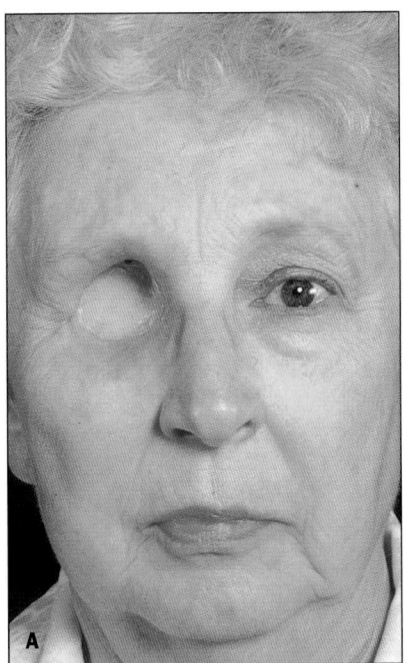
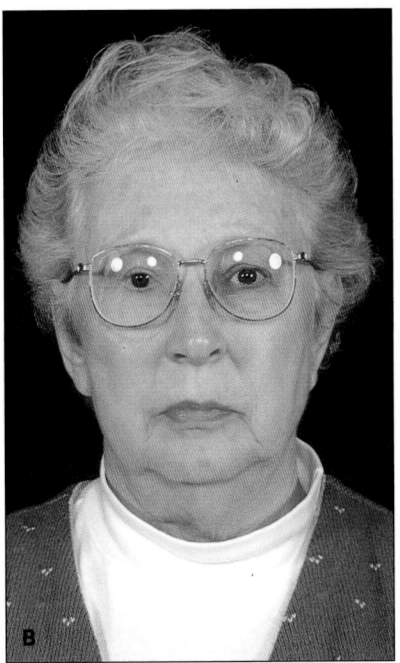

Fig 8-5 *A*, Orbital defect has undercut that provides mechanical retention in addition to the retention provided by adhesive. *B*, Prosthesis in place.

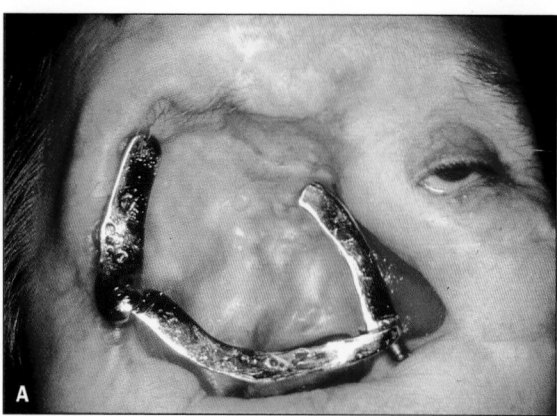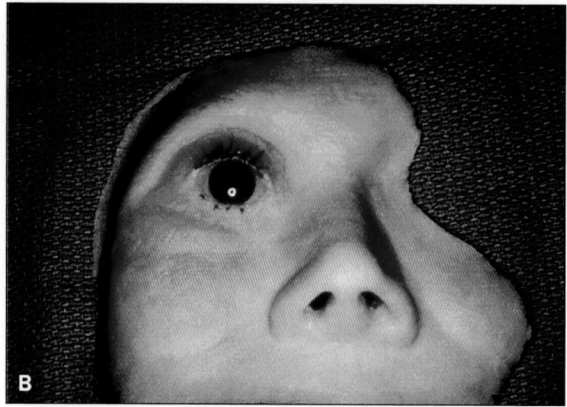

Fig 8-6 Large facial defect with limited opportunity for prosthesis extension suggests the potential benefit of endosseous implant use in retaining a large and heavy prosthesis. *A,* Connecting bar splint joins implants in right lateral orbital rim and the superior surface of the left maxilla to which *(B)* the facial prosthesis is attached. (*A* from Tolman DE, Desjardins RP, Jackson IP, Brånemark P-I. Complex craniofacial reconstruction using an implant-supported prosthesis: case report with long-term follow-up. Int J Oral Maxillofac Implants 1997;12:243. By permission of Quintessence Publishing Company.)

prominence could result in excessive bulk in the prosthesis—an unfavorable cosmetic result. Diagnostic impressions and prosthesis wax patterns assist the restorative team in determination of ideal implant location. Placement of implants in the superior and the lateral orbital rims may prevent insertion of a solid, one-piece infrastructure. Use of more than one bar splint may be needed to maximize implant placement for some patients.

Oral-Facial

Many facial defects are associated directly or indirectly with maxillary defects of various configurations. Nasal and orbital defects often communicate directly with maxillary defects. Although most facial defects are rehabilitated for cosmetic and psychosocial reasons,[27] oral defects require rehabilitation for physiologic reasons as well. A patient's inability to speak, swallow, and chew dictates the need to restore a separation between the mouth and the nasal and paranasal structures. Although this restoration of palatal continuity might be considered from a surgical perspective, separation of the mouth from the structures above is most commonly provided with an obturator prosthesis.[28] In addition, the facial support and resultant facial contour provided by an obturator prosthesis influence the fabrication and contours of a related facial prosthesis. For a consistent facial contour, retention and stability of the oral prosthesis are critical.

The design and resultant retention and stability of an obturator prosthesis depend on the location and size of the defect and the location and integrity of the remaining maxillary structures. If there is a small maxillary defect with many healthy maxillary teeth remaining, an obturator prosthesis likely will be well retained and stable. If the maxillary defect is large and there are no teeth remaining, an obturator prosthesis will be poorly retained and unstable.[29] The clinical status of most patients is between these two extremes, and the prosthodontist's ability to fabricate a retentive and stable prosthesis depends on the ability to design a prosthesis with sound prosthodontic principles of support, retention, and stability.

In many patients the absence of some or all of the teeth in the remaining maxillary segment seriously limits the prosthodontist's ability to fabricate an acceptable prosthesis. The configuration of the remaining hard and soft palate and the curvature of the maxillary arch in the remaining segment also influence retention and stability.[30] The potential for placement of osseointegrated implants into edentulous areas in the remaining segment or in bony remnants within the defect, such as the zygomatic arch, must be considered as a means to provide the optimal degree of retention and stability for an obturator prosthesis.

Consideration of placement of osseointegrated implants into the remaining maxillary segment must follow the same principles as placement of implants in conventional maxillary implant situa-

Table 8-1   *Adhesive-Retained Prostheses: Support and Retention*

Factor	Favorable	Unfavorable
Margin of defect	Wide margins Healthy skin Immovable tissue Devoid of facial, scalp, or eyebrow hair	Narrow margins Dry or irritated skin Movable tissue Hair extends into defect
Tissue within defect	Skin-graft lining Undercuts that may provide mechanical retention Immovable tissue	Mucosal lining Undercuts cannot be engaged Movable tissue Weeping tissue
Defect size	Small	Large
Tissue bed	Irregularities for orientation No therapeutic radiation to tissue bed Homogeneous color and texture	No orientation points History of therapeutic radiation to area Variation in color and texture

tions. Sufficient bone of good quality must be present in sites that allow placement of implants that can be acceptably used from the prosthodontic standpoint. It must be remembered, however, that these implants are likely to receive more stress from a large removable prosthesis than implants used to replace missing maxillary teeth only. The limited amount of available bone and the type 3 to 4 quality of bone suggest the need to maximize implant placement if possible.   Placement of onlay or inlay bone grafts in conjunction with the implants often may be needed.[31] Preoperative discussion between the surgeon and the prosthodontist is imperative to ensure the best possible result for each patient.

Conclusion

Facial prostheses may be retained by adhesive materials or through mechanical means (Table 8-1). Mechanical retention is possible if the defect presents undercuts that may be engaged with the restorative material or through the use of prosthetic connections to endosseous implants. The decision to use endosseous implants to assist in prosthesis retention should be made after a thorough evaluation of the patient and should be made in addressing the chief complaint (Table 8-2).

Table 8-2   *Tissue-Integrated Prostheses: Support and Retention*

Factor	Significant benefit from implant	Less benefit from implant
Defect size	Large Bulky prosthesis Heavy prosthesis	Small Light and thin prosthesis
Defect margins	Narrow margins, unfavorable for adhesive Adjacent muscular movement	Wide, hair-free margins Immovable tissue
Tissue bed	Few orientation points Lack of undercuts for mechanical retention	Multiple tissue tags or residual anatomy for orientation Tissue undercuts

Implant location is critical to ensure implant survival while also allowing the prosthetic retentive components to be located within the natural anatomic contours. Presurgical planning determines ideal implant location. Diagnostic procedures such as the making of facial moulage impressions, orientation of wax trial prostheses to facial planes, and the fabrication of surgical guides aid the surgical team in appropriate implant positioning.

Acknowledgment

The authors recognize the contributions of Scott R. Fehrenkamp, anaplastologist, Mayo Clinic and Mayo Foundation, in fabricating the facial prostheses illustrated in this chapter.

References

1. Ring ME. The fascinating story of maxillofacial prosthetics. Compendium 1993;14:194.

2. van Doorne JM. Extra-oral prosthetics: past and present. J Invest Surg 1994;7:267.

3. Fonder AC. Dental materials and skills in oral and facial prosthesis. J Am Dent Assoc 1955;50:636.

4. Bigelow HM. Facial restorations. J Am Dent Assoc 1943;30:509.

5. Tylman SD. Resilient and elastic resins: technique for their use in maxillofacial prostheses. Dent Dig 1944;50:260.

6. Bitonte JL. Prosthetic restoration of facial defects. Dent Clin North Am 1957 Nov:749.

7. Gonzalez JB. Polyurethane elastomers for facial prostheses. J Prosthet Dent 1978;39:179.

8. Sweeney WT, Fischer TE, Castleberry DJ, Cowperthwaite GF. Evaluation of improved maxillofacial prosthetic materials. J Prosthet Dent 1972;27:297.

9. Desjardins RP. Examination and diagnosis. In Laney WR (ed): Maxillofacial Prosthetics. Littleton, MA: PSG Publishing Company; 1979:41.

10. Hobkirk JA, Watson RM. Color Atlas and Text of Dental and Maxillo-Facial Implantology. London: Mosby-Wolfe; 1995:165.

11. Parr GR, Goldman BM, Rahn AO. Maxillofacial prosthetic principles in the surgical planning for facial defects. J Prosthet Dent 1981;46:323.

12. Shifman A, Levin AC, Levy M, Lepley JB. Prosthetic restoration of orbital defects. J Prosthet Dent 1979;42:543.

13. Clarke CD. Moulage prosthesis. Am J Orthod 1941;27:214.

14. Bulbulian AH. Facial prosthesis. Dent Dig 1945;51:380.

15. McComb H. Osseointegrated titanium implants for the attachment of facial prostheses. Ann Plast Surg 1993;31:225.

16. Holmes EM. Microtic ear. Arch Otolaryngol 1949;49:243.

17. Laney WR. Oral manifestations of systemic disease. In Laney WR, Gibilisco JA (eds): Diagnosis and Treatment in Prosthodontics. Philadelphia: Lea & Febiger; 1983;73.

18. McCormack RM. Skin cancer. In Rubin P (ed): Clinical Oncology for Medical Students and Physicians: A Multidisciplinary Approach, ed. 4. Rochester, NY: American Cancer Society; 1974:290.

19. Wiens JP. The use of osseointegrated implants in the treatment of patients with trauma. J Prosthet Dent 1992;67:670.

20. Wolfaardt JF, Wilkes GH, Parel SM, Tjellström A. Craniofacial osseointegration: the Canadian experience. Int J Oral Maxillofac Implants 1993;8:197.

21. Jacobsson M, Tjellström A, Fine L, Andersson H. A retrospective study of osseointegrated skin-penetrating titanium fixtures used for retaining facial prostheses. Int J Oral Maxillofac Implants 1992;7:523.

22. Parel SM, Tjellström A. The United States and Swedish experience with osseointegration and facial prostheses. Int J Oral Maxillofac Implants 1991;6:75.

23. Tolman DE, Desjardins RP. Extraoral application of osseointegrated implants. J Oral Maxillofac Surg 1991;49:33.

24. Parel SM. Diminishing dependence on adhesives for retention of facial prostheses. J Prosthet Dent 1980;43:552.

25. Parr GR, Goldman BM, Rahn AO. Surgical considerations in the prosthetic treatment of ocular and orbital defects. J Prosthet Dent 1983;49:379.

26. Beumer J III, Roumanas E, Nishimura R. Advances in osseointegrated implants for dental and facial rehabilitation following major head and neck surgery. Semin Surg Oncol 1995;11:200.

27. Thomas KF. Prosthetic Rehabilitation. Chicago: Quintessence Publishing Company, 1994:25.

28. Carl W. Preoperative and immediate postoperative obturators. J Prosthet Dent 1976;36:298.

29. Rahn AO, Goldman BM, Parr GR. Prosthodontic principles in surgical planning for maxillary and mandibular resection patients. J Prosthet Dent 1979;42:429.

30. Desjardins RP. Early rehabilitative management of the maxillectomy patient. J Prosthet Dent 1977;38:311.

31. Adell R, Lekholm U, Gröndahl K, Brånemark P-I, Lindstrom J, Jacobsson M. Reconstruction of severely resorbed edentulous maxillae using osseointegrated fixtures in immediate autogenous bone grafts. Int J Oral Maxillofac Implants 1990;5:233.

Osseointegration in the Irradiated Patient

9.

Gösta Granström, MD, DDS, PhD

- Review of the Current Literature
- Radiation Effects
- Radiation After Implant Surgery
- Radiation Before and After Implant Surgery
- Chemotherapy
- Factors of Importance Other Than Radiation
- Hyperbaric Oxygen Therapy

The osseointegration concept was established more than 30 years ago. It was developed originally for use in the oral cavity to replace lost teeth.[1] With time, it was adapted for extraoral use with the Bone-Anchored Hearing Aid.[2] It was further developed to anchor facial prostheses to cover defects in the craniofacial region.[3] The latest development within osseointegration research has shown that it is also possible to use the concept in orthopedic surgery for replacement of amputees' extremities and to replace malfunctioning joints.[4,5]

In the craniofacial area, defects of the auricle, orbit, nose, and midface are rare, but these are important areas to reconstruct with either autogenous tissue or a prosthesis. Naturally, if a reconstruction is possible to achieve with good cosmetic results by using the patient's own tissues, this would be the first option to choose. However, certain craniofacial defects might be difficult, if not impossible, to reconstruct by grafting techniques with a cosmetically acceptable result. Examples of difficult to reconstruct areas are the orbit, external ear, nose, and

midface. A prosthesis might be a better alternative in these cases; with the use of modern synthetic materials, a result close to the natural appearance can be achieved. Use of the osseointegration concept to anchor such prostheses has been widely documented to be effective.

Craniofacial defects might be inflicted by trauma or they might be congenital. The most common defects are, however, those obtained after tumor removal. Cancer surgery is, unfortunately, often extremely devastating, leaving the patient with large defects in critical areas. In my department, replacing lost parts of the craniofacial region after cancer surgery has been one of the most important fields for osseointegration reconstruction. One must expect that cancer patients will be irradiated as part of cancer treatment. In Sweden, it has long been a tradition to irradiate head and neck cancer patients before tumor surgery. The reason for this is to avoid destructive tumor removal in this sensitive area. As a consequence, a certain number of patients will be irradiated before radical cancer surgery is initiated. Later, when these patients are to be rehabilitated with use of the osseointegration concept, it is necessary to be aware of different factors influencing osseointegration, healing of the soft tissues, and the risk of severe side effects in the compromised tissues. This chapter deals with the possibilities and drawbacks from osseointegration in irradiated patients.

Review of the Current Literature

Irradiation originally was considered a contraindication to placement of implants.[6] The risk of inducing severe side effects was obvious. Such side effects include decreased healing rate of the soft tissue over the implants, fistulation, skin or mucosa infections, loss of implants, denuded bone around the implants, and even osteoradionecrosis. However, with more confidence regarding the possibilities of optimal rehabilitation in these patients, the attempts to insert implants in this group of patients increased. As a result of the gentle handling of the tissues and the surgical technique used, one would expect the risk for osteoradionecrosis development to be low.

It was soon evident that osseointegration could function in previously irradiated patients, even after high radiation doses.[7] In that study, 14% of extraoral implants inserted in nine patients were lost within 44 months of follow-up. At that time, this number was not regarded as an exceedingly high rate of implant loss. Reports of an increased loss of fixtures, however, came soon afterward and also ideas of how to possibly prevent such implant losses and to improve osseointegration with the use of hyperbaric oxygen (HBO).[8]

Parel and Tjellström[9] reported 39% losses for extraoral implants placed in previously irradiated facial bones compared with 5% losses in nonirradiated patients in the United States and Sweden. Lundgren et al[10] reported 9% losses of craniofacial endosseous implants inserted in irradiated bone compared with 7% in nonirradiated bone. Wolfaardt et al[11] reported losses of 5% of extraoral implants inserted in irradiated bone compared with 2% losses in nonirradiated patients in six Canadian centers. The differences in implant survival between these studies seem to be the result of different follow-up times; the longer the patient group has been followed, the higher the failure rate. Reports of intraoral implant placement in previously irradiated jaws are limited.

Albrektsson[12] reported 21 mandibular and 10 maxillary implants placed in previously irradiated jaws with no loss of implants at 1 to 5 years. Taylor and Worthington[13] reported on 21 mandibular implants placed in irradiated jaws, without any losses at 3 to 7 years. Fifteen of the implants were placed with adjunctive HBO. Franzén et al[14] reported on 20 mandibular implants placed without the use of HBO and without losses within 6 years of follow-up.

In my department, we placed osseointegrated implants in 946 patients from 1977 to March 1996. Most of these implants were related to the use of bone-anchored hearing aids in specific hearing disorders, but 382 patients had implants placed for rehabilitation of tissue defects in the craniofacial region. Of these 382 patients, 280 had defects in the face related to cancer surgery, and 89 of these (32%) were irradiated at the time implants were placed. It is from these patients that the following statistics have been calculated.

Radiation Effects

During the years that implants have been placed into irradiated patients, we have experienced several problems during and after implant surgery related to the fact that the patients had been previously irradiated. These problems are summarized in Table 9-1. Some of these complications could probably have been avoided; as our experience grew, the skin penetration site has been prepared in a better way, and the number of soft-tissue reactions has been reduced. Still, the most severe problem is related to the high number of implants lost during the follow-up period.

For extraoral implants,[15] there is a clear difference in how and when the osseointegration of the implant fails. Among the nonirradiated patients, most implants are found nonintegrated at the second-stage surgery or are lost during the first year. After this time, the remaining implants seem to be relatively well integrated and remain in the bone. The irradiated group of patients has a different course. Most of the implants are lost during the first 3 years, but implants are lost throughout the follow-up period; even up to 10 years or more after placement, osseointegration is lost.[15] If oral implants are also included, similar figures are found.[16,17]

Table 9-2 shows an extrapolation from known implant survival statistics in various bones of the cran-

Table 9-1 Complications in Irradiated Patients During 10-Year Follow-Up

Complication	Patients, %
Loss of implant	35
Slow wound healing	18
Fistula	15
Wound dehiscence	12
Soft-tissue infection	10
Osteoradionecrosis	2
Rupture of major vessel	0
Flap necrosis	0

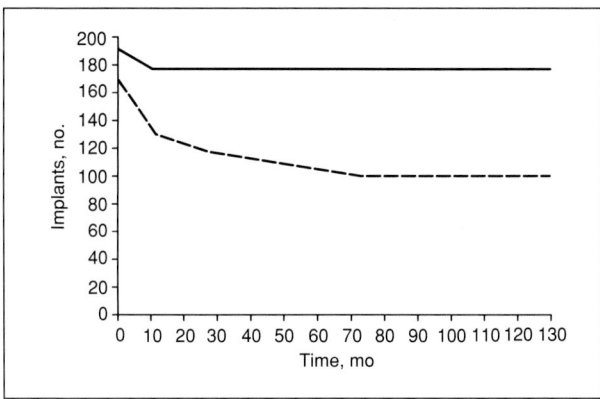

Fig. 9-1 Comparison of implant survival for nonirradiated *(solid line)* and irradiated *(dashed line)* patients reveals a significantly (P < 0.05) higher implant loss over time for the irradiated group after 4 years.

iofacial skeleton. Implant survival during the 30 years it has been studied in humans would be between 85% and 96% of implants placed in the maxilla, mandible, and temporal bone.[18-20] However, implants placed in the frontal bone behave in a dissimilar manner; 24% of implants placed were lost during a 15-year period.[20] The reason for the higher implant failure in this region (periorbital implants) seems to be that 80% of patients who have implants placed for orbital prostheses have been irradiated before implant surgery.[21] Thus, it seems reasonable to assume that irradiation per se is followed by a higher implant failure rate—loss of osseointegration.

If one follows two groups of patients, one irradiated and one nonirradiated, and compares the outcome of implant survival during a 10-year period, a graph like that shown in Figure 9-1 is obtained. The difference between the irradiated group of patients and the nonirradiated group of patients does not become significant until 4 years have elapsed. After this time, the difference between the two groups becomes more evident with increasing time.

Table 9-3 shows regional differences in implant failure and also the correlation between the irradiated and the nonirradiated patients. The highest implant failure rates are in the frontal bone, followed by zygoma, maxilla, and mandible, whereas the temporal bone seems more radioresistant.[16]

In a study investigating the possible effects of different irradiation procedures, it was found that radiation dose had a negative effect on the osseointegration process in two ways. First, in the high-dose region above 120 Gy (Table 9-4),[16] a high proportion of implants were lost. Second, in the low-dose re-

Table 9-2 Implant Survival According to Location

Location	Implant survival, %					
	5 yr	10 yr	15 yr	20 yr	25 yr	30 yr
Mandible	96	93	92	91	91	90
Maxilla	95	91	88	87	86	85
Temporal	95	93	92	90	—	—
Frontal	89	82	76	—	—	—

Table 9-3 Implant Failure According to Location by Group at 10-Year Follow-Up

Location	Implant failure, %	
	Irradiated	Nonirradiated
Frontal	49.4	25.0
Zygoma	50.0	20.0
Maxilla	25.0	9.6
Mandible	20.8	5.1
Temporal	25.0	6.8

gion, proportionally more implants were lost, whereas osseointegration in the medium-dose region showed minor effects.[15,16] The high frequency of implant losses in the high radiation dose region could be related to the irradiation effect per se, whereas the high losses in the low-radiation dose re-

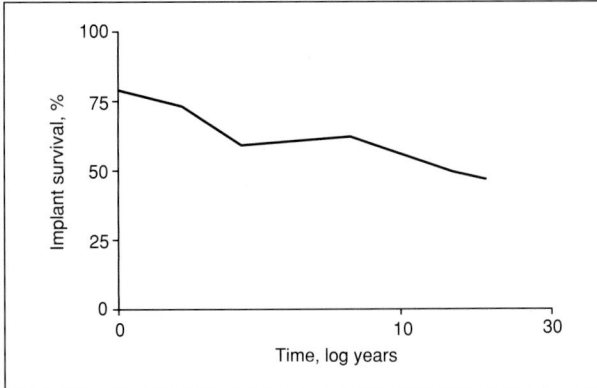

Fig. 9-2 Implant survival according to time of surgery after irradiation.

	Implants, no.	
Dose, Gy	Placed	Lost
15	8	6
25	20	10
35	11	4
45	52	23
55	37	8
65	25	2
75	15	2
85	12	3
95	10	2
105	5	1
115	4	0
125	8	0
145	2	2
165	2	2

Table 9-4   *Implant Failure According to Dose for Irradiated Patients*

gion are more difficult to explain. The probable reason for the higher implant failure in the low-dose region is believed to be that these patients also were irradiated the longest time ago: > 25 years ago.

If one makes a logarithmic comparison of implant survival related to time of osseointegration surgery after radiotherapy, the curve is like the one in Figure 9-2. With longer time from irradiation, more implants are lost. This is in accordance with what is known from irradiation effects in bone and soft tissues; the irradiation process induces a progressive endarteritis that becomes more evident with elapsing time.[22] From Table 9-4 and Figure 9-2 it seems logical to draw the conclusion that "full-course" radiotherapy per se is not a contraindication for osseointegration surgery. The very low-dose irradiation protocols (15-25 Gy) that produced higher implant failures with time are not used in modern radiotherapy. The extremely high-dose radiotherapy is only attained in patients with recurrent cancer or new tumor development; these patients are submitted to repeat radiotherapy. It seems logical, from the known higher implant failures among these patients, that patients with recurrent tumor growth probably should be excluded from rehabilitation with the osseointegration concept until further knowledge is obtained about how the high-dose irradiated tissue should be handled to accept implants.

One other conclusion that can be drawn from these figures is related to the time when irradiated cancer patients can be rehabilitated. It is actually those patients rehabilitated earliest after the radiotherapy course who show the highest implant survivals (Fig 9-2). This has stimulated us to perform implant-related surgery as soon as possible after tumor removal, and today we actually insert most of the implants at the time of tumor removal. This has the advantages that the patient is rehabilitated early and implant survival is higher. The negative aspects could be that tumor recurrences might appear during the following years, necessitating more radiotherapy and the removal of the implants at a time of extended tumor removal. On the other hand, the use of a prosthesis anchored by osseointegration enables the surgeon or oncologist free access to the tumor cavity and hence early detection of tumor recurrences. One other side effect could be the risk of inducing osteoradionecrosis or other complications due to too early surgery in an irradiation field. This has not yet been the case in our patient material, and one possible explanation for this could be that the osseointegration concept uses a tissue-gentle surgical technique with low drill speeds and extensive cooling, thus enabling the bone and soft tissue to recover from the surgically induced trauma.

With the known high implant failure rate in the irradiated patients and the knowledge that bone healing can to some extent recover with time after radiotherapy,[23] we have also extended the time from first- to second-stage surgery. That is, in the normal

Table 9-5 *Cutaneous Reactions of Irradiated Patients*

Follow-up, mo	Observations, no.	Cutaneous reaction, no.*				
		Gr. 0	Gr. 1	Gr. 2	Gr. 3	Gr. 4
3	80	65	5	6	4	0
6	73	61	4	7	1	0
9	66	55	9	2	0	0
12	65	45	4	6	0	0
18	47	41	3	3	0	0
24	40	34	4	1	1	0
30	36	30	6	0	0	0
36	37	33	2	2	0	0
42	34	28	2	3	1	0
48	30	25	1	3	1	0
54	27	23	1	1	2	0
60	23	21	1	1	0	0
66	19	19	0	0	0	0
72	19	19	0	0	0	0
78	16	16	0	0	0	0
84	16	14	1	1	0	0
90	13	12	1	0	0	0
96	12	12	0	0	0	0
102	11	10	1	0	0	0
108	8	8	0	0	0	0

Gr., grade.

*Grade 0, no irritation; grade 1, slight redness; grade 2, red and slightly moist tissue; grade 3, red and moist tissue, revision necessary; grade 4, infection, removal necessary.

nonirradiated patient we generally wait 3 to 4 months between the different stages, but with an irradiated patient we have doubled that time to 6 to 8 months. Because cancer patients might have large tissue defects from cancer surgery, different grafting procedures might be necessary before osseointegration.[24] This has been particularly so in the patient with a mandibular defect.[25,26] The possibility of bringing in nonirradiated bone and soft tissue to an irradiated craniofacial defect and rehabilitating that part of the face with the osseointegration concept that cannot be reconstructed without an implant-supported prosthesis seems logical.

The immediate question one might ask after having seen the high implant failure rate in the irradiated patients is, "What could be done to improve osseointegration in these patients?" Or, is there an "osseointegration stimulator" that can help us to improve osseointegration? The solution we have chosen is to use HBO, the results of which are discussed below.

The soft tissues around the abutments showed specific reactions in the irradiated patient (Table 9-1). With a clinical scoring system,[27] the following tissue reactions were found (Tables 9-5, 9-6, and 9-7), where grade 0 = clinically normal skin, grade 1 = red skin around the abutment, grade 2 = red and moist, grade 3 = granulation tissue forming around the abutment, and grade 4 = soft-tissue reaction leading to removal of the abutment or grafting of new skin. In the irradiated group of patients, there were more grade 1 and 2 reactions during the first postoperative year compared with the control patients.[15] Examples of soft-tissue reactions in irradiated patients are shown in Figure 9-3. Many of the adverse skin reactions seen in the early irradiated patients have been handled by repeated surgery, with thinning out of the subcutaneous tissues or grafting the skin. It is, however, important to use a gentle surgical technique to avoid too thin skin without the necessary blood flow, because the risk for complete flap necrosis is evident. Nevertheless, with time we also have noticed that the number of grade 3 skin reactions is increased in the irradiated patients compared with a control group.[28] HBO therapy seems to be beneficial for the irradiated group.

Table 9-6 *Cutaneous Reactions of Nonirradiated Patients*

Follow-up, mo	Observations, no.	Cutaneous reaction, no.*				
		Gr. 0	Gr. 1	Gr. 2	Gr. 3	Gr. 4
3	72	67	1	3	1	0
6	64	61	1	1	1	0
9	62	55	3	2	2	0
12	57	51	4	0	2	0
18	54	48	4	1	1	0
24	47	40	3	4	0	0
30	42	39	2	1	0	0
36	36	35	0	1	0	0
42	33	31	2	0	0	0
48	33	32	1	0	0	0
54	28	27	1	0	0	0
60	23	23	0	0	0	0
66	19	18	0	1	0	0
72	16	16	0	0	0	0
78	13	12	1	0	0	0
84	11	10	0	1	0	0
90	10	9	1	0	0	0
96	7	7	0	0	0	0
102	6	6	0	0	0	0
108	6	6	0	0	0	0

Gr., grade.
*Grade 0, no irritation; grade 1, slight redness; grade 2, red and slightly moist tissue; grade 3, red and moist tissue, revision necessary; grade 4, infection, removal necessary.

Table 9-7 *Cutaneous Reactions of Irradiated Patients With Hyperbaric Oxygen*

Follow-up, mo	Observations, no.	Cutaneous reaction, no.*				
		Gr. 0	Gr. 1	Gr. 2	Gr. 3	Gr. 4
3	68	66	1	1	0	0
6	64	63	1	0	0	0
9	64	61	3	0	0	0
12	62	60	2	0	0	0
18	56	55	1	0	0	0
24	43	43	0	0	0	0
30	38	38	0	0	0	0
36	33	32	1	0	0	0
42	24	24	0	0	0	0
48	19	19	0	0	0	0
54	18	18	0	0	0	0
60	15	14	1	0	0	0
66	14	14	0	0	0	0
72	12	12	0	0	0	0
78	12	12	0	0	0	0
84	12	12	0	0	0	0
90	12	12	0	0	0	0
96	12	12	0	0	0	0

Gr., grade.
*Grade 0, no irritation; grade 1, slight redness; grade 2, red and slightly moist tissue; grade 3, red and moist tissue, revision necessary; grade 4, infection, removal necessary.

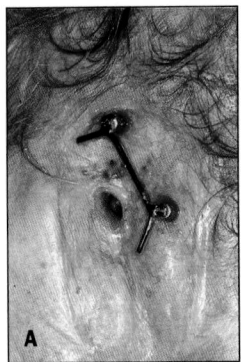 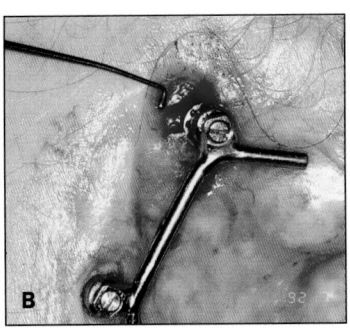 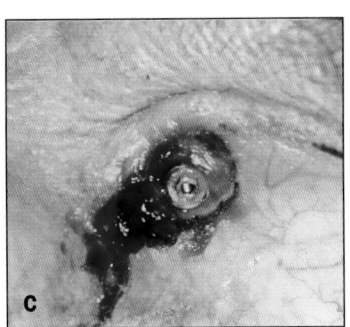 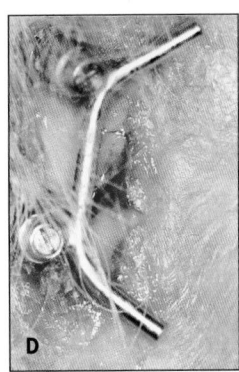

Fig. 9-3 Soft-tissue reactions in irradiated patients. *A*, Grade 1 (slight redness), result of inadequate hygiene. *B*, Grade 2 (red and slightly moist) with a bony pocket dorsal to the superior implant. *C*, Grade 3 (red and moist), revision required. *D*, Grade 4 (infection, with purulent drainage) resulting in loss of implants.

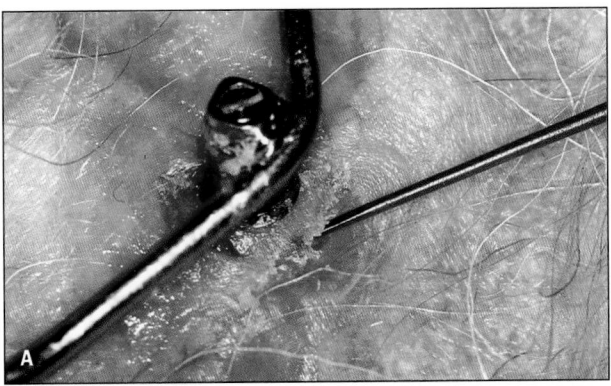 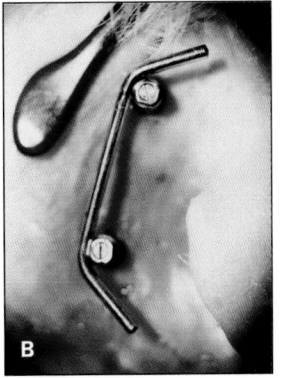 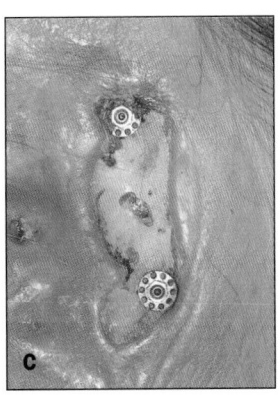

Fig. 9-4 Soft-tissue reactions in irradiated patients after implant placement. *A*, Progressive bone loss beneath flange of implant. *B*, Dehiscence anterior to abutment. *C*, Osteoradionecrosis in patient who received both preoperative and postoperative irradiation (total of 165 Gy). (*C* from Granström and Tjellström.[35] By permission of Quintessence Publishing Company.)

Radiation After Implant Surgery

In Sweden there is a long tradition of irradiating cancer patients before tumor surgery; in other countries tumor surgery might be performed before radiotherapy and postoperative radiation can be given at other doses and other intervals compared with preoperative radiotherapy. Radiotherapy with a metal object in the radiation field induces backscatter and front scatter effects from a radiation beam "bouncing" on the metal framework.[29] These scatter effects depend on the energy and source of irradiation, the distance from the metal to the tissue, and the atomic number of the metal. For the titanium used in the osseointegration procedure, it is considered that the backscatter effect is approximately 11% in the region 1 to 2 mm nearest the implant site when cobalt-60 radiation of 20 MeV is used.[30] Possible effects of the increased radiation dose in the delicate interface zone between an implant and the bone or between the abutment and the skin are not completely understood. In certain patients it could be the cause of implant loss and skin reactions, but in other patients it also could stimulate cell turnover.[31]

My department has experience with 15 patients treated with radiotherapy after implant placement. Doses from 50 to 115 Gy were delivered to patients with implants situated in the irradiation field.[32,33] During a 6-year follow-up period, overall implant failure rates have not been exceedingly high (11%), although longer follow-up times might influence the implant failure rate. In certain patients, a progressive bone loss in conjunction with implants has been noticed (Fig 9-4*A*). Whether this phenomenon will result in higher implant failure rates is not known. On the other hand, we have experienced more soft-tissue-related problems as skin dehisces around the implants (Fig 9-4*B*). These skin reactions were more common among patients

Table 9-8 *Implant Failure in Irradiated Patients According to Location* *

	Implants, no.	
Location	Placed	Lost
Frontal	6	4
Zygoma	4	2
Maxilla	2	1
Temporal	2	2

*Some patients irradiated before implant placement, whereas others irradiated after because of recurrent tumor.

after implant irradiation with the abutments and prosthetic bar in the irradiation field. As a consequence, we have recommended that as much of the metal as possible be removed before radiotherapy. However, we are of the opinion that removal of the implants before radiotherapy is not necessary and might even be contraindicated. Because an integrated implant is impossible to simply unscrew, removal necessitates a surgical procedure (trephining), which inflicts a considerable amount of trauma to the bone. Such trauma in the period 1 month before irradiation is known to increase the risk for osteoradionecrosis development.[34] Post radiotherapy the patient is left without a prosthetic retention, which from the psychologic point of view is infelicitous. My colleagues and I instead removed the superstructures (abutments and bars) but left the implants and covered the flange implants with skin or mucosa. After radiotherapy, when the acute tissue reactions have declined (4–8 weeks after irradiation), we have exposed the implants, reattached the abutments and bar, and remade the prosthesis. So far this regimen has worked in our department.

Radiation Before and After Implant Surgery

In three of our cases, an irradiated cancer patient with implants placed for rehabilitation of a tumor defect developed a tumor recurrence and had to be reirradiated as part of cancer treatment. Generally, one must expect that the tissues can reach extremely high radiation doses in a situation like this, thus challenging the limits for osseointegration. In our material, we have experienced a high implant failure rate: 64% in a 3-year follow-up period[35] (Table 9-8).

Our only case of osteoradionecrosis that developed in conjunction with osseointegrated surgery also is related to this group of patients (Fig 9-4C). We have concluded that if an irradiated patient who has osseointegrated implants needs reirradiation, the prosthetic device cannot depend solely on implants for retention; other types of retention must be considered.

Chemotherapy

A certain number of patients have chemotherapy included as a part of tumor treatment. Because this treatment is often combined with radiotherapy, the individual effect of chemotherapy on osseointegration might be difficult to determine. We[36] established that chemotherapy before implant surgery had no deleterious effect on osseointegration. However, chemotherapy after implant surgery would be assumed to negatively affect osseointegration. Although individual patients actually lost all implants in such a situation, the overall statistics could not verify such an association. Only among patients who had osseointegrated implants placed at the same time as they received chemotherapy treatment were implant failures statistically increased. The negative effects from chemotherapy on osseointegration are limited to a short and specific time when implants are placed and early in the osseointegration process. It is advisable to plan the surgical procedure for placement of osseointegrated implants to avoid installation in conjunction with chemotherapy treatment.

Factors of Importance Other Than Radiation

In a study performed to evaluate factors of importance for osseointegration other than irradiation per se, we found that implant survival also depended on the length of the implants (Table 9-9). The shortest

Table 9-9 *Implant Failure According to Implant Length*

Length, mm	Implants, no.	
	Placed	Lost
3	48	18
4	225	55
5	12	6
7	56	10
10	66	8
13	90	10
15	70	6
18	28	4
20	8	0
22	4	0

Table 9-10 *Implant Failure According to Abutment Length*

Length, mm	Abutment, no.	
	Placed	Lost
2	14	3
3	56	15
4	205	55
5.5	102	12
7.0	72	9
8.5	67	10

Table 9-11 *Implant Failure According to Prosthetic Anchorage by Group*

Anchorage	Nonirradiated, no.		Irradiated, no.	
	Placed	Lost	Placed	Lost
Bar with clips	45	2	56	17
Magnets	24	7*	38	16†
Ball	3	0	8	3
Bar, clips, and magnets	11	3†	15	11*

Statistically significant: *P < 0.005, †P < 0.05.

Table 9-12 *Implant Failure for Type of Orbital Cavity by Group*

Type	Nonirradiated, no.		Irradiated, no.		Irradiated, with HBO, no.	
	Placed	Lost	Placed	Lost	Placed	Lost
Open	11	3	60	34	23	0
Closed	17	6	18	3	3	0

HBO, hyperbaric oxygen.

implants, 3-mm-long flange implants, showed a statistically higher loosening rate than the other types of implants used (all implants studied were of the Brånemark type, Nobel Biocare, Göteborg, Sweden). We found no difference in loosening rate if abutments of different lengths were used (Table 9-10). One would expect that longer abutments could induce unfavorable loading forces on the implants, but such an effect could not be proved.

The retention of the prosthetic device could significantly affect the survival of implants (Table 9-11). In our patients we found that prostheses anchored on a bar construction with an extended arm for a magnet showed higher failure rates. This could probably be ex-

plained by cantilever effects induced on implants by the extended arm. We also found higher implant failure rates among patients with "single" implants where the prosthesis was anchored by individual magnets. This higher implant failure is believed to be induced in part by the patients themselves by retightening the magnet keepers without firmly holding the abutment.[15]

The effect on implant survival of an open orbit cavity with possibly other types of microbial flora compared with the closed orbit cavity with ordinary skin flora was investigated (Table 9-12). We found no correlation among different implant survival rates. We also investigated the possibility that the surgeon's experience affected our results; surgeons

Table 9-13 *Implant Failure Related to Experience of Surgeon*		
	Implants, no.	
Experience, yr	Placed	Lost
1–5	42	7*
6–10	35	8
11–15	95	16
16–20	50	20
21–25	36	12
*Statistically significant (P < 0.05).		

Table 9-14 *Implant Survival According to Use of Hyperbaric Oxygen*		
	Implants, no.	
Group	Placed	Lost
Nonirradiated	225	26*
Irradiated	193	73
Irradiated with HBO	191	5†

HBO, hyperbaric oxygen.
*Nonirradiated group had significantly (P < 0.005) lower failure rate than irradiated group.
†Irradiated, HBO-treated group had significantly (P < 0.001) lower failure rate than irradiated group.

operating in the temporal bone had a higher implant survival rate compared with surgeons operating in the midface and periorbital bone (Table 9-13).

Hyperbaric Oxygen Therapy

In 1988 we started a clinical trial to study possible effects on osseointegration of HBO treatment. Since that time, we have treated 36 patients according to the protocol: 20 sessions at 2.5 atmospheric pressure preoperatively and 10 postoperative sessions. We have been able to treat 36 of 89 irradiated patients (40%). This technique has considerably improved the results of osseointegration (Fig 9-5). Implant survival has been improved, especially in the difficult periorbital region. The improvement is statistically significant when comparing irradiated, HBO-treated patients with irradiated patients (*P* < 0.001) and with nonirradiated patients (*P* < 0.005) (Table 9-14).

The reason that not all of our patients have been treated with HBO is that we have avoided delaying tumor surgery while awaiting the HBO procedure. The patients who had implants placed at the time of tumor removal were not pretreated with HBO. Some patients included in the analysis were rehabilitated with the osseointegration concept before HBO became of practical use in our department. With time, it is expected that those patients not pretreated with HBO before implant surgery will lose more of their implants, necessitating placement of more implants under HBO coverage.

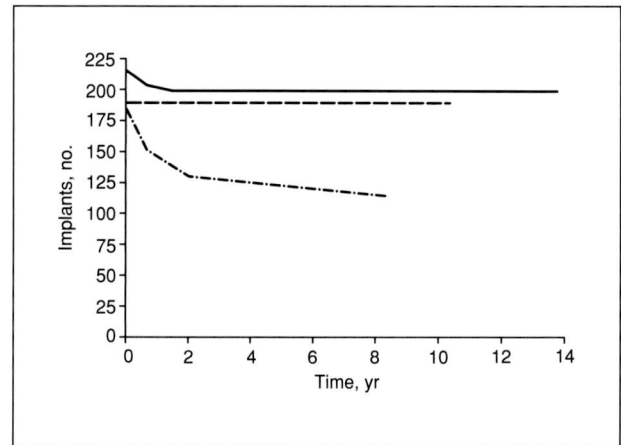

Fig. 9-5 Implant loss as a function of time by group: nonirradiated (solid line), irradiated (dashed line), and irradiated plus hyperbaric oxygen (dotted line).

Is HBO Therapy Really Necessary to Obtain Osseointegration in an Irradiated Patient?

An often repeated statement among surgeons and in the literature is that there have been no randomized, controlled double-blind studies performed to show that HBO really has a significant osseointegration stimulating effect in irradiated patients (eg, reference 14). One might argue that there are likewise few similar studies performed to prove the efficacy of surgical procedures in general. A critical analysis of the value of HBO is strongly supported by the present author. However, it might be hazardous to draw any specific conclusions from a group containing only 20 implants in five patients followed for 3 to 6 years. A complete loss of the implants in only one of these patients would significantly affect the statistics in such a group, and there are several clinical studies that actually reported such a complete implant loss in irradiated patients. Such failures can also appear a long time after implant placement. There are other reports indicating that in irradiated tissues without increased implant losses, HBO is of limited value.[37]

Our basic knowledge of HBO effects in relation to osseointegration is from animal studies in which controlled experiments can be performed in a manner not possible in humans. Our clinical studies show that with reasonable estimations and comparisons with available control groups, the improvement of osseointegration by HBO is significant (Fig 9-5). It is also possible to measure clinically some of the effects induced by HBO. In a study performed to standardize blood flow measurements by the laser Doppler technique, it was found that irradiated patients showed lower values compared with nonirradiated patients.[38] Points in the medial part of the orbit showed extremely low blood flow values, which might be related to the fact that this region also shows the highest implant failure scores. Irradiated patients who were preoperatively treated with HBO showed higher blood flow values compared with irradiated patients[38] (Table 9-15). Another technique that we have used to measure superficial blood vessels is infrared photometry. In Figure 9-6 this technique is shown in a patient under rehabilitation for an orbital defect. It is not realistic to assume that HBO would have an effect on major blood vessels, but the microcirculation can be affected by this treatment.

Why Was HBO Chosen in Relation to Osseointegration Surgery?

HBO was chosen because the current literature gave strong support for the positive effects of intermittent and surplus oxygen delivered to soft tissue compromised by irradiation (for review see references 39 and 40). The biologic effects that can be measured in irradiated tissue that has undergone HBO treatment are improved blood vessel content,[41,42] improved bone turnover,[42-44] and improved osseointegration—i.e., increased removal torque[45,46] and increased metal to bone contact.[46,47] The target cells influenced by oxy-

Table 9-15 Blood Flow According to Implant Location

Location	Flow (mean ± SD)*		
	Nonirradiated	Irradiated	Irradiated and HBO
Mandible	7.2 ± 0.6	3.3 ± 0.5	6.7 ± 0.5
Maxilla	6.9 ± 0.3	3.2 ± 0.2	8.5 ± 1.1
Zygoma	7.2 ± 0.4	3.5 ± 0.2	8.6 ± 0.8
Frontal	6.9 ± 0.2	3.5 ± 0.2	7.9 ± 0.8
Temporal	5.2 ± 0.3	4.0 ± 0.2	11.4 ± 0.5

HBO, hyperbaric oxygen.
*Flow in mL/min in 100 g of tissue.

gen seem to be nondifferentiated mesenchymal cells in the callus or granulation tissue that has the ability to differentiate into chondroblasts or osteoblasts, depending on the oxygen tension of the tissue. In an anoxic bone-forming tissue, more chondroblasts are found, whereas in a hyperoxic tissue, more osteoblasts are found.[48,49] In a healing soft-tissue wound, the granulation tissue exposed to hyperoxia will form angioblasts, leading to improved angiogenesis.[50] Both of these factors are important for the osseointegration process, especially in compromised tissue.

Are There Enough Hyperbaric Chambers?

Worldwide there are estimated to be approximately 2,900 hyperbaric chambers:[51] Russia has 1,200, China and South Korea have 350 to 360 each, Europe and the United States have 330 to 340 each, Japan has 325, South America has 25 to 50, Asia has 15 to 25, and Africa has 10 to 20. Generally, one could expect to find hyperbaric chambers along coastal regions, because their main purpose is to treat people who have had diving accidents. There are two different systems in use: the multiplace chamber used to treat more than one patient at a time and the monoplace chamber used for individual treatments. The basic differences are that a multiplace chamber is pressurized with air and oxygen is delivered with a face mask or head tent system. The monoplace chamber is completely pressurized with oxygen.

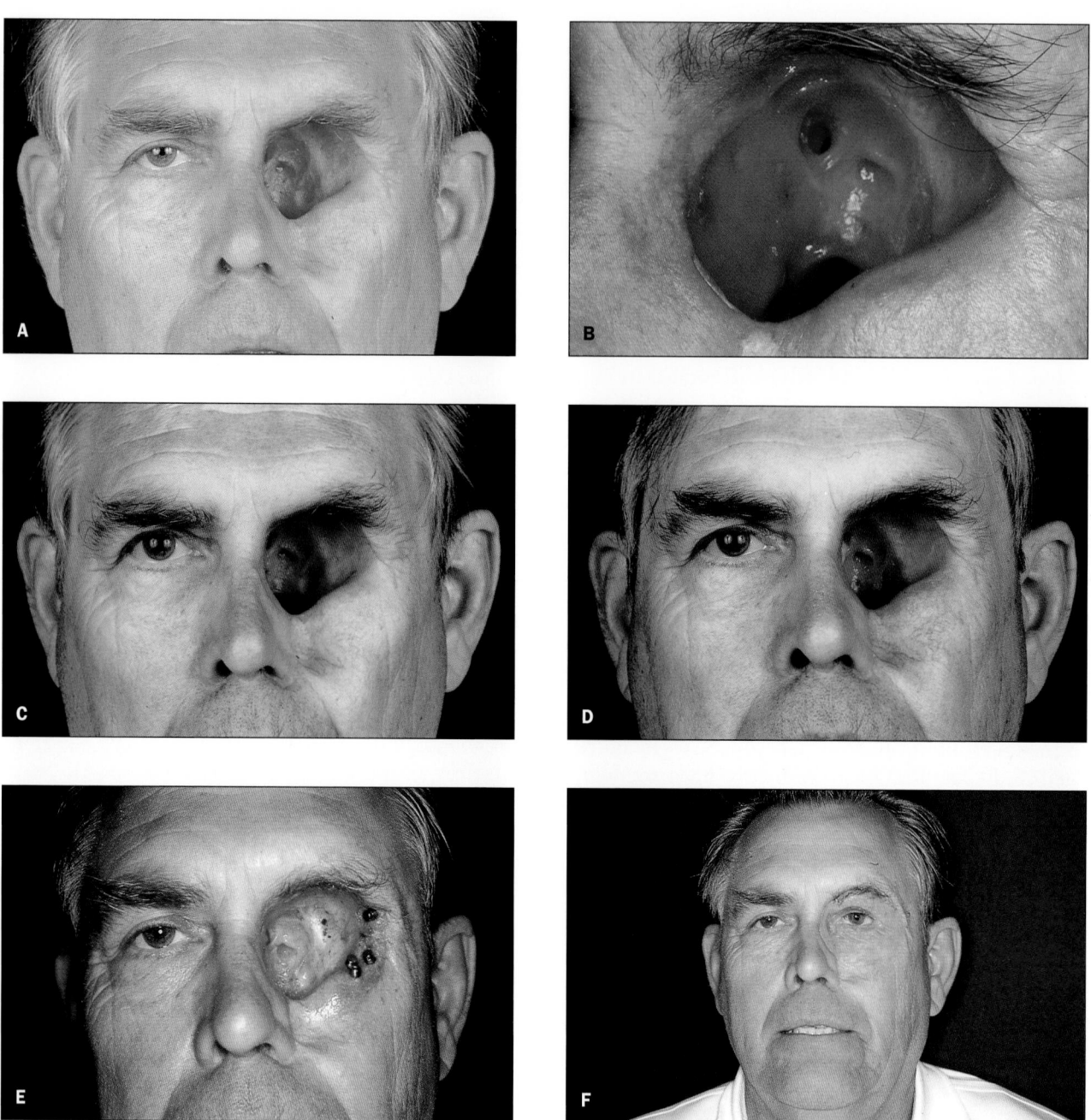

Fig. 9-6 Treatment sequence for orbital prosthesis. A, Defect after orbital exenteration followed by cobalt-60 irradiation (total dose 70 Gy). B, Close-up view of defect. C, Infared photograph before hyperbaric oxygen (HBO) treatment. D, Infrared photograph after 20 HBO treatments (2.5 atmospheric pressure for 90 minutes daily) shows superficial blood vessels below infraorbital rim. E, After placement of implants. F, Completed prosthesis in place.

Is HBO Therapy Expensive?

To discuss the costs for a specific procedure is always difficult, because background factors for cost analysis might differ throughout the world and prices for the actual treatment will differ among countries. HBO has often been regarded as an expensive procedure. Even today, the cost for one treatment might differ significantly among centers. We have been fortunate to have our own hyperbaric chamber, which of course affects the total cost of the procedure. When we estimated the installation and service costs, depreciation of the chamber, and cost for staff, a charge of 960 Skr (143 USD, in 1996 bank rates) per treatment was obtained. For the 30 treatments needed for implant placement, the total cost was 28,800 Skr (4,290 USD). The cost for HBO in the complete osseointegration procedure for rehabilitating a person with an ear defect would be approximately 50% of the total procedure. The corresponding figure for an orbit defect would be approximately 30%; for a midface defect, approximately 20%; and for a mandibular reconstruction, approximately 10%. One might therefore be tempted to place four implants in the temporal region without HBO and expect to lose one or two implants with time. On the other hand, if one induces osteoradionecrosis by implant surgery, the cost for these patients (only measuring monetary costs) is extremely high. In 1992 prices, it could be estimated that the cost to treat one patient with osteoradionecrosis would be equivalent to treating 40 patients with the proposed 30-dive HBO protocol.[52]

Are There Alternatives to HBO Therapy in Compromised Tissue?

The possibilities for avoiding complications when performing surgery in irradiated patients involve pharmacologic factors such as calcium, phosphorus, vitamin D, and calcitonin supplementation in osteoporotic patients; supplementation with gestagen or estrogen in postmenopausal women; anabolic steroids in cachectic cancer patients; synthetic oxygen transporters; and different growth factors.[40] All of these factors are important, but the clinical value of synthetic oxygen transporters has not yet been shown. Different growth factors such as the bone morphogenetic protein, transforming growth factor-beta,[53] seem to be interesting substances probably available in the future but not yet ready for clinical trials. What we therefore chose was to use HBO treatment, which is the only known treatment modality that has proven effects counteracting some of the negative effects from radiotherapy in the tissues. This modality has been used in clinical practice since the 1930s. Its function and detailed mechanisms of action are well described in more than 30,000 scientific articles. Its side effects and drawbacks are equally well known, and reports from all centers using HBO have proved that it is a safe and predictable modality.

References

1. Brånemark P-I, Hansson BO, Adell R, et al. Osseointegrated implants in the treatment of the edentulous jaw. Experience from a 10-year period. Scand J Plast Reconstr Surg Suppl 1977;16:1.

2. Tjellström A, Lindström J, Hallén O, Albrektsson T, Brånemark P-I. Osseointegrated titanium implants in the temporal bone. A clinical study on bone-anchored hearing aids. Am J Otol 1981;2:304.

3. Tjellström A. Osseointegrated systems and their applications in the head and neck. Adv Otolaryngol Head Neck Surg 1989;3:39.

4. Linder L, Carlsson Å, Marsal L, Bjursten LM, Brånemark P-I. Clinical aspects of osseointegration in joint replacement. A histological study of titanium implants. J Bone Joint Surg Br 1988;70:550.

5. Carlsson LV. On the Development of a New Concept for Orthopaedic Implant Fixation. Thesis, University of Göteborg, Sweden, 1989.

6. Dental Implants. National Institutes of Health Consensus Development Conference Statement, 1988;7:3.

7. Jacobsson M, Tjellström A, Thomsen P, Albrektsson T, Turesson I. Integration of titanium implants in irradiated bone. Histologic and clinical study. Ann Otol Rhinol Laryngol 1988;97:337.

8. Granström G, Tjellström A, Brånemark P-I, Fornander J. Hyperbaric oxygen treatment can increase the osseointegration rate of titanium fixture implants in irradiated bone. Proceedings of the XVIIth EUBS Meeting, Heraklion, Greece, 1991;415.

9. Parel SM, Tjellström A. The United States and Swedish experience with osseointegration and facial prostheses. Int J Oral Maxillofac Implants 1991;6:75.

10. Lundgren S, Moy PK, Beumer J III, Lewis S. Surgical considerations for endosseous implants in the craniofacial region: a 3-year report. Int J Oral Maxillofac Surg 1993;22:272.

11. Wolfaardt JF, Wilkes GH, Parel SM, Tjellström A. Craniofacial osseointegration: the Canadian experience. Int J Oral Maxillofac Implants 1993;8:197.

12. Albrektsson T. A multicenter report on osseointegrated oral implants. J Prosthet Dent 1988;60:75.

13. Taylor TD, Worthington P. Osseointegrated implant rehabilitation of the previously irradiated mandible: results of a limited trial at 3 to 7 years. J Prosthet Dent 1993;69:60.

14. Franzén L, Rosenquist JB, Rosenquist KI, Gustafsson I. Oral implant rehabilitation of patients with oral malignances treated with radiotherapy and surgery without adjunctive hyperbaric oxygen. Int J Oral Maxillofac Implants 1995;10:183.

15. Granström G, Bergström K, Tjellström A, Brånemark P-I. A detailed analysis of titanium implants lost in irradiated tissues. Int J Oral Maxillofac Implants 1994;9:653.

16. Granström G, Bergström K, Tjellström A, Brånemark P-I. Ten years follow-up of osseointegrated implants used in irradiated patients. Proceedings of the XXth EUBS Meeting, Istanbul, Turkey, 1994;308.

17. Granström G. Rehabilitation of irradiated cancer patients with tissue integrated prostheses. Adjunctive use of HBO to improve osseointegration. J Fac Somato Prosth 1996;2:1.

18. Adell R, Lekholm U, Röckler B, Brånemark P-I. A 15-year study of osseointegrated implants in the treatment of the edentulous jaw. Int J Oral Surg 1981;10:387.

19. Adell R. Long-term treatment results. In Brånemark P-I, Zarb GA, Albrektsson T (eds): Tissue-Integrated Prostheses: Osseointegration in Clinical Dentistry. Chicago: Quintessence Publishing Company; 1985;175.

20. Bergström K, Tjellström A, Granström G. Development of implant retained facial prosthesis based on 15 years of experience. Proceedings of the First International Congress on Maxillofacial Prosthetics, Indian Wells, California, 1994;250.

21. Granström G, Tjellström A, Brånemark P-I, Fornander J. Bone-anchored reconstruction of the irradiated head and neck cancer patient. Otolaryngol Head Neck Surg 1993;108:334.

22. Marx RE. Osteoradionecrosis: a new concept of its pathophysiology. J Oral Maxillofac Surg 1983;41:283.

23. Jacobsson M. On Bone Behaviour After Irradiation. Thesis, University of Göteborg, Sweden, 1985.

24. Neukam FW, Hausamen J-E. Microvascular bone grafting techniques in combination with osseointegrated fixtures. In Worthington P, Brånemark P-I (eds): Advanced Osseointegration Surgery: Applications in the Maxillofacial Region. Chicago: Quintessence Publishing Company, 1992;276.

25. Granström G, Bågenholm T, Edström S, et al. Mandible reconstruction in the irradiated patient using microvascularised osteomyocutaneous grafting and hyperbaric oxygen. Proceedings of the Joint Meeting on Diving and Hyperbaric Medicine, 3rd Swiss Symposium, XVIIIth Annual Meeting of EUBS, Basel, Switzerland, 1992:170.

26. Bågenholm T, Fagerberg-Mohlin B, Fogdestam I, Granström G. Mandibular reconstruction of the irradiated, tissue deficient patient who needs osseointegrated implants. Second International Congress on Maxillofacial Prosthetics, Seoul, Korea, 1996;99.

27. Holgers KM, Tjellström A, Bjursten LM, Erlandsson BE. Soft tissue reactions around percutaneous implants: a clinical study on skin-penetrating titanium implants used for bone-anchored auricular prostheses. Int J Oral Maxillofac Implants 1987;2:35.

28. Curi MM, Granström G, Tjellström A. Frequency of granulation tissue around titanium implants in the orbit. J Fac Somato Prosth 1998;3:1.

29. Scrimger JW. Backscatter from high atomic number materials in high energy photon beams. Radiology 1977;124:815.

30. Mian TA, Van Putten MC Jr, Kramer DC, Jacob RF, Boyer AL. Backscatter radiation at bone-titanium interface from high-energy X and gamma rays. Int J Radiat Oncol Biol Phys 1987;13;1943.

31. Rosengren B, Wulff L, Carlsson E, et al. Backscatter radiation at tissue-titanium interfaces. Analyses of biological effects from ^{60}CO and protons. Acta Oncol 1991;30;859.

32. Granström G, Tjellström A, Albrektsson T. Postimplantation irradiation for head and neck cancer treatment. Int J Oral Maxillofac Implants 1993;8;495.

33. Granström G, Tjellström A, Albrektsson T. Post-implantation irradiation of osseointegrated implants. Proceedings of the First International Congress on Maxillofacial Prosthetics, Indian Wells, California, 1994;292.

34. Marx RE, Johnson RP. Studies in the radiobiology of osteoradionecrosis and their clinical significance. Oral Surg Oral Med Oral Pathol 1987;64;379.

35. Granström G, Tjellström A. Effects of irradiation on osseointegration before and after implant placement. A report of 3 cases. Int J Oral Maxillofac Implants 1997;12;547.

36. Wolfaardt J, Granström G, Friberg B, Jha N, Tjellström A. A retrospective study of the effects of chemotherapy on osseointegration. J Fac Somato Prosth 1996;2;99.

37. Niimi A, Ueda M, Keller EE, Worthington P. A multicenter study of osseointegrated implants placed in irradiated tissues. Second International Congress on Maxillofacial Prosthetics, Seoul, Korea, 1996;106.

38. Granström G, Devge C, Tjellström A. Laser Doppler flowmetry for the intraosseous blood flow measurement after irradiation, bone grafting, and hyperbaric oxygen treatment. Proceedings of the XIXth EUBS Meeting, Trondheim, Norway, 1993;126.

39. Granström G. The use of hyperbaric oxygen to prevent implant loss in the irradiated patient. In Worthington P, Brånemark P-I (eds): Advanced Osseointegration Surgery: Applications in the Maxillofacial Region. Chicago: Quintessence Publishing Company; 1992;336.

40. Granström G, Jacobsson M, Tjellström A. Titanium implants in irradiated tissue: benefits from hyerbaric oxygen. Int J Oral Maxillofac Implants 1992;7:15.

41. Nilsson LP, Granström G, Röckert HOE. Effects of dextrans, heparin and hyperbaric oxygen on mandibular tissue damage after osteotomy in an experimental system. Int J Oral Maxillofac Surg 1987;16:77.

42. Støre G, Granström G. A morphologic and morphometric study of mandibular osteoradionecrosis. Proceedings of the XXI EUBS Meeting, Helsinki, Finland, 1995;105.

43. Nilsson P, Albrektsson T, Granström G, Röckert HOE. The effect of hyperbaric oxygen treatment on bone regeneration: an experimental study using the bone harvest chamber in the rabbit. Int J Oral Maxillofac Implants 1988;3:43.

44. Granström G, Magnusson BC, Nilsson LP, Röckert HOE. Biological effects on oral tissues by hyperbaric oxygen treatment. Proceedings of the XVth EUBS Scientific Meeting, Eilat, Israel, 1989;281.

45. Johnsson K, Hansson A, Granström G, Jacobsson M, Turesson I. The effects of hyperbaric oxygenation on bone-titanium implant interface strength with and without preceding irradiation. Int J Oral Maxillofac Implants 1993;8:415.

46. Granström G, Hansson Å, Johnsson K, Jacobsson M, Albrektsson T, Turesson I. Hyperbaric oxygenation can increase bone to titanium implant interface strength after irradiation. Proceedings of the Joint Meeting on Diving and Hyperbaric Medicine, 3rd Swiss Symposium, XVIIIth Annual Meeting of EUBS, Basel, Switzerland, 1992;151.

47. Larsen PE, Stronczek MJ, Beck FM, Rohrer M. Osteointegration of implants in radiated bone with and without adjunctive hyperbaric oxygen. J Oral Maxillofac Surg 1993;51:280.

48. Granström G, Nilsson LP, Magnusson BC, Röckert HOE. Experimental mandibular fracture. Effect on bone healing after treatment with hyperbaric oxygen. Proceedings of the XVth EUBS Scientific Meeting, Eilat, Israel, 1989;290.

49. Basset CA. Environmental and cellular factors regulating osteogenesis. In Frost HM (ed): Bone Biodynamics. Boston: Little, Brown and Company; 1964;233.

50. Marx RE. Angiogenesis and fibroplasia in irradiated tissue. In Kindwall EP (ed): Hyperbaric Medicine Practice. Flagstaff, AZ: Best Publishing Company; 1995;450.

51. Jain KK, editor. Textbook of Hyperbaric Medicine, ed 2. Seattle: Hogrefe & Huber Publishers; 1996;475.

52. Granström G, Fagerberg-Mohlin B, Lindström J, Mercke C. A comparison: retrospective and prospective management of osteoradionecrosis. Proceedings of the First International Congress on Maxillofacial Prosthetics, Indian Wells, California, 1994;309.

53. Rahal MD, Plyam R, Delorme D, Osmond DG, McCarthy GF, Clokie C. Effects of local administration of TGF-b1 on B-lineage cells in bone marrow of mouse femurs implanted with titanium. Fifth International Winter Seminar of the Biomaterials Club, Ischgl, Austria, 1995;9.

Part III

Soft and Hard Tissue Defects: Surgical Considerations

10.

Surgical Principles of Osseointegration

Kenji W. Higuchi, DDS, MS

- Definitions of Osseointegration
- Surgical Principles of Osseointegration
- Environmental and Clinical Differences Between Oral and Craniofacial Applications
- Multidisciplinary Team Approach
- Initial Implant Stability in Highly Variable Anatomy
- Skin Management at Abutment Penetration Site
- Implant Number and Location

The practice of surgery remains both art and science. Major defects involving aberrations of the soft and hard tissues of the craniomaxillofacial region have challenged the skills of reconstructive surgeons. In the past decade, significant advances have been made in the development of microvascular free-flap transfer of hard and soft tissue for reconstruction after oncologic resection in the oral cavity, mandible, maxilla, and midfacial regions. Similar developments have occurred using autogenous tissues to replace aesthetically challenging structures such as the nose and external ear. The results of these efforts are highly variable (Fig 10-1).

As an alternative to the significant surgical morbidity of autogenous reconstruction, osseointegrated craniofacial implant rehabilitation has proved to be a worthwhile and valuable addition in this area of head and neck surgery. The purpose of this chapter is to review basic surgical principles of osseointegration as applied specifically to the craniofacial region. As with any surgical procedure, good care requires an understanding and application of the basic sciences, including surgical anatomy, pathology, bio-materials, wound repair physiology, microbiology, and pharmacology. For patients with craniofacial defects, this scientific knowledge provides the framework for appropriate pretreatment evaluation, preoperative preparation, surgical methodology, selection of implant components, asepsis, and postoperative management. Specific discussions of these topics are provided in other chapters of this book. This chapter identifies basic principles of osseointegration surgery proved by long-term multicenter studies and related supporting research relevant to craniofacial implant reconstruction.

Although presently accepted as a routine therapeutic option, predictable and enduring direct implant to bone anchorage was not available until Brånemark introduced the concept of osseointegration.[1,2] It was his appreciation of the response of highly differentiated hard and soft tissues to surgical preparation and the placement of titanium components into minimally traumatized bone that has opened a new era of reconstructive possibilities based on this anchorage concept. Since 1965, a standardized two-stage surgical procedure has been developed for implant rehabilitation of the fully and

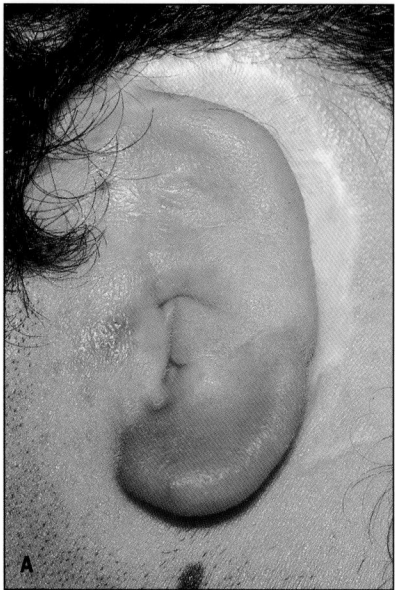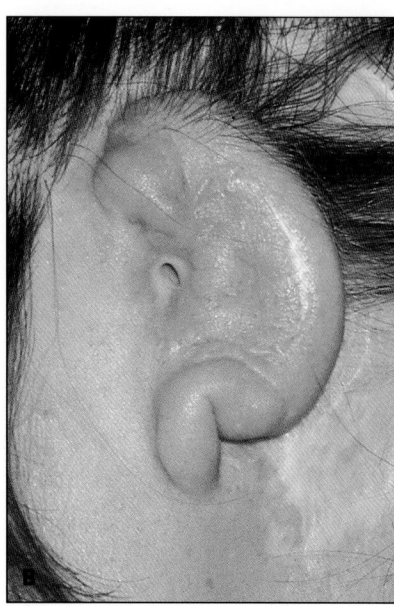

Fig 10-1. Autogenous ear reconstruction with variable aesthetic results.

partially edentulous jaw. In 1977, the first extraoral percutaneous application of osseointegration involved implant connection to a bone-anchored hearing aid. In 1979, again at the University of Göteborg, Department of Otolaryngology, auricular and other craniofacial prostheses were retained with skin-penetrating osseointegrated implants. Since that time, this approach has become a standardized alternative for surgical-prosthetic rehabilitation of hard- and soft-tissue defects in the craniofacial skeleton. To provide an understanding of factors important to favorable outcome in the extraoral environment, a review of criteria associated with successful osseointegration in the oral cavity is appropriate.

Definitions of Osseointegration

The end product of osseointegration is implant-bone anchorage, and it is this function that enables prosthetic restoration of missing anatomy. The creation and maintenance of osseointegration is the foundation of this form of reconstructive surgery.

Several theoretical and clinical definitions of osseointegration have been proposed since Brånemark first coined the term in 1977. Recent definitions have focused on clinical aspects, stressing biomechanical behavior of the implant-bone interface during loading conditions.

"Osseointegration in theory and practice is defined as continuing structural and functional coexistence, possibly in a symbiotic manner, between differentiated, adequately remodelling, biologic tissues and strictly defined and controlled synthetic components, providing lasting, specific clinical functions without initiating rejection mechanisms."[3]

"An implant is said to be biomechanically osseointegrated if there is no progressive relative motion of living bone and implant under functional levels and types of loading for the entire life of the patient."[4]

"A process whereby clinically asymptomatic rigid fixation of alloplastic materials is achieved, and maintained, in bone during functional loading."[5]

Predictable osseointegration is not an accidental event and involves many factors that influence prognosis and long-term results. Albrektsson and colleagues[6] identified the following decisive prerequisites for osseointegration: 1) implant material, 2) implant design, 3) implant finish, 4) status of the bone, 5) surgical technique, and 6) implant-loading conditions.

After selecting an implant hardware system, the surgical-prosthetic team expresses a preference for implant material, implant geometry, and implant surface finish. This choice should be based on a review of well-designed multicenter studies examining clinical outcome. The only system specifically intended for extraoral craniofacial application that has established documentation of safety and effectiveness is the Brånemark craniofacial implant. Long-term multicenter reports[7-15] have validated

112

high regional success rates in the craniomaxillofacial skeleton by following a standardized surgical protocol. After choosing the appropriate implant components, the remaining three factors involving the status of the bone, surgical technique, and implant-loading conditions are still under the control of the treating team. Bone morphology, bone quality, and other local conditions of the recipient site have been recognized as anatomic features affecting implant stability, position, and successful osseointegration.[2,16,17] With the exception of preoperative and postoperative hyperbaric oxygen therapy, it is difficult and usually unnecessary to alter the status of the bone greatly in the craniofacial patient. The surgical team, in most situations, learns to work with the existing bony anatomy and carefully applies basic principles of osseointegration surgery to produce successful anchorage.

Surgical Principles of Osseointegration

In 1977, Brånemark et al[2] identified the following factors as important for obtaining osseointegration in the treatment of the edentulous jaw: 1) inert, noncontaminated material; 2) minimal preparation trauma; 3) immobilized unloaded implant; 4) intact mucoperiosteum, sealed site; and 5) undisturbed bone healing. Based on three decades of experience with the oral cavity, multiple authors[16] have confirmed Brånemark's concepts and have suggested several additional requirements for predictable outcome: 1) sterile operating room conditions, 2) standardized recommended surgical equipment for implant placement and abutment connection, 3) correctly manufactured implant and abutment noncontaminated components, 4) experienced trained surgeon using meticulous tissue handling and a gentle surgical technique, and 5) thoroughly evaluated and prepared patient.

These general concepts have been incorporated into a standard protocol for routine osseointegration surgery in oral and craniofacial rehabilitation. Although the principles of osseointegration surgery for the oral cavity and jaw bone can be applied generally to the extraoral environment, certain modifications and refinements of these tenets are now recognized as important.

Surgical considerations unique for craniofacial rehabilitation include the following. 1) A complete, well-trained multidisciplinary team is imperative. 2) Use specifically designed craniofacial implant components proven to be safe and effective. 3) Secure primary implant stability in highly variable conditions. 4) Minimize skin mobility at the abutment site by subcutaneous tissue reduction. 5) Determine the number and position of implants according to the anatomic region treated and the design of the planned epithesis.

Before a specific discussion of these principles, a review of environmental and clinical differences between oral and extraoral applications of osseointegrated bone-anchored prostheses is useful.

Environmental and Clinical Differences Between Oral and Craniofacial Applications

Although it is tempting to extrapolate the experience gained from the oral cavity to external defects of the craniofacial region, obvious differences exist between these two areas (Table 10-1).

Intraoral implant-abutment units and their attached prostheses penetrate keratinized and nonkeratinized oral mucosa bathed in saliva and are

Table 10-1 Differences Between Oral and Craniofacial Rehabilitation

Oral cavity-jaw bone	Craniomaxillofacial extraoral environment
Saliva	Air exposure
Oral microflora	Skin microflora
Mucosal covering	Skin covering
Teeth, plaque	Keratin, sebum, sweat, hair
Increased bone volume	Typical reduced bone volume
More standardized anatomy	Highly variable local anatomy
Longer implant lengths	Shorter implant lengths
Higher loading forces	Reduced load demands
Majority of patients nonirradiated	Higher incidence of radiation therapy
Varying aesthetic demands of prosthesis with emphasis on function	Highly dependent on aesthetics

associated with a mixed microflora specific to the oral cavity. In the healthy environment, cocci and motile rods predominate, with approximately equal numbers of facultative and anaerobic species.[18] In the mouth, the hydrating effects of saliva protect against desiccation and ulceration while encouraging soft-tissue repair by reducing clotting time and accelerating wound contracture. Saliva also plays an important role[19] in the maintenance of ecological balance by débridement and lavage, aggregation and reduced adherence by both immunologic and nonimmunologic means, and direct antibacterial activity.

In contrast, skin is exposed to the drying effects of the external environment and is constantly contaminated by exogenous organisms. Skin dryness, reduced pH, and epithelial cell turnover provide an unfavorable environment for colonization by exogenous bacteria, which are usually displaced by the normal flora.[20] The normal microbiota of skin varies according to the age of the patient and location in question. *Staphylococcus epidermidis* constitutes more than 90% of the normal flora. Certain areas of the craniofacial skeleton support specific bacterium such as *Propionibacterium acnes*, found in facial areas containing numerous sebaceous glands. Moist skin areas are associated with gram-negative rods such as *Klebsiella*, *Escherichia coli*, and *Proteus*. Skin appendage structures such as eccrine, apocrine, and sebaceous glands as well as hair are not seen in oral mucosa. In the area where the abutment penetrates the skin, similar to the oral counterpart where the abutment penetrates mucosa and where plaque accumulates and must be removed, various byproducts of the skin must be cleansed. The cells from the cornified layers are shed from the skin surface. Sebum from sebaceous glands and sweat from eccrine and apocrine glands contribute to this debris. Additional differences involving bone volume, implant lengths, loading forces, irradiation, and prosthesis design will be elaborated in the following sections.

Multidisciplinary Team Approach

A team approach has proved to be effective in applying osseointegration for oral rehabilitation. In the majority of cases, the team is composed of a surgeon for implant and abutment operations and a restorative dentist or prosthodontist for prosthesis construction. The management of defective craniofacial anatomy resulting from acquired or congenital causes requires a more extensive multidisciplinary team. Using the example of oncologic resection of the midfacial structures, including the nose and maxilla, necessary team specialists might involve the following: 1) oncologic surgeon; 2) ear, nose, and throat surgeon; 3) oral and maxillofacial surgeon; 4) plastic and reconstructive surgeon; 5) maxillofacial prosthodontist; 6) anaplastologist; 7) dental technician; 8) speech pathologist and hearing specialist; and 9) psychologist. It is obvious that the decision to provide craniofacial implant rehabilitation should be made only if a qualified team complete with appropriate specialties is available. Communication and collaboration among team members are necessary for proper planning and execution of the desired surgical-prosthetic plan to achieve optimal results. The final goal of a craniofacial implant-retained epithesis is to replace prosthetically facial structures surgically resected, lost through trauma, or congenitally missing. Patient acceptance of this treatment option is related directly to the appearance and stability of the prosthesis, and therefore it is important that the multispecialty team include a skilled anaplastologist and maxillofacial prosthodontist capable of producing an aesthetically acceptable and lifelike epithesis. Communication among surgical and prosthetic team members should extend from presurgical assessment to delivery of the prosthesis. Preresection planning that anticipates the desired surgical-prosthetic plan can be helpful in maintaining potential anchorage sites. As recognized in oral rehabilitation, a diagnostic wax up of the final prosthetic configuration and position permits the development of a surgical placement guide (Fig 10-2 and 10-3).

In craniofacial implant rehabilitation, the extremes of age encountered range from the child with Treacher Collins syndrome to the elderly patient with a resected squamous cell carcinoma of the midface. Careful and regular short-term and long-term follow-up are important commitments of the treating team. Assessment of implant anchorage function, examination of soft- and hard-tissue status, inspection of the integrity of implant and prosthetic components, and evaluation of the aesthetic and retentive function of the prosthesis are all necessary. In children receiving treatment, ongoing follow-up may extend for 6 to 7 decades. Qualified surgical and prosthetic specialists working in collaboration form the foundation of the team approach. Concentrating craniofacial implant rehabilitation in regional centers seems to be advantageous in the development of provider experience and for refinement of the technique.

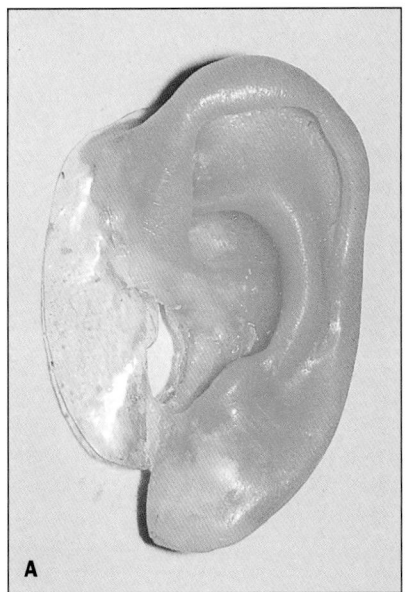

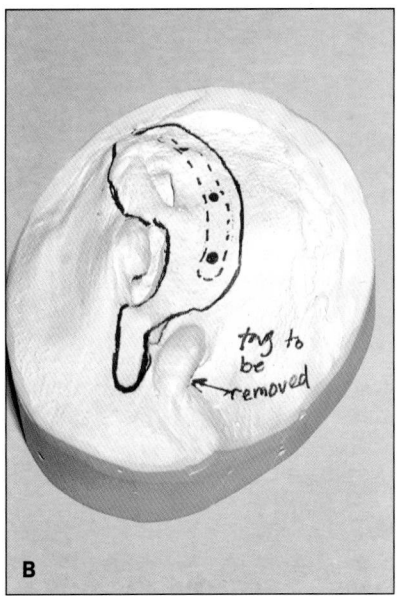

Fig 10-2. Diagnostic wax up of auricular prosthesis constructed on moulage cast.

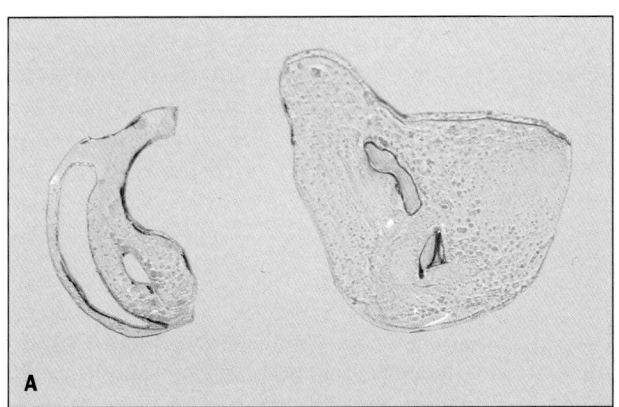

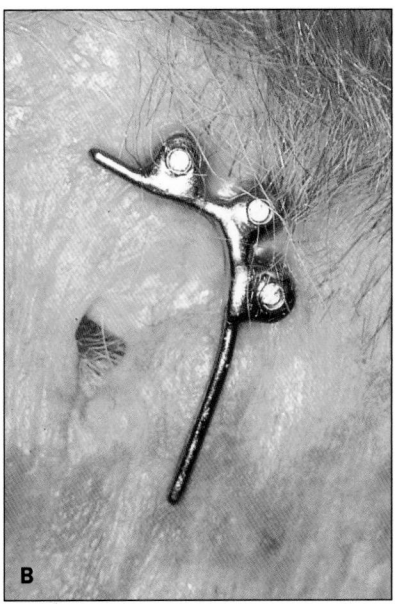

Fig 10-3. Surgical placement guide used to achieve compatible implant placement.

Initial Implant Stability in Highly Variable Anatomy

Surgical-prosthetic implant reconstruction of the craniofacial region is classified according to affected regional sites: auricular, nasal, orbital, and complex, which includes oral involvement. Congenital malformations, traumatic injuries, and margins in oncologic resection are associated with a wide range of skeletal and soft-tissue defects. Careful clinical examination and appropriate imaging studies are important in defining the highly variable volume and morphology of these tissues to achieve optimal implant stability.

With severe congenital deformities, especially for children, computed tomographic imaging is recommended. In the child who has Treacher Collins syndrome, the position of the dura mater of the middle cranial fossa may be unusually low and at risk for penetration. The stylomastoid foramen and facial nerve position can vary and have been observed more laterally and superiorly. Cranial bone less than 3 mm thick in the temporal region also is a risk factor for penetration of the dura mater; however, careful, deliberate, and precise bone depth preparation minimizes this risk.

Securing initial implant stability is a basic requirement in establishing favorable osseointegration between bone and implant and is highly dependent on the quality and volume of anchoring bone. Bone quality is directly proportional to the amount of compact bone present. Implant placement into basal bone and, when possible, bicortically enhances the initial stability. In children, especially those with craniofacial anomalies such as Treacher Collins syndrome or hemifacial microsomia, thin cranial bone of lesser quality in the temporal region is not uncommon, and this type of bone combined with mastoid air cells requires care to avoid overcountersinking and excessive torque during implant placement. Selection of alternative adjacent implant sites avoiding air cells but still compatible with prosthetic design usually solves the problem. The temporal, orbital, and nasal regions typically have smaller amounts of bone volume for implant placement. For this reason, craniofacial implant lengths are standardized to 3.0 mm and 4.0 mm, with a diameter of 3.75 mm. Reduced amounts of anchoring bone and shorter implant lengths underscore the importance of gentle nondamaging surgery in obtaining primary implant fixation.

Tjellström and colleagues[21] measured the removal torque of osseointegrated craniofacial implants after 3 to 4 months of healing and reported an average removal torque of 42.7 N·cm (range, 26-60 N·cm) in the temporal bone of nine volunteer patients. Ueda and associates[22] observed that insertion torque levels consistently were higher than removal torque in human cadaver temporal bone, with a maximum insertion torque exerted without causing a break in bone threads of 70 N·cm in bicortical bone and 50 N·cm in monocortical bone. Fracturing of the bony threads during insertion occurred at 77 N·cm in bicortical and 57.7 N·cm in monocortical bone. These observations suggest that overtightening during implant placement is a risk factor and that placement torque values should be reduced in lesser quality bone. Excessive tightening during implant placement may accidentally break or damage the recipient bone threads tapped before placement, resulting in reduced implant stability. Johansson and Albrektsson[23] demonstrated in the rabbit tibia that increased torque removal values and percentage of bone in direct contact with implant surfaces increase with increasing periods of healing after implant placement. Under suboptimal conditions, it may be advisable to consider an extended period of healing before abutment connection. Surgical technique associated with excessive trauma can decrease the repair capacity of bone formation at the interface and theoretically affect the likelihood of osseointegration.

In contrast to certain implants placed in the oral cavity, craniofacial implants usually are not subjected to premature loading forces. After implant placement, a period of undisturbed healing is crucial in developing osseointegration. Excessive loading force on an implant soon after placement is associated with the formation of a fibrous connective tissue capsule at the implant-bone interface.[24] The vast majority of patients rehabilitated with craniofacial implants had been treated using the well-defined two-stage approach. Since 1989, Tjellström[25] has used a one-stage surgical protocol in the temporal region. He recommended that the two-stage procedure be applied routinely, especially in areas other than the mastoid region and in compromised tissue such as after irradiation with poor bone quality. Detailed description of the one-stage technique is provided in Chapter 11.

Skin Management at Abutment Penetration Site

There are histologic differences between oral mucosa and skin that have clinical implications. The epidermal layer of skin is stratified squamous epithelium composed of a keratinocytic system as well as melanocytes, Langerhans' cells, and Merkel cells. The dermis is a layer of connective tissue, mainly collagen with varying amounts of elastic tissue. The adnexal structures (sebaceous glands, sweat glands, hair), blood vessels, and nerves are located in the dermis and subcutaneous tissues. The reduction of skin thickness at abutment connection involves excision of a portion of dermal and subcutaneous tissues. This excision often includes removal of the adnexal structures, muscle, blood vessels, and nerves. Consequently, in addition to fixing the skin to periosteum to minimize mobility, glandular components are removed. Often local soft-tissue surgery such as removal of skin tags, eyebrow suspension, or alteration of contour is done to facilitate facial epithesis construction and can be accomplished as part of the implant placement or abutment connection procedures. The conditions present where the abutment penetrates the skin are critical factors in avoiding subsequent soft-tissue problems. Multiple authors[26,27] have advocated the following implant conditions at skin-penetration sites: 1) subcutaneous skin reduction; 2) fixed, nonmobile skin; and 3) absence of hair. Brown et al[27] stated: "Fastidious adherence to these principles, at least in the temporal region, will almost always guarantee a favorable skin reaction, but contravention of them will almost as surely result in an unfavorable reaction." To achieve these goals, grafting of non-hair-bearing skin to periosteum frequently is required around the abutment.

The general sequence of wound healing in the oral cavity is similar to that of skin. One significant difference is that in the repair of skin a combination of dry epidermis and dermis and dry exudate (scab) forms over the fibrin clot deeper in the wound. Epithelialization is more rapid in the mucosal wound as the cells migrate directly onto the exposed surface of the fibrin clot.[28] In skin, the epithelial repair proceeds at a lower speed under the protection of the dried scab. The adverse effects of irradiation on wound healing are well known and are discussed in Chapter 9. In addition to the acute and delayed effects of irradiation, tumoricidal chemotherapy is known to impair wound healing. However, these effects appear to be transient, and incisions made a few weeks after chemotherapy seem to heal with normal or nearly normal tissue tensile strength.[29] In contrast, the effects of irradiation seem to be progressive and irreversible, perhaps because of permanent structural alteration of cellular DNA.[30]

Implant Number and Location

As a general rule, the number of implants planned to support a facial epithesis varies according to the affected site. Tjellström and associates[26] recommended that two well-spaced implants 15 mm apart are adequate for an auricular prosthesis compared with three to five for the orbit. Nasal and complex oral-facial defects are planned according to the residual bone available and the prosthesis design. Although the loading forces from a lightweight facial epithesis are not of a high magnitude, short craniofacial implants are often placed into compromised bone, making the number and location of implants important biomechanical considerations. Implant placement is dictated by the existing defect anatomy and should be compatible with the planned design of the facial epithesis. As previously mentioned, a diagnostic wax up is useful in preparing a surgical guide.

Conclusion

The surgical principles of osseointegration identified by Brånemark et al[2] in 1977 and by Adell et al[16] for use in the oral cavity were transferred to the craniofacial region with appropriate modifications. Tjellström and others[26,27] described these accommodations for skin-penetrating connection to the craniofacial region, with numerous international studies verifying the soundness of this approach.

The legacy of the pioneering group from Sweden is that a predictable and effective system has been provided that improves quality of life for patients suffering from craniofacial disfigurement. A precise road map guiding us toward this goal is available, and it is the responsibility of those traveling on this highway to use it.

References

1. Brånemark P-I, Adell R, Breine U, Hansson BO, Lindström J, Ohlsson Å. Intra-osseous anchorage of dental prostheses. I. Experimental studies. Scand J Plast Reconstr Surg 1969;3:81.

2. Brånemark P-I, Hansson B, Adell R, et al. Osseointegrated Implants in the Treatment of the Edentulous Jaw: Experience From a 10-year Period. Stockholm: Almqvist and Wiksell; 1977.

3. Brånemark P-I. Cited by Rydevik B et al(4).

4. Rydevik B, Brånemark P-I, Skalak R (eds): International Workshop on Osseointegration in Skeletal Reconstruction and Joint Replacement. Göteborg, Sweden: The Institute for Applied Biotechnology; 1991.

5. Albrektsson T, Zarb B. Cited by Sennerby L. On the Bone Tissue Response to Titanium Implants. Thesis, University of Göteborg, Göteborg, Sweden, 1991:42.

6. Albrektsson T, Brånemark P-I, Hansson HA, Lindström J. Osseointegrated titanium implants. Requirements for ensuring a long-lasting, direct bone-to-implant anchorage in man. Acta Orthop Scand 1981;52:155.

7. Tjellström A, Rosenhall U, Lindström J, Hallén O, Albrektsson T, Brånemark P-I. Five-year experience with skin-penetrating bone-anchored implants in the temporal bone. Acta Otolaryngol (Stockh) 1983;95:568.

8. Albrektsson T, Brånemark P-I, Jacobsson M, Tjellström A. Present clinical applications of osseointegrated percutaneous implants. Plast Reconstr Surg 1987;79:721.

9. Parel SM, Tjellström A. The United States and Swedish experience with osseointegration and facial prostheses. Int J Oral Maxillofac Implants 1991;6:75.

10. Granström G, Jacobsson M, Tjellström A. Titanium implants in irradiated tissue: benefits from hyperbaric oxygen. Int J Oral Maxillofac Implants 1992;7:15.

11. Wolfaardt JF, Wilkes GH, Parel SM, Tjellström A. Craniofacial osseointegration: the Canadian experience. Int J Oral Maxillofac Implants 1993;8:197.

12. Arcuri MR, LaVelle WE, Fyler E, Jons R. Prosthetic complications of extraoral implants. J Prosthet Dent 1993;69:289.

13. Granström G, Bergström K, Tjellström A, Brånemark P-I. A detailed analysis of titanium implants lost in irradiated tissues. Int J Oral Maxillofac Implants 1994;9:653.

14. Roumanas E, Nishimura R, Beumer J III, Moy P, Weinlander M, Lorant J. Craniofacial defects and osseointegrated implants: six-year follow-up report on the success rates of craniofacial implants at UCLA. Int J Oral Maxillofac Implants 1994;9:579.

15. Tolman DE, Taylor PF. Bone-anchored craniofacial prosthesis study. Int J Oral Maxillofac Implants 1996;11:159.

16. Adell R, Lekholm U, Brånemark P-I. Surgical procedures. In Brånemark P-I, Zarb BA, Albrektsson T (eds): Tissue-Integrated Prostheses: Osseointegration in Clinical Dentistry. Chicago: Quintessence Publishing Company; 1985:211.

17. Adell R. The surgical principles of osseointegration. In Worthington P, Brånemark P-I (eds): Advanced Osseointegration Surgery: Applications in the Maxillofacial Region. Chicago: Quintessence Publishing Company; 1992:94.

18. Newman M, Flemmig T. Bacteria-host interactions. In Worthington P, Brånemark P-I (eds): Advanced Osseointegration Surgery: Applications in the Maxillofacial Region. Chicago: Quintessence Publishing Company; 1992:67.

19. Mandel ID. The functions of saliva. J Dent Res 1987;66:623.

20. Peterson L. Microbiology of head and neck infections. Oral Maxillofac Surg Clin North Am 1991;3:247.

21. Tjellström A, Jacobsson M, Albrektsson T. Removal torque of osseointegrated craniofacial implants: a clinical study. Int J Oral Maxillofac Implants 1988;3:287.

22. Ueda M, Matsuki M, Jacobsson M, Tjellström A. Relationship between insertion torque and removal torque analyzed in fresh temporal bone. Int J Oral Maxillofac Implants 1991;6:442.

23. Johansson C, Albrektsson T. Integration of screw implants in the rabbit: a 1-year follow-up of removal torque of titanium implants. Int J Oral Maxillofac Implants 1987;2:69.

24. Brunski JB, Moccia AF Jr, Pollack SR, Korostoff E, Trachtenberg DI. The influence of functional use of endosseous dental implants on the tissue-implant interface. I. Histological aspects. J Dent Res 1979;58:1953.

25. Tjellström A. One stage surgical procedure: a modified method. Nobelpharma Int Updates 1994;1:3.

26. Tjellström A, Jansson K, Brånemark P-I. Craniofacial defects. In Worthington P, Brånemark P-I (eds): Advanced Osseointegration Surgery: Applications in the Maxillofacial Region. Chicago: Quintessence Publishing Company; 1992:293.

27. Brown AM, Proops DW, Wake MJ. Avoiding complications with craniofacial implants. In Laney WR, Tolman DE (eds): Tissue Integration in Oral, Orthopedic, and Maxillofacial Reconstruction. Chicago: Quintessence Publishing Company; 1992:294.

28. Giglio J, Abubaker A, Diegelmann R. Physiology of wound healing of skin and mucosa. Oral Maxillofac Surg Clin North Am 1996;8:457.

29. Kolb BA, Buller RE, Connor JP, DiSaia PJ, Berman ML. Effects of early postoperative chemotherapy on wound healing. Obstet Gynecol 1992;79:988.

30. Drake DB, Oishi SN. Wound healing considerations in chemotherapy and radiation therapy. Clin Plast Surg 1995;22:31.

Surgical Technique for Craniofacial Defects

11

Anders Tjellström, MD, PhD
Per-Ingvar Brånemark, MD, PhD

- One-Stage Surgical Technique for Auricular Implant Placement
- Postoperative Care
- Other Craniofacial Defects

The first patient treated with a craniofacial prosthesis retained on skin-penetrating osseointegrated implants was operated on by the authors in 1979. This was a patient who was missing his right external ear as a result of tumor surgery. The surgical technique was based on the intraoral procedure developed by Brånemark. Four implants were placed in the mastoid process and allowed to integrate without any load for 3 months. The second-stage procedure was performed, skin-penetrating abutments were connected to the bone implants, and a silicone rubber prosthesis made. The preliminary result was good, and soon more patients with different types of facial defects were treated with this technique.

This two-stage procedure was used until 1988. At that time, more than 750 implants had been placed in the mastoid process and only 10 had been lost. Of these 10, 5 were in younger patients with a thin cortical bone, in some cases only 1.5 mm thick. Two implants were lost owing to direct trauma, and only three lost their integration without any obvious reason.

The forces on implants in the oral cavity during chewing are in the range of 50 to 200 N. Forces up to 2,000 N have been measured. The force on an implant for the retention of a facial prosthesis is only the weight of the prosthesis and the force produced when the prosthesis is put in place and removed. The static force from the weight is small (range, 0.1–1 N). The torque bending force at the moment when the prosthesis is put in place and removed is more difficult to evaluate and depends on several factors. The stiffness of the retention elements as well as the dexterity of the patient are some of these factors. The design of a bar construction is also of importance, especially the length of any extension. However, even if these forces could reach high values, they are applied only for a few seconds and often only twice a day, when the prosthesis is put in place in the morning and when it is removed at bedtime. Based on this knowledge and the good clinical experience during a 10-year period, a study using a one-stage procedure started in 1989. When the technique was introduced in 1979, four implants were used for the retention of

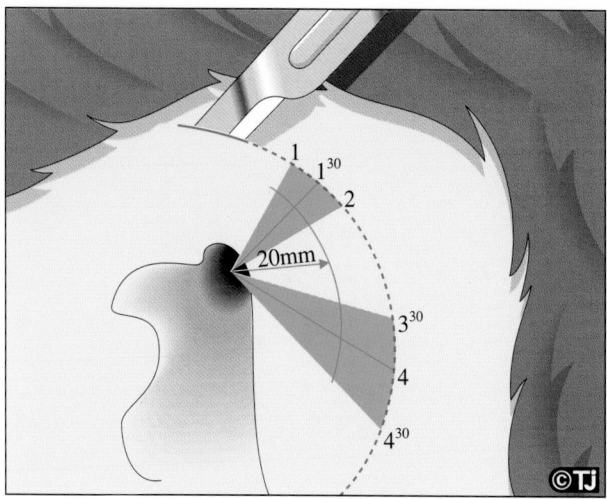

Fig 11-1. The distance and directions for placement of implants for an auricular prosthesis.

an auricular prosthesis. In some cases there was not room for four, and only three and in some cases only two implants were used for the retention. We noted no higher rate of implant losses in these cases. We also noted some important advantages with the use of only two implants. It was much easier for the patient to clean the implant area, which is important to avoid adverse skin reactions. The skin bridges between the implants were, in cases with four implants, often too narrow and more vulnerable, resulting in a risk of adverse skin reactions.

One-Stage Surgical Technique for Auricular Implant Placement

The surgical procedure for implants in the mastoid process will be described in detail. This technique could be considered as the baseline for extraoral implant surgery, and the differences between this and the technique used in the orbit and midface will be commented on below.

Implant Site Selection

In Figures 11-1 through 11-12 the artist's view of the technique is shown. The first step is to decide on the optimum sites for the implants. This must be done before the patient is taken to surgery and draped, otherwise there is a risk that the implants will be placed in the wrong position. A good cosmetic result could be jeopardized. Two different situations are possible. One is when the defect is caused by trauma or tumor surgery; the other is in patients with congenital malformations. In the former situation it is often easier to decide where to place the implants than in the latter. The external ear canal is a good landmark. The ideal placement is 18 to 22 mm from the center of the external ear canal opening, and on the left-hand side it is between the 1- and 2-o'clock positions for the most cranial implant and between the 3:30 and 4:30 positions for the caudal implant (Fig 11-1). The reason for this is that the implants and the bar construction will then be located underneath the anthelix ridge. This is important to be able to achieve an adequate depth and contour of the prosthesis. However, not only the distance from the ear canal opening but also the position within this radius is of greater importance. The ideal placement on the right-hand side is between the 10- and 11-o'clock positions for the most cranial implant and between the 7- and 8-o'clock positions for the caudal implant.

For the patient with a congenital defect, it is most important to make the marks for the implants before any draping for surgery is done. Even then it is often not that easy to find the best positions. Quite often there is a hemifacial microsomia in these patients. The mandible may be hypoplastic as well as the mastoid process. The opposite, if normal, side should be used for topographic reference when the level of the implant placement is decided. The possibility of using some external ear remnants for a tragus should be discussed. A rudimentary external ear canal cul-de-sac might need to be repositioned. The surgeon should be aware of the possibility of and abnormal route of the facial nerve. Sometimes the nerve can be close to the bottom of some of the deep pits. The stylomastoid foramen can be positioned more cranial and more lateral than its normal position.

For a good cosmetic result, removal of tags found and remnants of an external ear is often suggested. It is most important to discuss this with the patient well in advance. This is even more important in younger patients who may not fully understand the consequences. Once removed, replacement of the remnants is not possible. As will be discussed below, a two-stage procedure is suggested in younger patients when the bone is soft. In these cases, the tags and remnant are not touched at the first surgical procedure when the implants are placed in the bone. The reason for this is that the patients do not need to change their appearances between the first and second stage. Also, if they change their minds between the procedures, no visible alteration is made; the patients will look the same as before.

Marks are made with surgical ink where the implants should be placed, and the patient is cleaned and draped in the usual way. The incision line, usually 7 to 10 mm behind the intended implant sites, is marked, and the field is covered with a plastic draping. The reason for this is to avoid even sterile fragments from contaminating the implant sites and jeopardizing osseointegration. Ten milliliters of 2% lidocaine with epinephrine is injected, and the incision is made through the draping and down to the periosteum. That flap is folded anterior and kept in place with two self-retaining retractors.

Implant Placement

The positions of the implant sites are checked and marked in the periosteum. It is suggested that one start with the lower implant site first. In the mastoid tip area the air cells are larger and the cortical shell sometimes is fairly thin. A 6-mm-wide incision is made in the periosteum and the drilling with a guide drill is started (Fig 11-2). During all drilling procedures, generous cooling with saline solution is imperative. If the cortical shell is thin, a new implant site close by could be tried. It is important not to divert too much from the position in relation to the external ear canal opening. The hole is widened slightly to give the surgeon a good view of the bottom of the implant site. At the caudal implant site, the wall of the sigmoid sinus might be encountered. This happened in our patients in 9.6% of the drilled holes.[1] By widening the diameter of the hole, an injury to the wall of the vessel could be reduced. However, if the wall of the sigmoid sinus is damaged, the bleeding often is easy to manage. Because the pressure in the sinus is low, a pedicle periosteal flap will stop the bleeding. We do not suggest the use of bone wax or other loose autogenous or alloplastic material because of the risk of embolus. Knowledge of the route of the sigmoid sinus is essential in choosing a new implant site in a situation like this.

If the wall of the sigmoid sinus is identified at a depth of less than 2 mm, another implant site is tried.

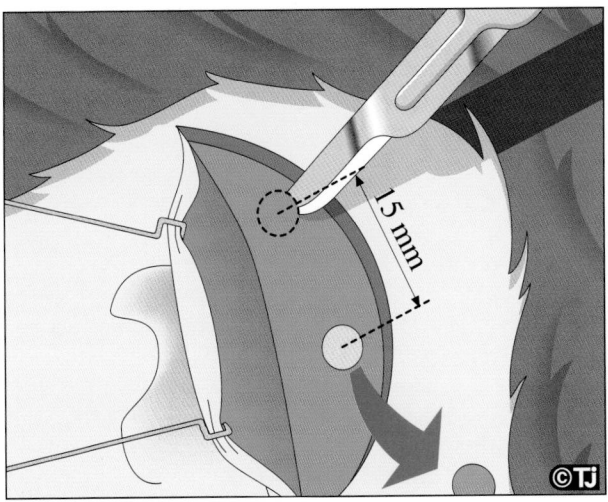

Fig 11-2. The periosteum is exposed and two 6-mm-wide holes are made in the periosteum.

If the wall is seen at a depth of 3 mm, a 3-mm implant is used. When the wall is present at 3.5 mm, a 4-mm implant could be used. We have used these guidelines whether the wall is injured or only exposed.

Another observation relates to entering the air-cell system during surgery, which happened in 13.5% of the drilled holes in the mastoid in our practice. If the cortical bone was more than 2 mm, we often tried to find a new implant site. If this was not possible without moving too far away from the ideal position, such an implant site still was used. Quite often the lower part of the implant gets support from some of the bony trabeculae in the air-cell system. Entering the air cells does not seem to influence the possibility of achieving a stable implant. In adult patients, we perform the implant surgery as an outpatient procedure using local anesthesia. If the air cells are opened, suction in the hole should be avoided because this will cause an instant retraction of the drum, which could be uncomfortable. The irrigation fluid enters the middle ear through the air-cell system and could cause a slight hearing impairment for a day or two. Bone grafting to close this opening has not been tried by the authors. In some cases in children with thin bone we have used a tissue-generating membrane technique. The use of this in the mastoid process is still under investigation.

When the caudal implant is in place, the position of the cranial implant is selected. The distance between the two implants should be at least 15

121

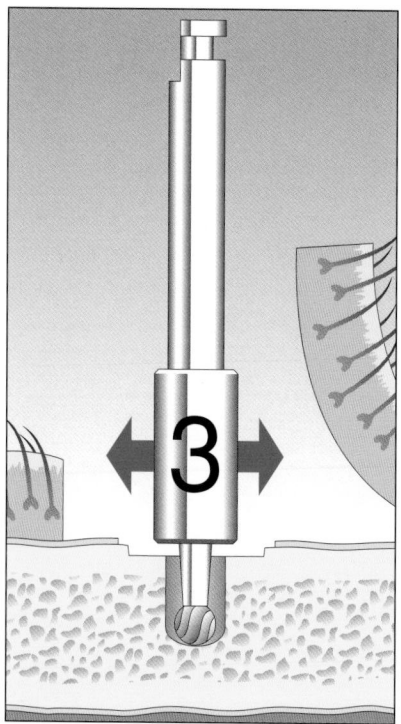

Fig 11-3. The drilling starts with a guide drill with a sleeve to protect from drilling deeper than 3 mm. (From Craniofacial Rehabilitation: Operating Theatre Manual. Göteborg, Sweden: Nobelpharma AB; 1995:13. By permission of the publisher.)

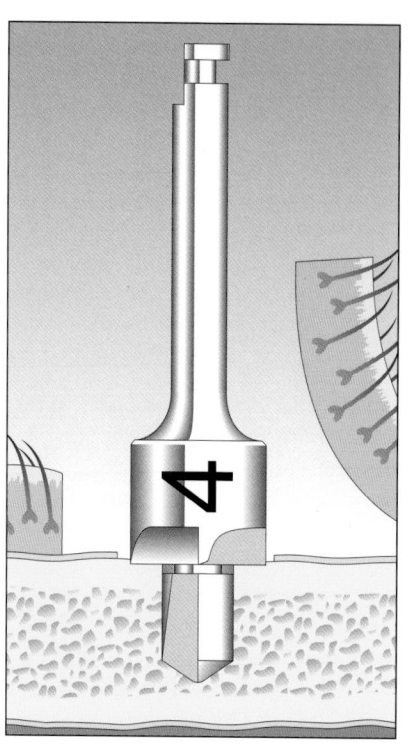

Fig 11-4. Spiral drill with a countersink gives the final dimension and direction of the hole. (From Craniofacial Rehabilitation: Operating Theatre Manual. Göteborg, Sweden: Nobelpharma AB; 1995:14. By permission of the publisher.)

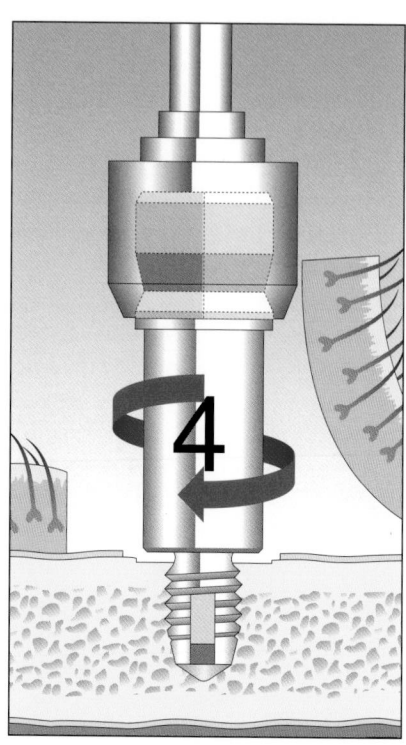

Fig 11-5. A titanium tap is used to make the threads of the hole at low speed (8 to 15 rpm). (From Craniofacial Rehabilitation: Operating Theatre Manual. Göteborg, Sweden: Nobelpharma AB; 1995:14. By permission of the publisher.)

mm, and 15 to 20 mm is preferred. The position of the cranial implant often will be in the linea temporalis where the bone in most cases is dense and thicker than 4 mm. Above the linea temporalis the bone could be 1 mm thick or less. In some patients, especially in those with congenital malformations such as Treacher Collins syndrome, this anatomic landmark is not well defined or is even absent. The close relationship to the dura mater of the middle cranial fossa should be kept in mind. When drilling holes for the top implant for an auricular prosthesis, we exposed the dura in as many as 11.2% but only once was the dura damaged during drilling. Placement of a titanium implant on the dura seems not to cause any problem. If the dura is torn during drilling and cerebrospinal fluid leakage occurs, the hole should be widened and the surgeon must make sure that no vessel is bleeding inside the tear. Two implants, which at the time of insertion were in touch with the dura, have been explanted as a result of direct trauma in automobile accidents. When examining these patients we found newformed bone in the bottom of both holes.

The drilling in the cranial site is started with a 3-mm guide drill (Fig 11-3). It is imperative that generous cooling is maintained during all drilling procedures. If bone is still found in the bottom, a drill that will provide space for a 4-mm implant is used. When bone is found in the bottom, it is important to make sure that the whole length of the guide drill has gone down. The reason is that the next drill, which is the spiral drill with a countersink edge, is not cutting at the tip (Fig 11-4). No bone will be cut away at the bottom. When working in soft bone (e.g., in children), the spiral drill should be used with care because the countersink edges are sharp and may be pushed too deep if too much force is used. The drills are made of stainless steel and 1,500 to 3,000 rpm is used. The next steps are made at slow speed, 8 to 15 rpm, and with titanium instruments. The titanium tap is brought from its sterile glass container to the titanium tray without being touched directly even by the sterile gloved hand or by anything but titanium instruments. The tap is picked up, with the connector placed in the low-speed handpiece (Fig 11-5). The tap is kept over the entrance and the direction is

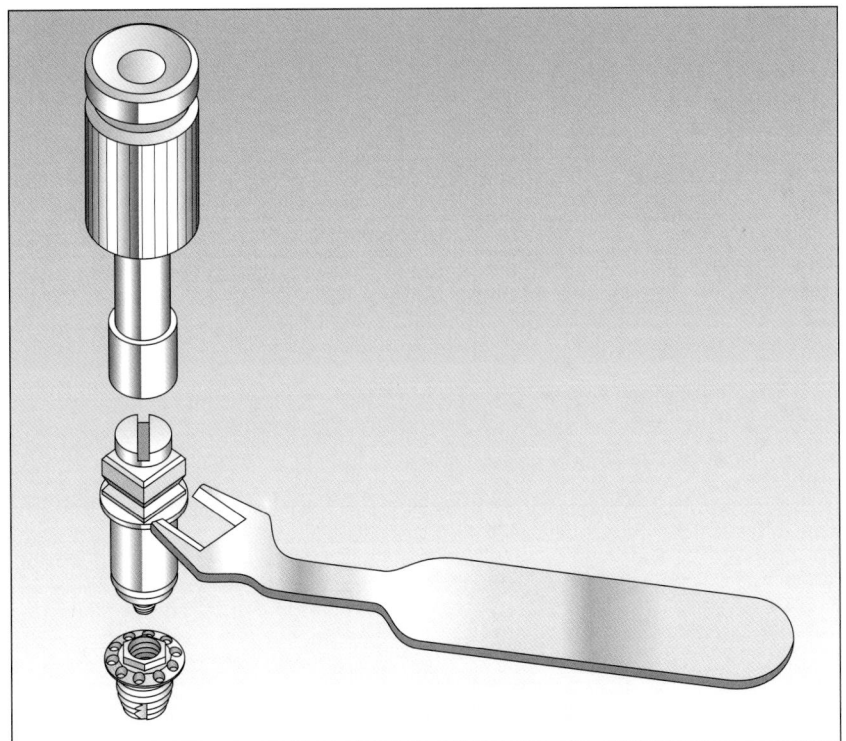

Fig 11-6. An implant mount is screwed onto the implant. (From Craniofacial Rehabilitation: Operating Theatre Manual. Göteborg, Sweden: Nobelpharma AB; 1995:15. By permission of the publisher.)

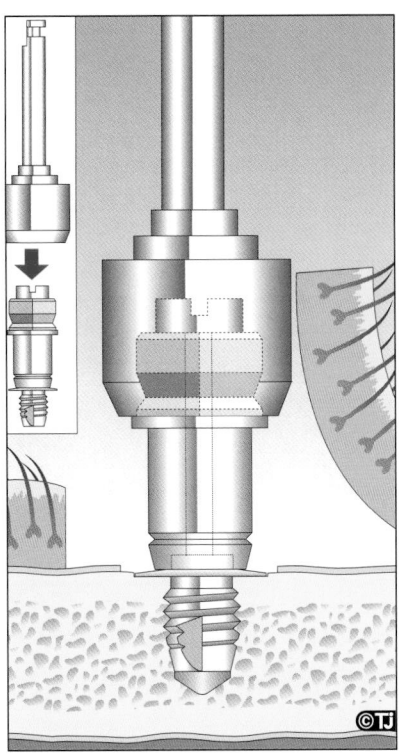

Fig 11-7. The implant mount with implant is picked up with the adapter of the handpiece and introduced with light pressure into the hole.

checked carefully. A slight pressure is applied, but when the first threads have engaged the bone, no further pressure is needed. When the tap approaches the proper depth of the site, the speed is decreased to not get the tap stuck in the bone, which might produce some unnecessary trauma to the bone tissue. Adequate cooling is used when the tap is removed.

The implant is inserted in the threaded hole. The implant comes sterile packed in its glass cylinder. The implant really must be in the bottom part of the container. When the glass container is broken it is important to keep it vertical and over the titanium tray. The waistline of the ampoule is cracked, and the top part is lifted straight up without dislodging the implant. If the implant is dislodged, it could still be used if it stays on the titanium tray but not if it is contaminated with the draping around the surgical field. If contaminated, the implant has to be discarded and reprocessed according to a special cleaning program. The implant, with or without the titanium tube it was delivered in, is transferred to the titanium tray using titanium instruments, but never by the gloved hand directly.

The implant mount is picked up with the fork-shaped instrument and the screwdriver. The implant mount is screwed on top of the implant. The hexagonal top of the implant must be fitted properly into the hexagonal indentation of the implant mount (Fig 11-6). If not, the hexagon might be damaged and it will not be possible to place the skin-penetrating abutment on the implant. How hard the screw of the implant mount should be tightened depends on the quality of the bone. In dense cortical bone it should be tightened fairly hard. If the screw is tightened too hard in relation to the texture of the bone, the implant site may be traumatized excessively during removal of the implant mount from the implant.

The implant site is cleaned of soft tissue and bone fragments by flushing with saline and using a blunt dissecting instrument. The implant mount with the implant is picked up with the adapter on the handpiece of the drill and kept immediately over the hole. The direction is checked. With the drill at low speed, the implant is allowed to find its way into the threaded hole using slight pressure (Fig 11-7). The small notches at the tip of the implant are allowed to

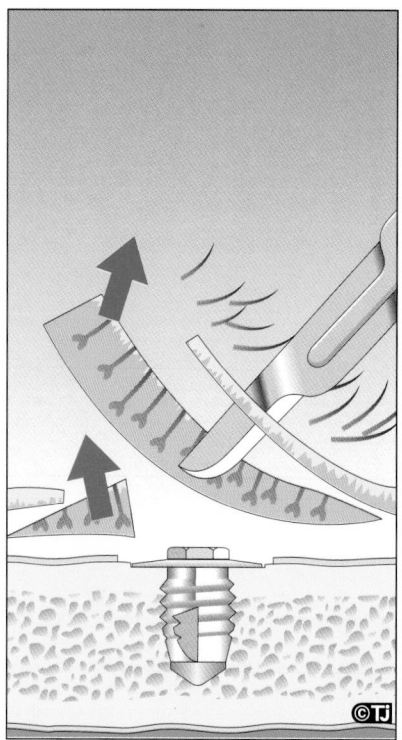

Fig 11-8. Subcutaneous tissue reduction with removal of all hair follicles at the implant area.

Fig 11-9. The hairless, thin-skin flap sutured in place.

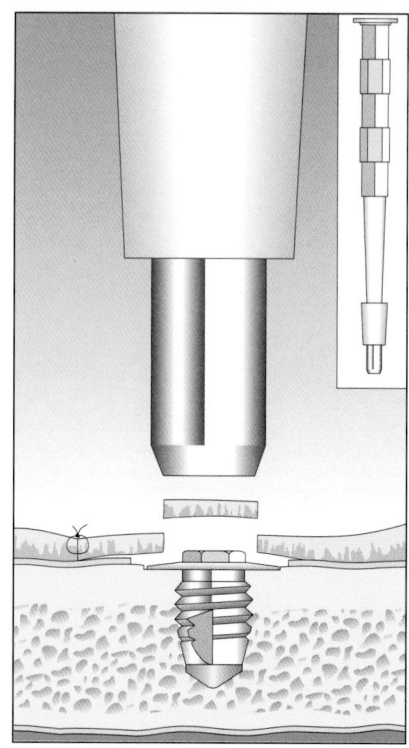

Fig 11-10. A hole is made with a disposable skin punch. (From Craniofacial Rehabilitation: Operating Theatre Manual. Göteborg, Sweden: Nobelpharma AB; 1995:17. By permission of the publisher.)

engage the threads before irrigation is started. The reason for this is that saline should not seep into the implant site, because it could lead to increased intraosseous pressure and induce unnecessary trauma to the implant site.

When the flange is almost down onto the countersink surface, the speed is decreased to minimize tissue trauma from torque in the surrounding bone. When the implant is all the way down, the handpiece is turned slightly counterclockwise to release the implant mount from the connector. It is important not to tilt the implant mount when disconnecting it from the handpiece. The implant mount is then removed from the implant. If the bone is loosely textured (e.g., in a child) or the stability is not perfect, the skin flap is sutured in place with some resorbable subcutaneous sutures and monofilament nylon sutures in the skin. In these situations the implant is left 3 to 6 months before the second-stage procedure is performed. The same delay is used in irradiated tissue. However, in most adult cases it is possible to continue and attach the abutments and make the skin penetration at the same time.

Soft-Tissue Management

Our experience is that two steps in this second part of the surgery are of great importance in achieving a lasting, reaction-free skin penetration. The first is production of immobility of the skin close to the implants relative to the underlying bone and the abutment. This is achieved by making a subcutaneous tissue reduction at the implant site. The second prerequisite is that no hair follicles are present in the skin at the implant site (Fig 11-8). A radius of at least 7 mm from the abutment should be hairless. This facilitates the daily cleaning procedures, which are of great importance. These two goals can be achieved by using a split-thickness skin graft or by reducing the thickness of the flap in the same way. The main reasons for adverse skin reaction in our experience are inadequate soft-tissue reduction and the presence of hair follicles at the implant site as a result of inadequate surgery. One also must ensure that the patient has adequate hygiene routines. The skin edges toward the implant site are trimmed to get a gentle slope down to the abut-

Fig 11-11. The abutments are put in place and healing caps are attached to the abutment screws.

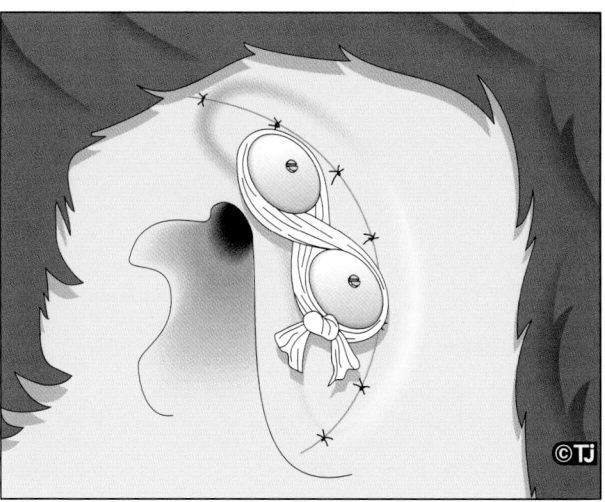

Fig 11-12. Ointment-soaked gauze keeps the skin down and prevents postoperative hematoma and swelling.

ments. In obese patients, this subcutaneous tissue reduction has to be quite extensive.

Abutment Connection

When the flap has been thinned and the hair follicles removed or the hairless skin graft has been harvested, the implant is covered with the thin skin and sutured in place (Fig 11-9). With a 4-mm disposable skin punch, a hole is made immediately over the implant (Fig. 11-10), and the abutment is secured to the implant with an internal screw (Fig 11-11). The nonalloyed titanium is soft and cross-thread damage is possible. Gentle handling is important in all these procedures. To get a stable arrangement, the hexagonal indentation of the abutment cylinder must fit the hexagon, and no soft tissue is allowed to be interposed. When the fit is established, the abutment screw is tightened firmly.

Healing caps are then attached to the abutments to keep ointment-soaked gauze down toward the skin to avoid postoperative hematoma and swelling (Fig 11-12). This packing should not be too firm and not interfere with the blood supply during the healing phase. The surgical procedure is finished by applying a firm mastoid dressing for 1 day. After this, only a light dressing is needed.

Postoperative Care

Five to seven days after the operation, the healing caps and the gauze are removed. At this stage some of the stitches are removed, and the surgical field is left open for 30 minutes. The healing caps are put back in place and a fresh gauze with ointment is loosely packed under the caps. After 5 to 7 days, the packing and the healing caps are removed and the surgical field is left open. A mild antibiotic ointment is prescribed and the patient is told to use that for a week or two and then just occasionally. Three weeks after operation the patient may start to clean the area with soap and water. In the beginning, the cleaning should be very gentle as the healing continues on the microscopic level. Less and less ointment is being used during this period. Later on, most patients use the ointment only occasionally, some never, and a few more regularly. Patients have to find their own routines in taking care of the implant area. The implants are left without any load for 3 months. This is important because even minor movement of the implant could result in fibrous encapsulation instead of osseointegration. As discussed in Chapter 8 on Prosthetic Considerations, the soft-tissue swelling has to settle completely before the prosthetic work can start. In our experience, the impression of the defect area, which is the first step in making a prosthesis, is taken after 3 months.

The patients are instructed to remove their prostheses at night to let air into the implant area. If this is not done, humidity underneath the prosthesis may cause irritation. There are few restrictions. The patients may swim with the prosthesis in place, take a sauna, or dye their hair. We know from our data that if this routine is followed, the frequency of adverse skin reactions is low. Sixty percent of our patients have never had a single episode of adverse skin reaction around the implants. A small group, 15%, is responsible for more than 70% of all adverse skin reactions.[2] During the last few years these figures seem to have improved.[1] This is probably due to a learning process regarding the surgical technique, the most important factors being the amount of subcutaneous tissue reduction and the handling of hair-bearing skin. Another reason may be an improvement in the selection of patients. Our experience is that this is most important for a good result. Patients must be well motivated for this type of treatment. In the preoperative work-up, the patients must be well informed about the requirements of daily hygiene, handling of the prosthesis, and the follow-up routines.[3,4]

Other Craniofacial Defects

The surgical procedure for other defects in the craniofacial skeleton is less uniform than for auricular defects. There are several differences that have to be taken into consideration, which are discussed in other chapters of the book. Has the implant area been exposed to irradiation (dose, fractionation, when)? Is the patient free of tumor or will the patient receive irradiation after implant surgery? Has the patient received cytotoxic drugs? What bone structures are available for the placement of the implants? The surgical technique is, however, basically the same as described above. One important difference is that we always use a two-stage procedure in irradiated tissue and also often in patients with midface defects who have not been irradiated. There is often a need for a combination of intraoral and extraoral implants to achieve a stable and passive framework for the retention.

References

1. Tjellström A, Granström G. One-stage procedure to establish osseointegration. A zero to five years follow-up report. J Laryngol Otol 1995;109:593.

2. Tjellström A. Osseointegrated implants for the replacement of absent or defective ears. Clin Plast Surg 1990;17:355.

3. Tjellström A, Jansson K, Brånemark P-I. Craniofacial defects. In Worthington P, Brånemark P-I (eds): Advanced Osseointegration Surgery: Applications in the Maxillofacial Region. Chicago: Quintessence Publishing Company; 1992:293.

4. Tjellström A, Granström G, Bergström K. Osseointegrated implants for craniofacial prostheses. In Weber RS, Miller MJ, Goepfert H (eds): Basal and Squamous Cell Skin Cancers of the Head and Neck. Baltimore: Williams & Wilkins; 1995:313.

Management of Soft Tissue

Ian T. Jackson, MD

- Ear
- Orbit
- Nose
- Maxilla
- Mandible

When planning soft-tissue reconstruction or rearrangement related to an osseointegrated prosthesis, the reconstructive surgeon must, to some extent, change philosophy. The surgeon must accept initially that the planned reconstruction will result from a discussion with the maxillofacial prosthodontist, who will have specific requirements depending on the area to be reconstructed and the prosthesis to be applied. External aesthetic reconstruction is required up to the site where the prosthesis is attached, but beyond that correct physical conditions of the implant region must be provided for implant placement. The latter situation is easier to achieve extraorally than intraorally.

Extraoral osseointegrated prostheses are no different from those used in the past with other methods of fixation. They are ideal for replacement of the ear, the nose, and the orbital area, provided the underlying bone is adequate. Lips, cheeks, and other areas of the face are best reconstructed with soft-tissue transfer.

Intraorally, it is necessary to supply good bone and, if possible, a thin soft-tissue cover. If these requirements can be met, excellent reconstruction can be achieved.

Extraoral soft-tissue reconstruction is required for congenital, traumatic, and post-tumor excisional defects. In the last category, it is complicated in some cases by the patient having had preoperative or postoperative radiotherapy.

Ear

Congenital

In congenital microtia, the patient may have had no previous surgery or there may have been an attempt, or frequent attempts, to create an ear from local and imported tissue.

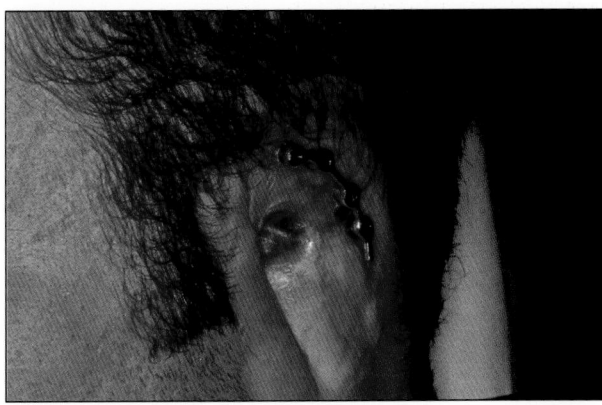

Fig 12-1. Post-traumatic ear loss. Osseointegration has been performed through a split-thickness skin graft placed directly on the periosteum of the mastoid area.

If there has been no previous surgery, all portions of the ear that are present should be removed. On some selected occasions, the prosthetist may wish to preserve the lobule, but generally this is not too advisable. Fortunately, the subcutaneous tissue surrounding the ear remnants is usually thin and thus provides a good local environment for implant placement.

In the patient previously operated on, there may be some of the reconstruction remaining and this should be excised. Whether or not this is the case, there is frequently a great deal of scarring and this leads to dense adhesions of skin to bone. This represents an ideal situation for osseointegration (Fig 12-1).

Post-Traumatic

In this situation, any ear remnants should be excised and the residual defects closed directly. The post-traumatic scarring, as mentioned above, frequently provides a suitable environment for placement of implants.

Post-Tumor Resection

When the resection of an external ear tumor is being considered, the decision rests on whether an ear of adequate size can be maintained. In addition to this, the patient's age and wishes should be considered. An elderly patient may wish to have only a structure that will allow wearing glasses comfortably. In this situation, part of the ear will be retained. Where the resection is significant and the patient wishes to have a reconstruction, it is best to remove the ear totally and reconstruct using an osseointegrated prosthesis. The residual skin is usually satisfactory for implantation.

Unsatisfactory Skin Cover

This can occur in any of the three categories above but is more likely with tumor and less likely after trauma.

If there is exposed bone covered with viable periosteum, a split-thickness skin graft can be done directly. In this situation, the graft take is usually satisfactory and thus provides the skin cover and stability required for implant placement.

If the periosteum is not present, a vascular cover must be provided to allow a split-thickness skin graft to be applied. There are three possibilities available to provide this type of cover and also to provide the required environment for placement of implants. These are the temporal galea,[1] occipital galea,[2] and the temporalis muscle, the last being the least satisfactory. Unfortunately, the superficial temporal vessels are often damaged in trauma or tumor resection, and this option may not be available. It is rare to have the occipital vessels damaged, and thus the occipital galea may be the structure of choice. The galea is transposed as a flap based on its vascular pedicle, and it is covered with a split-thickness skin graft. Although these may be thick initially, they become thinner with time and provide a satisfactory cover to allow placement of implants (Fig 12-2).

If these options are not available, a thin free flap may be transferred. This could be the temporalis galea from the other side; the superficial temporal vessels would be anastomosed under the microscope to whatever vessels are available on the traumatized side. In some tumor cases, a more significant bulk may be required and a radial forearm flap would be chosen. This is a thin flap that is not ideal for osseointegration because it lacks the stability of a skin graft on periosteum or galea, but nonetheless osseointegration is possible.

Complications

Loosening of implants necessitates removal, as does infection. Perhaps the most common problem related to soft tissue is the development of exuberant granulation tissue (Fig 12-3). This may respond to curettage or fulguration, but frequently it does not.

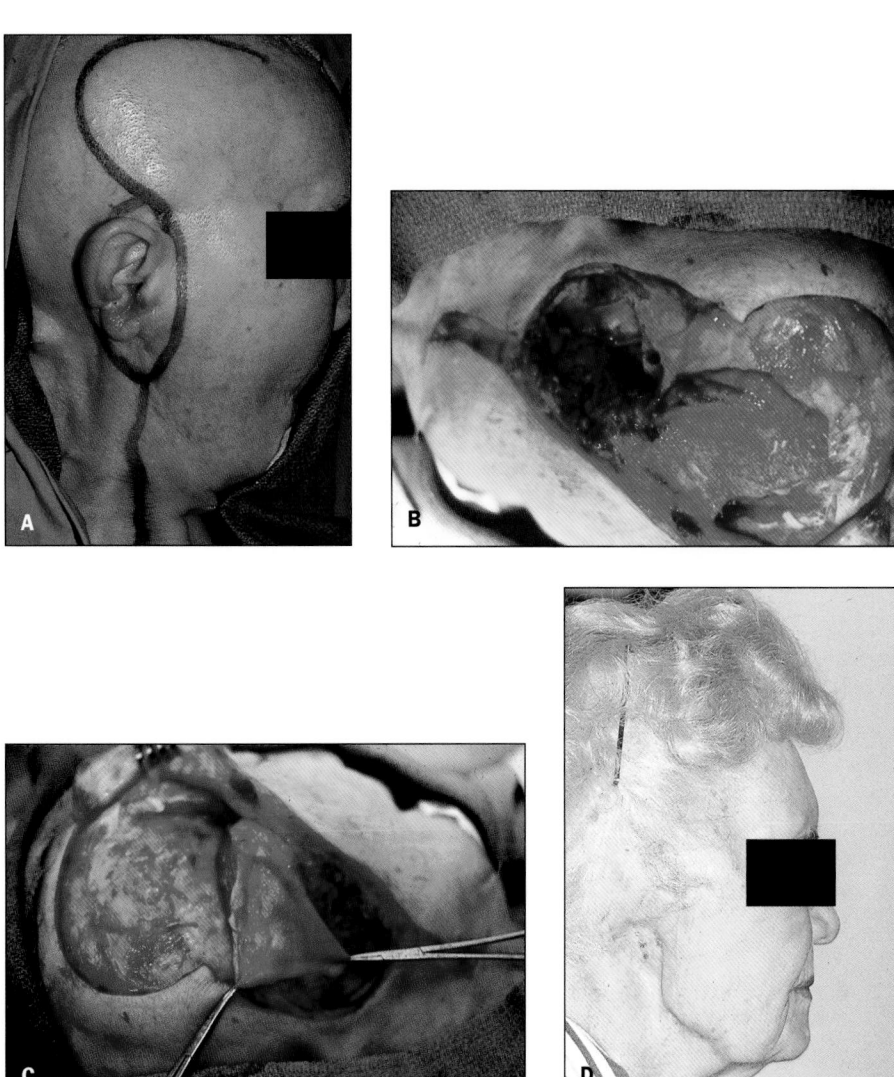

Fig 12-2. Use of temporalis muscle. *A*, Penetrating basal cell carcinoma of right ear. *B*, Resection of basal cell carcinoma; temporalis muscle flap elevated. *C*, Temporalis muscle in place. *D*, End result. Patient ready for osseointegration.

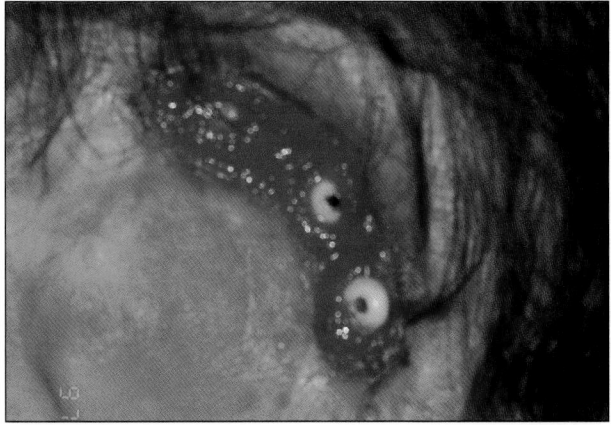

Fig 12-3. Complication of implants in ear reconstruction. Hypertrophic granulation tissue around implants. In some areas the implant is covered over by the granulation tissue.

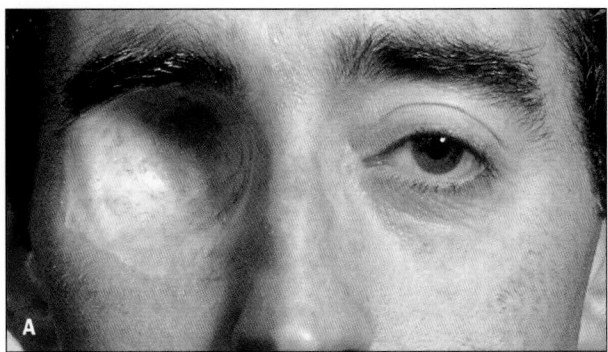
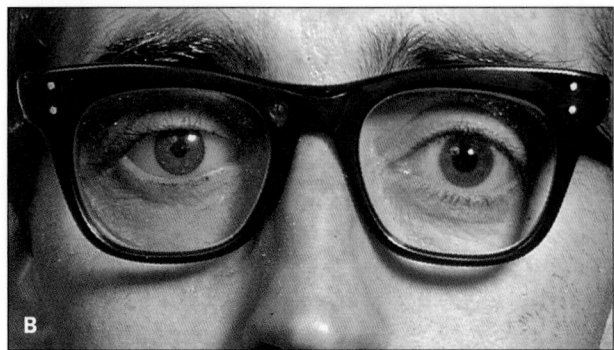

Fig 12-4. Boundaries in orbital reconstruction. *A*, Patient with resection of malignant melanoma. The orbital split-thickness skin graft, which has been placed on the periosteum, comes to the proper boundary with the cheek. *B*, The boundary area is covered with the prosthesis to give the best aesthetic result.

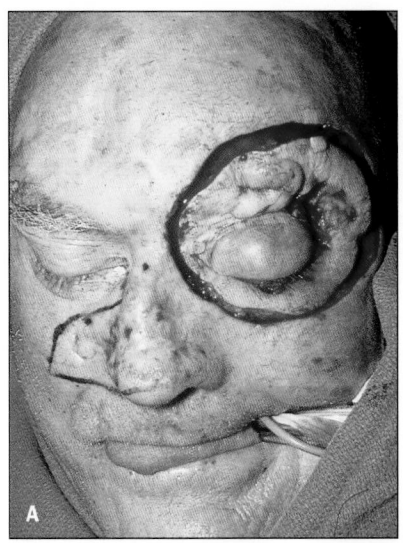
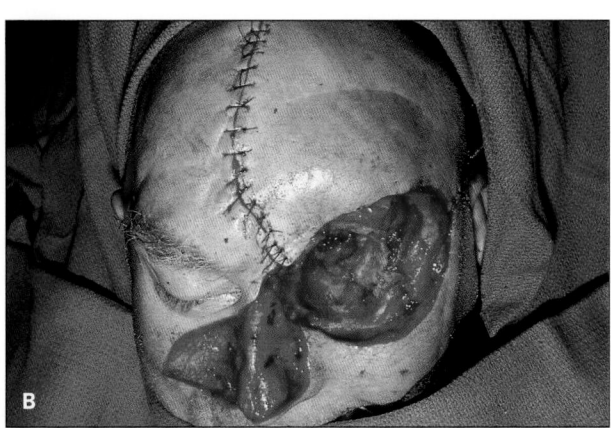
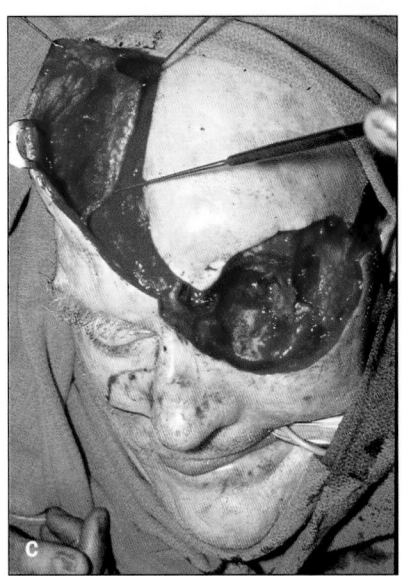
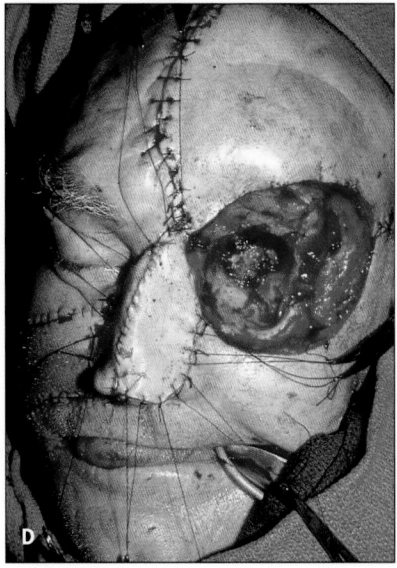
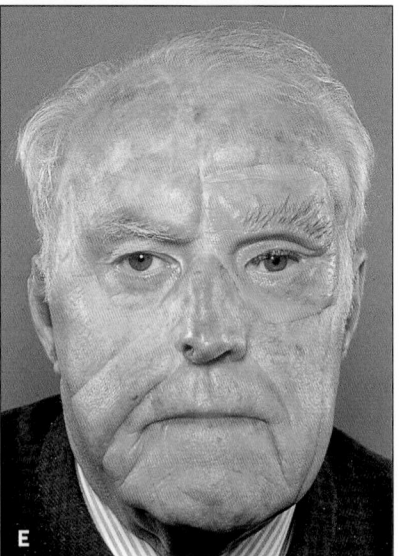

Fig 12-5. Use of galea in obliteration of sinus. *A*, Basal cell carcinoma involves left orbit and nose. *B*, Resection of basal cell carcinoma. *C*, Elevation of frontal galea. *D*, Galeofrontalis flap used to occlude and pack the left frontal sinus. *E*, Prosthesis covers boundary areas.

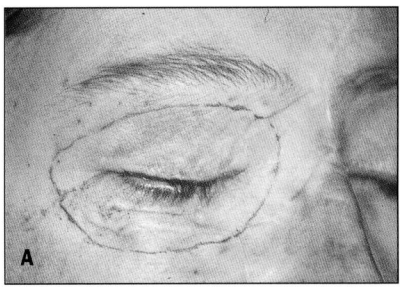
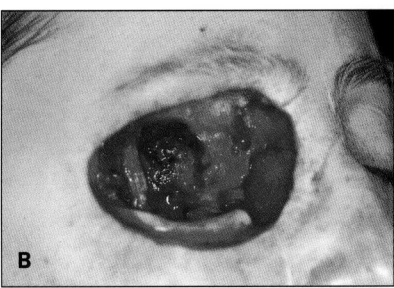
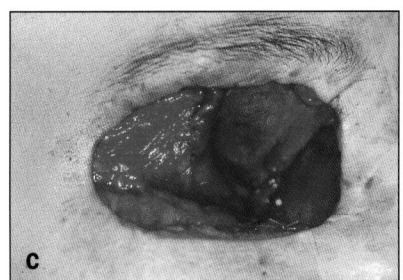

Fig 12-6. Use of temporalis muscle in orbital reconstruction. Extension of squamous cell carcinoma of lacrimal duct (previous duct resection). *A*, Outline of resection. *B*, Resection completed. *C*, Temporalis muscle to cover exposed orbital rim. *D*, End result with defect into nasopharynx for future inspection. Ready for prosthetic rehabilitation.

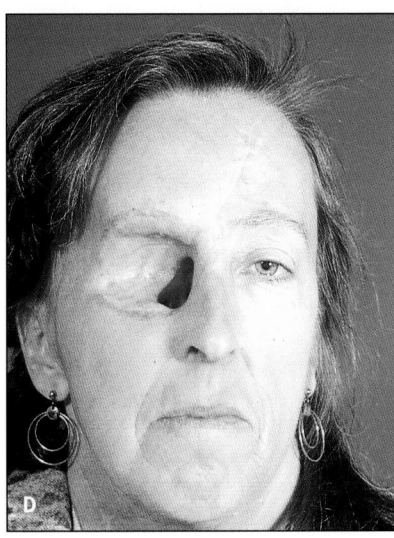

A combination of triamcinolone cream 1% and bacitracin 0.5% frequently flattens off the granulation tissue and allows it to accept a thin split-thickness skin graft. The skin graft should be dressed in such a way that there is pressure on the graft right up to the edge of the implant. In this situation, only this type of meticulous care gives any chance of success. When this is achieved, there is usually no further problem. If the overgranulation persists, it may be necessary to remove the implant, allow everything to heal, follow with skin grafting if necessary, and then start all over again.

Orbit

In orbital reconstruction, in addition to stable bone cover, there is the concept of boundaries. In the orbital area, the boundary is as close to the bony orbital rim as possible. Within the boundary is skin graft or scar tissue or both; outside the boundary the soft tissue should be as normal as possible in terms of texture and color (Fig 12-4).

The origin of orbital defects is congenital malformation, trauma, and post-tumor excision. What makes rehabilitation in this area difficult is the presence of the neighboring sinuses, especially the ethmoids. Any opening into the sinuses produces a chronic discharge. If such a situation exists, the sinus concerned can be obliterated or the opening can be closed over. Obliteration can be achieved with the galeal frontalis flap,[3,4] which usually includes the periosteum (Fig 12-5). This flap is supplied by the supraorbital and supratrochlear vessels. It is packed into the frontal or the ethmoid sinuses, and a split-thickness skin graft is placed on top of it. An alternative to the temporal galea is to use temporalis muscle (Fig 12-6).

If there is good sinus drainage, the orbital defect in continuity with the sinus, whether it be frontal or ethmoid, can be closed with a local forehead transposition flap.

Congenital

The skin around the orbit is often atrophic and takes implants well. A bone graft may be necessary to bring the surroundings of the orbit into the same

131

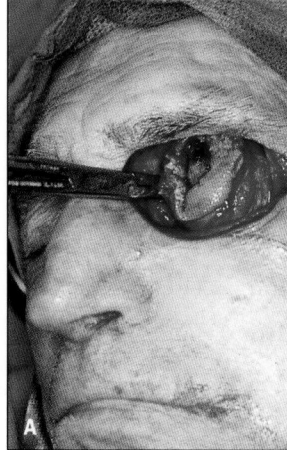
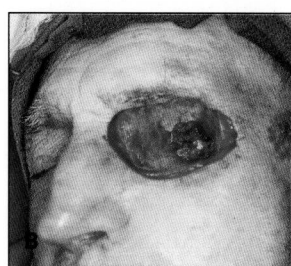
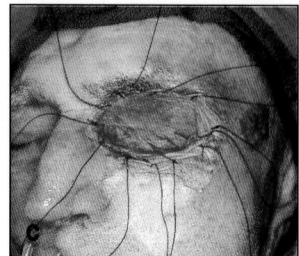
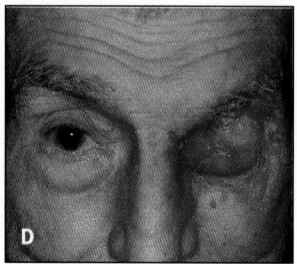

Fig 12-7. Orbital exenteration. *A,* Start of exenteration of orbit. *B,* Exenteration completed. *C,* Split-thickness skin graft to line the orbit is placed directly on the orbital bone. *D,* Good take of skin graft.

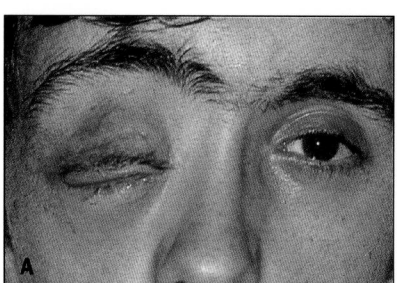
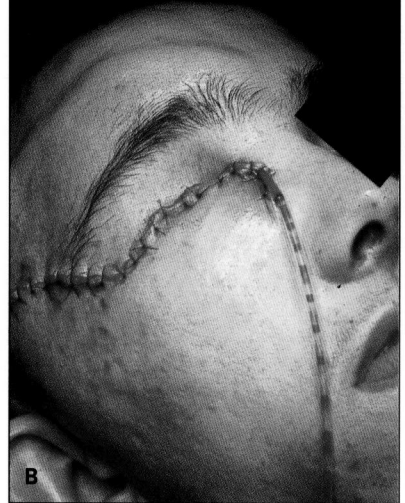
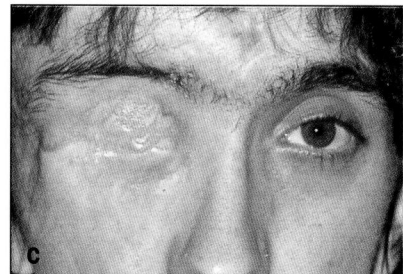

Fig 12-8. Use of local flap to reconstruct orbital defect. *A,* Neurofibroma of right orbit with blind eye. *B,* Orbital exenteration with reconstruction of bony orbit. Advancement cheek flap to reconstruct soft tissue. *C,* End result. Patient ready for reconstruction with orbital prosthesis.

anatomic situation as the contralateral normal side. Any rudimentary eye, conjunctiva, and lids should be removed; otherwise, there will be secretion under the prosthesis. This can produce an unpleasant odor. It is probably best to remove the orbital contents and place a split-thickness skin graft in the orbit. The orbital bones will accept a split-thickness skin graft without the necessity of having periosteal cover. This gives a stable situation for the prosthesis. The graft should be taken over the orbital rim, the amount being indicated by the prosthodontist. In this way, a deep orbit and a satisfactory boundary are obtained.

Trauma

In trauma, unless it is massive, a total orbital prosthesis rarely is required. If this is necessary, usually bony orbital reconstruction is indicated. When this has been done, local flaps may be needed to obtain skin cover. These should be as thin as possible. If they are not satisfactory for implant placement, after several months they can be replaced with vascularized temporal galea covered with a split-thickness skin graft.

Management of open sinuses was described above.

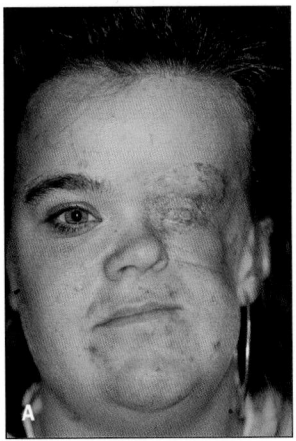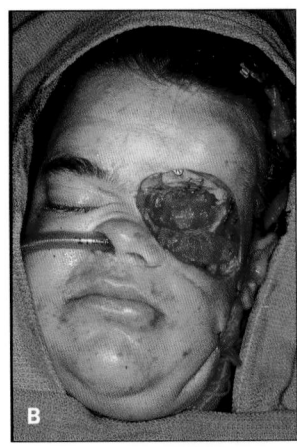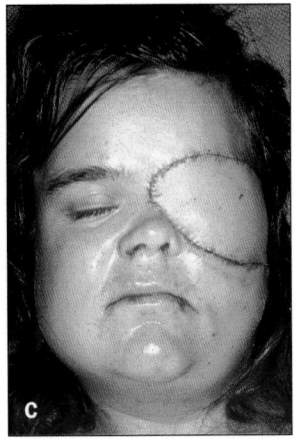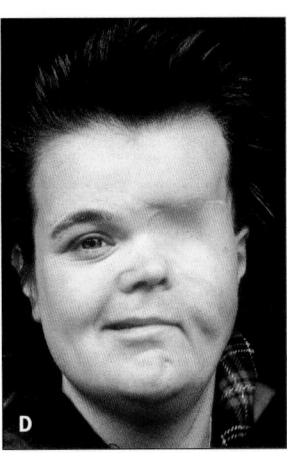

Fig 12-9. Reconstruction of bony orbit. *A,* Severe facial deformity resulting from radiation therapy for retinoblastoma in childhood and previous surgical procedures. *B,* Appearance after reconstruction of left cranium, left orbit, maxilla, and mandible. *C,* Orbital defect covered with rectus abdominis free flap. *D,* Flap has been thinned. Patient ready for rehabilitation with orbital prosthesis.

Tumors

In tumor surgery confined to the orbit, an exenteration is performed and a split-thickness skin graft is placed directly on the bony orbit, as described above. This is the ideal situation for prosthetic rehabilitation (Fig 12-7).

In more massive resections involving cheek or forehead (or both) and nose, there will be immediate soft-tissue replacement with local or free flaps[5] (Fig 12-8). This may pose problems in prosthetic rehabilitation because of the absence of true boundaries. In this situation, a large prosthesis may be necessary to cover the cheek area. Again, modification of the soft tissue with vascularized fascia and a split-thickness skin graft may be necessary to obtain a more ideal basis for implantation and prosthesis fitting. Occasionally, bony reconstruction will be required to give an orbit of adequate size to accept the prosthesis (Fig 12-9).

Any open sinuses should be obliterated or closed, as described above.

Nose

As with the orbit, boundaries are important in nasal rehabilitation. There are the static surrounding boundaries of the glabella, medial canthi, and the cheek, but in addition there is the lip, which is mobile and relatively unsupported. Occasionally the lip must be sacrificed, especially in tumor surgery. It is essential to reconstruct the boundaries if possible. The area that should be skin grafted is the glabellar region and around the pyriform aperture to allow implant placement if necessary.

The lip can be reconstructed with local flaps by variants of nasolabial, locoregional (e.g., deltopectoral), or free flap (e.g., radial forearm) (Fig 12-10).

In the vast majority of cases the nose can be reconstructed with facial tissue.[6] Lining is provided by local skin flaps, support is obtained by a cranial bone graft, and the external reconstruction is from the forehead. This should be the method chosen if the tissue is available and if the patient is agreeable; otherwise, prosthetic replacement is a satisfactory alternative (Fig 12-11).

In congenital absence of the nose and in traumatic loss, prosthetic replacement is not indicated. In tumor resection of the total nose, this method is indicated when local tissue is not available or when the area needs to be inspected for the possibility of recurrence. If possible, the boundaries should be created for aesthetic reasons, but this may be contraindicated for oncologic reasons. In this situation aesthetics take second place and the implants are placed in the most favorable position possible.

Maxilla

Although there are congenital intraoral anomalies that require reconstruction with implants, the main

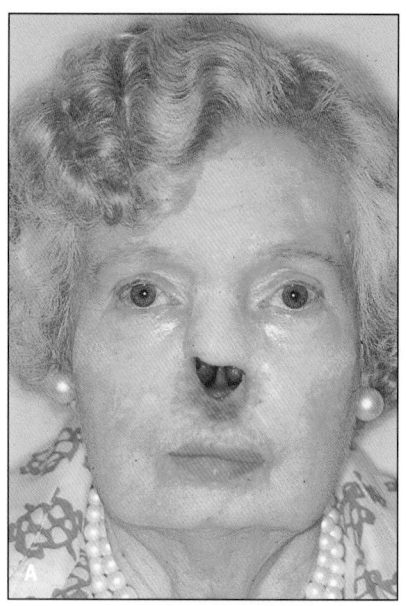
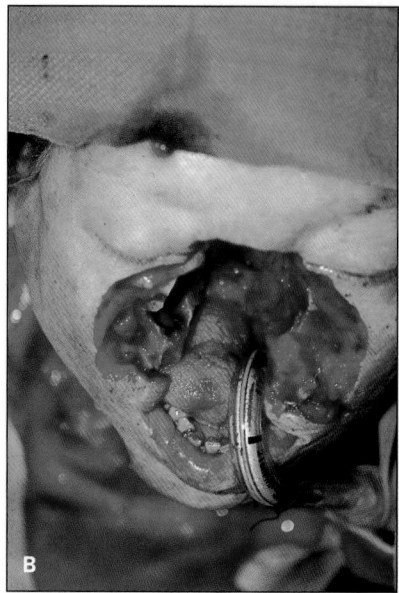
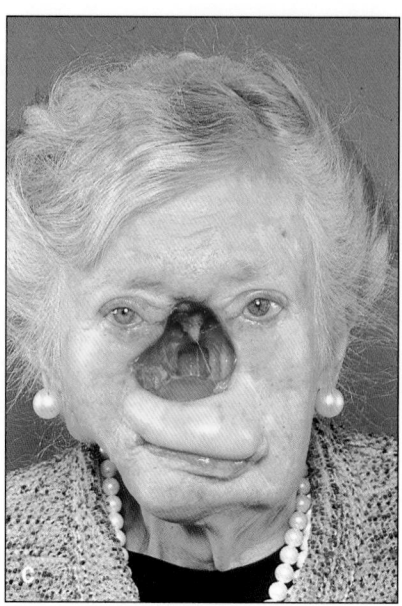

Fig 12-10. Management of nasal and labial squamous cell carcinoma. *A*, Preoperative appearance of patient with penetrating squamous cell carcinoma who had multiple previous procedures. *B*, Wide resection together with palate and upper lip. *C*, Reconstruction of lip with deltopectoral flap. Good boundary zones for placement of nasal prosthesis.

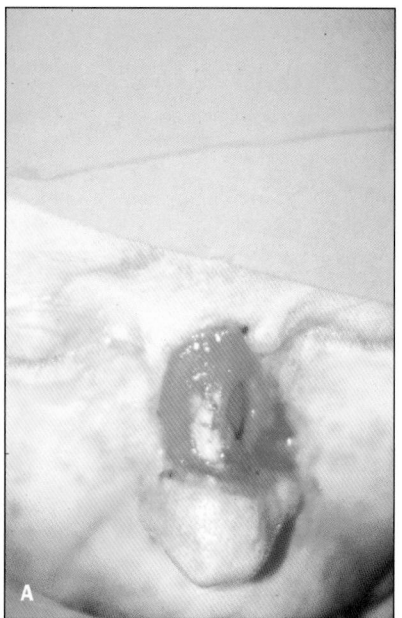
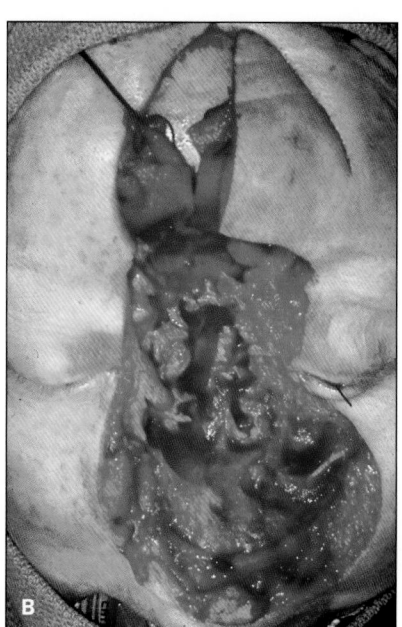
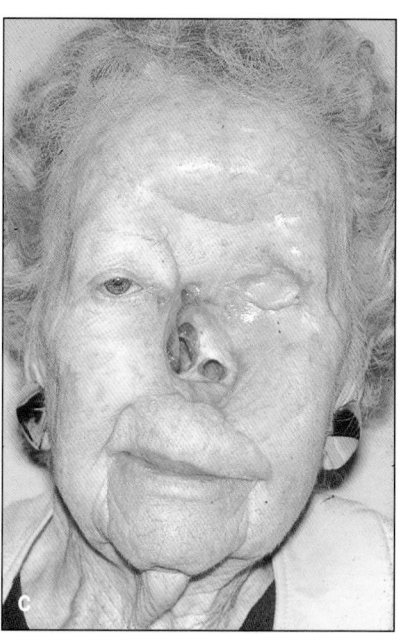

Fig 12-11. Naso-orbital basal cell carcinoma. A, Preoperative appearance. B, Resection of midface, which later proceeded to resection of orbital contents. C, End result with good tissue for placement of implants.

indications are post-trauma and after resection for carcinoma. In partial loss of the maxilla from trauma or resection for malignancy, exposed bone can be grafted with split-thickness skin grafts. Ideally, a dental impression is taken before maxillectomy, and a surgical obturator prosthesis is constructed. After resection, an accurate impression of the defect is made using the surgical obturator covered with dental compound. Mastisol (liquid adhesive composed of gum mastic, styrax liquid, methyl salicylate, and alcohol) is applied to this modified obturator to assist in holding the skin surface of the split-thickness skin graft against the obturator. The obturator is then put in the defect and wired in place. This is removed in 1

Conclusion

In the past the criteria for soft-tissue replacement before placement of implants were strict. Obviously, a thin stable cover over bone was ideal. However, with experience this has become less critical. A degree of subcutaneous fat with its attendant mobility is not a contraindication (e.g., the radial forearm flap or the fibular osseocutaneous flap).

A good cosmetic result is the optimal goal of an external prosthesis. An excellent prosthesis can be spoiled if its surrounding boundary area is aesthetically unacceptable. It is essential that a careful plan is established by the prosthodontist and the surgeon preoperatively to provide the optimal situation from technical and aesthetic viewpoints.

References

1. Har-Shai Y, Fukuta K, Collares MV, et al. The vascular anatomy of the galeal flap in the interparietal and midline regions. Plast Reconstr Surg 1992;89:64.

2. Sharma RK, Kobayashi K, Jackson IT, Carls FR. Vascular anatomy of the galeal occipitalis flap: a cadaver study. Plast Reconstr Surg 1996;97:25.

3. Jackson IT, Adham MN, Marsh WR. Use of the galeal frontalis myofascial flap in craniofacial surgery. Plast Reconstr Surg 1986;77:905.

4. Potparić Z, Fukuta K, Colen LB, Jackson IT, Carraway JH. Galeo-pericranial flaps in the forehead: a study of blood supply and volumes. Br J Plast Surg 1996;49:519.

5. Edington H, Ramasastry S. Microvascular flap transfer in cranial base surgery. Probl Plast Reconstr Surg 1993;3:207.

6. Burget GC, Menick FJ. Aesthetic Reconstruction of the Nose. St Louis: Mosby–Year Book; 1994.

7. Jackson IT. Calvarial bone for head and neck reconstruction. Recent Adv Plast Surg 1992;4:93.

8. McGregor IA. Reconstructive techniques of the oral cavity. In McGregor IA, Howard DJ (eds): Rob & Smith's Operative Surgery, Head and Neck, ed 4, part 1. London: Butterworth-Heinemann; 1992:215.

9. Chen ZW, Yan W. The study and clinical application of the osteocutaneous flap of fibula. Microsurgery 1983;4:11.

10. Hidalgo DA. Fibula free flap: a new method of mandible reconstruction. Plast Reconstr Surg 1989;84:71.

Auricular Defect: Treatment Options

13.

Gordon H. Wilkes, BScMed, MD
John Wolfaardt, BDS, MDent, PhD

- Issues in Ear Reconstruction
- Osseointegrated Implant Ear Reconstruction: Advantages and Disadvantages
- Autogenous Ear Reconstruction: Advantages and Disadvantages

- Additional Issues
- Treatment Selection in Auricular Deformities

Few areas of reconstructive surgery generate as much controversy as the selection of appropriate treatment of major auricular defects. Controversy has persisted for centuries.

The history of ear reconstruction dates back to 900 BC when *Susruta*, an Indian text of ancient medicine, mentioned partial reconstruction of the earlobe with a cheek flap. In 1597, Tagliacozzi of Italy transferred a flap from the arm to reconstruct the auricle of a monk. Two hundred fifty years later, Dieffenbach repaired a traumatic defect of the ear with a mastoid flap folded on itself. Roux and many of his contemporaries of the mid 19th century considered reconstruction of the auricle a surgical impossibility. In the early and mid 20th century, reports were published of use of an assortment of cartilage homografts and heterografts with dismal results.[1,2] The modern era of auricular reconstruction using autogenous tissue began with Tanzer's descriptions in 1959[3] and continued with major contributions by

Brent in 1980.[4,5] Further development of this field also was made by notable surgeons such as Fukuda and Yamada,[6] Cronin,[7] Bauer,[8] Yanai et al,[9] Isshiki et al,[10] and Nagata.[11] With improved techniques, more consistent autogenous results could be achieved.

The use of facial prostheses dates back to antiquity.[12] One of the major problems in achieving satisfactory results with ear prostheses was long-term successful retention of the prostheses. Adhesives have, until recently, been the primary means of retaining facial prostheses. Adhesives resulted in inconsistent bonding of the prosthesis to skin, skin damage, difficulty with prosthesis positioning, and a decrease in the life of the prosthesis.[13,14] These limitations led to inconsistent use of facial prostheses by patients. With the successful development of osseointegration biotechnology by Brånemark, previously unavailable treatment opportunities arose for the craniofacial region. Historically, a further compromising factor in constructing an aesthetically and functionally acceptable facial prosthesis was the limitation of available materials. With the introduction of silicone materials in the 1960s, a resilient and durable prosthesis was possible.[15] Since that time, many materials have been investigated but silicones have remained the materials of choice.[16] More recently, innovations in coloring and techniques of facial prosthesis construction have advanced greatly in aesthetic and functional value.

Osseointegration biotechnology was first used to retain an auricular prosthesis in 1979 in Göteborg, Sweden.[17] Reports followed documenting the success of this approach in terms of individual implant success,[18-23] skin response,[22,24-26] and patient response to treatment.[23] The challenges of prosthesis retention, difficulty with prosthesis positioning, and skin and prosthesis damage by the adhesives were resolved.[14] An ear prosthesis with consistent performance and superior aesthetics was now a viable option for the patient with a major auricular defect.

The current situation provides the patient and clinician with osseointegrated and autogenous options for ear reconstruction. Unfortunately, these fundamentally different approaches are frequently presented as competing technologies. At times, an almost adversarial relationship has developed between proponents of each approach based on differences in surgical specialties and lack of understanding of the relative value of the two treatment modalities. This has led to a situation that is not in the patient's best interest, with the consequence that the patient is not completely informed of treatment options or is left out of the decision-making process. Osseointegration and autogenous reconstruction techniques are complementary and must be presented in this manner.

Although there are still areas where treatment selection remains contentious, appropriate guidelines for treatment selection are becoming accepted. This chapter examines the many issues driving treatment selection, presents the current state of the art in ear reconstruction, and discusses the advantages and disadvantages of each approach. Finally, the rationale for treatment selection is considered. There is an obligation, both morally and medicolegally, for proponents of each approach to understand the full spectrum of treatment modalities available and to present them in a balanced manner to their patients. In many challenging auricular defects the ultimate aesthetic result using autogenous techniques will be compromised, and this can be predicted before initiation of treatment. If the option of using osseinte-

gration provides the patient with enhanced potential for a superior result, then this option must be brought to the patient's attention. The most important question in treatment selection is "What is best for the patient?" and not "What can I provide?"

The first stage in treatment selection must begin with a discussion with the patient and family. The family often expresses a sense of guilt and a need for urgent treatment of the deformity. These concerns must be addressed at an early stage by the clinician, and it is important to distinguish between the needs of the pediatric patient as opposed to the desires of the parents. This is followed by careful analysis of the defect. This includes an assessment of the underlying bony architecture; overlying soft tissue; residual ear remnants; quality of the skin; absence of scars, grafts, or flaps; position of the hairline; patency of the superficial temporal vessels; and three-dimensional spatial relationship of the site for placement of the auricle relative to the underlying cranial skeleton. All these factors may play a role in selecting the appropriate reconstructive technique. So what then are the factors that influence the possible ultimate treatment selection for an individual patient?

Issues in Ear Reconstruction

Clinician-Driven Issues

The discipline of training received may bias the clinician to favor a particular approach to the treatment of auricular defects. Most commonly, plastic surgery has favored autogenous reconstruction whereas otolaryngology and oral and maxillofacial surgery appear to have used osseointegrated prosthetic reconstruction. If the various specialties do not cooperate, then the resulting referral patterns will likely dictate ultimate treatment choice rather than appropriateness of available techniques. This has generated increasing friction in some geographic locations as surgeons fear losing the patient to a surgeon of a different specialty. This situation is counterproductive to meeting the patient's needs and is not conducive to the further evolution of ear reconstruction. The development of a recognized multidisciplinary team providing all aspects of auricular treatment results in an overall increase in the number of patients for all members of the team.

A clinician who is exposed to unfavorable treatment outcomes that are not presented in context may well hold a biased and poor opinion of the treatment modality. Thus, a poor autogenous result or recurrent skin problem around osseointegrated implants presented out of context likely results in a clinician viewing that treatment modality in a negative manner. As a result, distorted perceptions held by clinicians will continue to foster a lack of understanding by the medical community and the public of available treatment modalities for ear reconstruction. With current techniques, the results of autogenous auricular reconstruction should provide acceptable results in appropriately selected cases. However, even in the best hands, the ultimate aesthetic results show greater variability in anatomic form than with an auricular prosthesis. An all too common scenario is a surgeon with little appropriate training attempting a few autogenous reconstructions. This results in many operative procedures with poor results and unhappy patients. Ultimately, the surgeon stops performing autogenous reconstructions but leaves a legacy of dissatisfied patients and attending clinicians who view auricular reconstruction poorly. It is these results that may be presented as evidence of autogenous auricular reconstruction being an unacceptable procedure.

In many locales, a multidisciplinary team with facial prosthetic skills is not readily available. The skills of the multidisciplinary team are necessary to proceed with osseointegrated auricular reconstruction. The roles of the prosthodontist, dental technologist, and anaplastologist are not well appreciated in the medical arena. Members of these disciplines need to be full members of the team and must be involved with treatment planning before surgical placement of implants, intraoperative decisions, construction of prostheses, and long-term follow-up of patients. These team members have the same role to play in autogenous auricular reconstruction.

Patient-Driven Issues

Patients can be influenced by the physician who makes the initial referral. The physician's comments, particularly if ill informed, may influence the patients' views to the point where they will not consider all potential options presented to them. Patients will quickly have an intuitive response—pro or con—to an osseointegrated implant or an autogenous approach. Very seldom do patients change their minds after further discussion. This can lead to a situation in which the patient's ideal treatment selection differs from the reconstructive team's treatment of choice and can eventually result in less than optimal treatment.

There remain a considerable number of patients who are not satisfied with their autogenous auricular reconstruction. The result of treatment has failed to meet their expectations for several reasons. Often, these dissatisfied patients have no interest in considering any further autogenous option. These patients have often undergone numerous surgical procedures at considerable expense and are left with a feeling of great disappointment. Osseointegration offers this group an excellent opportunity to obtain a satisfactory result.

The functional or social demands on an individual in terms of occupation may contribute to choice. Accessibility to treatment with osseointegrated implants, the requirement for maintenance visits, and replacement of prostheses may make osseointegrated implant reconstruction difficult in certain cases. Psychosocial issues can contribute to treatment selection. Osseointegration requires a compliant patient who understands a lifetime commitment. No matter how ideal the auricular defect for implant reconstruction, the patient's ability to understand and comply with instructions is vital for care of the implant skin-penetration site. Problems with patient understanding may result in a different treatment choice or no treatment options being offered.

System-Driven Issues

The variety of health care systems in the world modifies approaches to auricular reconstruction. A brief overview of auricular reconstruction in several geographic locations illustrates an inconsistency of approaches to treatment. In the United States before 1995, the use of implants for auricular reconstruction was limited pending approval by the Food and Drug Administration. The vast majority of patients with auricular defects were then presented with either autogenous options or an adhesive-retained prosthesis. Approval by the Food and Drug Administration of the Brånemark craniofacial implant system on January 13, 1995, broadened the spectrum of potential treatment options available in the United States. The challenge in the United States appears to be related to both the short- and long-term costs associated with osseointegration and the ability of the system to adapt to the long-term commitment needed for each patient. How the medical community and the medical insurance industry in the United States view craniofacial osseointegration remains to be seen.

In Canada, provincial governments have paid for any autogenous alternatives without restrictions. The introduction of craniofacial osseointegrated implants has been a problem because, historically, the provincial funding agencies have not supported prosthetic costs. As a result, these agencies will fund only the direct surgical costs, which are a portion of the overall cost of treatment. This has resulted in an economic reason for some patients to favor an autogenous option when their better choice may have been an osseointegrated approach if their particular provincial funding agency does not offer equal coverage.

Sweden has been the leader in treatment of auricular deformities with osseointegrated implant-retained prostheses. The Swedish plastic surgery community appears not to have aggressively pursued autogenous reconstruction, so the vast majority of auricular deformities are treated with implant-retained prostheses. There has been satisfactory government support for implant-retained prosthetic reconstruction under the Swedish health care system.

Great Britain has both options available; however, there appears to be a preponderance of auricular reconstructions using implant-retained prostheses.

In Japan, although there is an interest in osseointegration, the majority of procedures have been autogenous.

In countries where ear deformities are treated, most are now in the process of reevaluating treatment selection for auricular reconstruction. These decisions are based not only on the introduction of new technologies but also on the many local clinical and nonclinical factors currently influencing medical decisions.

Medicolegally Driven Issues

As with most aspects of medicine, medicolegal implications of treatment selection must be considered. Patients must be advised of their choices, benefits, risks, limitations, and costs. They also need to be advised of the commitment, financial or otherwise, of their treatment options. Patients also need to be aware that, in most circumstances, the placement of implants and removal of auricular remnants make future autogenous options poor. The patients need to be aware of the standard of care in their local community, the skills and resources present, and where to obtain alternative treatment options. This

too may contribute to the ultimate treatment selection by the patient. The statute of limitations, which may vary from jurisdiction to jurisdiction in each country, and its medicolegal implications may have an effect in the future on appropriate treatment choices, particularly in the pediatric population.

Osseointegrated Implant Ear Reconstruction: Advantages and Disadvantages

The osseointegrated implant ear reconstruction has several distinct advantages. The surgical procedures are relatively short and more straightforward and can be performed on an outpatient basis. There is less pain and less potential morbidity. The procedures can be performed, if necessary, during local anesthesia, and there has been increasing success in certain circumstances with a one-stage procedure.[27] The technique is less demanding of the surgeon and so potentially is more widely available if suitable prosthetic support can be obtained. It offers an alternative to patients who are poor operative or anesthetic risks. It may benefit older patients likely to have calcified costal cartilage, which makes autogenous framework construction difficult. The prosthesis has a greater similarity in form and projection to the normal ear than can be achieved with autogenous reconstruction. If the prosthetic ear is unsatisfactory, another prosthesis can be constructed in an attempt to correct any shortcomings. Patients do not have difficulty incorporating a well-retained prosthesis into their body image.[23]

A major disadvantage of the osseointegrated prosthetic approach is the need for significant, ongoing long-term commitment from the patient and the health care providers. Daily care of the implant sites, regular maintenance visits, and replacement of the prosthesis make the osseointegration team and the patient lifelong partners. Distance from the osseointegration center does not appear to be a major problem in well-motivated patients. There may be a greater alteration in lifestyle, including limitation of body contact sports and removal of the prosthesis at night and in certain water sports. Poor manual dexterity, lack of family support, and unrealistic expectations may contraindicate an osseointegrated implant approach. Maxillofacial prosthetic skills are necessary for planning and completing an osseointegrated implant approach. This makes a team approach a necessity compared with autogenous reconstruction where, if necessary, a surgeon can function relatively independently. The final disadvantage is the decreased potential for later autogenous reconstruction. The removal of ear remnants at the second stage of osseointegration surgery converts the area to an anotia with superimposed scar. This severely compromises future autogenous options. There have been attempts to place the implants outside the area of reconstruction and then to have the prosthesis cover the ear remnants. This approach results in compromise of an acceptable outcome of treatment.

Autogenous Ear Reconstruction: Advantages and Disadvantages

The major advantage of autogenous ear reconstruction is that it follows the basic tenet of reconstructive surgery of using a patient's own tissue whenever possible. It usually produces a stable long-term result with no maintenance, little risk of late complication, and minimal alteration in lifestyle. The reconstruction readily becomes part of self and the cartilaginous framework has been shown to grow with age.[28] There are no ongoing costs and minimal need for long-term compliance from the patient. Improvement in ancillary procedures, such as soft-tissue expanders[29] and temporoparietal fascial flaps,[30] has increased the options available for patients with more severe local scarring or trauma.

The disadvantages are longer surgical procedures with more stages necessary and greater potential surgical morbidity. Although the final reconstruction may be aesthetically pleasing, it is anatomically less similar to a normal opposite ear than a sculptured prosthetic ear. Overall, there is greater variability in form with this approach but less variability in color.

Additional Issues

In considering the two treatment approaches to ear reconstruction, other issues require discussion. The time of treatment differs with each approach.

For a microtia reconstruction using implants, the time from initial operation with a one-stage approach to a completed prosthesis is approximately 4 to 5 months. The time from first procedure in an autogenous reconstruction to final procedure is usually 9 to 12 months. Costs and their implications vary from country to country. In a government-run system in the province of Alberta, Canada, the initial costs of the two techniques are similar; however, there are ongoing maintenance and prosthesis replacement costs associated with osseointegration. Because the Alberta government fully funds osseointegrated ear reconstruction, costs are not a factor in treatment selection. This is the ideal circumstance.

The use of an adhesive-retained prosthesis as a trial approach in no way mimics the definite advantages of an osseointegrated implant-retained prosthesis. With autogenous and implant techniques now available, the indications for adhesive-retained prostheses are limited at best.

An important consideration is the view of the patient. Patients usually, in any discussion of treatment options on ear reconstruction, state an early preference based on personal intuitive feelings. Some do not want several operations and a scar on their chest wall. Others do not want ear remnants removed, no matter how severely the remnant compromises appearance. Frequently, the patient will inquire if the remnant can be used to serve as a foundation for ear reconstruction. Although many patients find the idea of high biotechnology exciting, others are completely opposed to use of alloplastic materials. No matter what the best choice may be from a purely objective point of view, subjective personal preferences may supersede all other factors. Occasionally, this may put the patient and multidisciplinary team in conflict over which is the most appropriate way to proceed.

Treatment Selection in Auricular Deformities

A major indication for osseointegrated implant reconstruction is after major cancer resection (Box 13-1). This indication usually arises in older patients with calcified costal cartilage, making autogenous reconstruction difficult. Where significant

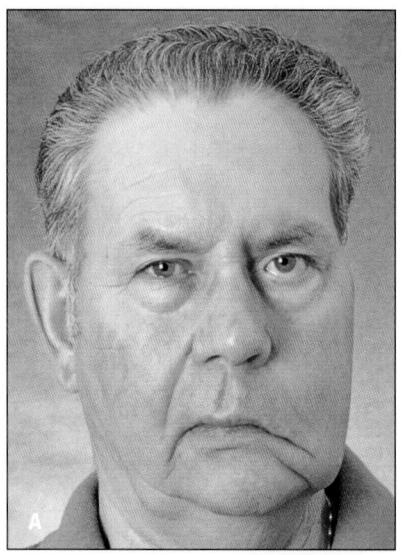
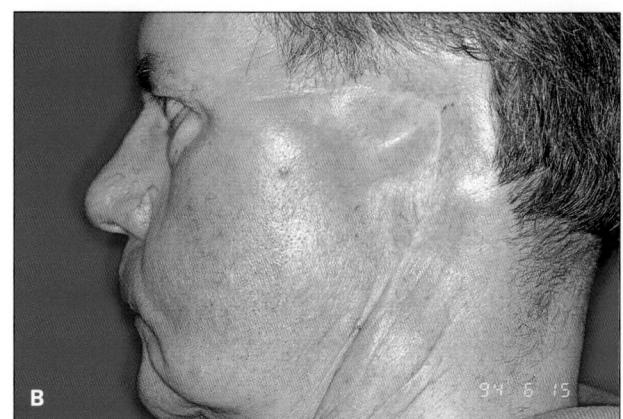

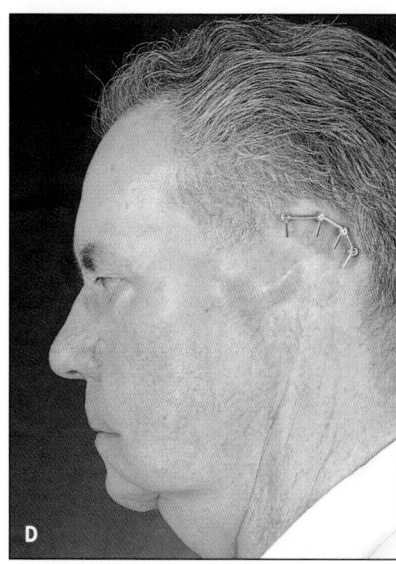
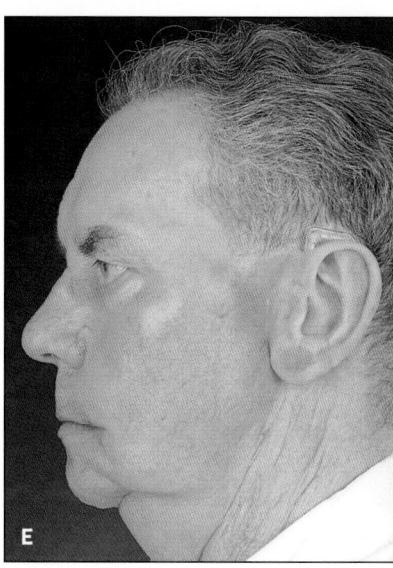

Fig 13-1 (case 1). A 70-year-old man underwent temporal bone resection, removal of the external ear, and postoperative radiotherapy because of recurrent squamous cell carcinoma. He had hyperbaric oxygen, osseointegrated implants placed, and a static facial sling. *A* and *B,* Preoperative. *C* through *E,* Postoperative.

Box 13-1 **Osseointegrated Alloplastic Ear Reconstruction: Indications**
Major cancer resection
Radiotherapy
Absence of lower half of ear
Severely compromised tissue
Patient preference
Failed autogenous reconstruction
Potential craniofacial anomaly
Poor operative risk
Microtia (controversial)

portions of the ear are removed, further compromise results and autogenous options are precluded. Higher osseointegrated implant loss rates have been reported where implants have been placed in irradiated bone. Studies have shown that, with hyperbaric oxygen therapy, implant survival rates are improved significantly.[22,31] For patients who have been irradiated in the temporal region, the use of hyperbaric oxygen therapy and osseointegrated implants is the only treatment alternative for auricular reconstruction. Case 1 (Fig 13-1) is a 70-year-old man who had removal of the external ear, temporal bone resection,

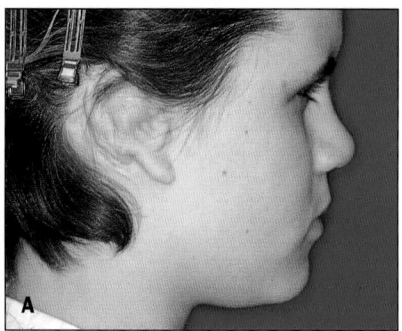 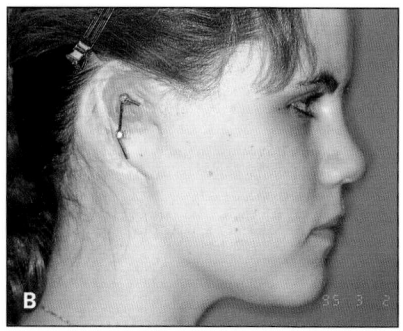 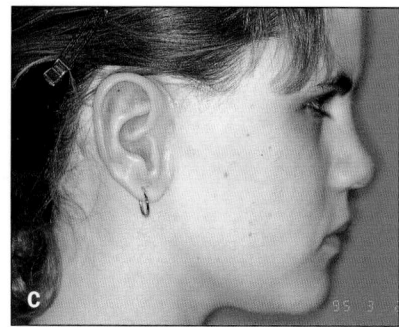

Fig 13-2 (case 2). A 14-year-old girl previously had an autogenous reconstruction using a Silastic framework. The ear was removed and replaced by an osseointegrated prosthesis reconstruction. *A*, Preoperative. *B* and *C*, Postoperative.

and postoperative radiotherapy because of recurrent squamous cell carcinoma.

Some of the patients benefiting most from craniofacial osseointegration are those for whom autogenous reconstruction has failed. This provides the reconstructive surgeon with the opportunity to salvage disappointed and disillusioned patients and turn them into satisfied and positive individuals. Unfortunately, as a result of inconsistent results with autogenous reconstruction, this group is not as small as it should be. Furthermore, if the autogenous reconstruction does not yield an acceptable result at the first attempt, revisional surgery frequently fails to improve the result. Case 2 (Fig 13-2) is a 14-year-old girl who previously underwent autogenous reconstruction using a Silastic framework. The reconstruction was removed and implants were placed.

A relative indication for implants is severely compromised tissue from trauma or burns.[3,10] Case 3 (Fig 13-3) is a 31-year-old man who lost his ear and suffered a major soft-tissue injury after a burn in a motor vehicle accident. Case 4 (Fig 13-4) is a 51-year-old man who had his ear avulsed in a motor vehicle accident. If absent, the lower half of the ear is particularly difficult to reconstruct, and so this is a further indication for an osseointegrated implant approach.

Theoretically, implants could be placed in children with significant craniofacial anomalies. The prospect of multiple facial surgical procedures makes judgment as to siting ear reconstruction difficult. With facial changes during growth, the ear prosthesis could be moved relative to the site of the implants. Also, if these children require implant placement for a Bone-Anchored Hearing Aid (BAHA)

and require ongoing care and commitment for this implant, then consideration could be given to placing the additional implants required for an auricular prosthesis, thereby giving the child satisfactory ear reconstruction with minimal further surgery. This applies particularly to children with Treacher Collins syndrome. The BAHA is a significant advance over conventional bone-conduction hearing aids, which are held in position with an uncomfortable, over-the-head spring assembly. With the success of BAHA, middle ear and external canal reconstruction, with all their attendant risks and complications, can be obviated.

The most controversial area of treatment selection is the child with microtia. In this situation, there is no definite right answer and most clinicians will have a strong opinion. Case 5 (Fig 13-5) is a 15-year-old boy with a classic microtia who wanted to undergo an osseointegrated prosthetic reconstruction. The proponents of osseointegration maintain that the patients will obtain a more pleasing result with less surgery and less morbidity. These clinicians claim many of the results of autogenous ear reconstruction are poor.[32] Unfortunately, most of the successful autogenous reconstructions are not seen by this group of clinicians because the patient has no need of their services. Although this group of clinicians understands that long-term commitment is required, they typically contend that the potential for significant implant or skin problems is low and is not a contraindication to osseointegrated implant treatment.[24]

The proponents of autogenous reconstruction believe the patient is better off if he or she can have reconstruction with autogenous tissue that mimics ab-

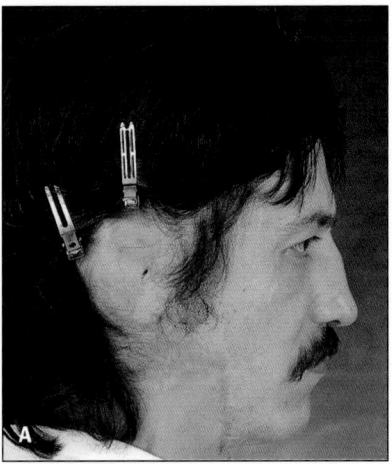
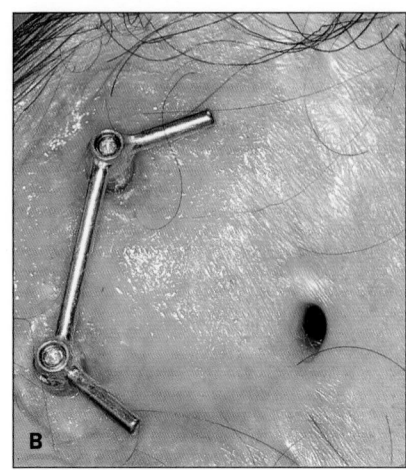
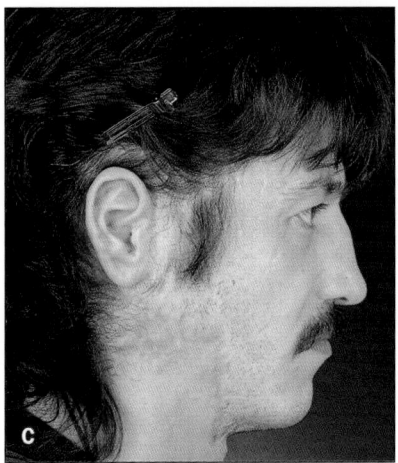
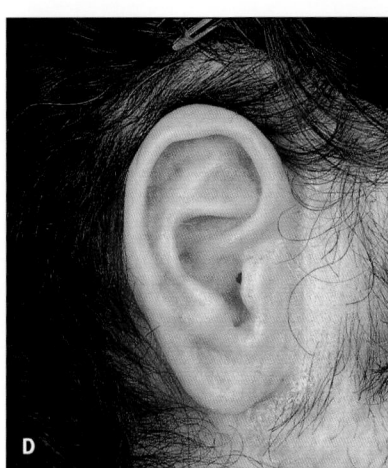

Fig 13-3 (case 3). A 31-year-old man lost his right ear and suffered a major soft-tissue injury. Reconstruction used an osseointegrated prosthesis. *A*, Preoperative. *B* through *D*, Postoperative.

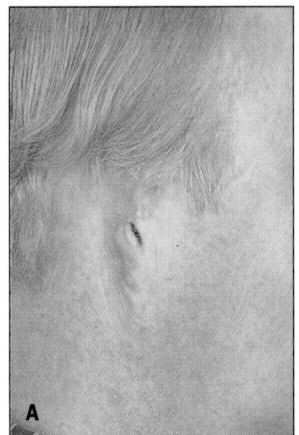
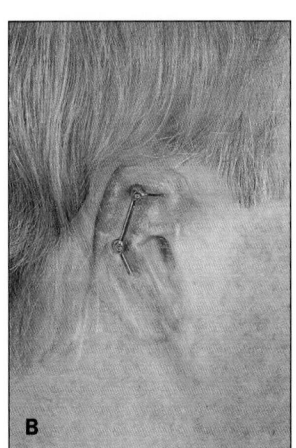
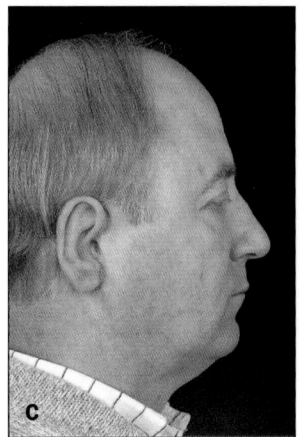
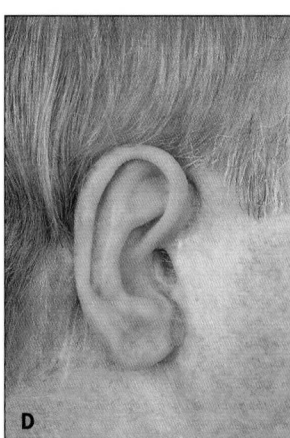

Fig 13-4 (case 4). A 51-year-old man lost his ear in a motor vehicle accident. He underwent osseointegrated prosthesis reconstruction. *A*, Preoperative. *B* through *D*, Postoperative.

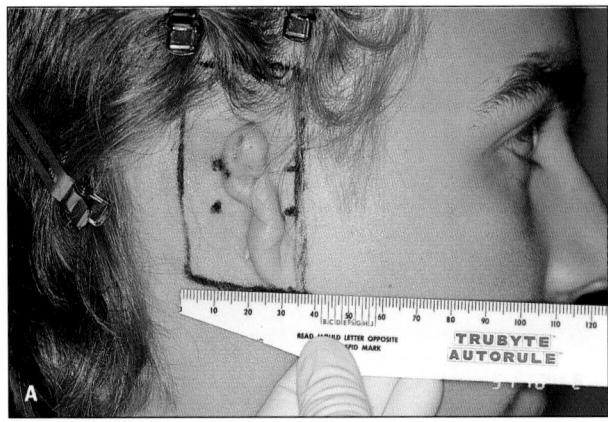

Fig 13-5 (case 5). A 15-year-old boy with classic microtia wanted an osseointegrated prosthetic reconstruction. *A*, Preoperative. *B* through *D*, Postoperative.

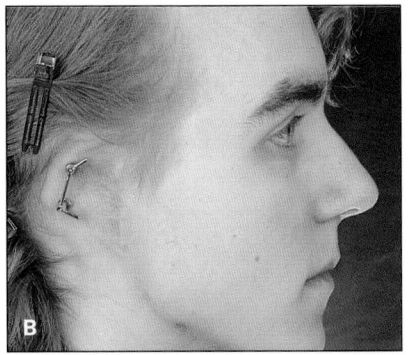
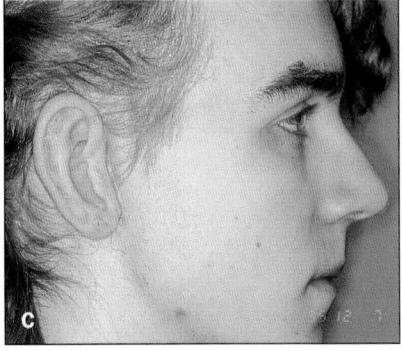
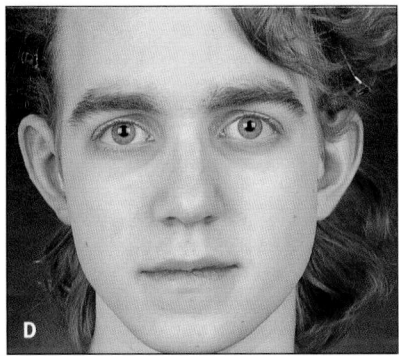

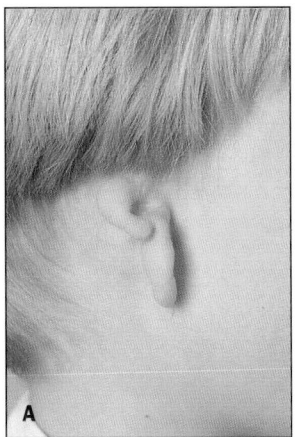
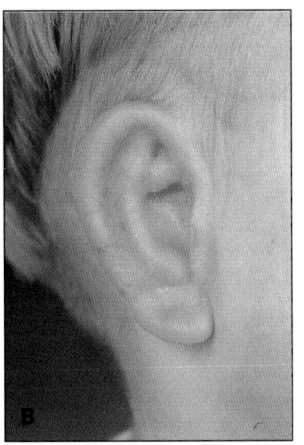
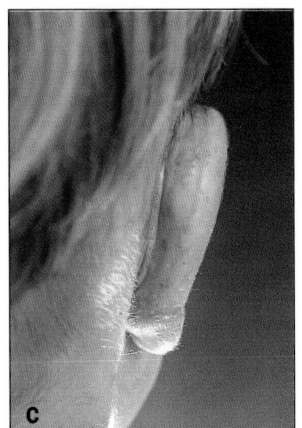
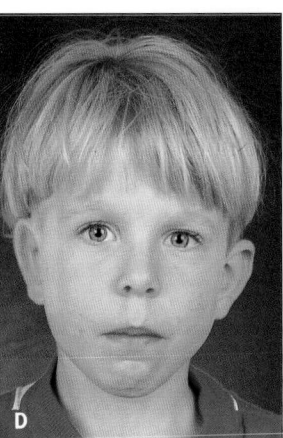

Fig 13-6 (case 6). A 6-year-old boy with classic microtia underwent an autogenous auricular reconstruction. *A*, Preoperative. *B* through *D*, Postoperative.

sent or lost ear tissue (Box 13-2). Case 6 (Fig 13-6) is a 6-year-old boy with classic microtia who underwent reconstruction with autogenous costal cartilage. The completed reconstruction can then be displaced from consciousness and the patient can resume life in a normal manner. There is no ongoing cost or commitment. There remains the option for future osseointegration if the autogenous result is not satisfactory.[5]

Box 13-2 Autogenous Ear Reconstruction: Indications
Classic microtia
Lower third of ear intact
Patient preference
Less compliant patient

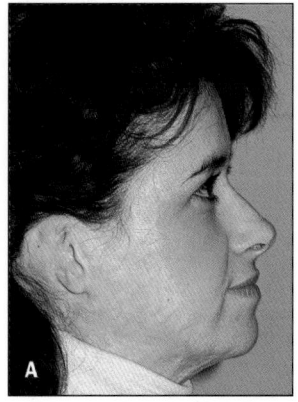
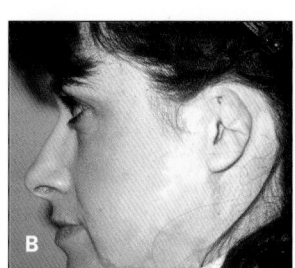
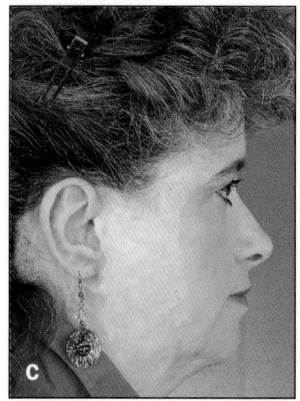
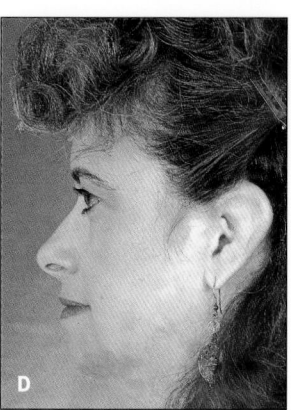

Fig 13-7 (case 7). A 41-year-old woman suffered a burn to her face and both ears in childhood. On the right, little ear remnant remained, so she opted for an osseointegrated prosthesis reconstruction. The lower half of the left ear was preserved, so it was reconstructed with a temporoparietal fascial flap and costal cartilage and skin graft. *A* and *B*, Preoperative. *C* and *D*, Postoperative. (From Wilkes G, Wolfaardt J. Osseointegrated alloplastic versus autogenous ear reconstruction: criteria for treatment selection. Plast Reconstr Surg 1994;93;967. By permission of American Society of Plastic and Reconstructive Surgery.)

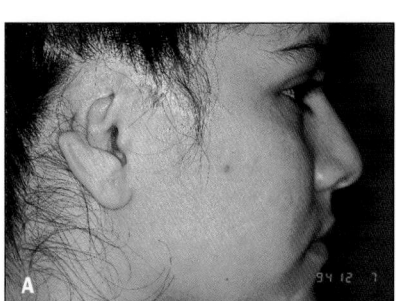
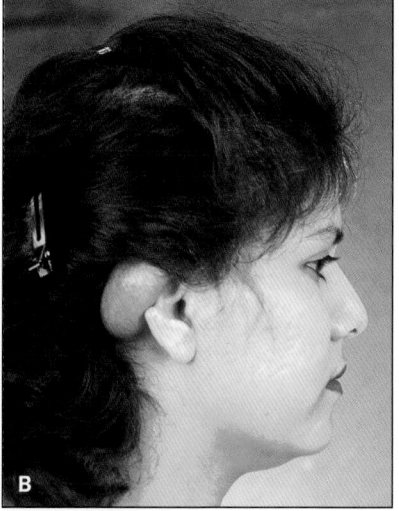
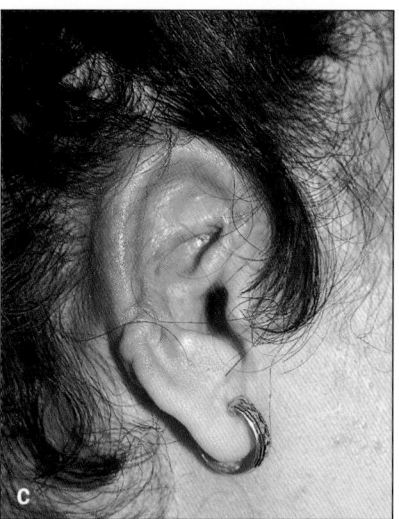

Fig 13-8 (case 8). A 29-year-old woman lost the upper half of her ear in a motor vehicle accident. Reconstruction used costal cartilage and a soft-tissue expander. *A*, Preoperative. *B*, With soft-tissue expander. *C*, Postoperative.

Although initial results with implants in children are encouraging, follow-up is relatively short. The long-term treatment outcome of implants over a lifetime and any long-term side effects are not yet known with certainty. There is also concern over the possibility of implants interfering with growth and the potential for surgical complication as a result of proximity of vital organs. There is the opinion that removal of ear remnants and implant placement at as early as age 3 years is far too young to commit a patient down an irreversible path. It is believed by some that the patients should be old enough to give their own informed consent before autogenous options are irretrievably removed. This school of thought holds that in appropriately trained hands, the level of patient satisfaction with autogenous ear reconstruction is predictably high.[33]

The placement of implants in a classic microtia patient and retention of the ear remnants does not give the patient the same chance for later autogenous success as in a case of surgically untouched microtia.

Nasal Defect: Treatment Options

14.

Denton D. Weiss, MD
Julian J. Pribaz, MD
Elof Eriksson, MD, PhD

- History
- Anatomy and Physiology
- Surgical Algorithm
- Autogenous Nasal Reconstruction
- Nonautogenous Nasal Reconstruction

History

Throughout the ages the nose has been adored as an object of beauty and a symbol of strength. Michelangelo's Sistine Chapel depiction of God with his nostrils flaring as he creates the sun and the moon brings home the essence of power. The amputation of the nose, the center of the facial universe, has been the bitter price of social dishonor and military conflict throughout history. The earliest accounts of nasal surgery were for the treatment of nasal fractures in the Edwin Smyth Surgical Papyrus (circa 3,000 BC). Nasal reconstruction has been credited to Indian tilemakers (circa 600 BC). *Sushruta Samhita*, one of the Brahman holy books, described the use of a cheek flap for the reconstruction of the nasal tip.[1] Brancas, in 1430, and later Tagliacozzi, in 1597, described the arm flap as a means of reconstructing nasal injuries secondary to dueling wounds.[2] Ambroise Paré mentioned in his 16th century writings that prosthetic noses were made of silver. The Sultan of Turkey was known to supply his soldiers with silver noses after their faces had been mutilated by Bulgarian warriors during the Russian-Turkish war in 1876.[3]

Joseph C. Carpue, a London surgeon, wrote the classic text about restoring a lost nose, which was published in 1816.[4] He described two cases in which the forehead flap was performed for nasal reconstruction. His work was most likely stimulated by the famous B.L. letter from Cowasjee where, under the authorization of Lieutenant Colonel Ward of the India service, an Indian artist from Poona was credited with reconstructing the noses of four native soldiers after they were amputated by an enemy sultan.[3,4]

In the 19th century, French surgeons began experimenting with sliding cheek flaps and several German surgeons began to perfect nasal reconstruction with the arm flap and the forehead flap. Nasal reconstruction began to be described as the Indian rhinoplasty (forehead reconstruction), French rhinoplasty (cheek advancement), and Italian rhinoplasty (arm flap) based on the origin of the technique. Johann Friedrich Dieffenbach, in his 1845 edition of *Die Operative Chirurgie,*[5] described several detailed variations of nasal reconstruction. He is credited with popularizing many of the basic tenets of nasal reconstruction still used today. Jonathan Mason Warren of Boston was one of the first American surgeons to study and perform Dieffenbach's technique.[6]

The nasal lining was initially addressed by Volkmann, who turned down skin from the nose, and later by Lossen, who in 1898 used split-thickness skin grafts.[3] Although other individuals had addressed the nasal lining, Keegan,[7] from his reconstructive experience in India, pioneered the concept of lining the new nose to prevent contracture and nasal collapse.

In 1828, Rousset wrote a thesis in which gold or silver frameworks were fixed to the nasal cavity and used to prevent collapse of the newly reconstructed nose. He boldly stated that a Roman or Carthaginian nose could be created.[3] Additionally, in the late 1800s, several individuals attempted to use nonremovable metallic supports, which included an unknown metal by Despres, aluminum by Lotievant, and platinum by Martin of Lyon. Ellison was noted to be the first author to describe the perforation of these fixed implants.[3] In 1925, the nasal prosthesis was again presented as a viable alternative to autogenous reconstruction by Kazanjian,[8] who used vulcanite and gold-plated fittings.

Autogenous tissue reconstruction of the nasal framework was addressed separately by Konig and by Helferich. Each transferred frontal bone with the forehead flap. Von Mangold, in 1900, was the first to describe the use of costal cartilage for saddle nose repair. Nélaton placed the cartilage graft under the forehead flap before rotating the flap into position.[3,9]

World War I brought in the age of modern weaponry and with it the severely disfiguring wounds of high-ballistic trauma. Sir Harold Gillies,[10] a well-known surgeon during the war, reported the use of a tube flap pedicled from the neck and chest to reconstruct the nose and facial soft-tissue deficits. He later went on to describe many techniques used in facial reconstruction. He described the "up and down" forehead flap and the use of chondrocutaneous graft implantation before rotation of the forehead flap. This provided support and lining to the ala and nasal tip.

In 1925, Blair[11] and Ivy,[12] and later Kazanjian[13] and Millard,[9] popularized and refined the forehead flap for reconstruction of partial and complete nasal defects. During the last century, their techniques and several other nasal reconstructive techniques have been advocated. More recently there have been further refinements. Burget and Menick[14,15] emphasized the aesthetic subunit concept of nasal reconstruction. Several authors[16-19] have described microsurgical free tissue transfers, and Brånemark and co-workers[20] have pioneered and refined osseointegrated nasal implants.

We present a view of nasal anatomy, the aesthetic subunit concept, our functional subunit concept, the tenets of partial and complete autogenous nasal reconstruction, and the current principles of nonautogenous nasal reconstruction.

Anatomy and Physiology

The nose can be viewed as a pyramid with the apex at the nasal tip and a support beam (the nasal septum) diagonally crossing underneath. The external pyramid is made up of the four triangles of the nose. The mirrored inferior triangles are made up of the columella, the combined soft triangle and ala lobule, and the nasal sill. The mirrored superior triangles are made up of the nasal dorsum, the nasal facial crease, and the ala lobule. The internal support structures of the nose include the nasal spine, septum, and floor. The structures involved in nasal function but not support are the superior, middle, and inferior turbinates located on the lateral walls of the internal nasal chamber. The nasal spine is the cornerstone supporting the anterior septum. The nasal septum can be divided into the septal cartilage, the perpendicular plate of the ethmoid bone, and the inferiorly positioned vomer. The floor of the nose is made up of the maxillary and posteriorly the palatine bones.

The nasal cartilages are the paired upper lateral cartilages, the paired lower lateral cartilages (or ala cartilages), and the anterior half of the nasal septum (membranous septum). The lower lateral cartilages are divided into three portions: the lateral crura, which are the lateral wings of the cartilages; the middle crura, which make up the tip projecting points; and the medial crura, which are found within the columella.

Many authors use the rule of thirds when discussing nasal deformities. Although this terminology is for the external appearance of the nose, understanding the bony and cartilaginous landmarks that make up these thirds is essential. The upper third represents the area from the root of the nose (nasion, a bony cephalometric point) to the junction point of the nasal bones and the upper lateral cartilages (rhinion, a bony cephalometric point). The middle third extends from the rhinion to the anterior tip of the upper lateral cartilages. The lower third of the nose is called the lobule and is made up of the nasal tip, the paired ala, and the columella. The soft triangle often is included in aesthetic discussions of the lobule, and it is the region of skin bridging the ala and the columella.

The arterial blood supply to the nose should be divided into the external and internal systems. The internal system is supplied by the anterior ethmoidal artery, the posterior ethmoidal artery, and the maxillary artery. The maxillary artery is the major vascular source to the internal system and to part of the external system. The maxillary artery passes through the pterygopalatine fossa and gives off branches to the lateral nasal wall and alveolar branches to the teeth, via the sphenopalatine and the greater palatine arteries, respectively. The greater palatine artery passes through the incisive foramen and supplies the anterior inferior septum. The sphenopalatine artery supplies the superior and posterior septum. These arteries with their accompanying veins form a vascular plexus as they anastomose in the anterior septum (Kiesselbach's plexus). The anterior and posterior ethmoid arteries also supply the superior and anterior lateral nasal wall. The arterial supply for the nasal skin and subcutaneous tissues comes from the facial, infratrochlear, and infraorbital vessels, which form a rich vascular plexus. The

facial artery branches to form the anterior facial artery, the angular artery, and the labial artery. The most common anatomic finding is that the anterior facial artery terminates as the lateral nasal artery and the angular artery forms a separate connection between the facial artery system and the ophthalmic system. Less than 25% of the time the lateral nasal artery connects directly with the angular artery (Fig 14-1 and 14-2).

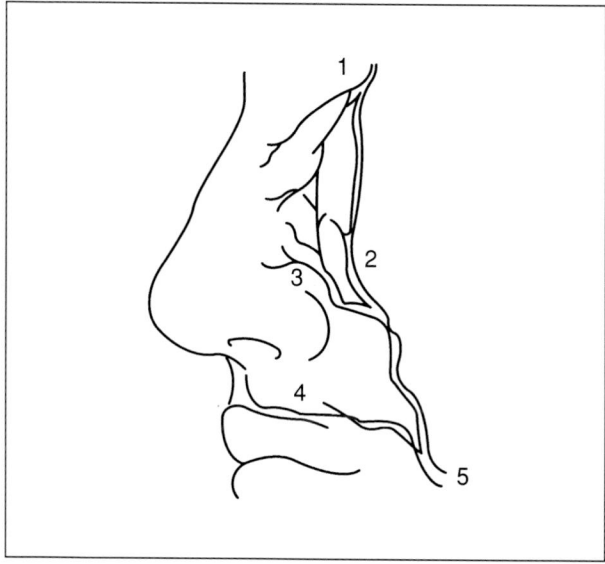

Fig 14-1. The external nasal vascular supply. *1,* Dorsal nasal artery (from ophthalmic artery); *2,* angular artery; *3,* lateral nasal artery; *4,* labial artery; and *5,* facial artery.

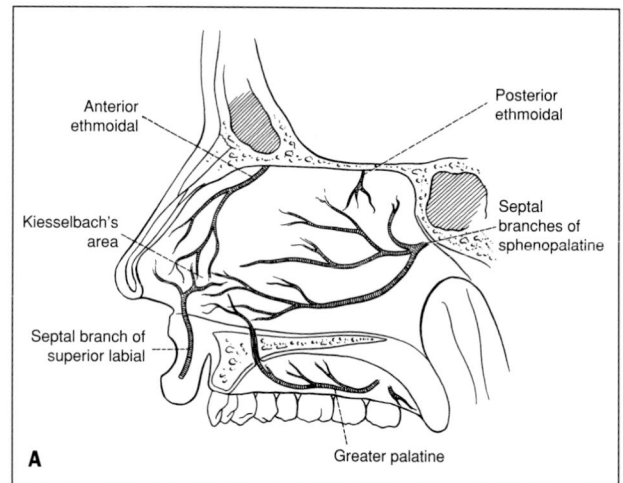

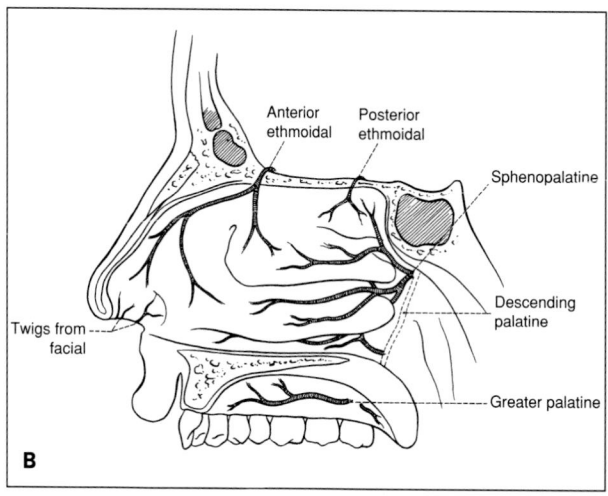

Fig 14-2. *A,* The lateral nasal wall and vascular supply. *B,* The nasal septum vascular supply. (From Hollinshead WH. Anatomy for Surgeons. Vol 1: The Head and Neck, ed 3. Philadelphia: Harper & Row Publishers; 1982:223. By permission of Lippincott-Raven Publishers.)

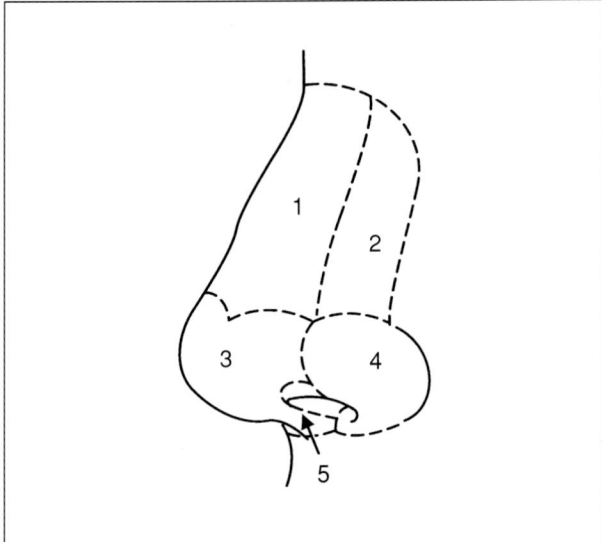

Fig 14-3. The aesthetic units per Burget and Menick. *1*, Dorsum; *2*, lateral nasal; *3*, tip; *4*, alar lobule; and *5*, soft triangle.

Aesthetic Units

The aesthetic units of the nose were originally presented by González-Ulloa[21] and later modified by Millard.[22] Burget and Menick further divided the lobule of the nose into subunits.[14,23] The external portion of the nose is divided into the dorsum, sidewalls, tip, ala lobules, and soft triangles. The Burget and Menick concept is to enlarge a defect to encompass an entire subunit if 50% or more of the aesthetic unit is involved and the enlargement does not exceed the dimensions of the future flap[14] (Fig 14-3).

Functional Units

Attention should also be directed to the functional units of the nose in nasal reconstruction. The functional units of the nose are the septum, anterior nasal valve, inferior turbinates, middle turbinates, superior turbinates, middle meatus, and posterior nasal valve. The anterior nasal valve is located 1.5 to 2 cm posterior to the anterior nares. This region represents the narrowest portion of the nose and the point of the mucocutaneous junction (limen nasi). The limen nasi represents the region where the nasal lining changes from keratinizing squamous epithelium to the ciliated pseudostratified columnar (respiratory) epithelium that lines the entire nasal cavity.

The mucosa of the nasal cavity is essential for humidification, cleaning, airway patency, and olfaction. The turbinates increase the surface area of the nasal cavity, thereby increasing the function of the mucosa. The inferior and middle turbinates are considered the major filters of the nose. The middle meatus is the entrance to the sinuses. When the mucosa is damaged or not properly reconstructed, the nasal lining dries. A tenacious mucous drainage from the sinuses develops that leads to obstruction, recurrent sinus infection, and often decreased olfaction. If the nasal lining is allowed to dry even further, the patient develops ozena (a chronic fetid odor noted by the patient).

The anterior nasal valve is formed by the nasal mucosa underlying the attachment of the upper and lower lateral cartilages and nasal septum. Inferior to the valve is the nasal floor and, inferolaterally, the anterior portion of the inferior turbinate. The posterior nasal valve is the second narrowest region of the nasal airway. This valve is defined by the posterior choanae. Airflow passes through the anterior nasal valve at the greatest speed. Once the airstream passes through the valve, it disperses into the larger chamber of the nose and then funnels through the posterior nasal valve. With minor changes in the architecture of the anterior nasal valve, the airflow patterns are significantly decreased or redirected. The patient often complains of recurrent nosebleeds and inability to breathe through the obstructed side. The nasal mucosa dries, and bleeding may occur from the anterior vascular plexus of the septum (Kiesselbach's plexus). The posterior nasal valve rarely is involved in nasal reconstruction, but the surgeon must keep this region in mind when anterior obstruction is not seen in a patient complaining of chronic anterior nasal drainage and decreased patency. The most common defects at the posterior nasal valve region are a posterior nasal septal deviation or obstructing adenoid tissue.

Olfaction is achieved largely through the smell receptors found on the superior aspect of the middle turbinates, superior turbinates, and superior portion of the nasal septum and cavity. The nasal mucosa covering these functional subunits should be moist and airflow must be allowed through the region.

Surgical Algorithm

The goal of nasal reconstruction is to reconstruct an aesthetically pleasing and functional nose.

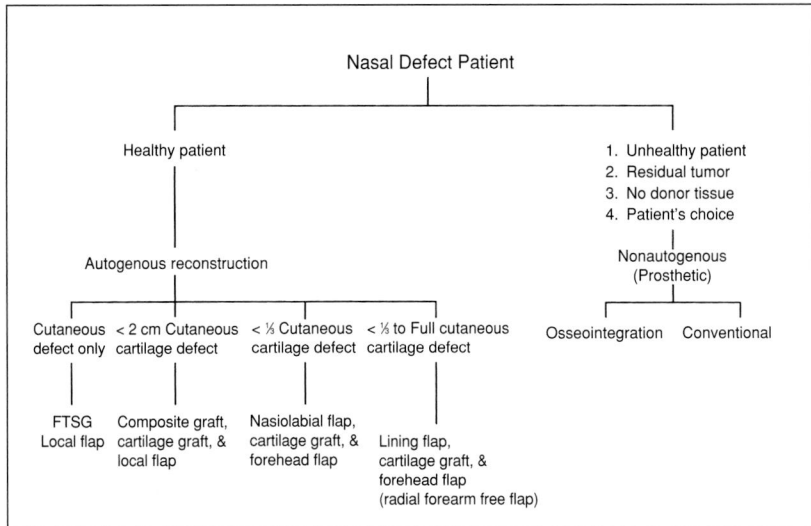

Fig 14-4. Nasal reconstruction algorithm.

Reconstruction with autogenous tissue is ideal in the relatively healthy patient. The nose is a laminated structure, and reconstruction must address the layers of cutaneous coverage, underlying support, and nasal lining if the goals of reconstructing the aesthetic and functional subunits are to be achieved. For those individuals who have poor health, residual tumor, or limited donor tissue available, nonautogenous reconstruction is considered. Manson et al[24] described an algorithm for autogenous nasal reconstruction. We propose an expanded algorithm based on the patient's health, the aesthetic and functional units, and the rule of thirds (Fig 14-4).

Before reconstruction, an accurate assessment and diagnosis of the defect must be made. All the options for reconstruction can be considered, and the reconstruction can be individualized to best address the presenting problem. In each case, it is best to break down the reconstruction into the repair of each layer requiring reconstruction. Occasionally, when composite grafts or flaps are used, more than one layer can be reconstructed simultaneously.

In general, the best aesthetic results occur when the reconstruction is a one-stage procedure. The tissues are more pliable and easier to contour, but the risk of tissue loss and subsequent scar contracture can be high. Staged procedures, in which the lining and support are prefabricated into the future cutaneous coverage, have less risk of tissue loss and greater likelihood of preserving function, but they are not as aesthetically pleasing. The edema from the staged procedures is thought to affect the long-term aesthetic contours of the reconstruction. With this in mind, we recommend that large defects be reconstructed in a staged fashion and small defects be closed in a single stage. If the patient has residual tumor in the area of the defect, is unreliable, or is unable to provide consent, neither autogenous reconstruction nor osseointegrated reconstruction is indicated. The patient probably is served best by a conventional glued-on prosthesis in this case. If the patient's general health does not permit autogenous reconstruction or the patient cannot tolerate the donor sites, does not want to have the procedure done, or has no donor sites for autogenous tissue, an osseointegrated reconstruction becomes the choice.

Autogenous Nasal Reconstruction

Cutaneous Coverage

The majority of nasal defects involve only the skin. The proximal two-thirds of the nose is covered by thin mobile skin with a limited number of sebaceous glands. The skin on the distal one-third of the nose is thick and relatively nonmobile, with an abundance of sebaceous glands. These characteristics make the distal one-third of the nose technically difficult to reconstruct.

Full-Thickness Skin Graft. Full-thickness skin graft (FTSG) from the postauricular or preauricular region is ideal for reconstruction of the proximal two-thirds of the nose because the color and texture are similar. These grafts are poor for the lower one-third because they are often too thin and a depressed scar results. Distal one-third defects usually are repaired best with flaps. FTSGs from the nasolabial region have been used, but the donor scar may be suboptimal. González-Ulloa[21] measured the skin thickness of the nasal dorsum and lobule and compared it with the skin of the postauricular, supraclavicular, submental, and nasolabial region. The dorsal skin was similar in thickness to the postauricular and supraclavicular skin, whereas the lobule was similar to the submental skin.

FTSG with some attached subcutaneous fat can be used sometimes in the thicker skinned, lower one-third of the nose to minimize a depressed scar.

Composite Grafts. Small defects of the nostril margin may be repaired with auricular composite grafts. These grafts were described initially by Konig[25] in 1902 and popularized by Gillies.[26] The helical margin is the most commonly used composite graft, although Argamaso[27] advocated the root of the helix. Rees et al[28] obtained better than 94% survival in chondrocutaneous grafts cooled 5° to 10°C. The largest graft that survived was 2.8 × 3.0 cm. We recommend that composite grafts be no larger than 1.5 cm and the raw surface interface be maximized to enhance survival. There is always some atrophy of these composite grafts, and it is advisable to make these grafts 10% larger to allow for this.

Local Nasal Flaps. Various local flaps have been described for nasal reconstruction using adjacent tissue or proximal nasal tissue.

Banner Flap. Elliott[29] introduced the banner flap in 1969. This flap is made of a transverse triangular flap of skin that is rotated from the nasal dorsum adjacent to the defect. Masson and Mendelson[30] placed the banner flap on the side opposite the nasal defect. This effectively lengthened the flap reach and helped achieve symmetry of the reconstruction by elevating both nostrils slightly. This flap can be used to close defects less than or equal to 2.5 cm.

Bilobed Flap. This flap is designed by rotating a flap of skin three-quarters the size of the primary defect no more than 90° into the wound. A second flap one-half the size of the primary flap is rotated into the initial donor site. The second donor site is closed in a linear fashion. The bilobed flap is ideal for nasal tip defects no greater than 2.5 cm (Fig 14-5).

Glabellar Flap. Because the glabella skin is lax, the glabellar flap transfers skin easily onto the root and upper one-half of the nose (Fig 14-6).

Axial Frontonasal Flap. The axial frontonasal flap (Miter flap) is a modification of the Rieger flap.[31] Marchac and Toth[32] concluded that this flap was an axial flap based on a branch of the angular artery. The flap consists of an inverted V incision that extends along the nasal facial crease to the tip defect. The incision continues superiorly along the contralateral nasal facial crease. The donor site often is modified with a Burow's triangle in an attempt to equalize the two sides of a Y closure.

V-Y Advancement and Extended V-Y Advancement Flaps. The V-Y advancement and extended V-Y advancement flaps are based on the transverse branch of the angular artery and are used to reconstruct lateral nasal defects (Fig 14-7). The basic design of the V-Y flap is a flap length that is 1½ times the longitudinal diameter of the defect. The long axis is in the direction of maximal mobility. Distal nasal defects of the lateral region ideally are closed by sliding a myocutaneous flap from the upper alar crease. The standard V-Y flap from the alar crease region can be advanced approximately 1.25 cm and is effective in defects no larger than 2 cm. The extended V-Y flap differs from the standard V-Y flap in width. A limb of the extended V-Y flap passes along the side of the defect at approximately the same distance as the width of the defect. This extension is rotated down into the open wound covering the distal end of the defect (Fig 14-8).

Even though most of the tissue in the V-Y flap comes from the upper part of the nasolabial area, the flap is designed so that after transfer the flap lies within the nasal subunit with the "Y" closure along the upper nasolabial fold. This avoids a flap that straddles the nose-cheek subunit, which is unsightly. The mobility of the V-Y flap comes from the more mobile skin above the lateral aspect of the ala cartilage, extending into the nasolabial fold. The V-Y flap should not compromise the alar base but advance and rotate around the relatively immobile ala, pre-

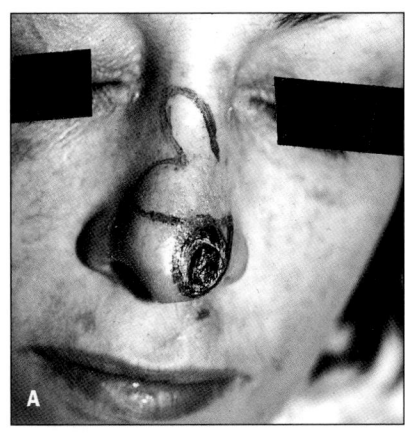
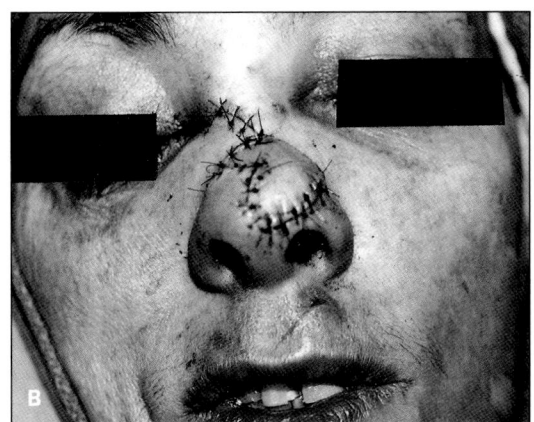
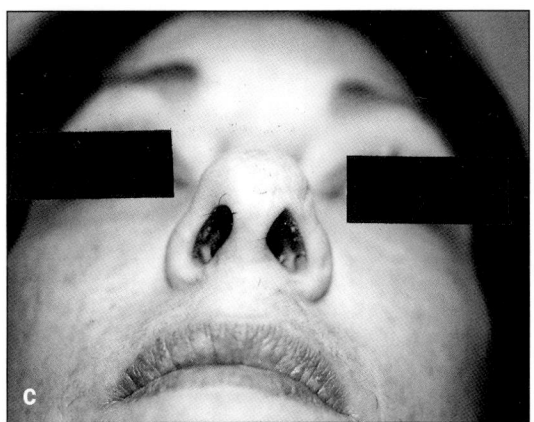
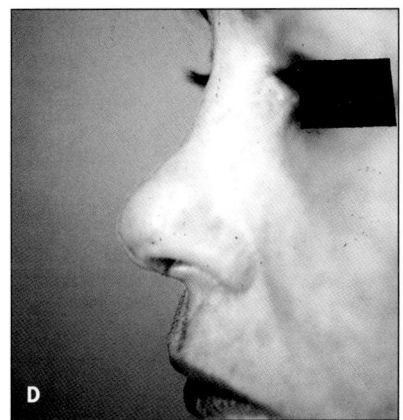

Fig 14-5. *A*, Post–traumatic alar defect reconstruction with a bilobed flap. *B*, Immediate postoperative view. *C* and *D*, Postoperative views at 3 months.

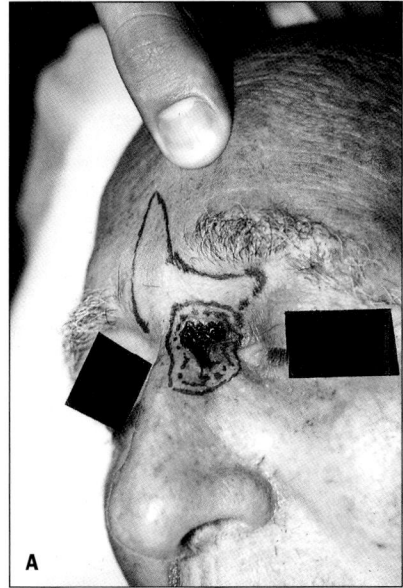
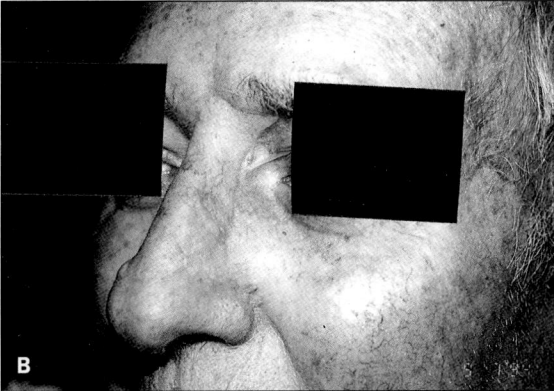

Fig 14-6. *A*, Bilobed glabella and upper eyelid flap used for reconstruction of an upper nasal and medial canthal defect after excision of a basal cell cancer. *B*, Postoperative view at 3 months.

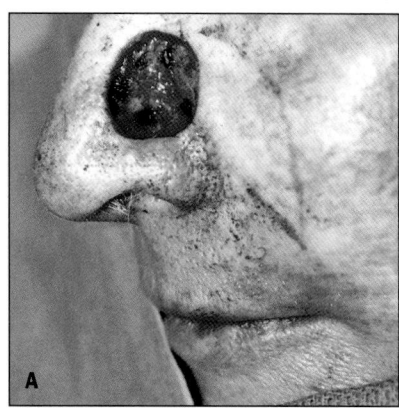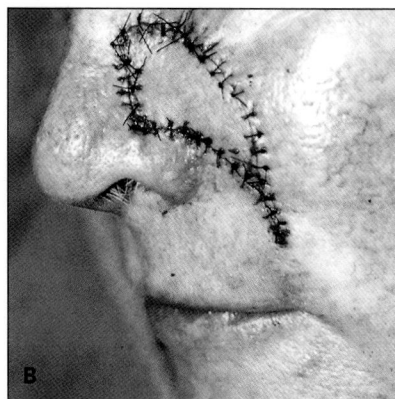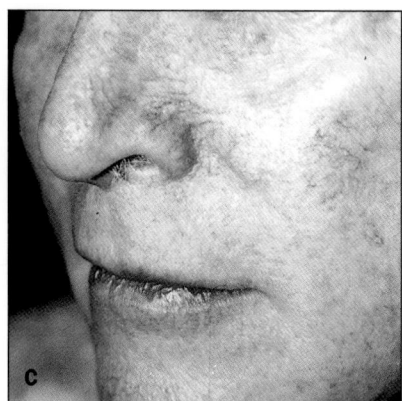

Fig 14-7. *A*, V-Y flap designed in the upper nasolabial area for reconstruction of the lateral nasal defect after excision of a basal cell cancer. *B*, Immediate postoperative view. *C*, Postoperative view at 6 months.

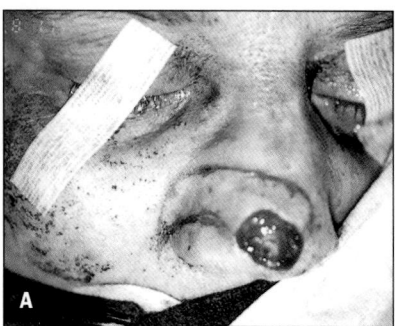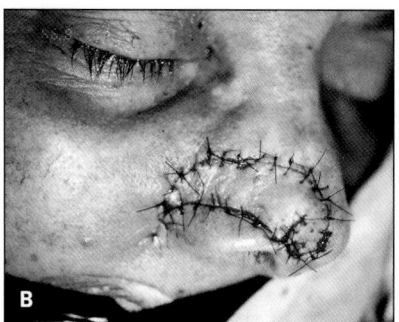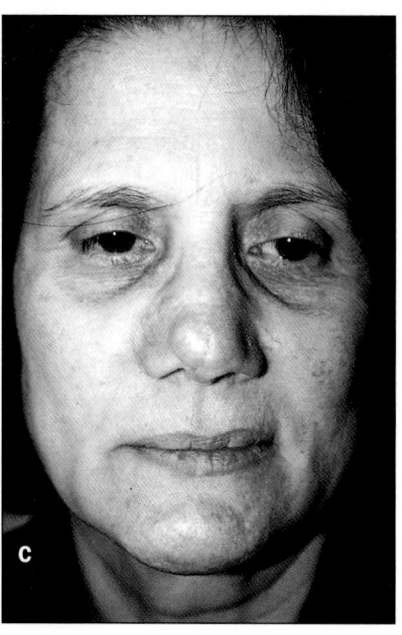

Fig 14-8. *A*, Patient with anterior alar defect after excision of a recurrent basal cell cancer, and design of an extended V-Y flap. *B*, Immediate postoperative view. *C*, Postoperative view at 6 months.

venting distortion to this important anatomic landmark.[33] V-Y flaps may also be used to reconstruct nasal tip defects with the flap based on the soft tissue and anterior septal artery between the medial crura of the alar cartilages (Fig 14-9). Another useful application of a V-Y flap is in the upper nasal area adjacent to the medial canthus, where a transverse V-Y flap may be used (Fig 14-10).

Cheek Advancement Flap. The cheek advancement flap often is used to repair defects up to 2.5 cm in the lateral nasal region. This is an ideal flap for the elderly patient with increased skin laxity. Skin from the paranasal and cheek area is advanced into the defect site after an incision is made along the proximal alar crease and nasolabial fold. The defect is closed in a linear fashion. The disadvantage of this flap is that the boundary between the lateral nasal wall and cheek has to be re-created in a second procedure.[34]

Nasolabial Flap. Dieffenbach[5] and other German surgeons were the first to popularize the nasolabial flap. The flap is designed off of the redundant skin of the nasolabial fold. The anterior facial and angular arteries send perforators through the levator labii muscle. These myocutaneous perforators provide the blood supply to the nasolabial flaps. The superiorly based flaps derive their blood supply largely from the angular artery perforators and the inferiorly based flaps from the anterior facial artery perfora-

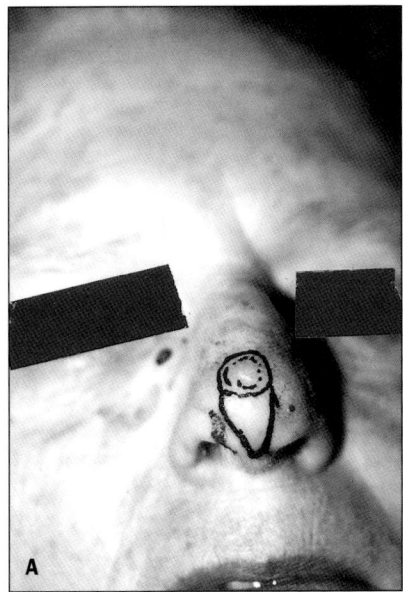

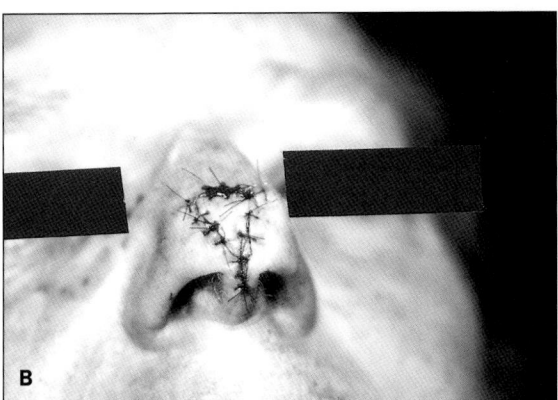

Fig 14-9. *A,* V-Y flap based on the septal vessels with the subcutaneous base between the medial crura of the alar cartilage. *B,* Immediate postoperative view.

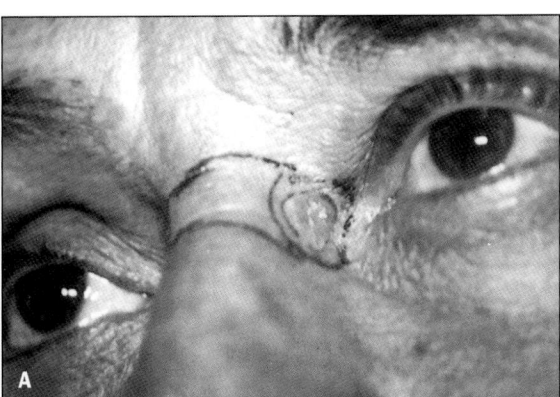

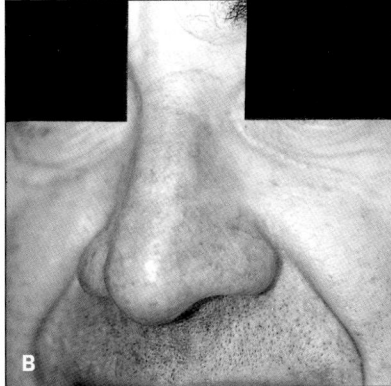

Fig 14-10. *A,* Transverse V-Y flap advanced across the nasal bridge for reconstruction of the medial canthal defect. *B,* Postoperative view at 1 year.

tors. The infraorbital artery sends perforators to the subcutaneous plexus of the cheek, and these perforators may be incorporated into the nasolabial island flaps. The nasolabial flap is one of the most commonly used flaps and can be designed as a transposition flap, island flap, or turnover flap.[35]

The nasolabial transposition flap is the basic standard for lateral nasal defects on or near the ala region (Fig 14-11). This flap commonly requires a two-stage procedure. Initially, the flap is elevated in a subcutaneous plane and transposed into the defect

site of 2.5 cm or less. Later, the pedicle is divided and the flap inset.

The advantages of the nasolabial flap are obvious. The flap is easy to raise, the scar is easily concealed in the nasolabial crease, and the flap has a good color match. The disadvantages of the nasolabial flap are that the flap often crosses the aesthetic subunits and, with its subcutaneous component, is thicker than nasal skin. Furthermore, a secondary procedure is needed to correct the bulge at the pivot point and to insert the flap.

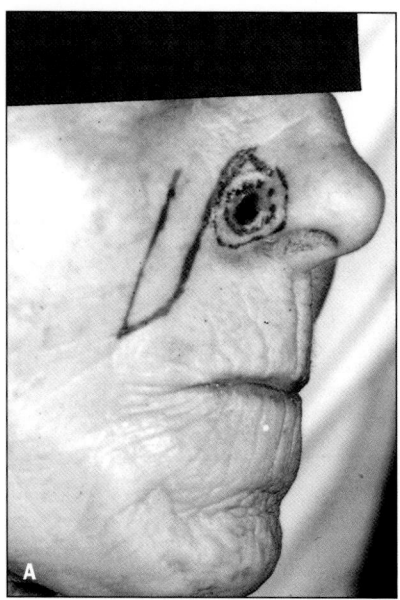
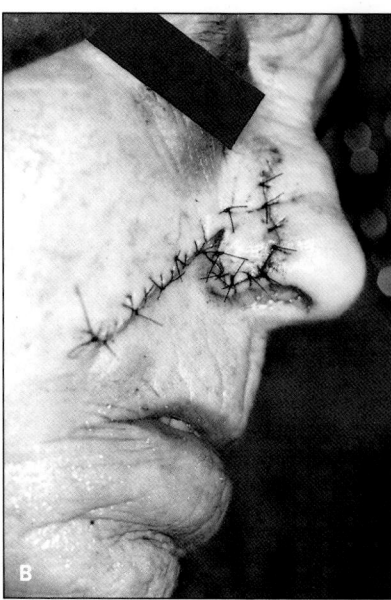

Fig 14-11. *A,* Superiorly based nasolabial flap used to reconstruct alar defect after excision of a basal cell carcinoma. *B,* Immediate postoperative view.

The nasolabial island flap is used primarily for reconstruction of the lateral nasal region above the ala; it is elevated from the nasolabial crease and pedicled on the subcutaneous tissue. The donor site is closed in a linear fashion. When the flap is used for lateral nasal defects above the ala, a disadvantage is postoperative contracture leading to pincushioning.

The nasolabial turnover flap is ideal for the repair of full-thickness defects of the ala. A superior-based subcutaneous flap is elevated to the level of the piriform aperture. The flap is rotated into the defect and rolled on itself so that both an inner lining and an external cover are formed. The donor site is closed in a linear fashion. The base of the flap should not be narrower than 1 cm, and the length of the flap should not exceed 6 cm. A second procedure is usually required for definitive inset.[35]

Regional Flaps

Forehead Flaps. 1) Midline forehead flap. The midline forehead flap has undergone several changes since its origin in ancient India. The flap initially was designed so a portion of skin from the central forehead region could be elevated in a subcutaneous plane and rotated down to the nasal tip. Although the base of the flap can be divided at 2 weeks, many surgeons prefer to perform some refinements and modifications, such as thinning or sculpting of the distal part of the flap before pedicle division and inset. The flap's vascular supply can be based on the supratrochlear or the supraorbital vessels. Millard[9] showed that a flap donor site of 3 cm could be closed primarily if the galea was scored and the surrounding skin was undermined. Although techniques have been described for defects > 3 cm, if a linear closure is not possible, healing by secondary intention is recommended.[13,36,37]

The classic midline forehead flap requires a forehead height of at least 7.5 cm if the nasal tip is to be addressed. A modification of this flap, called the "extended midline forehead flap," requires curving the flap along the hairline to achieve increased length.[35] The site is closed in a linear fashion. If closure is not possible with undermining and galea scoring, a relaxing incision can be made in the hair-bearing scalp. Another means of increasing length requires a portion of hair-bearing scalp be rotated down with the forehead skin[38] (Fig 14-12).

2) Skin expansion and the forehead flap. Tissue expansion has been used to overcome the difficulties of insufficient skin when a large forehead flap has been required.[39,40] Manders et al[39] showed that a midline forehead flap measuring up to 7.5 cm in width can be taken and the donor site closed in a linear fashion when tissue expansion has been done.

A major potential problem of expanded skin flaps is an unpredictable contracture of the reconstructed nasal skin, which can detract from the final aesthetic result.

3) Gull-winged flap. Millard developed a gull-winged flap as a modification of the midline fore-

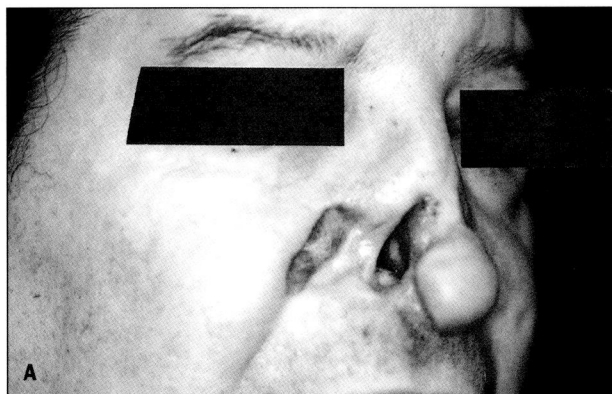

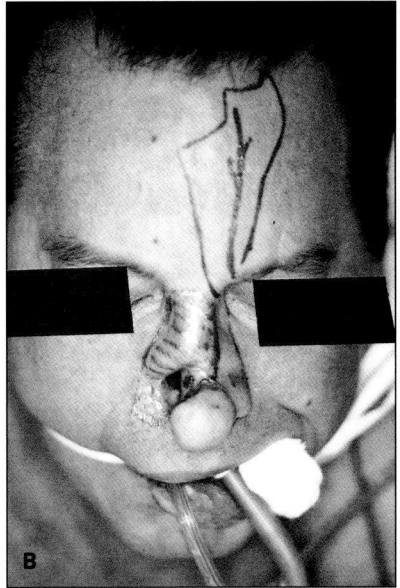

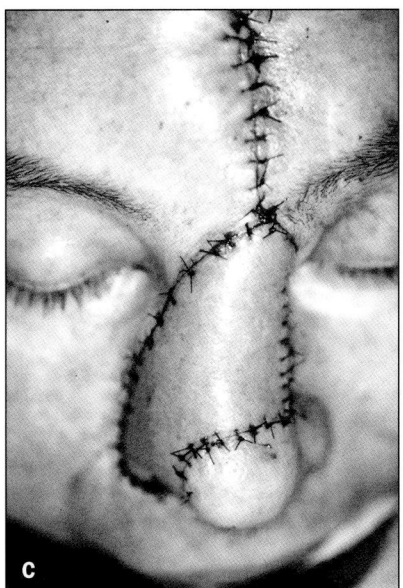

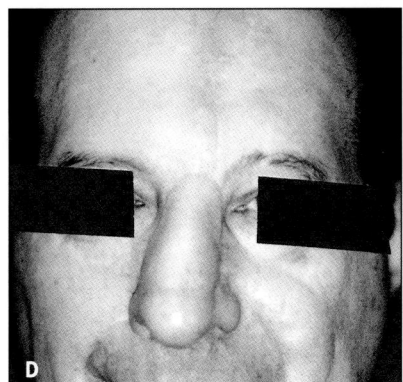

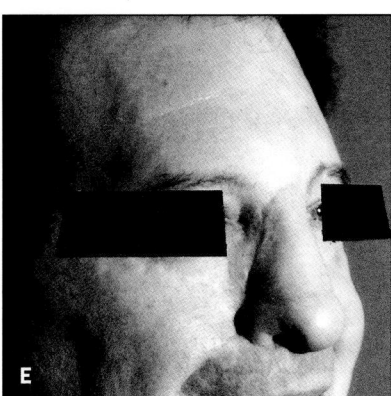

Fig 14-12. *A,* Patient with complex defect to the right side of the nose after a granuloma treatment. *B,* Intraoperative design of a forehead flap for heminasal reconstruction (lining was made with a local turn-in flap). *C,* Immediate postoperative view. *D* and *E,* After inset and one revision to define the alar crease.

head flap. A gull-winged flap was designed to allow better reconstruction of the nasal tip-alar base regions. The wings of the flap, which are used to make the ala, are made in the horizontal plane of the forehead. These wings form a cross with the vertical portion of the flap, and their donor site defect can be camouflaged into the natural skin creases of the forehead. Millard[41] allowed the donor site to granulate if a linear closure was not possible. Goldwyn and Rueckert[42] and others also advocated

healing by secondary intention and reported acceptable cosmetic results.

Millard[41] further modified the midline forehead flap by decreasing the initial skin pedicle to no more than 2.5 cm in width and at the time of division leaving the neurovascular pedicle intact. The result is a more defined narrow flap with less edema in the reconstructed nose after division and inset. Millard also advocated skin grafting to the underside of the forehead flap for lining.

4) Up-and-down flap. This rarely used flap was designed to overcome the initial problem of length with the midline forehead flap. The flap is a forehead flap that extends up into the scalp and then descends into the forehead. This technique allowed increased length so the nasal tip and columella could be reconstructed.[10] The problems with this flap were that the donor site could not be closed in a linear fashion and the poor vascularity of the distal part of the flap.

5) Scalping flap. Converse[43] presented the scalping flap as a modification of Gillies' up-and-down flap. This flap has three distinct advantages: 1) the majority of the incision line is placed in the hairline; 2) the permanent defect is left over the less obvious lateral aspect of the forehead; and 3) the flap has greater size and mobility than the midline forehead flap, which allows it to be rolled and tubed on itself more easily.

Initially, a pattern of the defect is made, and this is then drawn on the lateral aspect of the forehead. A coronal incision is made just behind the superficial temporal artery and extends across the midline. After crossing the midline, the incision curves downward past the scalp onto the lateral forehead region. Over the lateral forehead region a skin paddle is elevated, and the frontalis muscle is preserved. This facilitates graft take and ensures postoperative facial expression will be present in the grafted donor site. Once the skin paddle is elevated and the galea is reached, the galea is cut transversely 2 cm from the frontalis-galea junction. The dissection continues in the subgalea plane, elevating the galea and the frontalis muscle of the entire forehead except the skin paddle site. The flap is rotated into position and tubed on itself if warranted. The forehead donor site is covered with an FTSG from the retroauricular region. The temporary scalp defect is covered with a moist nonadhesive dressing. After 2 weeks, the skin paddle is divided and the remaining forehead skin and scalp are rotated back into their original position.[43]

Tempororetroauricular Flap. In 1926, Hunt[44] described the temporomastoid flap. Later, Washio[45] studied in detail the vascular supply to this tempororetroauricular flap and stated that the flap is based on the superficial temporal artery and its connecting vascular loop with the postauricular artery. Washio advocated this flap for ala reconstruction. Orticochea[46] described the use of bilateral Washio-type flaps for total nasal reconstruction.

A pedicle of 6 cm is marked in the preauricular region, starting just anterior to the helical root and extending upward slightly off vertical. From the superior aspect of the pedicle, an incision is made in a semicircular fashion, ending in the retroauricular region cephalad to the lobule. The skin and temporoparietal fascia are elevated as a unit off of the retroauricular region and rotated to the nasal defect. A portion of conchal cartilage can be taken with the fasciocutaneous flap if warranted for reconstruction. The donor site is covered with moist nonadhesive dressings, and after 14 days the pedicle is divided. The remaining soft tissue is rotated back into the original donor site.

Maillard and Montandon,[47] in their comprehensive account of this flap, described several advantages: 1) hairless thin auricular and thick mastoid skin for nasal reconstruction, 2) auricular cartilage availability for support reconstruction of the nose, and 3) no visible scars at the donor site when viewing the face. However, blood supply is random and may be insufficient, compromising the reconstruction.

Free Tissue Transfer. Head and neck donor site scars and lack of tissue have been the major problems with using local or regional tissue for nasal reconstruction. These disadvantages potentially are addressed by free tissue transfer, but with the benefits of free tissue transfer come the challenges as well. Ideal color match, skin thickness, and contouring are difficult to achieve.

Radial Forearm Free Flap. The radial forearm flap is based on the radial artery. The vascular pedicle can be as long as 10 cm. Before harvesting the flap, Allen's test is performed to ensure good vascular supply to the hand via the ulnar artery. The radial forearm flap can be harvested with a portion of the radius for nasal support. Baudet et al[48] and Costa et al[49] described separately a two-stage procedure in which they prelined a radial forearm flap with cartilage grafts and skin grafts to fashion a multilaminated flap. Silastic tubes were positioned to support the future nostrils, and 3 weeks later this composite free flap was transferred to the face for a total nasal reconstruction.[49]

Pribaz and Fine[50] described a case in which skin on the inner aspect of the arm was neovascularized by the insertion of a vascular pedicle supplying the latissimus dorsi and serratus anterior muscles to prefabricate a nose and forehead composite unit. After transfer of the prefabricated flap, the forehead component survived completely, while the distal part of the nasal reconstruction necrosed. They subsequently prelaminated a radial forearm flap, as described by Baudet et al[48] and Costa et al,[49] and used this for the nasal reconstruction[50] (Fig 14-13).

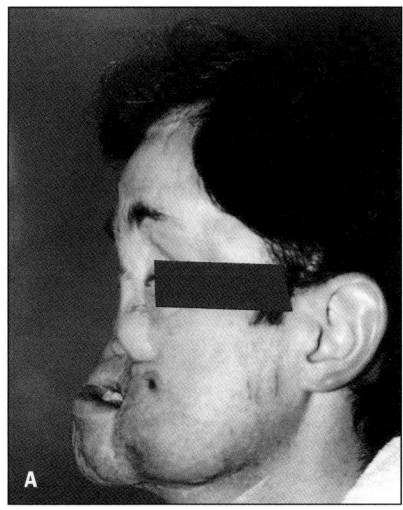

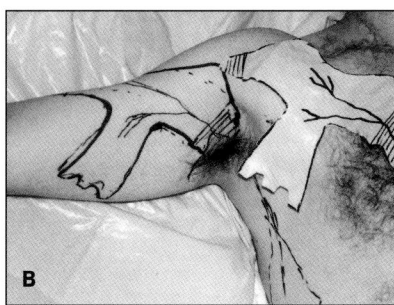

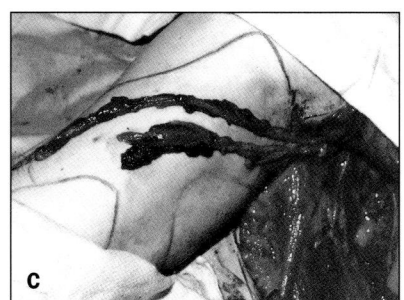

Fig 14-13. *A,* Patient with an absent nose and unstable forehead skin after a gunshot wound. *B,* Design of a prefabricated flap on the inner aspect of the right upper arm. *C,* Latissimus dorsi and serratus anterior vascular pedicle implanted beneath the inner arm skin. *D,* Six weeks later the prefabricated flap is raised and microsurgically transferred to reconstruct the nose and forehead. *E,* The distal part of the nasal flap necrosed. *F,* A prelaminated flap is prepared on the right forearm based on the radial vessels. *G,* The prelaminated flap has been prelined with skin grafts and cartilage grafts for distal nasal reconstruction. *H,* Postoperative view at 6 months. (From Pribaz and Fine.[50] By permission of John Wiley & Sons.)

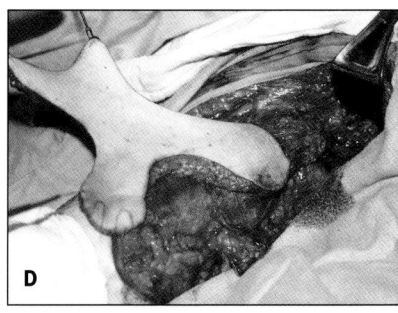

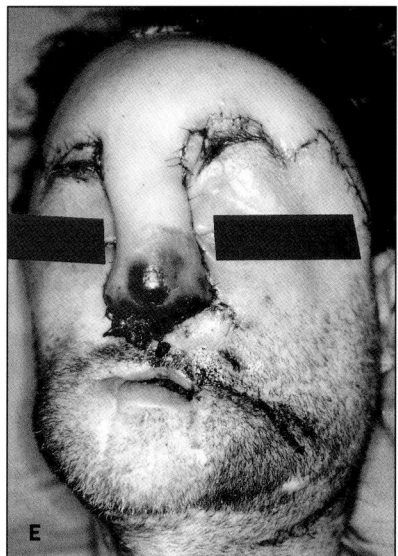

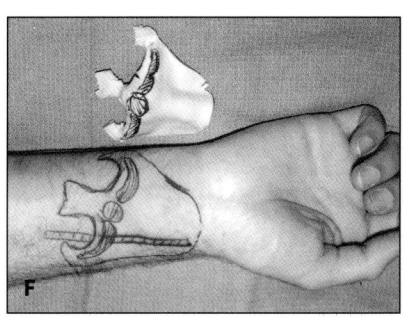

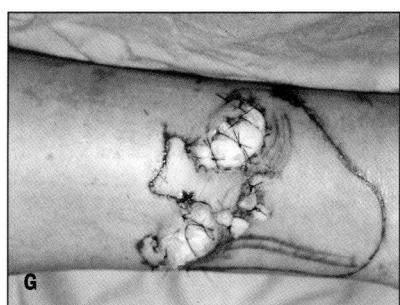

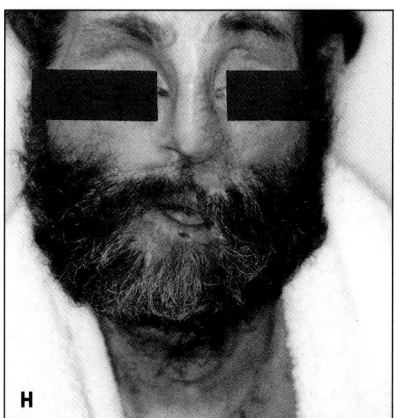

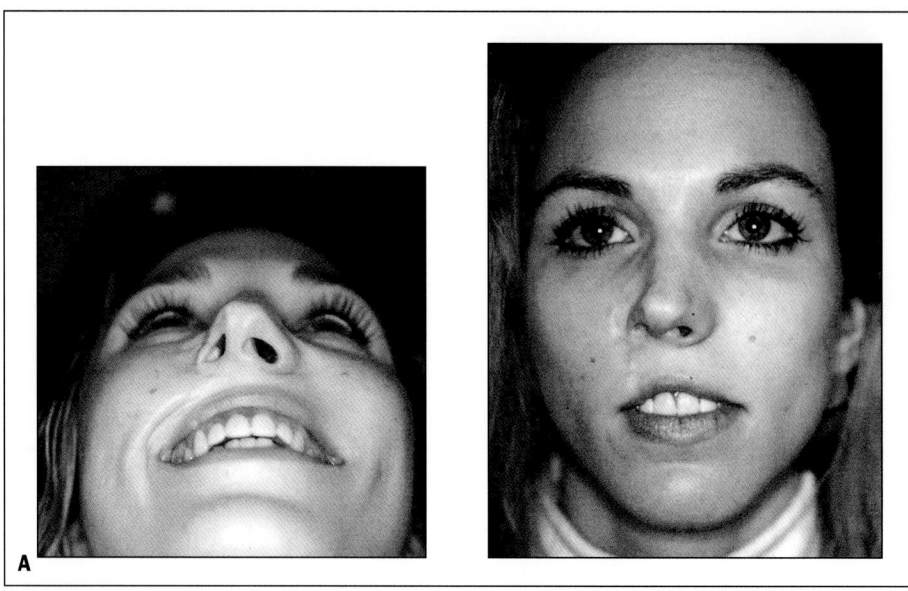

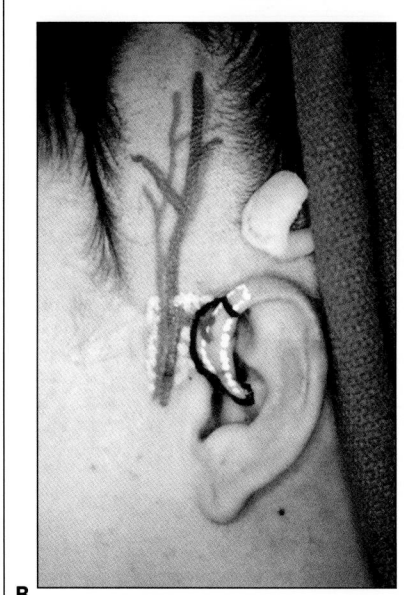

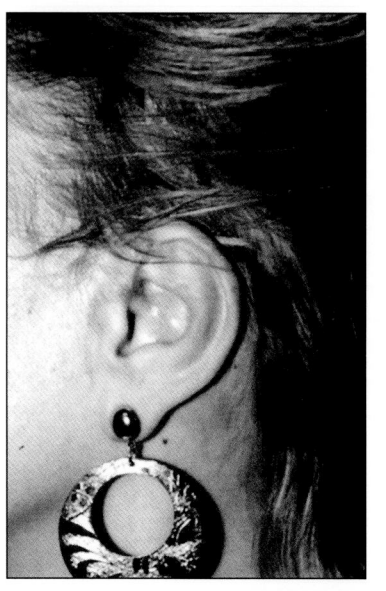

Fig 14-14. *A,* Patient with a right distal heminasal defect after a previous excision of a sarcoma and multiple failed reconstruction efforts. *B,* Design of auricular free flap from the left ear to reconstruct the alar and nostril sill. On the right, at long-term follow-up: the appearance of the ear after the flap harvest. *C,* Immediate and long-term results of the nose (inferior view). *D,* Long-term result (anterior and lateral views). (*A, B,* and *C* from Pribaz and Falco.[18] By permission of Lippincott-Raven Publishers.)

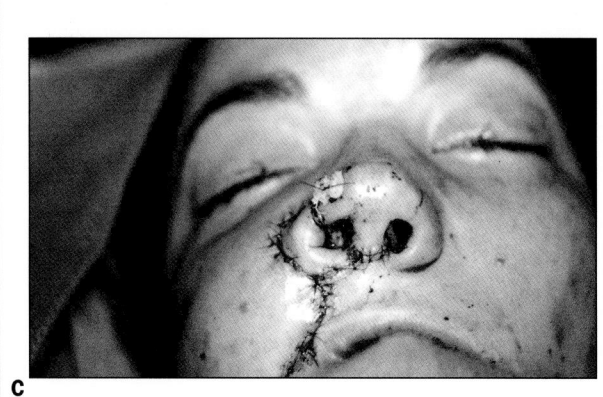

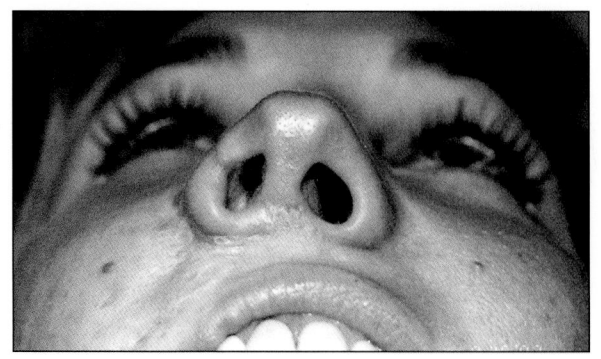

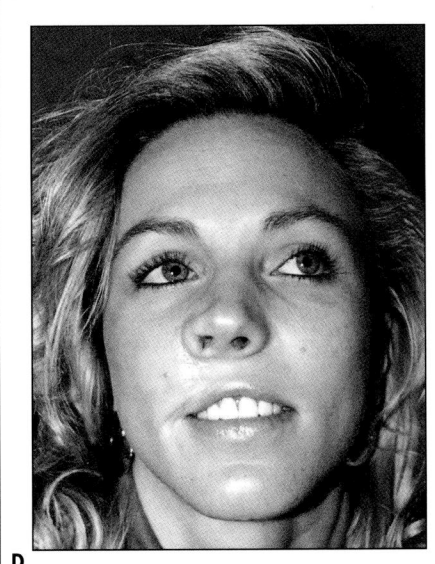
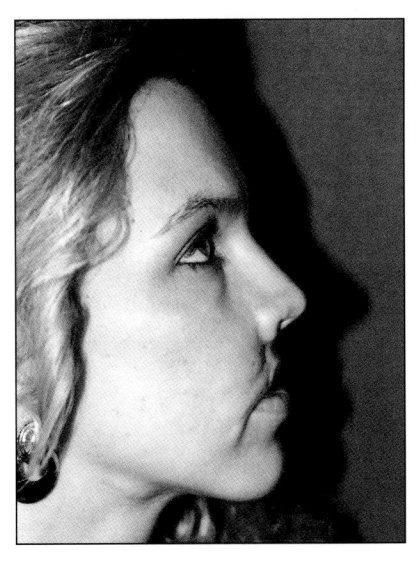

Dorsalis Pedis Free Flap. This flap based on the dorsalis pedis can be taken as an osseocutaneous tissue transfer. The flap's skin is thin and pliable. The disadvantages are the durability of the donor site skin graft and the potential decreased vascular supply to the foot.[16,17]

Postauricular Free Flap. Swartz[17] popularized the microvascular version of the Washio flap. In this case, the multistage component of the Washio flap is eliminated.

Auricular Free Flap. The auricular free flap is based on consistent branches of the superficial temporal artery, which supply the upper one-half of the ear. The ascending helix of the ear is composed of cartilage bound on each side with skin. This laminated flap is anatomically similar to the nostril rim and is ideal for lobule reconstruction. Pribaz and Falco[18] described using this flap for distal heminasal reconstruction, enabling the surgeon to reconstruct the nasal tip, columella, sill, and ala. The disadvantage of this flap is its lack of size. A 3 × 3-cm region of tissue can be transferred without distorting the remaining helix. The advantages are color match, contour, and ability to gain lining, support, and external coverage (Fig 14-14).

Lining and Support

To achieve the aesthetic functional nose requires the reconstruction of the lining and support as well as the cutaneous coverage. Once the soft tissues collapse as a result of scarring from poor support and lining, regaining aesthetics and function is nearly impossible.

Many extensive nasal defects commonly involve not only the lining of the nasal vault but also the other deeper functional components (i.e., turbinates, septum, posterior nasal valves). Maintaining an adequate airway, maintaining sinus drainage, preventing obstructive synechia, and providing a moisturized environment should be attempted. The efficacy of these functional aspects of nasal reconstruction depends directly on the quality of nasal lining and adequacy of the nasal support. There are many common problems in nasal lining and support reconstruction that can result from poor preoperative planning. Bulky flaps lead to obstruction. Inadequate support leads to nasal collapse and airway obstruction. Skin flaps and grafts used for nasal lining leave the nose dry. Currently in total nasal reconstruction, only the anterior septum supporting the nasal framework generally is reconstructed, leaving a unichambered nose. Lining this cavity with mucosa to moisturize the air is desirable for adequate airway function and olfaction.

For many years, nasal reconstruction focused on obtaining an aesthetically pleasing nose, with minimal regard for nasal function. We believe that it is important to evaluate the deeper functional subunits and reconstruct these as needed. These deep subunits, which are vital to the function of the nose (middle turbinate, middle meatus, superior turbinate, posterior nasal valve, and posterior septum), can be addressed by standard septoplasty and endoscopic techniques. The

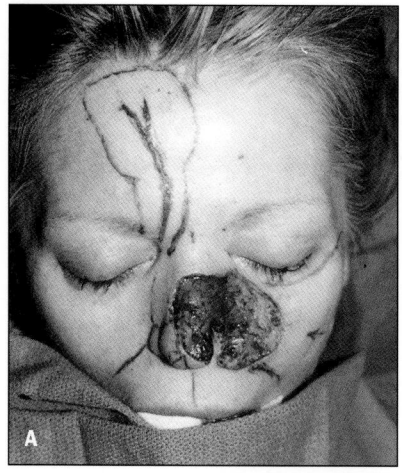
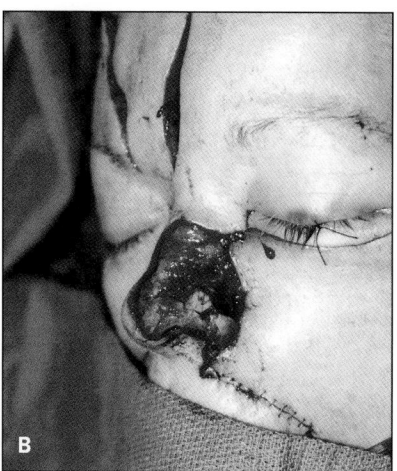
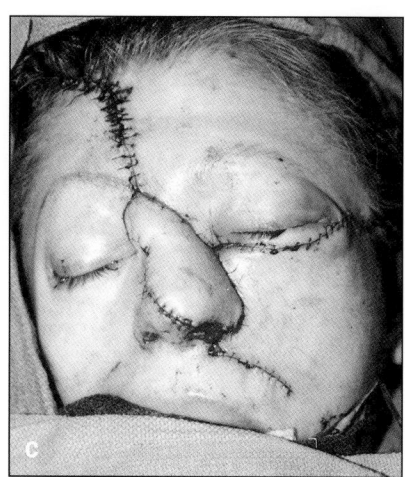
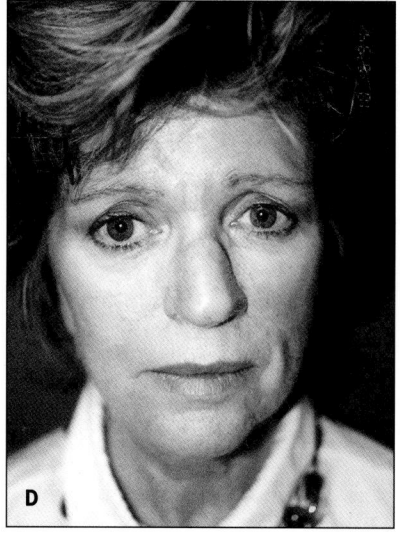
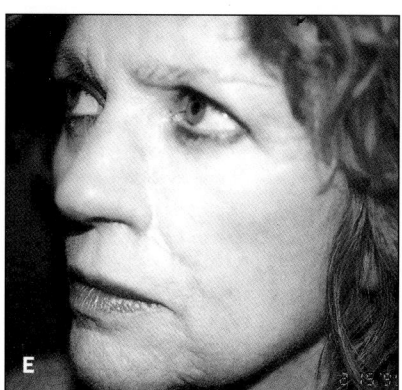

Fig 14-15. *A,* Nasal and cheek defect after Mohs' resection of a basal cell carcinoma. *B,* A cheek advancement flap has been advanced to the lateral aspect of the nose. A bipedicled mucosal flap has been used for nasal lining, and cartilage grafts have been sutured in place. *C,* After forehead flap closure. *D* and *E,* Long-term result after flap revision and inset.

middle and superior turbinates should be positioned off of the septum. Lateral nasal splints, which prevent adhesions from developing from the turbinates and the septum, should be used where indicated. The adjacent sinuses also are important for nasal function, and adequate drainage must be maintained. The middle meatus is the drainage pathway for frontal, maxillary, and ethmoid sinuses. The middle meatus may be preserved by placing Gelfilm in the meatus as the mucosa heals. This Gelfilm is removed if still present 7 to 10 days postreconstruction. Endoscopic or direct visualization of the nasal cavity allows the posterior

nasal valve to be monitored. The most common post-traumatic form of obstruction in this region is from a deviated posterior nasal septum, which if identified can be corrected easily by standard septoplasty techniques.

Support. Autogenous bone and cartilage are the mainstays of support material used in nasal reconstruction. More cartilage or bone is needed in the reconstructed nose than in the normal nose to overcome the contractile forces of the overlying soft tissues. The pyramid concept of the nose must be addressed when planning the support reconstruction (new support material often needs to be placed in positions not found in the original nose to support the new sidewalls, tip, or ala) (Fig 14-15).

Cantilever Graft. Cantilever bone grafts for midline support are designed such that the bone or cartilage is fixed to the frontal or nasal bones. If the bone is not fixed, a small notch in the frontal bone should be considered to lock the graft in place. The graft extends to the nasal tip, with either a perpendicular graft extending to the nasal spine (L strut) or no further underlying support. Many authors have advocated the use of autogenous bone for nasal reconstruction.[51-57] Bone from the iliac crest, tibia, rib, and calvaria has been described. Jackson et al[56] presented the results of 25 patients in whom calvarial bone was used in nasal reconstruction. They found there was minimal resorption and the contour was superior. The graft is taken as a split calvarial bone graft from the parietal region. Chait et al[57] thought the nasal support is best addressed by using osteochondral rib graft. Their work suggests that cartilage used to reconstruct the caudal support (perpendicular portion of the graft) below the tip allows the lobule reconstruction to be more pliable and natural. Only 1 of 25 patients developed long-term warping of the cartilage. Iliac bone graft for nasal support and contour is not as easily shaped and defined as other grafts, but when large amounts of bone are required, it becomes a viable option.

Hinged Septal Flap. In the hinged septal flap technique, an L strut is cut out of the remaining septum. The strut is left attached at the caudal aspect of the nasal bones and is hinged upward from this point. The short end of the L strut is sutured to the nasal spine.[35,41]

Lining. Reconstruction of the nasal lining is essential in re-creating a functional nose. Flaps and grafts containing keratinized squamous epithelium have been the main form of reconstruction in the past, but flaps and grafts of nonkeratinized pseudostratified epithelium (mucosa) are becoming more popular. The basic tenets of nasal lining we subscribe to are as follows. Each functional subunit needs to be addressed in the reconstructive plan. The mucosa of the nose is best reconstructed with like tissue. The primary functional goal should be airway patency and drainage followed by olfaction.

Turn-In Nasal Flaps. The turn-in flap is formed by using the skin adjacent to the defect. This flap is applicable in the established deformity and not in the acute setting. The skin flap is based on the healed scar at the defect margin. It is hinged on the edge of the wound and flipped over to line the defect cavity with squamous epithelium (Fig 14-12).

Folded Cutaneous Flaps. J.M. Delpech is credited with folding in forehead flap skin to cover and line the reconstructed nose.[35] Gillies[58] first described using nasolabial flaps for lining. This technique is hindered by the bulky nature and the lack of a moist lining.[35,59]

Skin and Cartilage Graft. Prelamination of forehead flaps before transfer can provide necessary lining. The undersurface of a forehead flap can be raised, and a skin graft or a composite graft can be placed. These composite grafts can be taken from the ear or nasal septum.[59] The conchal cartilage and retroauricular skin, anterior skin and helical rim cartilage, and conchal skin and vertical wall cartilage are options described by Barton.[60] Posterior septal mucosa and cartilage are valuable composite graft material if the anterior septum is intact.

Septal Pivot Flap. Burget and Menick[55] described an anteriorly based mucoperichondrial flap supplied by a septal branch of the superior labial artery. The flap is elevated off of the contralateral nasal mucosa and rotated forward as a mucosal cartilage graft. The hinge point is at the nasal spine, and a pedicle of 1.2 cm is required for survival. Once elevated and rotated, it can be turned to cover the inner surface of the lobule region or the entire undersurface of a dorsal graft.

Mucosal Advancement Flap. Mucosal advancement flaps can be rotated from the lateral wall and floor of the vestibule or the anterior septal mucosa (shortened version of the septal pivot flap). Septal branches of the superior labial artery supply both flaps. These flaps are ideal for covering small lining defects of the ala. The flap can be elevated as a bipedicled flap, a unilateral flap, or a contralateral flap that is passed through a septal orifice for contralateral coverage.[15] To prevent scar development around the anterior nasal valve, the mucosa should be left intact at the superior aspect of the valve (Fig 14-15).

Facial Artery Musculomucosal Flap. Pribaz developed the facial artery musculomucosal flap, which is based off of the facial artery. This flap is a mus-

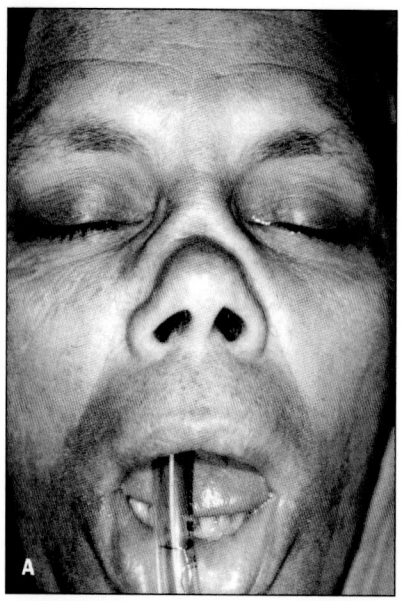

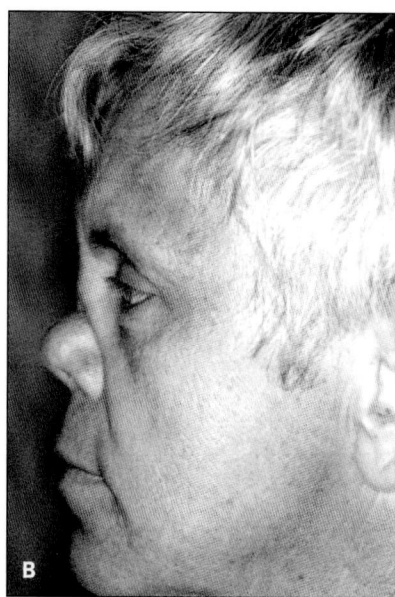

Fig 14-16. *A* and *B,* Patient with a nasal collapse due to Wegener's granulomatosis, with deficiency of nasal lining and support. *C,* Design of facial artery musculomucosal (FAMM) flap in left cheek. *D,* Bilateral FAMM flaps have been raised and placed into the nasal vestibule. *E,* Long-term appearance of a FAMM flap in the left nostril. *F,* Long-term appearance of the patient after restoration of adequate support with a cantilever bone and cartilage graft and bilateral FAMM flaps.

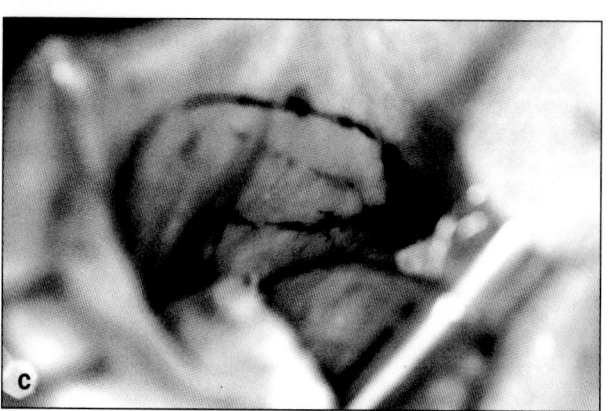

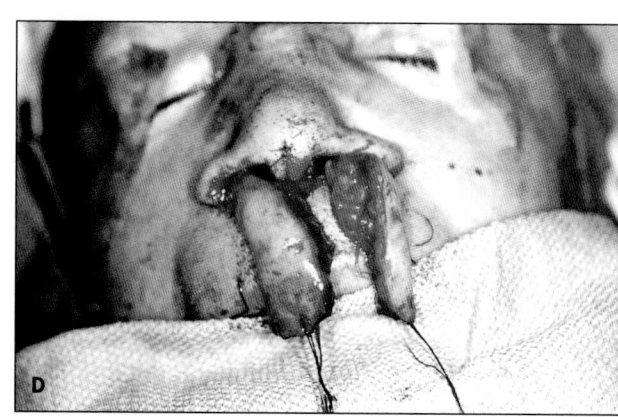

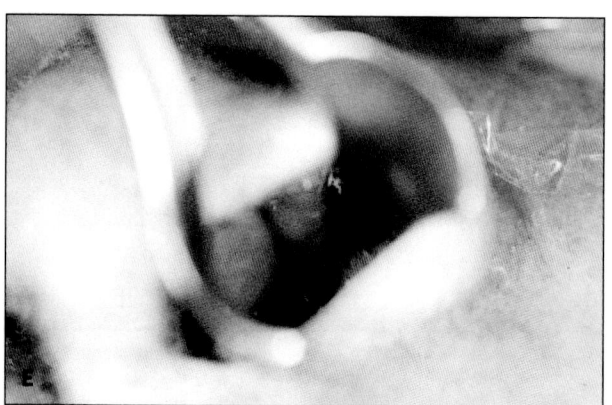

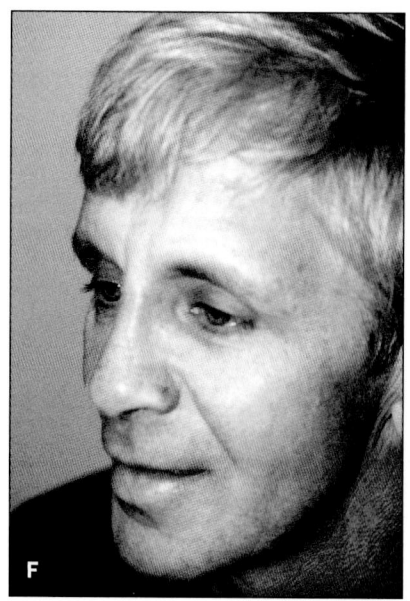

culomucosal flap that incorporates a segment of buccal mucosa and a small portion of the buccinator muscle. When this is based superiorly (retrograde flow), it can be used to reconstruct nasal lining.[61] Bilateral facial artery musculomucosal flaps may be needed for nasal lining in total nasal reconstruction. This flap is ideal for lining in patients with large defects because it replaces the nasal mucosa with a large amount of similar tissue[62] (Fig 14-16).

Nonautogenous Nasal Reconstruction

In 1969, Brånemark and collaborators published the first paper on osseointegrated implants for the attachment of dental bridges and teeth. To date, more than half a million patients have been treated according to the principles and techniques defined by Brånemark and others.[63-66]

In 1977, Tjellström started using osseointegrated implants for the attachments of hearing aids and later prostheses.[67-70] Osseointegration gained rapid acceptance in this area, and more than 3,000 patients have been treated to date. This work has also led to the development of better prosthetic devices with more detailed intrinsic anatomy as well as better interface with border tissues.

The goal of osseointegrated nasal reconstruction is stable osseointegration of a natural-looking nasal prosthesis with inconspicuous borders to the face.

Reconstructive Site

The preoperative assessment includes detailed radiographic analysis of the bones of the piriform aperture. In the total nasal defect, there is usually a sufficient amount of bone in the part of the maxilla that creates the inferior border of the piriform aperture. The same patient may or may not have a sufficient amount of bone for osseointegration in the naso-ethmoid area. If the nasal defect involves only the lower portion of the nose, one may accept only two osseointegrated implants inferiorly in the maxilla or do further resection of the remaining nose in the upper area to expose the nasal bones. The former alternative will not yield as stable integration as the latter.

If the defect involves more than the nose, special considerations will have to be made. If for instance part of the palate is missing, a palatal prosthesis can be attached at the same time. Similarly, if there is a need for a dental bridge in the upper jaw, the prosthesis may need to cover a portion of the face.

The quality of the bone varies from patient to patient, and it is sometimes necessary to place bone grafts to optimize the conditions for osseointegration of the implant. The soft-tissue anatomy of the area of the defect can be improved with flaps and grafts if necessary.[66]

Surgical Technique

Surgical procedures usually can be performed in a small outpatient operating room with local anesthesia and standard sterile procedures. If a bone graft or flap procedure is done at the same time, the operation is done in a larger operating room. It is preferable to use an operating table configured like a dental chair, with maximum flexibility in the positioning of the patient.

The planning of the procedure should be done in collaboration with the anaplastologist. It is important to carefully plan the placement of the implants and the abutments, so that the abutments and the connecting bar or magnets are concealed completely by the prosthesis. It is equally important that the components are placed so they will not cause pressure sores or erosions of the skin. The implants should be positioned to allow routine cleaning of the adjacent area.

The surgical principles are similar to the ones that govern the placement of the intraoral implants. Usually, there are scars in the areas where the implants are to be placed, and it is important that these scars are considered when the local flaps are being designed. Usually it is advisable to excise the scars narrowly to improve cosmesis and to increase the elasticity of the skin borders.

Stage I. The authors prefer to make incisions that pass through periosteum. The periosteum and skin are elevated together. The location of the implants is marked, and the actual placement of the implants is performed. A 4-mm flange implant usually is placed in the lower piriform aperture and 4-mm or 3-mm implants in the naso-ethmoid area. It is extremely important to use minimally traumatic technique, low-speed drilling, and copious irrigation. After placing the implants and the cover

Table 14-1 Cost of Surgery, Including Sales Tax, for Placement of Extraoral Implants (1989 Prices): Outer Ear or Nose

Item		Swedish krona*
Special drill equipment[†]		195
Personnel[†]		
Surgeon	45 min	180
Nurse	75 min	125
Assistant nurse	75 min	115
Materials[§]		
Implant + cover screw		4,280
Drill set and thread tap		510
Other: fixed costs		650
Total		6,055

*1989 exchange rate: 6.227 Swedish krona equaled US $1.00.

[†]The purchase cost of the equipment in 1988, according to Nobelpharma AB, was 80,000 Swedish krona, including sales tax. Life of 10 years, 11% internal interest. The annual number of implants is estimated at 200. The 1997 purchase cost, according to Nobel Biocare USA, Inc. (Westmont, IL) for drilling equipment, instrument set, and surgical items needed for implant placement is US $8,849.75. Additional cost for drills, implant (fixture), cover screw, and healing cap is US $1,241.25. These costs do not include prosthetic equipment, prosthetic instruments, or prosthetic materials, as discussed in Chapter 4.

[‡]Source: Anders Tjellström, University of Göteborg.

[§]Source: Nobelpharma AB.

Modified from Hallén et al.[64] By permission of The Swedish Council on Technology Assessment in Health Care.

Table 14-2 Cost of Surgery, Including Sales Tax, for Abutment Cylinders in Different Extraoral Applications (1989 Prices): Outer Ear or Nose

Item		Swedish krona*
Personnel[†]		
Surgeon	60 min	240
Nurse	90 min	150
Assistant nurse	90 min	135
Material[†]		
Skin-penetrating cylinders		2,346
Connection of hearing aid		
Other: fixed costs		650
Total		3,521

*1989 exchange rate: 6.227 Swedish krona equaled US $1.00.

[†]Source: Anders Tjellström, University of Göteborg.

[‡]Source: Nobelpharma AB.

Modified from Hallén et al.[64] By permission of The Swedish Council on Technology Assessment in Health Care.

Table 14-3 Cost, Including Sales Tax, of Production of Extraoral Prostheses (1989 Prices): Outer Ear or Nose*

	Swedish krona[†]	
Item	Initial production, including mold	Subsequent production
Material	3,000	800
Labor	5,229	2,900
Total	8,229	3,700

*Source: Anders Tjellström.

[†]1989 exchange rate: 6.227 Swedish krona equaled US $1.00.

Modified from Hallén et al.[64] By permission of The Swedish Council on Technology Assessment in Health Care.

screws, one must document their location in pictures and drawings to facilitate the second stage of the procedure. Some thinning of the flaps is done during this procedure, but the authors prefer to do the majority of the thinning in conjunction with the second stage.

Stage II. Approximately 3 months after the first stage, the second stage with the thinning of the flaps and the placement of the abutments is performed. The authors prefer simply to open the old incision and to expose the implants. Subsequently, the flaps are thinned and the wound is approximated loosely with a few temporary sutures. The holes for the penetration of the skin are created with a punch or a scalpel.

Subsequently, the temporary sutures are removed, the cover screws are removed, the abutments are placed, the skin flaps are replaced, and the incision is closed. Healing caps are applied, and a moderately compressive dressing is used to facilitate adherence of the flaps and to limit edema formation. The

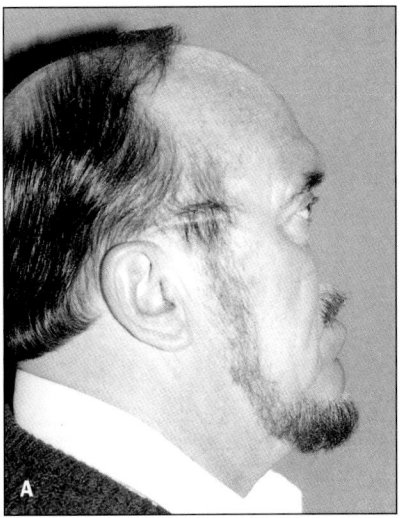
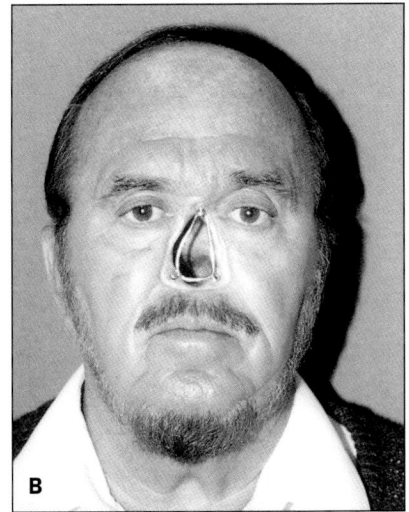
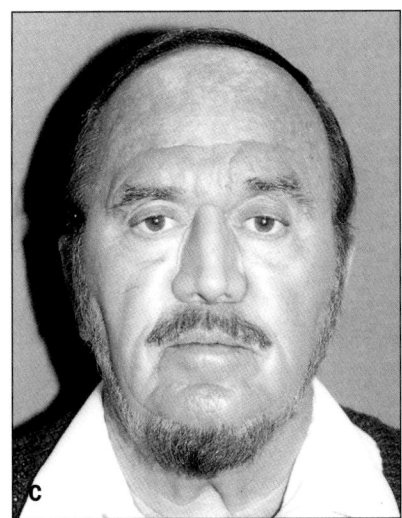

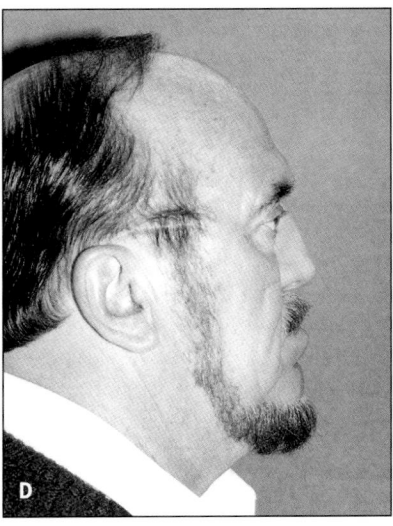

Fig 14-17. *A,* Patient with a total nasal loss after tumor excision. *B,* Osseointegrated implants and framework. *C,* Appearance with a nasal prosthesis (anterior view). *D,* Appearance with nasal prosthesis (lateral view). Fixation is stabilized by two implants.

wound is allowed approximately 2 weeks to heal before the prosthetic work is started. When determining the length of the abutments, measurements should be made such that the abutment extends approximately 3 mm above the skin.

Attachments

The anaplastologist usually makes the decision with the patient about using a metal bar to connect the abutments for a clip-on attachment or using individual magnets. In general, metal bars work better in the area of the nose. The bar has the additional advantage that it limits rotational forces on the implants. Once the metal bar or magnets have been placed, the work of attaching the prosthesis can be started.

Prosthetic Artwork

The details of this work are described in Chapter 19. The quality of the final appearance depends on the quality of the prosthetic work. Collaborate with the most interested and skilled anaplastologist available.

Outcomes

In general, patient satisfaction with these procedures is high. It is also relatively straightforward to care for the site of the skin penetration. In Tables 14-1 through 14-3, Tjellström and collaborators outlined the costs in Sweden.[64] Figure 14-17 illustrates a case of an osseointegrated nasal prosthesis.

References

1. Sushruta. Sushruta Samhita Based on Original Sanskrit Text. (English translation edited and published by Kaviraj Kunja Lal Bhishagratna.) Bose, Calcutta; 1907–1916.

2. Tagliocozzi G. De Curtorum Chirurgia per Insitionem. Venice: Gaspar Bindonus Jr; 1597.

3. McDowell F, Valone JA, Brown JB. Bibliography and historical note on plastic surgery of the nose. Plast Reconstr Surg 1952;10:149.

4. Carpue JC. An Account of Two Successful Operations for Restoring a Lost Nose from the Integuments of the Forehead. London: Longman, Hurst, Rees, Orme & Brown; 1816.

5. Dieffenbach JF. Die Operative Chirurgie. Leipzig: FA Brockhaus; 1845.

6. Warren JM. Rhinoplastic operations. Boston Med Surg J 1837;16:69.

7. Keegan DF. Rhinoplastic Operations, With a Description of Recent Improvements in the Indian Method. London: Ballière, Tindall and Cox; 1900.

8. Kazanjian VH. Treatment of nasal deformities, with special reference to nasal prostheses. JAMA 1925;84:177.

9. Millard DR Jr. Total reconstructive rhinoplasty and a missing link. Plast Reconstr Surg 1966;37:167.

10. Gillies HD. The development and scope of plastic surgery (The Charles H. Mayo Lectureship in Surgery). Bull Northwestern Univ Med School 1935:351.

11. Blair VP. Total and subtotal restoration of the nose. JAMA 1925;85:1931.

12. Ivy RH. Repair of acquired defects of the face. JAMA 1925;84:181.

13. Kazanjian VH. The repair of nasal defects with the median forehead flap. Surg Gynecol Obstet 1946;83:37.

14. Burget GC, Menick FJ. The subunit principle in nasal reconstruction. Plast Reconstr Surg 1985;76:239.

15. Burget GC, Menick FJ. Aesthetic Reconstruction of the Nose. St Louis: Mosby-Year Book; 1994.

16. Shaw WW. Microvascular reconstruction of the nose. Clin Plast Surg 1981;8:471.

17. Swartz WM. Microvascular approaches to nasal reconstruction. Microsurgery 1988;9:150.

18. Pribaz JJ, Falco N. Nasal reconstruction with auricular microvascular transplant. Ann Plast Surg 1993;31:289.

19. Zhou LY, Cao YL. Clinical application of the free flap based on the cutaneous branch of the acromiothoracic artery. Ann Plast Surg 1989;23:11.

20. Eriksson E, Brånemark P-I. Osseointegration from the perspective of the plastic surgeon. Plast Reconstr Surg 1994;93:626.

21. González-Ulloa M. Restoration of the face covering by means of selected skin in regional aesthetic units. Br J Plast Surg 1956;9:212.

22. Millard DR. Aesthetic reconstructive rhinoplasty. Clin Plast Surg 1981;8:169.

23. Burget GC. Aesthetic restoration of the nose. Clin Plast Surg 1985;12:463.

24. Manson PN, Hoopes JE, Chambers RG, Jaques DA. Algorithm for nasal reconstruction. Am J Surg 1979;138:528.

25. Konig F. On filling defects of the nostril wall. Berl Klin Wochenschr 1902;39:137.

26. Gillies HD. Plastic Surgery of the Face. London: Oxford Medical Publisher; 1920.

27. Argamaso RV. An ideal donor site for the auricular composite graft. Br J Plast Surg 1975;28:219.

28. Rees TD, Guy C, Wood-Smith D, Converse JM. Composite grafts. Excerpta Medica International Congress Series No. 66; 1964:821.

29. Elliott RA Jr. Rotation flaps of the nose. Plast Reconstr Surg 1969;44:147.

30. Masson JK, Mendelson BC. The banner flap. Am J Surg 1977;134:419.

31. Rieger RA. A local flap for repair of the nasal tip. Plast Reconstr Surg 1967;40:147.

32. Marchac D, Toth B. The axial frontonasal flap revisited. Plast Reconstr Surg 1985;76:686.

33. Pribaz JJ, Chester CH, Barrall DT. The extended V-Y flap. Plast Reconstr Surg 1992;90:275.

34. Converse JM. Reconstructive rhinoplasty. In Converse JM, McCarthy JG, Littler JW (eds): Reconstructive Plastic Surgery: Principles and Procedures in Correction, Reconstruction and Transplantation, ed 2. Vol 2. Philadelphia: WB Saunders Company; 1977:1040.

35. Barton FE. Nasal reconstruction. Selected Readings in Plastic Surgery 1994;7 No 13.

36. Sawhney CP. Use of a larger midline forehead flap for rhinoplasty, with new design for closure of donor site. Plast Reconstr Surg 1979;63:395.

37. Sawhney CP. A longer angular midline forehead flap for the reconstruction of nasal defects. Plast Reconstr Surg 1976;58:721.

38. Richardson GS, Hanna DC, Gaisford JC. Midline forehead flap nasal reconstructions in patients with low browlines. Plast Reconstr Surg 1972;49:130.

39. Manders EK, Schenden MJ, Furrey JA, Hetzler PT, Davis TS, Graham WP III. Soft-tissue expansion: concepts and complications. Plast Reconstr Surg 1984;74:493.

40. Adamson JE. Nasal reconstruction with the expanded forehead flap. Plast Reconstr Surg 1988;81:12.

41. Millard DR Jr. Reconstructive rhinoplasty for the lower half of a nose. Plast Reconstr Surg 1974;53:133.

42. Goldwyn RM, Rueckert F. The value of healing by secondary intention for sizeable defects of the face. Arch Surg 1977;112:285.

43. Converse JM. Clinical applications of the scalping flap in reconstruction of the nose. Plast Reconstr Surg 1969;43:247.

44. Hunt HL. Plastic Surgery of the Head, Face and Neck. Philadelphia: Lea & Febiger; 1926.

45. Washio H. Retroauricular-temporal flap. Plast Reconstr Surg 1969;43:162.

46. Orticochea M. A new method for total reconstruction of the nose: the ears as donor areas. Clin Plast Surg 1981;8:481.

47. Maillard GF, Montandon D. The Washio tempororetroauricular flap: its use in 20 patients. Plast Reconstr Surg 1982;70:550.

48. Baudet J, Rivet D, Martin KD, Boileau R. Prefabricated free flap transfers. Third Annual Meeting of the American Society for Reconstructive Microsurgery, San Antonio, Texas, September 12–13, 1987.

49. Costa H, Cunha C, Guimaraes I, Comba S, Malta A, Lopes A. Prefabricated flaps for the head and neck: a preliminary report. Br J Plast Surg 1993;46:223.

50. Pribaz JJ, Fine NA. Prelamination: defining the prefabricated flap—a case report and review. Microsurgery 1994;15:618.

51. Farina R, Villano JB. Follow-up of bone grafts to the nose. Plast Reconstr Surg 1971;48:251.

52. Wheeler ES, Kawamoto HK, Zarem HA. Bone grafts for nasal reconstruction. Plast Reconstr Surg 1982;69:9.

53. Gerrie J, Gloutier GE, Woolhouse FM. Carved cancellous bone grafts in rhinoplasty. Plast Reconstr Surg 1950;6:196.

54. Burget BC, Menick FJ. Nasal reconstruction: seeking a fourth dimension. Plast Reconstr Surg 1986;78:145.

55. Burget GC, Menick FJ. Nasal support and lining: the marriage of beauty and blood supply. Plast Reconstr Surg 1989;84:189.

56. Jackson IT, Smith J, Mixter RC. Nasal bone grafting using split skull grafts. Ann Plast Surg 1983;11:533.

57. Chait LA, Becker H, Cort A. The versatile costal osteochondral graft in nasal reconstruction. Br J Plast Surg 1980;33:179.

58. Gillies H. A new free graft applied to the reconstruction of the nostril. Br J Surg 1943;30:305.

59. Millard DR Jr. Reconstructive rhinoplasty for the lower two-thirds of the nose. Plast Reconstr Surg 1976;57:722.

60. Barton FE Jr. Aesthetic aspects of partial nasal reconstruction. Clin Plast Surg 1981;8:177.

61. Pribaz J, Stephens W, Crespo L, Gifford G. A new intraoral flap: facial artery musculomucosal (FAMM) flap. Plast Reconstr Surg 1992;90:421.

62. Duffy FJ, Rossi RM, Pribaz JJ. Reconstruction of Wegener's nasal deformity using bilateral facial artery musculomucosal (FAMM) flaps. Plast Reconstr Surg 1998;10:1330.

63. Brånemark P-I. Tissue integrated prostheses in oral and maxillofacial reconstruction. In Kagan AR, Miles J (eds): Head and Neck Oncology: Clinical Management. New York: Pergamon Press; 1989:121.

64. Hallén O, Magnusson S, Jacobsson M, Marké L-Å. Bone-Anchored Implants in the Head and Neck Region: Report From a Conference. Stockholm: The Swedish Council on Technology Assessment in Health Care, 1989.

65. McComb H. Osseointegrated titanium implants for the attachment of facial prostheses. Ann Plast Surg 1993;31:225.

66. Harris L, Wilkes GH, Wolfaardt JF. Autogenous soft-tissue procedures and osseointegrated alloplastic reconstruction: their role in the treatment of complex craniofacial defects. Plast Reconstr Surg 1996;98:387.

67. Holgers K-M, Thomsen P, Tjellström A, Ericson LE, Bjursten L-M. Morphologic evaluation of clinical long-term percutaneous titanium implants. Int J Oral Maxillofac Implants 1994;9:689.

68. Granström G, Bergström K, Tjellström A, Brånemark P-I. A detailed analysis of titanium implants lost in irradiated tissues. Int J Oral Maxillofac Implants 1994;9:653.

69. Henry PJ, Tjellström A, Beumer J III. Craniofacial Consensus Panel. Tissue Integration in Oral, Orthopedic, and Maxillofacial Reconstruction. Chicago: Quintessence Publishing Company; 1990:385.

70. Granström G, Tjellström A, Brånemark P-I, Fornander J. Bone-anchored reconstruction of the irradiated head and neck cancer patient. Otolaryngol Head Neck Surg 1993;108:334.

Orbital Defect: Tissue-Integration Reconstruction

15.

Keith D. Carter, MD
Jeffrey A. Nerad, MD

- Patient Selection
- Surgical Procedure
- Postoperative Care
- Prosthesis Fitting

Patients with orbital defects arising from trauma, congenital defects, or, more commonly, tumor ablation surgery are faced with the emotional stress of their condition and the hope for facial rehabilitation. These patients not only have to deal with their loss of vision and the inherent change in lifestyle but also a deforming facial appearance that is difficult to camouflage. Some patients attempt to cover their defects with various patches, whereas others may simply decide not to do anything. Efforts in orbital reconstruction involving various soft-tissue flaps may fill the orbital defect and in some cases create a resemblance to eyelids, but they lack the aesthetic qualities that allow these patients to function comfortably in society.

The development of facial prosthetic devices that allow the restoration of the facial appearance provided clinicians with another option for these patients. These devices provide the majority of patients with a satisfactory facial match that resolves their aesthetic concerns. Although these prostheses adequately address the aesthetic issues, the psychologic concerns of prosthetic retention often limit these patients' complete return to normal activities. To address these concerns, a facial prosthesis should be easy to remove and replace, maintain its position during normal physical activities, and be durable.[1]

Historically, different retentive methods have been used to retain these prosthetic devices. Skin adhesives or double-sided tape is capable of adequate retention but may lead to the complications of skin irritation, prosthetic margin integrity and discoloration, and misalignment.[2,3] Mechanical devices such as eyeglasses are useful, but they have limitations such as having to wear the glasses, prosthetic alignment, and movement of the facial muscles independent of the eyeglass frames.

179

The osseointegration technique allows the placement of titanium implants into the orbital bony rim that are capable of supporting a facial prosthesis.[4-6] The osseointegration procedure, as outlined elsewhere in this text, allows titanium implants anchored to bone to project through the skin, providing points of attachment for prosthetic devices. A stable titanium oxide coating of about 10 nm on the surface of the implant, actually preventing direct contact between the bone and metal, allows osseointegration to occur.[7] The effectiveness of osseointegration as a means of retaining prosthetic devices has been demonstrated for more than two decades. Brånemark initially performed this technique on edentulous patients in 1965.[8] The success rate after 10 years was better than 80% for implants in the upper jaw and 90% in the lower jaw.[4] Other studies have shown a success rate for this technique of approximately 97% in nonirradiated bone and between 61% and 94% in irradiated bone. The success rate in orbital bone has ranged from 92% to 100% in nonirradiated patients and 45% to 79% in irradiated ones.[9-11]

The osseointegration technique allows a patient to wear an orbital prosthesis with the confidence that the prosthesis will be retained securely and maintain proper alignment with normal physical activities.

Patient Selection

The reconstruction with osseointegration in a patient who has had exenteration of the orbit demands an economic and emotional long-term commitment on the part of the patient. Proper patient selection includes factors related to patient compliance, long-term proper hygiene, and necessity of regular prosthetic replacement, and need to undergo a second-stage procedure after the initial operation must be thoroughly explained to the patient. If any of these issues are a concern to the patient or to the surgical team, osseointegration should be reconsidered and another method of rehabilitation entertained.

The majority of patients who have undergone exenteration are being treated for life-threatening neoplasms or aggressive infections involving fungus.[12] The exenteration procedure consists of removal of the entire soft-tissue contents of the orbit, including the globe, extraocular muscles, fat, and periorbita. The remaining orbital volume, or depth of the socket, influences the options the facial prosthetist

has to offer the patient. Total exenteration allows adequate spacing for proper positioning of a prosthesis, including an anatomically retained prosthesis.[13] A subtotal exenteration or a partially filled orbit restricts the facial prosthesis to being thin, with a less natural appearance. Our preference is a total exenteration for optimal results. With the advent of microsurgical free tissue transfer, some surgeons have elected to fill the orbital defect entirely. Although this procedure may have some benefits to the patient, it eliminates the possibility of using osseointegration to secure an orbital prosthesis.

Preoperative radiologic studies and clinical examination help identify patients who will be good candidates for osseointegration. These studies should be evaluated to determine the position, quality, and quantity of the bony orbital rim. Because the orbital walls are thin, only the orbital rim is suitable for osseointegration of titanium implants. Clinically, the orbital rim should be digitally palpated to assess the contour, thickness, and continuity. The height of the eyebrow should be noted. Frequently, the brow will be pulled down toward the healing tissues of the exenterated socket. Efforts should be made to maintain the proper position of the brow at or slightly above the superior orbital rim at or before implantation. An eyebrow inside the orbital margin adds bulk to the superior orbital rim, therefore hindering proper prosthesis fitting and affecting the final cosmetic result. Correction of brow ptosis is an essential step during the first stage of the osseointegration procedure.

The use of titanium implants in patients who have undergone adjunctive radiation treatment after tumor resection has a higher risk of implant loss. The amount of irradiation that correlates with a poorer prognosis is unknown, but it generally is considered more than 50 Gy.[14] The mechanism for implant loss is thought to be secondary to insufficient bone vascularization over time, with the formation of a fibrous capsule around the implant.[15,16] Success rates for osseointegration in irradiated orbital bones range from 45% to 82%.[9,16,17] For unexplained reasons, orbital implants have shown a lower success rate than other facial implants in irradiated bone. Retention rates from 50% to 91% have been demonstrated in other irradiated facial bones.[14,16] The use of hyperbaric oxygen before and after implant placement has increased implant retention rates to more than 90%.[14,17] Hyperbaric oxygen stimulates the healing and remodeling of bone through capillary angiogenesis.[18] The use of hyperbaric oxygen in these patients is recommended but is not an absolute requirement,

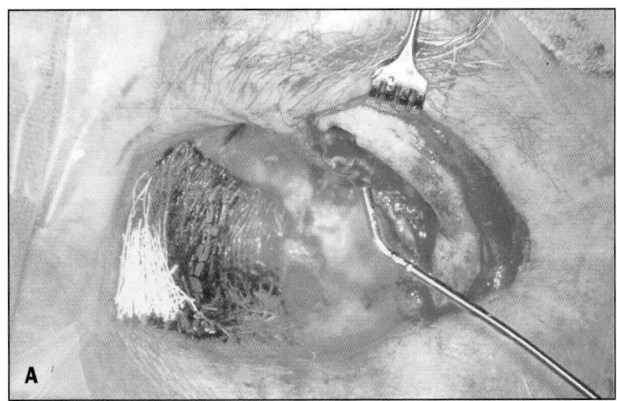 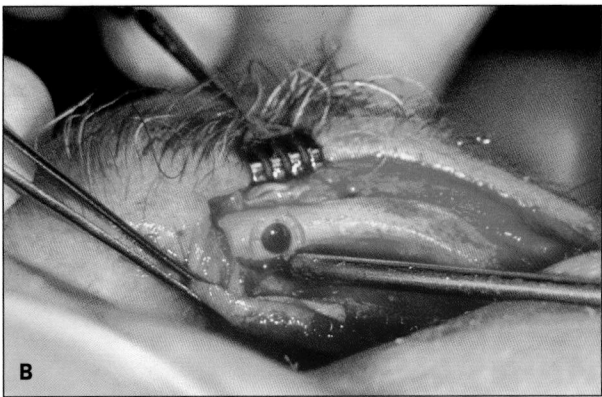

Fig 15-1. *A*, Anterior view of drill site with edge for flange seen along orbital rim. *B*, View of drill site shows the location and orientation on orbital rim.

because retention is achievable, albeit at a lower rate, when hyperbaric oxygen treatments are not used.

The placement of titanium implants in an irradiated orbit is not a contraindication to the osseointegration procedure. These patients should be informed of the slightly higher rate of implant loss compared with nonirradiated sites, but they should not be discouraged from having the procedure. The placement of one or two additional implants in these patients provides future optional sites if some of the selected implants fail to integrate or later become loose, allowing the majority of patients who have had radiation therapy to undergo successful osseointegration and rehabilitation.

Surgical Procedure

The osseointegration procedure[5,19] is performed in two stages. The first stage is the placement of titanium implants into the orbital rim. The superior, lateral, and inferior rims are all good sites for placement. The implants are allowed to bond to bone through osseointegration. The second stage is performed 3 to 4 months later when tissue-penetrating abutments are attached to the initial implants.

Stage 1

The first stage can be performed during general or local anesthesia. We prefer to use local anesthetic without epinephrine for this stage. A team approach is used in the operating suite, with the facial anaplastologist available for consultation on the desired placement of the implants around the orbital rim in some cases. A skin incision is marked with gentian violet or a marking pen along the orbital rim at the designated locations: superior, lateral, or inferior rim. The skin incision is made just anterior to the rim, and a flap of skin, muscle, and periosteum is elevated to expose the bony rim. Typically, three to four sites are chosen for implantation, with the superolateral and the inferolateral rim the more frequent sites.

Once the sites are identified and exposed, implant sites are drilled (Fig 15-1). Several features of the drilling are worth emphasizing. The drilling is performed with a slow drilling speed (1,200 to 1,500 rpm). Constant irrigation is used to control the temperature and to protect the bone from thermal injury. All of the instruments used should be particle free, and the implants should be handled only with the titanium instruments to prevent contamination that could inhibit the osseointegration process.

The initial drilling is done with an exploring cutting bur, which produces a small hole that allows the evaluation of the quality and depth of the bony rim. The orientation of this hole is important and should be directed toward the center of the orbit. This allows space for any bridging apparatus used and the future prosthesis. If the bone is adequate, a 3- to 4-mm spiral drill with a countersink is used to form the final hole diameter (Fig 15-2). The countersink will cut a flat edge on the rim that will later house the flange of the implant (Fig 15-2*B*). Next, the threading of the hole is done with the threading tap. This step is accomplished at the slow speed of 8 to 15 rpm that allows the precise cutting of bone needed for proper implant setting (Fig 15-2*C*).

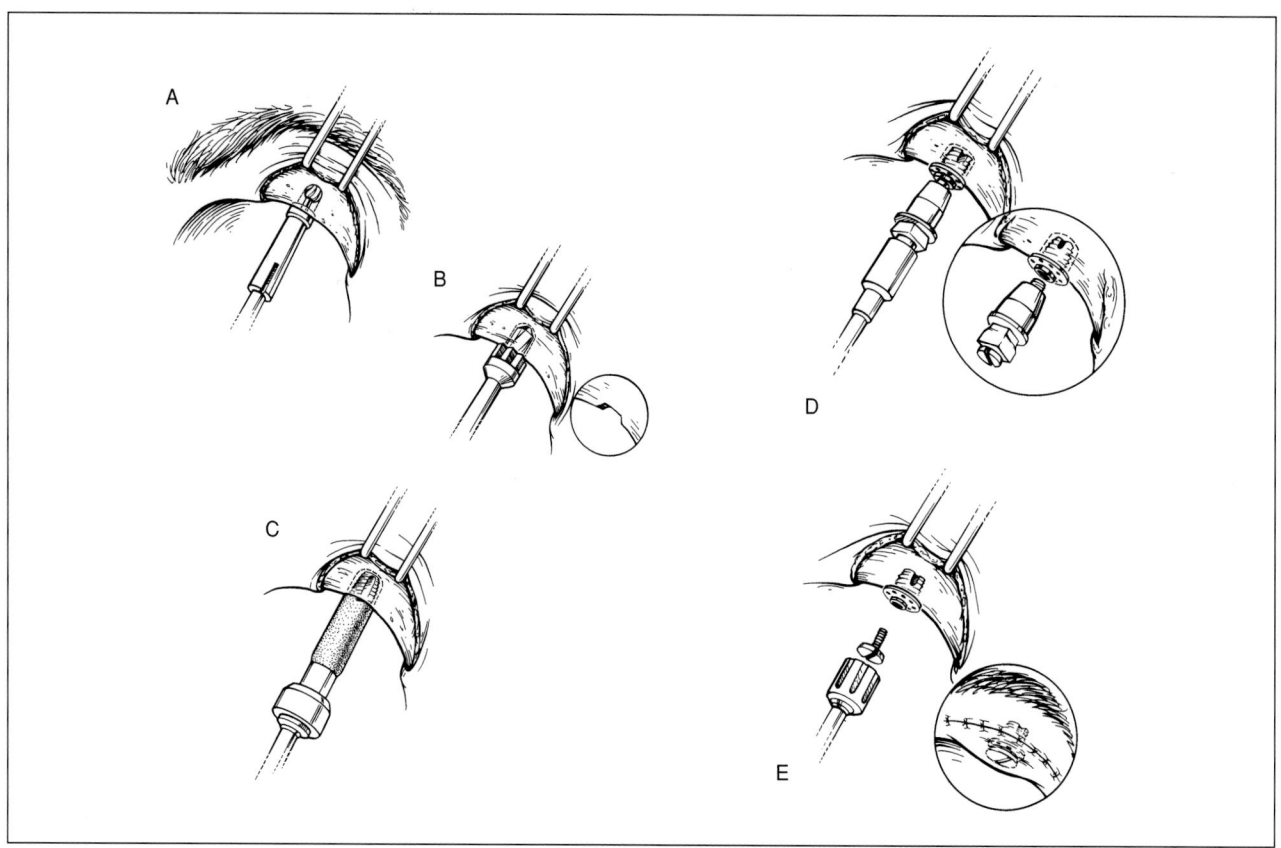

Fig 15-2. Schematic diagram of stage 1 of osseointegration technique. *A,* Cutting bur drills hole. *B,* Countersink creates final hole and edge for implant flange. *C,* Threading tap for creating threads for implant. *D,* Implant placed into drill site. *E,* Cover screw placed into implant. (From Nerad JA. Osseointegration for the exenterated orbit. In Bosniak S [ed]: Principles and Practice of Ophthalmic Plastic and Reconstructive Surgery. Vol 2. Philadelphia: WB Saunders Company; 1996:1150. By permission of the publisher.)

The titanium implant is selected for the hole depth (3 or 4 mm) and screwed into the threaded hole with an implant mount on the drill. Avoid the contamination of the implant before this placement into bone. The speed used for implant placement is 8 to 15 rpm. The end point for implant screwing is the appearance of bone shavings from the area of the countersink appearing in the holes of the flange of the implant (Fig 15-2*D*). The implant has a cover screw placed that is screwed into the internal threads of the implant (Fig 15-2*E*).

After placement of each implant as described above, the soft-tissue closure is done in a layered fashion. A minimum of cautery should be used to allow as much blood supply to the bone as possible. The periosteal flap is closed with interrupted 5-0 polyglactin 910 (Vicryl) sutures, followed by skin closure with interrupted 6-0 nylon sutures. A topical antibiotic is applied with a pressure dressing. This dressing is removed in 1 week.

Four to five implants are placed to compensate for the possibility of an implant failing to integrate properly with bone. Three of these implants are necessary for attachment of the implant. Any extra implants are buried for possible future use if one of the selected implants later fails.

Often these patients have undergone surgical resections that extend beyond the orbit and involve any of the orbital bones and midface. If the continuity of the orbital rim is disrupted, several options are available for bony reconstruction to create a bed for implant placement. Common sites for autogenous bone grafts are the calvarial bone, iliac crest, and fibula. The calvarial and iliac crest grafts require an additional procedure for graft placement, with stage 1 being done approximately 3 months later. One advantage described with the iliac crest graft is the ability to place the implants in an axial orientation, rather than the standard vertical position, allowing axial loading and thus reducing the torque with prosthesis

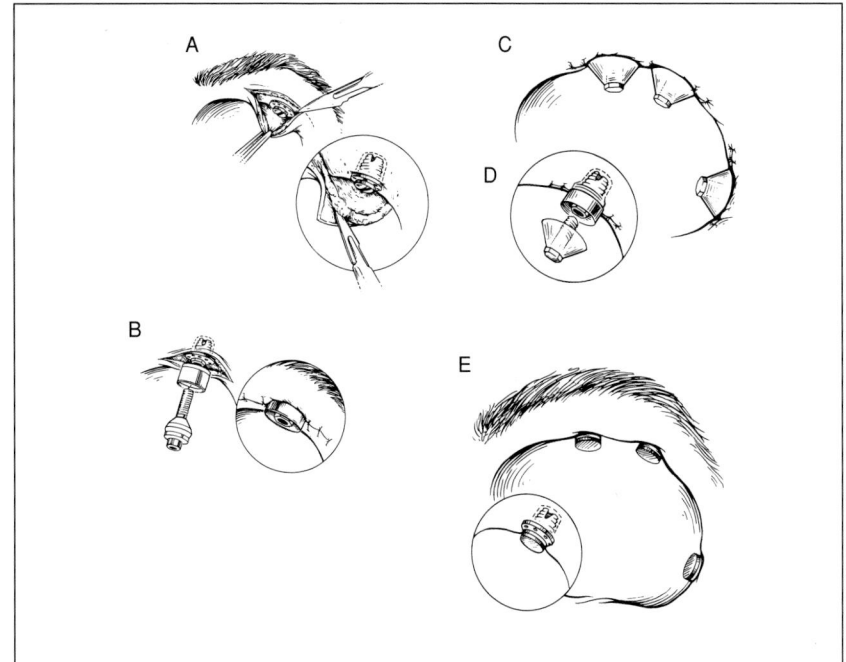

Fig 15-3. Schematic diagram of stage 2 of osseointegration technique. *A,* Implant exposed. *B,* Abutment attached to implant. *C,* Healing cap closes abutment. Healing caps in place. *D,* Healing cap insertion into abutment. *E,* Healing caps replaced with magnets for retention of the prosthesis. (From Nerad JA. Osseointegration for the exenterated orbit. In Bosniak S [ed]: *Principles and Practice of Ophthalmic Plastic and Reconstructive Surgery.* Vol 2. Philadelphia: WB Saunders Company; 1996:1150. By permission of the publisher.)

insertion and removal.[20] A folded fibular free flap can be used for reconstruction of midfacial defects that include the palatal as well as the orbital rim.[21,22] The advantages of this flap are that it is a single-stage procedure and provides vascularized tissue and stage 1 of implant placement can be performed in one sitting. This bone graft is pliable and can be molded to the natural contour of the inferior orbital rim. Unfortunately, contraction of the free tissue may change the orientation of the implant.

Stage 2

The second stage involves the placement of a titanium abutment. This stage can be done after 3 to 4 months. The important step in stage 2 is the proper thinning of the skin around the abutment, preventing movement of the skin adjacent to the abutment. This step prevents skin irritation and infection and allows integration of the skin with the abutment.[5,6] Stage 2 usually also is done during local anesthesia. The first step is locating the previously placed implants. This is done with the use of intraoperative photographs of stage 1, a skull radiograph, or a sharp probe or needle.

The skin is incised at the edge of the implant and elevated. The skin is thinned of its subcutaneous tis-

sue so the dermal layer will be in contact with the periosteum (Fig 15-3*A*). Any hair-bearing skin is removed and a skin graft of non–hair-bearing skin is applied if necessary. The thinned skin is placed over the implant. A trephine is used to cut an opening over the implant. An abutment is placed through the opening and attached to the implant with an internal screw. The abutment can be 3 or 4 mm in height (Fig 15-3*B*). The skin is closed around the abutment with interrupted 7-0 polyglactin 910 (Vicryl) sutures. The abutment is covered with a healing cap (Fig 15-3*C*). Antibiotic-soaked gauze is wrapped around the abutment to immobilize the skin. Four to five weeks after stage 2, the patient is ready for prosthesis fitting.

Postoperative Care

The goal in the postoperative period is to keep the skin around the abutments immobilized. The dressing is changed after 1 week. This dressing is reapplied and removed after an additional week. This 2-week period permits the skin to adhere to the underlying periosteum and the abutments. After this second dressing is removed, the abutments are kept clean and dry.

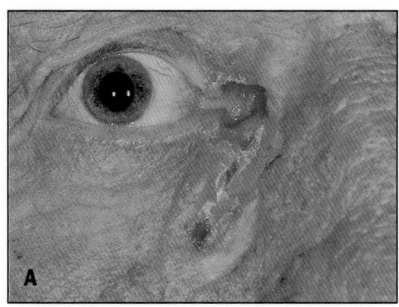

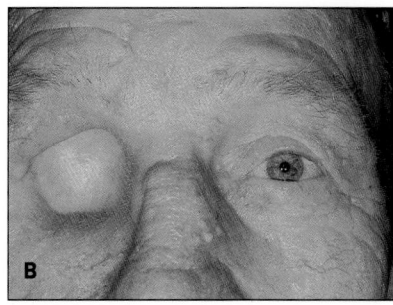

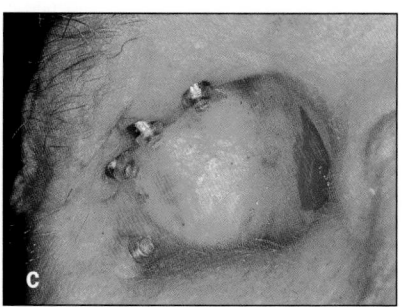

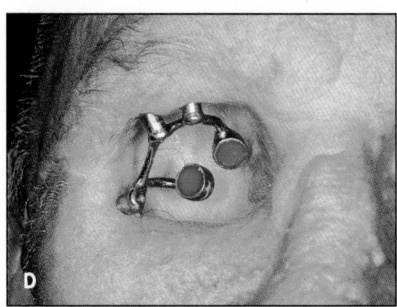

Fig 15-4. *A,* Extensive basal cell carcinoma with orbital extension requires an exenteration. *B,* After resection of tumor, well-healed right socket and cheek flap. *C,* Stage 2 osseointegration completed. Healing caps in place. *D,* Bar frame attached to integrated implants. Magnets attached to frame.

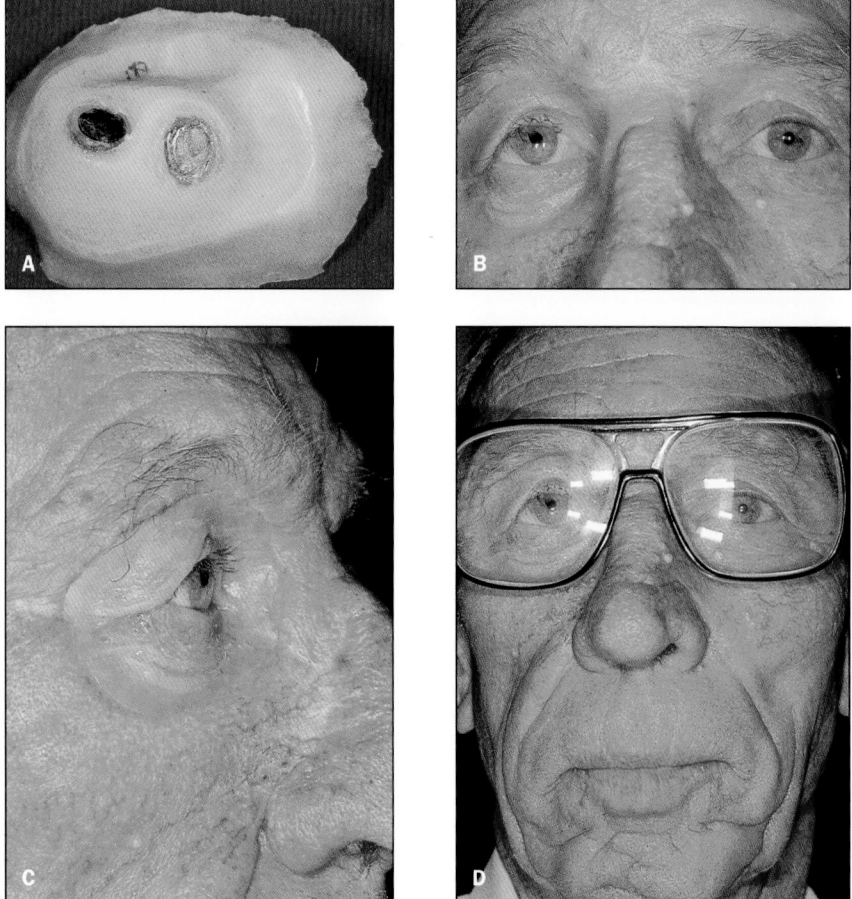

Fig 15-5. *A,* Posterior view of prosthesis with magnets cast in place. Same patient as in Figure 15-4. *B,* Prosthesis held in place by magnets. *C,* Edges of prosthesis blend well with surrounding soft tissue. *D,* Full-face view of prosthesis in place on right side with patient wearing glasses.

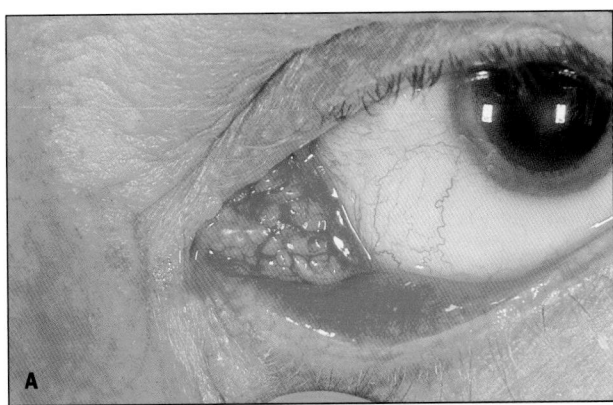 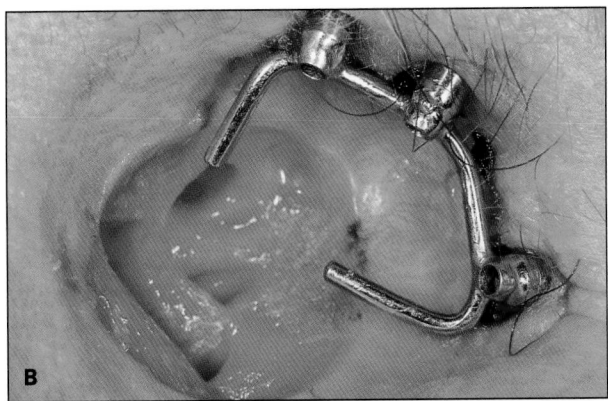

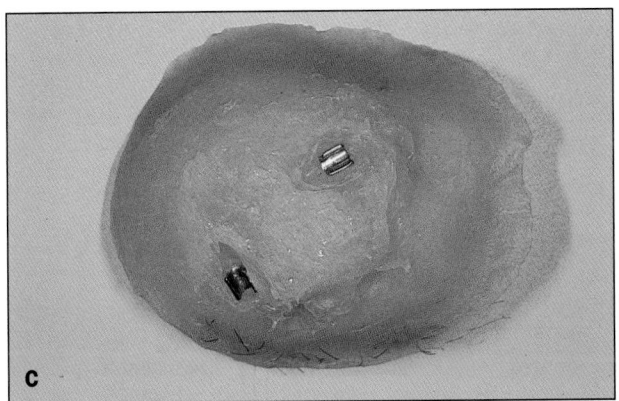 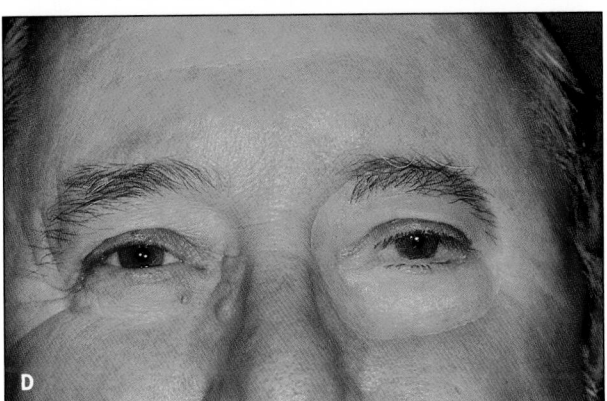

Fig 15-6. *A,* Sebaceous cell carcinoma of left medial canthus that required exenteration. *B,* Bar splint attached to integrated implants. *C,* Posterior view of implants with clips corresponding to the bar splint. *D,* Prosthesis in place on left side.

Prosthesis Fitting

The patient is ready for this stage of the process approximately 4 to 5 weeks after stage 2 or once the skin is healed around the abutments. A cast of the socket is made by the team prosthodontist and facial anaplastologist.[23] The cast is a negative impression of the socket, including the exact location of the abutment cylinders. This cast is used by the prosthodontist to create a metal bridge that will fit and join the abutments. Either magnets (Fig 15-4 and 15-5) or clips (Fig 15-6) are attached to this framework. Recently, rare earth magnets have been attached directly to the abutments, providing another option to this framework.[24] The decision of which retainment device to use is based on the judgment of the facial anaplastologist. The prosthesis is fabricated, and in most cases magnets of opposite polarity to the ones on the frame or abutments are cast into the back of the prosthesis.

The prosthesis is placed into position by bringing it up to the socket, allowing the magnetic forces to draw the prosthesis into position. This allows excellent prosthetic retention and alignment without other means of support.[23,25]

Conclusion

Osseointegration allows direct contact of living bone and a titanium implant that provides a permanent structure for prosthetic retention and alignment. Patient education and selection contribute to a good outcome. Care in intraoperative placement of implants yields a high integration rate. The implant success rate is good even in irradiated bone. The use of hyperbaric oxygen should be considered in these cases.

The technique of osseointegration in the orbit allows patients to wear a cosmetically acceptable facial prosthesis with the psychologic comfort that there is proper alignment and retention during daily activities. The orbital rim is conducive for implant placement, and the exenterated socket allows socket inspection and provides optimal space for the fabrication of a prosthesis. The prosthesis is easy to remove and attach. This technique should be recommended for all patients, after proper consultation, who have undergone orbital exenteration and wish a prosthetic device.

References

1. Shipman B, Finger IM, Guerra LR. Osseointegrated implants in facial prosthetics. Adv Ophthalmic Plast Reconstr Surg 1992;9:297.

2. Hamada MO, Lee R, Moy PK, Lewis S. Craniofacial implants in maxillofacial rehabilitation. J Calif Dent Assoc 1989;17:25.

3. Parel SM, Brånemark P-I, Tjellström A, Gion G. Osseointegration in maxillofacial prosthetics. II. Extraoral applications. J Prosthet Dent 1986;55:600.

4. Tjellström A. Osseointegrated systems and their application in the head and neck. Adv Otolaryngol Head Neck Surg 1989;3:39.

5. Brånemark PI, Adell R, Breine U, Hansson BO, Lindström J, Ohlsson A. Intra-osseous anchorage of dental prostheses, I. Experimental studies. Scand J Plast Reconstr Surg 1969;3:81.

6. Nerad JA, Carter KD, LaVelle WE, Fyler A, Brånemark PI. The osseointegration technique for the rehabilitation of the exenterated orbit. Arch Ophthalmol 1991;109:1032.

7. Albrektsson T, Brånemark PI, Hansson HA, Lindström J. Osseointegrated titanium implants. Requirements for ensuring a long-lasting, direct bone-to-implant anchorage in man. Acta Orthop Scand 1981;52:155.

8. Brånemark PI. Osseointegration and its experimental background. J Prosthet Dent 1983;50:399.

9. Parel SM, Tjellström A. The United States and Swedish experience with osseointegration and facial prostheses. Int J Oral Maxillofac Implants 1991;6:75.

10. Wolfaardt JF, Wilkes GH, Parel SM, Tjellström A. Craniofacial osseointegration: the Canadian experience. Int J Oral Maxillofac Implants 1993;8:197.

11. Tolman DE, Taylor PF. Bone-anchored craniofacial prosthesis study. Int J Oral Maxillofac Implants 1996;11:159.

12. Levin PS, Dutton JJ. A 20-year series of orbital exenteration. Am J Ophthalmol 1991;112:496.

13. Gion GG. Orbital prostheses. In Bosniak S (ed): Principles and Practice of Ophthalmic Plastic and Reconstructive Surgery. Vol 2. Philadelphia: WB Saunders Company; 1996:1134.

14. Granström G, Tjellström A, Brånemark PI, Fornander J. Bone-anchored reconstruction of the irradiated head and neck cancer patient. Otolaryngol Head Neck Surg 1993;108:334.

15. Marx RE, Johnson RP. Studies in the radiobiology of osteoradionecrosis and their clinical significance. Oral Surg Oral Med Oral Pathol 1987;64:379.

16. Jacobsson M, Tjellström A, Thomsen P, Albrektsson T, Turesson I. Integration of titanium implants in irradiated bone. Histologic and clinical study. Ann Otol Rhinol Laryngol 1988;97:337.

17. Johnsson K, Hansson A, Granström G, Jacobsson M, Turesson I. The effects of hyperbaric oxygenation on bone-titanium implant interface strength with and without preceding irradiation. Int J Oral Maxillofac Implants 1993;8:415.

18. Ketchum SA, Thomas AN, Hall AD. Angiographic studies of the effects of hyperbaric oxygen on burn wound revascularization. In Wada J, Irva T (eds): Proceedings of the 4th International Congress on Hyperbaric Medicine, Tokyo, Japan. Baltimore: Williams & Wilkins; 1970:388.

19. Albrektsson T, Brånemark PI, Jacobsson M, Tjellström A. Present clinical applications of osseointegrated percutaneous implants. Plast Reconstr Surg 1987;79:721.

20. Scherer UJ, Schwenzer N. A new implant site in iliac crest bone graft for retention of orbital epistheses: a preliminary report. Br J Oral Maxillofac Surg 1995;33:289.

21. Anthony JP, Foster RD, Sharma AB, Kearns GJ, Hoffman WY, Pogrel MA. Reconstruction of a complex midfacial defect with the folded fibular free flap and osseointegrated implants. Ann Plast Surg 1996;37:204.

22. Frodel JL Jr, Funk GF, Capper DT, et al. Osseointegrated implants: a comparative study of bone thickness in four vascularized bone flaps. Plast Reconstr Surg 1993;92:449.

23. Seals RR Jr, Cortes AL, Parel SM. Fabrication of facial prostheses by applying the osseointegration concept for retention. J Prosthet Dent 1989;61:712.

24. Thomas KF. Freestanding magnetic retention for extraoral prosthesis with osseointegrated implants. J Prosthet Dent 1995;73:162.

25. Lundqvist S, Carlsson GE. Maxillary fixed prostheses on osseointegrated dental implants. J Prosthet Dent 1983;50:262.

Maxillary Discontinuity Defects: Tissue-Integration Reconstruction

16.

Eugene E. Keller, DDS, MSD

> - Treatment Protocol
> - Congenital Maxillary Discontinuity (Unilateral or Bilateral Cleft Lip and Palate)
> - Acquired Maxillary Discontinuity

Discontinuity defects of the maxilla, whether congenital or acquired, challenge the diagnostic and treatment skills of the reconstructive oral and maxillofacial surgeon and the prosthodontist. The affected patients experience different degrees of functional disability of mastication, speech, and deglutition. Cosmetic compromise is substantial for most patients and adds to the overall difficulty in making an acceptable psychosocial recovery from congenital, post-traumatic, or postablative surgical deformities. These functional and cosmetic compromises primarily or secondarily potentially involve the dentition, oral-pharyngeal and facial soft tissue, perioral-oral-pharyngeal and masticatory musculature, nose, and eye.

The type of prosthetic reconstruction for maxillary discontinuity defects varies greatly and depends significantly on the size of the defect and the presence or absence of surrounding supporting structures, such as the natural dentition, tongue, lips, buccal mucosa, soft palate, opposing dental arch, and oral-pharyngeal osseous defect undercuts. The functional status of these structures, particularly the tongue, lips,

buccal mucosa, and soft palate, is of great importance in oral-pharyngeal treatment planning; they also significantly affect potential treatment outcome.

The oral and maxillofacial surgeon frequently is asked to close surgically a congenital or acquired osseous maxillary defect or to alter the surrounding soft and hard tissues to enhance the functional or aesthetic aspects of dentoalveolar-pharyngeal prosthetic reconstruction. When a critical number of natural dentition is present, it frequently is possible surgically to close small- or medium-sized maxillary discontinuity defects with bone grafts or soft-tissue flaps; the dentoalveolar reconstruction can be accomplished with natural tooth-supported fixed or removable partial dentures. When the natural dentition is missing or deficient, surgical closure of a discontinuity defect may complicate the prosthodontic treatment by reducing or eliminating prosthesis retention. In these patients, the osseous defect must be left open and the eventual obturator-type prosthesis stabilized by endosseous implants placed in residual bone, strategically placed bone grafts, or the opposing dentition.

187

Box 16-1   *Treatment Protocol*

I.   Congenital Maxillary Discontinuity—Unilateral or Bilateral Congenital Cleft Lip and Palate

    A.   Congenital cleft lip and palate defect closure: endosseous implants placed *with bone graft*

        1.   Routine bone grafting: autogenous bone followed 6 months later with endosseous implant (Fig 16-1 through 16-9)

        2.   Composite bone grafting: simultaneous autogenous bone graft and endosseous implants (Fig 16-10 through 16-12)

    B.   Congenital cleft lip and palate defect closure: endosseous implant placed *without bone graft* (Fig 16-13)

        (Simultaneous or delayed endosseous implant placement in residual bone)

II. Acquired Maxillary Discontinuity—Trauma, Sepsis, Oncologic

    A.   Hemimaxillectomy (or segmental) management *without defect closure* (Fig 16-14)

        1.   Endosseous implant in residual bone (Fig 16-15 and 16-16)

        2.   Bone grafting in residual bone or contralateral antrum

            Composite bone graft: simultaneous autogenous bone graft and endosseous implants (Fig 16-17)

            Routine bone graft: autogenous bone graft followed 6 months later with endosseous implant (Fig 16-18)

    B.   Segmental defect management *with defect closure*

        1.   Defect closure with bone grafting (Fig 16-10)

            Composite bone graft: simultaneous autogenous bone graft and endosseous implants (Fig 16-19)

            Routine bone graft: autogenous bone followed 6 months later with endosseous implant (Fig 16-20)

        2.   Defect closure without bone grafting (Fig 16-21)

        (Simultaneous or delayed endosseous implant placed in residual bone)

If the discontinuity defect is closed, bone grafts must be placed (primarily or secondarily) that will accommodate an adequate number of endosseous implants to support a full arch fixed, fixed-removable, or an overdenture osseoprosthesis. The most functional and aesthetic prosthesis in this group of patients obtains most, if not all, of its support from the osseous skeleton rather than the soft-tissue mucoperiosteum. Unfortunately, the mucoperiosteum and underlying bone continue to undergo functional remodeling when nonphysiologic functional loading is applied via

a soft-tissue-supported oral or facial prosthesis. For this reason, achieving adequate prosthetic skeletal fixation via osseointegrated endosseous implants is critically important for long-term load transfer and predictable prognosis of the osseoprosthesis.

In the early 1980s the benefit of Brånemark's osseointegration reconstruction in the craniofacial region became available in North America. Several surgical techniques have been described,[1,2] including a one-stage bone grafting procedure, which we modified and applied to other anatomic sites and defects.[3-13] This surgical technique uses autogenous corticocancellous bone grafts and simultaneous (or delayed) placement of Brånemark endosseous implants. In most patients, the endosseous implants first stabilize the fresh autogenous corticocancellous bone graft and secondarily, after 6 months of bone graft remineralization and revascularization and simultaneous implant osseointegration, function as skeletal fixation for the dentoalveolar osseoprosthesis (see Fig 16-10 and 16-14). In other patients, particularly those with larger defects with minimal residual bone or adolescents with small congenital defects (Fig 16-1), a two-stage procedure is done in which autogenous bone grafting and implant placement are separated by a 6-month healing period. The anterior medial ilium serves as the bone graft donor site in a majority of the patients because large segments of corticocancellous block grafts are needed and are harvested with minimal surgical and postoperative morbidity.[14]

Treatment Protocol

This chapter illustrates how the reconstructive surgeon strategically places endosseous implants, with simultaneous bone grafting or as a secondary procedure after bone graft healing and with or without defect closure, to assist the prosthodontist in providing a stable dental prosthesis for patients with congenital or acquired maxillary discontinuity.

Box 1 lists the endosseous implant and bone grafting surgical procedures (treatment protocol) used in this group of partially or totally edentulous patients. The endosseous implant used in all our patients is a commercially pure titanium, noncoated, threaded cylinder root form implant (Nobel Biocare USA, Inc., Westmont, IL). The bone graft is a fresh, autogenous, free, nonvascularized corticocancellous block harvested from the anterior medial ilium.

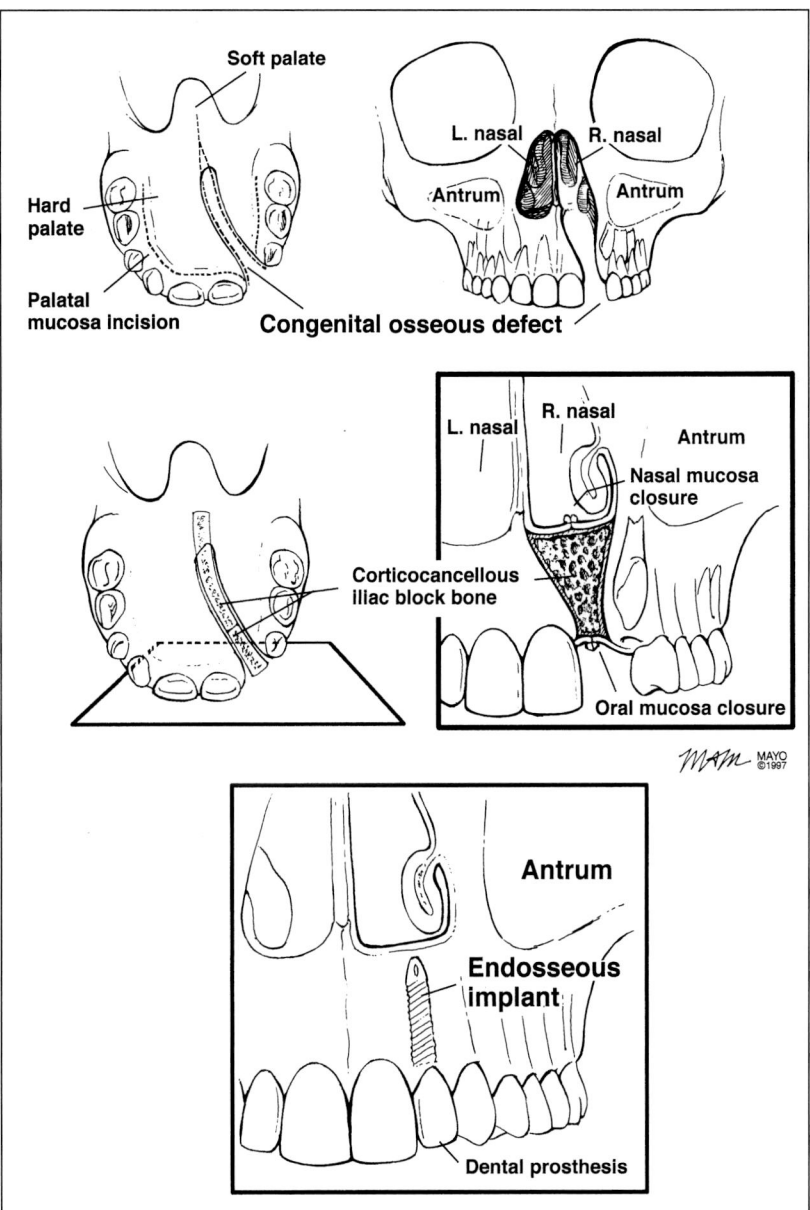

Fig 16-1. Autogenous iliac bone grafting and endosseous implant reconstruction in dentate congenital cleft lip and palate patient. Bone grafting and endosseous implant placement surgical procedures are separated by a minimum of 4 to 6 months for bone graft healing. Endosseous implant placement may be delayed for several years to allow for completion of dentofacial growth and development. *L,* left; *R,* right. (By permission of Mayo Foundation.)

Congenital Maxillary Discontinuity (Unilateral or Bilateral Cleft Lip and Palate)

Patients with congenital osseous and soft-tissue discontinuity (congenital cleft lip and palate [CLP]) benefit greatly from closure of the universally present oral-nasal communication, which is associated with significant nasal and oral functional and aesthetic compromises[15] (Fig 16-1 through 16-4). The surgical procedure to close this communication consists of oral and nasal mucosa closure and simultaneous placement of various types of bone graft materials to fill the nasal floor and aperture, hard palate, and alveolus bone defects. The surgical procedure is generally done during the growth and development years (age 4-12 years) or during adult life. Ideally, the initial osseous reconstruction is done after complete root development and eruption of the permanent central incisors and before downward movement of the permanent cuspid into the alveolar process (bone grafting in the infant is unpredictable and carries a significant risk of adversely altering maxillary growth and development).

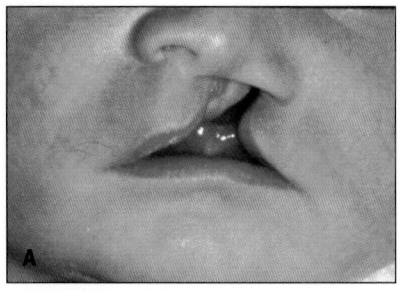 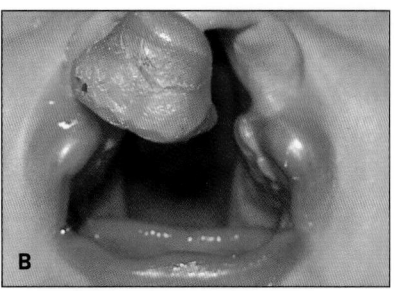

Fig 16-2. Oral-nasal deformity of unilateral (*A*) and bilateral (*B*) cleft lip and palate patients shortly after birth and before initial soft-tissue repair of lip, nose, and soft-palate discontinuity. In addition to the osseous and soft-tissue discontinuity, there frequently are missing (or deformed) deciduous and permanent lateral incisors on the cleft side.

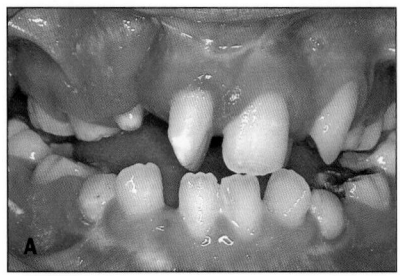 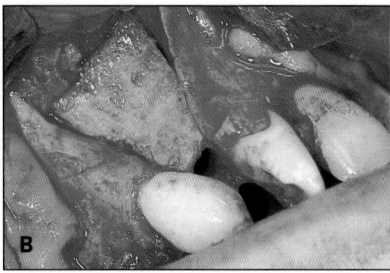

Fig 16-3. *A*, Unilateral cleft lip and palate patient at age 10 years, before bone grafting of the alveolar-palatal osseous cleft with simultaneous closure of the oral-nasal fistula. *B*, Placement of fresh, autogenous, corticocancellous block iliac bone graft into large bone deficit with only minimal clinical soft-tissue defect, as seen in *A*. Graft reconstructs the nasal floor and aperture, alveolus, and hard palate.

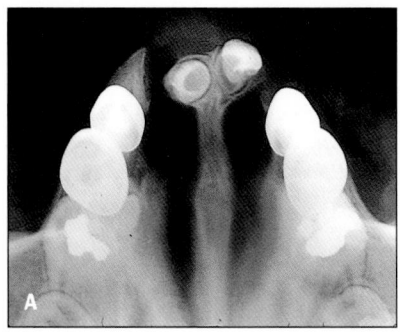 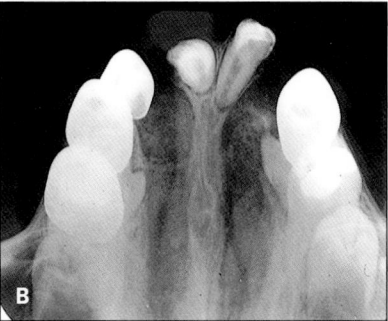

Fig 16-4. Intraoral occlusal radiographs show presurgical (*A*) and postsurgical (*B*) alveolar-palatal bone grafting of bilateral cleft lip and palatal bone discontinuity. Note congenital absence of lateral incisors and bone grafting of the secondary palate as well as the alveolus (same patient as in Fig 16-8).

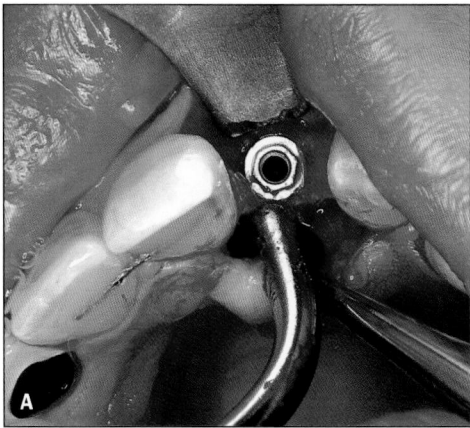 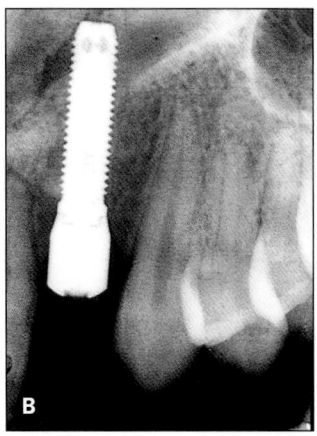

Fig 16-5. *A*, Endosseous implant placement in unilateral cleft lip and palate patient in whom bone grafting had been done previously (same patient as in Fig 16-6). *B*, Periapical radiograph of implant with healing abutment. Note piriform aperture, nasal floor, and alveolar bone reconstruction, which allows eventual adequate implant positioning and length to satisfy biomechanical and aesthetic requirements.

Fig 16-6. Unilateral cleft lip and palate patient. *A*, Clinical photograph at age 10 years, before bone graft and endosseous implant reconstruction; note osseous cleft on the patient's left. *B*, Radiograph before alveolar bone grafting at age 8 years. *C*, After bone grafting at age 12 years; note congenital absence of right and left permanent lateral incisors, high position of permanent cuspids, and osseous cleft on the left. *D*, Intraoral radiograph after endosseous implant and prosthetic reconstruction. *E*, Clinical photograph after prosthetic treatment. Both lateral incisors were reconstructed with osseoprostheses. Adequate bone in reconstructed osseous cleft allowed placement of a 15-mm-length self-tapping endosseous implant. Note typical low smile line in cleft lip patient.

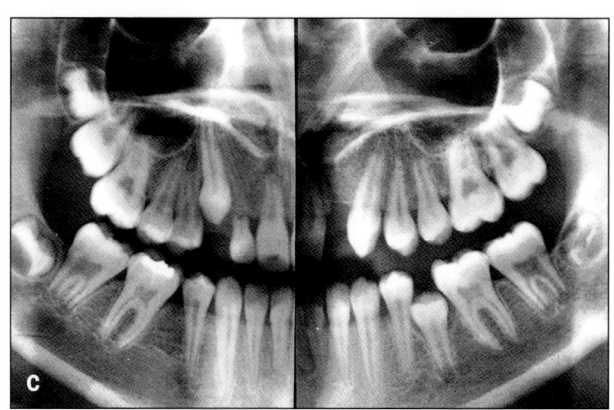

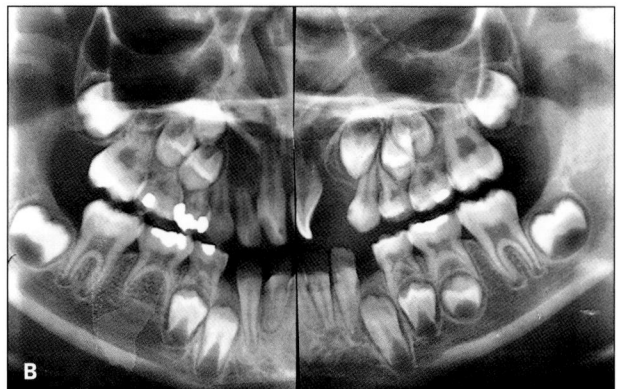

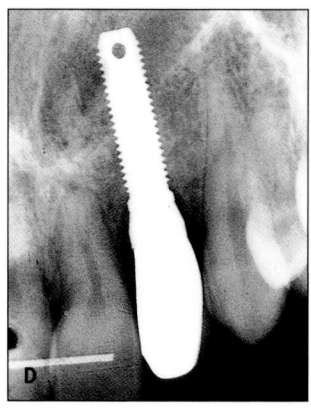

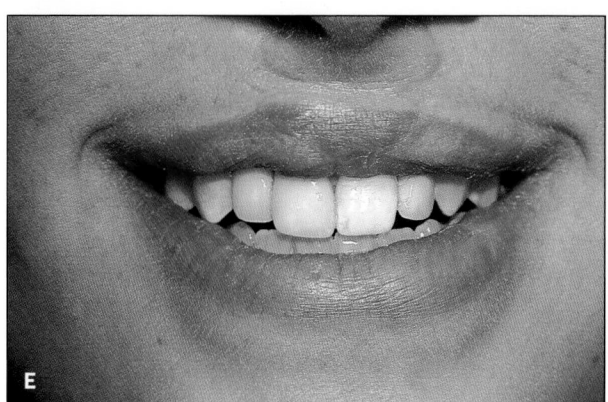

Surgical Procedure in Dentate Patient

The relatively small congenital osseous defect in most developing dentate patients and the presence of developing or erupted teeth dictate a two-stage procedure. The first stage is placement of fresh, autogenous, corticocancellous block bone grafts in a watertight soft-tissue (nasal and oral) repaired defect to replace *completely* the congenitally absent alveolar, nasal, and palatal bone (Fig 16-1). An anatomically complete bone graft reconstruction is critically important, because it allows for normal eruption of natural teeth or eventual placement of endosseous dental implants after complete graft healing (Fig 16-3*B*, 16-4). The second stage endosseous implant placement must follow completion of dentofacial (particularly alveolar) growth and development, because the implant is osseointegrated and acts as an ankylosed tooth and will not change in position with continued vertical or horizontal alveolar growth (Fig 16-1). The endosseous implant is placed secondarily at the appropriate time into the remineralized and revascularized bone graft (Fig 16-5). When indicated, orthodontic tooth repositioning into the healed bone graft may be accomplished and potentially obviates the need for prosthetic tooth replacement. (Patient examples Fig 16-6 through 16-9.)

(text continues on page 195)

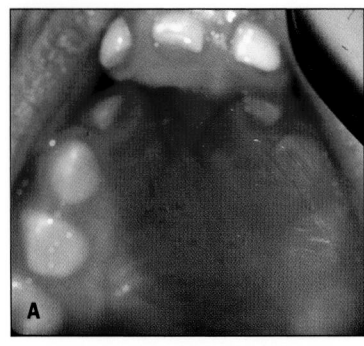
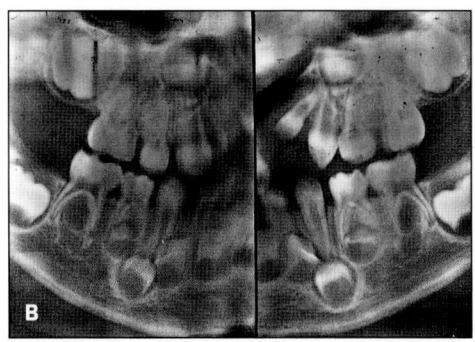
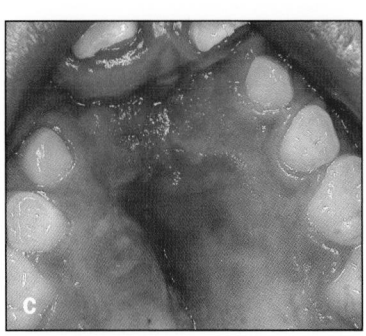

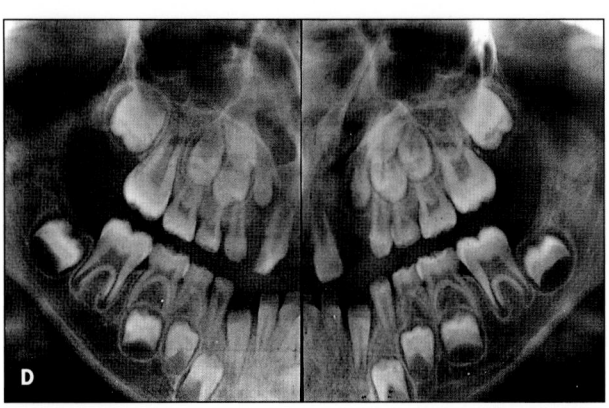

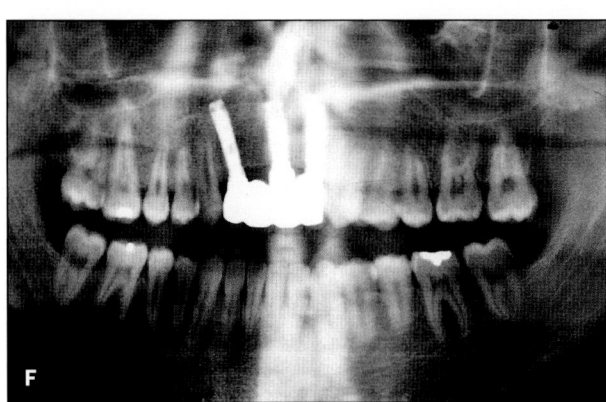
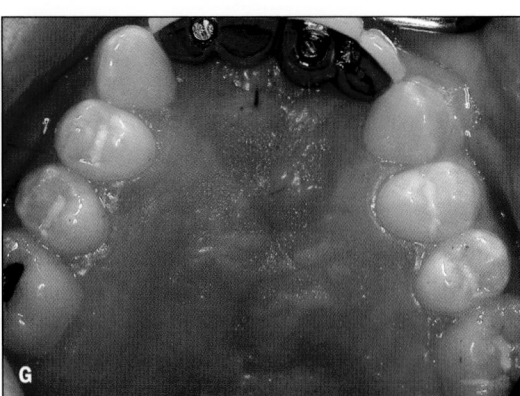

Fig 16-7. Bilateral cleft lip and palate patient. *A,* Clinical photograph and (*B*) radiograph at age 3 years, before bone graft reconstruction. *C,* Patient at age 8 years, after alveolar bone graft reconstruction. *D,* Radiograph illustrates dental and osseous deformity and osseous reconstruction before downward movement of permanent cuspids. Note bilateral congenital absence of lateral incisors and generalized enamel hypoplasia of central incisors. *E,* Patient at age 17 years, after endosseous implant and osseoprosthetic reconstruction. *F,* Radiograph after osseoprosthetic reconstruction; note central incisors were removed because their long-term prognosis was poor. Patient declined maxillary advancement osteotomy and was pleased with the cosmetic and functional result. *G,* Intraoral palatal view of reconstructed palate and fixed dental osseoprosthesis in place.

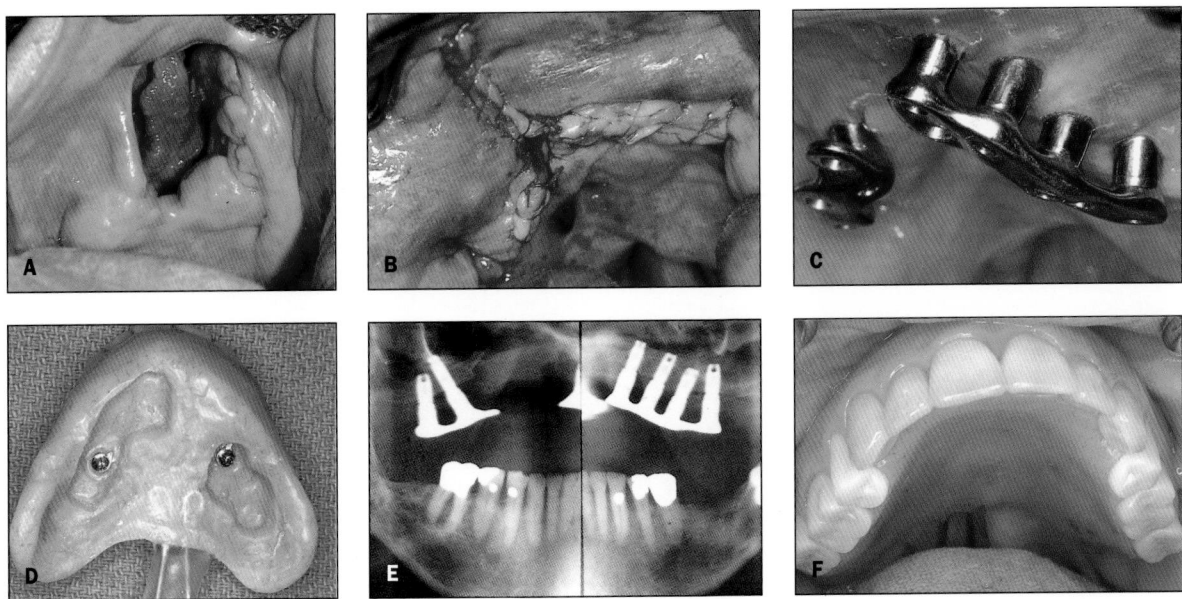

Fig 16-13. Edentulous unilateral cleft lip and palate patient. *A,* Clinical intraoral photograph of extensive oral-palatal-nasal defect. *B,* Surgical soft-tissue closure of oral-nasal defect *without* simultaneous bone grafting. *C,* After defect closure, six endosseous implants with bilateral implant-connecting metal bars. *D,* Fixed-removable overdenture dental prosthesis with oral pharyngeal obturator. *E,* Radiograph after prosthetic treatment; note bilateral implant connecting metal bars placed anterior and inferior to the bilateral antrum. *F,* Intraoral photograph after prosthetic treatment. Patient can now function without concern about prosthesis instability. (*A* from Keller EE. Maxillary-mandibular discontinuity reconstruction with composite grafts [autogenous free iliac bone and titanium endosseous osseointegrated implants]. Recent Adv Plast Surg 1992;4:109. By permission of WB Saunders Company; *D* and *E* from Tolman et al.[13] By permission of Quintessence Publishing Company.)

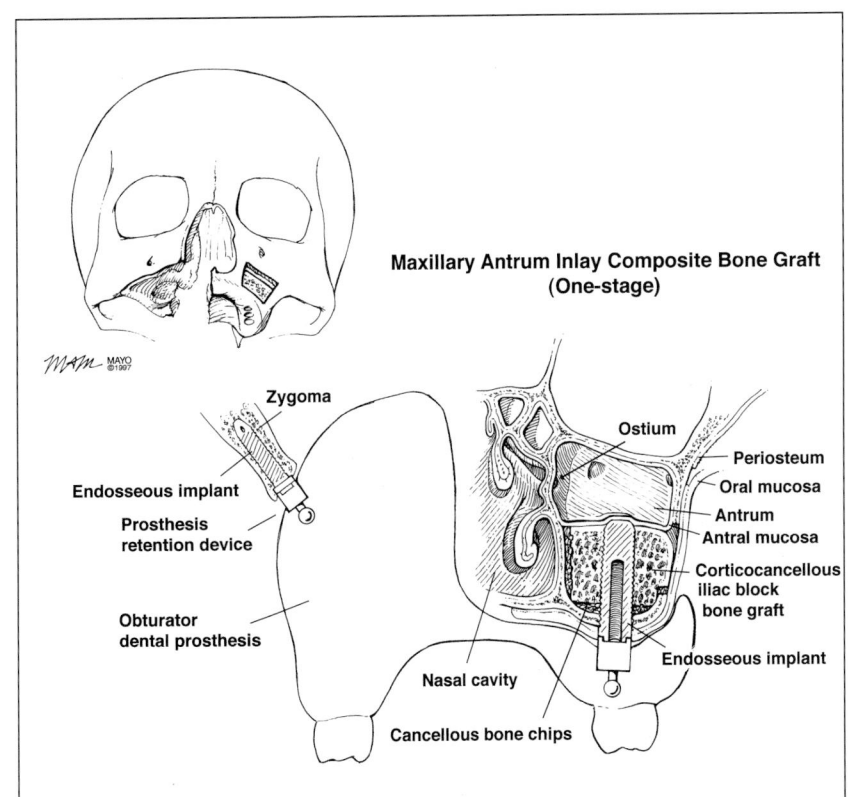

Maxillary Antrum Inlay Composite Bone Graft (One-stage)

Zygoma

Ostium

Periosteum

Oral mucosa

Endosseous implant

Antrum

Antral mucosa

Prosthesis retention device

Corticocancellous iliac block bone graft

Obturator dental prosthesis

Nasal cavity

Endosseous implant

Cancellous bone chips

Fig 16-14. Acquired maxillary discontinuity (hemimaxillectomy defect) reconstructive procedure. Note antral inlay bone graft procedure in contralateral defect side. (By permission of Mayo Foundation.)

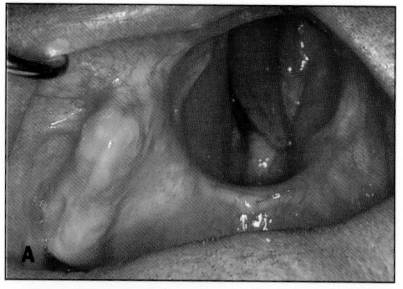
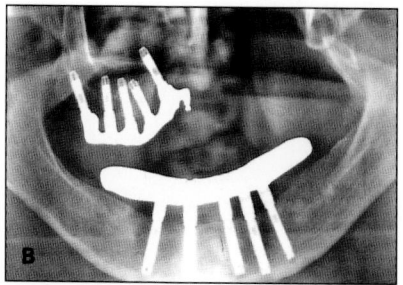
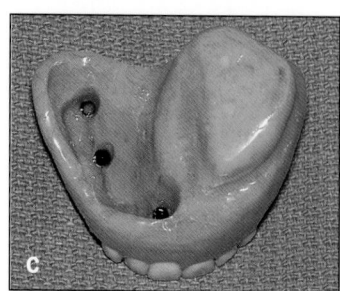

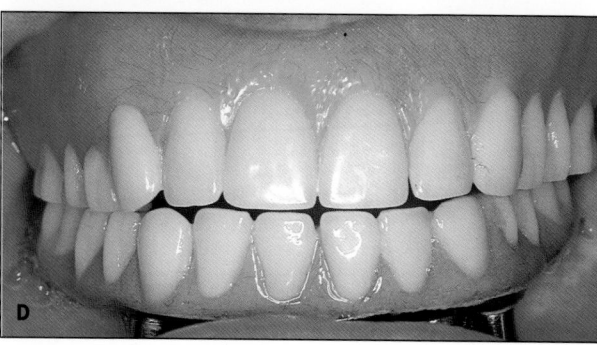

Fig 16-15. Postoncologic resection hemimaxillectomy defect. *A,* Intraoral clinical photograph shows large osseous and soft-tissue oral-nasal-antral defect. *B,* Post-treatment radiograph; note milled metal bar connecting the five maxillary endosseous implants. *C,* Obturator fixed-removable overdenture; note prosthetic retention device embedded in the prosthesis. *D,* Post-treatment photograph of occlusion of maxillary and mandibular dental osseoprosthesis.

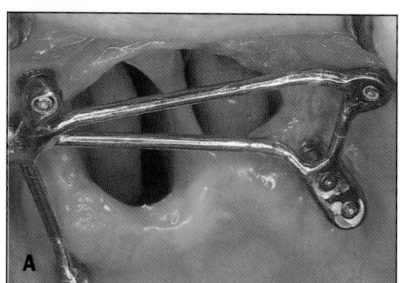
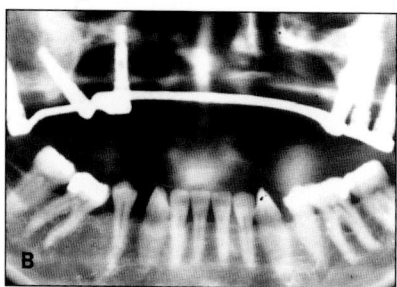
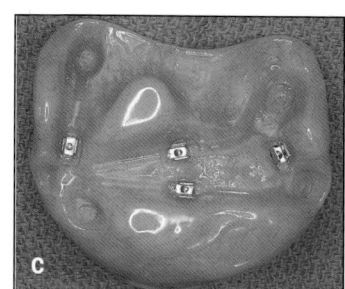

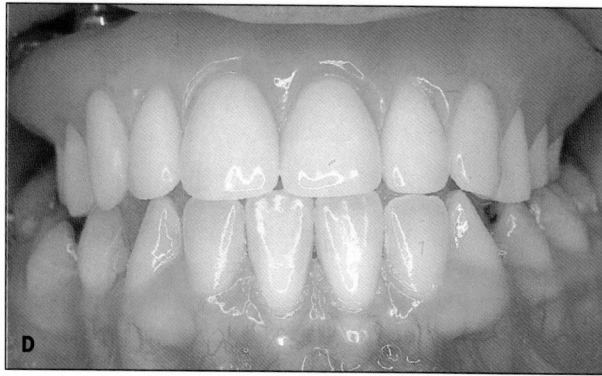

Fig 16-16. Postoncologic and postinfectious maxillary anterior segmental defect. *A,* After endosseous implant reconstruction. Intraoral photograph after implant uncovering, abutment placement, and cast bar placement on the six implants. Two implants were placed laterally into the zygoma body and two were placed in the tuberosity-pterygoid plate junction. Note almost complete lack of bone anterior to the maxillary buttress bilaterally. *B,* Post-treatment radiograph; pterygoid implants had been placed before loss of additional anterior maxilla. *C,* Obturator prosthesis (undersurface) with retentive devices. *D,* Intraoral photograph of dental osseoprosthesis in occlusion.

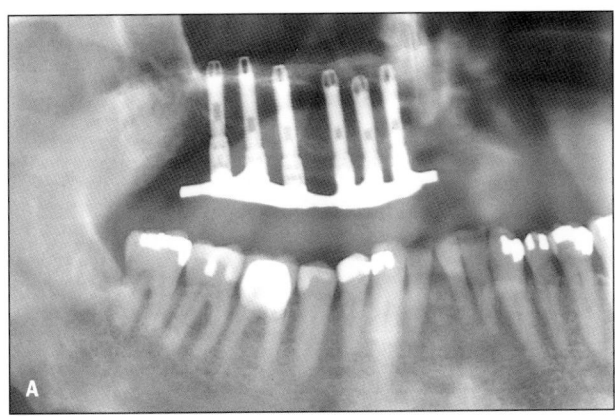

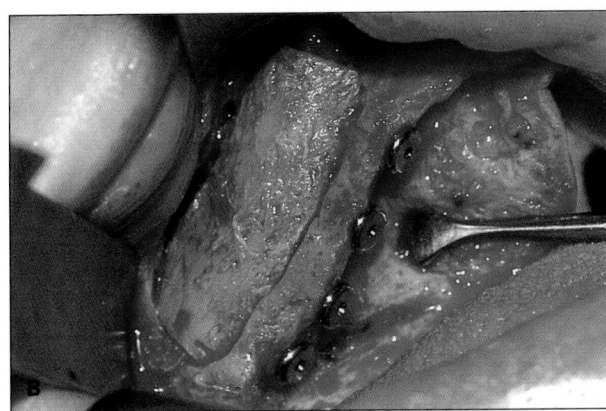

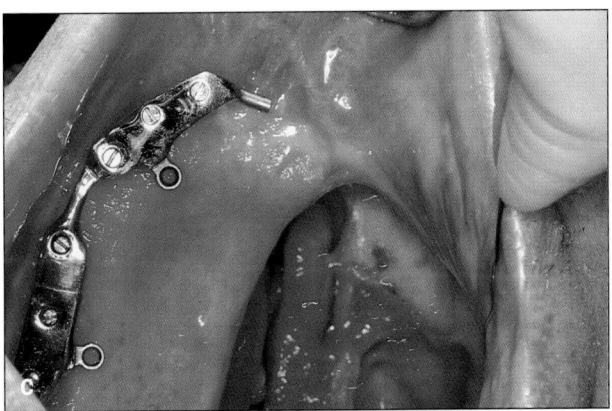

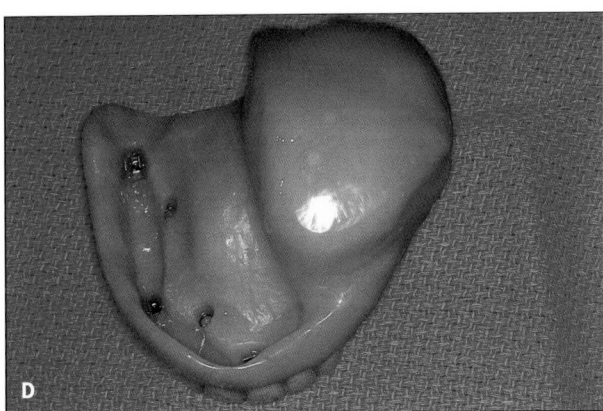

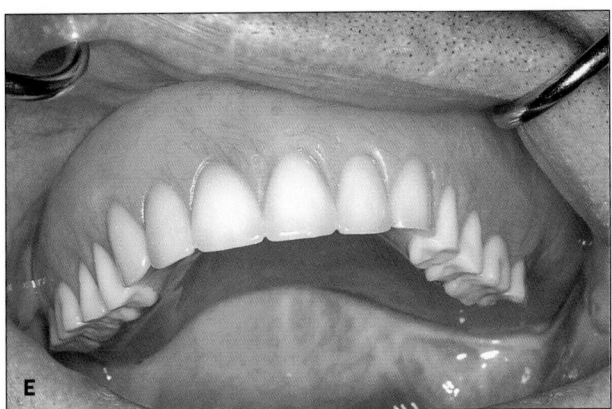

Fig 16-17. Postoncologic resection hemimaxillectomy defect. *A,* Post-treatment radiograph after one-stage antral inlay bone graft in contralateral antrum; note three endosseous implants anterior to antrum and three endosseous implants in antral bone graft reconstruction. *B,* Antral inlay bone graft reconstruction used in this patient; note implants extend through the residual alveolar ridge (antral floor) and through the corticocancellous block bone graft. *C,* Post-treatment intraoral defect; note the continuous implant-connecting metal bar. *D,* Obturator fixed-removable overdenture dental prosthesis; note prosthesis retention devices. *E,* Intraoral photograph of obturator denture in place. (*B* from Keller et al.[6] By permission of the American Association of Oral and Maxillofacial Surgeons.)

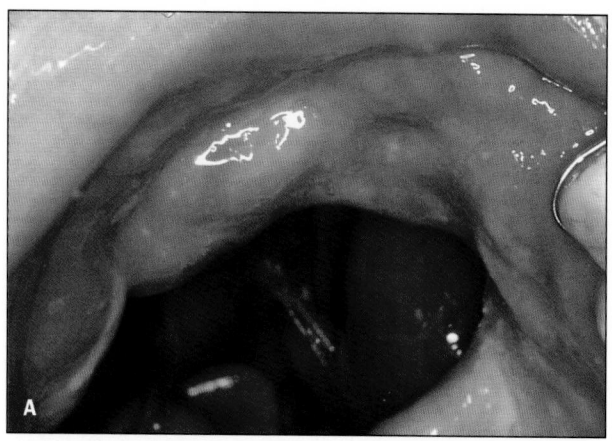

Fig 16-18. Post-traumatic anterior and posterior maxillary segmental defect. *A,* Intraoral photograph shows the large maxillary-zygoma osseous and soft-tissue defect. *B,* Pretreatment radiograph. *C,* Radiograph after bone grafting of alveolus and zygoma and after endosseous implant reconstruction. Note endosseous implant placement into zygoma was not accessible for prosthesis attachment. *D,* Post-treatment clinical photograph of implant-connecting metal bar. *E,* Post-treatment intraoral osseoprosthesis and occlusion. *F,* Post-treatment facial photograph. (*B, C, E,* and *F* from Keller.[12] By permission of WB Saunders Company.)

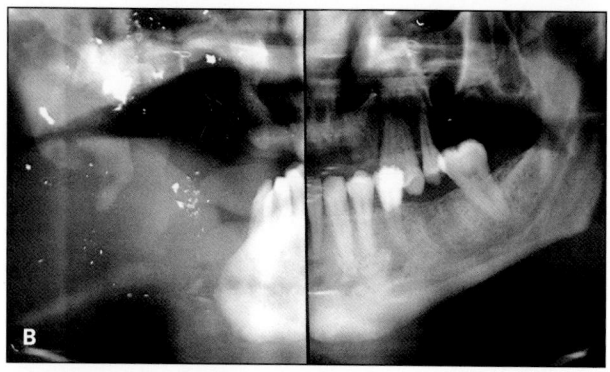

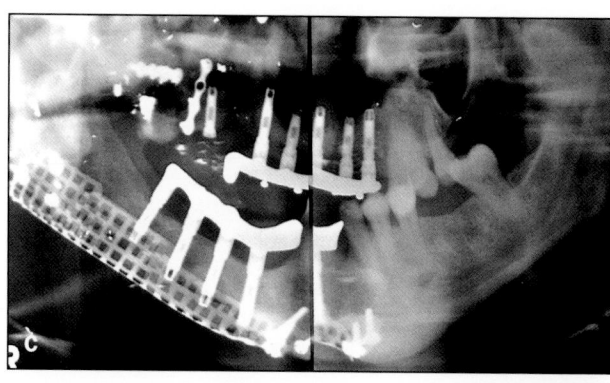

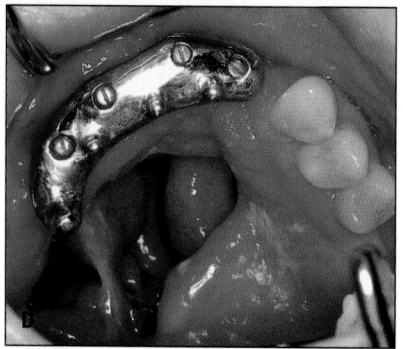

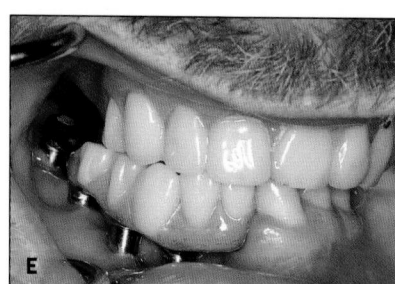

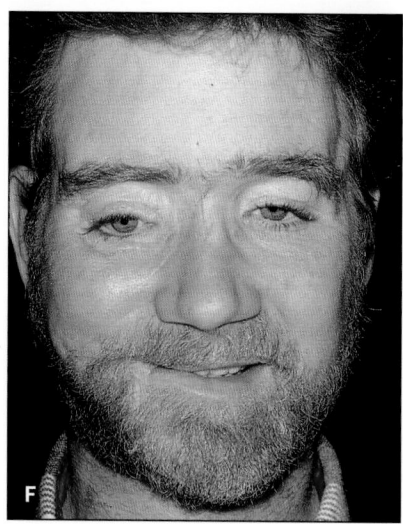

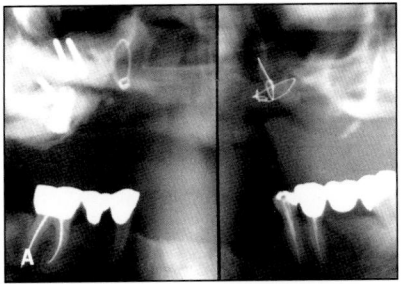 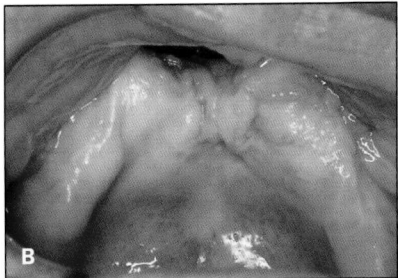 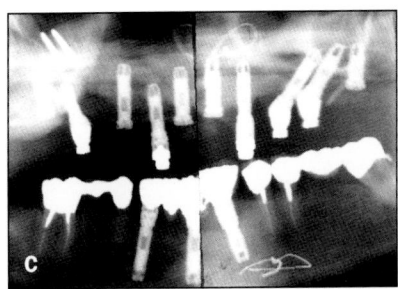

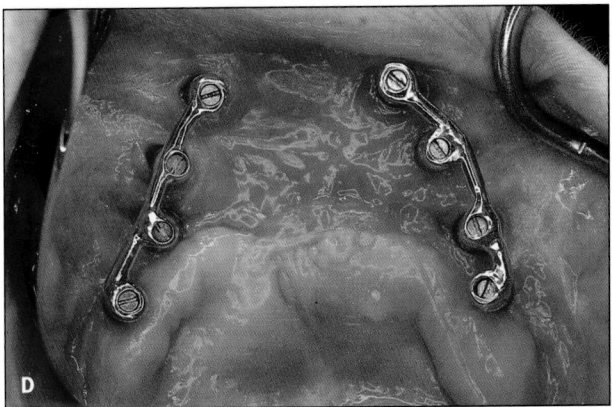 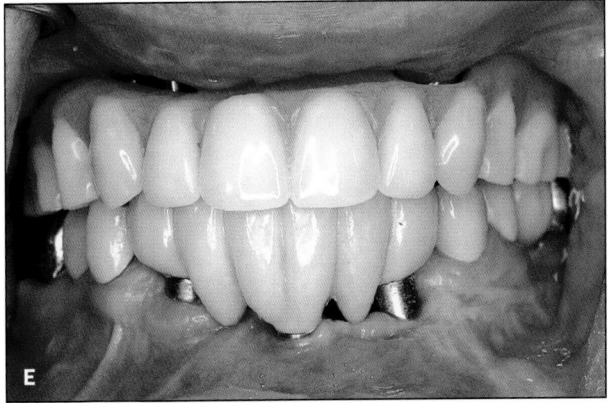

Fig 16-19. Post-traumatic anterior and posterior maxillary segmental defect. *A,* Pretreatment radiograph. *B,* Pretreatment intraoral photograph. Note extensive loss of maxillary bone anterior to bilateral buttress (patient had previous unsuccessful attempts at closure of oronasal fistula defect). *C,* Radiograph after one-stage bone graft reconstruction, endosseous implant uncovering, and abutment placement on five initially placed implants; note angulation of implants used to fix the bone graft to the zygoma bilaterally and the placement of four additional implants. *D,* For prosthesis support, four implants on each side were connected with a continuous metal bar; note distance between post-trauma ridge and most anterior implant. *E,* Post-treatment intraoral photograph; note normal position of anterior teeth, which restored lip and nasal alar position. Prosthetic treatment provided by Dr. Jonathan Wiens, Farmington Hills, Michigan. (*A-C* and *E* from Keller et al.[4] By permission of Quintessence Publishing Company; *D* from Keller.[9] By permission of WB Saunders Company.)

the threaded, cylindrical endosseous implants, which later function as skeletal support for a dental osseoprosthesis. Prosthetic treatment can be initiated shortly after uncovering the endosseous implants 6 months after the initial composite bone grafting procedure. (Patient examples Fig 16-11 through 16-13.)

In patients with large osseous defects, large blocks of bone graft are unsupported by residual bone. In this setting it may be necessary to place additional implants 4 to 6 months after the original bone graft procedure (Fig 16-19), because bicortical implant stabilization is not present at the initial procedure and implant loss was increased in these discontinuity defect sites in our initial patients. This secondary implant placement can be done 4 to 6

months after bone graft placement or at the time of uncovering of initially placed implants. The patient can wear an interim overdenture prosthesis with reduced function during the first or second implant healing period of 4 to 6 months.

Acquired Maxillary Discontinuity

Patients with acquired maxillary discontinuity differ in osseous or soft-tissue defect size, location, and etiology. Two major groups will be discussed based on the size of the defect: the large hemimax-

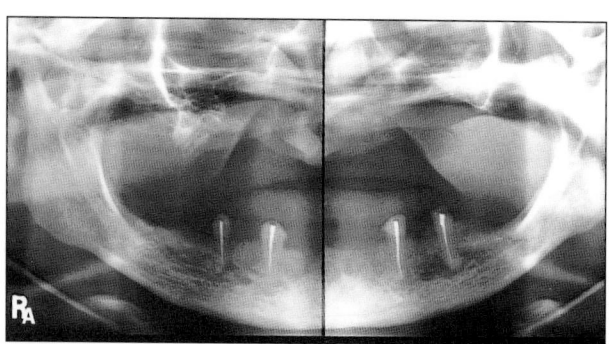

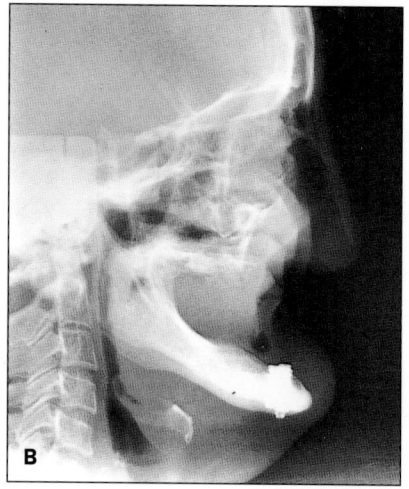

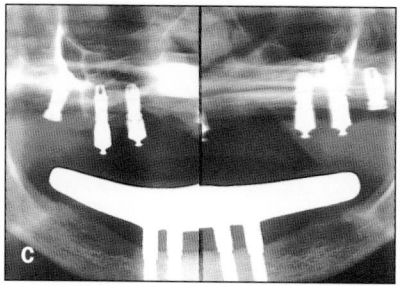

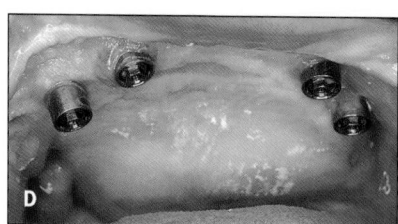

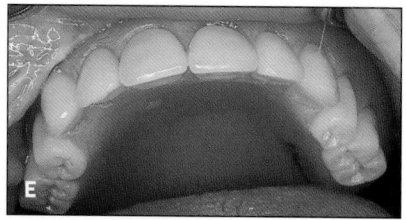

Fig 16-20. Postsurgical (septoplasty osseonecrosis) anterior and posterior maxillary defect. *A*, Pretreatment radiograph and (*B*) lateral cephalogram; note large osseous defect anterior to buttress bilaterally and severe relative mandibular prognathism. *C*, Post-endosseous implant reconstruction radiograph. The soft-tissue defect was closed with local flaps and skin grafted before the bone graft procedure. *D*, Intraoral photograph after abutment placement; note two posterior implants were not accessible then but could now be used with recent introduction of modified abutments. *E*, Post-treatment osseoprosthesis maxillary overdenture. *F*, Lateral cephalogram; note large anteroposterior discrepancy and significant cantilevering of fixed mandibular osseoprosthesis. Post treatment the patient was able to smile and masticate without concern about prosthesis retention. (*A* and *C* from Keller.[9] By permission of WB Saunders Company.)

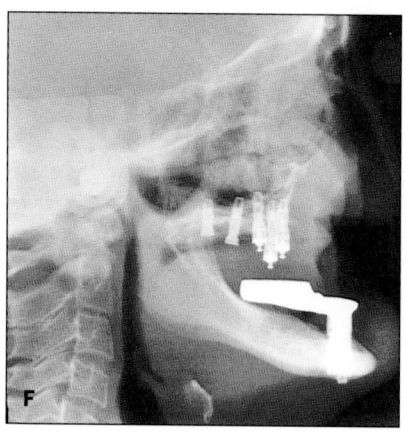

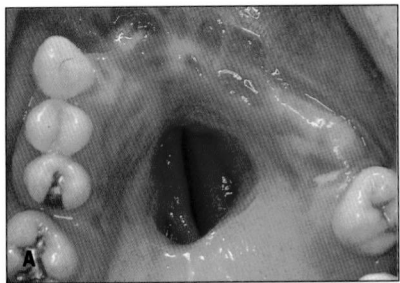 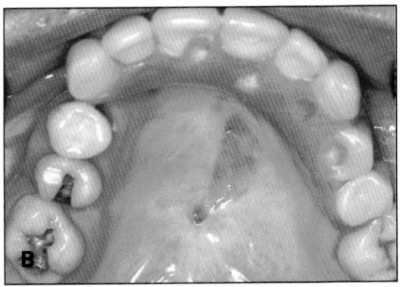 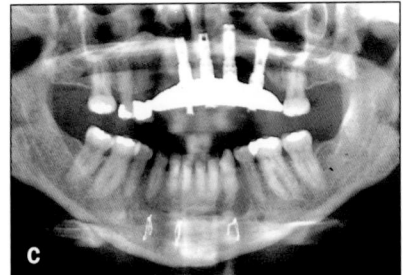

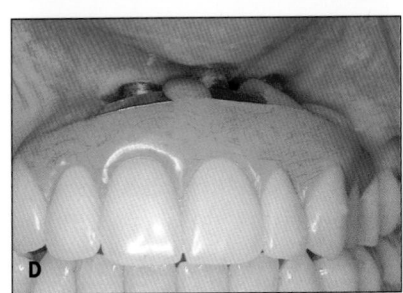

Fig 16-21. Postsurgical (Le Fort I osteotomy) osteonecrosis produced premaxillary and postmaxillary segmental defect. *A,* Intraoral photograph after sloughing, selective sequestrectomy and odontectomy, and soft-tissue healing of an avascular maxilla after multisegment osteotomy for skeletal malocclusion. *B,* Post-treatment photograph after soft-tissue closure, endosseous implant placement, and placement of the dental osseoprosthesis. *C,* Postoperative radiograph. *D,* Post prosthetic treatment; note osseoprosthesis height and anterior position, giving normal alar and upper lip position, and excellent peri-implant soft-tissue health. (*A-C* from Tolman et al.[13] By permission of Quintessence Publishing Company.)

illectomy defect of various etiologies in which the defect is not closed and is obturated by an implant-stabilized prosthesis (Fig 16-14 through 16-17) and the smaller segmental defect in which soft-tissue closure is done with or without simultaneous bone grafting or endosseous implant placement (Fig 16-18 through 16-21). In both groups of patients, it is common to do various nasal or antral inlay bone graft and endosseous implant procedures in areas of residual bone to provide additional bone anchorage for the eventual fixed, fixed-removable, or overdenture osseoprosthesis. These bone grafts may be placed via various approaches, including lateral window antrostomy,[6] Le Fort I down-fracture exposure,[8] or full arch or segmental arch onlay or inlay techniques.[4]

Surgical Management of Hemimaxillectomy Discontinuity

In this group of patients, the size of the defect, the oncology-radiation status of the patient, and the age and medical status of the patient dictate a surgical approach in which the defect is not closed. However, several surgical procedures (Fig 16-14) may be done to optimize the defect anatomy to receive an obturator prosthesis, including placement of endosseous

implants in the residual contralateral alveolar or zygoma bone or antrum-nasal cavity. Figures 16-15 through 16-17 illustrate endosseous implants and bone grafts placed to help stabilize an obturator dental osseoprosthesis.

Surgical Management of Segmental Defect Discontinuity

Segmental defects secondary to oncologic resection, sepsis, or trauma frequently are amenable to surgical closure with soft-tissue flaps or various bone grafting procedures (Fig 16-18 through 16-21). These defects in the edentulous or partially edentulous patient are managed in a manner similar to the congenital cleft discontinuity (Fig 16-1 and 16-10) for which one- or two-stage bone graft and endosseous implant procedures are done.[7,13] It is highly critical in this group for the surgeon and prosthodontist to accomplish coordinated treatment planning to be certain it is possible to close a defect and have an adequate number of teeth or implants in strategic positions to support the eventual prosthesis. Once a defect is closed, significant prosthesis retention and support are lost and must be replaced by skeletal anchorage via endosseous implants or natural teeth.

Conclusion

Composite bone graft reconstruction of congenital or acquired maxillary discontinuity has provided predictable skeletal fixation for a fixed, fixed-removable, or overdenture dental prosthesis that may or may not include defect obturation or velopharyngeal support. When the discontinuity can be closed surgically and the patient's medical or psychologic condition permits, the bone graft and simultaneous endosseous implant placement provide oral-nasal defect closure and simultaneous skeletal anchorage for a fixed or fixed-removable dental prosthesis. For discontinuity defects not amenable to surgical closure, strategic placement of endosseous implants or bone grafts and implants in the residual bone also provides skeletal anchorage or stability for a removable obturator-type dental prosthesis. Coordinated surgical and prosthodontic treatment planning is critically important to provide the appropriate surgical and prosthetic procedures for each discontinuity patient.

A careful and meticulous surgical technique is required for bone graft harvesting, donor site preparation, and endosseous implant placement. Donor and recipient site osteocyte viability is preserved by controlling heat production during osseous surgery. Careful handling of mucosal and periosteal soft tissues ensures uncomplicated soft-tissue integrity, which is an absolute necessity in composite bone graft reconstruction procedures. Fresh, autogenous bone grafting is highly predictable when a strict surgical protocol is followed, and associated endosseous implant survival has approached that for reconstruction of the noncompromised edentulous maxilla. Long-term dental prosthesis function theoretically occurs if nondisturbed implant healing and proper biomechanical implant loading are provided. Continuous and stable prosthesis service is predictable and approaches 100%. This is highly significant for a group of patients who have historically had to accept significant functional and aesthetic compromises and who have few treatment choices. The quality of life has been improved greatly in this select group of patients.

References

1. Breine U, Brånemark P-I. Reconstruction of alveolar jaw bone: an experimental and clinical study of immediate and preformed autologous bone grafts in combination with osseointegrated implants. Scand J Plast Reconstr Surg 1980;14:23.

2. Adell R, Lekholm U, Grondahl K, Brånemark P-I, Lindström J, Jacobsson M. Reconstruction of severely resorbed edentulous maxillae using osseointegrated fixtures in immediate autogenous bone grafts. Int J Oral Maxillofac Implants 1990;5:233.

3. Keller EE, Van Roekel NB, Desjardins RP, Tolman DE. Prosthetic-surgical reconstruction of the severely resorbed maxilla with iliac bone grafting and tissue-integrated prostheses. Int J Oral Maxillofac Implants 1987;2:155.

4. Keller EE, Tolman DE, Brånemark P-I. Surgical reconstruction of advanced maxillary resorption with composite grafts. In Worthington P, Brånemark P-I (eds): Advanced Osseointegration Surgery: Applications in the Maxillofacial Region. Chicago: Quintessence Publishing Company; 1992:146.

5. Keller EE, Jackson IT. Treatment of skeletal deformities in the cleft patient. In Bardach J, Morris HL (eds): Multidisciplinary Management of Cleft Lip and Palate. Philadelphia: WB Saunders Company; 1990:515.

6. Keller EE, Eckert SE, Tolman DE. Maxillary antral and nasal one-stage inlay composite bone graft. Preliminary report on 30 recipient sites. J Oral Maxillofac Surg 1994;52:438.

7. Keller EE. Composite graft reconstruction of advanced maxillary resorption: autogenous iliac bone, titanium endosseous implants. In Block MS, Kent JN (eds): Endosseous Implants for Maxillofacial Reconstruction. Philadelphia: WB Saunders Company; 1994:504.

8. Keller EE. The maxillary interpositional composite graft. In Worthington P, Brånemark P-I (eds): Advanced Osseointegration Surgery: Applications in the Maxillofacial Region. Chicago: Quintessence Publishing Company; 1992:162.

9. Keller EE. Skeletal-dental reconstruction of the compromised maxilla with composite bone grafts. Atlas Oral Maxillofac Surg Clin North Am 1994;2:41.

10. Keller EE. Composite bone graft reconstruction of acquired and congenital maxillary discontinuity. Proceedings of the First International Congress on Maxillofacial Prosthetics. Palm Springs, California, April 27 to 30, 1994.

11. Keller EE. Mandibular discontinuity reconstruction (endosseous implant placement in free autogenous bone grafts). Proceedings of the First International Congress on Maxillofacial Prosthetics. Palm Springs, California, April 27 to 30, 1994.

12. Keller EE. Mandibular discontinuity reconstruction with composite grafts. Free autogenous iliac bone, titanium mesh trays, and titanium endosseous implants. Oral Maxillofac Surg Clin North Am 1991;3:877.

13. Tolman DE, Desjardins RP, Keller EE. Surgical-prosthodontic reconstruction of oronasal defects utilizing the tissue-integrated prosthesis. Int J Oral Maxillofac Implants 1988;3:31.

14. Keller EE, Triplett WW. Iliac bone grafting: review of 160 consecutive cases. J Oral Maxillofac Surg 1987;45:11.

15. Bardach J, Morris HL (eds). Multidisciplinary Management of Cleft Lip and Palate. Philadelphia: WB Saunders Company; 1990.

Part IV

Soft and Hard Tissue Defects: Prosthetic Considerations

Materials and Artistic Conceptions

17.

Kerstin Bergström, CDT

- Preoperative Planning
- Materials
- Prosthesis Retention
- Artistic Concept

Facial disfigurements resulting from tumor and other disease, congenital malformation, or accident can be restored with facial prostheses using today's new materials and retention techniques, achieving a lifelike effect and good function. To achieve this, great effort must be put into replicating the missing anatomic part. Attention to harmony, texture, color matching, and blending of tissue interface is important for the aesthetic result.[1] The choice of retention systems is important to achieve a reliable and secure retention of the prosthesis. The choice of method of retention must also consider the anatomy of the prosthesis.

An osseointegrated prosthesis greatly improves the patient's quality of life. Many patients feel that the prosthesis is a part of themselves. For example, if someone touches an artificial pinna, the patient can feel this through the implants. Brånemark calls this osseoperception.

For the anaplastologist, osseointegration facilitates sculpting the prosthesis, because it is possible to position the prosthesis in precisely the same place during the sculpting process. This precise placement may make it more difficult in that there is less space to sculpt the correct anatomy of the prosthesis because the skin-penetrating abutments and retention elements take a given amount of space. Therefore, an optimal position of implants with respect to the anatomy of the prosthesis is critical.[2] The goal is to provide the patient with a realistic and natural appearance and good function of the prosthesis (Fig 17-1).

Preoperative Planning

In tumor surgery, it is of great value when the patient is seen by the prosthetic rehabilitation team before resection. For the prosthodontist or anaplastologist, obtaining a preoperative impression of the area facilitates the prosthetic reconstruction, especially when orbital, nasal, and midfacial defects are present. For the prosthesis to fit, the surgeon must plan a defect that provides space for implant placement, retentive elements, and materials of the prosthesis without the anatomy being compromised (Fig 17-2).

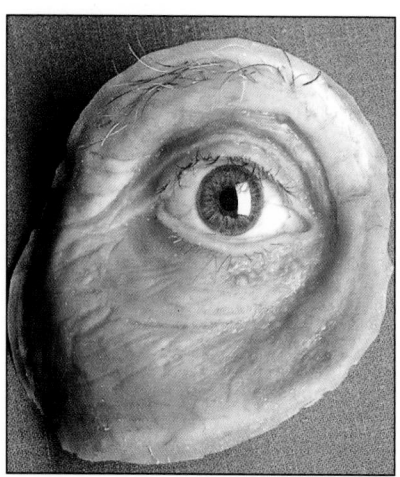

Fig 17-1. Orbital prosthesis for an elderly man shows details, intrinsic coloration, and thin margin of the prosthesis.

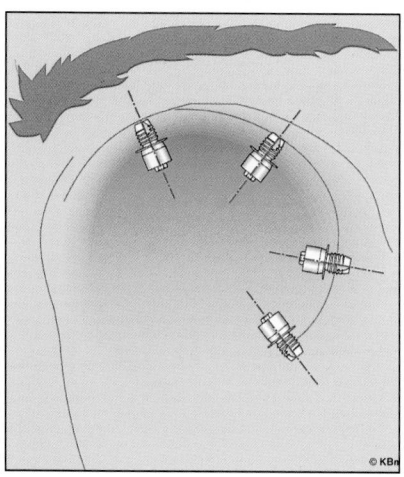

Fig 17-2. Ideal position and direction of implants in an orbital defect. (From *Craniofacial Rehabilitation: Operating Theatre Manual.* Göteborg, Sweden: Nobelpharma AB; 1995:6. By permission of the publisher.)

Preoperative planning for implant positions is crucial to the final outcome of the restoration. The anaplastologist should see the patient before implant surgery to plan implant position and direction. Close cooperation among the surgeon, prosthodontist, and anaplastologist is imperative. It is advantageous for the anaplastologist to attend implant placement surgery. If implants are angled in the wrong direction, their positions may make it impossible to achieve a good aesthetic result and optimal function of the prosthesis.

Materials

The ideal material for use in fabricating facial prostheses is silicone. There are many different brands and types of medical-grade silicone from which to choose. Important factors to consider when choosing silicone are biocompatibility, flexibility, translucency, color stability, and durability. Among the translucent silicones, some are more gray and some are more yellow or clear. These differences should be considered when mixing the colors.

When catalyst has been added to the elastomer, the material becomes fluid. A thixotropic additive can be used to thicken the material to make it easier to place the different colored parts of the material into the mold. As much intrinsic coloration as possible is included to achieve a lifelike prosthesis (Fig 17-3 and 17-4). Skin characteristics such as freckles and age spots are included. At least 7 to 10 different shades are mixed for an auricular prosthesis. Blood vessels can be added by using nylon fibers or by splitting sewing thread. Some extrinsic coloration can be made for final matching of the skin after vulcanization of the silicone.

The model of an implant-retained prosthesis usually is made in wax. Wax makes it possible to attach the model to the acrylic baseplate where the retentive elements are secured. With these parts integrated, the model may be placed on the patient in exactly the same position each time. The wax must not be too soft because the prosthesis prototype can be distorted during removal. A skin-colored wax is preferable because it is easier for the anaplastologist and for the patient to imagine the final look of the silicone prosthesis. The quality of the wax is important for the carving of lines, wrinkles, and surface texture. The wax should have plasticity and elasticity.

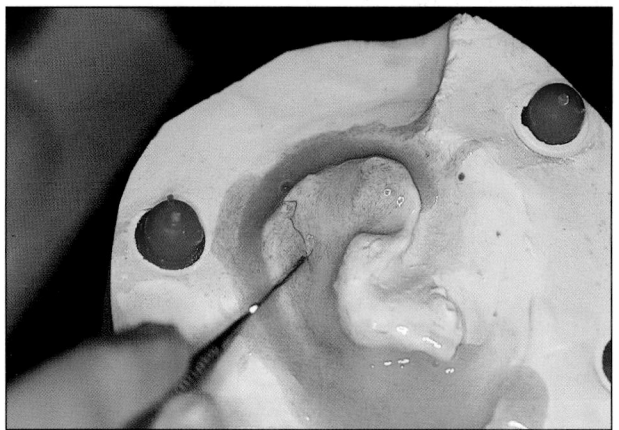

Fig 17-3. Intrinsic coloration of an auricular prosthesis.

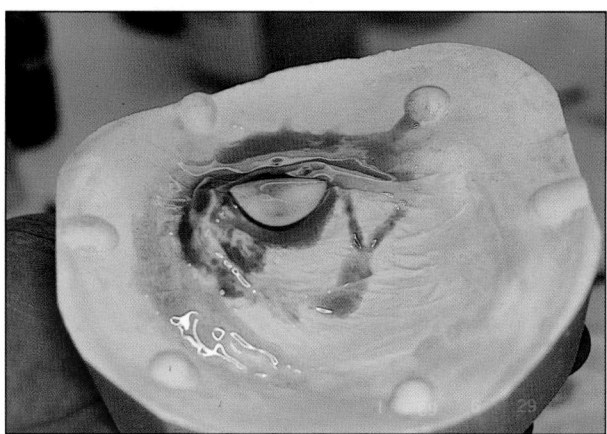

Fig 17-4. Intrinsic coloration of an orbital prosthesis.

Prosthesis Retention

There are different options to retain a prosthesis fixed with implants. The choice of retention depends on factors such as the size of the defect and the position, orientation, and number of implants. The most common types of retention used today are bar plus clips and individual magnets. When individual magnet support is used for retention, it is desirable to have a triangular arrangement of the implants. Load conditions are evaluated when designing and choosing a retention system. The load on the individual implants from the cantilever effect created through an extension of a bar construction should be considered. The movement of the face is another important factor.[3]

An acrylic baseplate is made to secure either clips or magnets inside the prosthesis. The silicone is bonded to the acrylic plate. To ensure a chemical bond between the acrylic plate and silicone, the acrylic must be prepared according to the recommendations for the primer to be used. For the best bond, the following are recommended.

1) Grind the acrylic plate. The surface that is going to be primed should be roughened with a stone grinding bit.
2) Thoroughly clean the roughened surface with solvent (acetone).
3) Apply the primer. Do not touch the primed surface with fingers because that will contaminate the surface.
4) The primer coat should be allowed to dry according to the manufacturer's recommendation before packing the mold with silicone (Fig 17-5).

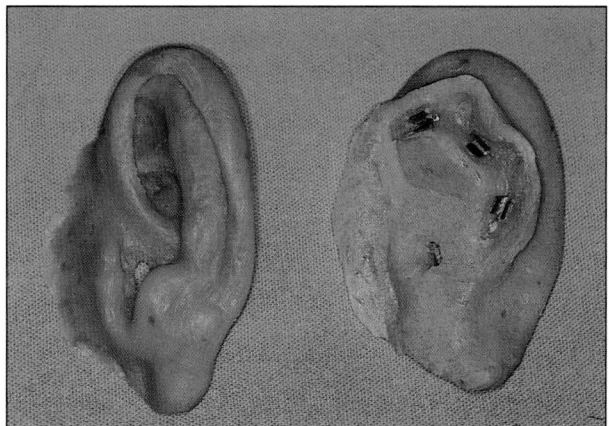

Fig 17-5. There is a chemical bond between the silicone and the acrylic baseplate.

Artistic Concept

Modeling

The process of silicone reconstruction of a facial defect includes making an impression of the normal and defective parts of the face, fabricating the retentive construction, modeling in wax to simulate the facial feature, making a mold, and packing the mold with intrinsically colored silicone to match the surrounding tissues. The final prosthesis is attached to the implants via the retentive elements.

To describe the artistic part of making a prosthesis in words is difficult. Artistically, the person making the prosthesis must use powers of observation and have a

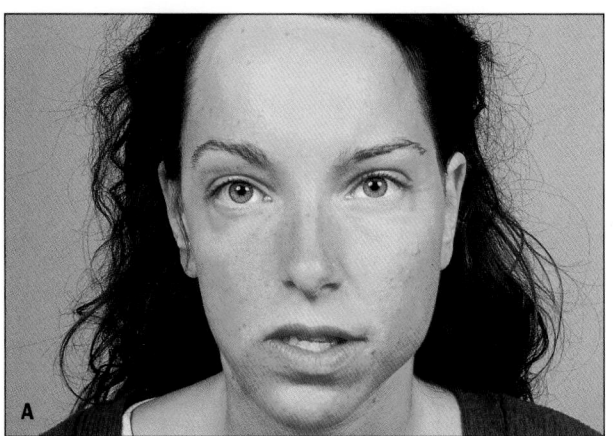
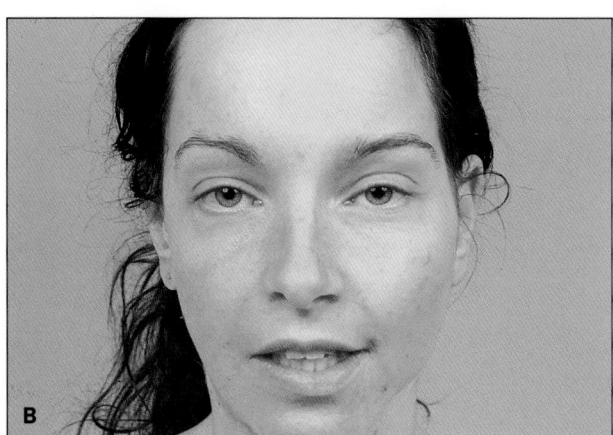

Fig 17-6. Before (*A*) and after (*B*) orthognathic surgery.

sense of aesthetics, including an understanding of form and proportion. It is important to learn how to look at things—to look in the right way. One must mentally translate and process the information seen. It is important to have the ability to imagine and to take an overall view. The anaplastologist must be able to visualize what the final result will be at the time of implant placement operation as well as when choosing a retention method.

Because the face moves in many directions, the prosthesis must be sufficiently large and flexible enough to cover the defect so there will be no gaps. The patient is asked to make facial movements such as smiling, chewing, and yawning. Proper evaluation of these movements ensures that they do not dislocate the prosthesis from the implants. An airspace should be left between the skin and the back of the prosthesis, and the margins should be left thin and flexible enough to allow for movements.

It is impossible to incorporate action into the feature being modeled, but the actions of the feature need to be taken into account.[4] It is important to catch the typical expression of the patient. When the patient and anaplastologist are satisfied with the overall shapes, contours, and proportions of the wax prosthesis, the final details are added. The texture of the prosthesis greatly influences the perception of realism in the prosthesis. In a young person, the skin is usually tight, smooth, and shiny, with few surface irregularities. The skin shows increased wrinkling and pigmentary changes with age. More surface irregularities, such as pores, veining, and raised spots, become apparent. Irregularities such as wrinkles and pores have to be exaggerated when inscribed in the wax model; otherwise, they will not show after vulcanization of the silicone. It is easier to achieve

a lifelike prosthesis for an elderly person because there are more characteristics in the skin.

Harmony

The patient is sometimes left with changes in the contour of the face as a result of tumor surgery or trauma. If nothing is done surgically to restore the contour, it is not possible to make a prosthesis that achieves symmetry. If the contour of the face is restored surgically, that helps achieve a good prosthetic restoration, although perfect symmetry is not the most important consideration. More important is to achieve harmony between the face and the prosthesis.

Faces of patients with congenital malformations often are asymmetric, so harmony and balance of the face are the goals. A good example of this is a young girl with hemifacial microsomia born with one ear missing and an asymmetric face. She received a bone-anchored auricular prosthesis that was sculpted and positioned to harmonize with the face. Because the defect side was much smaller than the normal side, it was not possible to use any measurements when positioning the ear. She was satisfied with her prosthesis and her face did not appear as asymmetric with the ear prosthesis in place. Some years later, the same girl had a jaw reconstruction and her appearance changed so that the prosthesis no longer harmonized with her face. It will be remade in accordance with her new appearance because of the now inappropriate size and position of the previous ear prosthesis (Fig 17-6).

In the case of orbit defects, sometimes the surrounding tissue is distorted, and the defect side is re-

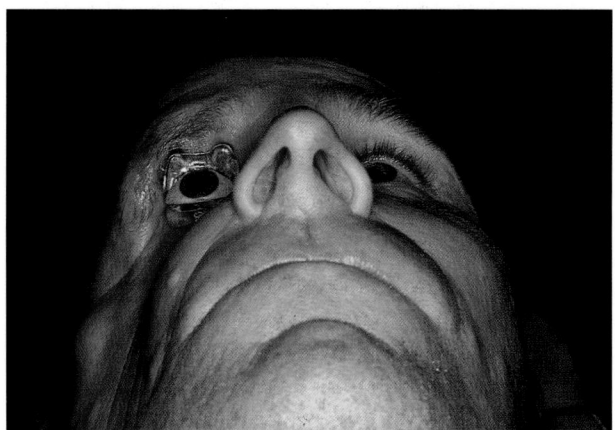

Fig 17-7. Positioning of the artificial eye before modeling of the orbital prosthesis.

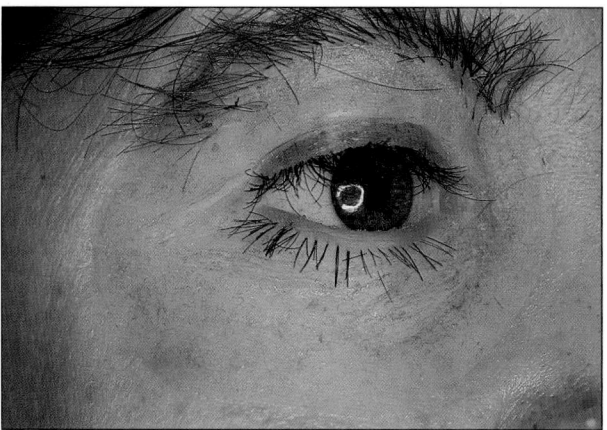

Fig 17-8. Orbital prosthesis in place (same patient as in Figure 17-7). Thin margins are imperative to allow the patient's own tissue to show through.

ceding more than the unaffected side. In such a situation it is not possible to build up symmetry with the prosthesis because it will be thick and bulky. The prosthesis has to be sculpted to fit the surrounding tissues and to harmonize with the other side. To achieve a lifelike look in orbital prostheses, the position of the artificial eye with regard to height, depth, and angle of inclination is important.[5] The positioning of the eye is determined with the patient in sitting and standing positions. The goal is to achieve a natural gaze when the patient is walking on the street and also to catch the most common expression of the patient's face. Repeated observations have to be made to catch the average configurations of the eyelids and skin surrounding the eye. It is the details that result in a realistic prosthesis (Fig 17-7). A thin edge on the prosthesis is necessary to allow the patient's own tissue to show through, thus avoiding a visible margin (Fig 17-8). Sculpting of the prosthesis should always be done with the patient present. The patient has to be involved and allowed to look in the mirror to give feedback regarding the wax model.

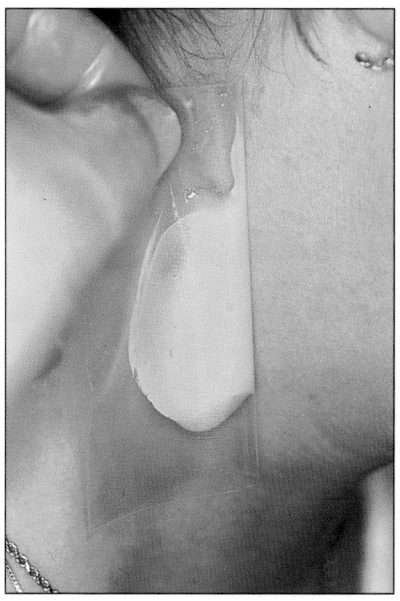

Fig 17-9. Attempt to match the basic skin color of a patient.

Color Matching

Color matching is one of the most important aspects of a successful prosthesis, but one of the most difficult to achieve (Fig 17-9). A thorough understanding of colors and how they are used is imperative.[6] To obtain realistic translucency of the skin, a translucent silicone material is used as a base. Pigments are added to the silicone to match the surrounding tissue of the prosthesis. Real skin has many heterogeneities,

including blushes, freckles, age spots, and veins. The silicone must show such variations to look realistic. Use of intrinsic coloration technique, to apply the various colors in multiple layers onto the textured surface of the mold, produces the most lifelike appearance of the prosthesis.[7] Because the silicone does not show shadows in the same way as natural skin, some parts of the prosthesis have to be colored to create shadow—for example, in the concha and underhelix of the ear (Fig 17-10).

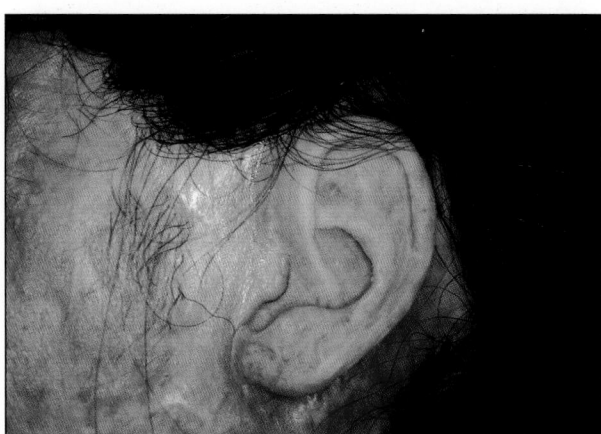

Fig 17-10. Auricular prosthesis for a burn patient.

The technique of applying the colors into the mold is important for achieving the desired effect of different shades flowing into each other. Avoid sharp lines between the different shades. Some extrinsic coloration of the prosthesis may be necessary to match the variations of the patient's skin. Because human skin changes with the season, some patients are provided with one summer and one winter prosthesis.

References

1. Sauerborn PJ, Weinberg FB. Maxillofacial prostheses as an adjunct or alternative to plastic surgery. In English GM (ed): Otolaryngology. Vol 4, chapter 65. Philadelphia: Lippincott-Raven; 1994:1.

2. Tjellström A, Jansson K, Brånemark P-I. Craniofacial defects. In Worthington P, Brånemark P-I (eds): Advanced Osseointegration Surgery: Applications in the Maxillofacial Region. Chicago: Quintessence Publishing Company; 1992:293.

3. Tjellström A, Granström G, Bergström K. Osseointegrated implants for craniofacial prostheses. In Weber RS, Miller MJ, Goepfert H (eds): Basal and Squamous Cell Skin Cancers of the Head and Neck. Baltimore: Williams & Wilkins; 1996:313.

4. Alison A. Principles of facial sculpting. In McKinstry RE (ed): Fundamentals of Facial Prosthetics. Arlington, Virginia: ABI Professional Publications; 1995:47.

5. Thomas KF. Prosthetic Rehabilitation. London: Quintessence Publishing Company; 1994.

6. De Grandis L. Theory and Use of Color. Englewood Cliffs, New Jersey: Prentice-Hall; 1986.

7. Erb RA. Intrinsic and extrinsic coloration of prostheses. In McKinstry RE (ed): Fundamentals of Facial Prosthetics. Arlington, Virginia: ABI Professional Publications; 1995:161.

Auricular Prosthesis

18.

Marcelo Ferraz de Oliveira, DDS

- Preprosthetic Plan
- Fabrication of Prosthesis
- Clinical Presentation

Congenital deformities, tumors, and trauma are the most common causes of a defect or loss of the auricle. Several techniques have been developed to rehabilitate this missing or deformed structure, enabling patients to rejoin society without the fear of being objects of mockery. Until 1977, when the osseointegration concept was applied to extraoral applications by Brånemark and colleagues,[1,2] the most common means of retention for prosthetic auricular reconstruction were adhesives, double-surface adhesive tape, or extraoral mechanical attachment (a metal band that gently clamps over the top of the head).

Unfortunately, these techniques have not proved to be retentive once the adhesive properties of the glue are impaired by perspiration and oil secretion, causing patients to sometimes endure social embarrassment due to prosthesis displacement. Another disadvantage of adhesive retention is that frequent application and removal of adhesives tend to cause deterioration of the thin margins of the prosthesis, reducing its durability. Furthermore, adhesives frequently are used on tissue surfaces compromised by adjunctive therapy (i.e., radiotherapy); therefore tissue damage may occur.[3-5]

Double-surface adhesive tape also provides retention but can be used only when there is a subsurface of polyurethane sheeting; it cannot adhere to silicone.

Extraoral mechanical attachments can hold the prosthesis in place but may compromise aesthetics because the metal band can be seen on the patient's head.

Preprosthetic Plan

Three factors are involved when planning the fabrication of a prosthesis: communication, skills, and careful treatment planning.

Regardless of the technique chosen for the fabrication of an auricular prosthesis, to achieve a successful aesthetic result, it is imperative that appropriate communication occur between the anaplastologist and the physician.

In addition to artistic and technical skills, the anaplastologist must have a broad knowledge in health sciences, such as head and neck anatomy (preoperative and postoperative), histology, physiology, and radiation oncology.

The area to be restored should be examined thoroughly. Any existing tissue tag that might compromise the final result of the prosthesis fit and aesthetics should be removed before fabrication of the prosthesis. If patients are to receive a bone-anchored prosthesis, it

213

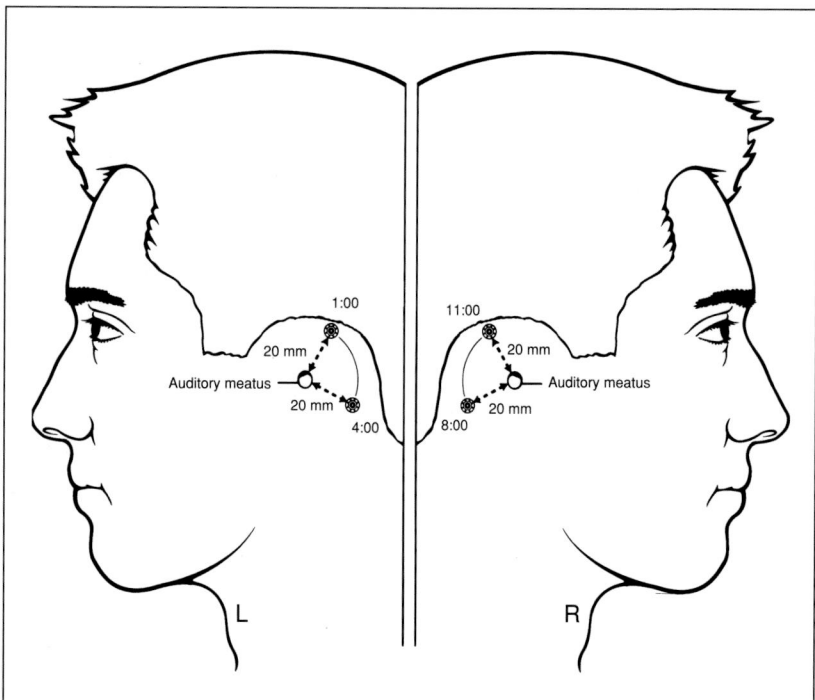

Fig 18-1. Ideal locations of implant placement.

is recommended that the tissue remnants be removed only at the second-stage procedure, because they might be useful if a skin graft has to be performed.

The number and location of the implants surgically placed determine whether the outcome of treatment will be favorable. It is known, for instance, that two implants normally are sufficient to provide retention for the auricular prosthesis, although more implants should be placed when in doubt about implant survival or in cases of poor quality or insufficient bone volume.

Because the position of the implants can facilitate or compromise the final aesthetic result, whenever it is possible, the implants should be placed 20 mm distal to the center of the external auditory meatus in the 8- and 11-o'clock positions for the right side of the face and the 1- and 4-o'clock positions for the left side (Fig 18-1). Presurgical templates should be used to guide the positioning of implants.

Unfortunately, when poor bone quality or insufficient bone volume compromises the ideal implant position and the distance from the ear canal is less than 20 mm, aesthetics will be compromised by having a prosthesis with a shallow concha, because the implants will be located right underneath it.

If the distance is more than 25 mm, then the acrylic plate will have to be fabricated with an extension so that the prosthetic ear can be positioned correctly (Fig 18-2 and 18-3).

With correct position of implants (20 mm from the ear canal and 15 mm between implants), the prosthesis support bar will be underneath the helix[3,6] (Fig 18-4 and 18-5).

Fabrication of Prosthesis

Impression and Bar Design

As described by Bergström,[3,7] the first step is to reproduce detailed anatomic information about the defect area and precise positions of the abutments. Impression copings with long guide pins are attached to the percutaneous abutments, and a thin layer of low-viscosity alginate is applied around the copings and over the area where the prosthesis will be fabricated. It is important not to cover the impression copings with alginate. Pieces of gauze are placed on the surface of the alginate. When the alginate has set, a layer of fast-set plaster is poured over the alginate. The plaster secures the impression copings in position and also stabilizes the alginate impression material. When plaster setting is completed, the guide pins are unscrewed and the impression is removed. Abutment replicas are connected to the impression copings, and the impression is cast in dental stone.

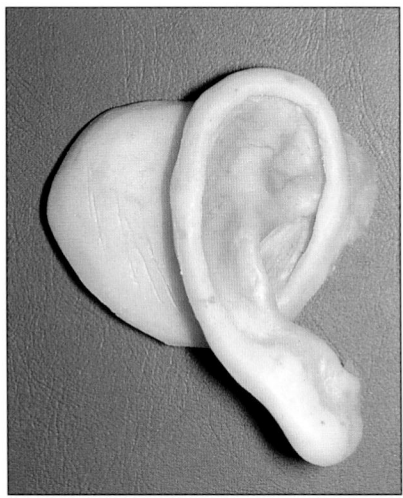

Fig 18-2. External surface of prosthesis shows extension of acrylic plate to allow correct positioning of prosthesis without ideal implant placement.

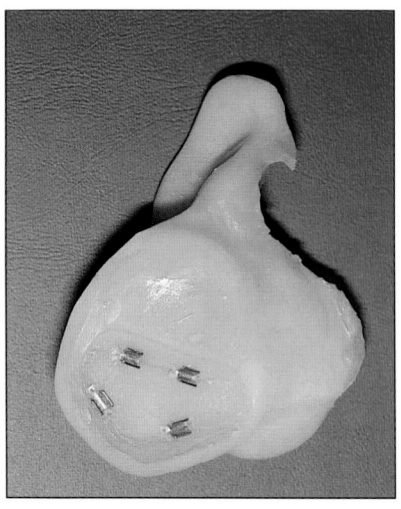

Fig 18-3. Undersurface of prosthesis (Fig 18-2) illustrates bulk required for coverage of implants and support elements.

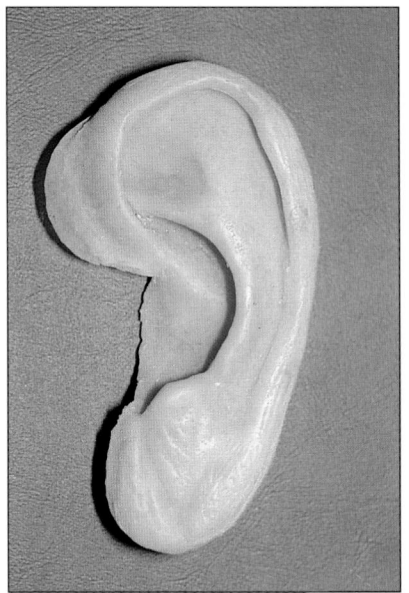

Fig 18-4. External surface of a prosthesis with ideal implant placement.

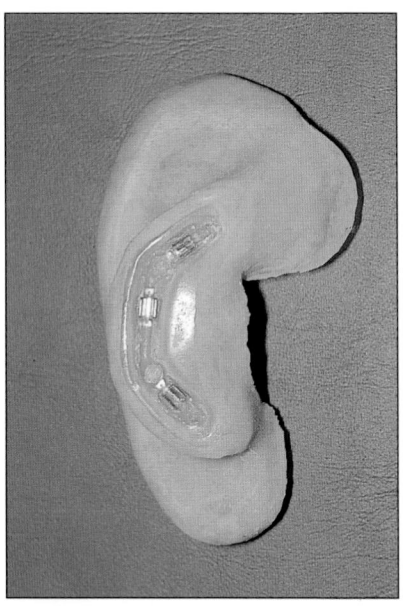

Fig 18-5. Undersurface of prosthesis (Fig 18-4) illustrates ideal position of support elements.

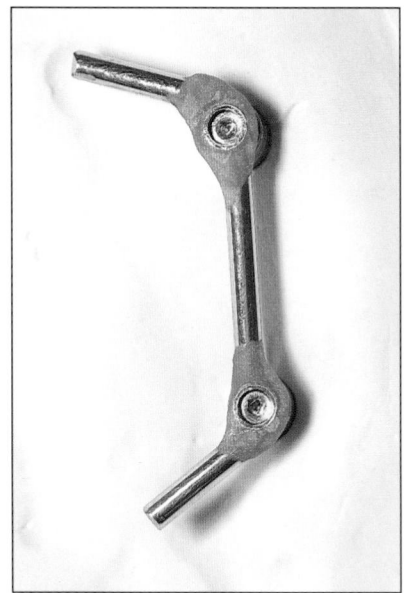

Fig 18-6. Gold bar ready for soldering.

Once the dental stone is set, the impression material is removed. The working model of the patient's defect, with the abutment replicas now in the same position, direction, and height as the skin-penetrating abutments, serves as a precise guide for the fabrication of the prosthesis.

Gold cylinders are placed on the abutment replicas of the working model, and a 0.2-mm gold bar is cut in three parts and attached to the gold cylinders with acrylic (Fig 18-6). For best aesthetic results, position the bar under the anthelix of the ear.

From the mechanical aspect, it is important that the cantilever not extend more than 8 to 10 mm beyond the abutments. The greater the distance from the abutments, the greater the bending moment ap-

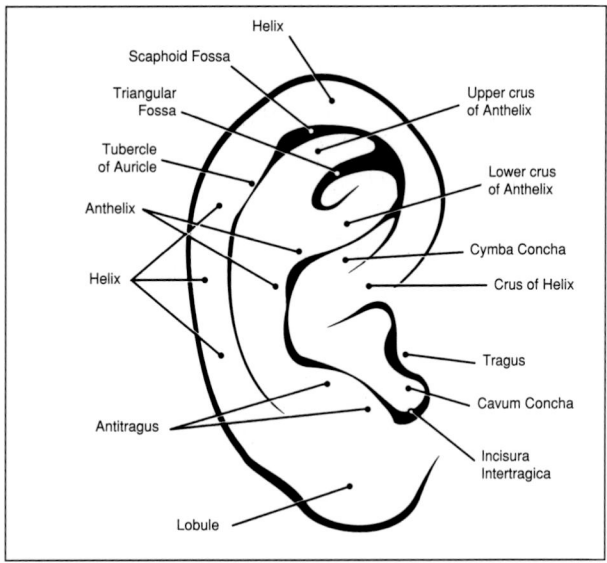

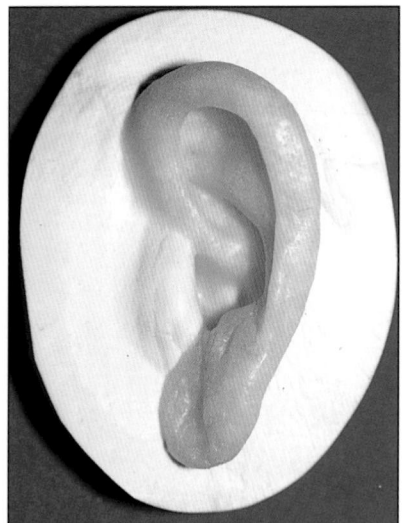

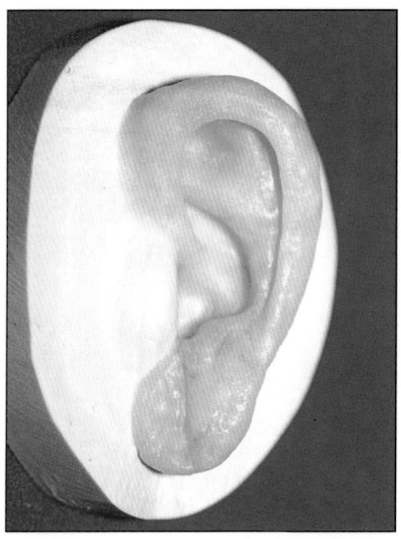

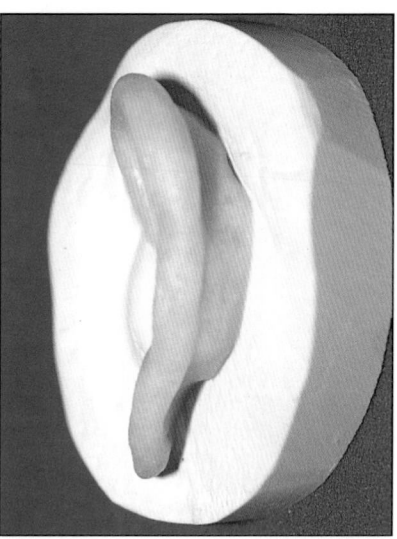

Fig 18-7. Anatomic details of the auricle.

Fig 18-8. Lateral view of sculptured prosthesis.

Fig 18-9. Anterior view of sculptured prosthesis; note space and depth beneath helix.

Fig 18-10. Posterior oblique view of sculptured prosthesis; note anatomy of helix.

plied to the implants will be, therefore possibly compromising the long-term success.[7,8]

After soldering, retention gold clips are positioned on the bar, and the acrylic plate is made with cold-cure acrylic. Fit and contour are checked in situ.

Sculpture

Special attention should be given when sculpturing, because the shape and texture of the prosthesis will look exactly like the wax pattern. The more anatomic details represented by the sculpture, the more lifelike the prosthesis appears. In addition, thin edges that

blend with the skin enhance the natural look. Therefore, to make an adequate sculpture, it is imperative that the anaplastologist knows the detailed anatomy of the auricle (Fig 18-7) and has the artistic skill to replicate it (Fig 18-8 through 18-10).

Understanding the growth pattern of the external ear is another important consideration for bilateral auricular absence, where there is no reference regarding the size of the auricle.

In a study by Adamson et al,[9] in the average child at age 3 years, 85% of ear development has been achieved. The remaining 15% occurs by age 20 years. Further small increases in length occur with advancing age and are related mostly to elongation of the lobule.[10]

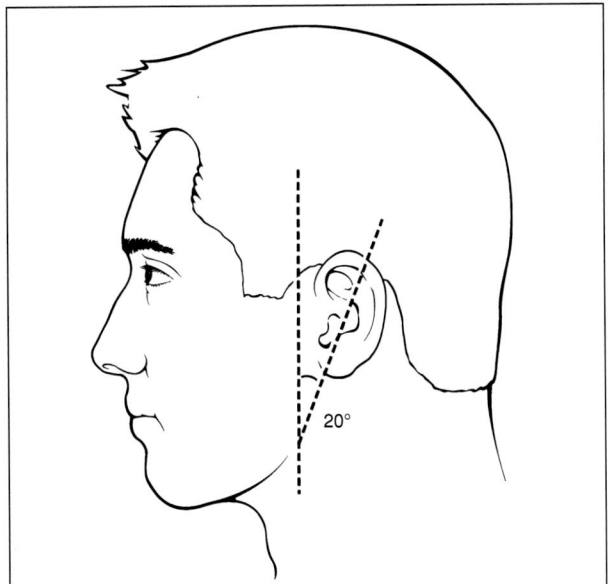

Fig 18-11. Ideal axis.

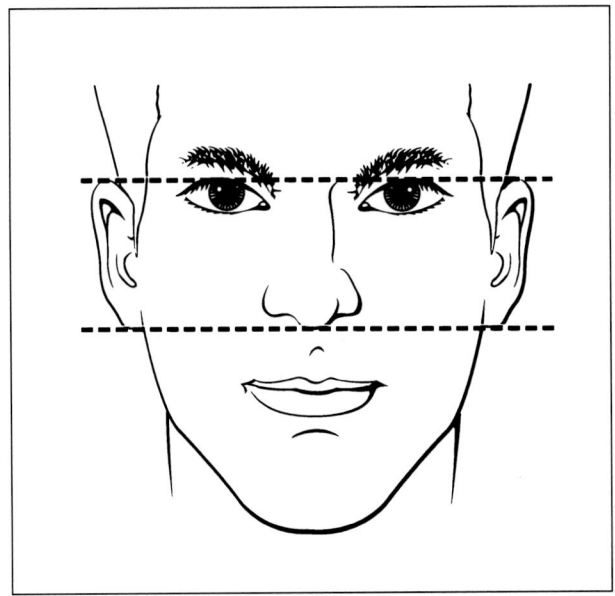

Fig 18-12. Ideal level with head in the anatomic vertical position.

Positioning of the Ear

The location of the prosthetic auricle is predetermined by first observing the topographic relationship of the opposite normal ear with facial features in cases of unilateral prosthetic reconstruction and then duplicating its position at the proposed reconstruction site. According to Tolleth,[10] three measurements must be correct to achieve a proper placement of the auricle: axis, level, and distance from the orbit.

Axis. It is difficult to define exactly the positioning of the axis, but it can be described as the "line of balance" through the long dimension of the ear. Some indicate the axis is parallel to the bridge of the nose; this is true in many cases, but it is of little significance in others, particularly in children. An angulation of 20° from the vertical position seems to be satisfactory (Fig 18-11).

Level. The level can be assessed with the head in the anatomic vertical position. The highest part of the helix is on a line roughly with that of the eyebrow, and the lowest part of the lobule is on a line at the base of the columella or slightly below that (Fig 18-12).

Distance From the Orbit. The ideal distance of the prosthesis from the lateral orbital rim is about one ear length, or 6.5 to 7.5 cm (Fig 18-13).

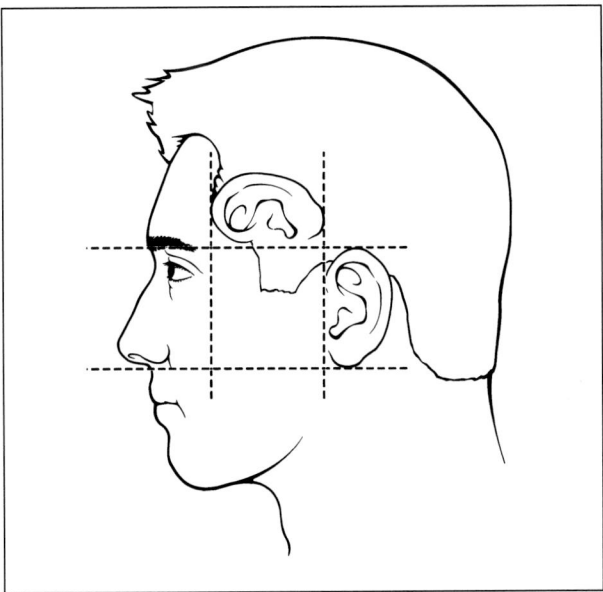

Fig 18-13. Ideal distance from the orbit.

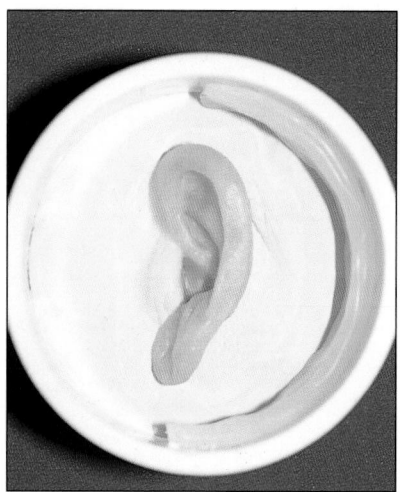

Fig 18-14. Part one of three-part mold; note stone is poured covering the bar fitted into the acrylic plate.

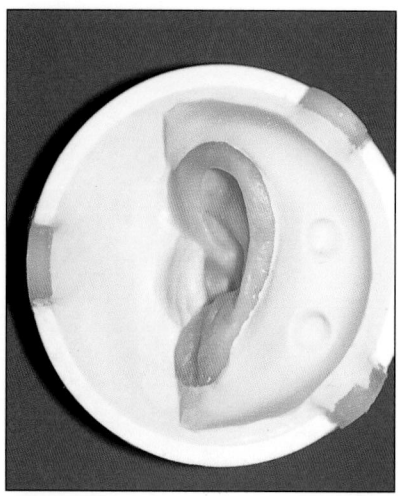

Fig 18-15. Part two of three-part mold; note stone poured until posterior part of helix and lobule are covered.

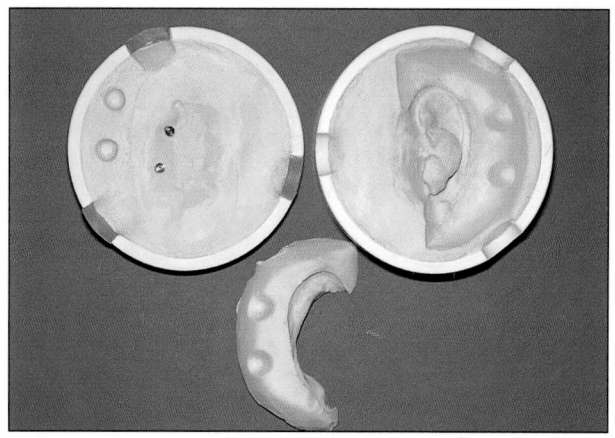

Fig 18-16. Part three of three-part mold; note stone poured to cover the entire sculpture.

Making the Mold

For an auricular prosthesis, a three-part mold seems to be ideal, because it facilitates the intrinsic painting and deflasking. Once the sculpture is refined, the bar is fitted into the acrylic plate located on the back of the sculpture and dental stone is poured, making the first part of the mold (Fig 18-14). When setting time is completed, the second part is made by pouring dental stone until the back part of the helix and lobule are completely covered (Fig 18-15). The third part is later made by pour-

ing dental stone until all the wax is covered (Fig 18-16). The stone should be allowed to harden for approximately 1 hour before the mold is dipped in hot water. The wax is thoroughly removed before packing the silicone.

Painting the Silicone and Packing

From dry pigments to oil paint, there is a great variety of materials that can be used for the coloration of silicones. In addition, rayon fibers are useful when one wants to create veins or modulate color.

Silicone should be mixed with paint until the basic color matches the skin color of the patient. At this stage, it is important to check the opacity of the mixture. Otherwise, the color may be correct but the reflection and refraction ratios cause metameric color shift of the prosthesis under different lighting. Next, all the other skin colors should be mixed. Most of the characterization should be done intrinsically, because any extrinsic painting is less durable.

Before packing the mold with silicone, the acrylic plate should be primed to create a chemical bond between the acrylic and silicone materials. The mold should be painted intrinsically in layers to represent the laminar characterization of the skin.

Once cured, the mold is opened and the prosthesis is trimmed and delivered. If necessary, extrinsic paint can be applied. With placement of the prosthesis, for aesthetic reasons, the patient can apply petroleum jelly under the thin edges. The petroleum jelly helps to blend the silicone to the skin by eliminating air between the prosthesis and skin.

Hygiene

For long-term success, the skin around the abutments must be properly cleaned on a daily basis. Therefore, it is imperative to motivate and convince the patients to do so. In most cases, patients can perform the hygiene procedures by themselves or they should be assisted by a local nurse twice a week.

The skin should be cleaned gently with a piece of gauze soaked in a solution of peroxide 3% and saline mixed in a ratio of 1:1 or soap and water. Dental floss can be used to clean around the abutments. Sharp in-

struments should be avoided, because they can traumatize the skin at the abutments. In addition, they can scratch the titanium surface, making cleaning more difficult in the future.

Clinical Presentation

Case 1

A 34-year-old man was diagnosed with atresia and deafness of the left ear. The patient was provided with a bone-anchored auricular prosthesis mechanically retained on two implants with a bar and clip system (Fig 18-17 through 18-20).

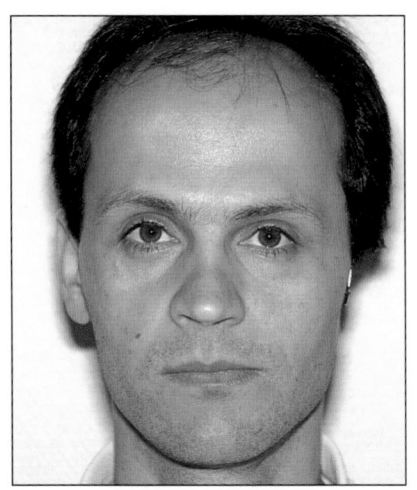

Fig 18-17. A 34-year-old man with atresia of left ear.

Fig 18-18. Completed prosthesis in place.

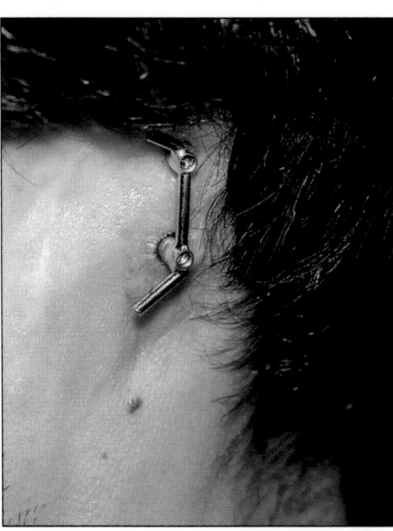

Fig 18-19. Support bar for the prosthesis.

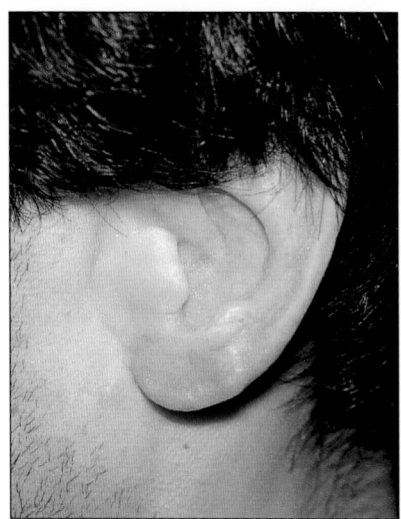

Fig 18-20. Lateral view of prosthesis in place.

Case 2

This man underwent left auricular resection for a squamous cell carcinoma (Fig 18-21 through 18-25).

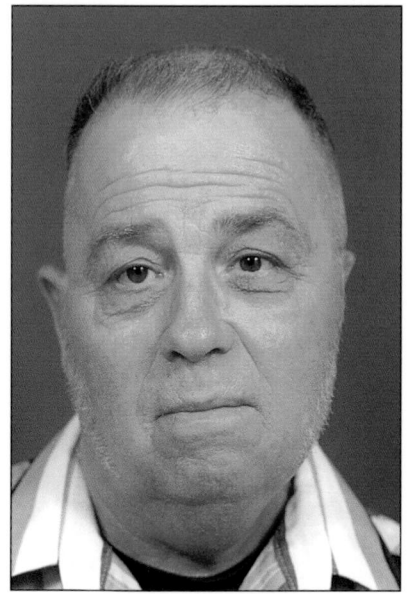

Fig 18-21. Left ear resected for squamous cell carcinoma.

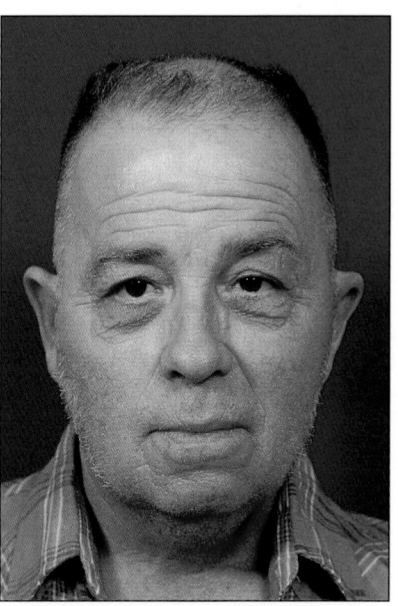

Fig 18-22. Completed prosthesis in place.

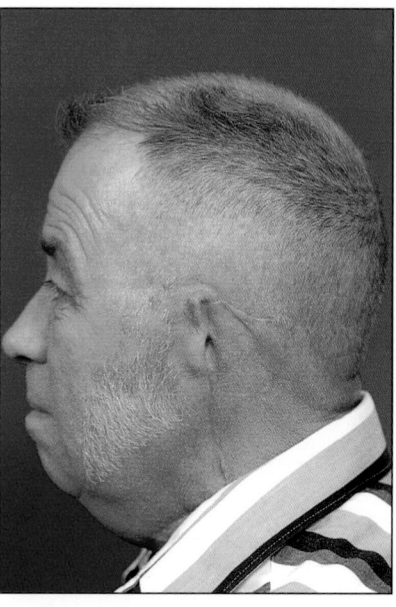

Fig 18-23. Defect before reconstruction.

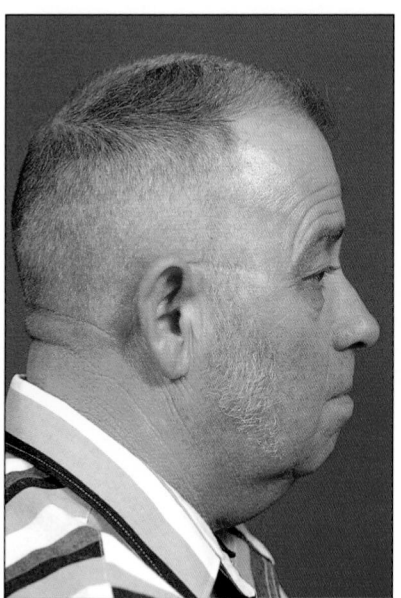

Fig 18-24. Lateral view of right ear used for comparison when sculpturing the prosthesis.

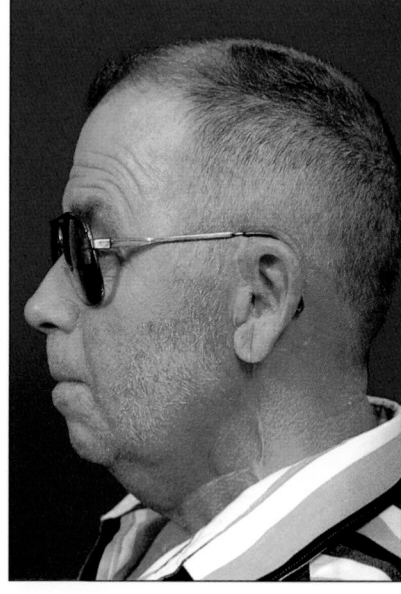

Fig 18-25. Prosthesis in place supporting eyeglasses.

References

1. Tjellström A, Jansson K, Brånemark P-I. Craniofacial defects. In Worthington P, Brånemark P-I (eds): Advanced Osseointegration Surgery: Applications in the Maxillofacial Region. Chapter 25. Chicago: Quintessence Publishing Company; 1992:293.

2. Hallén O, Magnusson S, Jacobsson M, Marké L-Å. Bone-Anchored Implants in the Head and Neck Region: Report From a Conference. Stockholm, Sweden: The Swedish Council on Technology Assessment in Health Care; 1989.

3. Tjellström A, Granström G, Bergström K. Osseointegrated implants for craniofacial prostheses. In Weber RS, Miller MJ, Goepfert H (eds): Basal and Squamous Cell Skin Cancers of the Head and Neck. Baltimore: Williams & Wilkins; 1996:313.

4. Del Valle V, Faulkner G, Wolfaardt J, Rangert B, Tan H-K. Mechanical evaluation of craniofacial osseointegration retention systems. Int J Oral Maxillofac Implants 1995;10:491.

5. Bulbulian AH. Facial Prosthesis. Philadelphia: WB Saunders Company; 1945:177.

6. Tjellström A. Osseointegrated implants for replacement of absent or defective ears. Clin Plast Surg 1990;17:355.

7. Bergström K. Anaplastological technique for facial defects. In Brånemark P-I, Oliveira MF (eds). Craniofacial Prostheses: Anaplastology and Osseointegration. Part II. Chapter 4. Chicago: Quintessence Publishing Company; 1997:101.

8. Rangert B. Biomechanical considerations for implant-supported orbital prosthesis. J Facial Somato Prosthet 1996;2:43.

9. Adamson JE, Horton CE, Crawford HH. The growth pattern of the external ear. Plast Reconstr Surg 1965;36:466.

10. Tolleth H. Artistic anatomy, dimensions, and proportions of the external ear. Clin Plast Surg 1978;5:337.

Nasal Prosthesis

19.

Ann Fyler, BS
William E. LaVelle, DDS, MS

- Treatment Planning
- Fabrication of a Presurgical Prosthesis Model and Implant Placement Guide
- Implant Placement and Abutment Connection
- Postsurgical Implant Impression
- Framework Design and Fabrication
- Fabrication of the Clip or Magnet Plate

- Adaptation of Sculpture to Postimplantation Model and Incorporation of Retention Clip
- Mold Fabrication
- Packing the Mold With Silicone
- Final Fitting, Patient Application Practice, and Hygiene Instructions
- Case Studies

The use of endosseous titanium implants with percutaneous abutments to retain facial prostheses greatly improves the outcome of facial prosthetic restoration.[1-6] The prosthesis is secured by retention clips or magnets that attach to a fixed bar that spans implant abutments or by supra-abutment magnets that screw onto the abutments.[7-9] The prosthesis is positioned easily and retained securely. Patient confidence in the retention of the prosthesis greatly increases.

The presence of moisture, mobile soft tissues, or lack of stable tissue support will not affect the retention of an extraoral prosthesis attached to the face by mechanical means to bone-anchored implants. Adhesives are no longer needed for retention; when the patient perspires, there can be no sudden loss of retention due to adhesive failure. Without the use of adhesives, the longevity of the prosthesis increases. Removal of adhesives, by either rubbing or rolling the adhesive off with fingers and thumb or using ad-

hesive solvents is no longer necessary; therefore, the prosthesis edges will be much less likely to tear. Prosthesis hygiene is simplified when the patient's task of applying and removing adhesive is eliminated. Extrinsic color characterization and the integrity of the prosthesis are better maintained with less handling. By eliminating the need for adhesive, a prosthesis can be designed to contact the skin as little as 2 or 3 mm in areas where there is a more or less vertical angle onto the skin or where the prosthesis can be tucked into a fold, as in the edge of the nostril in the nasolabial fold. Where the slope of the prosthesis blends tangentially onto the face, as in the bridge of the nose, less than 7 to 8 mm of skin contact is necessary. If there is less tissue contact by the prosthesis, then there will be less potential for friction or heat irritation to the skin.

Patients should be screened for candidacy for bone-anchored implants. Patients need to be ready psychologically for a facial prosthesis and have sufficient dexterity and visual acuity to apply the prosthesis and maintain hygiene around abutment sites and the prosthesis. A facial prosthetic restoration using bone-anchored implants requires a lifelong commitment from patient and practitioner to monitor and maintain the health of the periabutment tissues and the cosmesis and hygiene of the facial prosthesis. Periodic replacement of the prosthesis is necessary as the patient ages or changes weight and as the prosthesis degrades from environmental exposure and wear. Replacements of the silicone facial prosthesis, although not the retention mechanism, will be necessary at intervals of 2 to 5 years, depending on the patient's care of the prosthesis, the rate of postsurgical tissue remodeling and healing, and whether the patient smokes.

Patients should be made fully aware of the total cost involved in undergoing bone-anchored prosthetic restoration in advance of treatment. This includes team evaluation; diagnostic studies; two operations, including hospital and medical service charges, hardware fees, and biphase prosthetic service (retention bar or magnets and prosthesis); and follow-up. The patient needs to seek insurance approval that allows an extension of the normal 3-month limit to procedure scheduling and secure coverage for the total package, which will take longer than 3 months. Usually hospital and medical service charges are generated as service and treatment occur, so third-party insurance payers need to know these are related charges. Insurance approval of surgical implantation, but not the prosthesis, does not make sense, nor is it fair to the prosthodontist or anaplastologist who provide most of their services toward the end of the treatment plan. Unless approval is sought in advance, with an acknowledgment that these are sequential and unbundled fees generated from several health care providers, coverage for the total treatment plan may be incomplete. The patient needs to be clear about financial obligations for the initial treatment for implant placement and abutment connection, external fixation device, and facial prosthesis and the need for future replacement facial prostheses.

Treatment Planning

For patients needing nasal prosthetic restoration, the decision to undergo percutaneous osseointegrated implant surgery generally does not mean soft-tissue

surgical reconstruction could not be performed at a later date. Usually, implants are placed in the maxillary floor of the nasal antrum on either side of the septum, so that the abutments exit through attached immobile tissues.[10] If the patient decides not to wear a prosthesis, then the abutments and framework could be removed and the implants covered with soft tissue. Surgical tissue reconstruction of the nose could follow. This is contrary to auricular prosthetic restoration in which titanium implant placement involves significantly thinning the periabutment tissue or skin grafting at the time of abutment placement and perhaps eliminating autogenous bone graft or hydroxyapatite augmentation as an option. For nasal and auricular prosthetic restoration, however, the opposite is true: titanium implant placement can be a treatment option after unsuccessful autogenous grafts or unsuccessful hydroxyapatite surgical reconstruction.

Surgical preparation of the nasal tissues for prosthetic restoration can improve cosmesis, treatment execution, and retention. The following recommendations can be applied only as the surgeon judges appropriate, but, as a rule, the nasal spine should be left intact, because it is the only stable tissue at the base of the nose. Alar tissue tags should be removed or be reduced, because they act as levers that lift the prosthesis as they move away from midline during facial muscle flexion (e.g., when the patient smiles, depresses the upper lip, or grimaces). The nasal bones should be left intact. Exposed bone should be covered with a skin graft to accelerate the commencement of prosthetic restoration. The nasal septum should be reduced if it protrudes beyond the plane of the cheek to avoid potential abrasion and allow enough room for the sculpture on the tissue side.[11]

When a multidisciplinary treatment plan involves the sequential application of treatment and one stage affects the outcome of later stages, communication is especially important. The principal members of the osseointegration team are surgeon, prosthodontist, and anaplastologist. Patients undergo osseointegrated implant placement not for the implants, but as a means to anchor excellent facial prostheses. Implant placement should not be undertaken if the prosthetic team has not been included in the presurgical evaluation. The whole team should conceptualize the entire treatment plan presurgically, so that implants are placed in the best position for cosmesis and retention. To accomplish this, the patient is evaluated medically for implant candidacy, and the areas of suf-

ting problems may become apparent only at the completion of the bone-anchored silicone prosthesis.

Once the silicone prosthesis has been cured, gapping can be corrected by filling the gap with silicone, but the result is a thick and noticeable edge that is likely to delaminate over time. Pressure points can be relieved by drilling or cutting away the silicone with silicone burs, but this may risk tearing the silicone prosthesis. Either of these corrections compromises the integrity of the finished prosthesis. A better fabrication protocol includes an assessment of dynamic tissue action and the development of a prosthetic design based on that assessment before the mold is made. To accomplish these goals, a fitting template can be fabricated.

The purpose of the fitting template is to: 1) check the accuracy of the cast model, 2) evaluate muscle action and soft-tissue movement, 3) identify any tissue areas that may be sensitive to pressure, 4) serve as a temporary liner for the wax sculpture, and 5) visualize the location of the implant sites in relation to the defect and prototype prosthesis.

The template material used is 0.020-in. vacuumformable temporary splint material (Buffalo). Although the template is made of a thermoplastic material and is thin and somewhat flexible, it works well in this application. A silicone prosthesis is lightweight and also somewhat flexible, and it will respond to tissue movement in a similar manner as the template. The use of a fitting template eliminates the need for modifying a model or mold contour by guessing. The exact functional configuration of the facial tissues is analyzed and recorded, and there is little chance of fabricating a malfitting prosthesis.

After the stone model is trimmed, a sheet of 0.020-in. temporary splint material is vacuumformed over the model. The vacuum-formed sheet is removed easily from the model by cutting the edges with scissors and carefully removing it. The template should not be stored on the model, because the moisture in the stone will warp it. Replacement templates are easily produced by the anaplastologist during the analysis and sculpture development. The template is not meant to be a permanent part of the prosthesis, and it will be discarded before the wax edges are sealed to the stone mold during final margin shaping. The template is trimmed with scissors to cut away the areas over the airway and the areas beyond the widest possible theoretical margins of the prosthesis. Sandpaper can smooth any rough edges. The template is held in place on the patient's face and should fit the patient's face. Any difference between the fit

of the template on the model and the fit of the template on the patient is immediately obvious. A poor fit at this stage indicates a new impression should be taken. A good fit demonstrates the model is correct, at least in a passive facial expression.

If there is any blanching of the tissue, such as on the nasal spine, it is apparent immediately because the template is transparent. These tissues, other sensitive areas, or the nasal mucosa should not contact the prosthesis. Use a felt-tip pen to circle the areas on the template while the template is still in place on the patient's face. This information can be transferred to the stone model by cutting away the encircled area of the template and tracing the edges on the stone. The wax model can be relieved on the defect side in the areas circled on the template. The template provides a useful check because felt-tip pen marks can be seen from both sides.

Next, the patient is instructed to flex the face: smile, grimace, stretch the lip downward, or lift the forehead. Use a felt-tipped pen to outline the margin of the areas that gap under muscle flexion and extension; the gapping portion of the template, usually on the periphery, is cut off by scissors. Trimming is done in a gradual manner, functionally testing the template on the patient after each reduction. The template should be trimmed until it is almost completely stable when the patient makes these facial expressions. The final template shape is reduced greatly in size, especially in the area of the lip and nostrils where tissues are most mobile. This tests the functional accuracy of the model. First, it gives an accurate indication of where the tissue is stable and unlikely to be irritated by friction or gap. Second, it indicates where the tissue is movable, such as at the base of the nose, and therefore the template identifies the areas where the prosthesis is designed to contact the skin as minimally as possible. In most instances where there is substantial tissue movement, less tissue contact provides better retention than more tissue contact. If the prosthesis is thin in these areas, then the prosthesis will be more flexible and more likely to accommodate tissue movement. If there is a gap caused by extreme tissue divergence, as may occur in a big smile or wide open mouth, then part or all of the template can be relined to produce an improved model based on functional information.

If there is a need to reline the template, then the following procedure should be used. The template functions as a tray, but because it is not rigid it will need to be reinforced by plaster before removing the new impression. The template is perforated with a

229

fissure bur or small punch in the area to be relined. The back of the template is coated with vinyl polysiloxane adhesive where the impression material will be added. The adhesive is likely to warp the template slightly where it is applied, but that does not matter because the relining impression material corrects that. A thin coat of vinyl polysiloxane impression material is applied to the glue side of the template. The template is positioned gently in the proper orientation on the patient's face. If the original template fit everywhere and only gapped in the nostril and lip area during extreme functional divergence, then the patient is asked to smile or to open the mouth. The gap is filled with impression material. Excess impression material will ooze through the perforations. Do not apply too much impression material so that the soft tissues are compressed. Plaster is applied to the impression before removing it from the patient's face. The impression is poured up in the manner previously described. Another template is made from the new model and checked on the face to be sure the correction has been made.

Fabrication of the Wax Sculpture

Artistic talent is needed for the development of a realistic personalized feature. If the sculpture is crude, primitive in form, or inaccurate in anatomy, then it may be as noticeable and as undesirable as a bandage. The patient hopes for a realistic personalized feature. Failure on the practitioner's part to meet the best possible standards of aesthetics, given the limitations presented by a particular defect, is indefensible. Although obtaining excellent cosmesis is necessary, it is not enough. The sculpture and the resulting prosthesis must be retained and nonirritating. To accomplish these goals, the sculpture must be formed with consideration for its tissue or defect side. An excellent prosthesis is designed on its retentive or posterior side with as much care as for the aesthetic or anterior aspect. Sensitive or vulnerable tissues, nasal mucosa, or tissues with compromised vascularization should be avoided as a contact base for facial prostheses. Where there is a possibility that movement under the prosthesis could create irritation or tissue problems, the sculpture should be thinned or relieved on its posterior aspect to minimize tissue contact. After sculpture modifications, the fit is checked again during passive and active facial expression.

We prefer to use the fitting template, which is trimmed in a manner previously described, as a base for the wax sculpture. 1) The template registers more accurately to the skin and the model than wax alone. 2) The airway can be established quickly in the wax sculpture by the template pattern. 3) Tissues to be avoided are indicated clearly on the template and the wax can be relieved in these areas accordingly. 4) If wax distortion develops during the sculpture development, it is detected and corrected easily. 5) The template can be cleaned so wax shards are not incorporated inadvertently into the wax sculpture. 6) Glue or two-sided adhesive tape can be applied to the template-wax unit so the sculpture can be judged in situ from a distance and under its own weight.

The fitting template is a useful tool for the periodic check for distortion that may occur during sculpting. Practitioners who fit wax sculptures to the face tend to hold the wax where they want it to go, and they may not notice that a wax sculpture without a template backing has begun to rock slightly. Skin is pliable and accommodating to pressure and tends to hide this fabrication artifact when a sculpture of wax alone is held in place on the face. The template lining the sculpture makes fit comparison between the model and the patient easy. During the process of sculpting, if the wax has shrunk or warped or has been bent accidentally, a simple correction can be made. The vacuum-formed backing is popped off the wax. Then it is reseated on the stone model. The wax sculpture is positioned on top of it and heat sealed in place. Liquid wax is fluted into any area that gaps between the sculpture and template. The clarity of the backing allows the practitioner to understand the artifact and its correction precisely.

Because the backing is plastic it can be scraped clean before each trial fitting. Without it, wax shards can become attached inadvertently to the wax sculpture and change the practitioner's view of the work, resulting in overcorrection of form.

Another advantage to using the template and wax sculpture as a unit is that it can be glued or taped to the patient. The anaplastologist can evaluate the sculpture the way it will rest on the patient's face under its own weight. Attaching the wax-template unit to the face makes viewing it from all angles and distances easier. This eliminates the viewing error of holding the wax model where the practitioner wants to see it rather than where the wax model actually seats. It provides better viewing of the sculpture by the patient, because the practitioner's or patient's hand is not obstructing the view. It is easier to assess passive and functional facial expression with the sculpture held by adhesives in situ.

Either clay or wax can be used for the development of the nasal sculpture. We prefer wax because it can be boiled out of the mold cleanly, eliminating the risk to the mold of residual contamination from sulfur and oils that are left from clay that may inhibit the cure of platinum-cured silicones. The trimmed vacuum-formed template is seated on the stone model. A single sheet of pink baseplate wax is warmed and heat sealed to the plastic template. This gives the template an even reinforcement of wax and forms a smooth bottom layer of wax. Do not overheat the vacuum-formed template. Tissue-colored wax is melted to a liquid state and allowed to cool until it has the texture of soft clay. It is layered on top of the pink baseplate wax and heat melded to it. A rough shape of the patient's nose is shaped quickly on the template while it is still sitting on the stone cast. An airway is formed quickly by removing wax from behind. This is easily done when using the template, because the airway is indicated clearly by a central hole in the template. While the wax is still soft and warm, the wax-template unit is placed on the patient's face; a sagittal midline and a horizontal line for the upper edge of the nostrils are drawn in the wax with a tool. The wax sculpture is refined for symmetry, anatomic accuracy, and fit considerations. A prosthesis should appear to grow out of the face, not just sit on it. Thin edges grow from a face or the stone model of the face, not from the wax sculpture to the stone model; this is a key concept and a technique for making invisible or unnoticeable edges. The shape and contours present in the face lead into the sculptural form in a continuous manner, as though the anatomy was uninterrupted.

The sculpture unit is held up to light and carved from the back until sufficient and equal thinness of the wax sculpture are achieved. The walls of a nasal sculpture need not be more than 4 mm thick, and they should be much thinner where there is a need for flexure accommodation. Transillumination can be controlled in the mold-painting stage by thinly coating the defect side of the mold in the area of the nasal airway blockout with an opaque version of the base color. The wax-template unit is glued on the patient for a final check. In the preimplant sculpture of the nose, the edges need not be as thin as they would be for the final nose. Extremely thin edges are likely to break during the conversion of the wax sculpture to an acrylic surgical guide.

Fabrication of the Implant Placement Guide

The completed wax model can be reproduced in acrylic or polypropylene for use as an implant placement guide during implant surgery. These materials can be sterilized and are not broken easily. A simple two-piece mold of reinforced silicone is made of the wax sculpture-template unit. Clear, cold-cure acrylic resin is placed in the mold and cured in the usual manner. The acrylic replica is trimmed. An alternative method is to make an impression of the wax sculpture seated on the stone model to produce a stone cast. A surgical model of the sculpture can be created by vacuum-forming polypropylene (0.080-in. clear tray material) (Buffalo) on this stone cast. The first technique yields information about the airway and the areas of the special relief of the sculpture and the thickness of the prosthesis wall; the second technique yields information about the external shape less the thickness of the template material. At this point, consultation with the prosthodontist and surgeon about potential framework designs and implant placement occurs. The acrylic or polypropylene model is sterilized in preparation for its use as a reference during implant surgery. The same model or the wax sculpture is used later in the development of the retention framework and retention plate.[14]

Implant Placement and Abutment Connection

The surgical procedures for implant placement and abutment connection have been described extensively elsewhere and therefore will not be discussed here.[15] For support of the nasal prosthesis, the ideal site for implant placement is the anterior nasal floor, avoiding the roots of the anterior maxillary teeth. The periabutment soft tissue should be thin and immobile. The success rates of implants placed in the glabellar region are poor.[16] For aesthetic reasons, glabellar and lateral maxillary sites are poor choices for implants, because the external hardware and framework will interfere with the aesthetic formation of the nose.

Three to four months, or 6 to 8 months for irradiated tissues, is required between the implant placement and the abutment connection to allow for osseointegration. Four to six weeks is needed after abutment connection to allow complete healing of periabutment tissues before the commencement of the prosthetic procedures. If extensive skin grafting or thinning of skin was done during abutment connection, an additional delay of a few weeks may be necessary.

Postsurgical Implant Impression

The purpose of the postsurgical implant impression is to register precisely the implant location in the stone model of the midface. Any mucous debris should be removed before beginning the impression. In this impression the nasal opening *must* be occluded with moistened gauze to prevent the aspiration of mishandled hardware components.

Alginate, light body polysulfide impression material, and light body vinyl polysiloxane have all been suggested as appropriate impression materials. The use of alginate requires a dental floss lashing reinforced with DuraLay (Reliance Dental Co, Worth, IL) between the transfer copings, whereas the other materials are sufficiently strong to maintain the position of the transfer copings without reinforcement between abutments. All three impression materials are reinforced with plaster. We believe that soft-tissue considerations and the accurate transfer of implant position are of equal importance. Where there is extensive and recent skin grafting or thinning of tissues around the implant abutments, as is often the case in auricular implantation and sometimes the case in nasal implantation, alginate is the preferred impression material. Polysulfide and vinyl polysiloxane may lift the graft on the removal of the impression because of excessive surface tension. Subsequent periabutment tissue problems are likely to arise as a consequence. In the nose when recent grafting has not occurred, light body polysulfide and light body vinyl polysiloxane are the materials of choice. Alginate is less strong, and the patient is likely to react involuntarily to the chill of the moistened alginate.

The impression technique previously described is followed, with the addition of these instructions. First, the transfer copings are screwed onto the abutments with long transfer screws. The hardware components must be articulated properly. This impression should include the anterior surface of the septum, if present, in addition to the periabutment tissues and external perinasal tissues, because the septal relationship to implant location is crucial to

design of the framework. The inclusion of the anterior aspect of the septum in the impression helps to determine the vertical and coronal angles of the framework. Vinyl polysiloxane or polysulfide material should be extruded from a compound syringe around the abutments and transfer copings, covering an area of at least 10 mm beyond the abutments. The impression must be bubble free to maintain the accurate position of the transfer copings. The impression material is extended from the abutment area over the tissue of the external nose. The impression is reinforced with plaster. The tops of the transfer screws must be free of plaster so they can be unscrewed once the impression is set. To remove the impression, the transfer screws are loosened. Once the impression is removed, brass abutment analogs are attached to the transfer copings, which are still embedded in the impression, by tightening the transfer screws. Stone is poured into the impression, trapping the brass abutment analogs. To remove the impression from the master cast, the transfer screws are unscrewed, freeing the impression. The embedded abutment analogs are retrieved from the impression for reuse.

Framework Design and Fabrication

Framework design must consider: 1) space available under sculpture, including space allowance for retention clip plate or magnet plate; 2) establishment of sufficient airway; 3) access for cleaning periabutment tissues and nasal cavity; 4) length of framework extension from abutments and need for and location of cross-bracing stabilization; 5) amount of projection of the framework from the face in the coronal plane; 6) facial tissue movement that might affect the fit or retention of the nasal prosthesis; 7) ease of prosthesis application and patient capabilities; and 8) anticipation of nasal prosthesis mold design.

We avoid any retention design that engages the nasal mucosa or seats within the internal nose.

The completed framework must be checked for passive fit so torque is not placed on the implants, which could cause them to fail over time. A simple test is to tighten both sides, then loosen one side, and perform the same exercise on the opposite implant. If the framework does not lift or rock during unilateral tightening and is fully seated at all times, then the framework is judged to fit. A misfit requires the framework to be cut and corrected.

With the preimplantation sculpture or its clear acrylic or polypropylene replicate, it is easy to visualize the space available for the framework design and retention plate. To gain a profile view, the clear surgical template can be sectioned midsagittally. This view is useful in visualizing the retention bar and the dorsum of an articulated clip plate in relation to the inside of the dorsum of the sculpture.

To establish the space between the framework and the underlying septum, if present, a sheet of 0.150-in. clear mouth-guard material is vacuum-formed over the postimplant model. The abutment analogs are exposed by cutting a circular shape with a scalpel in the vacuum-formed spacer. The framework copings are screwed into the abutments. The framework model is developed using the spacer for support. If the septum has been removed surgically, then Reprosil Putty (L.D. Caulk) is shaped on the stone replica of the airway to the coronal plane desired for framework projection. The framework in its formation stage can be supported by this blockout.

For nasal prostheses, a midline clip and framework retention is best in most cases. The framework is designed to be cast in metal and is an upside down Y shape that has a cross brace between the widest part of the Y near the abutments. The advantages of this design are that it: 1) allows maximum bilateral airflow; 2) provides for vertical and horizontal clip orientation, preventing the misapplication of the facial prosthesis; and 3) provides adequate access to the nasal cavity and periabutment tissues for hygiene maintenance.

As part of the wax framework model, plastic sprues, 2 mm in diameter, are cut and positioned as the vertical stem and transverse brace of the inverted Y. It is on these segments of the cast metal framework that the clips will articulate. There should be enough vertical projection off the feet of the inverted Y, below the cross brace, so that the periabutment tissues can be accessed for hygiene maintenance. Also, the diagonal or triangular segments of the Y should be as far away from the walls of the nasal cavity as possible, so cleaning the turbinate and septal surfaces of the internal nose can be accomplished. The stem on the inverted Y should be as short as possible but still allow the attachment of a vertically oriented clip. The preferred clips are CM Rider for Hader bar (Attachments and Implants International, San Mateo, CA). These clips are resilient and retentive and can be tightened if the retention loosens slightly after extended wear.

Midline retention is preferred to lateral retention because of facial tissue movement considerations. Wherever there is a clip or magnet, that area of the nasal prosthesis will be thicker, because retention devices are embedded in acrylic and are usually further surrounded by silicone. A lateral location for magnet or clip attachment, near the external facial tissues, limits the flexibility and responsiveness to tissue movement of the prosthesis edge because thick silicone accommodates movement less. There is a greater likelihood that there will be tissue compression or abrasion during function, resulting in irritation or discomfort. There is an increased possibility that the prosthesis could become dislodged, because the stiff silicone form resting near areas of strong muscle function, such as the lip, could be lifted or pushed off its attachment. Placement of retention devices peripherally does not ensure there will be no gapping under the prosthesis, especially if no functional analysis has been made. In contrast, in midline attachment, the thickest part of the prosthesis is central. This allows the extensions of silicone toward the facial tissues to be formed thinly. By providing enough distance from the midline point of attachment to the skin, if the prosthesis is designed to be thin where movement is, the forces of leverage are reduced and tissue accommodation can occur. The use of a fitting template assesses areas of possible gapping during function, so that the sculpture can be corrected for a perfect fit. Furthermore, midline retention maintains bilateral air pathways and prevents diminution of airflow.

Magnets can be used within a cast framework but they must be strong and they may be larger than is ideal for designing a framework for the space available. Teflon-coated rare earth samarium cobalt magnets (Permag, Permag Central, Chicago, IL) are used. Because the Teflon coating on magnets is fragile and without it magnets are subject to corrosion in the moist nasal environment, these magnets are first embedded in clear cold-cure acrylic. Embedding magnets in acrylic reduces their effectiveness somewhat, but these magnets are so strong that embedding has not presented problems. For magnet embedding, a magnet is placed under a small piece of glass. Cold-cure acrylic is dabbed on top of the glass. Another magnet is placed in the acrylic puddle so that poles attract to the magnet under the glass. The top magnet is covered with more acrylic and then cured in a pressure pot. The result is a smooth, thin, level acrylic layer on the one surface of the embedded magnet. Any excess acrylic on the top or sides can be shaped or removed. The glass plate is flipped, and the same procedure is completed for the polar opposing magnet. In this way, matched magnet sets are made.

The wax model of a magnet cup is made during the wax framework fabrication. A stainless steel dipstick slightly larger than the magnets is dipped in melted casting wax until the wall of the wax cup is sufficiently thick. The wax is allowed to cool and is removed from the dipstick. It is attached to the rest of the wax framework design with additional wax. The wax design is cast in metal and polished. The prepared magnets are inserted in the cavity provided for them in the cast framework and are bonded to the magnet cup by DuraLay acrylic (Reliance Dental Co). Magnets placed in a framework must have the same poles facing in the same direction to provide the strongest retention. These kinds of magnets are brittle as well as being strong, so they are somewhat difficult to use without being embedded in acrylic. Extreme care should be used while drilling off the excess acrylic, because the magnetic force tends to grab the drill, causing the magnet to fly out of the practitioner's hand.

The principal design weaknesses in magnet retention within a cast metal framework are: 1) the framework may be bulky; 2) the magnets may dislodge because of lateral force on the projecting nasal prosthesis (e.g., if the nose is bumped), although our experience with these magnets is that this occurs infrequently; and 3) magnets are subject to force degradation at high temperatures, so the practitioner must be careful of their use during the mold-cleaning and silicone-curing stages in the fabrication of the silicone prosthesis.

Magnet frameworks are useful for circumstances in which there is significant movement and muscle action is able to disarticulate a clip. If a clip plate becomes partially disengaged in a nasal prosthesis, there is no force to reseat it, except by hand. This is not true for a denture, for example, when every bite could reseat a disarticulated clip. If magnets disengage slightly during tissue movement, they will reseat automatically if they are still within their force field. Magnet frameworks are helpful to patients with limited manual dexterity or vision. Application and orientation are effortless, because the prosthesis orients itself by magnet attraction. If magnets are used, we recommend a polyurethane sheet lining on the back of the silicone prosthesis to prevent moisture from penetrating the interface between acrylic and silicone.

An alternative magnet system is the use of the Technovent Limited (Leeds, England) or Factor II (Lakeside, AZ) Supra-abutment Magnacaps and magnets. These magnets do not require the fabrication of a framework. It is recommended that magnets with lips be used in the silicone nasal prosthesis. The lips lessen the possibility of disarticulation from an accidental bumping of the nose. The principal advantages of this system are simplicity of laboratory procedures and easy access to nasal and periabutment tissues for hygiene. Whereas these magnets are excellent in a cavity such as the orbit, the projection of the nose and the inferior placement of the implants compromise these magnets somewhat in nasal applications. The Technovent magnets are significantly smaller than the samarium cobalt magnet and the retentive strength is somewhat reduced.

Fabrication of the Clip or Magnet Plate

The purpose of the fabrication of a clip plate or magnet plate, which links the connecting components by encapsulating them in acrylic to form a single structure, is that this acrylic retention unit is more easily retained in the silicone prosthesis and a silicone-to-acrylic chemical and mechanical bond can be established. First, the framework is attached to the postimplant model. Undercuts under the bar are blocked out with wax or silicone putty. One clip is placed on the vertical stem and another on the horizontal cross bracing. Cold-cure acrylic is formed over the clips, entrapping them in acrylic. Sufficient acrylic is added to shape a fin, like the dorsal fin of a fish. When the acrylic is cured, it is disarticulated from the bar and shaped and trimmed. Space between the clips is relieved. The fin is shaped, and a transverse hole is cut into it. The purpose of the relief between the clips and the hole in dorsal extension of acrylic is to provide space for the silicone to entrap the clip plate. This gives additional mechanical reinforcement to the chemical bond between the silicone and acrylic provided by the primer. The size and shape of the clip plate are checked in relation to the preimplant sculpture or surgical model. For ease of clip plate replication for use in the fabrication of replicate nasal prostheses, the shape of the clip plate should be recorded by the fabrication of its own mold.

For opposing pole magnet articulation to a magnet framework, first the framework is secured in place on the model. Then 0.020-in. temporary splint material is vacuum-formed over the framework. This step aids in the release of the opposing magnets that

structed in hygiene for the periabutment tissues and the prosthesis. A follow-up schedule should be established before the patient leaves, so the practitioner can check for problems.

Case Studies

Patient 2 presented at the anaplastology clinic at age 72 years, after a total rhinectomy for the removal of basal cell cancer (Fig 19-3). An adhesive-retained prosthesis was fabricated and worn successfully for the next 6 years (Fig 19-4 and 19-5). At age 78 years, the patient returned to the anaplastology clinic for the evaluation for implant candidacy by the osseointegrated implant team. A preimplantation impression and sculpture were made for surgical study (Fig 19-6). Two implants were placed in the anterior nasal floor (Fig 19-7). They have been in place, under function, for 10 years without complication. After abutment connection, a wax model of the framework was fabricated. The vertical stem and horizontal cross

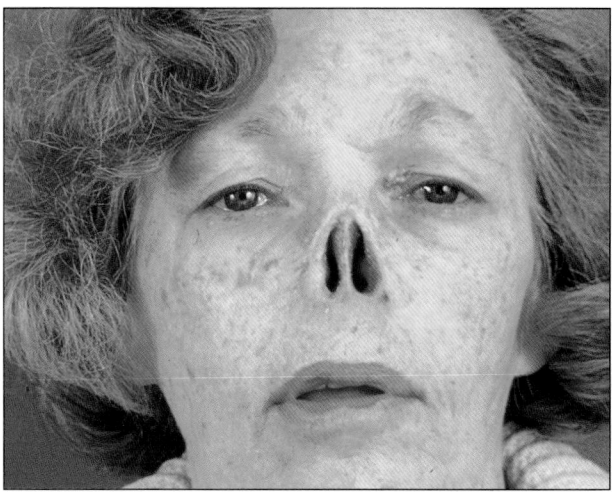

Fig 19-3 (patient 2). Patient at age 72 years, after total rhinectomy for basal cell carcinoma.

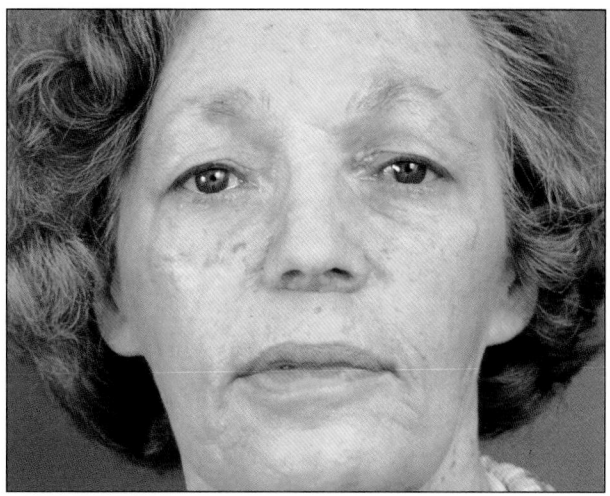

Fig 19-4 (patient 2). Patient wearing adhesive-retained silicone prosthesis, front view.

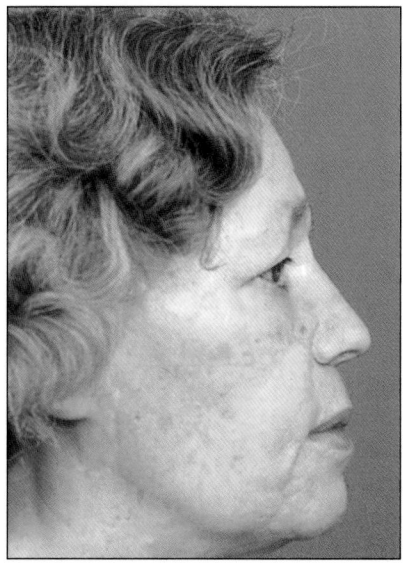

Fig 19-5 (patient 2). Patient wearing adhesive-retained silicone prosthesis, profile view.

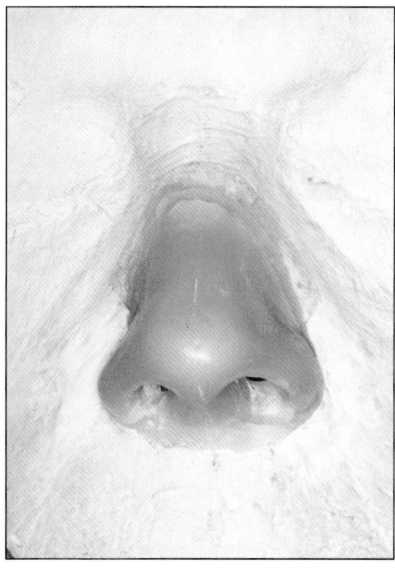

Fig 19-6 (patient 2). Presurgical wax model to be used as a reference for implant placement.

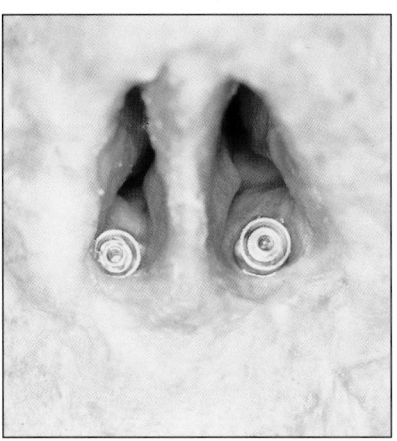

Fig 19-7 (patient 2). Patient at age 78 years, after abutment connection.

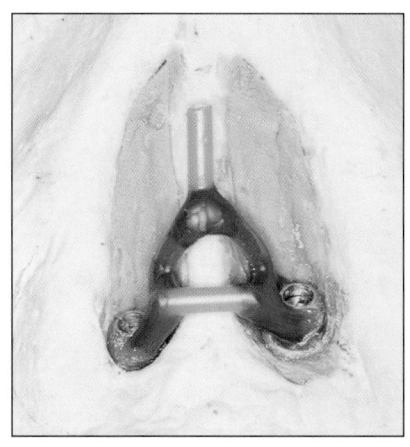

Fig 19-8 (patient 2). Wax framework design.

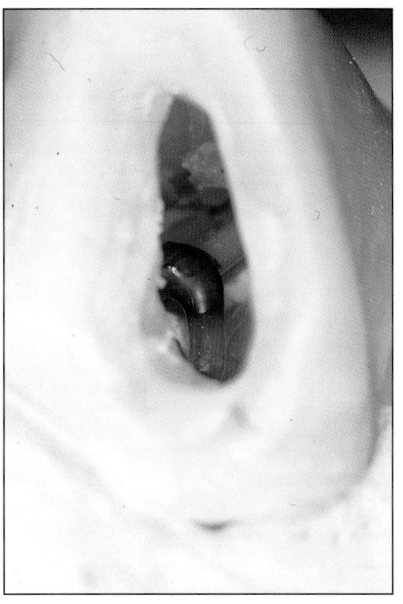

Fig 19-9 (patient 2). Evaluation of spatial relationship between wax sculpture and wax framework design.

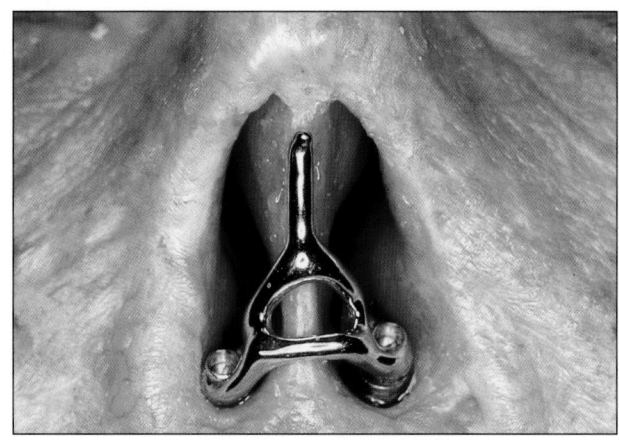

Fig 19-10 (patient 2). Retention bar, frontal view.

brace are green 2-mm plastic sprues that will become the sites for the articulation of retention clips in the metal (Fig 19-8). The dimensional relationship between the wax sculpture and the wax framework design was checked on the model (Fig 19-9). The cast framework is shown in frontal and profile views (Fig 19-10 and 19-11). A clip plate was fabricated and relieved on the underside to allow space for its entrapment by silicone (Fig 19-12). The clip plate is articulated to the inside of the wax sculpture using sticky

wax and slushy baseplate wax (Fig 19-13). The clip plate articulation is reinforced and the airway passage is refined (Fig 19-14). The wax sculpture with incorporated retention clips is tried on the patient to check fit and sculptural form (Fig 19-15). Oqvist clips (Sweden) were used on this prosthesis, because they are not as retentive as CM Rider clips. Our thinking at the time of fabrication, which we judge now to be an error, was that stronger clips might pull out of the silicone. These clips proved inadequate for retention

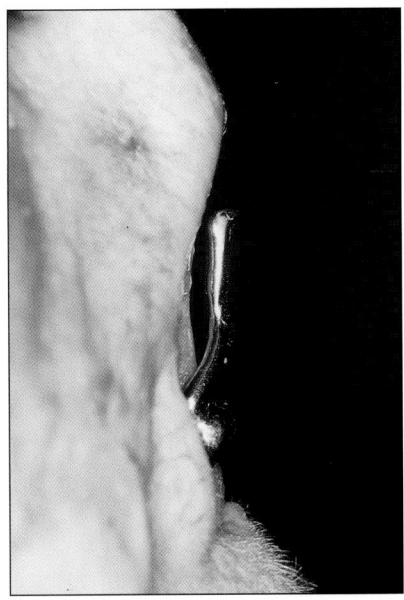

Fig 19-11 (patient 2). Retention bar, profile view.

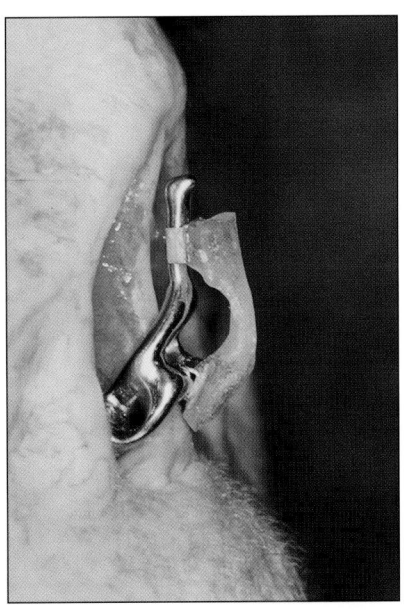

Fig 19-12 (patient 2). Retention clip plate articulated to retention bar.

Fig 19-13 (patient 2). Retention clip plate articulated to wax sculpture.

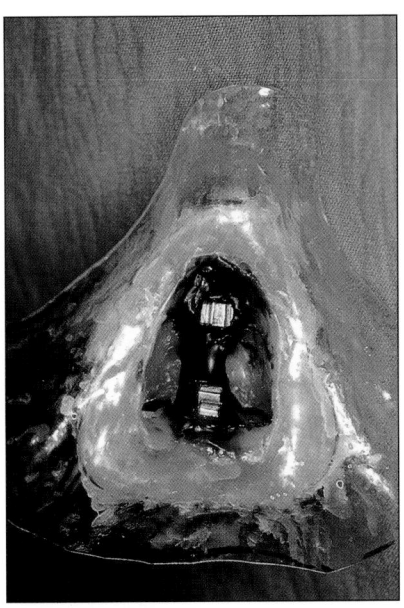

Fig 19-14 (patient 2). Refinement and reinforcement of wax around clip plate.

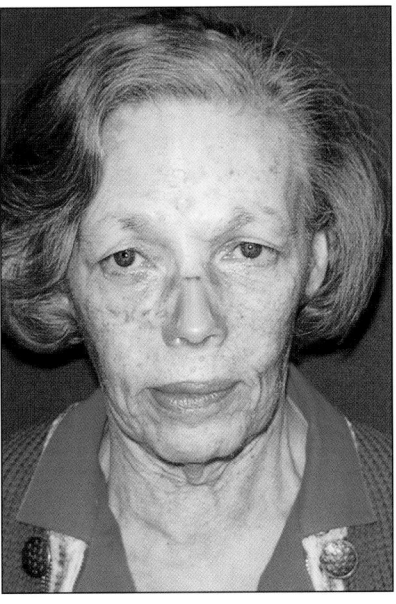

Fig 19-15 (patient 2). Wax sculpture held on face by clips for evaluation of form and fit.

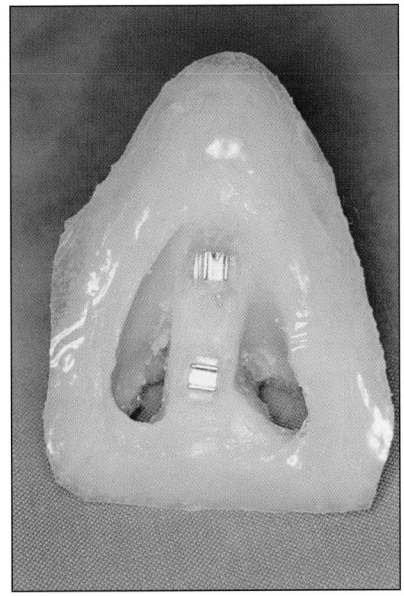

Fig 19-16 (patient 2). Back of silicone prosthesis shows clip position.

of the bottom clip because of strong and active movement of the lip. The posterior side of the Oqvist-retained prosthesis is shown (Fig 19-16). The clip-retained prosthesis is shown in place on the patient in Figure 19-17. A midline magnet-holding framework was designed to reseat the lower part of the silicone prosthesis actively, if lip movement dislodged it temporarily. The framework is shown in frontal and profile views in Figure 19-18 and 19-19, respectively. A polyurethane-lined silicone prosthesis was fabricated to protect the magnets from corrosion. The magnet-connecting view is shown in Figure 19-20. The magnet-retained facial prosthesis is shown in place in Figure 19-21.

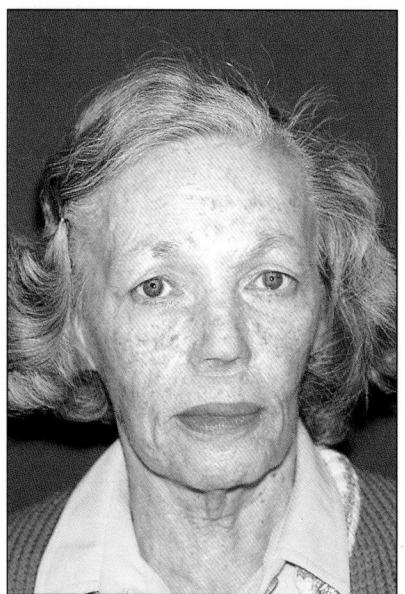

Fig 19-17 (patient 2). Clip-retained prosthesis on patient's face.

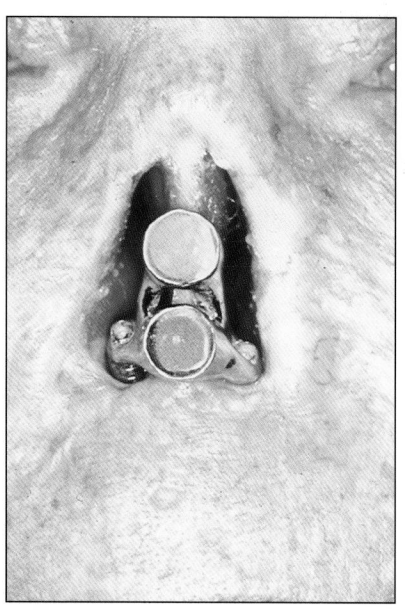

Fig 19-18 (patient 2). Magnet framework, front view.

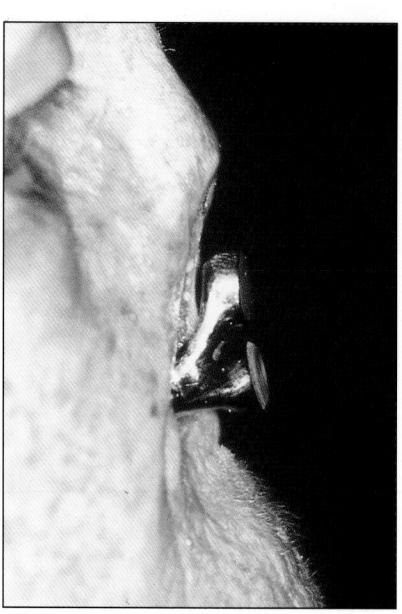

Fig 19-19 (patient 2). Magnet framework, profile view.

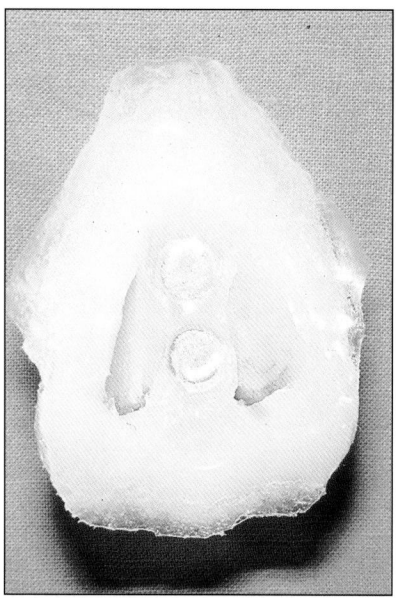

Fig 19-20 (patient 2). Back of magnet-retained prosthesis lined with polyurethane sheet.

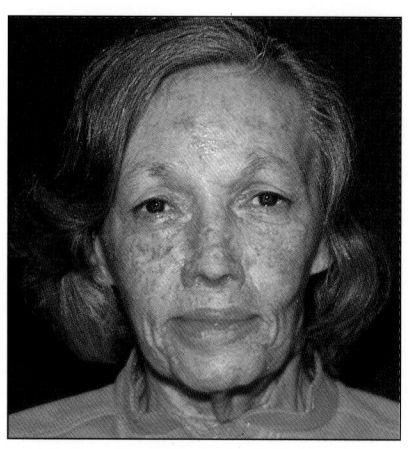

Fig 19-21 (patient 2). Patient wearing prosthesis retained by magnets.

Patient 3 had a traumatic amputation of his nose (Fig 19-22). During second-stage surgery, the perinasal tissue was debulked to improve chances for successful cosmesis in the nasal restoration (Fig 19-23 and 19-24). The nasal cavity is packed in preparation for the facial impression (Fig 19-25). The cast metal framework, inverted Y shape, is seated on the abutments. There was not enough room for a cross brace, given the small area of the nasal opening. Clip-retention sites were at the stem and the left oblique segment of the inverted Y (Fig 19-26). The profile and three-quarter views of the nasal prosthesis on the patient are shown in Figures 19-27 and 19-28, respectively.

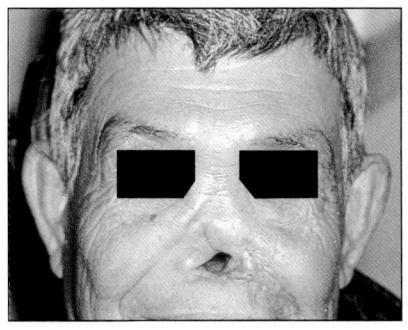

Fig 19-22 (patient 3). Presurgical photograph.

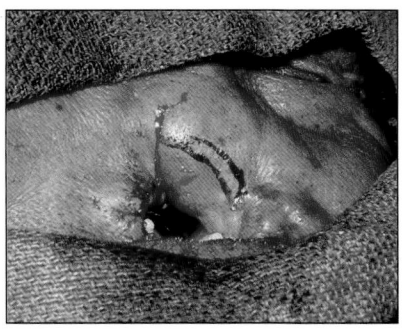

Fig 19-23 (patient 3). Tissue reduction indicated at second-stage surgery.

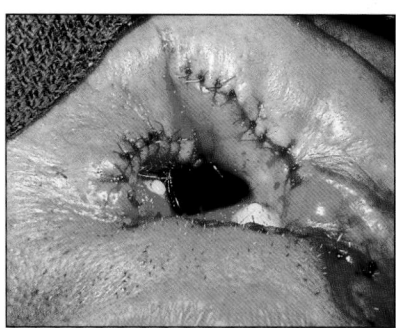

Fig 19-24 (patient 3). Tissue reduction sutured at second-stage surgery.

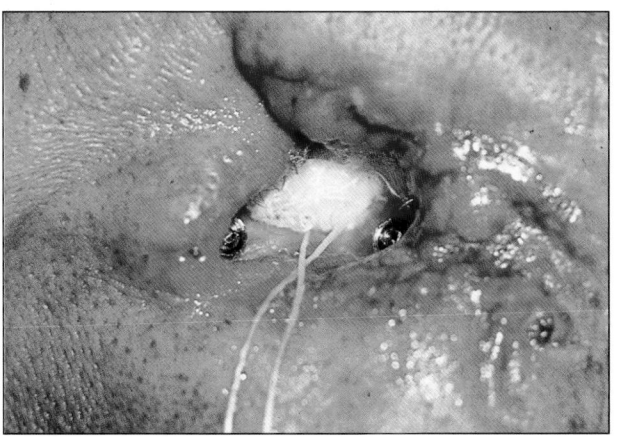

Fig 19-25 (patient 3). Nasal packing and nasal appearance at time of postimplant impression.

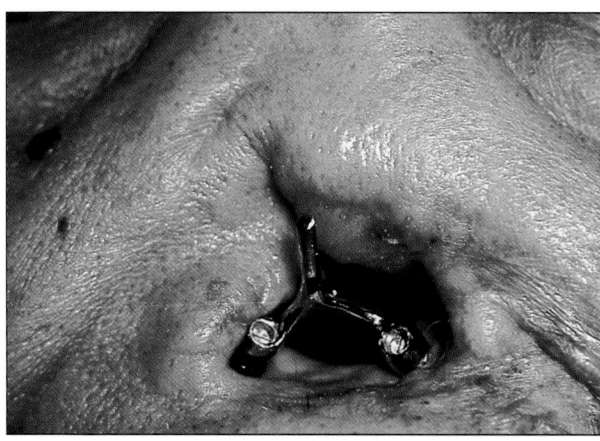

Fig 19-26 (patient 3). Cast metal inverted Y framework in place.

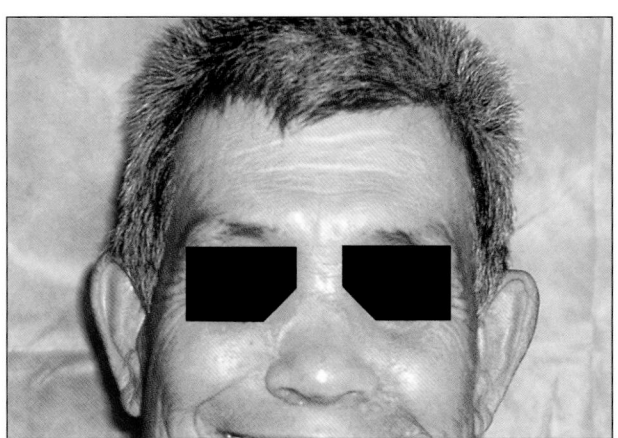

Fig 19-27 (patient 3). Silicone prosthesis in place on patient, front view.

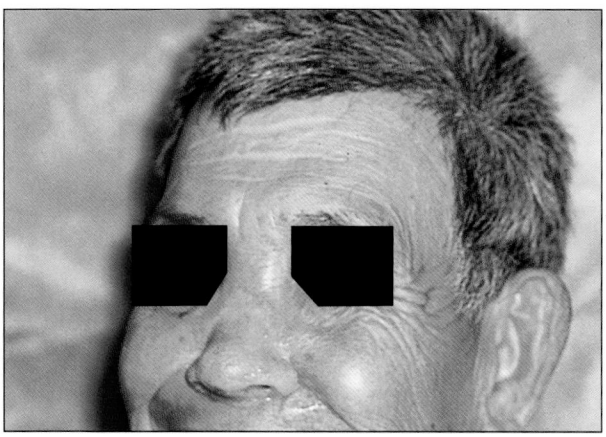

Fig 19-28 (patient 3). Silicone prosthesis in place on patient, three-quarter view.

Conclusion

Bone-anchored implant retention offers patients who wear facial prostheses increased security, especially with large defects or where the prosthesis rests on highly mobile tissues. Perspiration and vigorous physical activity will not affect the retention of bone-anchored prostheses. Independence from reliance on adhesives for retention frees the patient from the tedious task of applying and removing glue at each application and removal of the prosthesis. It prolongs the life of the prosthesis, because the edges are not subject to excessive handling.

The implant team must develop a coordinated treatment plan that is delivered in an efficient manner. The highest standards of aesthetics and retention should be met. As much attention should be paid to the fitting and care of soft tissues as to the issues of hardware articulation and registration. A commitment to follow-up for the clinical evaluation of implant tissues and the maintenance and periodic replacement of the facial prosthesis are a team responsibility and in the best interests of the patient.

References

1. Parel SM, Tjellström A. The United States and Swedish experience with osseointegration and facial prostheses. Int J Oral Maxillofac Implants 1991;6:75.

2. Tjellström A, Jacobsson M. The bone-anchored maxillofacial prosthesis. In Albrektsson T, Zarb GA (eds): The Brånemark Osseointegrated Implant. Chicago: Quintessence Publishing Company; 1989:235.

3. Tjellström A, Yontchev E, Lindström J, Brånemark P-I. Five years' experience with bone-anchored auricular prostheses. Otolaryngol Head Neck Surg 1985;93:366.

4. Wolfaardt JF, Wilkes GH, Parel SM, Tjellström A. Craniofacial osseointegration: the Canadian experience. Int J Oral Maxillofac Implants 1993;8:197.

5. Tolman DE, Taylor PF. Bone-anchored craniofacial prosthesis study. Int J Oral Maxillofac Implants 1996;11:159.

6. Jacobsson M, Tjellström A, Fine L, Andersson H. A retrospective study of osseointegrated skin-penetrating titanium fixtures used for retaining facial prostheses. Int J Oral Maxillofac Implants 1992;7:523.

7. Henry PJ. Maxillofacial prosthetic considerations. In Worthington P, Brånemark P-I (eds): Advanced Osseointegration Surgery: Applications in the Maxillofacial Region. Chicago: Quintessence Publishing Company; 1992:313.

8. Rubenstein JE. Attachments used for implant-supported facial prostheses: a survey of United States, Canadian, and Swedish centers. J Prosthet Dent 1995;73:262.

9. Thomas KF. Freestanding magnetic retention for extraoral prosthesis with osseointegrated implants. J Prosthet Dent 1995;73:162.

10. Beumer J III, Ma T, Marunick M, Roumanas E, Nishimura R. Restoration of facial defects: etiology, disability, and rehabilitation. In Beumer J III, Curtis TA, Marunick MT (eds): Maxillofacial Rehabilitation: Prosthodontic and Surgical Considerations. St Louis: Ishiyaku EuroAmerica; 1996:438.

11. Henry P. Mid-facial defects. In Proceedings of the 1st International Congress on Maxillofacial Prosthetics. New York: Memorial Sloan-Kettering Cancer Center; 1995:132.

12. Granström G, Jacobsson M, Tjellström A. Titanium implants in irradiated tissue: benefits from hyperbaric oxygen. Int J Oral Maxillofac Implants 1992;7:15.

13. Granström G, Bergström K, Tjellström A, Brånemark P-I. A detailed analysis of titanium implants lost in irradiated tissues. Int J Oral Maxillofac Implants 1994;9:653.

14. Reisburg DJ, Habakuk SW. Use of a surgical positioner for bone-anchored facial prostheses. Int J Oral Maxillofac Implants 1997;12:376.

15. Brånemark P-I, Zarb GA, Albrektsson T (eds). Tissue-Integrated Prostheses: Osseointegration in Clinical Dentistry. Chicago: Quintessence Publishing Company; 1985.

16. Nishimura RD, Roumanas E, Moy PK, Sugai T. Nasal defects and osseointegrated implants: UCLA experience. J Prosthet Dent 1996;76:597.

Orbital Prosthesis

20

David J. Reisberg, DDS
Susan W. Habakuk, BS, MEd

- The Orbital Defect
- Implant Placement
- Surgical Positioner
- Abutment Selection and Retention Systems
- Prosthetic Techniques

An orbital defect may be the result of a congenital anomaly (facial cleft), trauma (gunshot wound, motor vehicle accident), or surgery (tumor removal). Even with the advent of microvascular surgery and free tissue transfers, surgical reconstruction alone cannot fully restore this area. Prosthetic rehabilitation is needed.

Fabrication of an orbital prosthesis is the most challenging task in facial prosthetics. It covers and protects the site and restores normal tissue contours and appearance to provide a lifelike replacement. Most importantly, it can restore self-esteem to the patient.

Since 1979, osseointegrated implants have been used to retain facial prostheses.[1] This type of retention offers several advantages over an adhesive retention.

Because no adhesive is applied, a time-consuming and often messy step is eliminated. There is also less wear and tear on the prosthesis because there is no need to remove adhesive by rubbing the surface of the prosthesis. This preserves the color and permits thinner margins, which blend with the natural skin for a better aesthetic result.

The two most important advantages of the bone-anchored prosthesis are that proper positioning is easy and ensured and that retention is improved. The prosthesis can be seated in only one position, and this is guided by the retentive mechanism. This is particularly important because many patients are elderly and have compromised manual dexterity. In the case of an orbital prosthesis, it is even more critical because the patient's vision is affected by loss of an eye and acuity of the remaining eye may be compromised. Also, with an adhesive-retained prosthesis, the patient may need to have assistance putting on the prosthesis. The bone-anchored one gives these patients more independence.

The retention of the implant-retained prosthesis is more reliable than adhesive retention.[2] This is also of great psychologic benefit to the patient; many patients report that the bone-anchored prosthesis feels more like a natural part of them. There is no fear of it coming off in public.

Treatment with a bone-anchored orbital prosthesis requires a team approach. Ideally, the surgeon, maxillofacial prosthodontist, and anaplastologist should

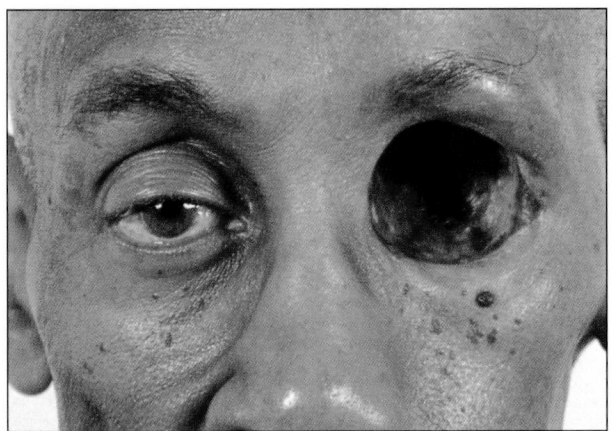

Fig 20-1. Ideal orbital defect.

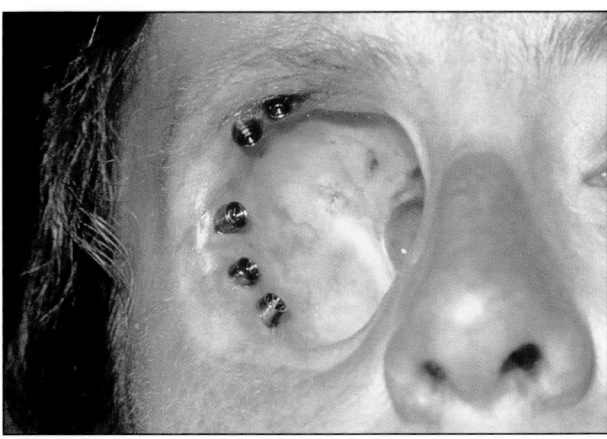

Fig 20-2. Implants in superior and lateral orbital rim. (Courtesy of Dr. S. Parel.)

meet with the patient before treatment to discuss the surgery, expected outcome, and considerations for later placement of osseointegrated implants and the prosthesis. Brochures, models, and photographs can be used to explain the procedure. At the same time, the patient should not be overwhelmed. At this preliminary meeting, rehabilitation is established as part of the overall treatment plan to build patient confidence and decrease anxiety.

The patient should be considered a member of the team. Patients need to understand the treatment and have realistic expectations of the outcome. They should realize their responsibilities for home care and follow-up visits and that this procedure involves a long-term commitment (see Chapter 23). Patient participation is critical for success.

The Orbital Defect

The ideal defect is circumscribed fully by the bony orbital rim. The eyebrow should be intact. The soft tissue defining the defect should be thin and immobile. Maintaining depth into the defect is critical to achieve a natural appearance of the prosthesis (Fig 20-1). The surface within the defect may be lined with a skin graft or even a free-tissue flap. This tissue must not be bulky or obliterate the defect or it will be impossible to set the ocular portion of the prosthesis to match the depth of the natural eye. Proper ocular position is the most important factor in creating a natural-looking prosthesis.

If the defect is more extensive, bone and soft-tissue grafting should be considered to restore missing portions of the orbital rim, zygoma, or temporal or midface regions before implant placement. The surgical restoration of contour can contribute to a less extensive prosthesis. The margins may then be confined to less-mobile soft tissue and be camouflaged more easily within the borders of eyeglass frames. Planning for such surgery involves the entire treatment team to ensure that the surgery will enhance the prosthetic result.

Implant Placement

Implants commonly are placed in the orbital rim—most often superiorly and laterally (Fig 20-2). Placement in the inferior rim is desirable if the shape of the defect and access permit. This improves the stability and retention of the prosthesis. In larger defects extending beyond the orbital rim, implants can be placed in the zygoma or maxilla. Even a single implant can help stabilize and retain a prosthesis, but more are desirable for support, stability, and retention.

The data from several studies indicate that the success rate for implants in the orbital region in nonirradiated patients was 91.8%,[3] 96.3%,[3] 96.6%,[4] 68%,[5] and 100%.[6] In irradiated patients, the success rate was considerably lower in two studies, 45.5%[3] and 56.8%,[3] and only slightly lower in two others, 96.4%[4] and 52.6%.[5] In two studies that

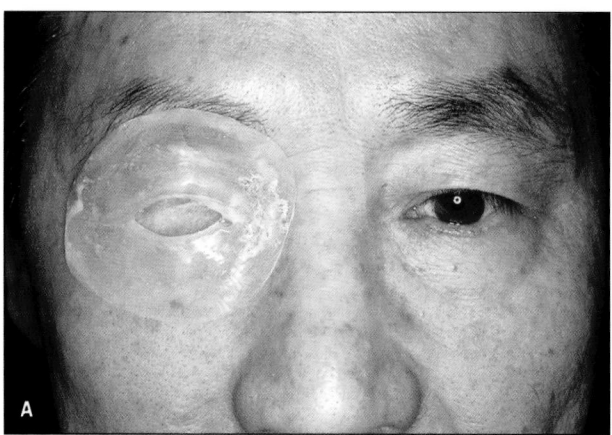
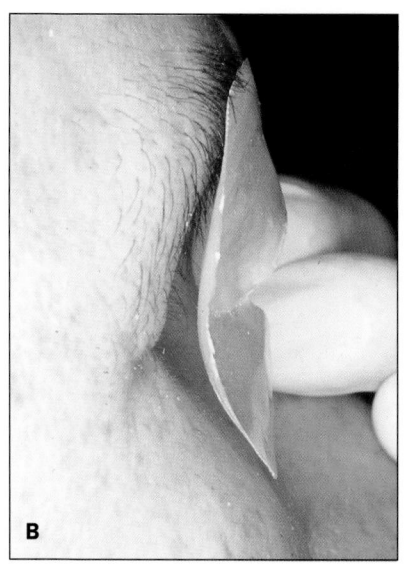

Fig 20-3. *A,* Frontal view of positioner. Note ocular opening for visual access into defect. *B,* Lateral view of positioner. Note visual access into defect. (From Reisberg and Habakuk.[7] By permission of Quintessence Publishing Company.)

used hyperbaric oxygen therapy before implant placement in orbital defects for irradiated patients, the success rate improved significantly: 100%[5] and 90%.[6] Based on these data, it is reasonable to conclude that as many implants as are feasible should be placed and that irradiated cases should be treated with hyperbaric oxygen therapy. Implants should be as long as possible.[5]

Surgical Positioner

Actual placement of the implants is guided by a surgical positioner.[7] This is an acrylic resin prototype of the prosthesis that is used intraoperatively. It indicates the ideal position for implant placement. It also serves as a guide for selection of the retentive mechanism and later as a timesaving reference for the shape of the prosthesis.

The surgical positioner also helps determine if preprosthetic surgery is needed before implant placement. Most often, the lateral superior aspect of the orbital rim needs reduction to place an implant at that location and remain within the guidelines of the positioner (Fig 20-3).

Implant angulation should parallel the frontal plane of the face or be inward slightly. A protrusive angulation can interfere with positioner contour and require compromise of the ideal shape of the prosthesis. At the same time, the implant should not be overangulated

inward or prosthetic access for fabrication of the retentive mechanism can be hampered. This is true especially in smaller shallow defects when a soft-tissue flap has been used to close the opening of the defect.

Abutment Selection and Retention Systems

The shortest abutment that protrudes 1 to 2 mm above the level of the skin should be selected at second-stage surgery (Fig 20-4). This can minimize stress to the implant and still allow for hygiene and prosthetic access. A shorter abutment takes up less space in conjunction with the retentive mechanism. At second-stage surgery, the gauze strip surgical dressing should be wrapped carefully around the abutments and under the healing caps so close adaptation of skin to the abutment and underlying bone is achieved (Fig 20-5).

Rubenstein[8] reported that orbital prostheses were fabricated with a wider variety of attachments than any other type of bone-anchored facial prosthesis: bar clips, magnets, ball studs, or a combination of types.

In a review of treatment centers, Rubenstein[8] found that magnetic retention represented nearly half of the attachments in the United States and Canada compared with only one-third of those used in

247

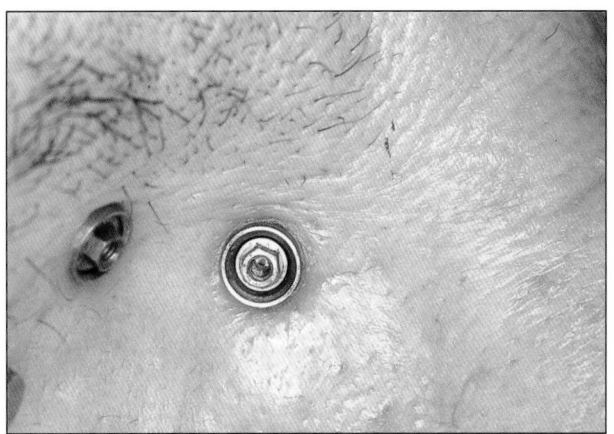

Fig 20-4. Abutment-skin relationship.

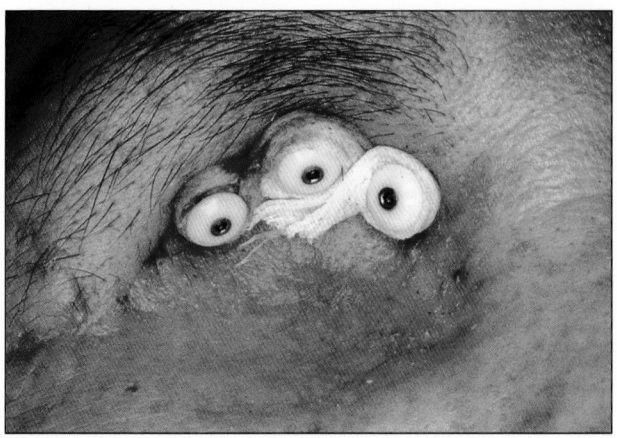

Fig 20-5. Gauze dressing wrapped around abutments for soft-tissue adaptation.

Sweden. Clips were used only 20% of the time in the United States, 33% of the time in Canada, and nearly 50% of the time in Sweden. Approximately 20% of orbital prostheses in the United States and Sweden used a combination of magnets and clips. Also, in 6 of 68 cases reported from Sweden and Canada, a ball attachment or stud type was used. Although this study reported on the popularity of retention systems, no long-term, multicenter results are available on the success of these systems with regard to orbital prostheses.

Bar-clip systems yield the highest retentive forces. They give good retention for large defects, especially when there are implants in only the superior orbital rim. When implants are splinted together by the bar, loading can be shared among them. This type of system permits retention and support beyond the actual position of the implant. These cantilevers must be limited in length or excessive bending moments can occur, which can endanger the implants. At least two implants must be used for this system, but three or more spread in a slight arch are preferred to control and distribute forces. Because this mechanism takes up more space than individual magnets, care must be taken that the bar does not interfere with the ideal position of the ocular prosthesis.

Extreme accuracy and a passive fit are requirements of the bar system so as not to stress the implants. Impression making and bar construction can be difficult, especially if the implants are excessively divergent (more than 35°) or widely distributed around the orbital defect. Asymmetric withdrawal of the prosthesis can result in amplification of loads to the implants.

Individual magnets attached to standard abutments offer the most ideal loading situation. The axial loads are most favorable, and horizontal ones can be avoided. This system is favored in a shallow defect where there is insufficient space for a bar construction. It is easy for the patient to place and remove the prosthesis, and hygiene is easier around the freestanding abutments than if a connecting bar is used.

Some divergence of implants is desirable to offer stability of the prosthesis against horizontal forces. If this cannot be achieved with magnets attached to standard abutments, then console abutments (Nobel Biocare USA, Inc., Westmont, IL) can be used. Such devices can alter the angle of one magnet with another and prevent sliding problems. However, because the magnets are offset from the axes of the implants, a small bending moment is introduced. Whether this is detrimental clinically to the implant is not known. Individual magnets can be used in conjunction with a bar when one implant diverges severely from the others that will be splinted with a bar.

Ball attachments also may be used with individual implants. They offer good retention and stability, and like the individual magnets, they take up little space behind the prosthesis. Their use is limited when the implants are divergent, and they can introduce forces that are not along the axis of the implants. Like the bar-clip system, a prosthesis with ball attachments can be more difficult for the patient to place than one with magnetic attachment. No retention system is ideal for all situations; each case must be evaluated to select the optimal one.[2,9,10]

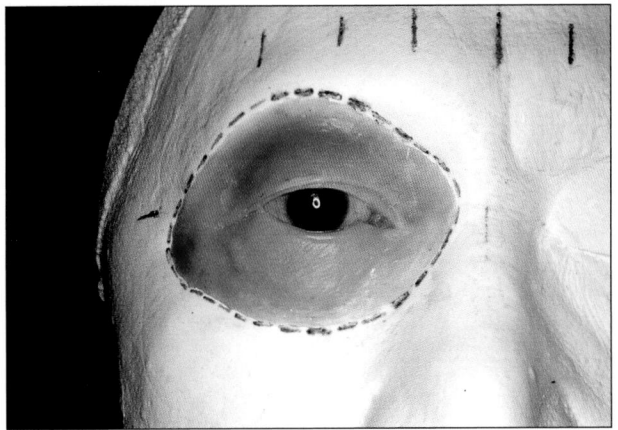

Fig 20-19. Wax prototype on cast.

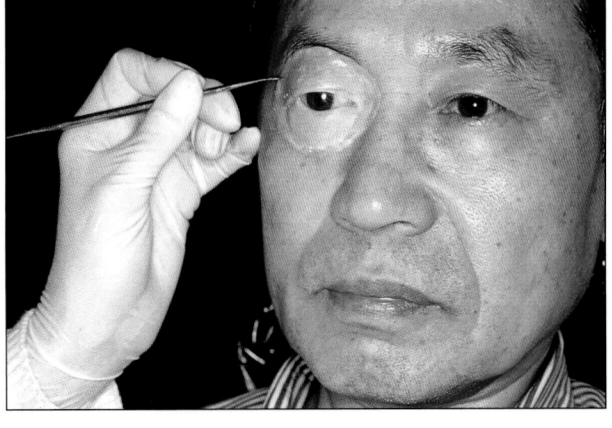

Fig 20-20. Sculpting on patient.

with wax, and 3 mm of wax is extended around the indexed surface of the eyepiece. This helps retain both in the silicone prosthesis.

One or more of the following are helpful in creating the wax prototype: surgical positioner, photographs, measuring devices (Boley and contour gauges, calipers), tissue conformer, computerized images, and the patient (Fig 20-19). A major advantage of the bone-anchored prosthesis is that much of the sculpting can be done directly on the patient (Fig 20-20). This saves time and also permits the patient and the anaplastologist to preview the form more easily. During the sculpting process, design considerations need to be made regarding tissue mobility and marginal extension as well as overall weight of the prosthesis.

The use of eyeglasses is required with an orbital prosthesis. They serve to camouflage the prosthesis as well as to protect the remaining eye. A larger lens opening is recommended to cover the margins of the prosthesis, if possible. The lenses should be tinted slightly to draw attention away from the prosthesis. The eyeglasses should be tried on during the sculpting process to ensure that they will be in harmony with the prosthesis.

Owing to the rigidity of the wax, it often is difficult to evaluate the marginal extension and adaptation of the prosthesis in relation to soft-tissue mobility. An aid in this determination is a tissue conformer. With transfer magnets on the cast, a thin layer of silicone rubber (2186 Silicone Elastomer-Fast, Factor II, Lakeside, AZ) is applied to the cast to incorporate the magnets and extend to the proposed margin of the prosthesis. Once the rubber is vulcanized, a thin layer of water-soluble lubricant (Surgilube, E.

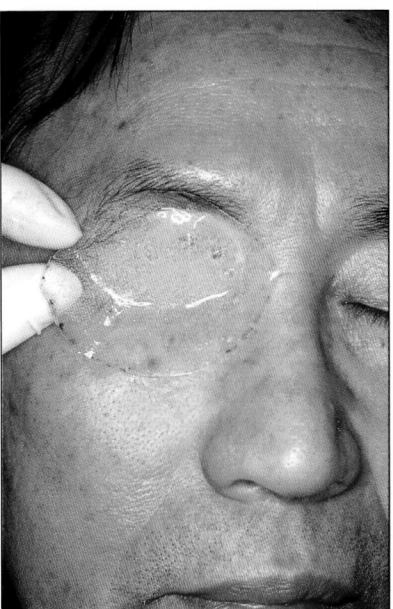

Fig 20-21. Conformer on patient.

Fougera, Melville, NY) is applied to the tissue surface and the conformer is placed on the patient, who is directed to simulate function and normal facial expressions. This helps determine if marginal placement must be changed because of gapping or dislodgement during facial movement or if the cast must be scored and sanded down to ensure close adaptation of the thin margins of the prosthesis (Fig 20-21).

The wax prototype should be sculpted so that the prosthesis will be lightweight with thin margins. It is not necessary for the wax to make complete contact with the soft tissue of the defect, only that the margins

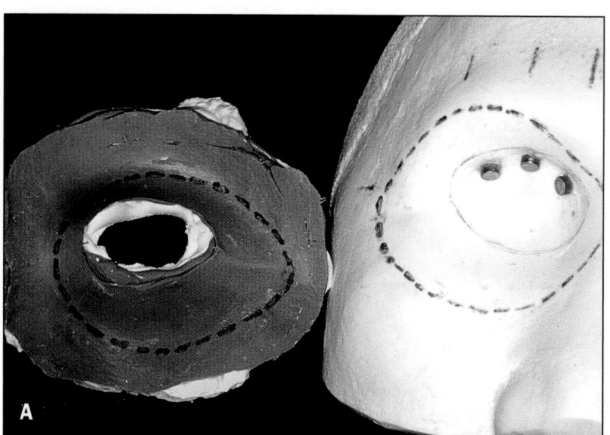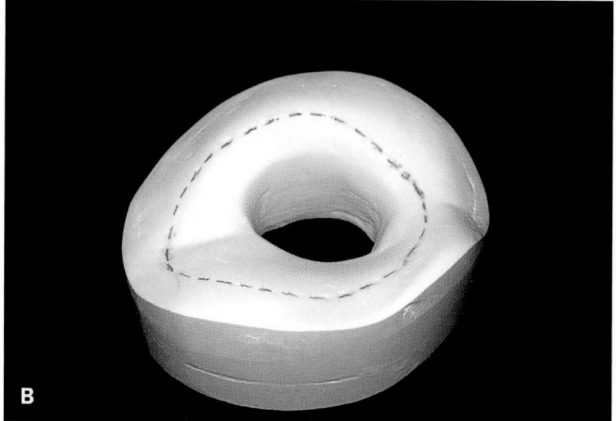

Fig 20-22. *A,* Impression of defect with transfer of margin of wax prototype. *B,* Stone cast of periphery of defect with transfer marks.

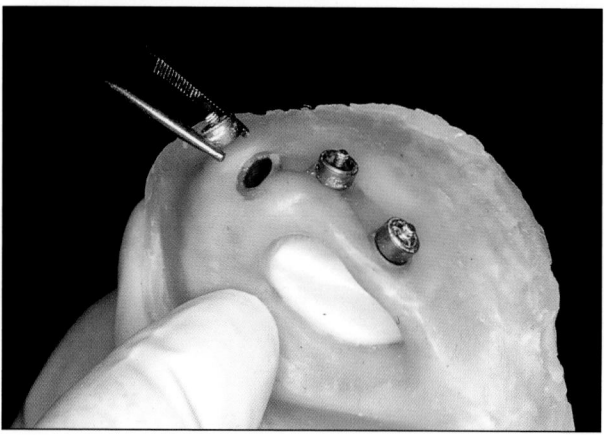

Fig 20-23. Tissue side of wax prototype with magnet analogs.

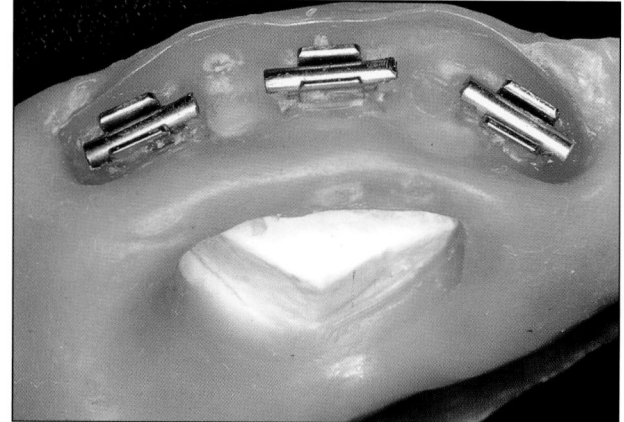

Fig 20-24. Tissue side of wax prototype with bar analogs.

are in contact. This decreases the weight of the prosthesis but still ensures close marginal adaptation and permits some underlying tissue movement. The areas of the eyelids, caruncle, and canthi must reproduce fine detail to achieve a lifelike quality. Final adjustments are made to the tissue side so the surface is smooth.

Mold Making

A three-piece mold of white improved dental stone (FujiRock, GC Fuji, Tokyo, Japan) is made: tissue side, eyepiece, and outer surface. Consideration is given to making a mold that can be reused so that replacement prostheses can be made without the patient having to go without the current prosthesis. This is particularly important if the patient is unable to come to the office for the replacement because of travel or health considerations.

Once the wax prototype is completed, its outline is marked on the cast with indelible pencil. An impression of the defect extending beyond the margins of the prosthesis is made with duplicating silicone elastomer (3110 RTV, Dow Corning, Midland, MI) or vinyl polysiloxane (Express, 3M, St. Paul, MN). It is reinforced with plaster backing. The periphery of this impression is poured in stone so that the center of the defect is left open (Fig 20-22). Registration keys are placed in the tissue side of the mold.

LAB-ANALOGUES of the magnetic caps are placed on the magnets within the resin plate (Fig 20-23). If a bar-clip system is used, segments of stainless steel wire the same gauge as the gold bar are cut so they are 4 mm longer than the length of the clip. The ends are undercut and placed into the clips so 2 mm extends beyond each end of the clip (Fig 20-24). The wax prototype is seated back on the cast by using the transferred pencil line as a guide for ori-

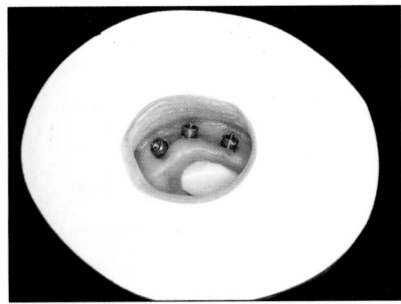

Fig 20-25. Back view of tissue side of mold with opening.

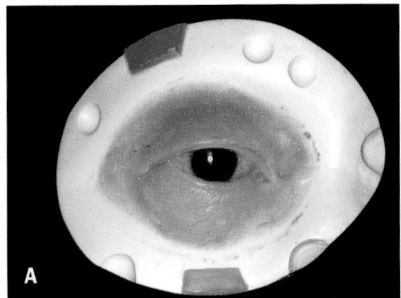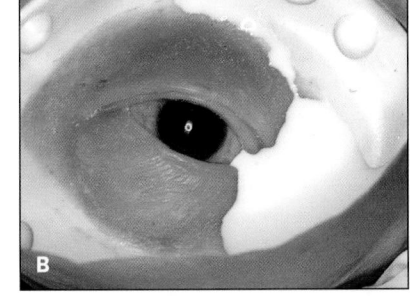

Fig 20-26. *A,* Wax spacers on tissue side of mold. *B,* Pouring top portion of stone mold.

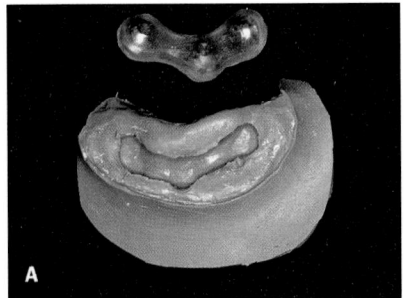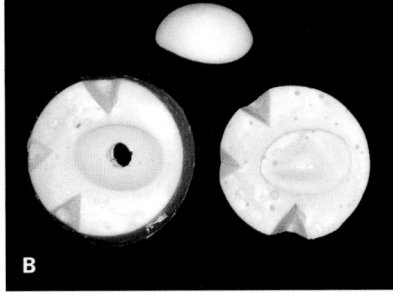

Fig 20-27. *A,* Mold of resin plate. *B,* Mold of ocular prosthesis and stone cast.

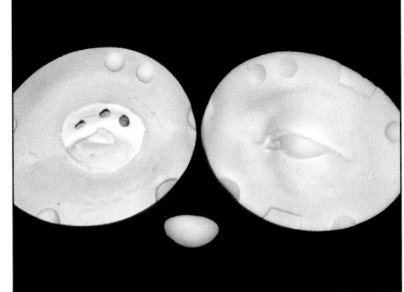

Fig 20-28. Three-piece mold, including ocular piece.

entation, and the margins are sealed. Skin surface detail can be refined at this time.

Stone is poured into the back of the wax prototype through the opening in the cast (Fig 20-25). Once set, wax spacers to facilitate later mold separation are placed in the first piece of the mold, a separator is applied to the stone surface, paper tape or wax is used to box the mold, and the top portion or outer surface of the mold is poured (Fig 20-26).

Once the stone has set, the mold is separated and the eyepiece and resin plate are removed. The mold is cleaned with boiling water and detergent to remove all wax residue.

Before casting the prosthesis, silicone elastomer (3110 or Express) is used to make a mold of the outer surface of the resin plate while it is in place on the tissue side of the mold. The impression material should be applied with a syringe around the edges to capture the ledge on the tissue side of the plate. Then a two-piece silicone mold is made of the eyepiece and this is poured in stone (Fig 20-27). This stone reproduction is used in the mold in place of the resin eyepiece during processing to protect it from damage (Fig 20-28). These steps allow the resin plate and prosthesis to be remade without the patient and the prosthesis present, when a replacement prosthesis is necessary.

Formulation of Skin Color

The intrinsic technique is used to color the prosthesis.[14] This method yields a prosthesis with more depth of color, simulating the translucency of skin. It also maintains the surface textures of the wax prototype for added realism.

A medical-grade room temperature vulcanization silicone elastomer (MDX4 4210 Medical Grade Elastomer, Dow Corning, or 2186 Silicone Elastomer, Factor II) is used to cast the prosthesis. If a polyurethane-lined prosthesis is to be made, Medical Adhesive Silicone Type A (Dow Corning) in combination with MDX4 4210 (Dow Corning) is used.[15] Pigmented solutions of silicone (Ferro, Factor II), rayon flocking (Factor II), and kaolin (Factor II) are added for color and characterization.

The coloring process requires knowledge of color theory as well as an ability to identify, evaluate, and simulate a wide range of skin tones in the patient's complexion. The process begins by determining the base shade. This is the lightest skin tone underlying the surface characterization of the skin. This is done by measuring specific quantities of the pigmented silicone elastomer and rayon flocking onto a mixing pad or in a plastic cup. Then shadow, highlight, and translucent

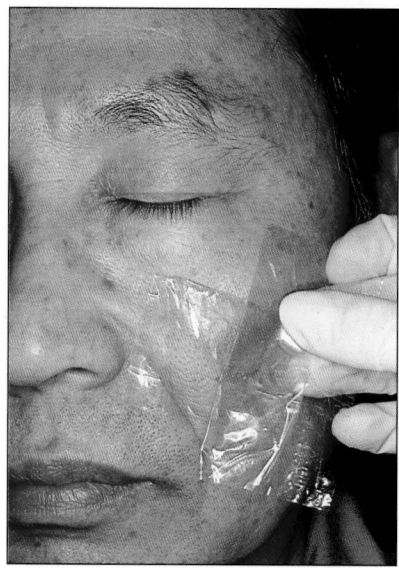

Fig 20-29. Color sample in plastic wrap to check color match to skin.

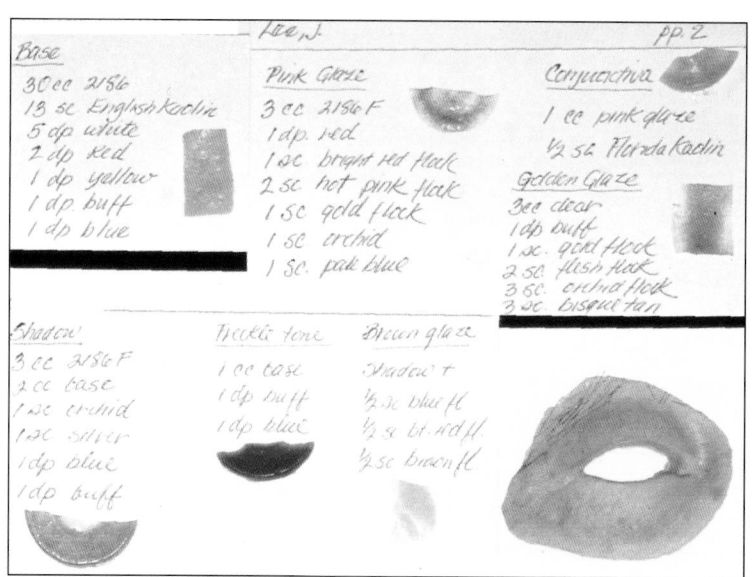

Fig 20-30. Color formula of skin tone.

glazes are mixed. Samples of each may be placed on a small piece of plastic wrap and held up for comparison to the patient's skin (Fig 20-29). Once satisfactory colors have been obtained, they are catalyzed and deaerated. These can be painted into a small sectional silicone impression of the mold and vulcanized to test for color match before casting the entire prosthesis.

The color formulas are recorded with a diagram on a card that becomes a part of the patient's record (Fig 20-30). This system works well when a replacement prosthesis is made and the patient is unable to come in for an appointment or if a replacement must be made by someone other than the person who made the original.

Processing the Prosthesis

To ensure adequate bonding to the resin plate, it must be thoroughly cleaned and primed. The surface of the plate is cleaned with acetone to remove any surface wax, oils, or other contaminants. Once dry, a thin layer of primer (92-023, Dow Corning) is applied to the outer surface and the ledge. This is allowed to dry for 20 minutes, and a second application is made. The plate is set aside until the pigmented silicone is ready to be painted into the mold. All portions of the mold must be clean and free of surface contaminants and coated with a separator.

Once the outer portion of the mold has been painted with the catalyzed skin colors, the resin plate

is fully engaged onto the retentive components in the mold, and the stone ocular piece is positioned in the mold. The base color is painted onto all surfaces of the plate and spatulated into the mold carefully to avoid entrapment of air. The mold is assembled and closed slowly in a vice. It is placed in an oven at 90°C for 2 hours to vulcanize. Samples of each color are placed in the oven in disposable aluminum foil dishes to be used as swatches for the color formula record.

After vulcanization, the mold is carefully separated and the prosthesis is retrieved. Gross flash is trimmed, the prosthesis is cleaned with a mild soap and water, and the ocular prosthesis is inserted.

Aesthetic Adjustments

The prosthesis is tried on the patient to evaluate retention, fit, and color. To aid in determining how much of the margin to trim, a thin layer of water-soluble lubricant is applied to the tissue side along the margin. Any edge that does not conform to the underlying soft tissue at rest or during facial movements is trimmed with a fine scissors.

Surface color may be modified by using the extrinsic technique.[16] Facial hair such as eyebrows, eyelashes, or sideburns can be added to the prosthesis to enhance multidimensionality and realism (Fig 20-31). Similarly, donor or synthetic hair can be used for eyebrows and sideburns.

Delivery of the Prosthesis and Follow-Up

This phase can elicit a wide range of expectations and emotions from the patient. To decrease anxiety, a family member or a close friend is encouraged to be present at this visit.

Adequate time should be allotted for demonstration of placement and removal of the prosthesis, and the patient should be instructed to do it alone. To prevent separation of the resin plate, a thumbnail should be inserted under the thickest part of the prosthesis near the plate to dislodge it from the retentive mechanism.

The patient is instructed not to wear the prosthesis during sleep. A demonstration and written instructions for the care of the prosthesis, retentive components, and the surrounding skin are given. The patient should return for a follow-up visit in 1 week (see Chapter 23).

With knowledgeable patient selection, treatment planning, prosthesis fabrication, and follow-up, the patient with an orbital defect can have a retentive prosthesis that provides an excellent aesthetic result (Fig 20-32).

Fig 20-31. Insertion of eyelashes.

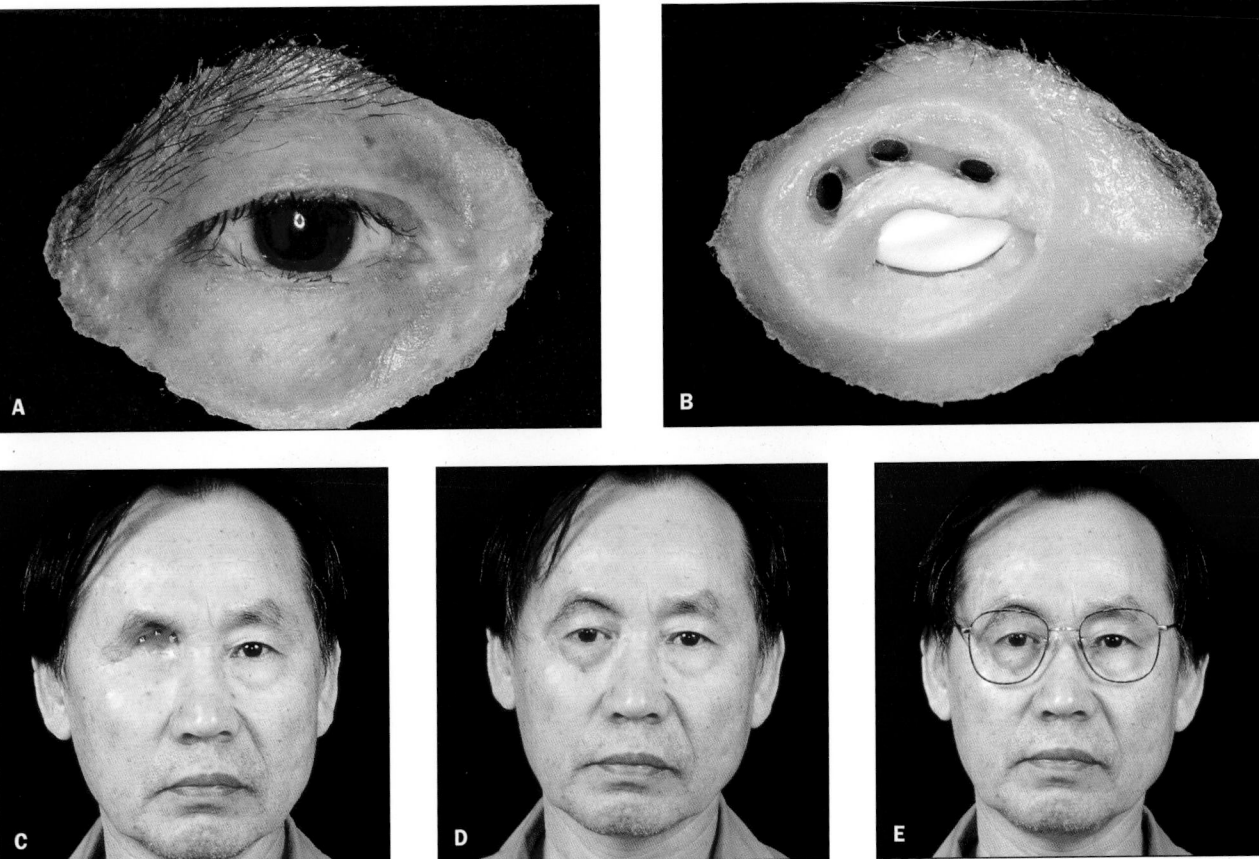

Fig 20-32. *A,* Completed prosthesis. *B,* Tissue side of prosthesis. *C,* Patient without prosthesis. *D,* Prosthesis in place. *E,* Prosthesis with eyeglasses.

References

1. Tjellström A, Yontchev E, Lindström J, Brånemark P-I. Five years' experience with bone-anchored auricular prostheses. Otolaryngol Head Neck Surg 1985;93:366.

2. Del Valle V, Faulkner G, Wolfaardt J, Rangert B, Tan HK. Mechanical evaluation of craniofacial osseointegration retention systems. Int J Oral Maxillofac Implants 1995;10:491.

3. Parel SM, Tjellström A. The United States and Swedish experience with osseointegration and facial prostheses. Int J Oral Maxillofac Implants 1991;6:75.

4. Wolfaardt JF, Wilkes GH, Parel SM, Tjellström A. Craniofacial osseointegration: the Canadian experience. Int J Oral Maxillofac Implants 1993;8:197.

5. Granström G, Bergström K, Tjellström A, Brånemark P-I. A detailed analysis of titanium implants lost in irradiated tissues. Int J Oral Maxillofac Implants 1994;9:653.

6. Tolman DE, Taylor PF. Bone-anchored craniofacial prosthesis study. Int J Oral Maxillofac Implants 1996;11:159.

7. Reisberg DJ, Habakuk SW. Use of a surgical positioner for bone-anchored facial prostheses. Int J Oral Maxillofac Implants 1997;12:376.

8. Rubenstein JE. Attachments used for implant-supported facial prostheses: a survey of United States, Canadian, and Swedish centers. J Prosthet Dent 1995;73:262.

9. Rangert B. Considerations for implant supported orbital prostheses. Nobelpharma Int Updates 1993;2:9.

10. Bergström K. Prosthetic techniques for orbital defects. Nobelpharma Int Updates 1993;2:5.

11. Cerullo L, McKinstry RE. Ocular prostheses. In McKinstry RE (ed): Fundamentals of Facial Prosthetics. Arlington, Virginia: ABI Professional Publications; 1995:99.

12. Thomas KF. Prosthetic Rehabilitation. London: Quintessence Publishing Company; 1994:169.

13. Habakuk SW, Potter-Ratzlaff E. Impressions for facial prostheses. In McKinstry RE (ed): Fundamentals of Facial Prosthetics. Arlington, Virginia: ABI Professional Publications; 1995:31.

14. Gion GG. Orbital prostheses. In McKinstry RE (ed): Fundamentals of Facial Prosthetics. Arlington, Virginia: ABI Professional Publications; 1995:121.

15. Udagama A. Urethane-lined facial prostheses. J Prosthet Dent 1987;58:351.

16. Allen R. Auricular prostheses. In McKinstry RE (ed): Fundamentals of Facial Prosthetics. Arlington, Virginia: ABI Professional Publications; 1995:147.

Prostheses for Complex Defects

21.

Patrick J. Henry, BDSc, MSD
Ronald P. Desjardins, DMD, MSD
William E. LaVelle, DDS, MS

- Treatment Opportunities
- Treatment Limitations
- Therapeutic Rationale

Residual facial defects that cannot be adequately reconstructed surgically may follow traumatic loss or more commonly result from the destructive effects of facial and oral cancer. In both types of patients, improvements in diagnostic imaging, surgical techniques, and treatment technologies have resulted in higher survival rates and extended longevity. Accordingly, health professionals in this area are increasingly called on to find solutions for residual defects in patients who hitherto would not have survived. The demands on personnel and resources for such patients can be huge. Because the time frame of extensive osseointegrated-based rehabilitation is long, maxillofacial prosthodontists and anaplastologists inevitably develop a close lifelong relationship with these patients, quite unlike anything seen elsewhere in dentistry and special even compared with most areas of medicine.[1]

Although life can be extended by medical science, the quality of that life is another consideration. Furthermore, it is inevitable that eventually that life will end, and toward the end, the demands made on the maxillofacial prosthetic therapist may be extreme, particularly in patients with cancer-related defects.

Treatment Opportunities

The patient presenting with combined intraoral and extraoral defects involving the middle one-third of the craniofacial skeleton is the greatest challenge. This situation implies loss of speech and masticatory function and aesthetic compromise. The aim of treatment is to give the patient the ability to communicate, masticate, and enjoy a level of social acceptance. Fundamentally, the patient must accept the treatment result in terms of a positive contribution to restoration of lost body parts and self-image. The central issue involved, and the most important goal, is communication.

259

Patients who have difficulty communicating because of extensive loss of intraoral or nasal structures do not cope as well as those who are permanently mute after surgery or trauma to the larynx. The permanently mute patients understand that speech will no longer be possible, whereas the others live in frustration and desperation because their sounds cannot be understood. Communication is important in our society. Persons living alone or physically restricted in their movements may be less helpless if they can communicate via the telephone, provided their speech can be improved with a prosthesis.

The requirements of treatment may be for separate internal and external prostheses or for complex combination devices. Because the ramifications at the assessment, diagnostic, and actual treatment stages may be many and varied, it is mandatory that case management be controlled properly. This control is achieved best by the appointment of a tissue-integrated prosthesis treatment coordinator, a role that can be fulfilled by any member of the team. In many cases the maxillofacial prosthodontist may be the most appropriate person to coordinate treatment because of the lifelong responsibility for maintenance that is inherent in this type of therapy. It is desirable in some cases to involve other professionals at the presurgical case conference level, depending on the nature of the case. Various oncologic personnel, social workers, audiologists, psychologists, and psychiatrists who have been, or should have been, involved with the case may be invited to participate as part of the team approach to rehabilitation.[2]

The tissue-integrated prosthesis team is organized to function when cases are referred to it for assessment. Such assessment may occur immediately before the anticipated placement of implants or can be used for preliminary evaluation with respect to long-range planning in cases involving revision surgical management or extensive surgery.

Treatment Limitations

Patients with complex problems and those with guarded prognosis benefit from evaluation and treatment with a team management concept. This concept is well established in major medical centers, but unfortunately it may not exist in remote or rural areas. To restore the complex craniofacial defect with bone-anchored prostheses requires a team for optimal management.[3,4] The potentially positive ramifications in the psyche of a devastated patient must be considered carefully when deciding on early rehabilitation treatment. Consideration also must be given to the immediate reconstruction at the time of tissue resection and to possible implant placement at this stage. The staging of these procedures depends on the patient's prognosis and desires, financial considerations, experience of the team members, and facilities available for care. In most medical centers, for those patients with cancer, the oncology board, with representation of all those involved in the total care of the patient, takes part in the decision-making process. Through this process, it is hoped that patients will not be referred to the prosthodontist by an isolated medical, surgical, or radiologic service with the consultation request to provide minimal care because no other treatment is available or indicated.

Videotape education, with or without the opportunity to talk to successfully treated patients, can be of enormous benefit to those devastated by the cancer diagnosis. Only people who have been there can truly appreciate what the videotape means. Such opportunities have impacted positively in selected circumstances, resulting in facilitation of the treatment plan with simplification of the logistics.

The use of osseointegrated implants for the anchorage of facial prostheses implies a lifelong commitment to maintenance on the part of the patient and the osseointegration team. Correct selection of patients is most important. The patient must demonstrate a high standard of personal hygiene and understand the necessity for continued cleanliness and care of the abutment sites. Immature and uncooperative patients are unlikely to maintain the necessary standards of home care or attend for long-term follow-up. Patients with significant physical disabilities may have difficulty in maintaining the areas of skin penetration.

A history of irradiation of the bone at the implant site does not preclude osseointegration. However, implant success rate in previously irradiated bone does decline to 85% compared with 99% for implants in nonirradiated bone.[5] The use of hyperbaric oxygen treatment in conjunction with implant installation is advocated and does give improved results.[6]

To obtain consent, the patient should be informed of the requirement for treatment in two stages, the mechanics of the prosthesis, and the necessity for long-term care. Realistically, an adequate prosthetic service capable of providing good quality prostheses must be available to patients. Prostheses may require renewal each year because of wear and tear on silicone rubber and because the color pigments are subject to ultraviolet degradation.[7]

Therapeutic Rationale

The number of long-term patients rehabilitated by extensive midface osseointegrated reconstruction is small, with most major centers recording only several. Nevertheless the accumulated patient load has demonstrated morphologic and management factors in common. As a result, important principles of treatment planning, recognizing the necessity for indefinite maintenance, have emerged. It is apparent that flexibility in planning so that modifications are possible, depending on changing circumstance, is fundamental to long-term success. Accordingly, careful patient counseling is advocated in this context, in light of the logistic and psychologic variables involved.

The aims and objectives of treatment are to restore masticatory function, phonetics, and aesthetics; to improve the patient's psyche; and to reestablish self-esteem. The overall prosthetic time frame involved is seldom less than 1 year and closer to 2 in patients requiring concentrated speech therapy after extensive palatal reconstruction. During and after treatment it is evident that the patient's condition generally impacts negatively on lifestyle. Lifestyle is compromised because involvement in sporting and leisure activities, such as swimming and boating, is significantly limited. Consequently, such individuals suffer considerable psychologic trauma, develop compromised behavior patterns, and sometimes believe themselves to be a burden, at the family level and on society in general.

Many of the previous limitations of conventional maxillofacial prostheses have been minimized or eliminated with the advent of direct prosthetic anchorage to underlying bone, as provided by the extraoral placement of implants. Problems with marginal integrity, skin reactions, placement misalignment, and prosthesis camouflage are minimized or eliminated. As a result, this group of patients can now be rehabilitated to a level hitherto considered impossible, and many such individuals enjoy greatly improved lifestyles.[2] Furthermore, the patients are able to perceive the attachment as part of their facial structure in the same way as a dental bridge be-

Table 21-1	*Midface Defect Classification*	
Zone and structures involved		
Aesthetic	Masticatory	Phonetic
Orbit	Maxilla	Palate
Nose	Mandible	Tongue
Orbit and nose	Maxilla and mandible	Palate and tongue

comes incorporated into the pattern of oral stereognosis.[8]

Midface defects involve a variable loss of facial continuity combined with partial or total maxillectomy, with or without mandibular involvement. At assessment the major concern expressed by the patient may be primarily a masticatory functional one or it may be that aesthetics is the crucial issue. Alternatively, as defects become more complex it is likely that both aesthetics and function are problematic, possibly with concomitant phonetic difficulties. The initial assessment should delineate the overall degree of difficulty of the treatment plan and include a list of all possible ramifications not only of the treatment phase but also with respect to long-term maintenance issues. Accordingly, the defect possibilities and therapeutic concerns are classified in Table 21-1. This table should be primarily interpreted vertically. Horizontal relationships may or may not be applicable. Long-term prosthetic treatment planning involves consideration of four areas: 1) requirements for prosthetic precision and predictability, 2) design flexibility and modification potential, 3) maintenance and monitoring, and 4) recurrent and terminal disease.

Requirements for Prosthetic Precision and Predictability

Several fundamental principles must be adhered to if the final prosthesis is to fulfill aesthetic and functional expectations precisely. Hence, the projected end result must be clearly visualized at the beginning of treatment and, wherever applicable, use of the diagnostic work-up and surgical template is mandatory if success is to be predicted.

Force Distribution on Implant Anchorage Units. In patients requiring extraoral and intraoral prostheses in combination, careful consideration must be

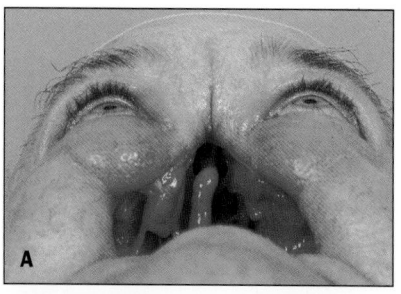
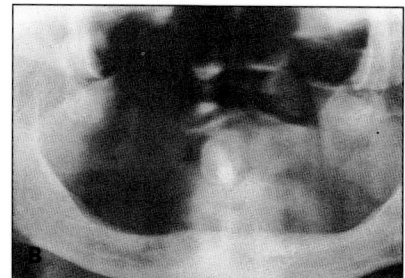
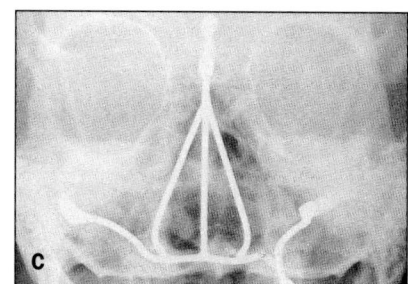

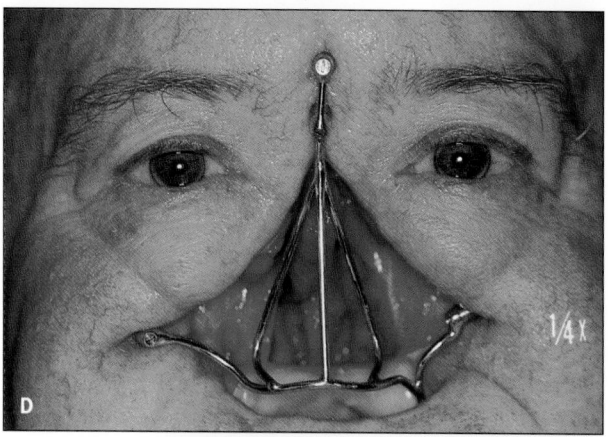

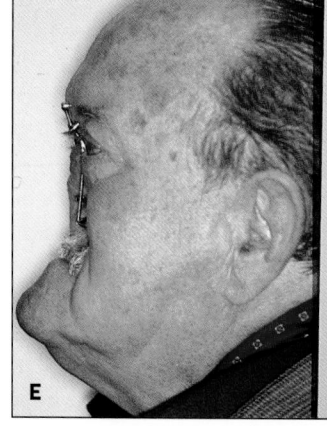
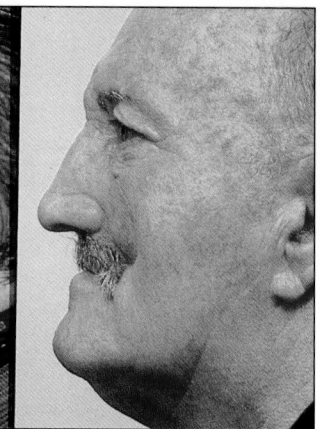

Fig 21-1 (case 1). Combined intraoral and extraoral prosthesis. *A,* Pretreatment condition after removal of nose, septum, and most of maxilla. *B,* Preoperative radiograph of defect. *C,* Radiographic visualization of bone-anchored bar structure. *D,* Clinical view of implant placement and bar design. *E,* Prosthesis attached, profile view. *F,* Frontal view at 10-year postoperative follow-up. (*B* through *F* from Henry.[2] By permission of Quintessence Publishing Company.)

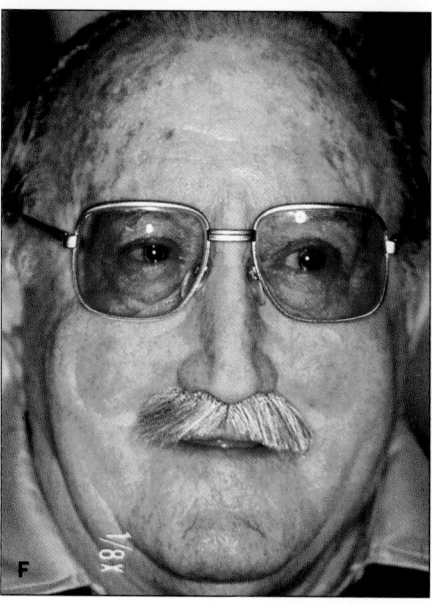

given to the leverage and force loads to which the prostheses will be subjected. Because the ultimate extraoral part of the prosthetic complex is essentially static when in position, no continuous stress is placed on the anchorage implants. However, anchorage designs that also contribute to fixed bridge or overdenture retention are subject to considerable loading not only from functional and parafunctional forces but also from leverage during placement and removal of the facial components. Such situations have to be planned carefully from the bioengineering viewpoint of providing a rigid anchorage system supported by implants placed in the residual bony skeleton wherever such anchorage is available (Fig 21-1).

Emphasis has been placed on the need to design such frameworks with an attempt to detail the stresses on individual implants and to distribute loads to the extent possible within the limits of available implant locations and anticipated degree of loading. Accordingly, there is an increasing awareness of the importance of including in the treatment team a biomechanical engineer capable of sophisticated stress analysis and appropriate model design.[9] Furthermore, difficult reconstructions must be planned, in the first instance, to provide excess anchorage potential where possible. This allows for complications. When the decision to treat with the osseointegration concept is made, it must not be to undertreat.[4]

Anchorage System Within the Periphery of the Prosthesis. Retention and support for the prosthesis must be planned within the peripheral extension of the appliance. Some restorations permit deviation of form if it is not visible. Overextension of nasal and orbital aspects of the prostheses are difficult to mask, and such compromise dictates a poor cosmetic result. Therefore, at operation, compromised implant placement should be selected internally away from the periphery because external placement can result in the anchorage point becoming prosthetically unusable.

The second-stage surgical procedure involving the skin is more critical than the second-stage procedure involving the oral mucosa. As opposed to the mucosal situation, it is imperative that the skin-abutment junction be in tissue that has been thinned as much as possible and with little capability for mobility. Adjacent hairbearing tissue is also problematic hygienically when it is in close proximity to the abutment. These problems can be eliminated by skin-grafting the area as an integral part of a modified second-stage surgical procedure, either with a split-skin or full-thickness skin graft. Procedures aimed at minimizing soft-tissue problems have been described and are now well established.[10-12] Detailed protocols of advocated techniques are given in Part III, Surgical Considerations.

Anchorage System Shallow to the Surface of the Prosthesis. The anchorage system together with its superimposed retention components must be placed sufficiently deep to provide adequate thickness for overlying prosthetic material, for reasons of structural durability and aesthetics. Again, the dimensional relationship of surface morphology to potential anchorage points is visualized using a transparent template developed from a diagnostic moulage wax up.

In the specific assessment of retention requirement, the principle of trade-off is frequently used,

whereby one area of advantage might have to be compromised in favor of other considerations. Structural wear and tear on rubber and plastic is accentuated with mechanical attachment systems providing firm and rigid anchorage. Alternatively, magnetic retention can be used without a rigid acrylic resin substructure, resulting in greater flexibility and thus facilitating removal of the prosthesis with less force. Flexible appliances have the additional advantage of being able to use available undercuts for additional stability in large complex defects.

In most cases, the retentive requirements for the prosthesis can be met by either mechanical or magnetic attachment systems or by hybrids of both. However, in these appliances or where retention is required peripherally, magnets require a greater dimension of contour to house the magnet, its anchorage component, and the overlying camouflage material. In such situations, low-profile clip systems can be used to advantage because the overall thickness requirement to use the attachment is about half that of currently available magnets.

Anchorage System Designed for Rigidity and Stress Distribution. The support and retention system must be designed to be absolutely rigid to avoid stress concentration at biologic and mechanical levels. This rigidity poses no problem for the simple ear, eye, or nose replacement. However, large midface defects and combination intraoral-extraoral cases can create considerable design problems. Implants have to be placed within the available residual skeleton in sufficient number and location to ensure rigidity of the proposed bar anchorage system. Whenever possible, retention of the maxillary tuberosity and posterior palatal rim should be considered fundamental. These structures aid in establishing a posterior peripheral seal for the denture and also provide important implant location sites for the placement of the pterygomaxillary implant option.[2] Implants placed horizontally into the palatal process can be used to advantage from the engineering point of view in formulating strategically placed anchorage points.[13,14] The angulation and direction of implants are of minor importance with respect to the overall engineering design of the retentive system because angular deviations can be overcome by using custom-designed prosthetic components, if necessary. It is fundamental that only bar systems with optimized physical properties are used to achieve maximum rigidity.

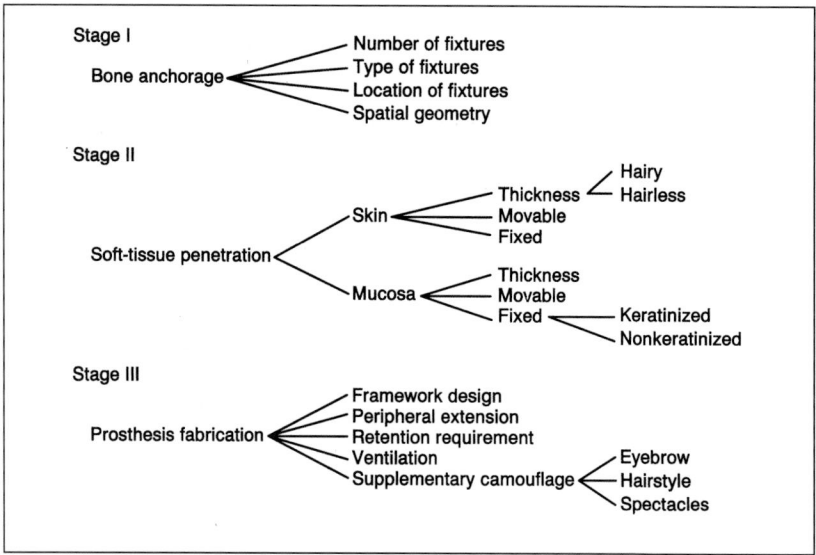

Fig 21-2. Prosthetic considerations in the treatment planning process. (From Henry.[2] By permission of Quintessence Publishing Company.)

Edges of Resection Optimized for Prosthetic Construction. Although conservation of tissue must be a basic surgical consideration, the success of the final rehabilitation is most important in planning. The edges of resection in midface defects should be prepared so as to conceal the prosthetic margin. This approach implies attached tissue with minimal mobility where possible.[15] It is advantageous to retain the upper lip wherever possible to achieve a contiguous defect and aid in minimizing the extent of the prosthesis. In maxillectomy patients with midface resection, the retention of the lip is fundamental in achieving optimal aesthetic, phonetic, and functional results. It also helps to minimize saliva dribbling and is of paramount importance with respect to lip function and social behavior.

Conversely, access has to be possible for prosthetic instrumentation and placement of awkward and cumbersome prosthetic bar systems in extensive resections. If such resections are largely internal with minimal residual external defect, it can be possible to conduct the prosthetic anchorage phases without surgical intervention to open the field. Careful consideration must be given to the necessity for tissue removal to ensure prosthetic access and maintenance.

Site-Specific Indications for Preprosthetic Revision Surgery. Anatomic variation can pose local tissue management problems that are site specific with respect to cosmetic requirements. Complex cases can often benefit from preprosthetic plastic or oral surgery (or both) to repair and simplify the defect as much as possible. Surgical main-

tenance or reconstruction (or both) of the maxillary lip profile is critically important to establish a lip seal and to minimize saliva dribbling. A functional closure of lower lip against an upper lip prosthesis is always poor. The inability to kiss is a severe social stigma, particularly for older patients and their relationships with children and grandchildren. In male patients, the ability to grow a moustache, thus blending the inferior border of the prosthesis with prosthetic and facial hair, is a major rehabilitative factor.

Repair of facial defects is planned on the basis of uniquely individual case requirements, and implants are placed where bone is available because the prime requirement is fixation. Resultant abnormalities of contour can often be compensated for by prosthodontic artwork. In the final analysis, the overall benefits of treatment often grossly overshadow the minor defects of form. An overview of prosthetic considerations in the treatment planning process is shown in Fig 21-2. Site-specific surgical guidelines for the midface defect are illustrated in Table 21-2. These guidelines indicate general principles that of course require modification in the assessment of each individual case.

Design Flexibility and Modification Potential

In light of the limited accumulated experience and because such cases show considerable variation, each patient is somewhat unique. Consequently, a certain

Table 21-2 *Site-Specific Surgical Guidelines for Midface Defects*

General principles	Orbital extensions	Nasal and midfacial extensions
Establish hard-tissue continuity	After exenteration, grafting technique should prevent tissue regrowth, which could result in inadequate depth for the correct positioning of the ocular prosthesis and obliteration of the bony orbital rim	In cases of missing lip, reconstruction to help fluid control; if necessary, a cosmetic lip could ride over the tissue flap
Remove plates and fixation wires from areas that radiographically mask implant sites	Maintain the level of the eyebrow	Leave nasal spine if possible, because it provides the only area of stability to the inferior edge of the nasal prosthesis
Bone graft sites of inadequate bone volume for strategic placement of implants	Remove eyelids and eyelashes or denervate the muscle and excise the eyelashes	Reduce the septum if it remains protrusive
Undercontour peripheral augmentation procedures	Reduce excess tissue on the temporal aspect	If the surgical excision extends too close to the vermilion border, re-create a keratinized tissue base at the inferior edge of the defect
Remove abnormal or asymmetric tissue tags	Fixate tissue inferior to the eyebrow to prevent tissue travel during forehead skin movement associated with facial expression. This will avoid superior and lateral "gapping" around the prosthesis margin	Remove floppy alar tags
Establish access for abutment and prosthetic instrumentation	Close ethmoid sinus or, if that is impossible, create a tissue drain to prevent pooling of body fluids on the socket floor, possibly by redirection into the sinus	Save the bony bridge if possible
		Graft exposed bone
		In hemimaxillectomies, do not obliterate areas of potential implant installation by filling in the area with myocutaneous flaps
		Maintain facial soft-tissue symmetry

Modified from Henry.[2] By permission of Quintessence Publishing Company.

degree of trial and error must be superimposed on the basis of established principle. Furthermore, the possibility of implant failure, treatment setback, or recurrent disease dictates the necessity for flexibility in planning with modification potential. The combined craniofacial experience indicates that implants placed in different sites have different anatomic success rates.[16-18] It is prudent to place additional implants wherever possible, especially in areas subject to high failure rates such as the orbital rim, posterior maxilla, and nasal bone locations. Areas such as the residual zygomatic buttress and pterygomaxillary region often are available after radical tumor resection for implant placement. Special instruments are required for the placement of long implants in these regions. The success rate of these implants has been high, and the angular placement is well suited to offset the load and torque of the prostheses.

It is important to ensure that, whenever possible, single-piece engineering bar system designs are used. If limited access dictates that segmental designs are to be used and subsequently united in situ, then the risks of stress concentration, fatigue, and fracture become high. Such designs jeopardize the long-term result, and precision, predictability, and prognosis are inevitably compromised. Furthermore, if there is insufficient access for prosthetic instrumentation, there is insufficient access for patient home care hygiene and maintenance.

However, large complex defects may have to be treated by segmental framework designs. These may remain segmented or may be joined to form an overall engineering design. In the latter circumstance it is imperative that the individual segments are placed to be self-sustaining, if required, as well as the structure in its entirety. In the event that modification becomes necessary, a fallback position should be readily available at the segmental level for independent interim anchorage for the facial prosthesis if an intraoral complication occurs, and vice versa.

Figure 21-3 illustrates a 52-year-old woman severely injured and disfigured as a result of a motor vehicle accident. Among the extensive intraoral defects were loss of palate and hemimaxillectomy, hemimandibulectomy, and partial glossectomy. After 62 surgical procedures, the patient sought evaluation

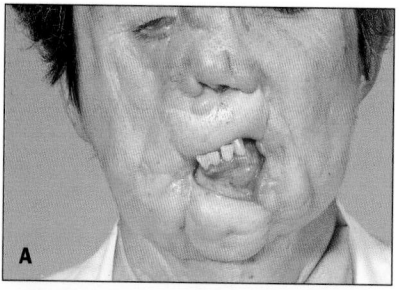 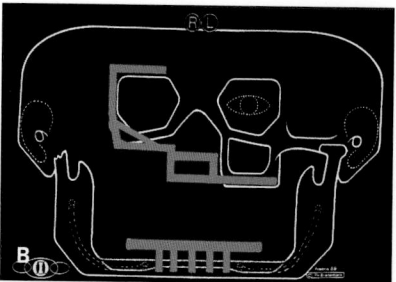 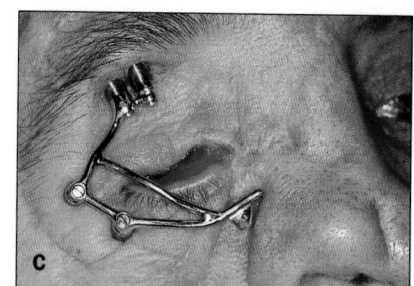

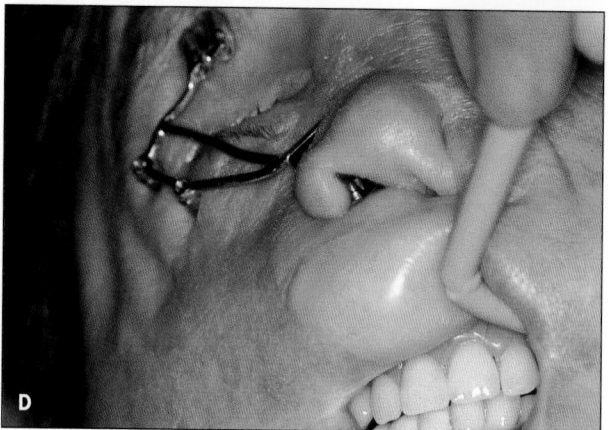 

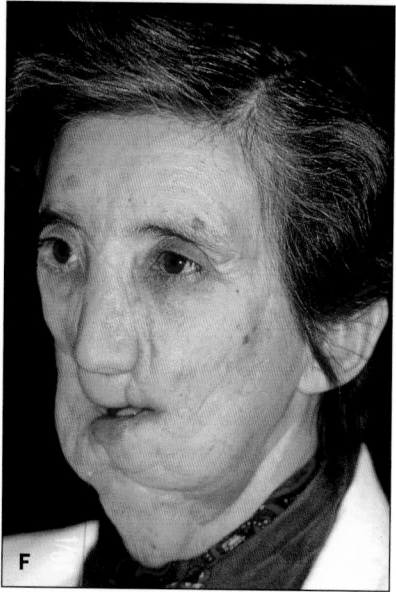

Fig 21-3 (case 2). Motor vehicle accident trauma. *A*, Pretreatment appearance. *B*, Implant treatment plan prescription for orbital facial prosthesis, maxillary overdenture, and mandibular fixed bridge bar design. *C*, External orbital bar connected to internal maxillary section by a rigid screw joint. *D*, Frontal view of intraoral rehabilitation. *E*, Remake of internal section as a speech appliance obturator to replace failed overdenture. *F*, At 5-year postoperative follow-up. (*B* modified from Henry.[2] By permission of Quintessence Publishing Company. *C* and *F* from Henry.[2] By permission of Quintessence Publishing Company.)

for reconstruction using the osseointegration concept. When asked what her chief problem was, her poignant reply—written on her notepad—read, "I want to be able to communicate." An extensive program of bone-anchored prosthetic rehabilitation was conducted in conjunction with intensive speech therapy. The patient can now talk on the telephone and go shopping. However, treatment was not without complications. The palate was restored initially with

a bone-anchored segmented overdenture opposing a lower jaw implant bridge, but implant loss in the residual maxillary segment resulted in its demise 1 year later. The palate subsequently was replaced with an obturator, using the extended bar of the orbital anchorage system for retention. This restored speech and communication for the second time, using the principle of flexibility of treatment planning and fallback position philosophy. Such difficult conditions

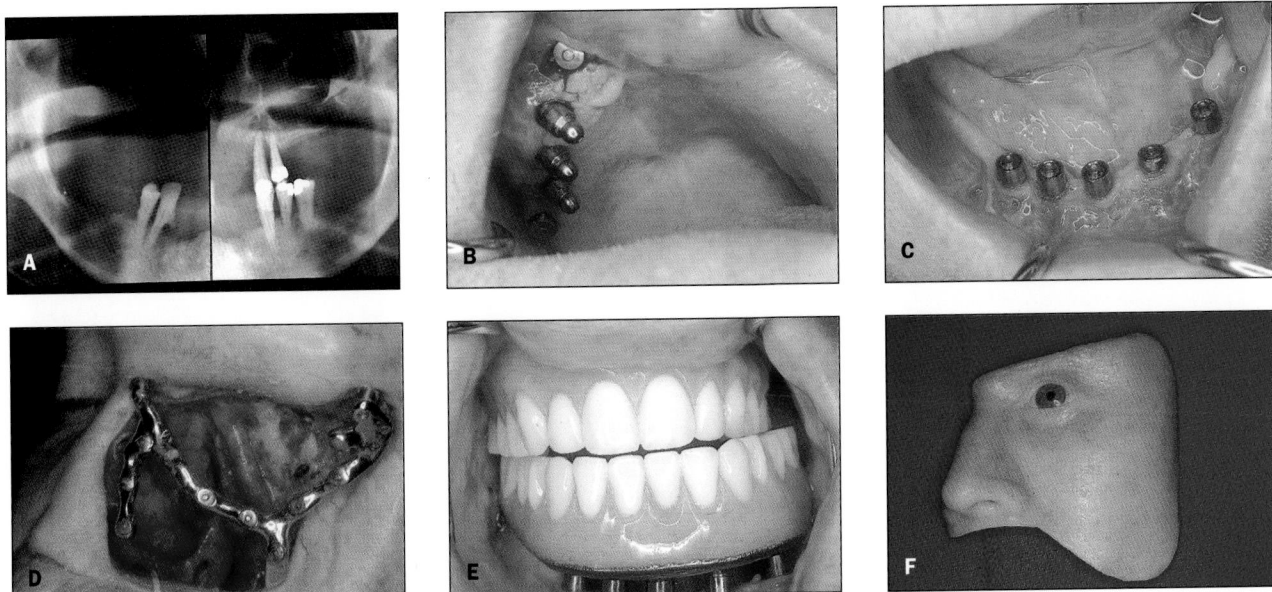

Fig 21-4 (case 3). Combined intraoral and extraoral prosthesis. *A,* Radiographic view of terminal dentition. *B,* Soft-tissue coverage, maxillary defect, with implants in place. *C,* Implants placed in anterior mandible. *D,* Implants placed into left orbital rim and nasal bone, with connecting bar splint. *E,* Fixed mandibular prosthesis with removable maxillary overdenture prosthesis. *F,* Facial prosthesis.

must be planned, in the first instance, to provide excess anchorage potential where possible.

This type of patient is at risk primarily with respect to mechanical overload of implant support. However, the potential for more frequent review, modification, and remake exists in cancer rehabilitation with respect to the additional risk of local disease recurrence. This need for long-term maintenance in light of altered prognosis is described in four case histories (Fig 21-4 through 21-7).

A 42-year-old man initially had a basal cell carcinoma surgically removed from the left side of the nose. Four years later recurrence on the left side of the nose and the forehead was managed with Mohs' technique. Recurrence in these same sites 1 year later was removed and reconstructed with a forehead flap. A further recurrence the next year resulted in resection of the left side of the nose and the maxilla with exenteration of the left orbit. As part of the maxillary resection, the oroantral communication was closed by attaching the buccal mucosa to the midpalatal resection site. Two years later, recurrence was evident in the ethmoid and sphenoid sinuses, the frontal sinus, the frontal bone, and the base of the skull. Irradiation (60 Gy) in fractionated doses was given at that time.

A large defect was evident when the patient first was seen for maxillofacial prosthetic consultation after the third recurrence. Intraorally, two maxillary and five mandibular teeth remained, all of which had se-

vere periodontal bone loss (Fig 21-4*A*). The soft tissue covering the maxillary defect was distended at rest but somewhat displaceable (Fig 21-4*B*). Surgical management included removal of the remaining teeth, placement of five osseointegrated implants in the maxilla in conjunction with an iliac crest antral bone graft (Fig 21-4*B*), placement of five implants in the anterior mandible (Fig 21-4*C*), placement of three implants in the left lateral orbital rim, and placement of three implants in the left nasal bone (Fig 21-4*D*). After osseointegration of the implants, oral prostheses constructed included a fixed mandibular hybrid prosthesis and a maxillary removable overdenture retained with three ball attachments and two magnets (Fig 21-4*E*). A two-piece magnetic alloy bar splint was made to join the orbital and nasal implants (Fig 21-4*D*). The facial prosthesis was made of a silicone elastomer with an internal acrylic resin substructure, which included multiple magnets for attachment to the magnetic alloy bar splint (Fig 21-4*E* and 21-4*F*).

Seven years after placement, the implants in the lateral orbital rim and the superior implant in the nasal bone were lost. The bar splint was revised to permit continued use of the facial prosthesis, with magnet retention medially and skin adhesive retention laterally. The patient died of disease after a further 2 years.

A 58-year-old woman had an initial diagnosis of facial basal cell carcinoma at age 23 years. During the next 35 years she had more than 60 surgical pro-

267

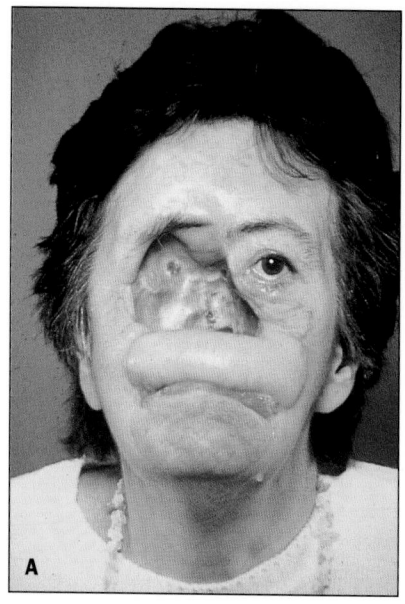

Fig 21-5 (case 4). Combined intraoral and extraoral prosthesis. *A,* Surgical reconstruction of upper lip. *B,* Implant placement into right orbital rims, with connecting bar splint. *C,* Magnetic attachment of facial prosthesis. *D,* Implant placement into bone graft in left antrum. *E,* Magnetic alloy bar system. *F,* Remaining lone maxillary molar. *G,* Obturator prosthesis. *H,* Completed restoration. *I,* Remake of facial bar splint. *J,* Remake of obturator prosthesis. (*A* and *C* from Laney WR, Tolman DE. The Mayo Clinic experience with tissue-integrated prostheses. In Albrektsson T, Zarb GA (eds): The Brånemark Osseointegrated Implant. Chicago: Quintessence Publishing Co; 1989;165. By permission of publisher. *B* from Tolman and Desjardins.[11] By permission of American Association of Oral and Maxillofacial Surgeons. *D, E, G* through *J* from Tolman et al.[12] By permission of Quintessence Publishing Company.)

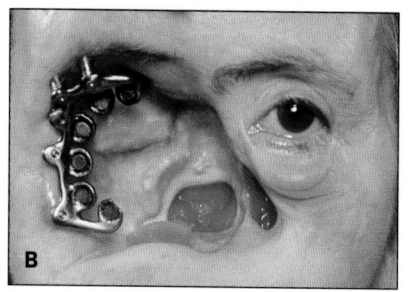

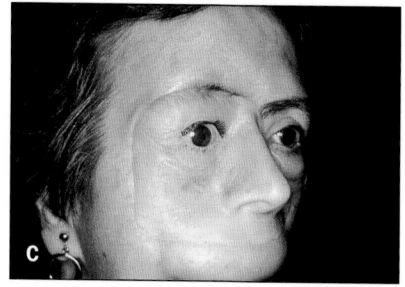

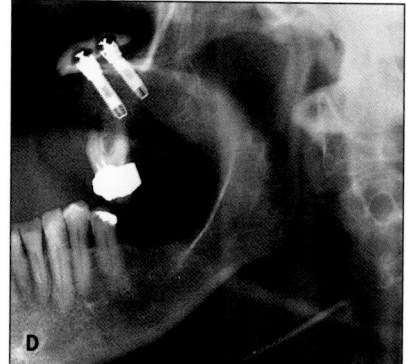

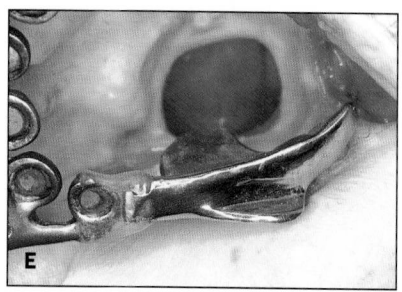

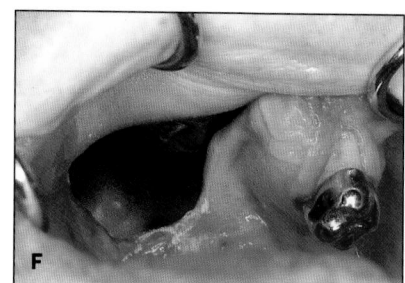

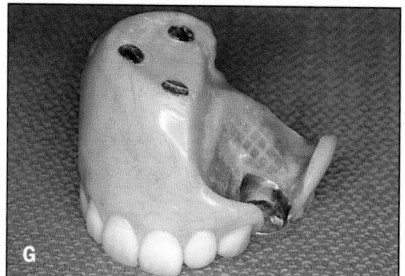

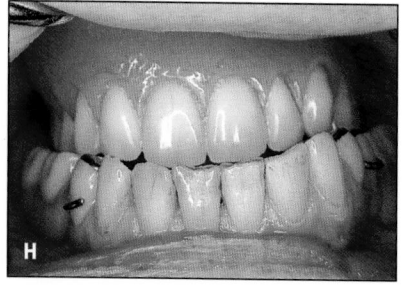

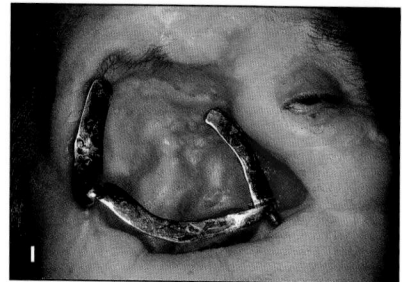

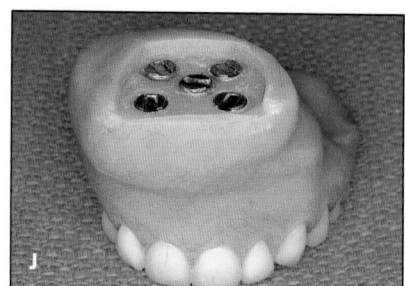

cedures, including a right orbital exenteration. On presentation she required a maxillary resection, which extended from the right pterygoid plates to the left second premolar region and included removal of the nose, lower half of the right orbit, ethmoid sinuses, medial wall of the left orbit, cribriform plate, upper lip, and right oral commissure. The upper lip was reconstructed with tongue and delto-pectoral flaps (Fig 21-5A). A temporary obturator prosthesis was retained by soft-palate extension and clasping of the lone maxillary left molar. With the midface resection and lip reconstruction the occlusal relationship was prognathous, with natural mandibular incisors contacting the reconstructed upper lip.

Four months after resection, five implants were placed into the right superior and lateral orbital rims. Six months later the implants were uncovered and were joined together with a bar splint to which a facial silicone elastomer prosthesis was magnetically attached (Fig 21-5B and 21-5C). The temporary obturator prosthesis was maintained.

After a further 3 years an iliac crest bone graft was placed into the maxillary antrum and supported with two implants placed from the superior approach (Fig 21-5D). Seven months later these osseointegrated implants were uncovered and a definitive obturator prosthesis was made opposing a mandibular, bilateral, distal extension partial denture. The bar splint joining the previously placed orbital rim implants was extended to the left maxillary implants. This revised bar was made of a magnetic alloy and included a horizontal section over the oronasal opening, that permitted incorporation of magnets into the superior surface of the obturator (Fig 21-5E). The lone maxillary molar remained and assisted in retention of the obturator prosthesis (Fig 21-5F through 21-5H). The facial prosthesis was remade at that time.

Recurrence 2 years later resulted in removal of a portion of the residual left maxillary alveolus, which included the lone molar and the most anterior implant of the two previously placed. The obturator prosthesis was revised. Two years later the two superior implants in the orbital rim loosened and were removed. Subsequently, the most inferior implant in the orbital rim was also lost. Two additional implants were placed in the orbital rim and one was placed in the superior surface of the left maxilla. Six months later the facial bar splint, obturator prosthesis, and facial prosthesis were remade (Fig 21-5I and 21-5J).

Ten years after her initial presentation, the upper lobe of the right lung was removed for adenocarcinoma. The following year an adenocarcinoma of the sigmoid colon with metastases to the lung and liver was diagnosed. Treatment included surgical resection of the sigmoid colon followed by chemotherapy. Various oral side effects from chemotherapy were managed symptomatically without significant change to the prostheses. The patient died of metastatic adenocarcinoma 18 months after the diagnosis of lung and liver metastases. This patient had more than 11 years of improved quality of life with her tissue-integrated prostheses.

Figure 21-6 illustrates a 36-year-old woman with surgical resection for a midface fibrosarcoma with a total rhinectomy and medial maxillectomy causing a significant cosmetic and functional defect. The medial half of her left eye was supported by a soft-tissue sling, compounding the difficulty of fitting this prosthesis. Significant muscle action resulted in changed tissue contours on the superior, left inferior, and lower right regions of the defect.

Her first immediate postsurgical prosthesis was retained by adhesive and was not satisfactory to this patient. Her second combination intraoral and extraoral restoration relied on a ball and socket attachment to the maxillary existing partial denture. Although this prosthesis was worn for 6 years, the problems associated with movement and moisture accumulation caused chronic telangiectasia and tissue irritation. This patient continued to have sociologic and psychologic rehabilitation problems.

The patient desired a bone-anchored restorative attempt. Bone-anchored intraoral and extraoral prosthetic rehabilitation was offered to minimize the existing problems and restore the patient's confidence in prosthetic retention, stability, and cosmetic result. Three Brånemark implants were placed: one in the left molar area, one in the right molar area, and one in the palatal shelf. These implants were 13 mm long. A fourth implant 15 mm long was placed in the nasion region. A rigid triangular bar was constructed and placed, ensuring that the midface restoration was stable. The intraoral prosthesis used natural dentition and the anterior bone-anchored bar to obturate the defect and provide lip contour before the construction of the facial prosthesis. The facial prosthesis was then constructed utilizing three clips for retention to allow tissue contact with minimal pressure. The patient's rehabilitation was accepted functionally and cosmetically, restoring her ability to return to school and continue her lifestyle.

Figure 21-7 illustrates a 64-year-old patient with postsurgical resection for multiple basal cell carcinomas. The planned osseointegrated reconstruction for combined intraoral and extraoral prosthesis was

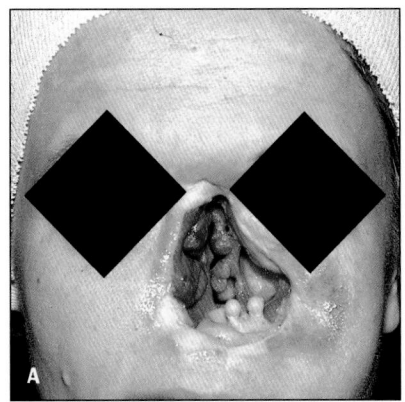
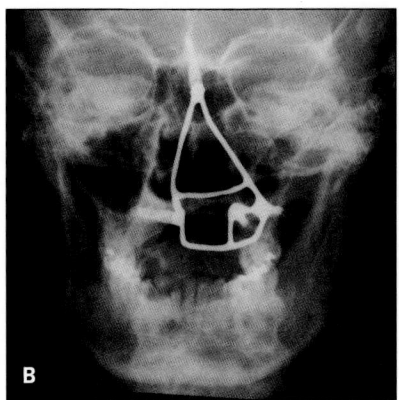
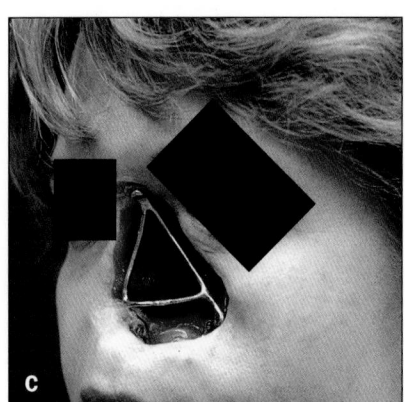

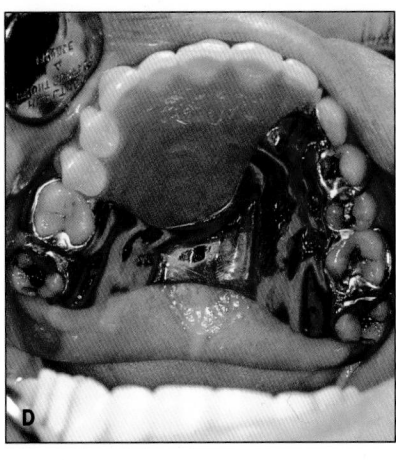
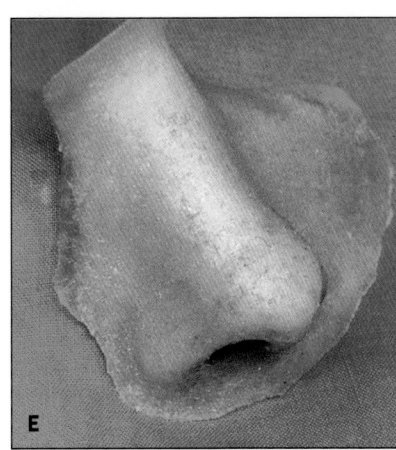
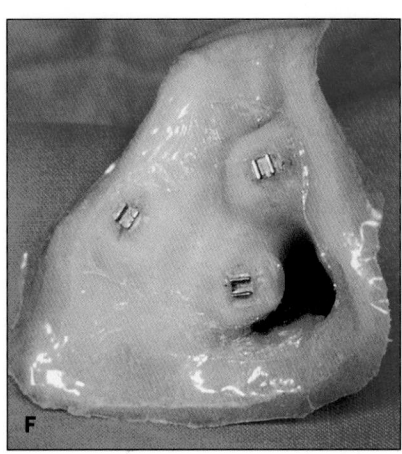

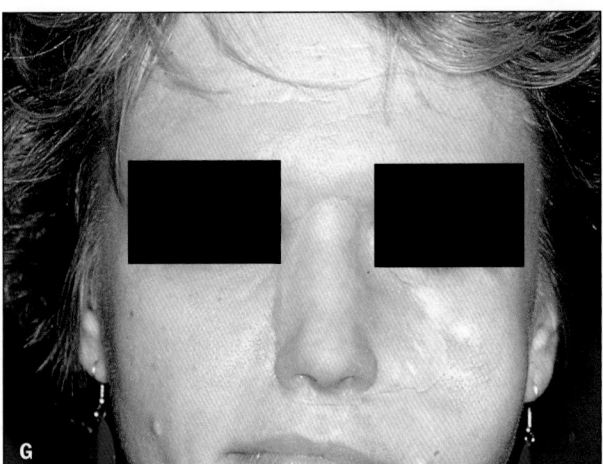

Fig 21-6 (case 5). Combined intraoral and extraoral prosthesis. *A,* Pretreatment condition after surgical resection of nose and anterior maxilla. *B,* Postimplant radiograph. *C,* Bone-anchored bar structure. *D,* Intraoral prosthesis. *E,* Facial prosthesis external surface. *F,* Facial prosthesis internal surface. *G,* Final photograph with prosthesis in place.

Part V

Soft and Hard Tissue Defects: Post-Treatment Considerations

Possible Complications

22.

Kajsa-Mia Holgers, MD, PhD
Per-Ingvar Brånemark, MD, PhD

- Complications of Percutaneous Implants
- Histologic Findings Around Percutaneous Implants
- Percutaneous Implants in the Craniofacial Region
- Histologic, Immunohistochemical, and Ultrastructural Findings
- Important Factors for the Outcome of Skin-Penetrating Titanium Implants
- Future Application Areas

Permanent skin-penetrating implants have many different medical applications (e.g., catheters for peritoneal dialysis, intravenous catheters, or attachment of prostheses for amputated limbs or craniofacial defects). In principle, a skin-penetrating implant is a foreign body penetrating the skin through a defect created during surgery.

Four basic types of biomaterials are used: metals, ceramics, polymers, and carbon (and composites). Biomaterials are also classified by their activity in living tissue: bioactive, bioresorbable, or inert. However, the term "inert" should be discussed. When an implant is permanently placed in the body, there always will be an inflammatory reaction in the tissue and the biomaterial is affected by the tissue response.[1,2] When the biomaterial also penetrates the skin, additional load is applied on the system. Because the skin barrier is broken, exogenous agents more easily penetrate into the tissue.[3]

In nature there are two epithelial penetrations, antlers and teeth; horn, nails, and hair are epidermal specializations and should not be considered as skin-penetrating formations. The antlers are attached firmly to the underlying skull and separated from the epidermal cells by a basal laminalike layer. In the dermis, collagen fibers penetrate into the antler and this arrangement seems to function as a seal from the external environment.[4] Around teeth, the junctional epithelial cells are anchored to the enamel via a basal lamina and by hemidesmosomes. In the subepithelial connective tissue, collagen fibrils connect the cementum to the bone.[5] From the natural epidermal penetrations, we can conclude that the following may be important for the function of epithelial penetrations: a tight contact between the epithelium and the penetrating implant; no relative motion in the interface area, by anchorage (e.g., to the underlying bone); the surface architecture of the implant; the material; and the status of the connective tissue.

Complications Associated With Percutaneous Implants

Percutaneous implants, in general, can be associated with many problems, and different failure modes were described by von Recum.[6] Failure of percutaneous implants may be due to only one or a combination of modes.

Marsupialization

This was described as an encapsulation of the implant by proliferating epidermis forming a sinus tract along the implant and is due to the free edge effect of the epithelial cells.

Avulsion

The skin around percutaneous implants is subjected to forces that lead to mechanical disruption of the interface, with microhematomas and subsequent microfoci of acute inflammation. This is considered to be a mechanically induced failure mode.

Permigration

The health and the maturity of the connective tissue are of great importance for the epidermis. Immature connective tissue cannot nourish the epidermis, which will permigrate deeper down around the skin-penetrating implant. This failure mode is related to implants with a porous surface. The soft connective tissue and the epidermis migrate into the implant and continue throughout the entire porous extent of the implant.

Infection

When an infection is established around an implant, this may have serious effects and usually leads to removal of the implant. The interactions between bacteria and the implant depend on the properties of both the implant and the bacteria and on the host defense.[7,8]

The major pathogen in infections around metal implants is considered to be *Staphylococcus aureus*.[9] However, few studies are available. Infections associated with external pin fixation of fractures were caused most commonly by *S aureus*,[10] and in experimental studies *S aureus* has been shown to colonize metal alloys (titanium-6-aluminum-4-vanadium) preferentially, whereas *S epidermidis* prefers polymer surfaces.[11] Coagulase-negative staphylococci, in particular *S epidermidis*, seem to be the most common agents in infections related to implants of polymers.[7,12]

Delayed Hypersensitivity

Another important reaction, especially for metal implants, is delayed hypersensitivity or contact allergy. This is well known for non-skin-penetrating implants of nickel, chromium, and cobalt.[13-16] Reports indicating hypersensitivity to titanium are rare and will be discussed further.

Histologic Findings Around Experimental and Clinical Percutaneous Implants

Only a few studies of the histologic and ultrastructural findings associated with percutaneous implants in experimental or clinical situations have been published, and these studies have involved a limited number of implants.[17-20] However, skin-penetrating implant materials have been researched extensively: polytetrafluoroethylene (Teflon), polymeric silicone (Silastic), and polyethylene terephthalates (Dacron)[21-25] as well as carbon,[19,26-29] hydroxyapatite,[18,19,30-32] titanium,[17,19,27,28,33-37] and stainless steel.[28,37]

Observations Around These Different Implants

The epithelium has a tendency to grow down along the skin-penetrating implant to a varying extent, and such an epithelial downgrowth is a common finding. A total epithelial downgrowth, marsupialization, is one of the failure modes described by von Recum.[6]

Formation of a connective tissue capsule around the percutaneous implants also is a common finding. Often the fiber orientation is parallel to the implant or oriented circularly around the hydroxyapatite implants.[19] In general, inflammatory cells are present in the connective tissue around the implants (carbon and titanium), even in the absence of clinical signs of inflammation.[26,27]

Relationship Between Histologic Findings and the Surface of Implants

Within porous implants, the connective tissue was less mature.[38] Gangjee et al[39] described a decrease in connective tissue maturity increasing the rate of epithelial permigration.

The surface topography appears to influence the morphology of the connective tissue as well as the behavior of the epidermis.[17,40] An attachment of epithelial cells to the implant surface via hemidesmosomes and a basal lamina structure was reported. This attachment was suggested to stimulate connective tissue ingrowth and correlated with an inhibition of epithelial downgrowth. However, the time of observation was limited. The experimental implants were placed for only 7 to 10 days to up to 3 weeks.[34]

Another factor of importance is the mobility of the implant, which can be related to the microsurface of the implant. The number of inflammatory cells seems to be low around titanium, carbon, or hydroxyapatite implants with decreased mobility,[19,30,33] particularly if the epidermis is attached to the implant, as described by Jansen et al[19] in an ultrastructural study of hydroxyapatite-coated titanium and sintered hydroxyapatite.

Percutaneous Implants in the Craniofacial Region

Few reports are available on percutaneous implants in the craniofacial region. In a clinical trial by Klomp et al,[29] percutaneous devices of carbon for electric stimulation of the cochlea or visual cortex (eight patients) were evaluated. One patient had an implant for 3 years. Histologic examinations were not performed. In another clinical study, including 42 patients with skin-penetrating cochlear implants of carbon, the clinical skin status around the implants anchored to temporal bone was followed up to 48 months with respect to local complications.[41] No histologic evaluation was reported. Histologic evaluations have been done on skin-penetrating implants in the craniofacial region.[3]

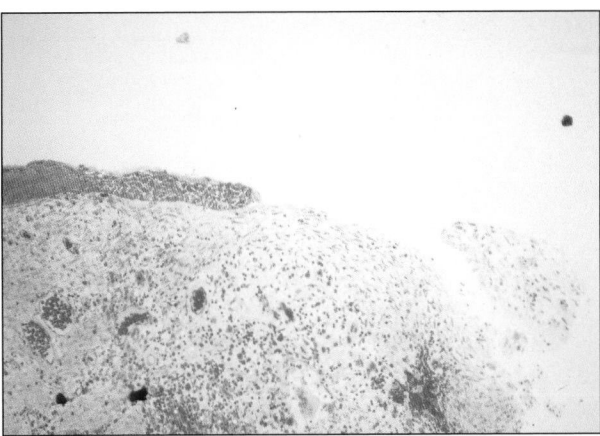

Fig 22-1. Photomicrograph from a patient without clinical inflammation. There is an epithelial downgrowth at the interface. There are inflammatory cells present: lymphocytes, macrophages, and plasma cells at the interface. (Richardson's solution; 1-μm section.) (×138.)

Clinical Percutaneous Titanium Implants

Percutaneous titanium implants have been in clinical use for anchorage of bone-conductive hearing aids and craniofacial prostheses since 1977 at the Otorhinolaryngology Department at Sahlgren's Hospital. Adverse skin reaction was observed in 10% of the observations and in 25% of the patients.[42] The incidence of adverse skin reaction reported by Parkin[41] was 36% for percutaneous implants of carbon.

Histologic Analyses of Clinical Percutaneous Titanium Implants

Biopsy specimens were investigated from the soft tissue around skin-penetrating titanium implants for anchorage of auricular prostheses and bone-conductive hearing aids from more than 30 patients. Histologic analyses were performed, including morphometry.[3] Whether or not clinical inflammation was present, inflammatory cells were always present at the area facing the implant (interface area). The epidermis migrates downward at the site of the implants. This epithelial downgrowth also was present in clinically irritated and clinically nonirritated specimens and was not keratinized and lacked rete pegs (Fig 22-1).

In contrast to the findings around subcutaneously placed implants, no fibrous capsule was present around the implants and the collagen was not

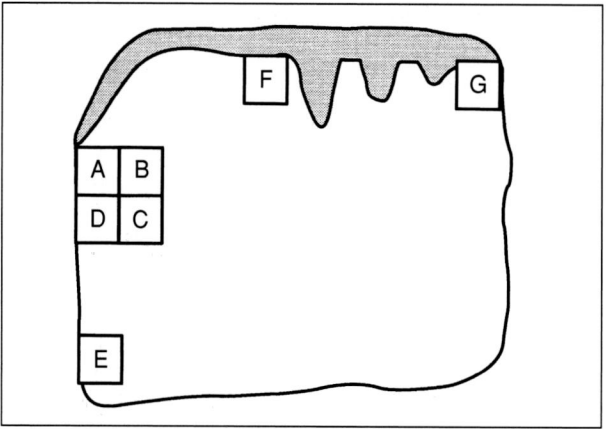

Fig 22-2. Schematic of skin biopsy specimen from skin-penetrating titanium implants for anchorage of bone-conductive hearing aids or auricular prostheses. The areas chosen for morphometry are indicated. (Not drawn to scale.) (From Holgers et al.[43] By permission of Elsevier Science.)

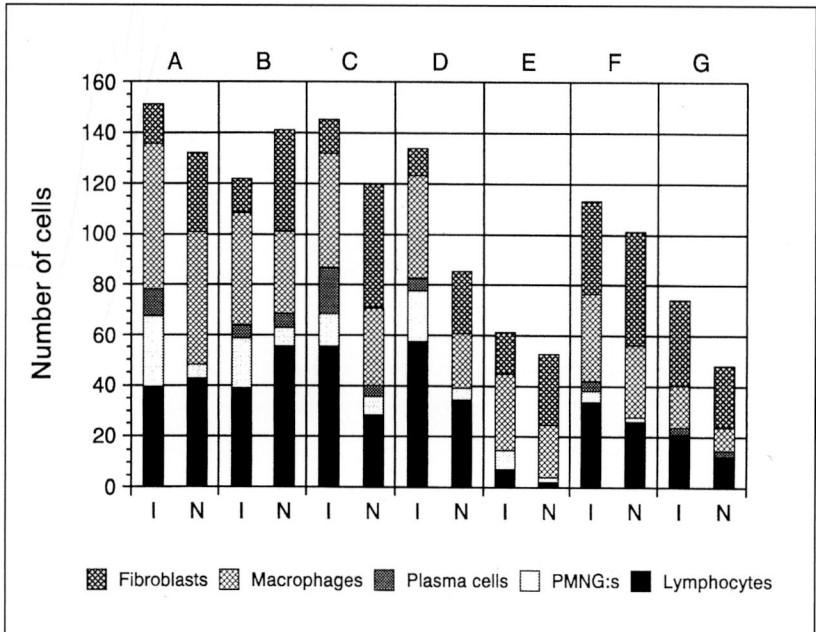

Fig 22-3. The distribution of inflammatory and immunocompetent cells around skin-penetrating titanium implants for anchorage of bone-conductive hearing aids or auricular prostheses. Specimens with clinical signs of inflammation (*I*) or without clinical signs of skin reaction (*N*). *PMNG:s*, polymorphonuclear granulocytes. (From Holgers.[3] By permission of University of Göteborg.)

arranged in any specific way in relation to the skin-penetrating part of the implant.

Morphometric data showed that in both groups there was a significantly higher number of inflammatory and immunocompetent cells in the areas close to the interface than at a distance and significantly more cells close to the epidermis compared with deeper portions.

A higher number of inflammatory cells was found regularly in biopsy specimens taken from patients with clinical signs of inflammation than in biopsy specimens from patients without clinical signs of inflammation. Figure 22-2 and 22-3 show the morphometric data and location of the analyzed areas.

The morphologic evaluation was confirmed by an immunohistochemical analysis, which also revealed that the number of B lymphocytes was significantly higher in the group with clinical signs of skin reaction compared with the group without clinical skin reaction.[43]

Bacteriologic Findings Around Skin-Penetrating Titanium Implants

The presence of a polymicrobial flora was evident around the implants. However, *S aureus* was the most commonly isolated microbe in skin with and without clinical inflammation.[44] In another investigation, coagulase-negative staphylococci were the most common isolates. Anaerobic isolates were detected from patients with or without skin inflammation but there were more anaerobes in the group with clinical inflammation (Holgers K-M, Ljungh Å, unpublished data). In this study, the skin condition in the clinically inflamed group was less severe.

There were no hydrophobic isolates; however, the isolates from clinical inflammation had a lower cell surface hydrophilicity than isolates from noninflamed tissue. High cell surface hydrophobicity is considered to be a virulence factor and related to clinical infection.[45] Another factor of importance is the difference in hydrophobicity or hydrophilicity of different implants. Metals have a hydrophilic surface whereas polymers often have a hydrophobic surface. For extracellular matrix proteins, binding to a hydrophobic surface is even more energetically favorable than binding to a hydrophilic surface. The influence of these factors on the adhesion potentials of the microbes probably is significant.

When clinical infection occurs around skin-penetrating titanium implants, the condition often is treated sufficiently with soap and water. This might be the result of the hydrophilicity of the microbes around titanium implants with no or moderate clinical infection (Holgers K-M, Ljungh Å, unpublished data).

Delayed Hypersensitivity

Metal sensitivity is typically a cell-mediated immune response, with metal ions acting as haptens.[14] In delayed hypersensitivity tests, salts of metals are used, but titanium salts have low solubility at neutral pH.[46] Tests for titanium sensitivity usually have been performed with solid titanium disks. In a case report, it was suggested that a patient with a titanium-encapsulated pacemaker had hypersensitivity to titanium.[47] Further, Lalor et al[48] reported on five patients with failure of total hip replacements (titanium alloy) and suggested a possible hypersensitivity to titanium. In their immunohistochemical study, a large number of T lymphocytes but few B lymphocytes were demonstrated. None of their patients showed a positive reaction to titanium salts used in patch tests, but two of four patients tested had a positive reaction to a titanium-containing ointment.

To investigate if a delayed hypersensitivity reaction to titanium was a possible cause for observed inflammatory reaction in patients with skin-penetrating titanium implants, a broad panel of potential allergens was examined by patch tests.[49] No contact allergy was found to titanium, but in both groups a higher incidence than expected was found of delayed hypersensitivity to *other* substances in the test panel.[49] One patient in the group without inflamed skin showed a suspect positive reaction to the titanium test disk, but the reaction disappeared when the titanium disk was thoroughly cleaned.[49] This patient was allergic to nickel, and the positive reaction might have been due to contaminants. This particular finding indicates the importance of a thorough cleaning of the disk with the same technique as used for the clinical implants. Our observations indicate that the positive reactions in the patients tested by Lalor et al[48] using a titanium-containing ointment could have been due to other constituents or contaminants (e.g., the container).

In patients with percutaneous implants, a puncture of the skin is present at the site of penetration, and this could increase the risk for delayed hypersensitivity reaction to other substances. Craniofacial patients with nickel earrings also have a puncture of the skin, and nickel sensitivity may result.[50,51] The precise relationship between history of delayed hypersensitivity and propensity to develop a skin reaction around percutaneous implants and, in turn, the risk of acquiring hypersensitivity to other presumably unrelated substances is not known. This may be important to examine further and information could be of value for the selection and treatment of patients.

Histologic, Immunohistochemical, and Ultrastructural Findings Around Implants

Several authors have reported a basal laminalike structure around intraoral implants to which epithelial cells attach by hemidesmosomes. This is present between the junctional epithelium and the surface of implants of different compositions such as aluminum oxide, various metals including cobalt-chromium alloys,[52] titanium,[53] epoxy resin,[54] and titanium-sprayed surfaces.[55]

Collagen fibers also have been described as firmly attached to intraoral implants.[55] In experimental studies on beagle dogs, collagen fibers were oriented perpendicular to the implant surface.[56]

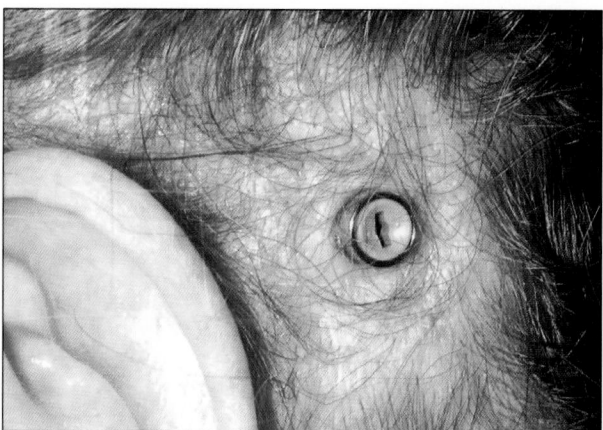

Fig 22-4. Photograph of a patient with skin-penetrating titanium implant for anchorage of bone-conductive hearing aid. The implant had been in place for 52 months and the soft tissue was judged as grade 0 (without clinical sign of infection).

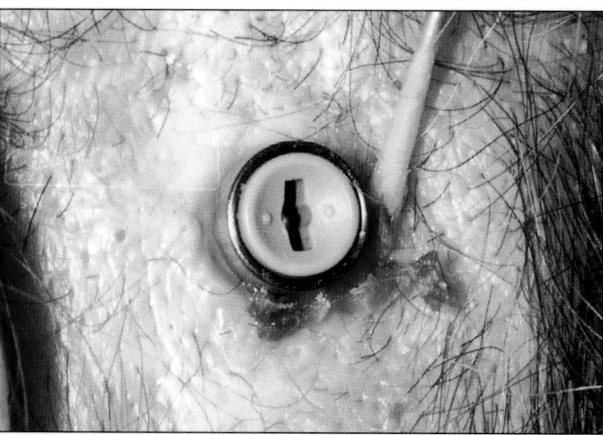

Fig 22-5. Photograph of the same patient as in Figure 22-4. Crusts are present around the implant.

In specimens from skin-penetrating titanium implants, the tissue surface adjacent to the implant from nonirritated as well as irritated skin was covered by a discontinuous layer of fibrin. Hemidesmosomes were never found. The collagen fibers were not arranged in any specific way, and we did not obtain any evidence for a direct contact between the connective tissue and the implant or between the epithelium and the implant surface, as seen around intraoral implants.[20] The depth of the epidermal downgrowth varied and was not correlated with time of placement.

The inflammatory cells around the percutaneous implants were located mostly in the superficial portion of the junction between the epithelium and the implant material. A possible explanation for this location is that exogenous factors (e.g., microorganisms and bacterial products) were located at this site and provided stimuli for leukocyte recruitment. The significantly increased number of B lymphocytes in the group with clinical inflammation suggests the induction of an antibody-mediated response by bacterial antigens.

The absence of a fibrous capsule around the percutaneous implants was a rather unexpected finding, because the formation of such a capsule appears to be an unavoidable event whenever an implant is surrounded by soft connective tissue.[1,2] One reason for this may be that the wound created when the abutment is placed is not sealed off from the external environment, which may lead to a lack of direct cell-implant contact. Signals leading to fibroblast proliferation and stimulation are not elicited. A crevicular fluid is likely to exist around the percutaneous implants, similar to the gingival crevicular fluid that acts as a barrier against disease. A crust formation always is present around the clinical titanium implants at clinical follow-up when the skin around the implants is examined with otomicroscopy. This reveals the presence of a fluid space in the interface area in the clinical situation (Fig 22-4 and 22-5).

However, there are differences between the intraoral and the extraoral situations. The epidermal migration seems to stop at the depth of 2 mm in the intraoral situation, but extraorally the depth of the epidermal downgrowth varies. There is a difference in the microbiologic findings around successful dental implants, similar to the findings in healthy sulci. The findings around the failing implant are similar to the microbiota of periodontal disease. A bacterial reservoir around the teeth has been suggested as a source of reinfection of the implant sulcus by periodontal pathogens.[57]

Soft-tissue reduction during implantation surgery seems to be favorable for the clinical outcome extraorally.[58] In contrast, this is not considered to be favorable intraorally, because epithelial migration of 2 mm occurs with or without soft-tissue reduction (Berglundh T, personal communication). The corresponding experimental analysis has not been performed in the extraoral situation.

When infection occurs around orthopedic implants (e.g., hip prostheses), the complications related to the infections may lead to reoperation and removal of the device.[7,8] In contrast, when inflammation and infection occur around percutaneous implants of titanium, these may be treated efficiently with nonsurgical topical application of cortico-steroids and antibiotics, reducing the number of skin-penetrating implants to be removed as a result of skin problems to 1.5%.[42] This difference may be because the non-skin-penetrating implant is sealed off from the environment, and when infection occurs, high concentrations of inflammatory signals develop, causing severe complications.

Possible Important Factors for the Clinical Outcome of Skin-Penetrating Titanium Implants

The skin-penetrating implants have good clinical acceptance. Because there is no evidence of a strong physical barrier between the soft tissue and the exterior, the nature of the seal seems to be a dynamic barrier of inflammatory cells. This dynamic seal depends on the load on the implant site from the host response to the implant material, surface, and stability; exogenous agents; and mechanical factors. Stable fixation of the implant is of great importance. Implant mobility was associated with failure.[33] This also has been shown in an experimental model in rats.[42]

An obvious aspect of the clinical outcome of percutaneous implants is the status of the patient. Patients with end-stage renal disease[59] receiving percutaneous devices of polymer, for peritoneal dialysis, are severely ill. The health status of the patient is an important factor for the host response to the implant. Patients receiving implants for attachment of auricular prostheses may, except for the hearing impairment or lack of an auricle, be healthy.

A group of patients with a clinical history of severe skin reactions[49] had psoriasis or seborrheic eczema, indicating that the skin disease influenced the development of inflammation around their implants. The hygiene of the patient is important, and the cleaning procedure is facilitated by the lack of hair at the skin-penetrating site, because a hair-free skin graft is placed around the implant. The cleaning procedure decreases the load of potentially exogenous inflammatory stimuli.

Patients with implants and previous treatment with radiotherapy have a high incidence (35%) of loss of the bone-anchored titanium implants.[60] Hyperbaric oxygen treatment is effective and decreases the failure of the implants.

Smoking has been suggested to be a negative factor for the maintenance of intraoral titanium implants.[61] A recommendation might be to stop smoking before implantation. Age; sex; and use of antidiabetic medication, supplemental female hormones, or corticosteroids did not correlate with increased failure of intraoral implants.[62]

Future Application Areas

Because 25% to 30% of the patients with skin-penetrating titanium implants sometimes have had clinical infections around the implants, there is room for improvement.[35,63] If the frequency of infection can be reduced, then there is the possibility of wider application of this percutaneous skin-penetrating technique. An important area is orthopedic implants for attachment of artificial limbs, developed by Brånemark at the Brånemark Osseointegration Center in Göteborg. The mechanical forces applied to these implants are of a totally different magnitude compared with the implants for hearing aids and craniofacial prostheses and are of great importance for the clinical outcome.

Patients with severe hearing loss have a difficult situation, but by acoustical improvements achieved by getting the stimulation closer to the target (the cochlea), their situation might be improved. Acoustical improvements could be made with a percutaneous coupling to a semi-implantable hearing aid or by achieving improved transmission of energy for cochlear implants. For these functions, a safer skin penetration is required.

Conclusion

Titanium has been reported to possess favorable properties owing to the stable titanium-oxide layer covering the metal. The hydrophilicity of the surface may be important. Further investigations on protein adhesion to the different materials are of great interest; perhaps we could change the surface to a less benign surface for the microbes and prevent adhesion of pathogens.

Irregularities on the surface could be beneficial for the connective-tissue attachment and this has been considered in manufacturing the present implants. Further analyses are necessary to improve the seal around the implant. Several observations indicate that the phagocytic cells have an altered function at biomaterial surfaces and that this change may be of profound importance for an efficient handling of the bacteria.[64,65] For achieving a safer skin-penetration it is of importance to better understand the mechanisms involved in the regulation of the host response to the implanted material.

References

1. Black J. Biological Performance of Materials: Fundamentals of Biocompatibility, ed 2. New York: Marcel Dekker; 1992.

2. Thomsen P, Ericson LE. Inflammatory cell response to bone implant surfaces. In Davies JE (ed): The Bone-Biomaterial Interface. Toronto: University of Toronto Press; 1991:153.

3. Holgers K-M. Soft Tissue Reactions Around Long-Term Clinical Skin-Penetrating Titanium Implants. Monograph, University of Göteborg, Göteborg, Sweden, 1994.

4. Grosse-Siestrup C, Affeld K. Design criteria for percutaneous devices. J Biomed Mater Res 1984;18:357.

5. Listgarten MA. Electron microscopic study of the gingivo-dental junction of man. Am J Anat 1966;119:147.

6. von Recum AF. Applications and failure modes of percutaneous devices: a review. J Biomed Mater Res 1984;18:323.

7. Christensen GD, Baddour LM, Hasty DL, Lowrance JH, Simpson WA. Microbial and foreign-body factors in the pathogenesis of medical device infections. In Bisno AL, Waldvogel FA (eds): Infections Associated With Indwelling Medical Devices. Washington, DC: American Society for Microbiology; 1989:27.

8. Gristina AG, Naylor PT, Myrvik QN. Biomaterial-centered infections: microbial adhesion versus tissue integration. In Wadström T, Eliasson I, Holder I, Ljungh Å (eds): Pathogenesis of Wound and Biomaterial-Associated Infections. London: Springer-Verlag; 1990:193.

9. Gristina AG. Biomaterial-centered infection: microbial adhesion versus tissue integration. Science 1987;237:1588.

10. Green SA, Ripley MJ. Chronic osteomyelitis in pin tracks. J Bone Joint Surg Am 1984;66:1092.

11. Barth E, Myrvik QM, Wagner W, Gristina AG. In vitro and in vivo comparative colonization of *Staphylococcus aureus* and *Staphylococcus epidermidis* on orthopaedic implant materials. Biomaterials 1989;10:325.

12. Bisno AL, Waldvogel FA. Infections Associated With Indwelling Medical Devices. Washington, DC: American Society for Microbiology; 1989.

13. Benson MK, Goodwin PG, Brostoff J. Metal sensitivity in patients with joint replacement arthroplasties. Br Med J 1975;4:374.

14. Merritt K, Brown SA. Metal sensitivity reactions to orthopedic implants. Int J Dermatol 1981;20:89.

15. Elves MW, Wilson JN, Scales JT, Kemp HB. Incidence of metal sensitivity in patients with total joint replacements. Br Med J 1975;4:376.

16. Carlsson AS, Magnusson B, Möller H. Metal sensitivity in patients with metal-to-plastic total hip arthroplasties. Acta Orthop Scand 1980;51:57.

17. Chehroudi B, Gould TR, Brunette DM. A light and electron microscopic study of the effects of surface topography on the behavior of cells attached to titanium-coated percutaneous implants. J Biomed Mater Res 1991;25:387.

18. Jansen JA, de Groot K. Guinea pig and rabbit model for the histological evaluation of permanent percutaneous implants. Biomaterials 1988;9:268.

19. Jansen JA, van der Waerden JP, van der Lubbe HB, de Groot K. Tissue response to percutaneous implants in rabbits. J Biomed Mater Res 1990;24:295.

20. Holgers K-M, Thomsen P, Tjellström A, Ericson LE. Electron microscopic observations on the soft tissue around clinical long-term percutaneous titanium implants. Biomaterials 1995;16:83.

21. Al-Nakeeb S, Pearson PT, Cholvin NR. A thoracic percutaneous lead system: development and evaluation. J Biomed Mater Res 1972;6:245.

22. Feldman DS, von Recum AF. Non-epidermally induced failure modes of percutaneous devices. Biomaterials 1985;6:352.

23. Mladejovsky MG, Eddington DK, Dobelle WH, Brackmann DE. Artificial hearing for the deaf by cochlear stimulation: pitch modulation and some parametric thresholds. Trans Am Soc Artif Intern Organs 1975;21:1.

24. Winter GD. Transcutaneous implants: reactions of the skin-implant interface. J Biomed Mater Res 1974;8:99.

25. Uretzky G, Appelbaum J, Sela J. Inhibition of the inductive activity of demineralized bone matrix by different percutaneous implants. Biomaterials 1988;9:195.

26. Mooney V, Predecki PK, Renning J, Gray J. Skeletal extension of limb prosthetic attachments—problems in tissue reaction. J Biomed Mater Res 1971;5 Suppl 2:143.

27. Mooney V, Schwartz SA, Roth AM, Gorniowsky MJ. Percutaneous implant devices. Ann Biomed Eng 1977;5:34.

28. Kadefors R, Herberts P, Almstrom C. A comparison of materials for percutaneous connectors. Ann Biomed Eng 1974;2:274.

29. Klomp GF, Womack M III, Dobelle WH. Percutaneous connections in man. Trans Am Soc Artif Intern Organs 1979;25:1.

30. Jansen JA, van der Waerden JP, de Groot K. Development of a new percutaneous access device for implantation in soft tissues. J Biomed Mater Res 1991;25:1535.

31. Aoki H, Akao M, Shin Y, Tsuzi T, Togawa T. Sintered hydroxyapatite for a percutaneous device and its clinical application. Med Prog Technol 1987;12:213.

32. Jansen JA, von Recum AF, van der Waerden JP, de Groot K. Soft tissue response to different types of sintered metal fibre-web materials. Biomaterials 1992;13:959.

33. Brånemark P-I, Albrektsson T. Titanium implants permanently penetrating human skin. Scand J Plast Reconstr Surg 1982;16:17.

34. Chehroudi B, Gould TR, Brunette DM. The role of connective tissue in inhibiting epithelial downgrowth on titanium-coated percutaneous implants. J Biomed Mater Res 1992;26:493.

35. Holgers K-M, Bjursten LM, Thomsen P, Ericson L. Clinical and experimental studies on percutaneous maxillofacial devices. Symposium on Angio- and Peritoneal Access in Uraemia. Billingehus Conference Center, Skövde, November 6, 1987.

36. Lundgren D, Axelsson R. Soft-tissue-anchored percutaneous device for long-term intracorporeal access. J Invest Surg 1989;2:17.

37. Pfingst BE, Albrektsson T, Tjellström A, et al. Chronic skull-anchored percutaneous implants in non-human primates. J Neurosci Methods 1989;29:207.

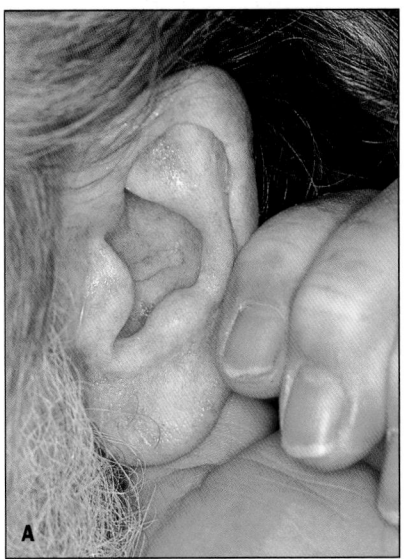

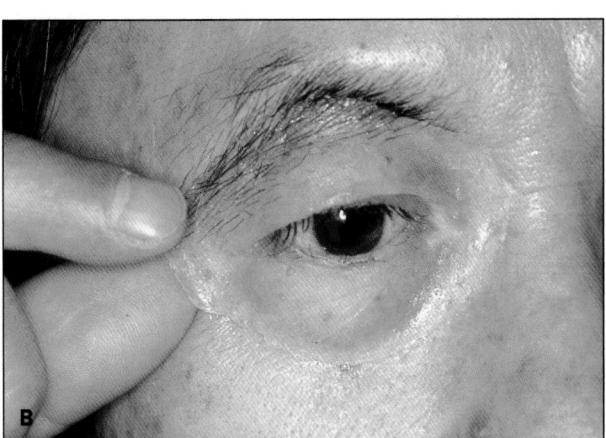

Fig 23-4. *A,* Proper removal of auricular prosthesis. *B,* Proper removal of orbital prosthesis.

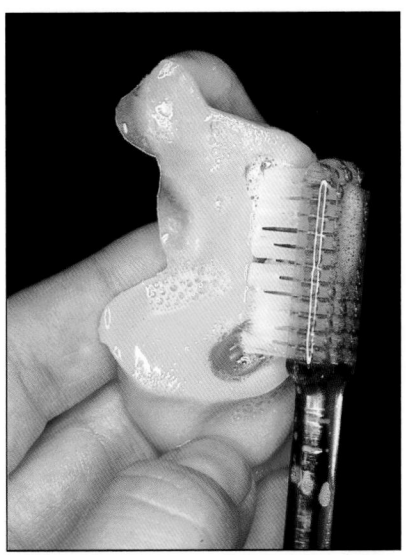

Fig 23-5. Gentle brushing of the prosthesis.

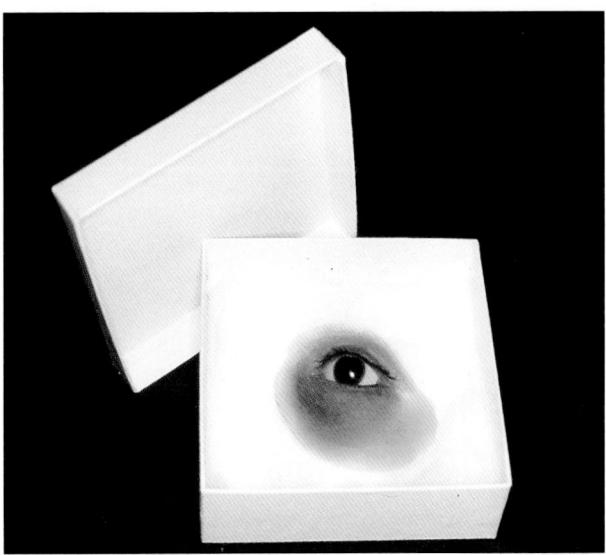

Fig 23-6. Storage of prosthesis.

and the silicone rubber does not separate from the resin plate. For an auricular or nasal prosthesis, proper removal by grasping a thick portion of the prosthesis and slowly disengaging the retentive elements should be demonstrated and performed several times by the patient (Fig 23-4*A*). For an orbital prosthesis, an outer margin should be lifted carefully until a thicker portion can be grasped to lift the prosthesis (Fig 23-4*B*).

At night, the prosthesis should be removed and cleaned. The patients should wash their hands first to decrease chances of soiling the prosthesis during handling. All surfaces of the prosthesis should be cleaned gently with a soft, nylon-bristle toothbrush and mild soap and water. Care should be taken not to damage or dislodge any simulated facial hair such as sideburns, eyelashes, eyebrows, or mustache. For an orbital prosthesis, cleaning with alcohol should be avoided because it can cause crazing on the surface of the ocular prosthesis. Special attention should be paid to cleaning at the retentive areas in case any debris has accumulated (Fig 23-5). The prosthesis should be patted dry with a towel and placed in a covered container. A denture cup or similar type of covered container can be used (Fig 23-6). It should be stored away from extreme heat or direct sunlight,

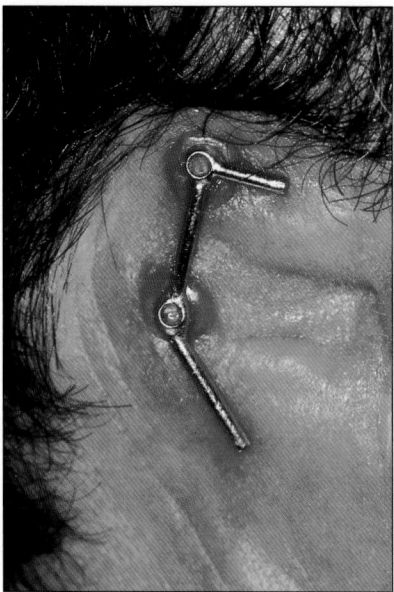

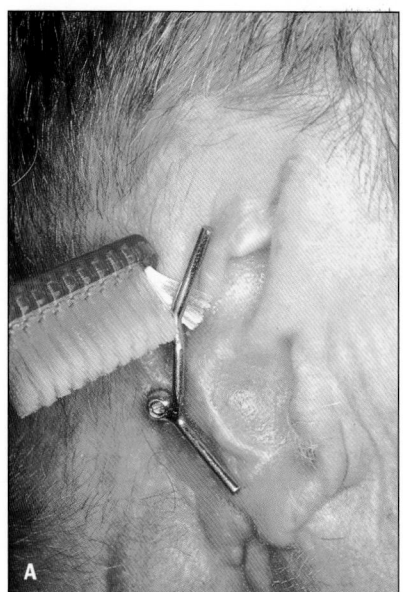

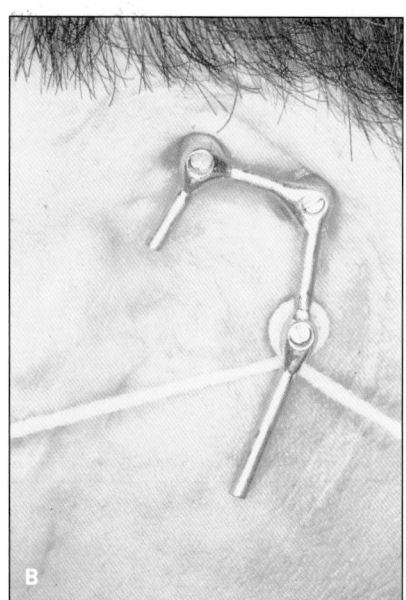

Fig 23-7. Severe skin inflammation from continuous wearing of prosthesis.

Fig 23-8. Cleaning under bar with toothbrush (*A*) and Super Floss (Oral-B Laboratories Inc., Redwood, CA) (*B*).

which can cause degradation and discoloration of the prosthetic material. It should also be kept out of reach of household pets.

The prosthesis should not be worn during sleep so that air can circulate around the abutments to help maintain skin health. If it is worn continuously, the dark moist environment underneath the prosthesis and around the abutments is ripe for bacterial and fungal growth, leading to inflammation and infection (Fig 23-7). Unfortunately, the bone-anchored prosthesis has created a problem in this regard. Because it is so retentive and patients are so pleased, many feel as though the prosthesis is a natural part of them and they are reluctant to remove it. Nevertheless, the importance of daily removal and hygiene should be stressed.

The patient should continue to clean the abutments and surrounding skin on a daily basis, as previously instructed. If the abutments are connected by a bar, this may be slightly complicated. However, the same technique of brushing or flossing around the abutments and under the bar should be recommended and demonstrated (Fig 23-8).

Office Care After Prosthesis Placement

The first follow-up visit should be 1 week after prosthesis delivery. At that time, the condition of the prosthesis, implants, and abutments and the health of the skin should be assessed. Any difficulties the patient has in placing or removing the prosthesis should be addressed. Subsequent follow-up visits should be scheduled at 1 and 3 months and then at regular 6-month intervals. Because of the required follow-up and maintenance for a bone-anchored facial prosthesis, if a patient moves from the area, it should be the responsibility of the treatment team to find a treatment center near the patient's new home.

Follow-up management is meant to ensure a retentive, natural-looking well-fitting prosthesis and healthy implants and soft tissue. At each follow-up visit, the prosthesis should be checked for retention, marginal tears, delamination of the silicone rubber from the resin plate, fracture of the resin

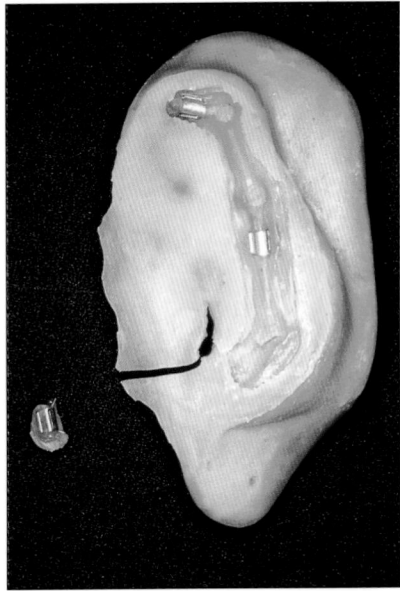

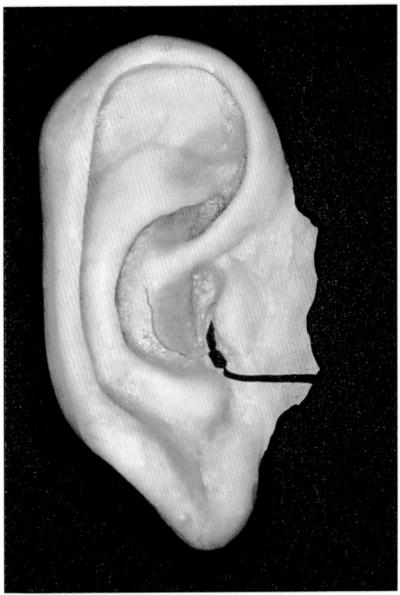

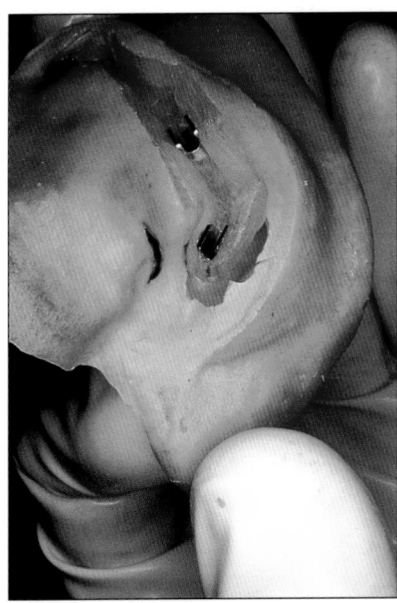

Fig 23-9. Clip broken out of resin plate. Note also marginal tear in prosthesis.

Fig 23-10. Marginal tear in prosthesis.

Fig 23-11. Delamination of silicone rubber prosthesis from resin plate.

plate, loosening or loss of retentive components, and discoloration. The retentive components attached to the abutments, the abutments themselves, and the implants should be checked for tightness and stability, and the condition of the soft tissue should be monitored.

The degree of retention of a clip is adjustable. It can be increased by squeezing the walls with a How pliers (American Orthodontic, Sheboygan, WI). Retention can be decreased by spreading with the tip of a pliers.

Management of Prosthesis Complications

Retention Elements

If magnets or ball or stud attachments are used, components may need periodic replacement to maintain adequate retention. The portion in the abutment can be removed by unscrewing it with its appropriate seating tool. An abutment clamp should be placed on the abutment during this procedure to prevent it from unseating. The retentive component in the resin plate should be loosened by grinding around it with a small round laboratory bur. The

new component can be seated in the plate and attached with autopolymerizing polymethyl methacrylate resin (L.D. Caulk, Milford, DE). The prosthesis can be seated on the master cast during polymerization to ensure correct position of the new retentive component.

If a clip, magnet, or ball or stud loosens or comes out of the resin plate (Fig 23-9), it can be reattached with self-curing resin in the same manner as previously described for replacing an attachment in the resin plate. If an attachment must be replaced and the cast is not available, this can be done directly on the patient. All undercut areas should be blocked out with soft wax or a visible light cure resin such as Barricaid (L.D. Caulk), and care must be taken not to cause irritation to the skin.

Prosthesis Margins

A tear in the margin of the prosthesis (Fig 23-10) may be repaired with A-6400 Dispersion (Factor II, Lakeside, AZ) while the prosthesis is placed back on the master cast. This repair material is strong enough so that there is no need to embed any reinforcing material that would create a thicker margin.

Delamination of the resin plate from the silicone rubber prosthesis (Fig 23-11) can be repaired by roughening the resin surface with a bur and preparing it with acetone and a primer (Dow Corning,

Midland, MI) and by using Medical Adhesive Silicone Type A (Dow Corning) to reestablish the bond. Once again, this must be done on the cast to ensure proper relationships.

Resin Plate Fracture

Fracture of the resin plate can be repaired by grinding a 3- to 4-mm-wide trough along the fracture site and using autopolymerizing acrylic resin or visible light cure resin (L.D. Caulk) to fill the gap. The delamination repair procedure is followed if there is also separation of the resin plate from the silicone rubber.

Prosthesis Replacement

Because no adhesive is used to retain the prosthesis, handling of it is decreased and cleaning requires less vigor. With normal use and proper care, the prosthesis should last 24 to 36 months. The guiding factors are discoloration as a result of breakdown of the pigments within the silicone rubber and care by the patient. Although the intrinsic technique is preferred to provide more stable color, extrinsic coloring can be used periodically to touch up modest color changes and prolong the life of the prosthesis. Work environment and personal habits such as smoking can cause more rapid discoloration of the prosthesis (Fig 23-12).

Molds should be designed with remaking the prosthesis in mind. A new prosthesis with resin plate and properly oriented retentive components should be able to be made without need of the existing prosthesis (see also Chapter 20).[1] In this way, the patient will not have to be without the prosthesis while a new one is being made.

The retention elements attached to the abutments should be evaluated for stability at each follow-up visit. If a bar is used, it should be removed to evaluate each individual abutment and implant. Each abutment should be checked to see that it is seated fully and tight.

Although soft-tissue response does not correlate directly with implant success, the condition of these areas should be monitored and their health maintained. From a general health standpoint, the existence of inflammation or infection is of concern. In addition, adverse soft-tissue reaction can affect the fit of the prosthesis, comfort of the patient, and the patient's overall ability to wear the prosthesis.

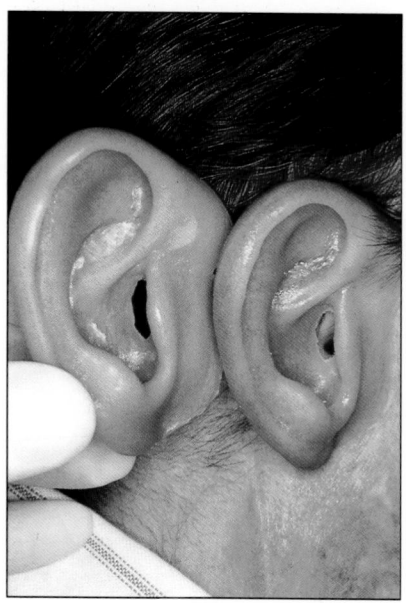

Fig 23-12. Prosthesis on left after 1 year. Note severe discoloration. Patient worked outdoors without a hat. Prosthesis in place on patient's right side.

Soft-Tissue Problems

There have been many studies to evaluate the soft-tissue response to percutaneous implants.[2-10] All of these reported a high success rate, even in irradiated cases. Tjellström,[6] Gitto,[7] and Nishimura,[8] and their associates acknowledged that while this success rate was high, no patient was able to maintain a consistent level of soft-tissue health for an extended period. They stressed the importance of continuous, regular follow-up visits to reinforce home care and hygiene. For the sake of comparison from visit to visit, it is helpful to photograph the implant sites and to describe the soft-tissue response with a standardized grading system, such as the one by Holgers et al.[3]

Common soft-tissue problems ranged from crusting of cellular debris (Fig 23-13*A*), to various grades of inflammation (Fig 23-13*B*), to frank infection (Fig 23-13*C*). Daily home care and reinforcement at regular follow-up visits are meant to minimize these problems. In addition, Tjellström and associates[2] recommended guidelines for implant placement and soft-tissue conditions that will aid the patient in maintaining health of the surrounding areas. These include placement of implants in a hair-free zone of skin. Most importantly, the soft

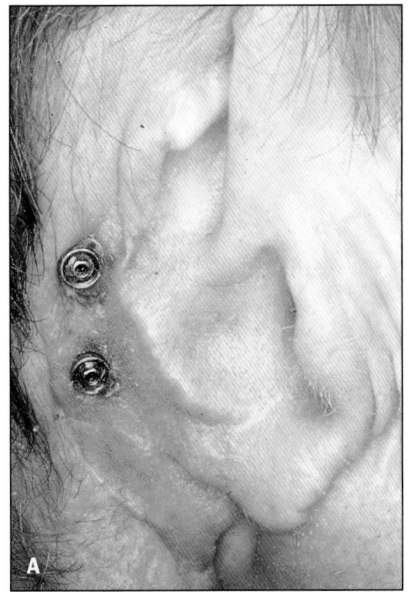 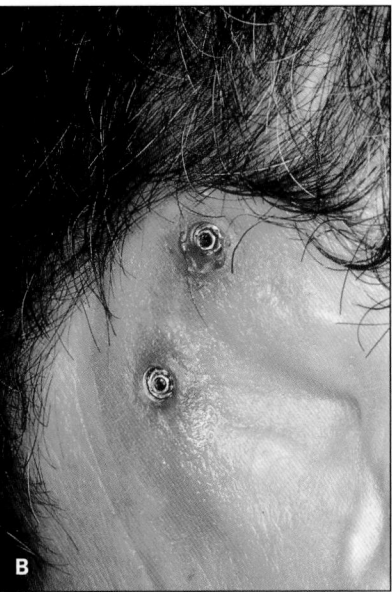 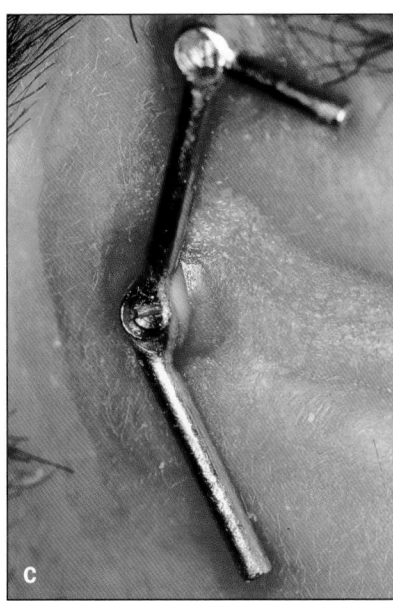

Fig 23-13. *A*, Dried cellular debris around abutment. *B*, Severe inflammation with granuloma around abutment. *C*, Frank infection at abutment.

tissue at the penetration site should be thin and fixed. If, during follow-up visits, it is noted that a severe, adverse skin response persists, postprosthetic soft-tissue grafting may be required to manage this problem (Fig 23-14).

Implant Failure

Failure of an implant is the most severe complication. Healing of the site should be monitored on a weekly basis until it is certain that normal wound closure is occurring. This is particularly important in patients who have undergone radiation therapy (Fig 23-15).

Depending on the number of implants remaining and the design of the retentive mechanism, the prosthesis may need to be modified. If two or more implants remain and the retention design is not compromised, the prosthesis can be stable and retentive. If a bar-clip system is used and implant loss means that there is now inadequate support for the bar, then individual magnets (Technovent Limited, Leeds, England) or ball or stud attachments (Nobel Biocare USA, Inc.)/(Attachments and Implants International, San Mateo, CA) need to be used. This involves mod-

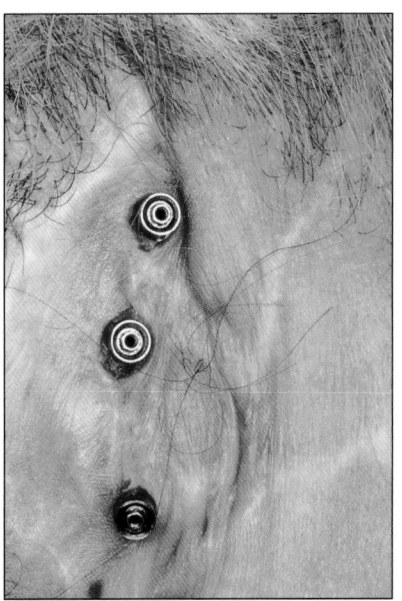

Fig 23-14. Skin graft placed to manage chronic severe inflammation around abutments.

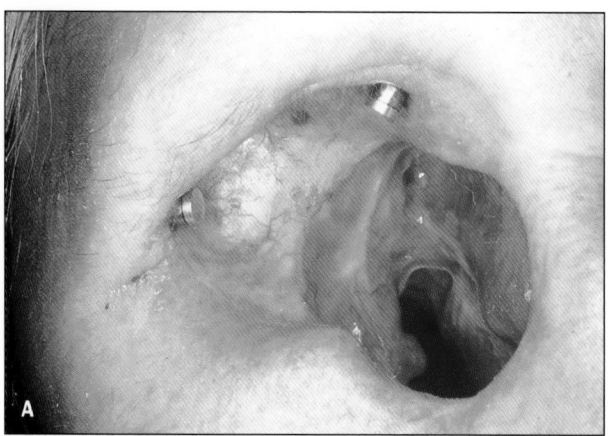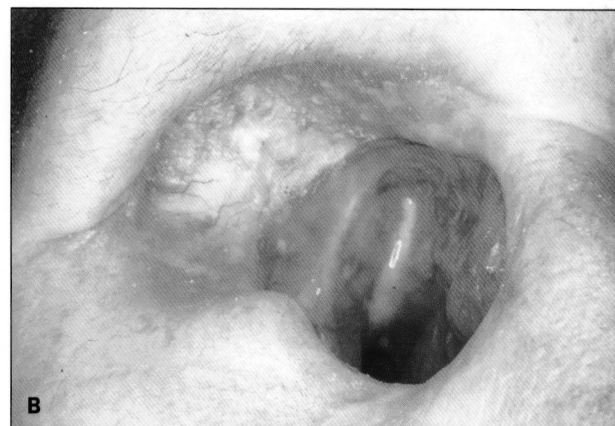

Fig 23-15. *A,* Two periorbital implants in irradiated patient. *B,* Loss of implants. Skin has healed normally.

ification of the resin plate, which can be accomplished without need for a new prosthesis.

If all implants are lost or if only one remains, the patient probably will need to rely on skin adhesive to provide adequate retention. The patient should be given written instructions and a demonstration of its use.

To attempt conversion of the bone-anchored auricular prosthesis to an adhesive-retained prosthesis, the resin plate with retentive elements is removed. A clear medical-grade silicone elastomer (382, Dow Corning) is used to refit the prosthesis on the patient. The refitting material is placed on the tissue side of the prosthesis, and the prosthesis is seated fully on the patient. Excess material should be wiped away at the margins to ensure complete seating of the prosthesis. The added material will make an impression of the defect and serve as an index to facilitate proper positioning of the adhesive-retained prosthesis. The added elastomer material can be colored extrinsically to blend with the existing prosthesis. An orbital or nasal prosthesis should already have an adequate margin overlying the peripheral skin to provide enough adhesive contact for retention. Evaluation on future follow-up visits for tears along the margins is in order because these areas were not originally designed for adhesive use.

The success of bone-anchored facial prostheses has added a new dimension to craniofacial rehabilitation. It is the responsibility of the patient as well as the treatment team to maintain the health of the implants and penetration site and the condition of the prosthesis. Follow-up management is a way of monitoring these conditions and managing problems to provide a healthy and successful prosthetic experience.

References

1. Wolfaardt JF, Coss P, Levesque R. Craniofacial osseointegration: technique for bar and acrylic resin substructure construction for auricular prostheses. J Prosthet Dent 1996;76:603.

2. Tjellström A, Rosenhall U, Lindström J, Hallén O, Albrektsson T, Brånemark PI. Five-year experience with skin-penetrating bone-anchored implants in the temporal bone. Acta Otolaryngol 1983;95:568.

3. Holgers KM, Tjellström A, Bjursten LM, Erlandsson BE. Soft tissue reactions around percutaneous implants: a clinical study on skin-penetrating titanium implants used for bone-anchored auricular prostheses. Int J Oral Maxillofac Implants 1987;2:35.

4. Holgers KM, Tjellström A, Bjursten LM, Erlandsson BE. Soft tissue reactions around percutaneous implants: a clinical study of soft tissue conditions around skin-penetrating titanium implants for bone-anchored hearing aids. Am J Otol 1988;9:56.

5. Tjellström A, Jacobsson M. The bone-anchored maxillofacial prosthesis. In Albrektsson T, Zarb GA (eds): The Brånemark Osseointegrated Implant. Chicago: Quintessence Publishing Company; 1989:235.

6. Tjellström A. Osseointegrated implants for replacement of absent or defective ears. Clin Plast Surg 1990;17:355.

7. Gitto CA, Plata WG, Schaaf NG. Evaluation of the peri-implant epithelial tissue of percutaneous implant abutments supporting maxillofacial prostheses. Int J Oral Maxillofac Implants 1994;9:197.

8. Nishimura RD, Roumanas E, Moy PK, Sugai T. Nasal defects and osseointegrated implants: UCLA experience. J Prosthet Dent 1996;76:597.

9. Granström G, Bergström K, Tjellström A, Brånemark PI. A detailed analysis of titanium implants lost in irradiated tissues. Int J Oral Maxillofac Implants 1994;9:653.

10. Tolman DE, Taylor PF. Bone-anchored craniofacial prosthesis study. Int J Oral Maxillofac Implants 1996;11:159.

Part VI

The Hearing Impaired

Pretreatment Evaluation

24.

Anders Tjellström, MD, PhD

> - The Bone-Anchored Hearing Aid
> - Indications for a BAHA
> - Contraindications

Hearing through bone conduction means that the sound is reaching the hair cells of the inner ear via vibrations of the skull. This is a natural way of hearing. In normal conditions the sound of one's own voice reaches the inner ear through two routes. One is via air conduction, as the sound waves go out of the mouth, into the air, and into the external ear canal. The eardrum starts to vibrate, and by transmission of vibrations through the malleus, incus, and stapes in the oval window, the sound is transferred to the fluid of the cochlea. In the cochlea, the mechanical energy is transferred into electrical impulses by the hair cells. The impulses are transmitted via cranial nerve VIII to the hearing center in the temporal lobe. The other route is via bone conduction. The sound produced in the oral cavity causes vibration of the surrounding bone, skull base, maxilla, and mandible. The sound is propagated through the bone and stimulates the inner ear. These sound waves cause deformation of the enchondral bone of the inner ear spaces. Because the compartments of the inner ear have different dimensions, the hair cells of the scala media are stimulated and the mechanical energy is transformed into electrical impulses in the same way as when they are stimulated through air conduction. When listening to one's own voice from a tape recorder, only the air-conducted sound reaches the inner ear, and this is the reason we do not recognize our own voices from a recording.

Bone conduction is a normal way of hearing. This was demonstrated by von Békésy.[1] He presented a sinusoidal wave tone in the external ear canal through a probe. The same sinusoidal wave also was presented to the test person through a transducer placed over the mastoid process on the same side. The sound was adjusted to a comfortable level. von Békésy then changed the phase of the sinusoidal wave presented through the transducer 180° and the sound could not be heard any longer. Through this cancellation effect, he showed that sound reaching the cochlea through bone conduction is not different from air-conducted sound. The significance of this study is that a bone-conduction hearing aid has the same quality as an ordinary air-conduction aid.

Bone-conduction aids have been used for many years. The transducer is pressed against the mastoid process via a headband (steel spring over the head) or via heavy frames of glasses. These arrangements have several drawbacks. The two most commonly experienced by the patient are the discomfort due to the pressure applied and the poor sound quality. This poor quality of the sound is the result of attenuation of the sound energy in the soft tissue over the mas-

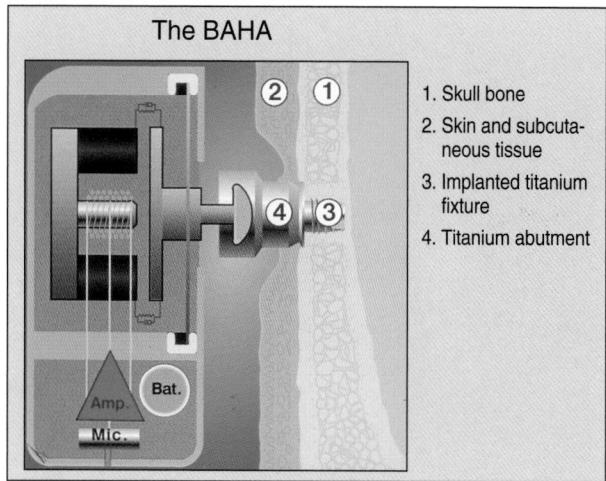

The BAHA

② ①
④ ③

1. Skull bone
2. Skin and subcuta-
   neous tissue
3. Implanted titanium
   fixture
4. Titanium abutment

Amp. Bat.
Mic.

Fig 24-1. The principal design of the Bone-Anchored Hearing Aid (*BAHA*). *Amp.*, amplifier; *Bat.*, battery; *Mic.*, microphone.

toid process. When the sound reaches the skull, the propagation of the sound wave is fairly good and without much distortion.[2] The attenuation of the sound in the soft tissues is most pronounced in the high-frequency range. It is in this high-frequency range that the consonant sounds, which are most important for speech understanding, are found. This is the physiologic reason for the advantage of direct bone conduction bypassing the soft-tissue attenuation. In selected patients in need of sound amplification, a Bone-Anchored Hearing Aid (BAHA) is a treatment alternative.

The Bone-Anchored Hearing Aid

The BAHA is an impedance-matched hearing aid attached to a skin-penetrating coupling that is secured to an osseointegrated implant in the mastoid process. The principal design of the BAHA and the coupling are shown in Figure 24-1.

Indications for a BAHA

In the pretreatment evaluation, two factors must be taken into account. What are *medical conditions* in which a BAHA could be offered as a treatment alternative? What are the *audiologic limitations*?

Medical Conditions

There are four main medical indications for a BAHA.

Bilateral External Ear Canal Atresia. In patients with bilateral external ear canal atresia, this malformation is sometimes not suitable for reconstructive surgery. Because the ear canal and middle ear develop during a different period of gestation than the cochlea, the inner ear function is often normal. Owing to the atresia, the patient has a maximum conductive loss of 60 dB and a conventional air-conduction aid cannot be fitted.

The timing of implant surgery is important. A child with bilateral atresia often is fitted with a conventional bone-conduction hearing aid within the first weeks after birth. This is of utmost importance for normal mental and social development. The youngest child I have operated on was age 3 years. At this time the bone is still thin and soft, but the surgery could result in a lasting osseointegration. Within a year, this patient learned to put on his BAHA, take it off, and even to adjust the volume.

In children with bilateral atresia, the possibility of reconstructive surgery always should be evaluated. Sometimes the mastoid process and middle ear develop favorably as the child is growing. Reconstructive surgery, initially abandoned, is not jeopardized by early implant surgery. It is easy to remove an abutment, and the implant could either be left in or drilled out if needed.

Children with unilateral atresia seldom have any major problem with their hearing impairment, and implant surgery is indicated only rarely. However, in the adult patient bilateral hearing could be of importance. Individuals participating in meetings, conferences, and teaching activities may suffer from their hearing impairment, and a BAHA could be of great benefit.

Chronic Ear Disease. In spite of the refinement of surgery for chronic ear disease during the last several decades, it is not always possible to get a dry ear free of infection and with good hearing. To help these patients is still a challenge. Within this group, there are three conditions in which a BAHA could be discussed. The first is those patients whose ears are draining most of the time. An air-conduction aid often aggravates this drainage and causes discomfort and a foul smell. The function of the aid is often less good, as the mold is clogged easily by the discharge. Another common situation in patients with chronic ear disease is that a dry ear starts to drain as soon as the external ear canal is occluded with an air-conduction mold. The third situation includes patients who have had ear surgery and have a radical cavity, a wide external auditory meatus. These patients often experience acoustic feedback from a conventional air-conduction hearing aid because it often is hard to get a good fit of the hearing aid mold into the meatus. This is especially true if the patient needs high amplification.

External Ear Canal Irritation. Some patients in need of sound amplification experience irritation in the external ear canal in spite of a closed middle ear cavity. There are several different materials from which to make a mold, but some patients cannot tolerate any of these. The irritation in the external canal in these patients also could be due to an occlusion effect, and a BAHA that leaves the external ear canal opening free solves this problem.

Maximum Conductive Loss. Many patients with a predominant conductive loss could have successful reconstruction with conventional middle ear surgery. However, a patient with a conductive loss in the only hearing ear presents a special problem. Because the risk of cochlear damage, even total deafness, due to ear surgery is a reality, most otologic surgeons have a conservative attitude in this situation and avoid ear surgery if possible. In patients with a maximum conductive loss, such as a total fixation of the stapes in otosclerosis or tympanosclerosis, an air-conduction aid may not be enough. In such a situation, a BAHA could be a good alternative.

Audiologic Limitations

In the pretreatment evaluation, the audiologic limitations must be appreciated by the treatment team. The BAHA is not suitable for the patient with poor or no cochlear function. A cochlear implant could be the treatment of choice for that patient. Based on our experience, my colleagues and I suggest that the cochlear reserve should be at least 45 dB for the speech frequencies (500-3,000 Hz).[3,4] A patient with a hearing threshold that poor should be informed that the ear-level device, the HC 300, may not be strong enough. There is a stronger aid available, the HC 220, which is a body aid. Some patients with a hearing impairment around 45 dB do not benefit even from the body aid. The air-bone gap is of no significance in the evaluation of the hearing level, unlike when an air-conduction aid is prescribed. A maximum conductive loss of 60 dB could thus be added to the cochlear reserve. This also means that the quality of the audiologic testing for bone conduction is of utmost importance.

One way to find out if the patient will benefit from a BAHA is to fit the patient temporarily with a conventional bone-conduction hearing aid. The patient is asked to ignore the discomfort and the cosmetic drawbacks and evaluate only the sound. If the patient experiences better hearing from this, the chances are good that the patient will benefit from a BAHA.

Another way to evaluate the possible benefit of a BAHA preoperatively is to use what is called the "test rod." An acrylic rod 10 mm in diameter and 60 mm long is fitted with a hearing aid coupling at one end. The piston of the BAHA is placed in the coupling, and the other end of the rod is pressed firmly against the mastoid process. If, when the hearing aid is put on, the patient's hearing improves, this is also a good sign. A comparison has been made of the capacity of the BAHA on the test rod and the BAHA on a bone-anchored implant.[5] In the low-frequency range there is not a great difference, but in the high-frequency range there is a significant improvement in favor of the integrated implant. If the patient experiences improved hearing with the test rod, the chances are good that surgery for the BAHA will be successful.

Because most of the patients considered for treatment with a BAHA have bilateral hearing impairment, the choice of side to place the implant on is an important part of the pretreatment evaluation. The general rule is that if there is a significant difference between the ears the implant should be placed on the side with the best cochlear function. This is based on my experience as well as studies on sound propagation through the skull by Håkansson et al.[2] If there are no or only marginal differences between the ears, the placement is directed more by the patient's social situation. If the patient often drives a car, it is better to place the BAHA on the side directed toward the front passenger seat. The dexterity of the patient also could influence which side to put the implant on. Figure 24-2 shows the skin-penetrating coupling and the hearing aid in place.

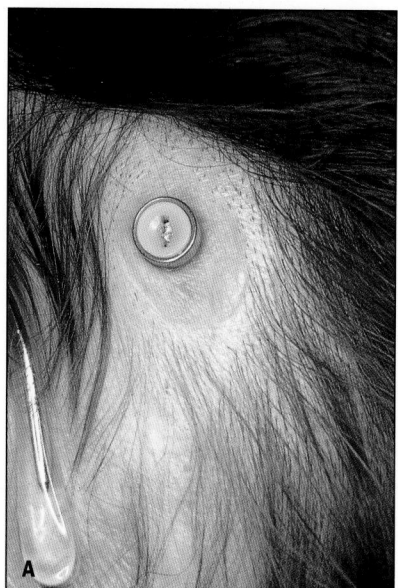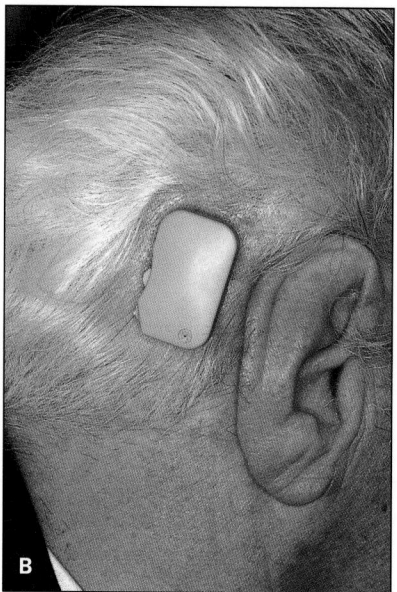

Fig 24-2. *A,* The skin-penetrating coupling with the plastic insert in place. Note the hairless area of skin around the implant. *B,* The Bone-Anchored Hearing Aid fitted to a patient.

Contraindications

There are few contraindications to providing a patient with a BAHA. The cochlea reserve should not be too poor (not worse than 45 dB). In evaluating the patient it is most important to make sure that the patient has understood the concept of the BAHA. The patient has to take part in a lifelong follow-up schedule. The most important reasons why a patient should not be treated with this modality are psychiatric disease, immature personality, and drug abuse. We have had the largest number of failures in these patients. If the patient's personal hygiene is at a low level, this is at least a sign of caution but may not be an absolute contraindication.

References

1. von Békésy G. Vibration of the head in a sound field and its role in hearing by bone conduction. J Acoust Soc Am 1948;20:749.

2. Håkansson B, Brandt A, Carlsson P, Tjellström A. Resonance frequencies of the human skull in vivo. J Acoust Soc Am 1994;95:1474.

3. Håkansson B, Lidén G, Tjellström A, et al. Ten years of experience of the Swedish Bone-Anchored Hearing System. Ann Otol Rhinol Laryngol 1990;Suppl 151:1.

4. Tjellström A, Håkansson B. The bone-anchored hearing aid. Design principles, indications, and long-term clinical results. Otolaryngol Clin North Am 1995;28:53.

5. Tjellström A, Granström G. One-stage procedure to establish osseointegration: a zero to five years follow-up report. J Laryngol Otol 1995;109:593.

Surgical Considerations

25.

Anders Tjellström, MD, PhD
Gösta Granström, MD, DDS, PhD

> • Surgical Procedure
> • Changes in the Surgical Procedure
> • Implants in Children

One of the key issues that Brånemark pointed out for achieving a lasting anchorage of an implant in the bone tissue was the two-stage procedure. When we introduced the Bone-Anchored Hearing Aid (BAHA) in 1977, this surgical protocol was followed carefully. After implant placement, 3 to 4 months passed before the coupling of the hearing aid was secured to the implant.

In 1989, when 750 implants had been placed in the mastoid process and only 10 had lost integration, we started a study on a modified one-stage procedure.[1] The rationale for this step was that the force on the implant-bone interface for the BAHA is of a much lower magnitude than the forces elicited during mastication. This modified one-stage procedure, which today is the standard procedure in the adult nonirradiated mastoid, means that the implant is placed in the bone according to the technique described below and the skin-penetration coupling is attached to the implant at the same time. However, we allow 3 to 4 months to pass before the patient is fitted with the BAHA.[2] The weight of the hearing instrument results in a force of only 5 N. Slightly higher forces are reached when the instrument is put in place and taken off.

When the plastic insert is placed, higher forces could be introduced. During the healing phase, the coupling is exposed to forces of everyday life, especially during sleep when the implant is in contact with the pillow. These risk factors do not seem to be of great importance because the frequency of implant loss is still low.[3]

The surgical technique, from marking the implant site to applying the mastoid dressing, is described in detail below. Changes in the surgical technique and the rationale for these modifications are discussed. Some remarks are presented on surgery for the BAHA in children.

Surgical Procedure

From the acoustic point of view, the position of the implant is not crucial, but the hearing aid should not touch the external ear because this could result in acoustic feedback. This is especially important if the cochlear reserve is low and high amplification has to be used. In the adult with a normal pinna, the mark

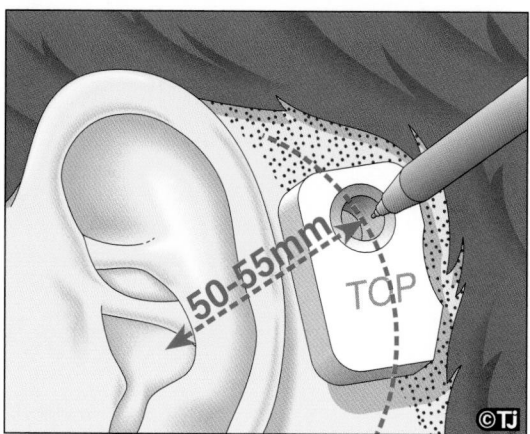

Fig 25-1. Marking the implant site.

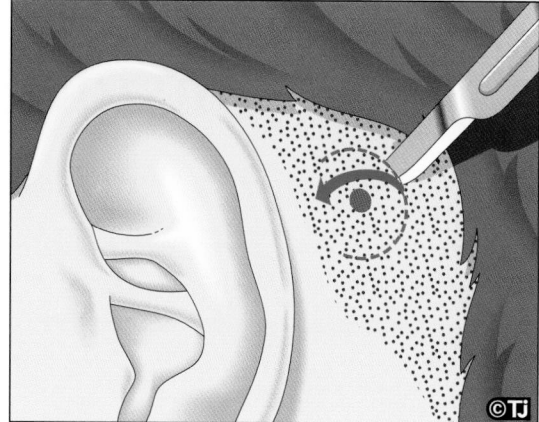

Fig 25-2. Incision.

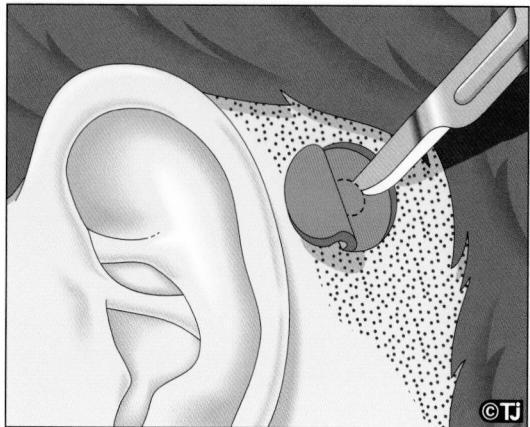

Fig 25-3. Hole (6 mm) made in the periosteum.

behind the mastoid cavity. On the other hand, in this area the sigmoid sinus could be close to the surface and the surgeon has to take this into account.

The site for the implant is marked with surgical ink. The area is draped with a plastic sheet. In doing this, the external ear is reflected anteriorly and a draining external ear canal or cavity is sealed off from the surgical field. In the adult patient, the procedure often is done during local anesthesia. We prefer 2% lidocaine with 12.5 µg/mL epinephrine. The same solution is used when the procedure is performed during general anesthesia because the homeostasis is good.

A semicircular-shaped incision is made 20 to 25 mm in diameter down to the periosteum but not through the membrane (Fig 25-2). Two small self-retaining retractors expose the surgical field, and an incision is made in the center of the periosteum (about 6 mm in diameter) (Fig 25-3). The size of the flange of the implant is 5.5 mm.

The drilling starts with a cutting guide drill, which is 2 mm in diameter (Fig 25-4). For safety reasons, the drill has a protecting shield that allows only 3 mm of penetration. The arrows in the illustration are the artist's way of indicating that the hole is made slightly larger than 2 mm. This facilitates inspection of the bottom of the hole where the dura, sigmoid sinus, or air cells might be found, and the surgeon is able to avoid any damage and, if necessary, find a new implant site. If, however, bone still is encountered at the bottom of the hole when the shield is all the way down, the 3-mm guide drill is exchanged for one that will make room for a 4-mm-long implant (Fig 25-5). This drilling is done at a speed of 2,000 to 3,000 rpm. Generous irrigation with room temperature saline solution is used during all drilling. The next step, which is also done at the same high speed, is to prepare the

of the implant site should be made before the pinna is reflected anteriorly with the plastic sheeting. In the child with a malformation, it is important to place the implant 50 to 55 mm from the place where the external ear canal should be or will be if reconstructive surgery is to take place later (Fig 25-1). In the cranial-caudal axis, we often place the implant 10 to 15 mm below the top part of the auricle. In this area it is often easy to identify the linea temporalis of the temporal bone. In the linea temporalis, the bone often is thick and has a dense solid structure. Cranial to this anatomic landmark, the bone can be thin and the dura of the middle cranial fossa can be only 1 to 2 mm below the surface. Below the linea temporalis, the mastoid air cell system is found and the bone is less thick. One of the indications for the BAHA is chronic ear disease, and many of these patients have already had mastoid surgery. This is, however, not a problem because the implant site almost always is

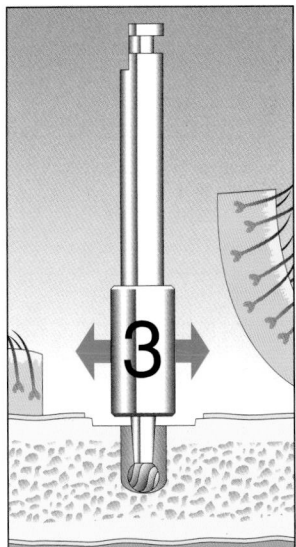

Fig 25-4. Guide drill (3 mm) with protecting shield. (From Craniofacial Rehabilitation: Operating Theatre Manual. Göteborg, Sweden: Nobelpharma AB; 1995:13. By permission of the publisher.)

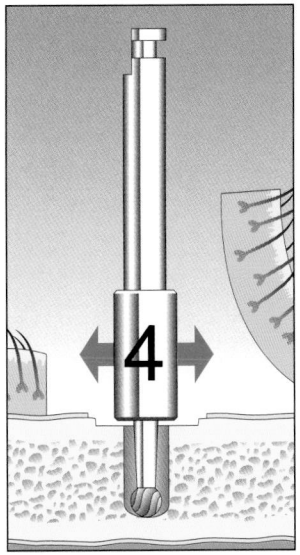

Fig 25-5. Guide drill (4 mm) with protecting shield. (From Craniofacial Rehabilitation: Operating Theatre Manual. Göteborg, Sweden: Nobelpharma AB; 1995:13. By permission of the publisher.)

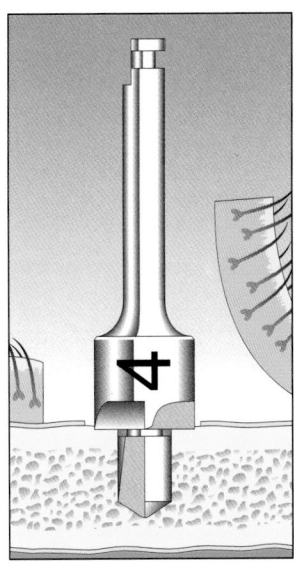

Fig 25-6. Spiral drill with countersink. (From Craniofacial Rehabilitation: Operating Theatre Manual. Göteborg, Sweden: Nobelpharma AB; 1995:14. By permission of the publisher.)

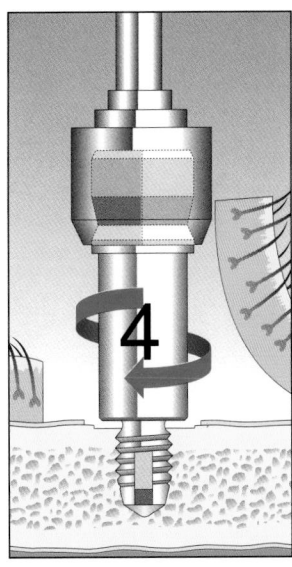

Fig 25-7. Titanium tap on adapter. (From Craniofacial Rehabilitation: Operating Theatre Manual. Göteborg, Sweden: Nobelpharma AB; 1995:14. By permission of the publisher.)

final dimension and direction of the implant site. A spiral drill with a countersink is used (Fig 25-6). This drill is blunt at the tip, so it is important that the hole from the guide drill is deep enough. If not, the drill produces heat without going down properly.

The next step, the tapping, is made with titanium instruments and with low speed (10 to 15 rpm) (Fig 25-7). The tap comes in two sizes (3 and 4 mm) and is sterile packed in a glass cylinder. The glass cylinder is broken and the tap is transferred to the titanium organizer where it will be picked up with the adapter, which has been placed in the low-speed handpiece. The tap is not touched with anything but titanium-clad instruments and never by the gloved hand directly. When the tap is to be unscrewed, the handpiece should not be lifted because there is a risk that the tap will be disconnected from the adapter.

The next step is to place the implant in the prepared implant site. The implant comes sterile packed in a glass cylinder. When the cylinder is broken it is important to keep it vertical and over the titanium organizer. The implant is short, and there is a risk that it will be dislodged when the glass is cracked. If it falls on anything but a titanium surface, it cannot be used. The implant is placed in one of the small holes in the organizer. By using a fork-shaped instrument and a screwdriver, the implant mount is

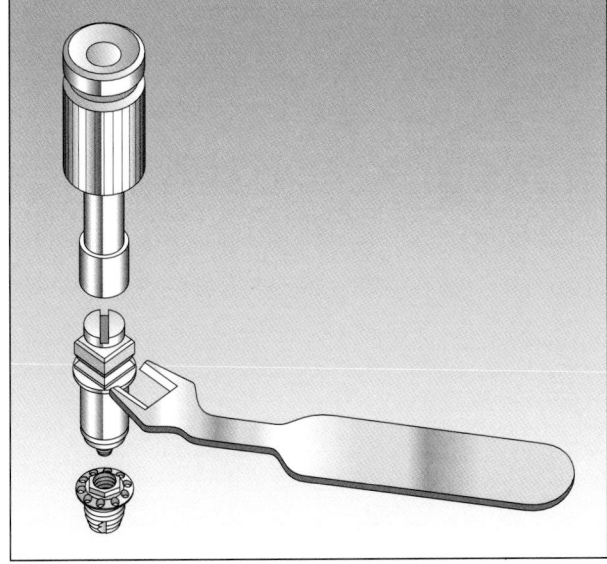

Fig 25-8. Instruments to attach the implant to the implant mount. (From Craniofacial Rehabilitation: Operating Theatre Manual. Göteborg, Sweden: Nobelpharma AB; 1995:15. By permission of the publisher.)

picked up, placed over the implant, and secured on the implant (Fig 25-8). The hexagon on top of the implant must be fitted properly into the hexagonal indentation of the implant mount. If not, the im-

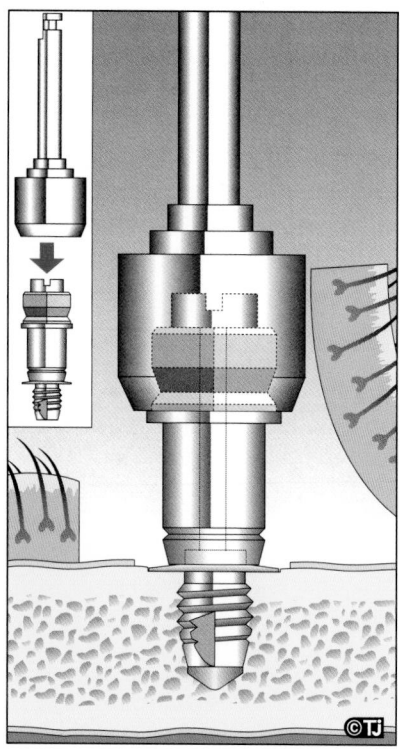

Fig 25-9. Implant mount with implant is picked up with the adapter.

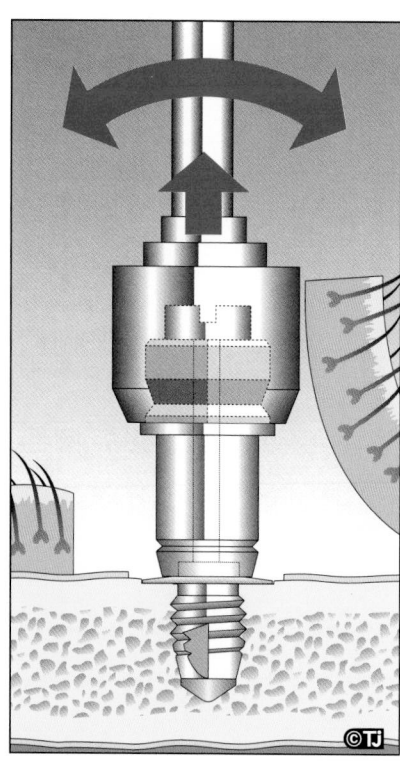

Fig 25-10. Adapter is removed from the implant mount when the implant is in place.

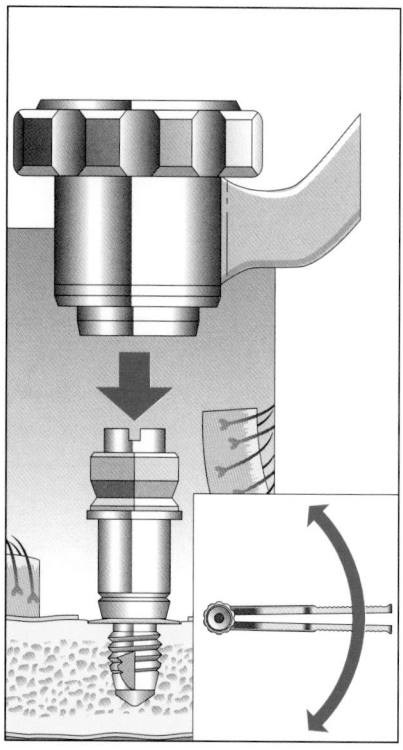

Fig 25-11. A ratchet wrench should be used with utmost care. (From Craniofacial Rehabilitation: Operating Theatre Manual. Göteborg, Sweden: Nobelpharma AB; 1995:15. By permission of the publisher.)

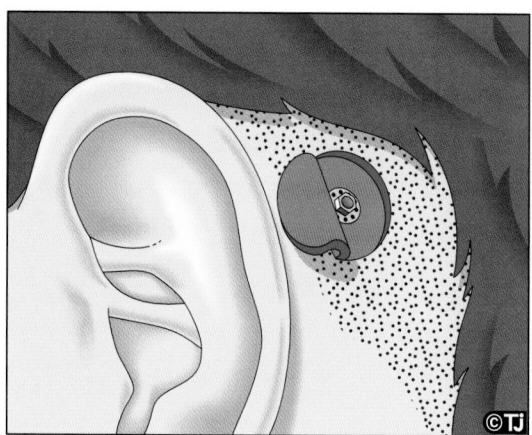

Fig 25-12. The implant in place.

plant hexagon can be damaged, and it will be impossible to attach the hearing aid coupling. For the same reason, the screw of the implant mount should be tightened firmly if the cortical bone is of good quality. In children with soft bone this tightening should be less firm because the threads in the bone could be damaged.

The implant mount with implant is picked up with the adapter and kept over the implant site (Fig 25-9). The proper direction is determined by discussion with the assistant, who often has another angle of observation. The implant is allowed to gently find its way down into the implant site without any pressure. When the flange of the implant approaches the bone surface, the speed is reduced to avoid high torque forces. A high torque could result in damage to the microcirculation at the interface and interfere with the healing capacity of the bone, resulting in less good implant-bone contact. The handpiece of the drill is rotated 30° to 45° counterclockwise to release the adapter from the implant mount (Fig 25-10). If manual tightening is needed, the ratchet

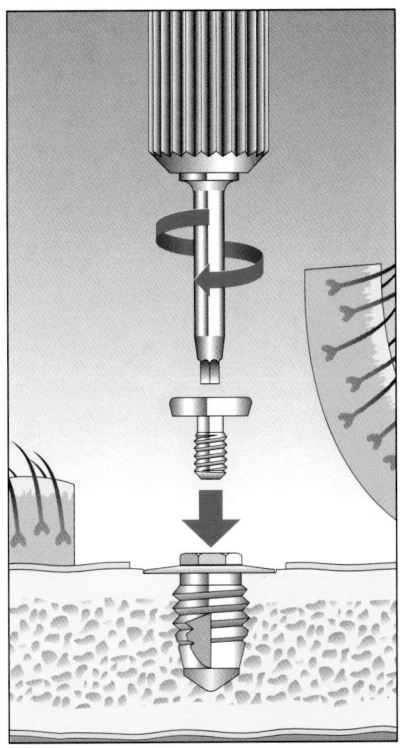

Fig 25-13. If a two-stage procedure is performed, a cover screw protects the internal threads of the implant. (Modified from Craniofacial Rehabilitation: Operating Theatre Manual. Göteborg, Sweden: Nobelpharma AB; 1995:16. By permission of the publisher.)

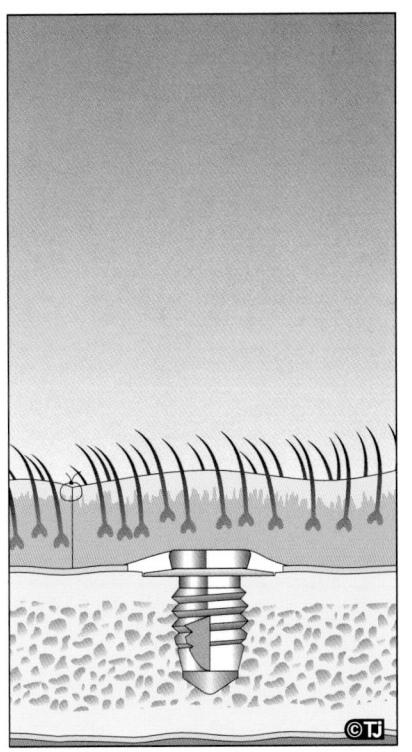

Fig 25-14. The skin flap is not reduced but put back in place during the phase of osseointegration.

wrench is used with utmost care for the same reason as above (Fig 25-11).

The open-end wrench is fitted to the implant mount and the fixture mount screw is unscrewed. The implant mount is removed from the implant, which is now in place (Fig 25-12).

In young children and if the quality of the bone is poor, a two-stage procedure is suggested. A cover screw is placed into the implant to protect the internal threads, and the skin flap is sutured in place (Fig 25-13 and 25-14). A mastoid dressing is placed, and the implant is left for 4 to 6 months to integrate without any load, according to the original recommendation by Brånemark. However, in most adult patients it is possible to continue directly after implant placement with the second stage and perform the abutment connection and skin penetration.

To have the best probability of a lasting, reaction-free skin penetration, two things have to be achieved: the relative movement of the skin in relation to the implant should be as minimal as possible and there should be no hair follicles at the implant area. This facilitates the everyday cleaning procedure, which is of great importance. The skin flap is thinned with a blade kept parallel to the skin surface; the thickness of the flap should be about 0.5 mm (Fig 25-15). The ideal thickness is that of a skin graft, and a dermatome can be used to achieve this thin skin at the implant site. If the flap has been made thin, it is easy to remove all hair follicles. The surrounding edges are thinned to get a gentle slope down to the implant area (Fig 25-16). If the subcutaneous tissue is thick, a larger amount has to be removed than in a slim patient. When this soft-tissue preparation is finished, that flap is sutured back in place with 5-0 monofilament suture (Fig 25-17). When the flap is in place, a hole is made over the implant with a 4-mm dermatologist punch (Fig 25-18).

The hearing aid coupling comes in a titanium cylinder. The protection screw is removed and the coupling is placed in the titanium bowl. The coupling screw, which secures the coupling to the implant, is made of

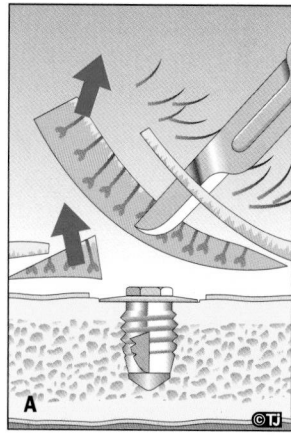

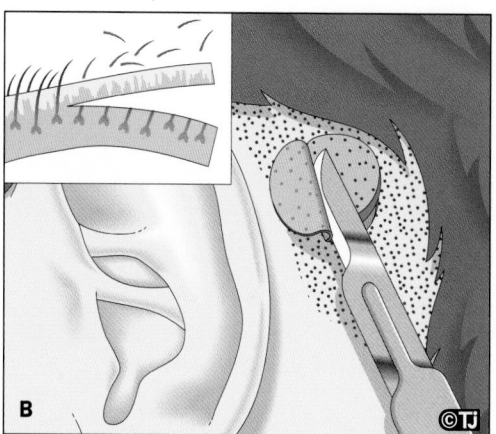

Fig 25-15. All hair follicles are removed and the flap is made thin.

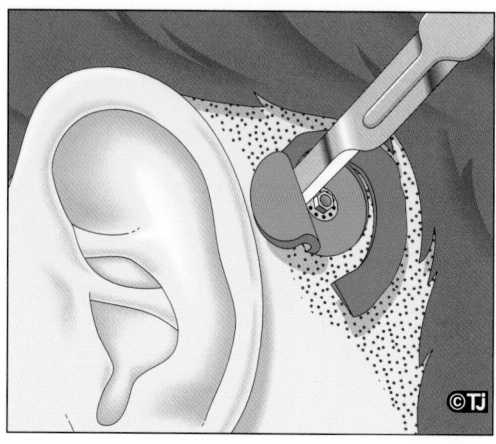

Fig 25-16. Soft tissue under the edges of the implant site is reduced.

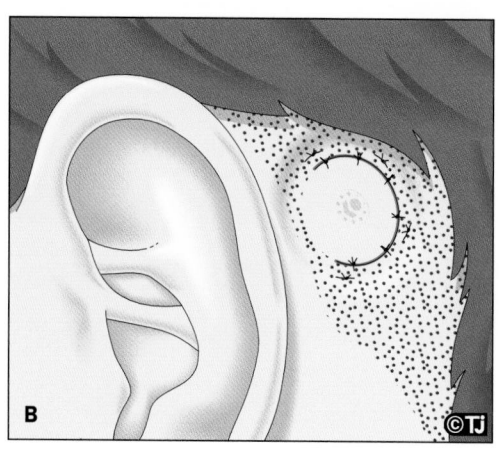

Fig 25-17. The flap is sutured back in place.

gold and comes sterile packed in a glass container. The coupling with its screw is picked up with the fork-shaped instrument (Fig 25-19). Slots that fit this instrument are made on the external side of the coupling and are parallel to the long axis of the rectangle inside the coupling. At the medial side of the coupling, 18

notches are made that will fit onto the hexagon of the implant. These notches allow a greater freedom in finding the best angle for the coupling. The coupling screw should be tightened firmly by using the fork-shaped instrument as a counterforce. If the screw is not tightened enough, there is a risk that the screw will

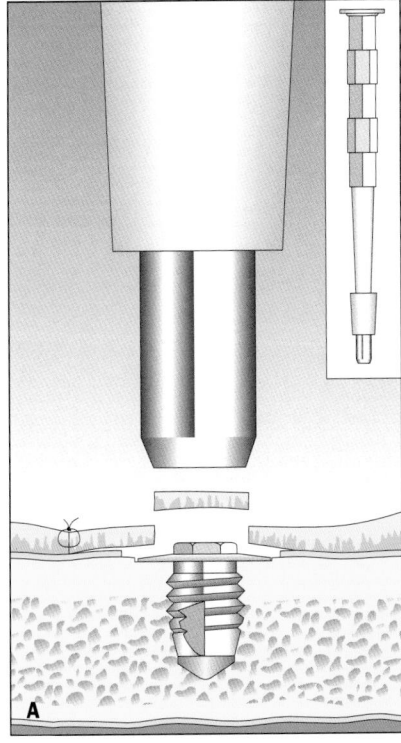

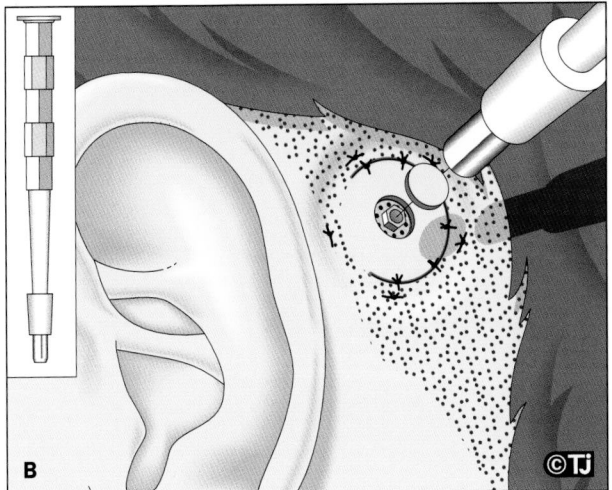

Fig 25-18. A hole is made over the implant with a 4-mm punch. (*A* from Craniofacial Rehabilitation: Operating Theatre Manual. Göteborg, Sweden: Nobelpharma AB; 1995:17. By permission of the publisher.)

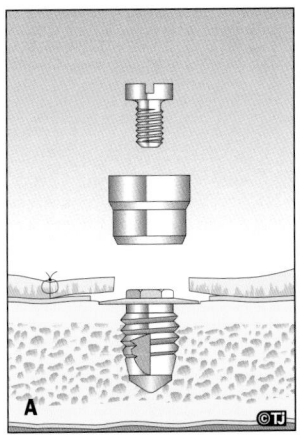

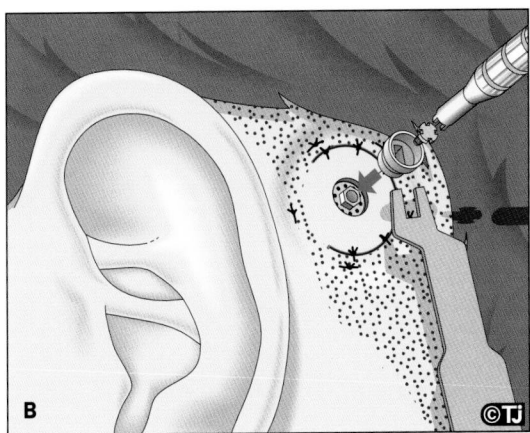

Fig 25-19. The hearing aid coupling is secured to the implant with an internal gold screw.

come loose, because the piston of the hearing aid is working directly on the head of this screw.

The surgical procedure is finished by placing a plastic healing cap over the hearing aid coupling (Fig 25-20). Ointment-soaked gauze is wrapped around the coupling (Fig 25-21). This wrapping should not be too tight because this could interfere with the blood supply to the flap and result in partial or total flap necrosis. An ordinary mastoid dressing is applied for 1 day.

The next day the dressing is removed, and only a small bandage is needed. Five to 7 days later, the patient returns for the first outpatient visit. The heal-

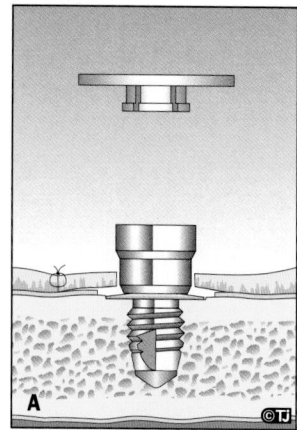
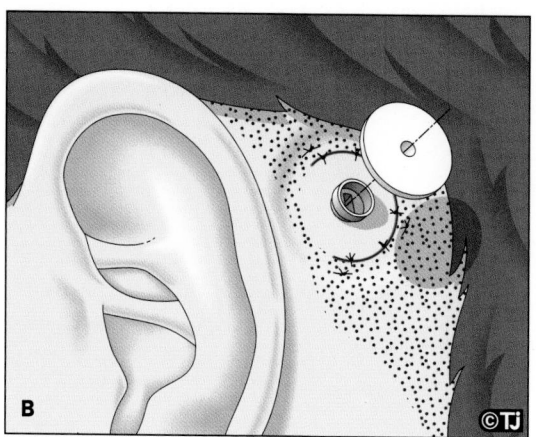

Fig 25-20. A healing cap is placed on the coupling.

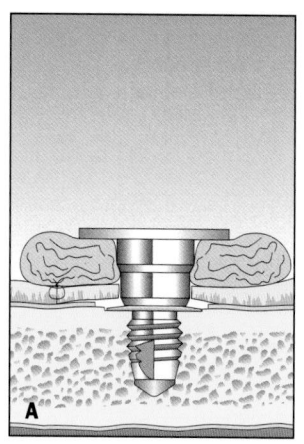
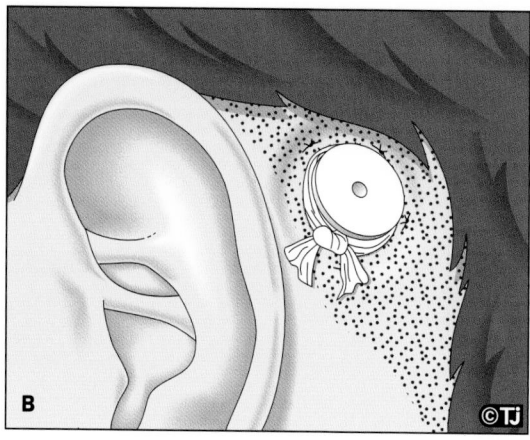

Fig 25-21. Ointment-soaked gauze is placed under the healing cap. (*A* modified from Craniofacial Rehabilitation: Operating Theatre Manual. Göteborg, Sweden: Nobelpharma AB; 1995:18. By permission of the publisher.)

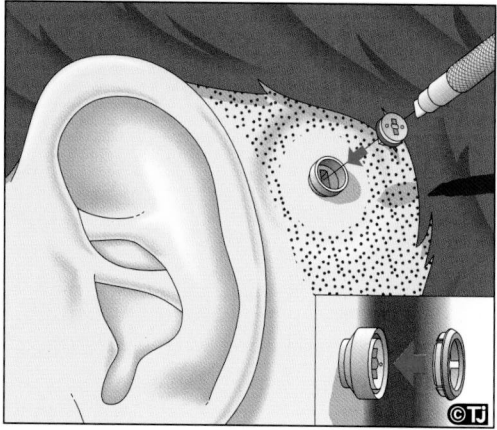
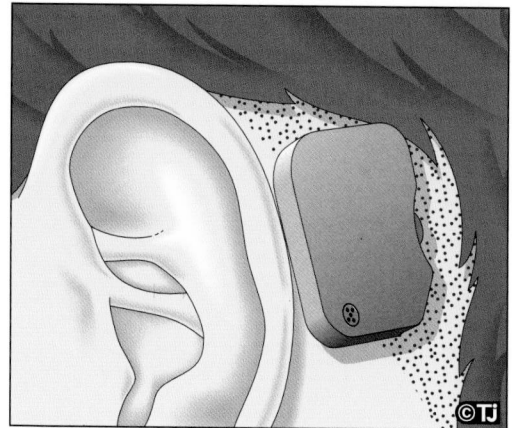

Fig 25-22. Three to four months after implant surgery, a plastic insert is placed into the coupling for retention of the hearing aid.

Fig 25-23. The hearing aid in place.

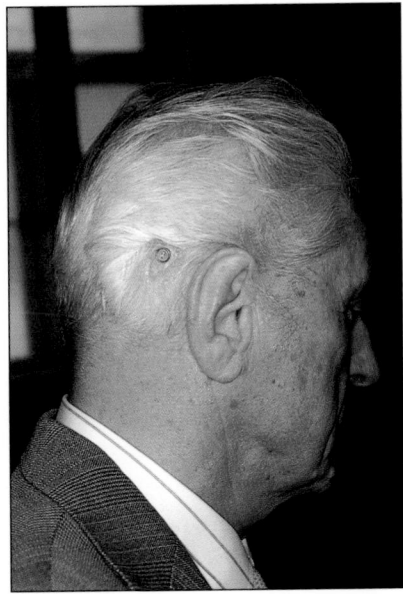

Fig 25-24. A patient with the skin-penetrating coupling.

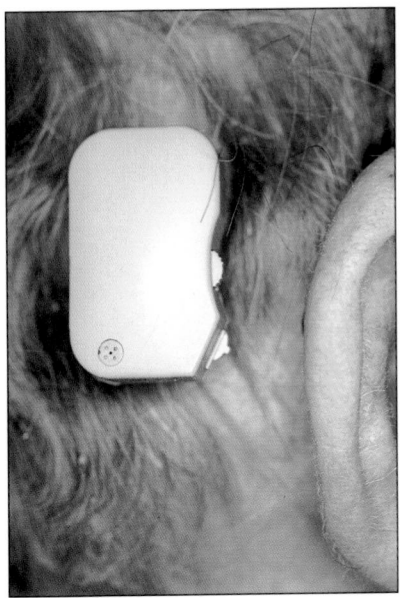

Fig 25-25. The Bone-Anchored Hearing Aid in place.

ing cap and the gauze are removed. If a lot of subcutaneous tissue reduction has been done, the healing cap is put back in place and a new gauze is applied under the cap for another 5 to 7 days. At this time, the stitches are removed and the implant area is left open. The patient is told to clean the site with some mild ointment. Soon the healing has reached a stage when the patient should start to clean the area with ordinary soap and water. Occasionally, some patients need to use the ointment, but the importance of daily cleaning as an integral part of the morning toilet should be stressed.

Three to 4 months later the healing often has reached the stage for the hearing aid to be fitted. A plastic insert with an O-ring is placed inside the coupling (Fig 25-22), and the hearing aid is fitted (Fig 25-23). Figure 25-24 shows the skin penetration in a patient, and Figure 25-25 shows a patient with the BAHA in place.

Changes in the Surgical Procedure

Since the introduction of this surgical technique in 1977, the following six procedures have been changed.

Number of Implants

Initially, two implants were placed for a BAHA. The reason for this was that we did not know the prognosis for an implant placed in the mastoid process. Today we know that the risk of losing an implant in this anatomic region is only about 2%, and we changed from placing two implants to only one.

Position of the Implant

To avoid acoustic feedback, the hearing aid must not touch the external ear. A good position for the implant is 50 to 55 mm from the center of the ear canal or, in the congenital defect, where the external ear canal opening is estimated to be. In the cranial-caudal axis, we suggest that the implant be placed just caudal to the top end of the external ear. From the acoustic point of view, it does not seem to matter where the implant is placed.

Insertion Torque

If the insertion torque is high, the removal torque will go down and vice versa. This indicates poor osseointegration. The probable reason for this is that, if a high torque is used, stress and compression of the bone interfere with the subtle blood supply in the bone close to the implant.

Soft-Tissue Handling

We believe that one of the most important steps in the surgical procedure to reduce the risk of adverse skin reaction is to minimize the relative movement of the soft tissue at the interface. The subcutaneous tissue reduction, not done at all originally, has become more and more extensive over the years. This is especially important for the tissue cranial to the implant. The soft tissue in this area has a tendency to sag down with time and can interfere with the coupling. Hair follicles are removed during surgery. Any left could be removed with electrolysis, using a thin needle in the follicle.

One-Stage Procedure

If the quality of the bone is good, the skin-penetrating coupling can be attached at the same time that the implant is placed. However, we still wait 3 to 4 months before the plastic insert is put in place into the coupling and the hearing aid is fitted.

Selection of Patients

One of the most important changes in this treatment modality is in patient selection. Every patient should be evaluated not only audiologically but also psychologically. Most patients who are not satisfied with the treatment have had some often minor and not detected psychologic abnormality. This has not always been obvious, and we believe that if the surgeon has any doubt about the patient's condition, the patient should be evaluated by a psychologist or a psychiatrist. Patients with a cochlear reserve close to 45 dB bone threshold should be informed that the ear-level device might not be strong enough and a body aid might be needed. The treating team should be aware that many patients, for psychologic reasons, do not want to wear a body aid, even if the amplification and sound quality are better.

Implants in Children

The youngest child we have provided with a BAHA was age 1.5 years. At surgery the bone was only 2 mm thick and soft. The dura of the middle cranial fossa and the wall of the sigmoid sinus are exposed more often than in the adult. The procedures were done in two stages, with an extended time interval between the implant placement and the abutment connection. We suggest 6 months at least. With this protocol, we have the same low frequency of implant loss as in the adult population. In children with a thin cortex of the mastoid, we have tried membrane techniques to generate new bone. Our initial experience with this technique is promising, but it is still too early for any general recommendation.

The soft-tissue reduction is done in the same way as in the adult, but the surgeon should be aware that soft-tissue proliferation in the young population is more pronounced than in the adult, and revision surgery of the soft tissue may become necessary.

References

1. Tjellström A, Granström G. Long-term follow-up with the Bone-Anchored Hearing Aid: a review of the first 100 patients between 1977 and 1985. Ear Nose Throat J 1994;73:112.

2. Tjellström A, Håkansson B. The Bone-Anchored Hearing Aid. Design principles, indications, and long-term clinical results. Otolaryngol Clin North Am 1995;28:53.

3. Tjellström A, Granström G. One-stage procedure to establish osseointegration: a zero to five years follow-up report. J Laryngol Otol 1995;109:593.

26.

The Bone-Anchored Hearing Aid

Bo E. V. Håkansson, PhD
Peder U. Carlsson, PhD

- Hearing by Bone Conduction
- Design History of the BAHA System
- Today's BAHA System
- Clinical Results and Patient Selection
- Ongoing and Future Projects

In 1977, a project was initiated at Sahlgren Hospital in Göteborg, Sweden, with the aim of developing a hearing aid system in which bone conduction (bc) via a skin-penetrating titanium implant would be used. With this new approach, we hoped that the drawbacks associated with conventional bc hearing aids could be reduced or completely eliminated. The Department of Applied Electronics at Chalmers University of Technology, Göteborg, Sweden, was invited to participate in the technical development of the device. A feasibility study, conducted in 1978 and 1979, showed that the use of a bone conductor rigidly attached to the skull via a skin-penetrating titanium abutment probably would be a good hearing aid alternative for some categories of patients.[1]

The first prototype of the single-housing design was constructed and tested on 10 patients from 1981 to 1983; the results were presented by Håkansson et al[2] in 1985. In that paper, the acronym BAHA was used for the first time to denote a Bone-Anchored

Hearing Aid of this type. Today this acronym is also the trademark used by Nobel Biocare USA, Inc. (Westmont, IL) for their bone-anchored hearing products. Some of the 10 patients had congenital defects with extensive conductive hearing loss, but with normal or nearly normal cochlear function; others had chronic middle ear disease with various degrees of sensorineural impairment. All 10 patients had one thing in common: they had been using a conventional bc hearing aid permanently or sporadically for many years. For these patients, the single-housing BAHA was superior to a conventional bc hearing aid in several respects. The most important improvements reported by the patients were improved wearing comfort, favorable aesthetic appearance, and improved quality of sound. The positive reactions from the first 10 patients corroborated our findings from the feasibility study that there is a real need for a BAHA; these positive reactions also gave us further motivation to immerse ourselves in the specialization of stimulation by bc.

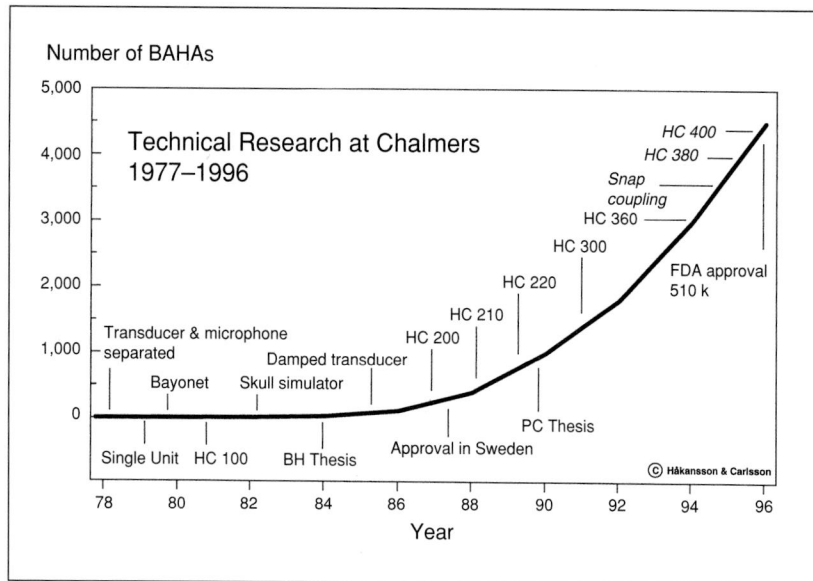

Fig 26-1. Important milestones in the history of the Bone-Anchored Hearing Aid (BAHA). BH, Bo Håkansson; FDA, Food and Drug Administration; PC, Peder Carlsson. (By permission of B Håkansson and P Carlsson.)

Many different models of the BAHA have been developed. More and more clinics have accepted this new treatment for selected patients, and today 250 clinics in 25 countries worldwide are prescribing the BAHA for their patients. The number of patients has increased from the first pilot group to 4,000 patients as of December 1996. Two important milestones in the history of the BAHA are the approval by the Swedish National Social Welfare Board, in February 1988, and the approval by the Food and Drug Administration (FDA) in the United States (US), in August 1996. Figure 26-1 shows the growth in number of patients as well as additional significant milestones in the BAHA history from 1977 to 1996.

Hearing by Bone Conduction

Bone Conduction Physiology

Extensive research on bc physiology was done between 1950 and 1970 by, among others, Bárány,[3] Kirikae,[4] von Békésy,[5] and Tonndorf.[6] Since then, the small number of publications on this subject probably can be explained by the extremely complex process of bc and by the attitude that conventional bc hearing aids were considered to be less than adequate. However, with the introduction of the BAHA, research in bc physiology has become more popular. The main reason for using a conventional bc hearing device is that the bone-conducted sound bypasses the impaired or diseased external or middle ear. With the introduction of the BAHA, a new type of excitation was introduced, namely, direct bc (dbc). Hearing via dbc is defined as sound transmission via bc without the skin and soft tissue being part of the vibration transmission path between the transducer and the skull.

Hearing by bc is a natural way of hearing. When listening to one's own voice, one is listening to both airborne and bone-conducted sound. The fraction of one's own voice transmitted by bc has been estimated to be of the same order of magnitude as the airborne component.[5] This phenomenon is the reason why most people do not recognize their own voices on a tape recording; the tape recorder records only the airborne component. From this observation one may conclude that bone-conducted sound is quite important, because most people do not experience their own voices as distorted.

The air-bone cancellation experiment, first done by von Békésy,[5] further indicates that bone-conducted sound is normal sound. This experiment showed that a pure tone transmitted via bc could be cancelled by simultaneously presenting an airborne tone of the same frequency and loudness level; cancellation occurred at a certain phase relationship

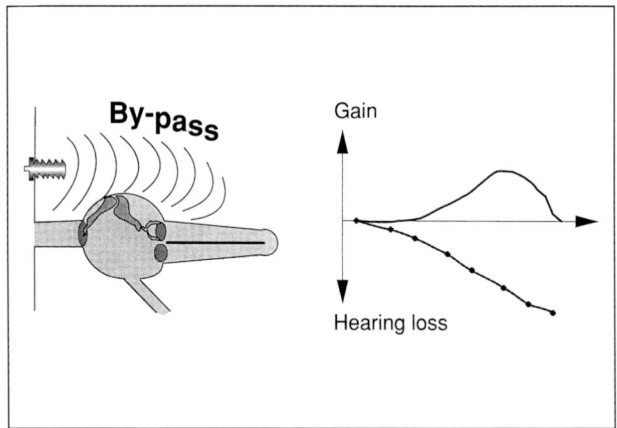

Fig 26-23. With the bypass channel, the hearing amplification can be matched to the hearing loss without affecting the low-frequency response.

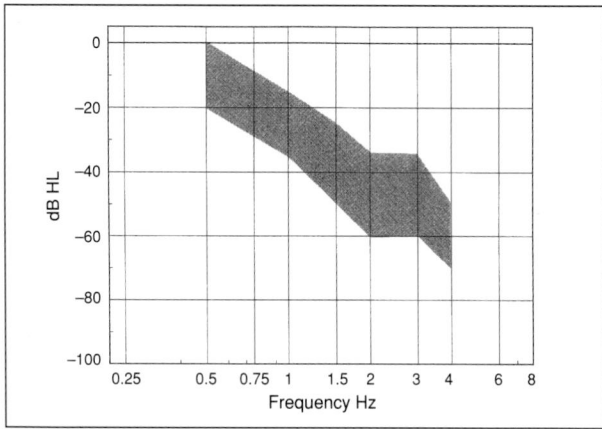

Fig 26-24. The shaded area shows the target hearing thresholds for patients with a pure sensorineural hearing loss participating in a feasibility study with the Bone-Anchored Hearing Aid HC 400.

ally good. Kochkin[22] found that 20% of the hearing aid owners were *very dissatisfied or dissatisfied with their device*, and of these, 12% *did not use their hearing aid at all*. Almost the same result was reported by Ovegård & Ramström,[21] who found that in a 1-year follow-up study of 50 new hearing aid users, 27% were *very dissatisfied or dissatisfied with their hearing aid*. It might be expected that the recently introduced completely in the canal devices have improved the satisfaction scores; however, a great number of patients are not satisfied with ac hearing aids for various reasons.

An important property that is used in connection with bc and dbc excitation is the bypass of the middle ear. A BAHA operates in parallel with, or bypasses, the middle ear; that is, the normal way of hearing is not affected by this type of hearing aid. At low frequencies, where the hearing ability usually is relatively good, the normal hearing by the ear canal is used (Fig 26-23). At high frequencies, the BAHA amplifies the sound and operates in parallel with the normal hearing. To achieve a good result with a miniaturized BAHA, it probably is important to attain an optimum direction of the mechanical excitation. Investigations are planned to examine the sensitivity in different directions. Today, the direction of the excitation is approximately perpendicular to the surface of the skull, a direction that has been chosen solely for practical reasons.

A feasibility study was initiated in 1994 as a joint project including the Department of Otolaryngology (Anders Tjellström and Gösta Granström) and the

Department of Audiology (Radi Jönsson, Gunnar Lidén, and Anders Ringdahl) at Sahlgren Hospital and the Department of Applied Electronics at Chalmers University of Technology. Preliminary results from five patients with a pure high-frequency sensorineural hearing loss (on average, 40 dB, Fig 26-24) indicate that the present solution of the BAHA (HC 400) offers some improvement in terms of wearing comfort compared with a conventional ac device. In terms of sound quality, the patients report subjectively that the BAHA (HC 400) offers a significant improvement over the unaided condition; however, preliminary investigations on a subgroup of patients indicate that a conventional ac device is better, especially in terms of power capability. Future modifications of the BAHA (HC 400) are needed to change this preference.

A Bone-Anchored Masker for Mitigation of Tinnitus

There is a great need of rehabilitation or mitigation for patients suffering from tinnitus. Some patients respond positively to using masking devices. Because a bypass device has some important advantages over an ac device, it might be a good idea to use a bone-anchored masker in patients suffering from tinnitus. Accordingly, in a planned future study, a bone-anchored masker will be investigated to see if it can offer some improved mitigation of tinnitus.

References

1. Tjellström A, Håkansson B, Lindström J, et al. Analysis of the mechanical impedance of bone-anchored hearing aids. Acta Otolaryngol 1980;89:85.

2. Håkansson B, Tjellström A, Rosenhall U, Carlsson P. The bone-anchored hearing aid. Principal design and a psycho-acoustical evaluation. Acta Otolaryngol (Stockh) 1985;100:229.

3. Bárány E. A contribution to the physiology of bone conduction. Acta Otolaryngol 1938;Suppl 26:1.

4. Kirikae I. An experimental study on the fundamental mechanism of bone conduction. Acta Otolaryngol (Stockh) 1959;Suppl 145:1.

5. von Békésy G. Experiments in Hearing. New York: McGraw-Hill, 1960.

6. Tonndorf J. Bone conduction: studies in experimental animals. Acta Otolaryngol 1966;Suppl 213:1.

7. Håkansson B, Brandt A, Carlsson P, Tjellström A. Resonance frequencies of the human skull in vivo. J Acoust Soc Am 1994;95:1474.

8. Håkansson B, Carlsson P, Brandt A, Stenfelt S. Linearity of sound transmission through the human skull in vivo. J Acoust Soc Am 1996;99:2239.

9. Håkansson B, Tjellström A, Rosenhall U. Acceleration levels at hearing threshold with direct bone conduction versus conventional bone conduction. Acta Otolaryngol (Stockh) 1985;100:240.

10. Håkansson B, Carlsson P, Tjellström A. The mechanical point impedance of the human head, with and without skin penetration. J Acoust Soc Am 1986;80:1065.

11. Håkansson B, Tjellström A, Rosenhall U. Hearing thresholds with direct bone conduction versus conventional bone conduction. Scand Audiol 1984;13:3.

12. Brandt A. On Sound Transmission Characteristics of the Human Skull In Vivo. Licentiate Thesis No. 611, School of Electrical Engineering, Chalmers University of Technology, Göteborg, Sweden, 1989.

13. Carlsson P, Håkansson B, Ringdahl A. Force threshold for hearing by direct bone conduction. J Acoust Soc Am 1995;97:1124.

14. Carlsson PU, Håkansson BE. The bone-anchored hearing aid: reference quantities and functional gain. Ear Hear 1997;18:34.

15. Håkansson B, McQueen D, Tjellström A. Analysis of the Mechanical Impedance and a New Transducer System for Bone Anchored Hearing Aids. Fifth Nordic Meeting on Medical and Biological Engineering, Linköping, Sweden, June 10-13, 1981, 1:204.

16. Håkansson B. The Bone Anchored Hearing Aid—Engineering Aspects. Thesis No. 144, School of Electrical Engineering, Chalmers University of Technology, Göteborg, Sweden, 1984.

17. Håkansson B, Carlsson P. Skull simulator for direct bone conduction hearing devices. Scand Audiol 1989;18:91.

18. Stenfelt S, Håkansson B. A miniaturized artificial mastoid using a skull simulator. Scand Audiol (in press, 1998).

19. Carlsson P, Håkansson B, Rosenhall U, Tjellström A. A speech-to-noise ratio test with the bone-anchored hearing aid: a comparative study. Otolaryngol Head Neck Surg 1986;94:421.

20. Tjellström A, Håkansson B. The bone-anchored hearing aid: design principles, indications, and long-term clinical results. Otolaryngol Clin North Am 1995;28:53.

21. Ovegård A, Ramström A-B. Individual follow-up of hearing aid fitting. Scand Audiol 1994;23:57.

22. Kochkin S. MarkeTrak III identifies key factors in determining consumer satisfaction. Hear J 1992;45:1.

Follow-Up Management

27.

David W. Proops, BDS

> • Evaluation
> • Maintenance of the Soft Tissues
> • Maintenance of the Abutment
> • Maintenance of the Hearing Aid

The advent of the Bone-Anchored Hearing Aid (BAHA) is a significant development in the rehabilitation of a group of hearing-impaired patients with bone-conduction hearing loss. The indications for the BAHA include congenital atresias in which the patient has no external ear or ear canal, bilateral mastoid cavities, chronic suppurative otitis media causing the ear molds of conventional aids to become soiled and blocked, and patients in whom the mere presence of an ear mold provokes irritation and discharge.

Wearers of conventional bone-conductor hearing aids are excellent candidates for the BAHA. Some patients with otosclerotic changes may find their particular needs are met best by the BAHA.

Evaluation

Patients should not be offered the BAHA until they have undergone a thorough preoperative evaluation. This should include audiometric, otologic, and general assessment, with particular attention to the patient's perception of the BAHA and willingness to maintain the health of the skin around the skin-penetrating abutment. Evaluation of the patient's personal hygiene can involve noting the care of the hair and nails and general physical appearance. Poverty is not the issue, but rather a consideration of the value the individual places on personal physical health. Questions to assess the motivation of the patient for this treatment may alert the provider that the patient is not a suitable candidate. The disappointment and loss of morale that both patient and provider suffer with repeated soft-tissue infections and local treatments could jeopardize the BAHA treatment.

The best setting in which to offer a BAHA is within the context of a total rehabilitation program. If evaluation revealed that only a BAHA is required, the patient may benefit from supplemental auditory training. If the patient has a congenital conductive loss, then it almost is axiomatic that there will be speech and language difficulties. These patients may be helped by speech therapy when improved audition is experienced by placement of the BAHA. Children with congenital absence of ears should be offered their BAHA as early as possible to provide the best opportunity for development of normal speech and language. Their prosthetic rehabilitation may not occur until some years later. Ideally, the surgical and

327

Table 27-1 *Grading (After Holgers) of Skin Reaction Around Titanium Abutments*	
Grade	**Reaction**
0	No reaction
1	Slight reddening
2	Granular and moist
3	Exuberant granulations
4	Loss of implants

Box 27-1 *Postoperative Management*

Leave the healing cap and dressing on for 10 to 14 days

Remove the dressing and the sutures

Leave wound uncovered unless there is an area of breakdown

Instruct patient and caregiver in skin management

Fit aid at 4 weeks

Continue conventional management of mastoid cavities

Box 27-2 *Management of the Skin and Abutment*

Daily cleaning of the skin around the abutment

Use of plastic implant scaler to remove any matter

Use of shaving brush and soap and water

Use of an antibiotic cream if the area becomes reddened and sore

prosthetic treatment are coordinated and performed by the same team.[1]

The goals of evaluation should be prevention as well as solution of problems.

Those fitted with the BAHA require lifetime follow-up evaluation. They require supervision of use of the BAHA and their underlying hearing problem. Long-term maintenance is required for the diseased ear, the abutment, the skin, and the aid itself. It is wrong, therefore, to offer patients this form of treatment and rehabilitation until the long-term maintenance has been discussed with the patient.

Maintenance of the Soft Tissues

The largest cause of problems with the BAHA is the soft tissue around the abutment.[2] The originating Swedish group,[3] the Dutch group from Nijmegen,[4] and the Birmingham group[5,6] have reported that the majority of patients (>75%) have no adverse skin reactions. Holgers et al[7] suggested a 5-point scale, which has been universally adopted to represent the skin reaction (Table 27-1). This should be recorded at every outpatient visit. In all series, a few patients have the majority of the problems.

The three key features for good long-term management of the soft tissues are good patient selection, adequate thinning of the skin flap and reduction of surrounding subcuticular tissues, and regular cleaning of the skin around the abutment.[5]

The long-term management should start with the first postoperative examination. In Birmingham, United Kingdom, a clinical nurse specialist is responsible for the soft-tissue maintenance and postoperative instruction of patients (Box 27-1). Printed instructions are given to each patient, which emphasize the importance of daily or regular care (Box 27-2). It is suggested that an important other person also be instructed by the nurse. In the case of a child, this is a parent, and for an adult, usually the spouse or another adult. The problem for patients is that they are unable to visualize directly the abutment and surrounding skin.

There are various methods to remove the skin debris and dried exudate that accumulate daily around the abutment. Plastic implant scalers are ideal for this purpose because they do not damage or alter the polished surface of the implant abutment (Fig 27-1). Other methods include the use of a soft brush, either a shaving brush or a toothbrush, with soap and water and, in some cases, the use of dental floss.

An antibiotic cream is prescribed for all patients, and they are encouraged to use it if the skin around the abutment begins to look red. Hair in the region should be trimmed; if it becomes long, it can wrap around the abutment and can provoke an inflammatory reaction.

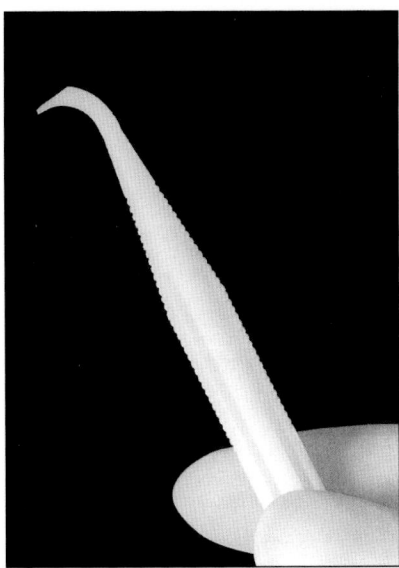

Fig 27-1. Photograph of plastic implant scaler to assist in removal of debris from around abutment. It may be sterilized by autoclaving for up to 10 cycles.

Maintenance of the Hearing Aid

Some individuals seem incapable of keeping or caring for their aids and lose them or leave them places where they are damaged. We have had aids returned that have been worn in the shower, chewed by the dog, or run over by the car. Others are simply lost. Depending on the health care system, some method needs to be in place for their timely replacement. The patient should be encouraged to have private insurance for the aid. If there is a real risk of accidental displacement, then a piece of fishing line can be attached to the aid through a small eye in the casing and the other end can be pinned to clothing. This can be useful particularly for small children or active teenagers and adults.

No electronic device works forever; however, the BAHA appears particularly robust. Nevertheless, a planned replacement system should be organized. A reasonable life expectancy of the BAHA appears to be 5 years.

The follow-up protocol for the patient requires several early visits. Instruction for care of the skin, abutment and hearing aid maintenance should be given and reinforced with written and pictorial presentations during these visits.

The first visit for the patient after surgery is at 10 days to remove the dressing and sutures and to check the viability of the skin flap.

When a one-stage surgical procedure is performed, the fitting of the hearing aid can be done 3 to 4 months after surgery. If the surgery is done in two stages, it is often possible to fit the BAHA 4 weeks after the second stage. After fitting of the hearing aid during the first year, follow-up should be at 3, 6, and 12 months. Thereafter, annual medical and audiologic examinations should suffice, provided the patient has access to the specialist nurse if problems occur.

The BAHA is an effective and rewarding form of rehabilitation for a group of hearing-impaired patients who previously were ill served.

The success of the BAHA depends on suitable patient selection, careful surgical management, appropriate postoperative care, and long-term follow-up management, which are provided by a coordinated team in close communication with the patient.

If an inflammation persists, despite supervised local treatment, the abutment may have loosened from the implant or it may be that the abutment is not properly seated on the octagon of the implant. In either case, there is dead space, which may become infected and act as a nidus for the inflammatory response. Removal of the abutment from the implant should be undertaken if there is any doubt about the seating of the abutment or concern about persisting inflammation. This is not a time-consuming procedure and there is no discomfort for the patient. It is suggested, therefore, that a set of instruments be kept in the outpatient department for this procedure.

Maintenance of the Abutment

The abutment problems of loosening or poor seating have been discussed. The plastic insert of the abutment rarely causes problems but may be lost. The patient should be provided with a spare. The O-rings that hold the plastic insert into the head of the abutment do require regular changing and the patient needs a spare supply and access to more. The newer mounting and demounting instrument has made this process easier for both patient and provider.

References

1. Stevenson DS, Proops DW, Wake MJ, Deadman MJ, Worrollo SJ, Hobson JA. Osseointegrated implants in the management of childhood ear abnormalities: the initial Birmingham experience. J Laryngol Otol 1993;107:502.

2. Tjellström A, Granström G. Long-term follow-up with the Bone-Anchored Hearing Aid: a review of the first 100 patients between 1977 and 1985. Ear Nose Throat J 1994;73:112.

3. Tjellström A, Håkansson B, Lindström J, Hallén O, Rosenhall U, Leijon A. Analysis of the mechanical impedance of Bone-Anchored Hearing Aids. Acta Otolaryngol (Stockh) 1980;89:85.

4. Mylanus EAM, Cremers CWRJ, Snik AFM, van den Berge NW. Clinical results of percutaneous implants in the temporal bone. Arch Otolaryngol Head Neck Surg 1994;120:81.

5. Proops DW. The Birmingham Bone Anchored Hearing Aid programme: surgical methods and complications. J Laryngol Otol Suppl 1996;21:7.

6. MacNamara M, Phillips D, Proops DW. The Bone Anchored Hearing Aid (BAHA) in chronic suppurative otitis media (CSOM). J Laryngol Otol Suppl 1996;21:38.

7. Holgers KM, Tjellström A, Bjursten LM, Erlandsson BE. Soft tissue reactions around percutaneous implants: a clinical study of soft tissue conditions around skin-penetrating titanium implants for Bone-Anchored Hearing Aids. Am J Otol 1988;9:56.

Index